RAIN OF
STEEL

RAIN OF
STEEL

Mitscher's Task Force 58,
Ugaki's Thunder Gods, and the
Kamikaze War off Okinawa

STEPHEN L. MOORE

Naval Institute Press

Annapolis, Maryland

This book has been brought to publication with the generous assistance of Edward S. and Joyce I. Miller.

Naval Institute Press
291 Wood Road
Annapolis, MD 21402

Library of Congress Cataloging-in-Publication Data
Names: Moore, Stephen L., author.
Title: Rain of steel : Mitscher's Task Force 58, Ugaki's Thunder Gods, and the Kamikaze war off Okinawa / Stephen L. Moore.
Other titles: Mitscher's Task Force 58, Ugaki's Thunder Gods, and the Kamikaze war off Okinawa
Description: Annapolis, Maryland : Naval Institute Press, [2020] | Includes bibliographical references and index.
Identifiers: LCCN 2020012670 (print) | LCCN 2020012671 (ebook) | ISBN 9781682475263 (hardcover ; alk. paper) | ISBN 9781682475317 (electronic)
Subjects: LCSH: World War, 1939–1945—Campaigns—Japan—Okinawa Island. | Mitscher, Marc Andrew, 1887–1947. | United States. Navy. Task Force 58—History. | Fighter pilots—United States—Interviews. | Ugaki, Matome, 1890–1945. | Kamikaze airplanes. | World War, 1939–1945—Aerial operations, American. | World War, 1939–1945—Naval operations, American. | World War, 1939–1945—Naval operations, Japanese. | World War, 1939–1945—Aerial operations, Japanese.
Classification: LCC D767.99.O45 M57 2020 (print) | LCC D767.99.O45 (ebook) | DDC 940.54/252294—dc23
LC record available at https://lccn.loc.gov/2020012670
LC ebook record available at https://lccn.loc.gov/2020012671

∞ Print editions meet the requirements of ANSI/NISO z39.48-1992 (Permanence of Paper).
Printed in the United States of America.

28 27 26 25 24 23 22 21 20   9 8 7 6 5 4 3 2 1
First printing

CONTENTS

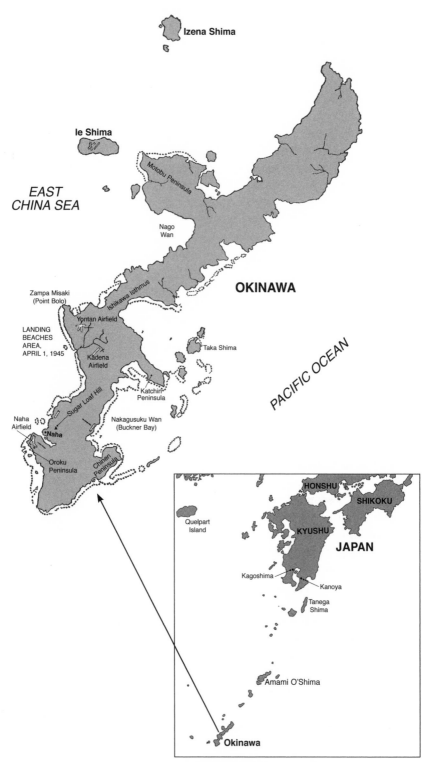

OKINAWA CAMPAIGN AREA, 1945

PROLOGUE

Marsh Beebe's blue eyes were sore as he blinked heavily into the blinding white light. His momentary confusion was replaced almost instantly by a sense of responsibility.

"What's the news?" he demanded.

The quartermaster's messenger looked perplexed as Lieutenant Commander Beebe scrambled from his stateroom bunk, demanding to know the latest overnight details about his five lost pilots. The young sailor said he was unaware and reminded him, "Commander, it's time to get up. You left a call for 0400."

Beebe rolled out of his bunk and mechanically crammed his five-foot-ten, 175-pound frame into his flight dungarees, left ready the night before so that he could dress in less than a minute. As the fighter-squadron skipper rushed to grab a cup of coffee, his mind ran through the events of the previous evening.

Five fighter pilots of his squadron, Composite Squadron 39 (VC-39), had taken off in the late afternoon of November 23, 1943, from the light carrier *Liscome Bay* (CVE 56) for a dusk patrol to intercept several bogies (enemy aircraft) indicated on the ship's radarscope. Beebe's pilots had encountered a severe storm en route, and all communication with them had been lost.

His pilots were like his children. A native of Anaheim, California, Beebe had been an aviator himself since earning his golden wings in 1937, and he found flying to be addictive. "Every time I climbed in an airplane, it was a thrill to me," he said. During college, Beebe had played varsity football and basketball, graduating with majors in mathematics and physics from Occidental College. He had been commissioned as an ensign in the U.S. Navy in March 1941 and had worked his way up the ranks until being promoted to lieutenant commander in 1943, whereupon he took command of VC-39 in August on board *Liscome Bay*.[1]

Unlike the Navy's larger fleet carriers, *Liscome Bay* was a small flattop, derisively handed such nicknames as "jeep carrier" and "Kaiser coffin." Such escort carriers, given the naval designation of "CVE," were typically half the length and a third of the displacement of full-sized "fleet" carriers, which displaced more than 27,000 tons. Once America was thrust into World War II, there was an urgent need to quickly build new aircraft carriers to replace those lost during the early naval actions of 1942. Shipbuilder Henry J. Kaiser soon won over President Franklin D. Roosevelt on the idea of his ability to rapidly construct smaller aircraft carriers, the earliest of these being hastened along by building upon modified merchant-ship hulls.

The Kaiser shipyards at Vancouver, Washington, cranked out new escort carriers at a pace far superior to the timeline generally required of larger flattops—but at a price. They were smaller, slower, lightly armored, and generally less able to withstand severe damage. Many of the escort-carrier crews would sarcastically remark that their ship's designation actually stood for "Combustible, Vulnerable, and Expendable." *Liscome Bay* displaced only 7,800 long tons, was 498 feet in length, and carried only twenty-seven aircraft—less than one-third the capacity of a fleet carrier.

Liscome Bay and Marsh Beebe's VC-39 air group had departed San Diego for the Pacific on October 21, 1943, arriving just in time to take part in the Central Pacific campaign to take Tarawa and Makin Islands in late November. Late on the afternoon of November 23, five of his Grumman F6F Hellcat fighters, sent to chase a potential "bogey," had disappeared from the radarscopes as massive thunderclouds swept the area. Long after dark Beebe's pilots still could not be raised via radio. Their skipper and the carrier division's chief of staff, Commander John Crommelin, had placed calls to other carriers in their task force, but they had received no word about the missing pilots. Beebe had spent anxious hours awaiting their return but knew nothing more of them before finally turning in close to midnight.

Unknown to Beebe at the time, his lost sheep had found refuge within another American carrier task force some sixty miles away. Lieutenant David C. Bagby, Lieutenant (jg) George McFedries, and Ensign Richard Cowger landed without incident on the fleet carrier *Yorktown* (CV 10) at 1843. A fourth *Liscome Bay* pilot, Lieutenant Foster J. Blair, overflew the flight-deck barrier and crashed into parked planes. Two *Yorktown* crewmen were killed, and eight other men were injured, including Blair and Cowger. The fifth VC-39 pilot, Lieutenant R. M. Wells, shuffled over to the carrier *Lexington* (CV 16) and landed safely at 1947.

As Lieutenant Commander Beebe sipped his coffee during the predawn hours of November 24, he still had no news of these five pilots. He decided that after his morning combat air patrols (CAPs) were launched, he would send out a search patrol at 0800 if Lieutenant Bagby's flight was still missing. He stopped by the ready room to ensure that his flight officer had the morning's pilot briefing well in hand. Beebe then scurried below to his quarters, a former linen locker located two decks below the flight deck and directly above *Liscome Bay*'s hangar deck, to gather his shaving gear and prepare for what might be a long day. Beebe grabbed his razor, slung a towel over his arm, and ducked into the nearby head to have his shave.[2]

He had scarcely entered the head at 0510 when he felt a tremendous rumbling throughout the ship. Almost immediately, a violent explosion of bright orange flames shot a thousand feet into the air above *Liscome Bay*. The little jeep carrier had fallen victim to a spread of torpedoes launched from Lieutenant Commander Sunao Tabata's submarine, *I-175*. One of the torpedoes detonated in *Liscome Bay*'s bomb-storage area, creating a secondary explosion so powerful that it virtually disintegrated the forward half of the carrier. Ready aircraft warming up on deck were thrown like toys two hundred feet into the black sky. Pieces of decking up to three feet long, oil particles, white-hot shrapnel, and human flesh showered the decks of the battleship *New Mexico* (BB 40) some fifteen hundred yards away.[3]

The violence of the explosions slammed Beebe into the ceiling of the head and knocked him momentarily senseless. When he came to, he found himself lying on the deck in pitch blackness. Fear gripped him as he found the exit to the head destroyed. Beebe groped his way through the dark, feeling his way farther in to the washbasins and toward the back of the shower stalls.

There's no way out of here! he realized.

The fighter-squadron skipper was trapped on a blazing, exploding carrier in a compartment far below the waterline. His thoughts turned to sailors who had been trapped below the waterline on the doomed ships when Pearl Harbor was attacked by the Japanese on December 7, 1941. But Beebe had little time to sulk in despair before another heavy explosion erupted, followed by others.

To his amazement, he suddenly saw a light in the distance, afforded to him by the mere fact that the explosions had blown down the adjacent bulkheads. Above him he could see fires raging on the hangar deck through the jagged holes in the upper bulkhead. Beebe scrambled quickly through the ragged steel into an adjacent bunkroom before making his way into an open passageway.

His mind became a blur in the minutes that ensued, and Beebe could later not recall just how he had picked his way through the wrecked corridors and flames to make it up to *Liscome Bay*'s flight deck. There he found the decks slippery with oil and his footing further insecure due to the 10-degree starboard list his carrier had already assumed. He paused long enough to carry a wounded sailor to a safer location. Around him other sailors played out firehoses to fight the raging inferno, only to find that no water pressure existed to fill their hoses. Those who had once jeered the satirical "combustible, vulnerable, and expendable" remark suddenly believed that description of the escort carrier was close to the truth.

Beebe ran into Commander Crommelin, who had raced naked from the shower when the carrier began exploding. Crommelin was clearly injured, but he passed orders for others to save themselves by abandoning ship. Men were dying all around as the fires cooked off bombs and ready ammunition for the antiaircraft guns. Beebe had no lifejacket, but he quickly remembered that each corner of the flight deck contained a rubber life raft that could be thrown over the side in the event of a plane crash during flight operations.

Beebe navigated the slanted deck and catwalk amid the exploding ammunition and ripped the life raft free. He slipped and fell heavily across one of his junior pilots, Ensign Danny Mack, nearly knocking him overboard. While shielding his face from the searing flames with his left hand, he helped Mack drag the raft to a point almost abreast of the forward part of the carrier's island. Beebe hoped to slide down a line from the catwalk nets to the ocean sixty feet below while clutching the raft. But his left arm, ripped by flying shrapnel, failed him, and Beebe plunged over the side, striking the water hard.[4]

As he floundered to the surface, he found his squadron's executive officer, Lieutenant John "Pete" Piegari, nearby. Together the two men began swimming away from their ship, towing their uninflated raft away from the blazing oil that surrounded the doomed vessel. The pair were joined by Ensign Mack, who helped them struggle farther away. After swimming for what seemed at least a mile to Beebe, he looked back and found that they had only moved fifty yards from the blazing *Liscome Bay*.

The trio flailed, kicked, and towed their raft another hundred yards before they simply floated in exhaustion. As Beebe gulped in lungfuls of air, he looked back again at his proud carrier, blazing as her gray bow began rising out of the water. "The rest of the ship was a sputtering inferno," he said, "bombs bursting from her innards, sending glowing fragments into the air like a gigantic 4th of July display."[5]

Within moments, *Liscome Bay* settled by the stern, sliding beneath the waves at 0533 with an evil hiss as the seawaters contacted her white-hot steel. When the rising cloud of steam drifted away with the light ocean breeze, Marsh Beebe's carrier was gone, descending to the bottom, just twenty-three minutes after taking the torpedo. The Imperial Japanese Navy (IJN) had robbed him of his command. Fourteen of the twenty-nine pilots of VC-39 perished in the sinking. The remainder were now clutching on to flotsam or struggling to find a life raft with room to spare.

Beebe's little raft was soon packed with survivors, and more than a dozen others clutched a line playing out behind it. Among those who reached this group was Lieutenant Bill Davis, one of *Liscome Bay*'s landing-signal officers. He was selflessly helping support Ensign Frank Sistrunk, a young VC-39 pilot who was fighting for his life. Unable to swim, Sistrunk had been wounded in the knee and leg before leaving the ship, where he had been lying in sickbay after having an emergency appendectomy the previous week. His fear of water and his freshly sewn gut only added to the pilot's challenges until others helped him into the raft.

Beebe and his comrades would drift for some two hours as the morning sun began to rise before they were hauled on board the destroyer *Morris* (DD 417). The loss of *Liscome Bay* and half of his squadron would sideline the lieutenant commander's chance of striking at the heart of Japan for nearly a year. During that time, he assumed command of another squadron, VF-17, and began plotting his opportunities for revenge until he could finally challenge his opponent in the air. While his new unit was rebuilt with a healthy dose of green young ensigns, it also included seven of his surviving VC-39 pilots, among them Sistrunk, McFedries, and Cowger. These men would need little motivation to fight, with the memory of 644 *Liscome Bay* shipmates who had perished burning in their brains.

When his Fighting Seventeen headed back to the Pacific War in late 1944, Marsh Beebe intended to make the Japanese pay heavily.

Chapter One

BALD EAGLE'S WINGS

The wrinkles in his pug face, chiseled from years of wind exposure and chain-smoking, creased as the short, frail-looking man tugged hard on another cigarette. A sly smile nipped at the corners of his mouth as the morning breeze rushed across the open air wing outside Flag Plot, his tactical control center high atop his flagship aircraft carrier. Sporting a signature duckbilled hat to protect his hairless scalp and shade his eyes from the sun, he was a staple figure, frequently sitting on a stool on the elevated island structure of his ship to watch the takeoffs and landings of the naval aviators he commanded.

He was a man of few words, and when he spoke, his voice was low and direct. Those who knew him well considered him both a brilliant leader and a bulldog of a fighter. He was in his element this day, in control of a vast armada that was standing forth to hand out vengeance to an old enemy with a bold new strike.

From the bridge of his flagship *Bunker Hill* (CV 17), Vice Admiral Marc Andrew Mitscher watched as sailors below toiled at recalling the flattop's anchor from the bed of Ulithi Atoll. Shaped like a fishhook, the group of islets composing the atoll were part of the Caroline Islands in the western Pacific and the staging area for the world's mightiest naval group—the U.S. Navy's Task Force (TF) 58. Ulithi's lagoon, one of the largest in the world, was eighteen miles long and nine miles wide. The date was February 10, 1945, and in short order the 28,000-ton carrier swung from her berth and pointed her mighty bow out toward the torpedo nets, which opened from the lagoon, and beyond to the vast ocean.

Mitscher was a seasoned carrier fighter. He had been through plenty already in three years of Pacific warfare. For the pilots he would order into harm's way in a matter of days, few could challenge the vice admiral's credibility. In January 1928 Mitscher had made the first aircraft landing on the old carrier *Saratoga* (CV 3). As fate would have it, "Sister Sara," as she was affectionately nicknamed by the sailors who crewed her, was among the sixteen carriers under his command as his TF 58 began its latest campaign.

Mitscher was a true "brown shoe," a pioneering naval aviator who had been along for the ride as the carrier forged its place ahead of the traditional battleship-led surface navy. Surface officers wore black shoes with their military uniforms, unlike the brown shoes worn by commissioned naval aviators. Any brown-shoe admiral leading a task force thus had a certain degree of respect from his aviators. His respect also ran to the highest levels of the Navy, including Admiral Chester Nimitz, commander in chief, U.S. Pacific Fleet. "He is the most experienced and most able officer in the handling of fast carrier task forces who has yet been developed," Nimitz said of him.[1]

Mitscher had a deep interest in his pilots. It was common for him to summon the first pilot to return from a mission to the bridge to question him from his swivel seat about it—without regard as to whether that man was a senior aviator or a squadron commander.

Born January 26, 1887, in Hillsborough, Wisconsin, Marc Mitscher was the grandson of a German cabinetmaker who immigrated to New York in the 1850s. Much of Marc's youth was spent in Oklahoma, where his father, Oscar, served as Oklahoma City's second mayor in the recent territory. By 1904 young Mitscher had secured a congressional nomination to the U.S. Naval Academy, where he narrowly achieved grades high enough to secure the start of what would be a long and colorful career.[2]

During his first fall semester, Mitscher was tagged with the nickname "Oklahoma Pete," in tribute to both his home state and a popular bilged-out former classmate. His sobriquet was eventually shortened to "Pete," and Mitscher began what would become an uphill battle to graduate. After two years at the academy, he was forced to resign due to scholastic difficulties and involvement in a fatal hazing incident. His father was able to have the same congressman reappoint him to Annapolis, but this meant that Pete's first two years of grades at the academy were wiped off the books.[3]

His naval schooling remained in jeopardy thereafter, as Mitscher collected demerits for smoking, drinking, playing cards, and other antics. During the summer of 1908, when he and a dozen fellow classmates were disembarked from *Olympia* (C 6) to relieve overcrowded conditions, they decided to "cement their common misery" by getting matching tattoos on their upper right arms. The bluish-colored buzzard, pierced by a bloody dagger, was a piece of body art that Mitscher would take pains to keep covered in his later career.[4]

Mitscher's first sea duty had begun in the summer of 1910 on board the armored cruiser *Colorado* (ACR 7). It was during this period that his courtship of young, brown-eyed Frances Smalley, daughter of a Tacoma lawyer, began. The couple first met at a wedding, and months later Frances was invited by Mitscher to join him for dinner on board *Colorado*. As a midshipman he was not allowed to marry for two years, but he wrote to Frances and asked for her hand in marriage when he returned. "I was nineteen. I didn't take it seriously enough," she admitted. "I did write to him, and continued to write to him." Mitscher was persistent and requested that they be married after he returned from a six-month cruise to Mexico on the gunboat *Vicksburg* (PG 11). When his ship was delayed a week, he rode a train to Tacoma and was married on January 16, 1913.[5]

During the first three years of their marriage, Frances spent only three months with her husband at different times due to his constant deployment. It was not until he was ordered to Pensacola for aviation training in October 1915 that the couple could enjoy a normal married life together in a home. Little by little she began to understand the complex yet quiet man who adored her. "I never knew when he was teasing me," she said. "He could tell me something with a completely straight face."[6]

Marc Mitscher was witness to the earliest significant events of naval aviation. He stood and watched the first catapult launch of an airplane from his armored cruiser *North Carolina* (ACR 12) and would be among the first thirteen Pensacola aviation students. His flight school was commanded by Lieutenant Kenneth Whiting, who had been taught to fly by none other than Orville Wright. On June 2, 1916, Lieutenant Mitscher earned his wings at the age of twenty-nine, with his head already nearly completely bald, and became the U.S. Navy's thirty-third aviator.[7]

The young officer became commander of Naval Air Station (NAS) Miami in 1918, while his wife remained with family in Tacoma, pregnant with their first child. She became gravely ill during the spring, fell into a coma, and lost the baby. When Mitscher learned that his wife would be unable to conceive again, he chose to never mention the subject of family again. The loss drew them closer together, and Frances was able to join him in Miami. She found his fondness for smoking stronger than any other vice: "The first thing in the morning when he woke up, he always awakened at dawn, you could hear the cigarette being lighted."[8]

In May 1919 Mitscher was among a group of naval aviators who attempted the first transatlantic crossing by air in Curtiss NC flying boats, but his NC-1 was forced to make a water landing near the Azores Islands. He and his five crewmen would spend hours adrift at sea before they were rescued by a Greek vessel. The fact that men went out of their way to search for and rescue him would not be forgotten by the future carrier admiral when his own aviators faced life-or-death situations during World War II.

During the next two decades, Pete Mitscher worked to advance naval aviation with assignments on the carriers *Langley* (CV 1) and *Saratoga* and the seaplane tender *Wright* (AV 1). When *Saratoga* was commissioned as the U.S. Navy's newest aircraft carrier, Mitscher made the first landing on her on January 11, 1928, in a Chance-Vought UO-1 fighter. Promoted to captain in 1938, he would spend the last two years prior to America's entry into World War II as assistant chief of the Bureau of Aeronautics. In October 1941 Mitscher assumed command of the newly commissioned carrier *Hornet* (CV 8) and was completing her fitting-out period when Pearl Harbor was attacked.

Captain Mitscher's *Hornet* would make history in April 1942 by transporting Vice Admiral William F. "Bull" Halsey and sixteen B-25 U.S. Army bombers to within striking distance of Tokyo. Lieutenant Colonel Jimmy Doolittle's raid against mainland Japan did little long-term military damage to that nation's mighty war machine, but the morale boost to the American psyche back home was immeasurable.

Less than two months later, Mitscher's *Hornet* participated in the historic Battle of Midway, in which U.S. carrier aviators sunk four Japanese flattops in a matter of hours. His Air Group 8 was the least experienced, and Lieutenant Commander Stan Ring, commander, Air Group (CAG) 8, chose a course that caused them to completely miss the Japanese fleet. Lieutenant Commander Jack Waldron, skipper of VT-8, defiantly radioed Ring, "the hell with you," and took his squadron straight to the enemy carriers. Left without fighter cover, Waldron's fifteen TBD Devastators were wiped out by Japanese fighters, and only one pilot would survive the ordeal. The Dauntless dive-bomber squadrons from *Enterprise* (CV 6) and *Yorktown* shared the glory of destroying four Japanese carriers on June 4, leaving Captain Mitscher stung by the loss of his entire torpedo squadron. No after-action reports were filed for *Hornet's* individual squadrons other than a joint report signed by Mitscher that was believed by some to be a cover-up to help protect his reputation.

Following Midway, Mitscher was moved from carrier command to shore duty as commander of Patrol Wing 2 in accordance with his prebattle promotion to rear admiral. He was left feeling that he was not in good graces with Admiral Nimitz and had been shelved for his performance at Midway. It was not until December 1942 that Mitscher edged one step closer to returning to the Pacific War when he was sent to the South Pacific as commander, Fleet Air, Noumea. Four months later his old comrade Halsey came to his rescue by placing him in command of all Army, Navy, Marine, and New Zealand aircraft in the air war in the Solomon Islands. "I knew we'd probably catch hell from the Japs in the air," Halsey later stated. "That's why I sent Pete Mitscher up there. Pete was a fighting fool."[9]

Admiral Mitscher handled the tough job of managing the constant air combat over Guadalcanal during 1943 with true professionalism. Nimitz and Halsey returned him to the Central Pacific by appointing him as commander, Carrier Division 3, on January 6, 1944. Now in charge of TF 58 as part of black-shoe Admiral Raymond Spruance's Fifth Fleet, Mitscher was in command of America's fast-carrier striking force, which he ably led on a rampage of operations through the Gilbert and Marshalls Islands in early 1944.

Mitscher's TF 58 conducted a series of raids on Japanese bases across the western Pacific, culminating in the climactic Battle of the Philippine Sea in June 1944. His carrier-based fighter squadrons devastated the best aviators of the IJN, shooting down more than four hundred aircraft in what became known as the "Great Marianas Turkey Shoot." On June 20 a large strike group sent out to hit the Japanese carrier fleet found itself returning long after dark, with the potential for heavy losses of airplanes and airmen. Mitscher brashly ignored the risk of enemy submarines and ordered all flattops to turn on their running lights, thereby saving countless lives and endearing himself to hundreds of aviators. The admiral did not see himself as a hero, and whenever the subject of this "turn on the lights" incident was brought up, it seemed to embarrass him. He was quick to dismiss the episode with, "It was nothing."[10]

Mitscher's care for his pilots was noted, and he became affectionately known as the "Bald Eagle"—which had also become his call sign within the fleet in 1944. His wife could see the effects of command stress on his five-foot-nine-inch body when he visited home late in the war. Pete looked weak and frail, with very white skin. She considered him "a very gentle man and very generous," but the effects of war had left him very thin. "He had absolutely no flesh on him at all," she said. "He seemed much smaller."[11]

As the war rolled into 1945, Allied plans were cooking to move the war right to the doorstep of Japan by seizing the islands of Iwo Jima and Okinawa. Mitscher was aware the enemy would pull out all the stops to slow his carrier force. During the Leyte Gulf campaign of October 1944, he had been introduced to the terrifying new tactic of kamikazes—planes flown by suicide pilots whose purpose was to dive directly into his warships.

As a result, the American carriers had doubled their fighter strength, as Mitscher explained to reporters at a Pearl Harbor press conference on December 28, 1944. Regarding kamikazes, he said, "They're damn hard to stop." He further explained, "The only way we have of stopping them now is to be more alert all the time on the guns and have more fighters in the air."[12]

Mitscher hinted to the press that attacks on the Japanese mainland were imminent and that he expected resistance to "be pretty stiff." He expected the enemy to continue retiring toward its homeland as the Philippines were taken. "By next summer," he hinted, "they will be sitting on a decidedly uneasy seat in the Empire." Admiral Nimitz was convinced that Pete Mitscher was the right choice to lead the offensive against the enemy's home islands. Months earlier, when he presented Mitscher with a Gold Star in lieu of a third Distinguished Service Medal, Nimitz had said of the Bald Eagle, "Ninety-one years ago, a Naval officer opened up the ports of Japan and now another officer is doing his damndest to close them."[13]

Admiral Mitscher's success was due partially to the first-rate staff he assembled, even if his relationship with some of his key men began a bit cold. Case in point was Captain Arleigh Burke, a stocky, popular forty-three-year-old destroyer-squadron commander who was better known as "31 Knot" Burke. Hand-picked as Mitscher's new chief of staff in March 1944 and advanced to the temporary rank of commodore, Burke had reported on board the admiral's flagship *Lexington* less than enthused to be part of the carrier command staff.

"Admiral Mitscher certainly did not want me," Burke later acknowledged, due to his being a nonaviator. "He didn't know me at all, but he took me as the lesser of the evils that he was confronted with." Burke felt that the admiral wanted to use him as a figurehead for potential surface actions and little else. "Admiral Mitscher would say 'good morning' to me in the morning when I came up and that was the end of it. He never sent for me. He talked to the junior people on the staff, but he never sent for me."[14]

Their first weeks operating together had been strained, as Burke "studied like hell." He did little to help his case with the Bald Eagle by hitching a ride as a rear-seat observer in the Dauntless dive bomber of Lieutenant Ralph Weymouth, skipper of *Lexington*'s VB-16, during the April 1944 raids on Hollandia. After buzzing that island's airfield, Weymouth and another pilot, Lieutenant Cook Cleland, decided the lack of visible enemy troops or gunfire would afford them the rare opportunity to do a "touch and go" landing on a Japanese-held airstrip. Encouraged by Burke to do so, Weymouth touched his wheels briefly on the strip and then pulled up. "When we got about above the end of the damned runway and we were climbing, a 40mm opened up and got our starboard wing," said Burke.[15]

According to Air Group 16's action report, "Lt. Cleland, in a foolhardy but interesting gesture, made a touch and go landing on the Cyclops runway." The same report makes no mention of Burke's SBD performing the same stunt (a show-off maneuver known among pilots as "flat-hatting"), perhaps due in part to the potentially fatal antiaircraft hit his plane sustained. According to Burke, Lieutenant Weymouth struggled to maintain control of his SBD on the flight back to *Lexington* due to aileron damage, and the jolt of their plane catching an arresting wire on the flight deck caused a chunk of the starboard wing to drop off. Mitscher, who watched the landings of the VB-16 planes, was waiting when his chief of staff reached the bridge "You're grounded," he announced to Burke. "You must have flat-hatted."[16]

During the next few months of carrier operations, Burke and Mitscher became increasingly comfortable with each other. During the Marianas battle, Burke was in support of Mitscher's decision to "turn on the lights" to save the pilots returning from the late attack on the Japanese carrier fleet. The Great Marianas Turkey Shoot proved to be a major turning point in the Bald Eagle's relationship with his chief of staff. "Admiral Mitscher

TG 58 chief of staff Commodore Arleigh "31 Knot" Burke (*left*) studies maps with Vice Admiral Marc Mitscher on board their flagship carrier, *Bunker Hill* (CV 17), in February 1945. *80-G-303981, NARA*

changed his feelings toward me and I changed my feelings toward him and toward his aviation," Burke confessed.[17]

Burke learned that Mitscher was an ardent reader of detective story novels who brought cases of such books on board his flagship at every opportunity. "Naturally, I, and most of the rest of the staff, became detective story addicts," said Burke. After a newspaperman broke a story on Mitscher that revealed his love for such trash literature, the admiral began receiving ample supplies of detective novels in each new mail delivery. "We never ran out again," said Burke. "Cigarettes, yes, bombs sometimes. Ammo and fuel we had to conserve carefully, but detective stories we had plenty of."[18]

In February 1945 Mitscher and Burke prepared to sortie TF 58 for the first carrier launches against Japan since the Bald Eagle had been captain of Doolittle's carrier in 1942. From Mitscher's new flagship *Bunker Hill*, Burke wrote a letter to his wife, Bobbie, that weeks of boredom were about to change: "There isn't much to do out here now, but there will be soon." Mitscher's new mission would be multistaged, starting with providing aerial support for the planned invasion of Iwo Jima, an eight-square-mile island of the Volcano Islands and closer to Japan than anything the Fifth Fleet's amphibious forces had assaulted to date. But to accomplish this, the carriers would first strike at Japan itself in mid-February to soften up dozens of airfields.[19]

The task was momentous, but Pete Mitscher had a task force surrounding him that he could scarcely have dreamed of in the spring of 1942. Then the number of American aircraft carriers available in the entire Pacific could be counted on one hand. By late January 1945 the Fast Carrier Force in the Pacific had grown to a dozen fleet carriers and a half-dozen light carriers. These eighteen carriers embarked a whopping 1,365 aircraft, with each light carrier averaging 27 planes on board and each fleet carrier having an average of 102 aircraft. Fleet defense had become the name of the game by early 1945, and nearly three-quarters of these 1,365 planes were fighters.[20]

The fleet carriers (CVs) were of the *Essex* class. The namesake of the class, *Essex* (CV 9) had been commissioned into the U.S Navy in December 1942, and by August 1944 eight more *Essex*-class carriers were in service. Each of these vessels displaced 27,000 tons, were 880 feet long, and were just wide enough to barely fit through the Panama Canal. Each was designed to operate an air group of thirty-six fighter planes, twenty-four dive bombers, and twenty-four torpedo bombers. By late 1944, however, this balance of plane types had been changed to increase the number of fighters on board each flattop.

The need for more carriers became urgent after the Japanese attack on Pearl Harbor, so President Roosevelt authorized plans for several cruisers then under construction to be converted to light aircraft carriers (CVLs) of the *Independence* class. Nine of these small carriers were in commission by November 1943. Each displaced only 11,000 tons, with short, narrow flight decks and space for an air group of only thirty planes.

As the Pacific War progressed, a third class of American carriers was forged by converting merchant ships to escort aircraft carriers (CVEs). These had fewer watertight compartments than other warships, were made of thinner steel, and were powered by inexpensive steam engines that did not conform to Navy specifications. Shipbuilder Henry J. Kaiser had promised that an escort carrier could be produced in a mere ninety days. These vessels thus were known by nicknames such as "Woolworth flattops," "jeep carriers," "Kaiser coffins," and "one-torpedo ships."

Pete Mitscher's fast carriers faced little threat of being overwhelmed by Japanese carrier groups. Each individual task group of his TF 58 had three or more carriers, stronger than any carrier task force America had sent into battle against Japan during 1942. While the U.S. war machine had immediately set to work cranking out dozens of new fleet carriers, light carriers, and jeep carriers by early 1944, Japan simply could not match this production. Four of the fleet carriers that had assailed Pearl Harbor—*Kaga*, *Akagi*, *Soryu*, and *Hiryu*—had been destroyed at the Battle of Midway.

During the Battle of the Philippine Sea in June 1944, U.S. submarines had disposed of two more Japanese fleet carriers, *Taiho* and *Shokaku*. The last of the six big flattops that had attacked Pearl Harbor, *Zuikaku*, was sunk at the Battle of Cape Engaño on October 25, 1944, along with three smaller carriers: *Zuiho*, *Chitose*, and *Chiyoda*. Japan's new-production flattops, more often than not, were taken out of the game before they entered it. The U.S. submarine *Archerfish* (SS 311) sunk the massive new *Shinano* with four torpedoes on November 29, 1944, just ten days after the 65,000-ton warship was commissioned. Just weeks later, on December 19, the U.S. submarine *Redfish* (SS 395) sunk the new 20,000-ton *Unryu* en route to the Philippines.

By January 1945 Japan simply lacked the raw materials, fuel supply, and qualified air groups to even send her remaining carriers out to sea to challenge the U.S. carrier fleet. America had thus already won the carrier war by February 18, 1945, when the light carrier *Ryuho* arrived at Kure Harbor at 0930, marking the end of the last wartime voyage of a Japanese flattop outside home waters.

The 16,700-ton *Ryuho* was one of only eight carriers Japan had available as Mitscher's fleet weighed anchor from Ulithi. None of the eight posed any immediate threat to the Americans. The smallest of them, the 7,470-ton *Hosho*, had become a training vessel for breaking in new carrier pilots. Two of the larger fleet carriers, *Amagi* and *Katsuragi*, arrived at Kure Harbor on February 15, after their carrier group had been abolished, and transferred their air groups ashore for other duties. The 24,000-ton *Junyo*, damaged by torpedoes in December 1944, was still undergoing repair work at the Sasebo Naval Yard. The 13,600-ton escort carrier *Kaiyo* was similarly operating from Kure for aircraft training.

Two new light carriers were nearing completion, including the 10,000-ton *Shimane Maru*, a tanker hull that was being converted to an escort aircraft carrier at the Kobe shipyards. The eighth carrier, the 16,119-ton *Yamashio Maru*, was a former merchant tanker being fitted with a 351-foot flight deck in Yokohama Harbor to become an escort aircraft carrier as well.

Japan's once mighty carrier fleet was a ghost of its former self.

Sixteen of Vice Admiral Mitscher's fast carriers were involved in the sortie from Ulithi on February 10. They were divided into five independent task groups, collectively composing TF 58, all ready to make an historic attack on targets that had not been touched in three years of war. The five task groups also included eight battleships, fifteen cruisers, and seventy-seven destroyers plus support ships carrying ammunition and fuel. In total the TF 58 armada steaming from Ulithi comprised 121 ships—the largest force to be sent against an enemy in U.S. Navy history.

Five carriers—*Bennington* (CV 20), *Randolph* (CV 15), *Bunker Hill*, *Belleau Wood* (CVL 24), and *Saratoga*—and their air groups had reported to TF 58 just prior to leaving Ulithi. In addition, *Cowpens* (CVL 25) had just received the new Air Group 46, and *Lexington* had taken on the new Air Group 9. *Wasp* (CV 18) had just received two new Marine fighter squadrons, VMF-216 and VMF-217.

The carrier crews were called to General Quarters and the warships began filing through Ulithi's torpedo net and into the open ocean. The first task group was labeled Task Group (TG) 58.1 and commanded by Rear Admiral Joseph James "Jocko" Clark, a colorful character who was a proud registered member of the Cherokee Nation thanks to his claim for one-eighth Cherokee ancestry. Known to be loud and profane, Clark was a brown shoe who had earned his wings of gold in 1925 and had worked his way through carrier commands during the next fifteen years. He had commanded the new carrier *Yorktown* shortly before he was promoted to rear admiral in January 1944 and assumed command of the task group. His carrier force standing out from Ulithi included the fleet carriers *Hornet* (CV 12), *Wasp*, and *Bennington* and the light carrier *Belleau Wood*.

The second task group heading for open waters was TG 58.4 under Rear Admiral Arthur W. Radford, a strong-willed, aggressive former aviator who had moved into carrier-force command in late 1943. His current group included the fleet carriers *Yorktown* and *Randolph*, and the light carriers *Langley* (CVL 27) and *Cabot* (CVL 28). His pilots were ready for action. *Langley's* VF-23 squadron history notes that the previous day, February 9, a Marine captain had lectured all flight personnel on escape and evasion. "Considerable emphasis was placed upon what could and could not be disclosed to Japanese interrogators. We still don't know where we are going but one thing is certain, the cloak and dagger boys expect that the areas will be loaded with Japs."[21]

Next to depart was TG 58.2, under brown-shoe Rear Admiral Ralph E. Davison, who had earned his wings of gold in 1920. Davison, who enjoyed his whiskey while in port, was considered to be quiet yet brilliant and cool in combat. He had commanded an escort-carrier division during the Gilberts and Marshalls campaign and had fleeted up to command one of Mitscher's carrier task groups in August 1944. In February 1945 his TG 58.2 included the fleet carriers *Lexington* and *Hancock* (CV 19), plus the light carrier *San Jacinto* (CVL 30), two battleships, three cruisers, and twelve destroyers.

Fourth of the carrier task groups to depart Ulithi was TG 58.3, under the direction of Rear Admiral Frederick Carl "Ted" Sherman, who had commanded the first carrier *Lexington* (CV 2) from 1940 until her loss in the 1942 Coral Sea carrier battle. An academy graduate of 1910, Sherman was aggressive and capable but was viewed by some as carrying a chip on his shoulder. His task group included the fleet carriers *Essex* and *Bunker Hill*, and the light carrier *Cowpens*. Sherman fully understood the task at hand with the push toward Japan, especially after Bull Halsey's Third Fleet and Vice Admiral John S. McCain's TF 38 suddenly became Ray Spruance's Fifth Fleet and Pete Mitscher's TF 58. "Each change of command brought a fresh fleet commander determined to outdo his predecessor and to get the most out of his forces," said Sherman.[22]

The last to leave the anchorage was Rear Admiral Matthias B. Gardner's night-fighting TG 58.5. It was spotlighted by the fleet carriers *Enterprise* and *Saratoga*, both veterans of the earliest days of Pacific fighting in 1942, accompanied by two cruisers and a dozen destroyers. Gardner had commanded *Enterprise* from November 1943 until his promotion to task-group commander, whereupon his "Big E" became the first fleet carrier to begin operations in late 1944 with a night air group. *Enterprise* operated with only fifty-four planes—thirty-four Hellcat fighters and twenty-one Grumman Avenger torpedo bombers—as part of her Night Air Group 90. Gardner's two flattops would operate nighttime CAPs and airstrikes while leaving the other four carrier task groups free to handle the traditional daytime operations.

Commander Jimmy Flatley, a fighter hero of 1942's early carrier battles, had been selected by Mitscher in September 1943 to be his staff training officer. He had spent considerable effort supervising the instruction of some sixty fighter, bomber, and torpedo squadrons into 1944, preparing each for deployment on fleet carriers and escort carriers. While the former Grim Reapers leader worked stateside, Mitscher carried out raids with his carrier forces through the Marshalls, New Guinea, the Marianas, and the Carolines in 1944. It was not until August 1944 that Flatley was ordered to become operations officer for the new carrier task force. He was highly recommended to Mitscher by another of his peers, Commander John S. "Jimmy" Thach, another fighter-squadron hero of the early 1942 actions.[23]

Mitscher considered Flatley to be "an outstanding officer in every respect." The commander arrived on board the flagship *Bunker Hill* on September 2, 1944, where he was cordially greeted by his new boss. Mitscher trusted his subordinates to take care of their duties, remarking once, "I tell them what I want, not how." Jimmy knew that the Bald Eagle had a solid grasp on how to utilize a multi-carrier force, but understood that Mitscher was not one to quickly change his thinking on all tactics. Among those was the admiral's reluctance to use night fighters, a strategy that Flatley would have to delicately prove to Mitscher in the coming months.[24]

Between Mitscher and Flatley in the order of command was Commodore Burke, with whom Mitscher had developed a stronger trust with in their past year of campaigning in the Pacific. Flatley took a liking to Burke, and the trio's respect for each other would make a force to be reckoned with by the time TF 58 departed for Tokyo in early 1945.[25]

Planning for the invasions of Iwo Jima and Okinawa had commenced in November and December of 1944, and included meetings in Pearl Harbor involving Mitscher, Burke, Flatley, and their key staff members. The captain had arrived at Ulithi on January 25, 1945, to join Mitscher's staff on the flagship *Bunker Hill*. He had spent considerable time reviewing the latest weapons available for the carrier aircraft and drafting plans for the missions ahead. Once at sea, Mitscher's staff of 130 officers and men put in long hours each day, fueled by coffee and cigarettes from 0315 into the late hours. The chain-smoking Mitscher was nearly matched by Flatley, who admitted to consuming an average of thirty cigarettes per day in 1945.[26]

As operations officer, Flatley drew up the plans for carrier-combat implementation, which were then modified or approved by Commodore Burke before he presented them to Mitscher. The Bald Eagle rarely consumed each report, instead nodding his assent to allow his trusted peers to carry forth the plans he was briefed on. When it came time to brief the squadron commanders, Flatley ran the show.

Once TF 58 hit the open waters, its mission was soon made available to sailors and aviators alike. The carrier pilots were aware of the air-support role for Iwo Jima's invasion, and all CAGs had received support briefings at Ulithi. Mitscher finally made his intentions known by having Commander Flatley post a memorandum titled "Air Combat Notes for Pilots" on the bulletin boards in each ready room. "The coming raid on Tokyo will produce the greatest air victory for carrier aviation," the admiral predicted. "The battle will be primarily a fighter combat. The enemy will be forced to come up to protect the capital of his empire. In his eagerness and inexperience will he meet his downfall in great numbers but only if you keep your heads and apply your teamwork to the utmost."[27]

Mitscher's notes included specific details on how to execute fighter sweeps, engage enemy aircraft, deliver bombs, conduct strafing runs, and effectively rendezvous following combat operations. "Over one-half of our air groups are inexperienced in carrier operations," the admiral warned. "Squadron commanders and experienced pilots must stress the little points that mean the difference between a smooth carrier operation and a sloppy one." He concluded: "Let's bear down every minute between now and the big day, which you alone can make the greatest day in history for naval aviation, AND THE SADDEST DAY FOR THE JAPS."[28]

In addition to Mitscher's memo, the plans for striking Tokyo were announced over the public-address system throughout the fleet on the afternoon of February 10. On *Bunker Hill*, the crew's reaction to Captain George A. Seitz's announcement was electric. "The cheers were so loud there was concern that the Japanese some 1500 miles away might hear us," said VMF-221 fighter pilot Ralph Glendinning.[29]

Ensign Tilman E. "Tilly" Pool, a member of *Hornet*'s VF-17 Hellcat squadron, also called Fighting Seventeen, had been impressed with the view of the vast armada departing Ulithi. The Tokyo destination announcement made by *Hornet* skipper Captain Austin K. Doyle was met with equal enthusiasm. "Everyone cheered at first," said Pool. "Then they kinda got quiet as we did some thinking about it. Those of us making the strikes were expecting wall to wall Japanese fighters to greet us."[30]

The conquest of Iwo Jima was the mission at hand, and the fleet included some reporters. The most famous of them was Scripps-Howard war correspondent Ernie Pyle, who landed on the light carrier *Cabot* with its air group. He was treated like a celebrity, even being presented in the wardroom with a large white cake whose pink icing read, "Welcome aboard, Mr. Pyle." He was amazed by the vast size of TF 58 as it was under way. "The eye could easily encompass the formation in which we were sailing," he wrote. On the third day at sea, Admiral Mitscher sent over a message to *Cabot* to check on Pyle. "How is Ernie getting along? Does he wish he was back in a foxhole?" *Cabot* messaged back that Pyle was happy, had not yet gotten seasick, and hoped that all his future foxholes could be as plush as his current one.[31]

Mitscher certainly made impressions on the people serving around him. Commander Flatley would later write that Mitscher was "the greatest combat Admiral of World War II."[32]

The hours and days ahead were consumed with final preparations, keeping most too busy to have time to worry. Yet the prospect of pushing so deep into enemy waters was never far from mind. A line from the bulletin of *Yorktown*'s posted plan of the day well summarized the mindset for this new offensive: "Underway for Indian Country."[33]

Appropriately enough for the upcoming action, TF 58 commander Pete Mitscher would use the call sign "Mohawk."[34]

Chapter Two

UGAKI'S THUNDER GODS

It was only fitting that on February 10, 1945—the very day that Marc Mitscher's U.S. carrier fleet got under way from Ulithi—his new chief antagonist was being commissioned by the emperor of Japan. Matome Ugaki woke at 0500, preparing himself for a fresh start to pull from the depressing weeks he had recently spent near his modest coastal hometown of Atami, located just sixty miles southwest of Tokyo. Balding and slight in stature, Ugaki carried himself with a stern, unsmiling composure that led some of his subordinates to nickname him "The Golden Mask," in reference to a Japanese comic superhero.[1]

Vice Admiral Ugaki seldom strayed from his strict, impassive nature except for when drinking sake, the rice wine of high alcohol content in which he indulged for relief from the stern Japanese code. With iron will and burning pride, he had served his emperor and country ably for more than three decades. He was willing to die for both, having no fears in doing so.[2]

Born to a family of samurai ancestors in the small city of Okayama on western Honshu, Ugaki had graduated from the Eta Jima Imperial Japanese Naval Academy in 1912, placing ninth out of 144 cadets. His early years of service were spent on cruisers and battlecruisers and as a destroyer gunnery officer. Ugaki rose to the rank of lieutenant commander in 1924 after graduating from the Naval Staff College. He later served as an instructor at the Naval War College and held a staff position with the Combined Fleet before commanding the cruiser *Yakumo* and then the battleship *Hyuga*.

15

Ugaki rose to the rank of rear admiral on November 15, 1938. A deeply religious man who read ancient Buddhist texts and practiced the nationalistic religion Shinto, he was appointed in late 1941 as the chief of staff for Admiral Isoroku Yamamoto, the supreme leader of the Combined Fleet. As he helped plan for the December 7, 1941, attacks on the U.S. Pacific Fleet at Pearl Harbor, Ugaki began to see the wisdom of his new boss: Japan could not survive a long war given its resource limitations. Ugaki thus pledged a death wish: he would not survive the war and would go down fighting.

Ugaki began keeping a diary in the fall of 1941, one that would grow into a fifteen-volume set by the end of World War II. In these journals he scrawled entries about his country's military progress, its setbacks, its strategies, regular updates on the weather, the progress of his adversaries, and personal reflections on his life's own high points and bitter losses. His thoughts—and often his prose—turned each April to mourning his wife, Tomoko, who died in 1940. As Ugaki approached the third anniversary of his wife's death, he narrowly cheated his own demise on April 18, 1943, when the two airplanes he and Admiral Yamamoto were traveling in were shot down by sixteen P-38 fighters of the 339th Fighter Squadron from Guadalcanal's Henderson Field.[3]

Although badly injured, Ugaki was one of only two survivors when his plane crashed violently into the ocean. "Contrary to my determination to sacrifice myself for the commander in chief, instead I lost him and survived," he lamented afterward, dreaming of vengeance during his months of recovery. "I should be resigned to my fate, deeming it God's will, and do my best to live and serve to repay God by carrying out revenge."[4]

While Ugaki convalesced, his country's early good fortunes were in decline. In the early months of World War II, the military forces of

Admiral Isoroku Yamamoto, commander in chief of the IJN's Combined Fleet, is seen at center in April 1943 at Lakunai Airfield near Rabaul, New Britain. To Yamamoto's left is Vice Admiral Matome Ugaki as the officers watch an A6M3 Zero fighter taxiing to takeoff. The planes carrying both Ugaki and Yamamoto would be shot down soon after this photo was taken. *Imperial Japanese Navy*

forty-one-year-old Emperor Hirohito—the 124th emperor of Japan, according to the traditional order of succession—had built an empire that stretched across twenty million square miles and included one-tenth of the world. But the mighty giant's control had begun to slip with a string of defeats beginning at Midway and Guadalcanal in 1942, after which the U.S. military began strong offensive operations in 1943 that would continue in a series of campaigns that slowly began to tax Japan's grip on its reign over the central and eastern Pacific.[5]

The vice admiral's first chance for revenge came with his appointment as commander of the 1st Battleship Division, which went to sea in February 1944 and included the world's largest battleships, *Nagato*, *Yamato*, and *Musashi*. The Japanese suffered heavily in both the Philippine Sea and Leyte Gulf naval actions that followed, the first proving to be devastating to their naval air arm and the latter being equally destructive in terms of warships. Although Leyte was a solid American victory, Admiral Halsey's carrier forces had been subjected to a new weapon that would soon become Ugaki's special personal project.

Translated as "divine wind," the term *kamikaze* gained considerable attention during the fall of 1944. The Divine Wind concept originated from a thirteenth-century typhoon that wrecked a Mongolian fleet, thus sparing Japan from an imminent invasion. Pilots undergoing training during 1944 had suicide tactics as part of their curriculum. "The idea that we were practicing to die" struck home with army aviation cadet Yasuo Kuwahara. "It was taken for granted that any pilot with a disabled plane would do his best to die in true samurai tradition, provided he couldn't make it back to home territory."[6]

Captain Motoharu Okamura was the first officer to propose intentional kamikaze-attack tactics in mid-June 1944. The Japanese credit the first official such strike to Rear Admiral Masafumi Arima, who led one hundred Judy dive bombers against the carrier *Franklin* (CV 13) on October 15, 1944. Although the admiral was killed in action, part of one of his planes struck the U.S. carrier; the attack leader was posthumously promoted to vice admiral. Just over a week later, on October 21, another Japanese aircraft deliberately crashed into the foremast of the heavy cruiser HMAS *Australia*, killing thirty and wounding sixty-four others.

On October 25 the Kamikaze Special Attack Force carried out a fully planned mission. Five Mitsubishi A6M Type 0 carrier fighter planes—known formally by the Allied code name "Zeke," but popularly called "Zero" by many U.S. pilots—led by Lieutenant Yukio Seki made suicide attacks on several U.S. escort carriers during the Battle of Leyte Gulf. Most were destroyed in their attacks on the carriers *Kitkun Bay* (CVE 71),

The escort carrier *St. Lo* (CVE 63) explodes after being hit by a kamikaze on October 25, 1944, off Samar during the Battle of Leyte Gulf. *80-G-270516, NARA*

Fanshaw Bay (CVE 70), and *White Plains* (CVE 66), but one Zero plowed into the flight deck of *St. Lo* (CVE 63). Its bombs created fires that detonated *St. Lo*'s bomb magazine, sinking the carrier. The Divine Wind was just beginning to blow.

By October 26, kamikazes from the Special Attack Force had hit more than forty other ships, including six escort carriers. In the month that followed, other kamikazes caused major damage to the fleet carriers *Intrepid* (CV 11) (twice hit), *Franklin, Belleau Wood, Lexington, Essex, Hancock*, and *Cabot*. Ugaki wrote of the kamikazes in his diary, "I'm glad to see that, as the situation becomes critical, this kind of attack method comes to the fore without compulsion, thus displaying our glorious way of warriors."[7]

These early successes fueled further development of the kamikaze program, and special units were formed to defend the Tokyo metropolitan area. Some pilots were even ordered to ram their aircraft into U.S. Army Air Force B-29s when they attacked Japan, but this proved to have little effect. The kamikaze program was in full swing as Vice Admiral Ugaki returned from the ill-fated Leyte Gulf naval actions. A major fleet reorganization in November 1944 disbanded his 1st Battleship Division, leaving him temporarily without an official assignment.

Japanese losses in the Pacific led to crisis mode within its naval leadership, especially as oil imports declined. The remaining IJN battleships were relegated to antiaircraft duty, and Hirohito's warships seldom ventured far from their homeports toward year's end. The struggle for Leyte had cost the country some 60,000 men dead from combat or from starvation and disease. Allied forces also clamped down on imports, resulting in food shortages that caused great suffering among Japanese civilians and the soldiers still holding various island conquests throughout the Pacific.[8]

"We have been pressed into a corner, and the rise and fall of the empire is now at stake," Ugaki wrote in early 1945. He felt despair during two months of relative inaction on his part, and his diary entries became less detailed as he toiled in gloom and depression. On February 9, as Ugaki was wasting away another afternoon in his modest Atami home over a bottle of sake, he received a phone call ordering him to meet with Emperor Hirohito the following morning. As fate would have it, U.S. Army Air Forces B-29 bombers forced the meeting to be called off by pounding the Nakajima aircraft factory at Ota.[9]

Although the ceremony was canceled, Ugaki was still appointed the new commander in chief of the IJN's 5th Air Fleet. That evening he enjoyed a dinner party with the navy minister and the chief of the Naval General Staff. "I'm now appointed to a very important post, which has the key to determine the fate of the empire, with the pick of the Imperial Navy available at present," Ugaki wrote in his diary.

While Japan's naval might had been greatly diminished by the end of 1944, the country's aircraft industry had still been capable of turning out almost 2,000 combat planes per month at midyear. This production rate began to decline during the fall of 1944 due to deteriorating economic conditions, the necessity to move aircraft construction underground, and the increase in American strategic bombing and naval bombardment against Japanese bases. Total aircraft strength as of January 1, 1945, was estimated at 4,100 planes, down 1,400 in quantity in six months.[10]

More alarming to Vice Admiral Ugaki than the decline in total available air strength was the fact that pilot flight-hour experience had plunged from an average of 700 hours flight time in early 1942 to less than 300 hours by January 1945. During the Leyte Gulf battles, Japan's carriers had served merely as sacrificial decoys, and by early 1945 the kamikaze corps—which had expended 650 suicide planes during the Leyte campaign—had almost entirely replaced the deployment of Japanese carrier-based striking forces.[11]

Aside from the traditional pilots who flew fighters and fighter-bombers into enemy shipping, Ugaki inherited a new weapon, whose pilots became known as the "Thunder Gods." The special suicide vessel was the brainchild of Special Service sub-lieutenant Shoichi Ota, a bearded, broadshouldered, young navigator who had penciled a crude drawing of a glide bomber with rocket-engine boosters that could be towed to a target vicinity beneath a twin-engine Mitsubishi G4M medium bomber (code-named "Betty" by the American military). Ota's superweapon project was given the codename Maru Dai. He pitched this manned suicide weapon to the general staff in July 1944 during the Marianas campaign.[12]

The first two aircraft emerged from production in early September. The Maru Dai planes were given the shorter name "Ohka," meaning "exploding cherry blossom," as the project moved forward. The first one hundred Ohkas were packed and loaded on board the new supercarrier *Shinano* on November 27, 1944, where they would be transported to the port city of Kure at the southern end of Kyushu for deployment to Formosa and the Philippines.[13]

En route to Kure, *Shinano* was intercepted by the U.S. submarine *Archerfish*. Hit by four torpedoes, the carrier plunged to the bottom hours later, taking down her load of Ohkas. This setback was only temporary, however, for by early December another production run of the wood-and-aluminum planes had been shipped to Kure for disbursement. The Thunder Gods program was further set back when the submarine *Redfish* torpedoed and sank the carrier *Unryu* on December 19, sending another thirty-eight unused Ohkas to the ocean floor. Another carrier, *Ryuho*, managed to dodge the deadly American "pigboats" to offload fifty-eight Ohkas at Formosa that same month. But the eager young Ohka pilots would sit idle through January and February 1945, awaiting their first chance to see action.[14]

The Thunder Gods Special Attack Corps had been officially organized on October 1, 1944. The unit—officially the 721st Naval Flying Corps—included a special-attack component plus Betty bombers (serving as Ohka transports) and fighter-escort squadrons. A sign attached to the front of the main gate at Konoike Airfield read "Kaigun Jinrai Butai" (Navy Thunder Gods Corps). Its members continued training even as the first Ohkas were lost to the American submarines.[15]

Admiral Soemu Toyoda, commander in chief of the Combined Fleet, came to Konoike in late December to visit the 721st's pilots, presenting each of them with a short sword and a white headband emblazed Thunder Gods in red Japanese characters. Supplementary pilots were transferred into the program during January, some fresh from the Naval Training School, others new graduates from the reserve-officer training programs. "They had finished only the most basic level of flight training and were barely able to maintain horizontal flight," said Lieutenant Hatsusho Naito, a technician involved in testing the Ohka planes.[16]

On January 20 Admiral Toyoda ordered the 11th Aviation Group—comprising the Thunder Gods Corps and the Kamikaze Special Attack Force—to move to Kyushu, the southernmost main island of Japan. Plans were made to deploy Ohka groups as widely as possible to bases on Kyushu and Taiwan to maximize their destructive effect. Kanoya Airfield would serve as the headquarters for the Thunder Gods Corps as plans were formulated on how best to defend against an impending invasion by the Americans. The Kamikaze Special Attack Force and the Thunder Gods Corps were both reorganized on February 10 into the 5th Naval Aviation Fleet (or 5th Air Fleet), placed under the direction of a new leader, Vice Admiral Ugaki. He alone would direct the final effort to stem the rising American tide in the Pacific.

Ugaki spent his first days in command attending combined table maneuvers of the fleets, naval stations, and bases while being briefed about his enemy's situation and strength. By Tuesday, February 13, he was aware that Admiral Mitscher's carrier fleet had gotten under way from Ulithi. The following afternoon Ugaki flew from Atsugi Airfield near Tokyo to the Thunder Gods headquarters at Kanoya, where he hoisted his command flag in a newly constructed base house. Search planes that afternoon located vessels of the U.S. amphibious force bound for Iwo Jima but failed to uncover the carrier task groups. "The probability of the enemy task force attacking the Tokyo area isn't small," Ugaki wrote on the fifteenth.[17]

The Japanese estimated the Americans would attempt an invasion of Okinawa by April 1, and they planned to challenge it strongly. More than four thousand aircraft were assembled for airstrikes to be launched from Kyushu, which would feature *tekko* (kamikaze) units to destroy the invasion force and its naval support. Formosa-based 8th Air Division of the Imperial Army and the IJN's 1st Air Fleet would be half of the two-pronged air campaign against American ships, while the balance fell to the IJN's 5th Air Fleet—the Kyushu-based naval wing under Ugaki.[18]

Japanese Army command was quick to write off Okinawa, while Navy leadership was eager to commit every ship and plane available to the operation. Isamu Cho, chief of staff to Lieutenant General Mitsuru Ushijima, believed that if kamikaze strikes could score heavily against enemy warships and transports, the Thirty-Second Army could potentially smash the American invasion. Ushijima, emboldened by these reports from Cho, issued three fighting slogans on February 15 for both his troops and the kamikaze boats and aircraft:

One plane for every warship.
One boat for one ship.
One man for ten of the enemy or one tank.[19]

The Kamikaze Special Attack Force and the Thunder Gods would factor heavily into the success or failure of the impending campaign for Okinawa. But Vice Admiral Ugaki correctly suspected that an American assault on Tokyo-area airfields would occur before his Divine Wind could take flight.

Chapter Three

HELLCATS, CORSAIRS, AND THE BIG BLUE BLANKET

The fighter squadrons of TF 58's sixteen carriers were filled with young men excited to strike at the Japanese mainland, but few more eager than Lieutenant Commander Marshall U. Beebe of *Hornet's* VF-17, also referred to as Fighting Seventeen.

Having survived the sinking of the escort carrier *Liscome Bay* in November 1943, Beebe carried more than a fair amount of desire for vengeance against the Japanese. His injuries sustained in the loss of his carrier had taken time to heal. "I was just one big blister from the intense heat," he said. During his recovery, he spent days peeling "just like a snake." Married in 1939, Beebe had been flying for years, including a stint in the Philippines, before war commenced for America. He briefly commanded an F4U Corsair squadron, VF-304, which was later dissolved, before being tapped to reorganize Fighting Seventeen for a second tour in the Pacific theater.[1]

Beebe assumed command of the new VF-17 on April 18, 1944, at NAS Alameda, California, with twenty veteran pilots under his charge. He pulled a handful of pilots from his former VC-39 *Liscome Bay* squadron, including Frank Sistrunk, Joe Farrell, George McFedries, and Dick Cowger. In addition, he retained a dozen veteran pilots from VF-18, which had served a Pacific tour on the carrier *Bunker Hill*.

Training consumed the balance of the year before VF-17 moved toward the combat theater. On January 11, 1945, Beebe's massive unit was broken into two thirty-six-plane squadrons, VF-17 and VBF-17. Beebe's executive officer, Lieutenant Commander Hugh Nicholson, an experienced dive-bomber pilot who had attacked Japanese carriers in 1942 during the

Battle of the Coral Sea, was tapped to take command of VBF-17. Two weeks later—ten and a half months after its formation—VF-17 and the rest of Air Group 17 went on board the carrier *Hornet* to replace its outgoing Air Group 11. Marsh Beebe knew that in mere days he would finally have the chance to avenge his lost *Liscome Bay* pilots and shipmates.

As with all carrier fighter squadrons, VF-17 would spend a considerable portion of its time flying combat air patrol (CAP) duty above the task group to protect the ships from enemy air attacks. Each fighter squadron could expect additional combat duties when the fast-carrier fleet went on the offensive during the upcoming Iwo Jima campaign, among them flying CAP duties above the island or above radar-picket ships, conducting fighter sweeps to knock down Japanese aircraft over their home airfields, and making strikes with bombs, rockets, and guns against enemy installations and shipping.

A fighter squadron's specialty was engaging enemy aircraft. Lieutenant Commander Beebe was commanding his third fighter squadron as the war entered its fourth year, but he had yet to engage an enemy aircraft in action. Many of his veteran pilots from VF-18 had scored aerial victories, but the skipper was still a combat virgin.

VF-17 was organized into twelve divisions of four pilots each. With more pilot divisions than the thirty-six planes allotted, Beebe was assured of always having fresh men to rotate out on missions each day. Each division included five pilots as a combat team, the one extra man allowing for some personnel rotation. The squadron's dozen divisions included one dedicated to aerial photography and one assigned to CAG 17 Edmond Konrad.

The first division of VF-17, called "Fighting One" by its pilots, was headed by Beebe and his regular wingman, Lieutenant (jg) Robert Chester "Bud" Good. Lieutenant Sistrunk led Beebe's second section of Fighting One with three substitute ensigns: Jack Davis, Leonard F. Mallon, and Dave Crist.

Beebe's other division leaders—with the exception of Lieutenant John McIntyre—had served either a previous combat tour with *Bunker Hill's* VF-18 or under Beebe on *Liscome Bay* in 1943. The division leader of "Fighting Nine" was Lieutenant Dick Cowger, from Loveland, Colorado, who had escaped *Liscome Bay's* loss by landing on another carrier the night before his ship's torpedoing. The "Fighting Four" division was led by twenty-six-year-old Lieutenant Ned Langdon, from Sherwood, Ohio, who had shot down one Zeke in November 1943 and was credited with probable destruction of a second one. Being older than many of the junior pilots and possessing a slow drawl in his speech, Langdon was tagged with the nickname "Grandma."

The division leader of "Fighting Two" was Lieutenant (jg) Tommy Harris, from Tamaroa, Illinois, who had scored one kill while with VF-18. The leading scorer of the squadron was Lieutenant Bob Coats from Delhi, Louisiana, who had achieved three kills while flying off *Bunker Hill*. Four other VF-17 division leaders were respected *Bunker Hill* fighter veterans— Lieutenant Millard Junior "Fuzz" Wooley, Lieutenant James Lano Pearce, Lieutenant (jg) Charles Edward "Billy" Watts, and Lieutenant Willis Parker Jr.

Watts, a rail-thin, slight twenty-three-year-old who hailed from the little East Texas settlement of Ben Wheeler, was VF-17's second-leading scorer with 2.25 confirmed aerial victories. In the air group's cruise book, Watts was known as "the lad with the face of a choir boy and the morals of a tom cat." He had been raised as a hard-working farm boy, and during his early childhood his grandfather had given him the nickname "Billy." Like many of his fellow pilots, Billy decided to enter flight training after the Japanese attack on Pearl Harbor. His mother was furious with him when he left East Texas State University after two years and hitchhiked with a buddy to Dallas to join the Army Air Forces. "I was a year too young," he recalled. Watts shuffled off to San Diego and worked for several months before returning to Dallas to enlist in the Navy's V-5 pilot-training program. He managed to pass primary flight training in the old Stearman biplanes before moving on to more-advanced training at NAS Corpus Christi.[2]

After enduring additional months of flight training, Watts was commissioned an ensign in the U.S. Navy on February 16, 1943. He was ordered to San Diego to join VF-18, then a new squadron that was checking out in the Navy's latest fighter plane, the Grumman F6F Hellcat. While waiting for delivery of the faster, more maneuverable Hellcats, Billy decided to try some flights in the F6F's predecessor, the F4F Wildcat.

Watts failed to correct for a stiff crosswind while attempting a landing at Cotati Airfield, a satellite asphalt strip of the Santa Rosa Auxiliary NAS. He consequently plowed the Wildcat into a steep drainage ditch, necessitating his accompanying the damaged fighter back to Alameda on a big flatbed truck. "My skipper, Sam Silber, was kinda teed off with me," Watts later admitted. "In our squadron briefing the next morning, he had someone present me with the Cotati Medal of Honor to embarrass me."[3]

In time Watts earned the respect of Lieutenant Commander Silber once Fighting Eighteen deployed to the Pacific theater on board *Bunker Hill*. His first aerial victory as a fighter pilot came on November 11, 1943, when Air Group 18 participated in a strike on Japanese-held Rabaul Harbor. Watts had accompanied an early strike and was back on board eating a fast lunch when orders came to escort a second strike mission.

Bunker Hill was still launching aircraft at 1325 when her task group was subjected to the several attacks by Japanese planes. Watts cleared the flight deck and was only fifty feet above the waves when he spotted an Aichi D3A "Val" dive bomber pulling out of its attack dive. "He came off at the same level right in front of me," recalled Billy. "I got a little excited. I started shooting even before I got my wheels or flaps up." His tracers tore through the Val. "He started burning and coming apart and splashed in the water. That was my first kill, on my first day of combat."[4]

By the end of the month, Watts had scored a second kill against a Nakajima E8N Type 95 "Dave" single-engine seaplane and shared one-quarter victory on the downing of a land-based Mitsubishi G4M "Betty" attack bomber. With senior division leaders like Watts, Lieutenant Commander Beebe had plenty of reason to feel confident in how his squadron would handle itself in combat during the coming week.

The same eagerness for action was felt within the fighter squadrons on fifteen other flattops moving toward the homeland of Japan.

Each carrier of TF 58 was bristling with fighter planes, a new tactical direction by the Navy to help ward off anticipated counterattacks and kamikazes. Vice Admiral Mitscher's staff air officer, Commander Flatley, already known for having helped develop effective aerial fighter tactics, now implemented a new defensive aerial strategy for the U.S. fleet. He was a veteran fighter pilot who had scored his first two kills flying from the first *Yorktown* at the Coral Sea battle in 1942. During the period of October 25, 1944, to January 13, 1945, some 137 ships were hit by kamikazes, of which 22 were sunk. Flatley soon found that Mitscher's thinking did not rapidly adapt to new tactics, such as the use of fleet night fighters. But the kamikaze threat finally had help convince the admiral to adopt a three-strike system designed to keep enemy planes on the ground when the fast-carrier fleet was operating near Japanese bases.[5]

This new anti-kamikaze doctrine, adopted in late 1944, was nicknamed the "Big Blue Blanket" by Vice Admiral John McCain's chief operations officer, Commander Thach, creator of the fighter tactic known as the "Thach Weave." Regarding kamikaze attacks, Thach once stated that Mitscher "liked to depend on antiaircraft fire and the fighters," tried-and-true tactics versus the new thinking being pushed by Flatley. The three-strike system first involved creating a fighter "blanket" over all enemy airfields within range of the task force, particularly those identified as posing a kamikaze threat. Second, the local Hellcat CAP was increased with twenty to twenty-four F6Fs above each task group, with low-level fighter sections positioned to intercept low-flying suicide aircraft that approached under the radar coverage. Third, pairs of radar-picket destroyers were stationed in the most likely direction of attack at least forty miles from the task force. Each picket group was covered by at least one fighter division overhead to provide forward interception of enemy aerial threats.[6]

Fighter sections and divisions were directed by the task group fighter-director officers (FDOs). Under the Big Blue Blanket doctrine, fighter direction was further relaxed to allow any ship with available fighters and enemy "bogies" (unidentified aircraft) on its radarscope to assume the contact and direct an interception.

This new curtain of fighter policy forced changes within carrier-air-group composition. The large *Essex*-class carriers changed their aircraft mix to include seventy-two fighters instead of fifty-four in December 1944. By February 1945 this was further changed to split the fighters into thirty-six VF and thirty-six VBF units. Within these carrier air groups, Grumman F6F Hellcats fighter planes represented 80 percent of the total fighter force.

The F6F was a great contribution to the Pacific Fleet. In three years Grumman's Long Island factory cranked out more than 12,000 Hellcat airframes. The plane proved to be easy to fly, well armed, and fairly easy to maintain on board a carrier at sea. Each was powered by an 18-cylinder Pratt & Whitney R-2800 Double Wasp radial engine that drove a three-bladed Hamilton Standard propeller. The Hellcat sported a bullet-resistant windshield, cockpit armor, and armor around its oil tank and oil cooler. Standard armament was six .50-caliber (12.7-mm) M2/AN Browning air-cooled machine guns, with 400 rounds available per gun.

Painted in an overall gloss blue finish, the Hellcats had a 250-gallon self-sealing fuel tank fitted into the fuselage and could carry an additional 150-gallon disposable drop tank to extend its range for long missions. Each F6F could carry a total bombload in excess of 2,000 pounds, split between the center-line and underwing bomb racks. Six 5-inch high-velocity aircraft rockets (HVARs) could also be carried, three tucked under each wing. The Navy preferred the flight qualities of the F6F compared to the superior speed of the Vought F4U Corsair, whose carrier-based testing had begun in 1940. The Corsair's design included inverted gull wings that folded directly over the canopy to allow extra space for transport below to the hangar deck on carrier elevators. The F4U began carrier operations in 1943, but the plane proved to be difficult to land on a pitching flight deck. Its stiff landing gear also created a damaging bounce in all but a perfect landing, while low-speed stalls often caused the plane's right wing to drop quickly.[7]

The first Navy squadron to receive the Corsair, Lieutenant Commander Joseph C. Clifton's VF-12, suffered a number of crashes and finally replaced the F4U with the more-readily available Hellcats before deploying to the Pacific. The second Navy Corsair squadron, Lieutenant Commander John Thomas Blackburn's VF-17, believed in the new fighter plane's potential and worked to make the F4U seaworthy for operation on *Bunker Hill*. Blackburn's pilots worked with Vought representatives to solve the F4U's landing-gear problem by experimenting with the oil level and air pressure in the gear strut to alleviate the jolt of landing and its consequent bounce.[8]

The Corsair was generally cast off from carrier operations, relegated to shore-based operations mainly with U.S. Marine units. But the F4U was found to be at least 50 miles per hour faster than the F6F, with a faster climb rate for aerial combat. By the end of 1944, several Marine squadrons took the Corsair back on board fleet carriers while Vought engineers worked at further modifications to the plane. A "tamed" F4U-1D model proved to be better suited for use from carriers, and by early 1945 it was being reintroduced into Navy operations. With top speeds of 413 miles per hour (355 knots) at 20,400 feet, the Corsair proved to be 55 knots faster than a Japanese Zeke.[9]

The move to add Corsairs to the fast-carrier striking force was taken all the way to Washington by Admirals Jocko Clark and Pete Mitscher. They succeeded in getting ten F4U squadrons authorized for carrier deployment, and during the first three months of 1945, five *Essex*-class carriers each received a pair of eighteen-plane Corsair squadrons. The first two Marine squadrons, VMF-124 and VMF-213, went on board *Essex* on December 28.[10]

The two *Essex* Marine squadrons did well, and before TF 58 sortied in February 1945, six more Corsair squadrons had been added to the fast-carrier striking force, with a total of 174 bent-wing F4Us spread among four carrier air groups. The eight Marine squadrons accounted for one-sixth of the total TF 58 fighter strength. *Bennington* hosted a pair of Marine units, VMF-112 and VMF-123, as did *Wasp*, with VMF-217 and VMF-216. Admiral Mitscher's flagship *Bunker Hill* actually hosted three Corsair squadrons: Navy unit VF-84, under Lieutenant Commander Roger Hedrick, and two Marine units, VMF-221, under Major Edwin S. Roberts, and VMF-451, under Major Henry Ellis. *Bunker Hill's* fighter complement was almost entirely Corsairs, with seventy-one of the newer F4U-1Ds allocated to its Air Group 84, with a mere six Hellcats on board to serve as photo-reconnaissance fighters.[11]

Each *Bunker Hill* Marine squadron included significant aces. Wyoming-born Captain Archie Donahue, who completed three years at the University of Texas before entering flight training, was VMF-451's leading ace. He flew both Wildcats and Corsairs while based at Guadalcanal in 1942 and 1943, during which time he amassed a record of fourteen Japanese planes destroyed, including five in a single mission.

Top scorer for VMF-221 was Captain Jim Swett, who had earned the Medal of Honor at age twenty-two on his first combat mission from Guadalcanal on April 7, 1943. Flying a Wildcat, he downed seven Val dive bombers before he was forced to ditch his battle-damaged fighter off Florida Island. Swett was wounded and became trapped in his cockpit as it sank underwater, but he somehow managed to extricate himself and be rescued. By the time his VMF-221, the "Fighting Falcons" squadron, deployed on *Bunker Hill*, Swett already had an impressive 14.5 aerial victories.

Despite the Falcons' record, Mitscher was not endeared to taking the gull-wing Corsairs on board *Bunker Hill*. The carrier's skipper, Captain Seitz, made it clear from the start that he did not want Marine fliers on his ship—that is, until they managed to convince him they had "the right stuff." As Swett recalled: "When we first flew out to the ship, we had our Corsairs coming aboard only about twenty seconds apart. That really impressed him [Seitz], and he finally agreed that we could handle it."[12]

Swett proved to be a key mentor to many of his younger Marine Corsair pilots, including twenty-two-year-old 2nd Lieutenant Dean Caswell. The young Texan had first boarded *Bunker Hill* at San Francisco for the carrier's transit to the Central Pacific while he was suffering from a nasty bout of flu. The rolling and tossing of a warship at sea did not agree with the young officer, whose first meal in the wardroom was less than settling. "If I was a natural sailor, it didn't show," noted Caswell.[13]

Being cast into a Navy ship did not suit Caswell at the start, having been trained to fly air support for fellow Marines on the ground. He and his comrades took every chance to ruffle the feathers of their Navy shipmates by using nonnaval terminology such as "left" and "right" versus "port" and "starboard" and by failing to use "ship" as the proper term for their vessel. "We always called it a boat in front of Navy personnel," recalled Caswell. "That made them pissed as hell."[14]

Caswell still held brown-shoe admirals in higher regard, particularly Mitscher for the boldness he had shown in turning on the carrier lights during the Philippine Sea battle to save returning air crews from ditching in the ocean. The lieutenant was pleased with the speed and maneuverability of his Corsair, even if it proved more challenging than an F6F to land on a carrier deck.

During training he had performed a violent evasive maneuver known as a snap roll, but the stunt had nearly been his last. Caswell had been assigned to be an enemy "bogey" in a simulated fight against Captain Swett's division. Swett quickly picked up Caswell's F4U closing on them in a dive that exceeded 400 miles per hour. As the captain turned left to counter the "enemy" plane, the lieutenant immediately snapped his stick right and kicked right rudder. "There was a tremendous jerk and the plane started spinning like a corkscrew," he said. His Corsair went into such violent spinning that Caswell momentarily thought of bailing out before he was able to regain control.[15]

Back on the ground, his division leader, Captain John Delancey, was astounded. "You did seven snap rolls in a row! How did you do that?"

"I didn't have the heart to tell him that I didn't even have my hands on the stick," recalled Caswell.

A handful of TF 58 pilots alternately flew both Hellcats and Corsairs during the spring of 1945. One of them was Pittsburgh native Lieutenant (jg) Edward Pappert, whose carrier sported both a VF Hellcat squadron and a VBF Corsair squadron. As pilots and planes were lost in his F6F unit, Pappert was occasionally tapped to fly rotation on F4U missions. "Both airplanes were tough," he noted. "Both returned with holes big enough to throw a basketball through. The Hellcat was easier to fly. It was more forgiving." During his first two carrier landings in a Corsair, Pappert floated in nose up until his arresting gear caught a wire on the deck, although his speed ripped the tail hook from his plane on one occasion.[16]

Task Force 58 thus stood to sea on the offensive with a mixed bag of seasoned and green Corsair and Hellcat pilots across the sixteen carrier air groups. Some squadrons were blooded, having seen action in late 1943 and into 1944. VF-30, for example, had achieved fifty aerial victories while based on the light carrier *Monterey* (CVL 26) through March 1944. For its second war cruise, the squadron was deployed on *Belleau Wood*, but its pilots would continue to build on their success. While *Lexington*'s VF-9 was returning to combat for a second tour, seven of the fast-carrier striking force air groups would be embarking on their first combat operations in February 1945. Regardless of their experience level, the airmen were enthusiastic about the chance to strike at mainland Japan.[17]

The mixed Navy and Marine air groups had a collective purpose as they readied for their first strikes on mainland Japan. What they might accomplish in the lead-up to what planners designated Operation Iceberg could make a significant difference in the Pacific War.

Chapter Four

OPERATION ICEBERG AND THE "MOWING MACHINE"

The fast-carrier fleet's move toward Japan was part of a larger plan, dubbed Operation Iceberg. The most powerful U.S. Navy push against mainland Japan in its history was a two-fold operation, to serve as both a diversion for the imminent invasion of Okinawa and to destroy Japan's ability to launch air assaults on the amphibious fleet bearing down on the Ryukyu Islands.

Almost a year before the invasion of Okinawa, Pacific-theater strategy had been discussed in San Francisco by Admiral Ernest J. King, chief of naval operations and commander in chief of the U.S. Navy; Admiral Nimitz, commander in chief, Pacific Fleet; and Admiral "Bull" Halsey, then commander of the Third Fleet. Arguments were made to bypass the Philippine Islands with an invasion of Formosa (present Taiwan), but strong opposition by General Douglas MacArthur to uphold his promise to return to the Philippines was taken into account by both Nimitz and President Roosevelt.

The Marianas campaign was in full swing by June 1944, and by August Saipan had been conquered. Nimitz advised King in early October that MacArthur should land on Luzon in the Philippines during December, while his naval forces would move first against Iwo Jima in the Volcano Islands and then against Okinawa by March 1, 1945. The overall campaign was dubbed Operation Iceberg, with the plan being that securing Iwo Jima and Okinawa would provide the Allies with bases from which to launch bombers and fighters for the final push to assault Japan itself before year's end.

The Ryukyu Islands form the majority of the Nansei Shoto group that run in a gentle curve between the southernmost of the Japanese home islands, Kyushu, and Formosa. Five major groups—Osumi, Torkara, Amami, Okinawa, and Sakishima Guntos (gunto meaning "group")—make up the 161-island chain, with Okinawa Gunto being the largest. Located 320 miles southwest of Kyushu, Okinawa is 64 miles in length and varies in width between 2 miles and 18 miles. Most of its coastline consists of limestone cliffs, while its interior is laced with rugged terrain rising to 1,500-foot ridgelines in places. Two significant Japanese airfields, Yontan and Kadena, lay on the central plains, with some 110,000 troops manning strong and well-prepared defenses on the island.

Seizing the Okinawa airfields was key, as violent air attacks on any invasion fleet were expected. The landing date for U.S. Marine and U.S. Army divisions was moved back to April 1, 1945, in what was expected to be the largest simultaneous amphibious assault of the Pacific War. Admiral Spruance, one of the heroes of the Battle of Midway, was now in charge of the Fifth Fleet forces that would support these landings. Just weeks before, on January 26, he had relieved Halsey as commander of the Third Fleet. Overnight, the carrier armada changed its name to the Fifth Fleet and designated TF 58. Vice Admiral Mitscher, as commander of the fast-carrier force, would direct the five carrier task groups.

It had been nearly three years since Halsey had led the first carrier strike against Japan proper. The second coming under Mitscher would be something to reckon with.

One of the veteran fighter pilots who planned to make a difference against Japan's aerial opponents was Lieutenant Gene Valencia, leader of a tactically polished division dubbed the "Mowing Machine."

Valencia had cut his teeth in dogfighting during his first tour with VF-9 on the carrier *Essex* during late 1943 and early 1944. In that time, he had shot down 7.5 enemy planes (one shared kill) and had received credit for damaging a Japanese Zeke fighter. He and his shipboard roommate, Lieutenant (jg) Bill Bonneau, had each scored their first confirmed kills against Zekes on November 11, 1943, over Rabaul Harbor.

He achieved ace status three months later on February 17, 1944, while participating in TF 58's raid on Japan's premiere shipping harbor at Truk Lagoon. Valencia tangled with aggressive Zeke fighters that landed 7.7-mm machine-gun hits in his F6F, but he knocked down three of his opponents. "I discovered at Truk that once you take the offensive, the Jap doesn't know

Lieutenant Gene Valencia of VF-9 would finish World War II as one of the Navy's top aces. Raised as Gene Powell, he would later discover both his true ancestry and a strong desire for aviation. His "Mowing Machine" Hellcat division (later known as the "Flying Circus") would serve on both the carriers *Lexington* (CV 16) and *Yorktown* (CV 10) during the Okinawa campaign in 1945. *80-G-329441, NARA*

what to do," he later stated. Valencia's confidence in the F6F Hellcat had been boosted tremendously by the end of his *Essex* tour with VF-9.[1]

Fighting Nine's war cruise wrapped up, with its pilots claiming 120 total aerial kills, another 8 probably destroyed, and 124 planes destroyed on the ground. Ten of those men had become aces, led by Lieutenant Hamilton McWhorter with 10 kills, Mayo Hadden with 8, and Valencia with 7.5 victories. Air Group 9 afterward returned to the States, where the pilots were offered a month's leave to reunite with their families before returning for their next assignments.

Valencia enjoyed the reunion in California with his wife, Jeanne Ann Doyle Valencia, the high school sweetheart he had married in 1943. Her father, Charles Michael Doyle, was a former aviator himself, having seen service during World War I. California had long been home to the Valencia family. Eugene Anthony Valencia had been born on April 13, 1921, in San Francisco into a family of Spanish and European descent. His parents were divorced when he was a year old, and Gene never saw much of his father, also Eugene Valencia, whose wealthy family owned extensive land grants in the San Francisco area. Gene's mother, Myrtle Eleanor (Loveing) Valencia, later married Ed Powell, and the couple quickly changed their young son's name to Eugene Powell. Gene's Spanish ancestry played little into his physical appearance, which trended more toward his European genes. He was light skinned, with black hair and brown eyes, and his face tended to freckle slightly.[2]

His birth name was kept secret from him for many years, as his mother feared her former husband's wealthy family might attempt to take him away. He went through Alameda High School as Gene Powell, graduated

Two of Valencia's VF-9 squadron commanders are seen in February 1944 with the squadron's scorecard. It includes kills of French Vichy planes downed during the unit's service in the North Africa campaign. Squadron skipper Herb Houck (*center*) took over Air Group 9 after Lieutenant Commander Phil Torrey (*right*) was killed in February 1945. *80-G-217606, NARA*

in 1939, and attended San Francisco Junior College for two years. There he participated in football and boxing, was president of the Associated Students of SFJC, and was a member of Phi Lambda Epsilon.

Gene had marveled at airplanes since he was a toddler and within years was building his own balsawood models. His first flight was at age twelve, but his formal flight training began in the Oakland Airport's Civil Aeronautics Authority (CAA) program while he was attending San Francisco Junior College. Valencia and three other students pooled their money to buy a Luscombe light plane. He completed his primary, advanced, and acrobatic courses with honors at Alameda by age nineteen, the youngest of thirty California students to do so. It was only when he applied for military service that the young man learned of his birth name, Valencia, which became the surname he used from that point onward.

One of Valencia's closest friends during the Oakland Airport CAA program was Bill Bonneau, who would later fly with him on two combat tours in VF-9. Shipboard roommates, Valencia and Bonneau were dubbed the Navy's "Flying Twins," as they had worked hard to be reunited again in 1942 after Valencia had been originally assigned to flight-instructor duties. Both had emerged from their first combat tour in 1944 as aces and were pleased to be reassigned together to the revamped Fighting Nine.

Valencia's time at home was all too brief before he received orders to return to VF-9, which reformed at NAS Pasco, Washington, on April 19, 1944. The new CAG 9 was Lieutenant Commander Philip Huston

Torrey Jr., and VF-9 was headed by Lieutenant Commander Herbert Norman Houck. Training for the thirty-six-plane Hellcat squadron began right away, and Valencia set to work.

At Pasco the returning ace was eager to perfect new tactics to exploit weaknesses in Japanese fighter-pilot techniques he had observed during his fights with the Zekes over Truk. Valencia formed a new division, built around three energetic young pilots. Ensign Joseph Howard Roquemore, a twenty-one-year-old who hailed from Ponca City, Oklahoma, became his trusted wingman. Valencia's second section was led by James Barber French, a blond-haired, good-looking Ohioan who had attended the University of California before joining the Navy in 1942. French's wingman was twenty-three-year-old Clinton Lamar "Smitty" Smith from Yazoo City, Mississippi. "I insisted on three men who really loved fighting, and I got 'em," recalled Valencia. "They called my new gang the three 'Eager Ensigns.'"[3]

French had taken up civilian pilot training at the age of eighteen. He had been encouraged by his grandmother, Dora C. Barber, after she had taken her first passenger flight across the United States while in her seventies: "She was so enthusiastic about it, she came back urging me to take up flying and said she'd take it up herself if she were younger." His father, Harold S. French, had been an Army pilot in France during World War I, where he was shot down and injured. Once he departed for the war zone, Ensign French would frequently send letters to his grandmother, kidding her for getting him into aviation but also giving her due credit.[4]

As the only blooded veteran of the new division, Valencia worked his men hard. During the six months they trained at Pasco, his division flew more than one hundred hours per month, one-third more hours than averaged by the balance of his squadron. The extra flight time required more fuel than was authorized, but his quartet found ways to trade for what they needed. "We just slipped the service crews a few bottles of booze," noted French, "and they filled up our airplanes for us."[5]

Valencia had learned at Truk that a tight offensive attack often threw off the Japanese pilots. In drilling his division in what he termed "mowing machine" tactics, he was able to keep one section always on the offense. The extra efforts and special tactical attention of Valencia's Mowing Machine division drew a certain amount of envy from the other pilots of Air Group 9.

One who took note of the hot-shot division was Ensign Harris Edlow "Mitch" Mitchell, a slight, five-foot-six-inch, brown-haired, twenty-two-year-old Texan who was flying Hellcats with Lieutenant Commander Arthur T. Decker's VBF-9. Mitchell and other pilots watched as Valencia's team practiced both day and night, honing their skills in dummy gunnery runs that focused on both offensive and defensive weave maneuvers. When Valencia's division returned to the airfield, they would buzz the strip in tight formation before sliding into a tight echelon. Each of the four pilots would brake sharply at close intervals as they came in for landings.[6]

Mitch found the division's pilots to be "as inseparable on the ground as they were in the air." Most junior pilots during their downtime drank cans of beer or the occasional bourbon or scotch with water. But Mitch found with Valencia's division, "there was always something special at the bar for that group, like Mint Julips in frozen glasses or champagne cocktails." Minor envy aside, Mitchell recognized the God-given leadership abilities of Lieutenant Valencia that enabled such an esprit de corps to be maintained among his chosen men.[7]

Air Group 9 left Pasco in the summer of 1944 and shifted to NAS Alameda, California, in preparations for deploying to sea on board the carrier *Lexington*. Roquemore, Valencia's wingman, was suffering with a severe case of pneumonia at the time, which on October 12 claimed his life. The lieutenant's premiere division was suddenly down one key member as the "Lady Lex" sortied with her task group the following day for the Hawaiian Islands. Adding to the loss of his wingman, Valencia also faced the prospect of a long separation from his wife, who was pregnant with their first child.

Air Group 9 would be based for two months in Hawaii at Kahului on Maui. There the VBF and VF squadrons were combined while Valencia tested out several new young pilots to become his wingman. In the end he settled on Harris Mitchell of VBF-9 as the newest member of his "Mowing Machine" division.

Growing up near the Lone Star State's Gulf Coast in Richmond, young Mitchell had often watched commercial airliners and mail planes flying overhead. On occasion a barnstormer would buzz the town, then land in a nearby field to be surrounded by both kids and adults. While others gazed in awe at the pair of aviators who typically emerged from these antiquated biplanes wearing their flight gear, leather helmets, and goggles, Mitch never felt the urge to cough up the nominal fee requested by the flyboys for the chance at a joyride in their bird.[8]

Mitchell's first flight did not happen for several more years until he was attending Sam Houston State Teachers College in Huntsville, Texas. He accepted a dare from his college roommate—who was taking civilian pilot training—to take a flight in a Piper Cub. Once the United States was swept into World War II, Mitchell began to realize that being a pilot wasn't such a bad option for a young man who was at the prime age to be drafted. "I felt flying an airplane would be easier than carrying a rifle with the infantry," he recalled.[9]

The young Texan entered the naval-aviation cadet program on May 27, 1942. He did his preflight training in Athens, Georgia, before moving on to three months of elimination basic training (E-base) at Olathe, Kansas. As his flight hours increased, so too did his confidence and love of flying. Fifteen months into his training, Mitchell received his commission as ensign and designation as a naval aviator on August 13, 1943, at NAS Pensacola. He continued through operational training in the Douglas SBD Dauntless dive bomber in Jacksonville, Florida, and was then sent to Glenview, Illinois, for carrier qualifications. His training ship on Lake Michigan was *Wolverine* (IX 64), a modified paddle-wheeler serving as a makeshift flattop, on which naval aviators had to "qualify" by making at least five successful landings.[10]

Upon completing this task and enjoying a short leave back home with family, Mitchell had reported to CASU-5 (Carrier Air Service Unit 5) at San Diego, California, for further assignment. In January 1944 he received orders to join VB-301 and trained for six months with the squadron in Santa Rosa, California, in Dauntless dive bombers. His thoughts were of vengeance, having "visions of splendor at being able to drop a bomb on some Japanese ship or shore installation."[11]

Mitchell's dive-bomber training came to an abrupt halt in April, when he received orders to VBF-9, a new fighter-bomber unit being commissioned under skipper Arthur Decker in Pasco, Washington. Mitch quickly made the transition from the Douglas SBD to a Grumman product, the F6F Hellcat. "It was a new concept which allowed fighters to act as bombers," he recalled of the aircraft. "As soon as you dropped your bomb, then you were a fighter." He found the F6F to be a powerful machine, and the feeling of firing its six .50-caliber, water-cooled machine guns was quite a rush.[12]

While Mitchell was comfortable flying the F6F Hellcat, he found all of his previous training to be easier than the newfound pressures he assumed upon joining Valencia's VF-9 division. Mitch realized that the lieutenant was tough on him, likely trying to overcome the months of training that had been lost with Roquemore's death. "Gene was quite critical of we young fledglings," recalled Mitchell. "My tendency was to become despondent but since I knew nothing of aerial combat and this was a military organization, I was hesitant to voice my grievances."[13]

The Texan learned that he must keep his wing within four or five feet of Valencia's horizontal stabilizer or face harsh words following a flight. "I discovered what the perfectionist he was." Mitch took the critique in stride, concentrating on becoming the best he could be. Valencia worked the ensign through the basics of the Thach Weave in Hawaii but incorporated a few refinements of his own design. The principles were basic: whichever way Valencia turned his Hellcat, Mitchell was to be in position to slide in and cover his tail, then the tables would turn as Gene covered Mitch's tail. "With these maneuvers, no Japanese airplane could attack our group without one or two of us having guns trained on them at the same time," noted Mitchell.[14]

Ample time during their Hawaiian layover was also spent in gunnery, rocket, and bombing practice, some against towed target banners in the air, others against targets ashore, and some against towed bombing sleds at sea. Each day the pilots reviewed a schedule sheet to see what activities were assigned to their air group. One day Fighting Nine was assigned to drop bombs on a sled towed far behind the carrier *Saratoga*. They received notice that a Marine division would be in the same area practicing amphibious-assault maneuvers on one of the usual bombing targets, Molokai Rock. All went well as planned until Valencia endured a hung bomb that he could not shake free from his racks.[15]

The manner in which Valencia handled the situation offered his new wingman some insight into his division leader's dark humor. Back at Kahului, the lieutenant quickly ordered some ordnance men to remove the hung bomb and stow it in the bomb-supply shelter. He then casually strolled into the operations building and reported that cover had obscured his target, so instead of wasting his bomb, he had dropped it on Molokai Rock before returning to base. Considerable confusion reigned over the potentially lethal mistake until Valencia finally fessed up that he was just teasing. As Mitchell saw it, "It took hours to get all the details verified and soothe the feathers of the High Priest (CAG), but it certainly put a little action into an otherwise routine day."[16]

The more time Mitchell spent with Valencia, the more he began to appreciate him. Over time he was able to find out little details of the man Eugene Valencia himself. The two pilots' childhoods had run a similar course. Mitchell's father had never been present since just after his son's birth, leaving him, his older brother, and his sister to be raised by his mother, Aileene Campbell Mitchell, who worked hard in the Fort Bend County office to make ends meet. Valencia later admitted that while in Hawaii Mitchell "had the toughest time of all, because he had all three of us riding him night and day." In time, though, he would admit, "I wouldn't fly without him."[17]

Knowing that his division leader had similarly been raised without the presence of his birth father helped Mitchell appreciate his sense of

This VF-9 Hellcat division, first dubbed the "Mowing Machine" and then later the "Flying Circus," would become the most successful U.S. Navy fighter division in history during the Okinawa campaign. *Left to right, in 1945:* Lieutenant (jg) Harris Mitchell, Lieutenant (jg) Clint Smith, Lieutenant (jg) Jim French, and Lieutenant Gene Valencia. *700016, VF-9 Folder, NARA*

humor. On another occasion weeks after the fake bombing incident, Valencia secured the use of a Grumman TBM Avenger that he and Mitchell flew over to Ford Island for the weekend. Before takeoff at the close of their R&R time, the lieutenant secured a number of rolls of toilet tissue and stuffed them in the bomb bay of their torpedo bomber. He climbed the TBM to several thousand feet after takeoff, circled around Pearl Harbor, calculated the wind, opened the bomb-bay doors, and dumped his load of toilet paper to float down over Ford Island. "People all over the base gathered to see what those objects in the sky were that were falling on the air strip," recounted Mitchell.[18]

Valencia's air group shipped out from Hawaii on December 21, 1944, and spent several weeks training on Ponam Island in the Admiralties. Air Group 9 boarded the escort carrier *Barnes* (CVE 20) on January 29, 1945, and reached Ulithi on February 3, just one week before TF 58's departure for Tokyo. Shortly after *Barnes* had anchored, Air Group 9 was ordered aboard the carrier *Lexington* to relieve Air Group 20.

There was little time to settle in, as briefings for VF-9 began immediately in Ready Room No. 1 on the invasion of Iwo Jima and the role that the task force air groups would play in support. With little time for beer parties ashore at Mog Mog Island, the Mowing Machine division found Valencia's work ethic to be contagious. Prior to entering the combat zone, the team had wanted to paint their Hellcats with purple lightning bolts, but they were denied such markings by naval regulations. The division instead individually decorated their flying helmets with striking logos. French opted for the ace of spades on his. Valencia and French always wore white helmets, while Smith wore yellow and Mitchell red.[19]

Ensign Mitchell was excited as Mitscher's TF 58 pounded toward Japan. He was thrilled to finally be assigned to a veteran air group on board a carrier with a solid record. "I was just about the proudest fellow in the whole U.S. Navy," he said. "This is the big league!"[20]

In between training flights, Mitchell learned his way around the maze-like corridors of the massive *Lexington*. Scuttlebutt ran rampant as to what exact targets his squadron would face. By the evening of February 15, TF 58 was plunging northward through stormy seas, low-hanging clouds, and rain squalls cold enough to be on the verge of snow. Briefings finally informed the squadron commanders what Japanese airfields they were to hit the following morning.

Vice Admiral Mitscher had wisely used foul weather to disguise his carrier fleet's approach to the Japanese mainland. "He was the best aerologist in the force," said his chief of staff, Arleigh Burke. "He would get up, smell the air, go around and look, look at the weather charts, look at the data." Mitscher wanted to offer his pilots the best opportunity for surprise and the greatest chance for success. "Everything he did revolved around the effectiveness of his pilots," observed Burke. "He estimated the speed of the front and we stayed with it. We went up there completely undiscovered behind a big wall of bad weather."[21]

Anticipating an early call to flight quarters the next morning, Ensign Mitchell finally stretched out in his bunk on *Lexington* to catch some rest that evening. He had learned that Valencia's VF-9 division would be among the second wave of fighters going over Japan on February 16, launching within sixty miles of the coast of Honshu.

"Adrenalin flowed very freely that night," said Mitchell.[22]

Chapter Five

ACES OVER KYUSHU

Breakfast came early for the aviators scheduled for the first flights on February 16. Duty messengers in sixteen aircraft carriers made the rounds around 0345 to rouse the fighter pilots who would make the first strikes on Tokyo in nearly three years. On *Bunker Hill* 2nd Lieutenant Ralph Glendinning of VMF-221 was pleased yet somewhat apprehensive when he took a seat in the wardroom with a plate of steak and eggs. *Beware, if you're ever in the Navy and they offer you something special for breakfast,* he thought.[1]

In dozens of ready rooms, eager aviators assembled to review the flight boards and copy key data to the navigational plotting charts they called their "Ouija boards." Among the most crucial information to record was Point Option—the precise spot in the ocean where a pilot's carrier could be expected to be found upon the air group's return from its strike. The weather forecast was bleak: wind speeds exceeded twenty-two knots, the seas had five- to six-foot swells, and the ceiling was a mere four thousand feet, with broken clouds hanging at one thousand feet. Visibility would be further hampered by rain and snow squalls, all driven by northeast winds.

Around 0630 the call to flight quarters sent the early strikers scrambling up cold steel ladders onto a flight deck that was shockingly frigid. Normal Pacific flight gear had been padded with thermal underwear by many of the pilots. Lieutenant (jg) Billy Watts of *Hornet's* VF-17 was struck by the irony of the moment. Nearly three years prior, the original *Hornet* had launched Doolittle's Army Air Forces B-25 Tokyo raiders on the first American offensive to pound mainland Japan. Now the second *Hornet* was turning into the wind sixty miles off the coast of Honshu to launch part of the greatest assault the people of Japan had yet endured.

The Bald Eagle hoped the foul weather had properly disguised TF 58's approach, but officially Mitscher reported that his "plan was premised on the assumption of no tactical surprise, and heavy airborne fighter opposition."[2]

A light rain was falling, mixed with snow flurries, as Watts picked his way across the slick, rolling deck to his ready Hellcat. His division was one of three scheduled to launch from *Hornet* before dawn. The pilots and their plane captains operated without flashlights or running lights to prevent their carrier from being an easier target for any lurking Japanese submarine. This precaution mattered little moments later once dozens of radial engines coughed to life with flashes of light and belching flames as propellers began twirling—slowly at first and then becoming deadly, whirling disks of high-speed propulsion.

Watts quickly checked the dimly lit instrument gauges to ensure proper order of all key components. Staged ahead of him were two other divisions of VF-17, the first being that of the squadron executive officer, Lieutenant Ned Langdon. Just after 0645 Langdon taxied up to the takeoff position, whereupon the flight deck officer whirled a flashlight in his right hand, signaling him to run his engine up to full power.

Langdon stood on his brakes, moved his throttle forward, and increased his rpms to 2,700. He saluted the launch officer, who dropped his arm and pointed down the flight deck. Langdon released his brakes and sped down the deck at 0647, followed less than thirty seconds later by his wingman, Lieutenant (jg) Eldridge J. "Nootsie" Courrege, a previous-tour veteran of *Bunker Hill*'s VF-18.

Two planes of "Grandma" Langdon's division suffered engine problems and had to be scratched from launching. Next off was Lieutenant Jim Pearce's division, followed rapidly by the four F6Fs of Watts' own division. Pearce, who had been raised in Detroit as the son of an automotive executive, had left a coveted spot at the prestigious General Motors Technical Institute to take up flight training.[3]

Once airborne, Pearce strained to pick up the wing and tail lights of other VF-17 planes. He was unable to locate the executive officer's lead section amid the skud and would not learn until later that Langdon and Courrege were busy making strafing runs on a Japanese picket boat they found just ten miles ahead of the task force shortly after launching. Langdon and his wingman were never able to rejoin their *Hornet* comrades in the darkness, leaving Pearce to finally assume leadership of the flight. Under radio silence, he moved forward and headed out, leading his own

A pair of *Lexington* SB2C-3 Helldivers seen above TF 58 en route to attack Tokyo-area airfields on February 16, 1945. *80-G-397938, NARA*

division, that of Watts, and two other Fighting Seventeen orphans, Lieutenants (jg) Jack "Chili" Crawford and Murry Winfield. They were followed in turn by a four-plane VBF-17 division under Lieutenant Commander Hugh Nicholson as well as fighters from two other TG 58.1 carriers: sixteen VF-82 Hellcats from *Bennington* and, from *Wasp*, five VF-81 F6Fs and seven VMF-216 Corsairs.

During the same time, Hellcats and Corsairs from the other task groups took to the air for the early fighter sweeps. TG 58.2 began its launches at 0645, only 115 miles southeast of Tokyo, with *Lexington* sending up a dozen VF-9 Hellcats, *San Jacinto* contributing eight from VF-45, and *Hancock* launching sixteen fighters from VF-12 and VBF-12. *Yorktown* and *Randolph* from TG 58.4 contributed another thirty-five fighters, while *Langley* and *Cabot*'s fighter squadrons handled CAP duties for their task group.

Low overcast, poor visibility, and rain squalls delayed TG 58.3's launches. *Bunker Hill*'s first fighter sweep—sixteen VMF-221 Corsairs under Major Ed Roberts, skipper of the "Fighting Falcons"—did not begin launching until 0705, twenty minutes behind the first two task groups. Rendezvous was planned with other TG 58.3 fighters launched from *Essex* and *Cowpens*, but Roberts and his pilots could not carry out the plan due to rain squalls.

The escort carriers handled much of the CAP duties during the dawn launches, their squadrons being tasked with preventing any enemy planes from molesting the carrier fleet. The Marines liked to brag about "being first," and in the carrier raids on Tokyo, *Bennington's* VMF-112 "Wolfpack" squadron was first to make a kill. Less than an hour after Major David Andre's division launched at 0635, it intercepted and destroyed an unsuspecting Mitsubishi G4M Navy Type 1 Betty, a twin-engine land-based attack bomber.

Throughout the Pacific War, the Allies had adopted reporting names to identify aircraft operated by the Japanese for reporting and descriptive purposes. In mid-1942 Captain Frank T. McCoy—a U.S. Army Air Forces military-intelligence officer—devised a simple method for identifying Japanese aircraft to avoid confusing nicknames that had alternately been tagged on the same planes by Army and Navy pilots. Enemy fighters took on boys' names, while the names of girls were given to all other aircraft types. In comical fashion McCoy used hillbilly names such as "Zeke" and "Rufe" that he had encountered while growing up in Tennessee, while the Mitsubishi bomber was named "Betty" in homage to a female friend.[4]

Second Lieutenants Robert B. Hamilton and Laurence Sowles set fire to the lone bomber's right engine, and they were followed by Major Andre and 2nd Lieutenant Carroll King. The green and brown Betty, with big red Rising Sun "meatball" insignias on its wings and fuselage sides, hit the ocean and exploded, marking Air Group 82's first victory that day.

The weather and a lack of additional airborne opponents would result in very little action for most of the TF 58 fighter pilots launched on the predawn sweep. The VF-17 contingent led by Lieutenant Pearce flew by instruments through the foul weather. Upon reaching the Japanese mainland, division leader Watts found conditions only slightly better: a solid overcast still prevailed, with broken clouds below four thousand feet mixed with rain and snow flurries.

When the *Hornet* planes reached Sagami Bay, they were greeted with heavy but inaccurate antiaircraft fire from the tip of the Chiba Peninsula. The strike group orbited over the channel for thirty minutes at 4,000–5,000 feet, with Fighting Seventeen flying high cover, waiting for the ceiling to raise or break up sufficiently to ensure a successful strafing attack on the primary target, Yokosuka. There were no Japanese fighters airborne that intercepted the *Hornet*, *Wasp*, and *Bennington* aircraft. The only VF-17 pilots to see action on this early sweep turned out to be Langdon and Courrege, who each managed to shoot down a Zeke fighter but were never able to rejoin their own carrier group.

After eternal circling, the *Wasp* contingent finally broke off at 0840 to climb through the overcast. Pearce led his *Hornet* fighters in shooting up aircraft and structures on the ground. By 0855, with the weather not clear-ing and gas supply becoming an issue, a dejected Pearce finally gathered his *Hornet* flock and headed back for base.

The only early morning strike groups to meet significant aerial opposition on February 16 were the squadrons from Task Group 58.2 as they oper-ated over the Chiba Peninsula on the east side of Tokyo Bay. About one hundred enemy aircraft were sighted there, and Navy Hellcats in a series of dogfights claimed more than forty kills.

Honors for being the most successful Navy fighter squadron of the morning fell on the "Vipers" of *Hancock's* Fighting Eighty. Air Group 80 had only arrived on board *Hancock* at Ulithi on January 27, with the Vipers led by Lieutenant Commander Leroy William James "Pete" Keith from Kansas City. Thirty miles off the coast of Honshu, around 0755, Keith sighted a lone Zeke and scored first for his squadron by sending it flaming into the ocean.[5]

"That was first blood for the day," noted VF-80's squadron diarist. "The ice was broken." Soon after leading his pilots in a rocket and strafing attack on Katori Airfield, he was greeted by an "Oscar" (Nakajima Ki-43 Army Type 1 fighter) coming head-on at him. Keith destroyed his opponent. In the hour of swirling dogfights that followed, Keith would add to his score with the destruction of another Oscar, a "Nate" (Nakajima Ki-27 Army Type 97 fighter), and a Val, plus probable credit for destroying a "Tojo" (Nakajima Ki-44 Army Type 2 fighter) and another Zeke. Keith emerged from the morning as VF-80's first "ace in a day," with five confirmed kills in a single mission.[6]

His Viper wingman, Ensign Fred Ackerman, downed four opponents and added a Zeke probable kill in the Katori area. Not to be outdone, Keith's second-division leader, Lieutenant William C. Edwards Jr., also achieved instant ace status on the morning of the sixteenth. "Buddy" Edwards had started the war as a Dauntless dive-bomber pilot at the 1942 carrier battles of Coral Sea and Santa Cruz before switching to Hellcats in 1944. Edwards added to his two previous 1944 kills by bagging two Nates, two Zekes, and an Oscar and damaging another Zeke. The morning sweep by VF-80 was credited with twenty-four total aerial victories and another five aircraft probably destroyed.

Lexington's VF-9 Hellcats were fully engaged with Japanese fighters beginning at 0800, soon after strafing and destroying aircraft on the ground at Katori Airfield. Lieutenant Commander Houck, Fighting Nine's skipper and the flight leader, found his squadron being assailed by a half dozen Nates and thereafter by some two dozen Zekes. Houck claimed probable destruction on a Zeke, but his F6F was damaged by direct hits in further dogfighting, and he was forced to return to base.

Within an hour, VF-9 pilots could claim fourteen aerial victories, six planes probably destroyed, and many others damaged. Lieutenant (jg) Henry Champion, struggling with only three working machine guns, still managed to achieve one kill, two probables, and four other enemy fighters damaged. "I fired on at least 12 airplanes, and should have gotten all of them!" he later wrote.[7]

Makeshift flight leader Pearce returned to *Hornet* with his early morning fighter-sweep Hellcats at 0948. Shortly after landing, he was summoned to the flag bridge, where Rear Admiral Clark waited to hear from the leader of the first returning strike to attack the Tokyo area. With Langdon still not yet returned, Pearce made his way to "Flag Country" to see the admiral. "Jocko was not in a merry mood," recalled Pearce. "He questioned me as to how many planes we had shot down, how many we had destroyed on the ground, [and] what facilities and vessels we had destroyed."[8]

Pearce did his best to describe the confused launch and the foul weather that forced his group to circle for so long, then made his best guess as to what damage the fighters had done to shore installations and parked aircraft. He added that no enemy fighters had been airborne to engage. Clark, oddly sipping on a glass of milk, was less than pleased at the meager report.

"What the hell do you think the taxpayers are paying for?" he barked. Clark commenced to chew out Pearce, telling him that he was grounded from further flights and was to remain in his stateroom for the day. The lieutenant realized that the admiral was incensed by radio reports coming from other carrier groups that were having more success with the morning's strikes, but for the moment the pilot could do nothing but sheepishly retire to his stateroom.[9]

Pearce later related to squadron mate Tilly Pool that Clark believed a more aggressive fighting nature from his VF-17 pilots might have resulted in more enemy losses. The incensed admiral even remarked that the fact that more of his carrier's pilots had not been lost in action was indicative of their lack of aggressiveness. Such sentiments did not sit well with any member of the air group.

"Next time you talk to Jocko," snapped Pool to Pearce, "you can tell him we're losing a hell of a lot more pilots out there than we are admirals!"[10]

◆◇◆

Lieutenant (jg) Mitchell could barely stand the anticipation. Minutes passed like hours as he sat in VF-9's Ready Room No. 1 on *Lexington*, listening to a Japanese standard radio broadcast on the ship's low-frequency radio. Around 0800 the chattering announcer very abruptly discontinued his routine broadcast. Moments later the station came back on the air with a string of excited phrases before the transmissions ceased altogether. "We knew that the first group was over Japan," Mitchell said.[11]

Shortly after 0930 *Lexington* turned into the wind, and Lieutenant Commander Houck was first to land, his F6F sporting bullet holes in its right fuel tank and aileron. He made his way below decks to Fighting Nine's ready room, where he began shucking his parachute harness, Mae West jacket, and other flight gear.

"How was it, Skipper?" someone called out.

Houck's answer was exhilarating and sobering to Mitchell. "There's Zeros all over the place!"[12]

In an instant, Houck was gone, racing to make his report to the flag bridge without further details of what his first fighter sweep over Japan had experienced. Mitchell and his comrades pumped the next fighter pilots to arrive for information as they entered the smoky room. The squadron's air-combat intelligence officers (ACIOs) moved in, documenting all details of the flight, including enemy targets, aerial combat, victories, and losses. On the negative side of the news, Mitchell learned that VF-9 had lost one pilot, Lieutenant (jg) Robert Lawrence Parker, whose Hellcat was last seen in a dogfight with a Zeke.

But Fighting Nine's first sweep over Japan had not come up empty. Houck and his fellow F6F pilots claimed fourteen kills in exchange for one pilot missing in action. *Lexington*'s flight deck was a flurry of activity as the freshly returned planes were ferried below decks on the massive aircraft elevators, where hangar-deck crews rapidly refueled and rearmed them for further flights.

"Pilots, man your planes!"

The pulse-pounding order blared through the loudspeakers at 1030. Mitchell snatched up his chart board, buckled on his bright red flight helmet, and sprinted out of the room on the heels of his division leader, Lieutenant Valencia. Mitchell's Hellcat was spotted in the sixth position on deck, next to Valencia's F6F. *Lexington*'s second fighter launch of the day, slated to hit Tokyo Target Area No. 4, was officially labeled Fighter Sweep 2D and consisted of three VF-9 divisions. The first division was led by Lieutenant Commander Phil Torrey, CAG 9. Spotted farther aft of Torrey's four Hellcats were the divisions of Lieutenants Valencia and Bill Bonneau.

Lexington's second fighter sweep launched at 1045 and effected a rendezvous with three fighter divisions of *Hancock*'s VF-80 and two VF-45 divisions from the light carrier *San Jacinto*. The pilots faced an undesirable light rain so cold that icing conditions were experienced as they formed up. As the American fighters approached the Japanese mainland while flying on instruments, Mitchell shivered despite the layers of flight gear he wore and his Grumman's little cockpit heater. Near the coastline, the eight-hundred-foot ceiling gradually lifted to eight thousand feet, and Mitch found his visibility increased to roughly fifteen miles.

"My first sight of Japan was a beautiful, snow-capped symmetrical peak which I immediately recognized as Mt. Fuji," he said. One of Japan's Three Holy Mountains, Mount Fuji is the highest peak in Japan, rising more than 12,000 feet, and on a clear day can be seen from Tokyo, sixty miles northeast. Mitchell and his VF-9 companions scanned the horizon for enemy fighters as they proceeded toward Imba Airfield, forty miles from Tokyo.[13]

The noon hour was fast approaching as the thirty-two shiny Hellcats from *Lexington*, *Hancock*, and *San Jacinto* moved inland. Torrey ordered a strafing and rocket attack on the target airfield. His fighters would sweep in at two hundred knots, moving from north to south, and retire over nearby Imba Lake. Torrey's lead division had just pushed over at 1140 when three different radio calls pierced the guarded radio silence. The traditional call of "tally-ho," first used in nineteenth-century fox hunting, had long become the standard radio cry for fighter pilots who had sighted their quarry.

"Tally-ho! Bandits approaching!"

Lieutenant Valencia, astern of his CAG, was the first to "tally-ho" a bogey at six o'clock. He had spotted what proved to be a single Tojo coming down fast in a steep dive from astern of his division. Other fighter pilots called out their sightings, soon to be estimated as a total of seven Japanese aircraft. Torrey's division pulled out of its approach and leveled off, passing orders to all F6F pilots toting HVARs to jettison (launch) them in the direction of the airfield.

It had been one year and one day since Valencia had scored his last aerial victory, and he was primed for the fight this day. He focused his attention on the incoming Tojo, ordering his division to make a hard, 180-degree turn. His turn was so abrupt that Mitchell was almost left sitting alone high and dry. Mitch instantly dropped his left wing, horsed back on the control stick with all his might, and pushed his throttle to the wall—applying full power. His division had commenced defensive weaving as the Texan quickly pulled back into position on the lieutenant's wing. He could clearly see a small speck in the distance that was the enemy fighter, coming head-on toward him.

Valencia jettisoned his rockets to prepare for the fight. Mitchell instinctively followed suit, sliding out to the side of his division leader to unleash his own rockets. He flipped the switch to arm the HVARs, took aim well above the Tojo to allow for gravity drop, and pickled off his load. "My rockets converged and were seen to fall what appeared to be just short of my target," he said.[14]

Mitchell then slid back under Valencia's wing. As he did, he spotted a small black puff of smoke arise from the underside of Gene's cowl. Valencia's F6F decelerated rather rapidly as he peeled off to the right. *My God, he's been hit!* Mitch thought.

The rapidly closing Tojo left him no time to ponder his comrade's fate. Mitchell turned the rheostat on his gun sight up to full blast, armed all six of his guns, took aim, and pressed the trigger. He fired one short burst to find his mark, then let loose with a longer burst of his .50-caliber machine guns. The result "was a beautiful sight," said Mitchell. "Pieces of metal began to fly through the air, and in the next instant the Tojo was burning profusely."[15]

As the flaming wreckage flashed past him, Mitchell saw the Japanese pilot bail out. He quickly rolled his Hellcat onto its back, heading down to search for his division leader. To his relief, Mitch found Valencia slightly below him and learned that Gene had exhausted the fuel in his belly tank, causing his Hellcat to plummet before he could switch back to his main tanks. Reunited, Valencia and Mitchell were soon in the sites of a Kawasaki Ki-61 Army Type 3 "Tony" fighter, which began a firing sweep from astern of them. Upon his completion, the Japanese pilot made the mistake of crossing the flight path of Valencia, who laid into him with a long burst of his six .50-calibers. Bullets ripped through the plane's cockpit, radiator, and the aft end of its fuselage. The fighter burst into flames and fell to the ocean.

Valencia's second section, Lieutenants (jg) Jim French and Clint Smith, were next to score. French blasted apart one Tony and had to maneuver violently to avoid a midair collision as its wreckage plunged toward the ocean. Smitty turned head-on into another Tony that was attempting a run on Valencia and Mitchell and set its engine ablaze. As the Japanese army fighter glided toward the water, Mitchell had a front-row view of the pilot as he dived from his cockpit and popped his chute. He momentarily marveled at the man's black flight suit, the white parachute, and the green-and-brown-camouflaged Tony spinning in flames all before a background of black antiaircraft puffs.[16]

Following the scrap, Valencia called for the flight leader for a rendezvous, but he received no answer. The balance of the fighter divisions had become equally embroiled in fierce fighter combat with Zekes and Tonys. Lieutenant Edward McGowan's section downed four opponents in the next half hour of dogfighting. It was not until 1215 that Valencia was able to spot the other divisions and effect a rendezvous.

The attacks ceased at 1225, after a lone Tony made a run on Lieutenant Commander Torrey. The formation then headed back toward Imba Lake, but within minutes Torrey's Hellcat was seen to make a series of steep dives and climbs from five thousand feet. The air-group commander was likely wounded, flying out of control, and his wingman lost sight of him at the bottom of his third dive. Torrey was never seen again. Bonneau's division retired from the area around 1230 but was subjected to fresh attacks by Zekes and Tonys, which downed the Hellcat of Lieutenant William Moulton Hilkene.

Two U.S. fighters had been lost in action, but the collective group had scored eight kills, two probable kills, and another fifteen enemy planes damaged. Valencia's VF-9 division had been efficient, accounting for exactly half of the kills—one for each pilot. His Hellcats landed back on *Lexington* at 1400, three hours and fifteen minutes after launching. Mitchell's self-confidence had been boosted by his first aerial victory, but his excitement was tempered by the loss of three men from Fighting Nine: Hilkene, Parker, and skipper Torrey, all officially listed as missing in action. More sweeps against mainland Japan were scheduled, during which Mitch hoped to even the score: "We vowed vengeance would be ours."[17]

Tilly Pool expected to see action on February 16. His division was regularly assigned to fly with that of VF-17 skipper Marsh Beebe, who had the luxury of penciling himself into flights where he believed he would have the best chance of engaging the enemy.

Ensign Pool, born and raised in the Heights area of Houston, Texas, was making his first carrier-based combat strike as a Navy fighter pilot. Ironically, he first tried to get into aviation via the Army's cadet program in 1942, when he learned that it might take eighteen months to reach the training pipeline. Checking with the Navy, Tilly found that he could enter flight training in six weeks, so he never returned to take the Army oath.

Pool left Southwest Texas University, earned his golden wings in the Navy, and spent much of 1943 flying Hellcats with land-based VF-39 from Majuro in the Marshall Islands. The stress of constant flight dwindled his six-foot-one, 178-pound body down to 138 pounds by the end of this tour. Following a thirty-day leave, the black-haired, blue-eyed Texan reported to Lieutenant Commander Beebe's revamped Fighting Seventeen, "still skinny as the dickens," and progressed through the squadron's training. It was not until early 1945 that the Army sent Pool an official notice that he was due to be sworn in. Tilly politely replied on official U.S. Navy stationery that he was now otherwise engaged, having received a better offer.[18]

Pool spent the early hours of February 16 in his *Hornet* ready room, waiting out the news from his fellow squadron mates already flying missions over Japanese airfields. *Hornet* sent off two more groups of fighters between 0735 and 0745. As with the early morning sweep, the second and third groups did some strafing but found few aerial opponents. One pilot, Lieutenant (jg) Monte D. Harouff, suffered damage to his Hellcat from ground fire, but he was promptly recovered by the destroyer *Sigsbee* (DD 502) after ditching near the task force.

Beebe hoped to change his squadron's luck as his pilots manned their Hellcats, each uniquely painted with a checkerboard on its tail and wings for friendly identification, for VF-17's fourth mission of the day. Only two of his men, Langdon and Courrege, had scored kills; one plane had been lost; and Lieutenant Pearce had been grounded by Rear Admiral Clark.

Launching at 0858, Beebe led his division and those of Lieutenant (jg) Tommy Harris and Lieutenant "Fuzz" Wooley, the latter being Pearce's shipboard roommate. The sixteen-Hellcat formation was filled out by a four-plane VBF-17 division. Tilly Pool was seventh to launch, serving as second-section leader of Harris' division. Skipper Beebe's own division included two of his VC-39 *Liscome Bay* survivors, Lieutenants (jg) Bud Good and Frank Sistrunk.

Good, wingman for Beebe, had gotten into aviation training by following in the footsteps of his older brother, who was then in New Guinea flying for the Army Air Forces. After graduating from Oregon's Eugene High School in 1939, he had worked on commercial fishing boats and with the Civilian Conservation Corps in Juneau, Alaska, until Pearl Harbor was attacked. Good earned the position of becoming the skipper's wingman via his shooting prowess. While training with VF-17 at NAS Alameda, Beebe approached him.

"I hear you're a good shot," said the skipper. Good, an above-average sportsman and bird hunter during his youth in Oregon, agreed to join him at the base range to shoot clay pigeons, betting a bottle of booze on the best score. Beebe shot twenty-three out of twenty-five skeet, but Good finished with a clean sweep of all twenty-five targets.

"I'm going to make you my wingman," the lieutenant commander announced. "If you can shoot skeet, you can shoot six machine guns and hit things, too."[19]

Good was plenty anxious to see his first combat this day. During some of the briefings prior to the Tokyo strike, the brass had made various promises. "You guys will either get you a Zero, become an ace, or you won't come back," Good recalled hearing. "The night before, I didn't sleep a wink, and I don't think anybody did."[20]

Hornet's fourth fighter strike rendezvoused with sixteen Hellcats from *Bennington* and set course for Hamamatsu Airfield. As they approached the Japanese coast, the group strafed a small merchant ship, leaving it burning and settling into the sea. Beebe was pleased to see more than thirty single-engine planes dispersed on the ground at Mikatagahara Airfield, while another forty or more—primarily twin-engine planes—sat on Hamamatsu's field. The American fighters set at least eight aircraft ablaze and damaged more in their strafing runs. Beebe found that the big twin-engine bombers when hit "made a very beautiful pyrotechnic display" as he led his men away from the antiaircraft fire to regroup.[21]

As they effected their rendezvous, the U.S. formation was jumped by eight Zekes and Tonys. Lieutenant Commander Beebe pulled up sharply and, with a full deflection burst, caught one Zeke squarely in the engine and cockpit. As the stricken fighter dove for the clouds below, Beebe pursued it to eight thousand feet, where his final machine-gun bursts sent it plunging downward in flames. His fellow pilots claimed damage or probable destruction to six other fighters in the air. The only damage sustained in the Hamamatsu raid was antiaircraft damage to the F6F of Lieutenant (jg) Harris, who suffered half of his horizontal stabilizer and elevator shot away. Tilly Pool and the other wingmen of Harris' division escorted him back to the ship, where he landed safely.

The *Hornet* contingent lost one plane when Ensign George Salvaggio's VBF-17 Hellcat exhausted its fuel near the task force, where the pilot ditched and was recovered by the destroyer *Taussig* (DD 746). Good, forced to make his own water landing months earlier during carrier-qualification landings, felt relief that Salvaggio had been rescued. "They had a saying," he recalled: "There are only two types of carrier pilots—ones that have gone in the water and ones who are going to."[22]

Landing back on board their carrier at 1240, Pool and Beebe did the usual debriefings in the squadron ready room. Beebe's divisions had downed or damaged more than a half dozen Japanese fighters, but it was not enough to please task-force commanders. "The whole task force was disappointed because we were not encountering the number of enemy aircraft that we had expected," remembered Beebe. "No one was more discouraged than Admiral Jocko Clark. Old Jocko was mad all the time, but I had never seen him as mad as he was after that mission."[23]

Two hours later eleven bomb-laden F6Fs were launched, again under Beebe's command. Tommy Harris borrowed another Hellcat to replace his damaged plane, leaving his division one plane short, with only Tilly Pool and Ensign Robert F. Cunningham accompanying him.

Joined en route by seven *Wasp* fighters, Beebe's pilots were again assigned to hit Japanese airfields in the Tokyo Bay area. Approximately fifteen miles inland from Sagami Bay, the VF-17 formation sighted enemy fighters above them at 20,000 feet. Three Zekes made a lazy pass at Beebe's lead division, recovered below the Hellcats, then proceeded to the northwest. After a five-minute chase, Beebe raked the trailing Zeke until he saw violent flames erupt in its cockpit and a portion of its elevator shear off. Lieutenant (jg) Good then finished the job, blasting off the Zeke's starboard aileron, which caused the plane to flip over to port and the pilot to eject.

Harris' division flamed a lone Zeke, marking his second aerial victory and his first with VF-17. His second-section leader, Tilly Pool, had the utmost confidence in his division leader. "Tommy was an excellent pilot and the best damn aerial gunner I'd ever seen," said Pool. "In gunnery training flights on towed targets, we would have 100 rounds dipped in different-colored paint so you could tell who hit the target. I thought I was pretty good, but Tommy would always come out a little ahead of me on the shooting."[24]

The determined pilot of a Mitsubishi J2M Navy "Jack" interceptor landed hits on Pool's wingman, Ensign Cunningham, before overrunning the F6F to make a pass on the leading Hellcat, Pool's. Cunningham pulled onto the Jack's tail and shot off chunks of its cowling. The Japanese fighter "split-S'd and went down in the clouds," said Pool. "I have no idea what happened to him." Harris reformed his division and then made strafing runs on Tateyama Airfield, where Pool shot up a parked Betty. Two pilots from Bob Coats' division destroyed a pair of Nakajima Ki-84 Army Type 4 "Frank" fighters before the entire *Hornet* group completed its action with rocket strikes against Otawa Airfield.[25]

Pool gained valuable experience in his first two strikes on Tokyo but was left yearning for his first aerial victory.

The Vipers of *Hancock*'s VF-80 turned in a big day over the Japanese airfields on February 16. The squadron's second fighter sweep of the day was led by Lieutenant Commander Albert O. "Scoop" Vorse Jr., CAG 80 and original Fighting Eighty skipper. His fourteen Hellcats mixed it up

Four of the six TF 58 fighter pilots who achieved "ace in a day" status on February 16, 1945. *Above, left to right:* Lieutenant William Edwards of VF-80; Lieutenant Commander Leroy "Pete" Keith, skipper of VF-80 of *Hancock* (CV 19); and Commander Gordon Eugene Schecter, skipper of VF-45 of *San Jacinto* (CVL 30). Schecter was killed in action over Okinawa on March 18. *Right:* Lieutenant Patrick Fleming of VF-80, who scored five kills and one probable near Imba Airfield outside Tokyo. *U.S. Navy*

between 0845 and 0915 with more than two dozen Japanese planes—mainly Zekes, Oscars, Nates, and Tojos—which quickly became easy victims for the skilled American pilots; Vorse alone dropped two Oscars in one firing pass. Before the action was complete, the commander had also downed a "Dinah" (Mitsubishi Ki-46 Army Type 100 reconnaissance plane) and a Nate for four total victories, raising his wartime total to 11.5 kills.

Collectively, the second VF-80 fighter sweep made 17 kills, raising the unit's daily total to 41 kills. *Hancock's* fourth fighter mission of the day was also productive, as a dozen F6Fs under Lieutenant Robert M. Bell engaged an estimated thirty-five Japanese fighters off the Chiba Peninsula between 1130 and 1220. Lieutenant Alexander L. Anderson, a Yale economics major who jettisoned his rockets at the start of the action, became the Viper's third "ace in a day" by downing a Zeke, two Oscars, a Tony, and a Tojo; he added another Tony as a probable and was credited with damaging a "Frances" (Yokosuka P1Y twin-engine fighter-bomber). Five other pilots from Bell's flight scored kills, bringing the tally to fourteen victories and seven probables and the squadron's daily running total to fifty-five kills.

At 1330 ten Viper pilots under Lieutenant Patrick D. Fleming engaged twenty Zekes, Oscars, and Tojos between Imba and Mobara Airfields. Fleming, already the leading ace of VF-80 with ten confirmed kills, made triple ace on February 16, downing five Zekes. His second-division leader, Ensign Elbert W. Parrish, knocked down an Oscar and three Zekes, while

Lieutenant Richard L. "Zeke" Cormier flamed another three A6M fighters. Collectively, Fleming's VF-80 sweep accounted for sixteen more kills.

By day's end, *Hancock's* fighters had recorded an astonishing seventy-one kills and fifteen probables, a record in U.S. aviation history. Even though boasting one massive fighter squadron not split into separate VF and VBF units like most other fleet carriers, VF-80 still accounted for one-quarter of the total daily aerial victories amassed by all the squadrons flying from TF 58 carriers.[26]

The Vipers had thus managed to have four pilots earn "ace in a day" honors on the sixteenth. Two other TF 58 pilots would achieve the honor that day, both from the light carrier *San Jacinto*. Commander Gordon Schecter, skipper of VF-45, gunned down three Zekes in the morning over Katori Airfield and earned half-credit kills on a Dinah and an ancient "Claude" (Mitsubishi A5M Navy Type 96 fixed-gear fighter). In the afternoon Schecter added an Oscar to raise his day's collection to five kills. The sixth "ace in a day" on February 16 was VF-45's Ensign Robert R. Kidwell Jr., who took down three Tonys, a Claude, and a Zeke in two missions. *San Jacinto's* fighters turned in twenty-eight kills for the day, giving them the second-best tally behind Fighting Eighty.[27]

Total aerial victories in the Tokyo region for February 16 were 291, of which only 27 went to Corsairs. The nine task-force F4U squadrons lost ten aircraft and eight pilots during the day. From *Bennington*, Major Everett Alward's VMF-123 "Flying Eight Balls" managed only one kill—by Alward—and lost three Corsairs in the day's actions. Major Jack Amende's VMF-217 "Bulldogs" from the carrier *Wasp* claimed a half dozen Japanese planes near the Hamamatsu Airfield, but the major was lost in the process.[28]

Bunker Hill's Fighting Falcons claimed two kills, including a Betty bomber downed by Captain William N. Snider and Lieutenant Donald MacFarlane during the early morning sweep. One of their young VMF-221 comrades, 2nd Lieutenant George Johns, was disappointed to not be slated for any morning action, so he jumped at the chance when a call was made in the ready room that afternoon for two pilots to escort a photo-reconnaissance flight. Johns and Lieutenant William M. Pemble launched at 1415 and proceeded to Honshu to document the bombing of an aircraft plant.

Twice Pemble and Johns managed to fight off attacks by intercepting Zekes, but when their formation dived on the Japanese target, they were left quite vulnerable to a swarm of fighters. "All hell broke loose, with enemy fighters all over the place," said Johns. He went into a frenzied series of skids and rolls to throw off his foes, three times managing to shoot pieces off Zekes that flashed past him. He finally screamed at the pilot of the photo Hellcat he was protecting, "Firewall the son-of-a-bitch and dive!"[29]

Together, the Corsair and Hellcat pilots escaped the firestorm and made their way back to the *Bunker Hill*. But Pemble did not survive the action; his F4U seen by a dive-bomber aircrewman to fly out of control before crashing into a hillside.

More than 2,700 combat sorties would be flown from the decks of TF 58 carriers by day's end. Combat and operational losses were expected, but the prospects of being recovered were greatly reduced by the proximity of the fleet's operations to the coast of Japan. In the case of a few lucky souls, their saving grace was the presence of U.S. submarines specifically placed offshore on lifeguard duty.

For his second mission of February 16, Lieutenant (jg) Watts was tasked with providing cover for nine VB-17 Helldivers and eight VT-17 Avengers, which in turn rendezvoused with other strike planes from the carriers *Belleau Wood* and *Bennington*. Billy's division launched at 1352, along with those of thirty-five-year-old Commander Ed Konrad, CAG 17, and Fighting Seventeen's executive officer, Langdon.

Konrad's flight strafed a Japanese destroyer en route to its Japanese Army Air Force (JAAF) target, Hamamatsu Airfield. His first division strafed more than two dozen enemy aircraft parked along the field, while Helldivers and Avengers made bombing runs against Hamamatsu's runways. The division under Watts was among the last to make strafing runs. Billy's six Colt-Browning M-2 machine guns chattered in quick bursts, unleashing hundreds of rounds of 709-grain .50-caliber bullets that chewed into the aluminum wings and fuselages of the immobile prey below. His F6F was fully loaded with twenty-four hundred rounds of ammunition, but he noted a lack of explosions and fire as his slugs shredded his target planes. Watts decided that the ground crews below had drained the fuel from their planes in anticipation of the Americans' arrival.

The *Hornet* strike group left many fuelless JAAF planes riddled and six others ablaze on the airfield, while also thoroughly strafing hangars, shops, and maintenance facilities. The heavy antiaircraft fire had failed to touch Watts' Hellcat, but as he retired over open water, the young lieutenant learned that his shipboard roommate had not been as fortunate. Lieutenant (jg) Joe Farrell, a native of Muskogee, Oklahoma, was one of Billy's closest friends on *Hornet*. Together they had endured flight training in Dallas back in 1942 and were reunited in late 1944 when selected to help form the veteran contingent of the revamped VF-17. By then Farrell was already leading something of a charmed life. In November 1943 he had been one of the survivors of the sinking of escort carrier *Liscome Bay*.

"Billy, come up here," Farrell called to his division leader as he broke radio silence. "I think I'm losing oil!"[30]

Watts could see precious oil blowing down the fuselage of Farrell's plane, which had taken a hit from antiaircraft fire during his strafing runs. Together they headed for open water, but after a half hour Farrell lost the battle to make it home. Billy saw his roommate's engine freeze up, with flames erupting along the cowling as the propeller windmilled to a halt. Farrell fought his powerless glider down to the wave tops at 1702 and slammed the F6F into the sparkling blue sea with a mighty splash. He scrambled from his seat as the icy water rushed in to the cockpit. The four-and-a-half-ton aircraft was gone in less than a minute, plunging toward the icy depths with a mighty belch of released air so fast that Farrell's life raft was pulled down with it.

Watts could see that that his friend's yellow Mae West lifejacket was releasing a bright green dye that helped him to be spotted from the air. He remembered that a notecard attached to his "Ouija board"—the navigational plotting board strapped alongside his seat—contained the lifeguard sub's codename and emergency radio frequency. Glancing about in excitement, Billy was frustrated to find the card had slipped from his board and down to the floorboards by his feet.

Strapped into his confined space, Watts simply could not reach the vital information. *Maybe I can float that thing up to me if I put some negative G's on this baby,* he thought. Watts pushed his Hellcat into a steep dive, the centrifugal force pressing his body solidly back into his seat. His ingenuity worked. "That little card floated right up toward my hand just like a waiter handing me a check," he said.[31]

Watts opened up on his radio, using the assigned codename "Full Holster" to call up *Pomfret* (SS 391). His transmission was acknowledged almost instantly by a radioman's voice at 1723. The sub's skipper, Commander John Hess, a veteran of eleven war patrols, estimated from Watts' coordinates that his boat would arrive within the hour. During the interim, Billy made two low-level passes to drop life rafts to Farrell. The winter snows dotting the distant Japanese mainland made the seawater so frigid that Farrell was too numb to swim for either raft. When *Pomfret* arrived forty-five minutes later, Watts coached the sub toward Farrell's position, but four-foot waves foiled the efforts of the pigboat's lookouts to locate the downed flier.

Watts cut his throttle, pushed the nose of his Hellcat down, and made a dive directly over his buddy to pinpoint his location. The sub crew still could not make out the drifting airman, so Billy pushed his F6F into another steep dive. As he did, his engine belched a fortuitous black cloud of smoke that lingered like a marker directly above Farrell. Watts smiled as *Pomfret* turned sharply and pushed a white feather of water as she raced to the downed VF-17 pilot. He soon watched two sailors dive into the freezing waters and help pull Farrell up on deck.

Darkness had settled over the ocean at 1812 as Watts banked his F6F back toward the decks of *Hornet*. He brought his plane down on the deck long after dark, feeling more satisfaction with having saved a friend than with the exhilaration he had felt in downing his first enemy aircraft. Commander Hess' *Pomfret* would also rescue a downed Japanese pilot and an American pilot (Ensign Robert L. Buchanan) from the carrier *Cabot* the following day. Such bold operations within spitting distance of Japan did not go without notice by the aviators and even by the media. Famed war correspondent Ernie Pyle devoted a column to the *Pomfret* rescues under the headline, "Even If You Was Shot Down in Tokyo Harbor, the Navy Would Be in to Get You."

By the end of February 16, Pete Mitscher's carrier fighters had downed 284 aerial opponents in addition to destroying numerous parked planes on the ground and damaging aircraft frame and engine plants. American losses had been substantial, with *Bennington*'s VF-82 and *Wasp*'s VF-81 each losing five Hellcats in dogfights, to antiaircraft fire, or to ditching.[32]

Once all returning aircraft were recovered at sunset, TG 58.5 launched a sweep of night fighters to cover the enemy airfields. The task force remained undisturbed during the night. With dawn on February 17, strikes on Tokyo-area targets resumed. The foul weather continued, dropping ceilings to as little as 150 or 200 feet over the task groups, so low that some CAP divisions were not even launched.

Lieutenant Pearce of VF-17, confined to his quarters after his encounter with Admiral Clark the previous morning, was visited by his Fighting Seventeen squadron commander, Marsh Beebe, and Captain Doyle, *Hornet*'s skipper. Doyle apologized for the outburst on the flag deck, saying Clark was keyed up over reports from other task groups attacking areas north of Tokyo, where they had found better weather and had shot down several planes. "The upshot of the visit was that I was ungrounded as quickly as I had been grounded," Pearce remarked.[33]

Enterprise and *Saratoga* began sending off their night fighters in the early morning darkness of February 17. At dawn the four daytime carrier task groups began launching deckloads of fighters and bombers to make sweeps over the airfields, followed by conventional bombing strikes by Helldivers and Avengers on the Tachikawa, Musashimo, and Tama plants near Tokyo.

Lieutenant Valencia's Mowing Machine division launched at 0715 from *Lexington*, whose fighter sweep was designated to hit Target Area No. 4, airfields east of Tokyo, once again. In the wake of the loss of Lieutenant Commander Torrey the previous day, Lieutenant Commander Houck stepped up as acting CAG 9, while Lieutenant Jack "Buster" Kitchen assumed the role of VF-9 skipper. Houck's first mission as air-group commander on the seventeenth would include fourteen Hellcats from Fighting Nine.

Two VF-9 fighters were forced to turn back, but a dozen effected a rendezvous with another twelve from *Hancock's* VF-80 and proceeded with the mission. The formation flew low over the water to avoid the heavy cloud cover, climbing as they approached land. "It was snowing and at times you couldn't see outside of the cockpit," recalled Lieutenant (jg) Mitchell. "That's an eerie feeling when you are jammed in a sixteen-plane formation."[34]

Houck's Hellcats broke through the foul weather at nine thousand feet and continued climbing until they neared the coast of Japan a few miles north of Mobara. Mitchell heard another pilot break radio silence with, "Tally ho land, two o'clock, five miles."

Another voice piped up, "I wonder what that is?"

"It sure as hell ain't San Francisco," called another pilot, whose comment drew a chuckle from many of the stressed pilots.[35]

The combined VF-9 and VF-80 flight found Kisarazu Airfield obscured with fog, so the fighters shifted to strafe parked aircraft at Mobara Airfield. Houck rendezvoused his Hellcats and climbed to 15,000 feet to head for Katori Airfield. En route some twenty enemy fighters were observed, scattered above, below, and on the same level as the American warplanes. Houck exploded a passing Zeke. Ensign Ralph J. Warner destroyed another Zeke, whose pilot Lieutenant (jg) Smith of Valencia's division saw bail out.

Valencia spotted another Zeke making a run on Houck's lead division and got in an effective long burst that caused smoke to pour from its cockpit. Lieutenant (jg) French, covering Valencia during the run, witnessed the Japanese pilot bail out. About five minutes later Valencia attacked an Oscar just off Naruto, landing hits all over it until the enemy fighter burst into flames and spiraled downward.

The *Lexington* flight returned to base without loss, although Smith was so low on fuel he had to pancake on *San Jacinto*. Valencia's three kills in two days combat over Japan raised his wartime aerial victories to 10.5, making him a double ace. Lieutenant Fleming of *Hancock*'s VF-80 destroyed four more fighters on February 17, adding to the five he had scored the previous day. His total score since November 1944 now stood at nineteen kills, making him the top ace in the task force. But as it turned out, Fleming had scored his final kills of World War II, while Valencia was just getting warmed up.

The two-day aerial clashes above mainland Japan provided ripe pickings for Lieutenant Commander Fritz Wolf's *Yorktown*-based VBF-3 squadron. Wolf, credited with four kills while serving a previous tour with the famed Flying Tigers, achieved ace status on February 16 by downing his fifth enemy opponent—his first while dueling in a Grumman F6F Hellcat.

On the seventeenth Wolf and eighteen of his VBF-3 pilots began engaging brownish-green Zekes, Oscars, "Hamps" (Mitsubishi A6M3 Navy Type 0 fighters), "Judys" (Yokosuka D4Y Navy Type 2 carrier attack bombers), and "Jills" (Nakajima B6N carrier-attack bombers) around 0830 near Ishioka Airfield. There were "meatballs all over the sky," according to Lieutenant (jg) Bob Rice. Wolf's squadron claimed a baker's dozen in kills, plus three probables, against no losses. Lieutenant (jg) James "Jake" Jones shot down an Aichi E13A Navy Type 0 "Jake" reconnaissance floatplane and an Oscar, becoming Air Group 3's first ace by adding to his three victories scored the previous day. Wolf's VBF-3 finished the two-day assault on Japan with 37.5 kills, placing them second on TF 58's leader board. *Yorktown*'s other Hellcat squadron, VF-3, under Lieutenant Commander Edward Howard "Buggsy" Bayers, added another 19 kills in this two-day action.[36]

Beebe's VF-17 turned in another solid performance on February 17. The squadron's first sweep of the day shot up bombers at Yokosuka Airfield. One pilot, Lieutenant (jg) Eugene George Fetzer, was forced to ditch twenty miles short of *Hornet*, but searches failed to find any trace of him. Skipper Beebe led Fighting Seventeen's second sweep of three F6F divisions. Tommy Harris' Hellcat was unable to launch, leaving his second-section leader, Ensign Pool, to lead Ensign Stanley Edward Smith and Lieutenant (jg) Harry Jules "Swede" Sundberg on the mission.

Beebe's Hellcats proceeded toward Tokyo Bay to make strafing attacks on Atsugi Airfield, where nearly five dozen planes were dispersed in the open and in revetments. Beebe was just passing ten thousand feet when an antiaircraft shell exploded in front of his F6F, disintegrating his cockpit and spraying the rest of his plane with shrapnel. "It seemed like a bomb had gone off right in my cockpit," he recalled. "The wind was blasting through and tearing at my helmet." Beebe regained his senses quickly as he saw the ground "coming at me terribly fast. I finally got straight and level just over the treetops, and fortunately I was headed for the coast and open water."[37]

The only aerial opposition was a Tojo that made a firing run on Sundberg's plane as the Americans began their strafing runs. Lieutenant (jg) John Theodore "Ted" Crosby and his wingman, Ensign Joe Friedman, ganged up on the fighter and chased it off. Crosby, a veteran of a previous Pacific tour with *Bunker Hill's* VF-18, hailed from Eureka, California, where he had attended Marin College, just north of San Francisco. After completing his pilot training, he resisted assignments to jeep carriers, fighting to gain a position with a large fleet carrier. "That's where the action was," Crosby reasoned. He was elated when a veteran pilot, Lieutenant James Bellows, helped him secure a coveted slot within the *Bunker Hill* squadron.[38]

Crosby was flying with Bellows in November 1943 when he got his first partial kill, a quarter credit for a Betty bomber from Rabaul. He gained battle experience over time and maintained a ritual of never keeping his Hellcat in one spot more than ten seconds while on strafing runs or in dogfights. "When I looked in my rear view mirror, I'd often see flak bursts where my plane had just been," said Crosby. His jinking kept his Hellcat bullet-free on February 17 as Crosby and his companions strafed parked aircraft at Atsugi, Otawa, and Tateyama Airfields around 0945.

Lieutenant Commander Beebe found the cold air blasting into his shattered cockpit almost unbearable as his division mates escorted him back toward *Hornet*. "After an hour of open-cockpit flying in below-freezing weather, I needed help getting out of the airplane upon landing," he said.[39]

Lieutenant Langdon led the next VF-17 strike off at 1110 for a special bombing and rocket attack after word was flashed to the task force that a Japanese escort carrier had been spotted in Yokohama Harbor. The other divisions were led by Watts and the newly reinstated Pearce. Watts was forced to send his second section back to *Hornet* after one F6F developed propeller-pitch problems. He was excited with the prospect of unleashing 500-pound bombs and 5-inch rockets against an enemy carrier, so he proceeded on the mission with only his wingman, Lieutenant (jg) Werner Gaerisch, and seven other VF-17 planes. Langdon's group, joined in flight by eleven *Wasp* fighters, encountered heavy antiaircraft fire as it neared

Tokyo. The carrier target was sighted inside the Yokohama breakwater, and the attack commenced at 1310, with the *Wasp* group going in first.

Their prey was the 15,864-ton *Yamashio Maru*, freshly commissioned on January 27, 1945. She had been partially constructed as a Type 2TL oil tanker but was one of two such ships Japan converted midproduction into an auxiliary escort carrier. *Yamashio Maru* carried only eight Kokusai Ki-76 planes and measured 485 feet long by 66 feet wide, with a 410-foot-long flight deck and top speed of fifteen knots.

Commander Frederick James Brush, CAG 81, led his Hellcats on their bombing runs from bow to stern to release their 500-pounders on *Yamashio Maru*. Brush claimed one direct hit on the stern and one close near miss, crediting additional bomb hits to six other pilots. To further punish the motionless flattop, Ensign William Alexander Grant Jr. landed two rocket hits, and Lieutenant (jg) Thomas Earl Bourdon piled on three more. The *Hornet* fighters observed many near misses and at least one direct hit amidships on the flight deck from the *Wasp* group before Grandma Langdon led his nine-plane VF-17 group down on the burning carrier.

Watts and wingman Gaerisch followed Langdon's division. Billy held his path, ignoring the incoming flak while drawing a careful bead on the flight deck to line up his rockets before firing them at about 3,500 feet. He had but a split second to visually trail the rocket streaks before he turned his attention to releasing his main bombload and pulling out over the harbor. His recovery from his attack left him no ability to judge the success of his bomb drop, but he felt certain that at least one of his rockets struck

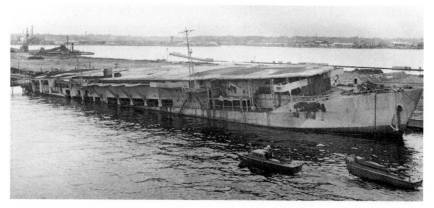

Six divisions of *Wasp* (CV 18) and *Hornet* (CV 12) Hellcats attacked the newly commissioned Japanese carrier *Yamashio Maru* on February 17, 1945, in Yokohama Harbor with bombs and rockets. The 15,864-ton auxiliary aircraft carrier sank alongside her dock, marking the only carrier destroyed solely by U.S. fighter planes during World War II. *SC-211765, NARA*

home in the flight deck of *Yamashio Maru*. Lieutenant Pearce then struck: "At the time of our dive, the ship was already afire, and I used the big fire in the middle of the flight deck as my point of aim for six rockets," firing two at a time. Division mates George Johnson and Winfield followed quickly with their own runs.[40]

The *Hornet* fighters rendezvoused over Tokyo Bay and noted the enemy carrier to be low in the water and burning violently, with flames shooting out of the hangar deck and curling over the flight deck. *Yamashio Maru* sank by the stern in Yokohama Harbor, prior to seeing any combat service at sea. Her loss marked the first Japanese carrier destroyed solely by Hellcat fighters.

When Pearce returned to *Hornet*, he was pleased that Jocko Clark did not summon him to the flag bridge again. Langdon went there instead, where the admiral congratulated him on a job well done and recommended him for the Navy Cross for helping sink a Japanese carrier. Each *Hornet* Hellcat pilot from the flight would receive a Distinguished Flying Cross, the third awarded in the case of Langdon. "I suspect the taxpayers had been appeased," noted Pearce.[41]

The Navy and Marine Hellcats and Corsairs of TF 58 knocked down another 84 Japanese planes during their second day of action against the mainland airfields. The lion's share of the aerial victories—some 371 total in two days by the count of fighter historian Frank Olynyk—went to Hellcat pilots, although Corsair fighters accounted for 31 kills. Another 190 enemy aircraft were listed as destroyed on the ground. TF 58 lost 60 planes in combat during these two days and another 28 as operational losses out of the 738 sorties that engaged the enemy from a grand total of 2,761 sorties of all types, including those for CAP duty.[42]

Seven pilots achieved ace status in two days of dogfighting, and six earned "ace in a day" honors. Lieutenant Fleming led the pack with 9 kills for VF-80, the *Hancock* squadron also taking top claims with 83 aerial victories over the two-day operation. *Yorktown's* VBF-3 followed with 37.5 kills in two days, with *Lexington's* VF-9 right behind at 32 total claims.

By midday on February 17, TF 58 was collecting its strike groups and steaming south from Japan to support the invasion of Iwo Jima. Lowering weather convinced Admiral Mitscher to move on to avoid more losses of his own pilots and planes. Two days of airstrikes and dogfights had seriously damaged the Japanese air arm, but TF 58's fliers were just beginning six months of hostilities. The freshly blooded aviators had a new mission at hand—flying support for the Iwo Jima invasion, slated to commence in only two days.

Top Scoring Fighter Pilots over Kyushu, February 16–17, 1945

Name	Rank	Squadron	Carrier	Kills	Probables
Fleming, Patrick Dawson	Lt.	VF-80	*Hancock*	9	—
Anderson, Alexander Lewis	Lt.	VF-80	*Hancock*	5	1
Edwards, William Clarence, Jr.	Lt.	VF-80	*Hancock*	5	—
Jones, James Murrell	Lt.(jg)	VBF-3	*Yorktown*	5	—
Keith, Leroy William James	Lt. Cdr.	VF-80	*Hancock*	5	2
Kidwell, Robert Riffle	Ens.	VF-45	*San Jacinto*	5	—
Schecter, Gordon Eugene	Cdr.	VF-45	*San Jacinto*	5	2
Sherrill, Hugh Virgil	Lt.(jg)	VF-81	*Wasp*	4.5	2
Ackerman, Fred Forrest	Ens.	VF-80	*Hancock*	4	1
Carmichael, Daniel Archibald, Jr.	Lt.(jg)	VBF-12	*Randolph*	4	—
Parrish, Elbert Willard	Ens.	VF-80	*Hancock*	4	—
Vorse, Albert Ogden, Jr.	Lt. Cdr.	VF-80	*Hancock*	4	—

Chapter Six

CRUEL FORTUNES AT CHICHI JIMA

V ice Admiral Ugaki found it "most regrettable to see that little improve-
ments . . . [had] been made" in defending against the type of TF 58–
based fighter sweeps that struck mainland Japan. He had been prepared
for the American carrier raids by moving many planes to the east ahead of
time, but the Kyushu bases had still been hit hard. Ugaki noted in his diary
that 150 Japanese aircraft had been destroyed on the ground.[1]

At the time of these raids, Ugaki's kamikaze forces were in the
process of being bolstered. Japan's aircraft carriers had made their final sorties from home waters by mid-February 1945, with the once lethal Carrier
Division 1 being abolished on the tenth. *Amagi's* Air Group 601 was
detached from its carrier when *Amagi* entered the docks at the Kure Naval
Base that day. Her airmen were assigned to air bases in Kyushu, including
some to a new *tokkotai* unit based at the Katori Airfield, from where they
would have their chance at striking the American carriers.

Despite the reorganization process, the headquarters of the Thunder
Gods Corps remained at Kanoya Airfield, along with the main forces of
Betty bombers and Ohka divisions. In the wake of Vice Admiral Mitscher's
carrier raids, Tokyo's English-language newspaper, the *Nippon Times*,
announced the attacks on its front page but offered the propaganda that
the country's antiaircraft forces had obtained favorable results. Ugaki now
held little hope that Japan could win the war, but he busied himself with
preparing for the next chance to punish TF 58 with Operation Tan, one he
described as "a suicide attack upon the enemy after it gets back to Ulithi."[2]

Ugaki's intelligence pointed toward American landings being prepared for Iwo Jima. On February 18 his search planes located a U.S. carrier task group only two hundred miles west of Chichi Jima. During the next two days, he closely monitored the Americans' progress in moving troops ashore on Iwo Jima. He noted with disgust in his diary how little he trusted his own army's confidence in being able to hold this key position. "If this island, noted for its fortification, should fall into enemy hands, the future of our main islands should be feared indeed."[3]

Commander Charlie Crommelin swung into his cockpit, ready for the mission at hand. His Air Group 12, based on the fleet carrier *Randolph*, would be leading Rear Admiral Radford's TG 58.4 strike force against the volcanic island of Chichi Jima on February 18. Air Group 12 was contributing forty-two Hellcats, Avengers, and Helldivers, while the light carriers *Cabot* and *Langley* each launched eight fighters for escort. Commander John T. "Jigger" Lowe—a veteran of 1942's carrier battles near Guadalcanal—led fleet carrier *Yorktown*'s Air Group 3 formation, which included twenty Hellcats of VF-3, fourteen SB2Cs of VB-3, and fifteen torpedo bombers of VT-3.

Randolph's strike force was led off the deck at 1045 by CAG 12 Crommelin, who hailed from a famous group of five Alabama brothers. Commander John Crommelin, a staff officer, had survived the sinking of the escort carrier *Liscome Bay* in November 1943. Their brother Henry was serving as commander of a destroyer task group, while Dick Crommelin was a fighter pilot, decorated for his actions in the 1942 Coral Sea and Midway carrier battles. Youngest brother Quentin Crommelin had spent most of 1942 as a gunnery officer on the carrier *Saratoga* before beginning his own flight training in 1943.

Charlie Crommelin was badly injured in November 1943 during air battles near the Marshall Islands when a 20-mm shell burst inches in front of his cockpit. Shrapnel and glass from his windshield peppered his body with more than two hundred wounds, including both eyes, leaving him with only partial vision in one of them. The resilient Crommelin managed to return to his carrier, *Yorktown*, and after recovering from his wounds, returned to air duty as commander of *Randolph*'s Air Group 12, nicknamed "Crommelin's Thunderbirds."

Mitscher's TF 58 steamed for Iwo Jima during the night of February 17–18, destroying four small Japanese picket boats en route. Two carrier task groups—Radford's TG 58.4 and Rear Admiral Jocko Clark's TG 58.1—

were directed to carry out sweeps during the morning of the eighteenth against Japanese-held Chichi Jima, located 150 miles north of Iwo Jima, to neutralize any enemy aircraft or shipping there.

Chichi Jima was heavily defended by antiaircraft batteries, which had proven adept at downing American planes during the past seven months. The island had become a regular target for attacks aimed at wrecking the anchorage, seaplane base, radio station, and weather station located there. Two task groups, including that of Clark, had raided Chichi, Iwo, Haha, and Muko Jima on July 4, 1944. Among the American planes shot down was that of VT-1's Lieutenant (jg) Owen Marsten Hintz from *Yorktown*.

Hintz perished, but his gunner, twenty-year-old ARM2c Lloyd Richard "Dick" Woellhof, parachuted out and landed just off of little Ani Jima. Although wounded, he struggled ashore and tried to resist his captors, only to be bayoneted through the shoulder. Woellhof was moved to Chichi Jima, where he was held with another downed aviator, Ensign William Laughlin "Bill" Connell from *Hornet*'s Air Group 2. Connell had been taken ashore and lashed to a tree while the Allied airstrikes continued, then was taken to the garrison's headquarters, where Woellhof was held.[4]

Both aviators were questioned, beaten, and finally separated. Connell spent seven days tied to a tree before he was flown in an old seaplane to Iwo Jima and then moved to the mainland Japan prisoner-of-war camp of Omori. He would spend the rest of the war as a prisoner. Although his treatment was not pleasant, he later learned of his unique distinction. "I was the last American [taken] off the island [Chichi Jima] alive" by the Japanese, said Connell.[5]

Woellhof's fate was not as kind. On August 5, 1944, Chichi Jima was hit by a fierce bombing raid in which a Navy B-24 Liberator crashed off the island. All aboard perished except the heavy bomber's navigator, Ensign Warren Arthur Hindenlang, who crawled out of the sinking wreckage alive. The infuriated Japanese commander had Hindenlang and Woellhof tied to trees in front of his headquarters, but Lieutenant General Yoshio Tachibana ordered them executed the next day for the Japanese lives that had been lost in the bombing. The two Americans were taken to a firing range, walked up a small hill, and blindfolded. They were then lashed to stakes driven into the ground, and Japanese soldiers repeatedly drove bayonets into their lungs and stomachs before a colonel stepped forward and beheaded the Americans with his sword. The Japanese command on Chichi Jima was only beginning to demonstrate its evil ways.[6]

Lieutenant (jg) George Herbert Walker Bush (a future president of the United States) narrowly escaped a similar fate when his VT-51 Avenger was shot down on September 2, 1944, while attacking the island. Bush's two crewmen perished, but he parachuted out with minor injuries and drifted in his raft toward Chichi Jima for two hours before being rescued by the lifeguard submarine *Finback* (SS 230).[7]

On February 18 Commander Crommelin overflew the Chichi Jima target area first at 1245 and decided there were few worthwhile targets for his *Randolph* air group to strike. He assigned the airstrip and other targets of opportunity to his respective squadrons. VBF-12 attacked the seaplane base as its primary target, while VB-12 went after an 1,800-ton cargo vessel in Futami Harbor with 1,000-pound bombs and caused it to settle. The Americans encountered savage antiaircraft fire. Ensign Clifford L. Fisher's Helldiver was hit in the starboard side of its fuselage, severely wounding his rear gunner, ARM2c William Duncan Crook. During the return flight, Crook conversed with Fisher, mistakenly opening up on the radio instead of using the internal intercom. "His cries of pain during the flight back and in the landing pattern were unforgettable," said Ensign John Morris of VB-12. After Fisher landed their SB2C on *Randolph*, Crook was hustled to sickbay, where the ship's surgeon managed to save his nearly severed leg.[8]

Randolph's VT-12 lost two TBMs to the intense antiaircraft fire during its attacks on the airstrip and shipping in Futami Harbor. The three-plane division of Ensigns Leland A. Holdren, Rudolf Frederick "Fred" Rohlfing, and Floyd Ewing Hall had circled while other bombers made their attacks. Holdren finally led his VT-12 division in at lower speed and a shallower dive angle than their predecessors had used. Rohlfing's Avenger was hit, burst into flames, and crashed before he or his two crewmen—ARM2c Carroll Curtis Hall and AOM3c Joseph Edward Notary—could escape.[9]

Ensign Hall's Avenger was also crippled by antiaircraft fire, but he managed to ditch in the harbor, where he took to his Mae West along with ARM3c Marve William Mershon and AOM2c Glenn Junior Frazier. They found themselves between Chichi Jima and Ani Jima, a small, uninhabited island that Frazier swam to. Mershon and Ensign Hall, however, swam to Chichi Jima, where they were helped from the freezing water by two fishermen and soon became prisoners of war, held at 308th Battalion headquarters.

Long before Admiral Radford's TG 58.4 strikers began returning to their carrier in midafternoon, a second assault on Chichi Jima had been launched by Admiral Clark's TG 58.1, beginning around 1240, at a distance of about 114 miles from the island.

Clark's strike group numbered 132 warplanes—41 from *Bennington*, 44 from *Wasp*, and 47 from *Hornet*—all under the direction of strike coordinator Commander Ed Konrad, CAG 17, of *Hornet*. Konrad's 23 fighters swept in on the Susaki Airfield around 1400 with bombs, rockets, and blazing machine guns but faced severe enemy ground fire in the process.

Ensign Willis "Bill" Hardy of Lieutenant Dick Cowger's VF-17 division found the antiaircraft fire to be particularly intense. Raised in rural Corning, California, on his grandfather's ranch, Hardy paid his way through college by milking cows before enlisting in the Navy. He started as an aviation machinist's mate, making enough money to be one of the few men on base with a nice car. "I didn't have trouble chasing the girls," boasted Hardy. "They were chasing me."[10]

As fun as the single life was, Hardy wanted to do something "more supportive of the war effort" after the Pearl Harbor attack. He took a discharge and a sharp drop in pay in order to become a reserve naval-aviation cadet, entering flight training in 1943 at the Sand Point NAS in Seattle. "I wanted to be a fighter pilot," he said. "I didn't want to be an enlisted and do secondary duties. I didn't want to be a bomber pilot, either." Hardy had earned his wings of gold by January 1944 and was well on his way to seeing the action he so desired as a fighter pilot.

At five-foot-eight Hardy found his height to be a challenge in seeing properly to land his first Hellcats. "I was just too short for the manufactured cockpit. I figured it must have been made for someone a minimum of five-foot-ten. I had to lean and twist sideways a bit to work the top of the rudder pedal and keep the plane slowed to 85 knots coming around the pattern for the last 180 degrees in the landing process," he explained. "That's why I liked the Corsair after we got them. On the trim tab, I didn't have to sit sideways in the seat to keep it slow."[11]

Hardy might have second-guessed his decision against becoming a bomber pilot as he swept in low over Chichi Jima's deadly gun crews at low altitude on February 18. The antiaircraft fire was heavy, and one of his VF-17 comrades suffered a badly damaged Hellcat from a 40-mm shell that exploded in its fuselage.

Konrad directed *Wasp's* Air Group 81—led by Commander Fred Brush—to attack the dock area at Omura town, on the northern coast of Futami Harbor. Many of the Hellcats, Corsairs, and Avengers dived on a small ship and an oil tanker there, finding out only upon pullout that the oiler was an already destroyed hulk. Two of *Wasp's* VMF-216 Corsairs were hit by ground fire but managed to return to base by 1640.

Bennington's Air Group 82 circled for some fifty minutes while the *Hornet* and *Wasp* planes staged their attacks. When Lieutenant Commander

Hugh Wood's dozen VB-82 Helldivers made their attacks, Lieutenant Arthur Wayne Lundblade's bomber was hit and crashed into the harbor, killing him and his rear gunner, ARM3c Edward James Gerber.

By the time Lieutenant Commander Ed DeGarmo's VT-82 pushed over into its dives on wharfs, buildings, and enemy shipping from eight thousand feet, Japanese gunners had their range. Ensign Robert Jay Cosbie's plane was hit by flak, which carried away half of his port wing, causing his TBM to flip over on its back and collide with the one flown by Ensign Robert T. King. Cosbie's plane spiraled to the ground in a violent spin, crashing and burning just inland from the north shore of Chichi Jima, killing him and his crewmen.

The collision tore a three-foot chunk out of the trailing edge of King's port wingtip and caved in the dorsal side of his fuselage for about four feet. Out of control, his plane began to lose altitude. Fearing a crash, King offered his crewmen—AOM3c Grady Alvan York Jr. and ARM3c James Wesley Dye Jr.—the chance to bail out, which they both did. The men were seen, with parachutes deployed, landing on the shore or within a few feet of it. King miraculously regained control of his *Bennington* torpedo bomber, however, and was escorted back to the ship by five *Wasp* fighters. In its after-action report the squadron reported, "The raid of Chichi Jima is a touchy subject with the pilots and aircrewmen of VT-82."[12]

It was exactly two years since Jimmy Dye had enlisted, but his first combat mission had ended terribly. Dye and Grady were taken to General Tachibana's headquarters, where the two nineteen-year-olds were badly beaten and interrogated the following day. Two of the captured *Randolph* aviators, pilot Floyd Hall and radioman Marve Mershon, were taken into Tachibana's offices as well that afternoon, having already endured considerable abuse. Additional time spent on Chichi Jima would not bode well for the downed U.S. aviators.

The task groups of Jocko Clark and Arthur Radford did not linger off Chichi Jima after recovering their final strikers on the afternoon of February 18. Pete Mitscher's TF 58 had an important role to play in the landing scheduled for Iwo Jima the following morning. Radford's TG 58.4 and Rear Admiral Sherman's TG 58.3 took stations west of Iwo that evening, while the other three task groups made rendezvous with fleet tankers to refuel south of the island.

The morning of February 19 was clear and bright as the assault on Iwo Jima commenced. Shortly after daylight Rear Admiral William "Spike"

With air support from TF 58 carrier planes, 5th Division Marines worm up the sandy slopes of Iwo Jima's beach on February 19, 1945, in full view of Japanese observers on the sides of the distant Mount Suribachi. *NH-104205, NARA*

Blandy's eight battleships, five heavy cruisers, three light cruisers, and ten destroyers opened fire in earnest to soften up Japanese defenses for the day's amphibious landings. Lieutenant General Holland M. "Howling Mad" Smith, commander of the expeditionary troops that would go ashore, was frustrated that TF 58 had been diverted to strike Japanese airfields over the previous days rather than committing them to softening up Iwo. Beaches, airfields, and the lower slopes of the prominent Mount Suribachi were pounded heavily by the naval guns until 0803, when a cease-fire was ordered to allow airstrikes to be finally made by the first planes from Sherman's and Radford's carriers.[13]

From west of the island, the fast-carrier task group launched twenty-four Corsairs and twenty-four Hellcats, all led by Marine lieutenant colonel Bill Millington of *Essex*. This marked the first Marine carrier-borne air-support operation for an amphibious landing. The pilots bombed, strafed, and dropped napalm on targets of opportunity on the eastern slopes of Suribachi, on high ground north of the landing beaches, and on the airfields in the island's center. At 0825 the surface ships resumed a heavy bombardment that continued until 0850, at which time carrier planes were allowed in again to strafe the beaches during the minutes leading up to the H-hour landings at 0900.[14]

The first Marines hit the beaches one minute ahead of schedule on the island's southeastern coast. While the men had expected a somewhat easy advance across excellent beaches, they found instead fifteen-foot-high slopes of soft black volcanic ash that did little to absorb fragments from the Japanese artillery bombardment that erupted with intense fury after Lieutenant General Tadamichi Kuribayashi allowed the Americans a one-hour respite to gather on the shoreline. A violent hailstorm of heavy artillery, mortar, and machine-gun fire began raining down on the crowded beaches, turning the area into a slaughterhouse.

Amtracs (amphibious tractors) made little progress through the black ash, forcing Marines to dismount and slog forward on foot. By nightfall the Japanese had lost their hold on Airfield No. 1, and other U.S. forces had driven to the base of Mount Suribachi. By the end of the first day of ground action, some 30,000 Marines had landed on Iwo Jima, with another 40,000 to follow. Casualties were heavy. Aboard his command ship, *Eldorado* (AGC 11), Howling Mad Smith was heard to remark on the slow progress of the ground forces, "the Japanese general running this show is one smart bastard."[15]

Mitscher's carriers were kept busy throughout the day with hundreds of combat sorties. *Hancock* and *Lexington* sent additional fighter sweeps to Chichi Jima and Haha Jima during the morning, losing six planes in the process. During the afternoon, Sherman sent more strike groups to work over targets on Okinawa with napalm bombs. The only Japanese aerial opposition on the nineteenth came late in the day, when two aircraft were splashed by the antiaircraft fire of several ships, including one downed by the battleship *Missouri* (BB 63).

Second Lieutenant Dean Caswell of *Bunker Hill's* VMF-221 had been pleased with his steak-and-eggs breakfast that morning but was a little concerned with his orders: "Go in and scrape your bellies on the beach." Caswell's sixteen Fighting Falcons dropped napalm, fired rockets, and shot up Japanese pillboxes in their assigned target squares. He felt fortunate to encounter only light antiaircraft fire and an absence of Japanese aircraft.[16]

Air operations continued around Iwo Jima for the next two days, with little enemy action that came close to harming the carriers. On February 20, aircraft from TF 58 and the escort carriers flew 545 sorties, expending more than 116 tons of bombs and 1,331 rockets. TG 58.4 and TG 58.3 operated about seventy miles west-northwest of Iwo Jima the following day, providing CAP and several bombing strikes. Admirals Sherman and Davison sent a strafing sweep to Chichi Jima to interdict the airfield so it would not be used for staging. Japanese air attacks aimed at the task groups during the overnight of February 20–21 failed to create any damage. TG 58.3's night carriers operated northwest of Iwo Jima to provide dusk CAP over the island, fighter cover overnight, and nighttime observers for naval gunfire.[17]

Saratoga's fighters had been busy. Ensign Richard E. Schwendemann, who had finished two years of junior college at Fort Dodge, Iowa, before joining the Navy, had taken part in the Tokyo raids the previous week and had since been tasked with CAP duties for the task force. His squadron, VF-53, was ready for action again the following day, having been briefed for a raid on Chichi Jima.

Prior to that strike, Saratoga had been detached from TG 58.3 on the afternoon of February 21 with orders to take three of her destroyers to provide nighttime fire cover for amphibious forces off Iwo Jima. Saratoga had just reached her operating area some thirty-five miles northwest of Iwo at 1628—Schwendemann was in VF-53's ready room—when word came for the ship's company to station General Quarters. Six bogies had suddenly appeared on radar about seventy miles to the northeast heading south.

Four of Schwendemann's VF-53 comrades, the division under Lieutenant Raymond W. Luke, intercepted the six Zeke fighters at 1650. Ensign Constantine Szymborski flamed one, and within three minutes Luke's flight had downed three more. Saratoga in the meantime had turned into the wind to begin catapult launches of fourteen more night fighters and one ready Avenger. The carrier was making sixteen knots at 1700 when six Japanese suicide planes dropped down from out of the clouds to the east. They were Nakajima B6N2 "Jill" carrier attack bombers, each carrying an 800-kg bomb, that had taken off from Hachijojima Airfield around 1400. Among those making his last flight was Flight Petty Officer 2nd Class Kunio Shimizu, a twenty-year-old member of the 2nd Mitate Squadron, Kamikaze Special Attack Corps, serving as a bombardier on one of the Jills. "Today, I will rush in to destroy the American fleet," he wrote in his final letter to his parents. "I will go and fall splendidly as a young cherry blossom."[18]

Saratoga's main batteries hit the leading Jill and set it on fire, but the bomber slammed through the starboard side of "Sister Sara," penetrated into the hangar deck, and exploded violently. A large gasoline fire ensued among the parked planes. The second Jill, also hit by antiaircraft fire, slammed into the ocean close aboard and bounced into the ship's starboard side at the waterline with a powerful explosion that caused flooding in several compartments. The third kamikaze was shot down clear of the ship, but the fourth Jill dropped its bomb into the anchor windlass through the port catapult before crashing into the water.

By 1703 Saratoga's catapults were wrecked, and she was unable to launch any additional aircraft. Schwendemann, caught in the ready room below, was forced to evacuate that space as acrid, black smoke began belching into the compartment. *Saratoga* took on a 5-degree list to starboard from the damage, requiring Schwendemann to feel his way along the slightly sloping passageways toward the ladder that led topside. By the time he reached the flight deck, the ship's 5-inch, .38-caliber main batteries were still firing away at the Japanese suiciders, forcing the pilot to seek refuge back down on the hangar deck.

The final two kamikazes were both hit and set afire as they bored in, but they were not stopped. The fifth plane headed toward the bridge, carrying away the ship's antenna and signal halyard before crashing into the port catapult and exploding. The final plane crashed into an airplane crane on the starboard side and dropped its bomb. Parts of the plane landed in the No. 1 gun gallery, while the rest of its wreckage carried over the side. The bomb exploded on the flight deck, creating a fifteen-foot hole that wrecked three staterooms.

In a matter of minutes, *Saratoga* had been hit by two bombs and four suicide planes. Below decks Schwendemann joined others to help fight the fires. *Saratoga*'s power plant was undamaged, so she built up to twenty-five knots while damage controlmen fought the fires. By 1830 the fires on the hangar deck had been knocked out, and another large fire was contained within another quarter hour. Her flight deck was in no shape to land her circling fighters, so they were directed to head for TF 58. Things were beginning to look up until parachute flares suddenly flared up at 1846 as five more kamikazes made a dusk attack.

Four of these were shot down clear of the carrier, but the fifth came in unobserved, dropping a bomb that exploded on or just over the flight deck, blowing a twenty-five-foot hole in the deck, as the Japanese plane bounced overboard. Schwendemann, having retired to his bunk room for a while to rest, was just heading for the junior officers' wardroom when this latest kamikaze hit. The ensuing explosion "creamed all of our bunks. From then on, back to Pearl Harbor, we slept wherever we could find a bed," he said.[19]

Saratoga was not alone in feeling the wrath of Japan's Divine Wind on the evening of February 21. Rear Admiral Calvin T. Durgin's TG 52.2, built around smaller escort carriers, had sortied from Ulithi on the fifth to help support the Iwo Jima landings. Durgin's task group included the jeep carriers *Makin Island* (CVE 93), *Lunga Point* (CVE 94), and *Bismarck Sea* (CVE 95) along with three destroyers. Operating about forty-five miles east of Iwo Jima that evening, the task unit scrambled its fighters to intercept Japanese kamikazes that approached shortly after *Saratoga* had been hit. A Jill dived into the net-cargo ship *Keokuk* (AKN 4), killing seventeen there, while another kamikaze lightly damaged an LST, but the escort carriers remained untouched. By 1825 all of the CAP had returned to base except one division of *Makin Island* fighters, which was unable to intercept a half dozen Jills that approached just after sunset.[20]

Task-force gunners tore into the attacking Jills, and *Lunga Point* was able to dodge at least three torpedoes. One of the Jill pilots narrowly missed the CVE's stern with his torpedo but pressed home his attack with his flaming torpedo bomber in true kamikaze fashion at 1845. The plane's gas tanks exploded just before impact near *Lunga Point's* after end of the island, its wreckage crashing across the flight deck and sliding over the port side. Damage-control crews quickly subdued fires on the flight deck, signal platform, and after end of the island, and *Lunga Point* was back in full operation by sunrise the following day.[21]

Another Jill made a run on *Bismarck Sea*, bearing in only twenty-five feet above the wave tops to slam into the ship abeam the after elevator. The elevator slammed to the hangar deck, and fires erupted there and below decks. Two minutes after this first kamikaze hit, a second plane dove vertically into *Bismarck Sea* just forward of her collapsed after elevator. This kamikaze exploded four loaded Wildcat fighters, wiped out a repair party stationed directly below the hangar deck, and caused ready ammunition to begin exploding in the hangar area. The after portion of *Bismarck Sea* became a raging inferno, sending brilliant flames high into a darkening sky already illuminated by the burning *Saratoga* on the distant horizon.[22]

At 1905 Captain John L. Pratt ordered his listing carrier abandoned, an evacuation that would consume an hour. During that time, *Bismarck Sea* was rocked by a violent explosion caused by her own ready torpedoes, the force of the blast enough to blow out both sides of the after hangar and remove the after section of the flight deck. Lieutenant (jg) Robert M. Campbell was blown from a railing and suffered a broken arm. As the fighter pilot stroked away from *Bismarck Sea's* hull with his one uninjured hand, he noted that his carrier's deck was "glowing very red."[23]

Another VC-86 fighter pilot, Lieutenant Roger Chambers, fished a life raft from an Avenger, jumped overboard, and pulled another sailor from the sea into his raft. The pair was unable to push free due to the force of the pyrotechnic wind, which kept them against the side of the blazing *Bismarck Sea*. Moments later a tremendous explosion on the carrier caused Chambers to lose his grip on the raft and tumble out. After struggling to the surface, he watched *Bismarck Sea* drifting away "with fireworks going off in every direction."[24]

The carrier's list stopped temporarily at 20 degrees, then increased at a faster rate. At 2007 *Bismarck Sea* lurched to starboard, hanging at an 80-degree angle for half a minute before her island structure snapped away and plunged beneath the water. The escort carrier continued rolling over until she disappeared stern first at 2015.

Task-unit vessels worked through the night to rescue 625 crewmen of *Bismarck Sea*, although 318 casualties had been created by the kamikaze strikes and ensuing explosions. The chilly 70-degree water claimed some of the sailors, and a Japanese plane killed others in a vicious strafing attack. One year and three months earlier, *Bismarck Sea* had stood by *Liscome Bay* as that ship was ripped apart, marking the first American escort carrier lost. Now, on the evening of February 21, it became the last escort carrier lost by the United States.

The badly damaged *Saratoga* survived her ordeal, and her damage controlmen had her flight deck patched up well enough by 2015 to resume landing aircraft on the after portion. Nevertheless, Luke's six CAP planes were forced to ditch after running out of fuel. Five of the pilots were recovered by task-group vessels, but Ensign John Philip Nelson, who had downed one of *Saratoga's* attackers, was never found.

Saratoga had lost thirty-six planes on board and six more by water landings. She also had sustained heavy casualties: 113 killed or missing and 192 wounded. Admiral Spruance ordered her to Eniwetok, where she arrived on February 25 for emergency repairs. *Saratoga* then proceeded to Pearl Harbor, offloaded her air group, and headed to the West Coast for extensive repairs that would keep her out of the war for three months. For surviving pilots like Schwendemann, it would be many weeks before they returned to Operation Iceberg for further action.

Pete Mitscher was stung by the loss of *Saratoga* and the casualties suffered by the sinking of *Bismarck Sea*. Days later he would take pride that his carrier fleet had helped support the bloody battle on Iwo Jima as fighting moved forward toward the key Japanese stronghold of Mount Suribachi. On February 23 a battle ensign from *LST 779* was raised by U.S. Marines atop the little mountain, a moment captured for history by Associated Press photographer Joe Rosenthal. What became one of the most famous photos of the Pacific War was also a triumphant moment for Mitscher, who called his task-force commanders to his flagship to show them a copy of the print. It was a ground victory materially supported by the efforts of everyone in TF 58.[25]

Admiral Mitscher, not overly impressed with the performance of his night air groups, opted not to further develop other such units for service. For the operation at hand, and for the coming months, *Enterprise's* Night Air

Group 90 would be the only one in operation, following the loss of service of *Saratoga*'s air group. It remained an open question whether the performance of her pilots would change Mitscher's mind on such operations.[26]

Night Air Group 90 was under Commander William Inman Martin, an enthusiastic pilot who had cut his teeth in dive bombers off Guadalcanal in 1942 before taking command of VT-10 for a second combat tour, which stretched through much of 1944. Martin had helped guide the use of aerial radar in torpedo bombers, and when he took command of his night-flying air group, he retained a number of his senior pilots, including Lieutenant Russell F. "Kip" Kippen, skipper of VT(N)-90.

"Bill Martin started night flying operations while we were part of Torpedo Ten," recalled turret gunner Don Warner. "We were doing night bounce drills before anything was even thought of by the Navy as far as night flying goes. We were the pioneers of night operations." Warner and other veteran VT-10 men volunteered to join Commander Martin for the stateside training required for his new Night Air Group 90. While at NAS Barbers Point in Hawaii, the VT(N)-90 Avengers were modified to remove the turret guns in favor of a bucket seat for a radar officer to man the TBM's aerial set during fights. Gunners like Warner were shuffled to support roles within the squadron versus actual flight duty.[27]

Under Bill Martin, Kip Kippen, and Lieutenant Commander Robert McCullough—skipper of VF(N)-90—*Enterprise*'s night fliers made raids against Luzon in the Philippines and against Japanese shipping in the South China Sea in early January 1945. Such pioneering night operations came with casualties. During a strike on Formosa on January 22, VT(N)-90 skipper Kippen was lost with his crewmen while making an attack run. His former turret gunner, Don Warner, considered Kip "the greatest guy in the world and a great pilot."

Kippen's replacement was former VT-10 pilot Lieutenant "C B" Collins from Silver City, New Mexico, another respected Avenger jockey who would not be long in the driver's seat. Collins allowed his VT(N)-90 pilots to let off some steam on the evening of February 18 as the task force retired from the Tokyo area, his men mourning the loss of the crew of an Avenger that had crashed without survivors. Two of the larger staterooms became the scene of a rum-punch party attended by Bill Martin and the lion's share of the torpedo squadron. "The rooms became so packed that it was impossible to move, smoke so thick you could walk on it, and heat so oppressive that it weighed tons," logged VT(N)-90's unofficial history. There were few sober airmen standing when festivities broke up in the early morning hours.[28]

Such escapades were not permitted on most fleet carriers in Admiral Mitscher's force, but the officers of "Big E" were known to sidestep protocol on occasion to allow their aviators to unleash pent-up steam. C B Collins and his night torpedo squadron was all business again in time for the Iwo Jima landings. But their losses would continue.

In addition to enemy aircraft and antiaircraft fire, the night-flying crews were stressed more so than the fleet's daylight air groups. One recurring challenge involved returning to the task force via radar, finding *Enterprise* in the dark with its one red light displayed, and then being coached into the groove as they dropped altitude. "To me, this phase of night carrier flying was the most hazardous thing a Navy pilot could ever experience," recalled pilot Bill Balden. "It is really a miracle that any of us survived!" Joe Hranek, the radioman for Lieutenant Gilbert S. "Gibby" Blake's Avenger, could only watch the dark water coming up and record the altitude as his TBM settled in for each landing. Hranek was "never sure where we were until he [Blake] cut the engine and the deck lights suddenly appeared. All in all, it was sheer terror."[29]

During the night of February 22, Commander Martin's "batmen" were tasked with flying night coverage for the fleet after the departure of *Saratoga*. A division led by Lieutenant Collins was taken under fire by friendly warships that night, and two VT(N)-90 Avengers were shot down. Ensign Henry G. Hinrichs and his crewmen were recovered by an American sub-chaser, but Collins and his two crewmen were lost. Command of the badly shaken night torpedo squadron passed to its third skipper in a month, Lieutenant Charlie Henderson, another veteran of the old VT-10 squadron from 1943 and 1944.

Henderson's luck was better than that of his predecessors, and *Enterprise's* night fighters soon set a new fleet record for continuous flying from a carrier. Commencing at 1630 on February 23, Big E's aircraft compiled a record of 174 consecutive hours flying CAPs, sweeps, and intruder missions over Chichi Jima and Iwo Jima both night and day. McCullough's night Hellcats averaged fifty flights every 24 hours. During that extended period, Lieutenant (jg) Cliff Largess even flew a staff officer to hand-deliver messages to the Marines fighting on Iwo Jima, affording Largess the chance to visit briefly with his Marine brother ashore.[30]

Enterprise would remain in night operations off Iwo until March 10, when she was officially relieved by the escort-carrier groups. Big E retired to Ulithi lagoon on March 12, where she rejoined TF 58 in preparation for the next big offensive off Okinawa. In the course of those 174 hours of consecutive flights, Martin's enterprising night fliers had effectively delivered a message to Admiral Mitscher on the merits of their worth.

Mitscher's TF 58, in the meantime, had remained busy with almost-continual flights in support of the Iwo Jima campaign. Two carrier task groups had alternatively taken on fuel on various days, leaving the others to maintain the daily support missions.

Lieutenant Valencia's VF-9 division flew its first mission over Iwo Jima carrying napalm belly tanks on the morning of February 22. A collective *Lexington* and *Hancock* group, led by Lieutenant Commander Herb Houck, CAG 17, orbited ten miles south of Mount Suribachi until the aerial coordinator assigned them specific troop entrenchments upon which to unload their napalm. Valencia's wingman, Ensign Harris Mitchell, found that his first napalm bomb "skidded across some emplacements in a blaze of glory." It was impossible to assess the true damage caused by this mission, but Mitch and others could see several fires burning in their target area as they retired from the island.[31]

Mitscher's carriers provided vital support for the Marines on Iwo Jima, but the aerial threats coming from mainland Japan proved deadly to a number of his ships. Plans were drawn to conduct more strikes on the Tokyo area on February 25, so much of TF 58 spent the twenty-third refueling prior to shaping a northerly run toward Japan. Jocko Clark's TG 58.1 was the exception that day, with his group making another strike against Japanese defenses on Chichi Jima.

Bennington began launching a dozen VMF-123 Corsairs at 0950 on February 23 to strike the Susaki Airfield and to perform a reconnaissance of nearby Haha Jima. Led by Major Everett Alward, skipper of the Flying Eight Balls, *Bennington*'s Marine fighters rendezvoused with a dozen Hellcats of *Wasp*'s VF-81. The combined group began their attacks on Chichi Jima's airfields at 1115, encountering no flak until *Bennington*'s Corsairs made bombing and rocket attacks on the planes parked along the runway. As VMF-123's third flight came in, 2nd Lieutenant Warren Earl Vaughn's aircraft was struck by flak at three thousand feet. Vaughn pulled straight up before his Corsair went into a violent vertical spin that ripped off the remainder of his damaged wing. He bailed out at five thousand feet and finally deployed his parachute at one thousand feet before drifting down east of the bay, inland and north of the highest mountain peak on the island.[32]

Lieutenant (jg) Billy Watts, leading a VF-17 division from *Hornet* over Susaki Airfield hours later, nearly experienced the same fate as Vaughn. As Watts swept in low over wrecked airfield planes, a 40-mm shell smashed into his Hellcat, taking away the outboard half of his starboard aileron and ruining his radio. Shrapnel tore through the starboard side of his cockpit, shattering the Plexiglas of his canopy and sending a two-inch chunk of shrapnel that ripped his right side about seven inches below his armpit.

Watts had his division jettison their rockets before his wingmen escorted his damaged F6F back to *Hornet*. Anxious shipmates, having

Lieutenant (jg) Billy Watts of *Hornet's* VF-17 receives a Purple Heart for shrapnel wounds he sustained in action over Chichi Jima on February 23, 1945. *Charles Watts*

heard that Billy was wounded, were waiting as the division landed. "That got everyone's attention," said Ensign Tilly Pool, who watched as the plane captain on deck helped the bloodied VF-17 pilot from his cockpit. Watts was taken to sickbay, where Doctor Ashley removed the shrapnel splinter, stitched him up, and removed him from flight duty for the remainder of the day. Days later Billy would receive a Purple Heart from Admiral Clark. He would carry the piece of shrapnel with him for decades to remind him of how fortunate he had been to survive his first attack on Chichi Jima.

Fate was not as kind to the TF 58 aviators taken prisoner by the Japanese on Chichi Jima. The latest, Marine Warren Vaughn, was collected on February 23, joining four other carrier aviators who had been downed during the February 19 strikes: pilot Floyd Hall and airmen Jimmy Dye, Marve Mershon, and Grady York. One other airman, Glenn Frazier, remained alive, hiding on desolate Ani Jima. Frazier surrendered on the twenty-third to two fishermen and was taken to Chichi Jima's army headquarters, where a drunken Captain Noburu Nakajima beat him to death by bashing his head with a club.[33]

Vaughn, Dye, Mershon, and York were lashed to trees on Chichi Jima that afternoon. The Japanese commanders decided to execute another American aviator and marched radioman Mershon, his hands tied, up a hill to a small cemetery. He was allowed to smoke a last cigarette before he was blindfolded and made to kneel over a freshly dug grave. Lieutenant Hironobu Morishita stepped forward and swung his sword nearly through the American's neck, the crumpled body then falling into its final resting place.[34]

By Saturday, February 24, Lieutenant General Tachibana's staff was aware of the fierce fighting on Iwo Jima. Joined by Major Sueo Matoba, the hard-drinking 308th Battalion commander, Tachibana accepted the

Second Lieutenant Warren Earl Vaughn of VMF-123 of *Bennington* (CV 20), seen in the cockpit of his Corsair, was shot down over Chichi Jima on February 23, 1945. His Japanese captors would later be tried for war crimes committed on the island by beheading captured American aviators and even practicing cannibalism on them. *U.S. Navy*

invitation of Colonel Takamune Kato, commander of the 307th Battalion, to spend that evening drinking sake in his headquarters. Soon Tachibana was fully drunk, and he decided that his officers should build their fighting spirit by eating some human liver from one of the recently murdered American aviators. A battalion surgeon was sent with a team to exhume Mershon's body, from which the doctor cut out his liver and a large chunk of his thigh, which were soon delivered for cooking in a sukiyaki frying pan. Major Matoba and General Tachibana ate much of this human meat, telling their junior officers that they must demonstrate "necessary courage."[35]

Radioman Dye, gunner York, and pilot Vaughn remained tied to trees outside Tachibana's headquarters for four days. On Monday, February 26, Vaughn was sent to where Hall was still being kept alive for questioning, while York was sentenced to be executed by the 307th Battalion in response to the number of casualties Colonel Kato's command had recently suffered. That afternoon, short, black-haired Grady—who weighed barely 100 pounds—was tied to a telephone post and blindfolded. Two bamboo spears and three bayonets were used to puncture his chest repeatedly until his lifeless body was dumped into a shallow grave and buried. Roughly ninety minutes later, Dye was marched from the radio station where he was being detained and ordered to kneel before a fresh grave. Two officers slashed the American's neck with swords before a doctor was summoned to cut him open and remove his liver before burying his body. That evening, a drunken Imperial Japanese Navy captain, Shizuo Yoshii, ordered his officers to join him in eating some of Dye's liver.[36]

By day's end on February 26, only two U.S. pilots, Hall and Vaughn, remained alive on Chichi Jima. They survived several more weeks, but Allied firebombing attacks on Tokyo and the eventual fall of Iwo Jima spelled the end for these unfortunate prisoners of war. On March 17 Vaughn was decapitated above a bomb crater, his body also dissected so his liver could be eaten. Hall was spared only two more days before he was given a final cigarette and a glass of whiskey as he sat on the edge of another bomb crater. Japanese soldiers partially decapitated him before plunging bayonets into his expiring body, which was then dissected for examination. Hall's liver was removed for consumption at Major Matoba's cannibalistic headquarters.[37]

The last American prisoner on Chichi Jima had been killed.

Two days after making more raids on Chichi Jima, TF 58's carriers were turning into the wind on February 25 to launch a new wave of strikes against airfields on the Japanese mainland. By 0715 Vice Admiral Mitscher's flat-tops were about 190 miles southeast of Tokyo. The weather was as bad as it had been during the first strikes on Japan on the sixteenth.

VMF-123, which had lost 2nd Lieutenant Vaughn two days prior during the Chichi Jima strikes, suffered again on February 25, losing two Corsairs. Major Everett Alward, the Flying Eight Balls skipper, led twenty of his *Bennington* F4Us in attacks on inland targets before moving over Tokyo Bay to attack a 7,000-ton freighter. "Let's sink it!" Alward shouted over the radio to his comrades. General-purpose bombs straddled the ship and created a fire on its bow.[38]

As VMF-123 completed strafing runs on the damaged vessel, the squadron was jumped by about ten Zekes, "Georges" (Kawanishi N1K-J Navy interceptor fighters), Tojos, and Jacks. In the swirling dogfights that followed, Alward was seen to plunge to his death in Tokyo Bay after a Zeke ripped his Corsair's fuselage. Another Eight Ball pilot, 2nd Lieutenant Vincent A. Jacobs, was seen to make a safe water landing, but he was never recovered after attempts to raise a lifeguard submarine went unanswered.

Hornet's early fighter sweep was more productive, particularly in the case of VBF-17's Hellcats, led by the squadron executive officer, Lieutenant Edwin S. Conant. Seeing that Tokyo Bay was socked in by foul weather, Conant led his twenty-two fighters north up the Chiba Peninsula to attack snow-covered Yachimata Airfield, where they strafed hangars, antiaircraft emplacements, a Hamp fighter on the ground, and even a locomotive sitting on the tracks southwest of the field.

As Conant's flight recovered from its strafing runs, the *Hornet* fighters were attacked by twenty Zekes, Tojos, and Oscars. Conant and Lieutenant (jg) James H. Cales—a former Dauntless rear gunner who had seen action at the Coral Sea and Guadalcanal carrier battles in 1942—each downed a pair of enemy fighters. Three other fighters were downed by VBF-17 before the strikers returned to *Hornet*. Their only loss was the F6F of Lieutenant (jg) Sverre O. Bach, who was forced to ditch his damaged Hellcat alongside the radar-picket destroyer *Ringgold* (DD 500).

In contrast to this action, a fifteen-plane sweep from *Hornet's* VF-17, launched at 0736, encountered no enemy fighters over its assigned areas. Flight leader Ned Langdon then led his divisions past Tokyo Bay to attack the Tateyama NAS and the field on Hachijo Jima. Lieutenant (jg) Werner Gaerisch suffered a 40-mm antiaircraft hit in his port wing during these attacks. His division leader, Billy Watts, had seen another division-mate downed near Tokyo during Fighting Seventeen's previous visit, so he helped escort Gaerisch back to the carrier.

Second Lieutenant Dean Caswell launched from *Bunker Hill* at 0825 as part of a major strike against the Nakajima aircraft-assembly plant at Neisumi. Led by Major Ed Roberts, the *Bunker Hill* group included twenty F4Us of VMF-221, thirteen SB2Cs of VB-84, thirteen TBMs of VT-84, and four VF-84 Hellcats. For Caswell, the mission could easily have been his last.

En route, Major Roberts led his Corsairs up to high altitude for advantage over any enemy fighters the strike force might encounter. Above ten thousand feet the fighter pilots were forced to switch to their oxygen masks, whereupon Caswell soon found himself in a predicament. His oxygen hose became disconnected from his mask, and he began slipping into hypoxia—losing consciousness from oxygen starvation. In his groggy state the Marine pilot only vaguely noted his division leader, Captain John Delancey, yelling at him to maintain formation.[39]

"Fortunately, I came to my senses just enough at around 15,000 feet to reconnect the hoses and attempt to rejoin my flight," Caswell said. Due to the foul weather, the flight leader opted to change his target from the Naka-jima Musashino plant to the alternate bad-weather target, the Nakajima Koisumi factory. The bombing attack commenced at 1030, during which Captain Delancey successfully bombed one of the hangars.

Caswell, still separated from the *Bunker Hill* formation, ran the risk of being picked off. Major Roberts reported five or six Japanese fighters shadowing the main formation around this time. Caswell avoided a pair of Franks and took a few potshots at what appeared to be a Tony that passed by him. He was only able to rejoin his squadronmates as they pulled out from their attack runs on the aircraft-assembly factory.

"I was still a little groggy and not very proud of my first combat flight against the enemy," Caswell admitted. Landing and trapping on the deck in

Ensign Ardon Rector Ives of VBF-9 struggles to escape his Hellcat's cockpit. *Lexington's* flight deck erupted into flames on February 25, 1945, after arresting cables ripped open the belly tank of his F6F. *U.S. Navy*

a snow squall topped off the young pilot's tough day, but he was relieved at least to live to fight another day.

Yorktown's VF-3 claimed ten aerial victories over Tokyo and many more planes destroyed on the ground in exchange for two F6Fs forced to ditch near task-force destroyers. Returning pilots in the afternoon reported few worthwhile targets available, freezing guns and gun cameras, and especially lousy weather, prompting Mitscher to curtail any further strikes. TF 58 pilots thought they destroyed 160 planes, only 37 of which were shot down, against their own losses of 9 carrier planes. Mitscher's second strike on Tokyo had thus been less effective than the first.[40]

Lexington's deck crews endured dramatic moments during the return of some of her fighter-bombers. Ensign Ardon R. Ives of VBF-9 ruptured Hellcat No. 23's centerline fuel tank upon landing, and gasoline began gushing out onto the flight deck. Shipboard photographers captured the whole incident as the fuel ignited into a blazing orange inferno. Ives hurriedly extricated himself from the cockpit and scurried across his F6F's starboard wing to safety. Firefighters rushed to extinguish the blazing fuel belching black smoke to prevent a deadly explosion.

Mitscher decided to strike Nagoya on February 26, but heavy wind and seas forced him to cancel this operation as well. But *Enterprise's* Night Air Group 90 made another heckler run against Chichi Jima during the early morning hours and very nearly provided more prisoners of war for the island's garrison. Lieutenant Jim Moore of VT(N)-90 had just released his HVARs at 0705 when his TBM's engine was struck by a 25-mm shell. His windshield was immediately fouled with oil, and his engine ran wildly for a mere fifteen seconds before it quit cold.

Moore glided east across Chichi Jima at ninety knots, preparing to make a water landing three thousand yards off the east coast. He called to his crewmen, Lieutenant (jg) Robert B. Hadley on the radar and ARM1c Tom Watts on the radio, to prepare for ditching. Moore and Hadley suffered no great shock thanks to their shoulder landing straps, but Watts was thrown into his radio gear, wrenching his back, tearing muscles in his chest, and inflicting minor lacerations and bruises about his legs and body.[41]

Hadley and Moore broke out their Mark 4 life raft and emergency gear before helping the dazed Watts escape their bobbing Avenger. The downed crew rigged a makeshift sail and paddled throughout the morning until the destroyer *Gregory* (DD 802) was coached in to their position around 1442 to pick them up. Moore, Watts, and Hadley, treated to hot showers, a stiff shot of brandy, and dry bunks, would eventually make their return to *Enterprise*. "The quick and efficient action taken by the Air-Sea rescue people in this instance has done much to bolster the morale of the entire squadron," noted VT(N)-90's historian.[42]

Enterprise, the flagship of Rear Admiral Gardner's TG 58.5, continued to launch night and day strikes against the Chichi Jima airfield while also providing CAP fighters for Iwo Jima during the following week. Admiral Radford's TG 58.4 was detached to the fleet anchorage at Ulithi on February 27, while the other three "day carrier" task groups steamed westward to make a strike on Okinawa.[43]

The U.S. carrier force had first conducted airstrikes against the airfields on Okinawa in October 1944 during the Philippines campaign, at that time more as a feint to confuse the Japanese than to cause significant damage. This time Admiral Spruance ordered Mitscher's carrier air groups to hit every airfield in the Ryukyus chain on March 1, exactly one month from the planned invasion of Okinawa. TF 58 reached a position about seventy miles southeast of the "Great Loochoo" (as Okinawa was sometimes called, being the largest of the Loochoo Islands, another name for the Ryukyus) during the early morning hours of March 1.

The strike groups enjoyed tactical surprise and found little aerial opposition. Photo Hellcats were sent to perform low-level reconnaissance missions over Okinawa and the other islands of the Ryukyus, and for once the weather proved favorable enough that excellent photographic intelligence was gathered for the operations planned for the coming weeks. Lieutenant Valencia's VF-9 division flew what would prove to be its final combat sortie from *Lexington* that day. Valencia departed with only Ensigns Mitchell and French on his wings, along with three other three-plane VF-9 divisions, to secure photographic coverage of Kikai and Tokuna Islands, Amami Gunto, Nansei Shoto.

The group flew low passes over Kikai before moving on to Tokuna Island, where a low ceiling prevented effective photography. Valencia's division strafed revetted planes on the island's airfield, where the lieutenant was credited with destroying a single-engine aircraft, French with damaging another, and Mitchell with damaging an Oscar. During his run, the bulletproof windshield of Mitchell's plane was hit by a 20-mm shell, which shattered the glass but left it intact.

Captain Jim Swett led VMF-221's first fighter sweep from *Bunker Hill* on March 1, attacking first Suba Harbor and then the airfield on Ie Shima. He then led his two divisions in an attack on Okinawa's Yontan Airfield, where Captain Don Balch burned a Betty bomber tucked into an aircraft revetment. During an attack on antiaircraft batteries northwest of the field, Lieutenant Fred Brigg's Corsair lost more than a third of its port wing to an antiaircraft burst, but Briggs managed to bail out successfully near a task-force destroyer.

Second Lieutenant Caswell participated in VMF-221's second mission of the morning by providing escort to a trio of *Bunker Hill* photo Hellcats over southern Okinawa. At Yontan Airfield he joined his division leader, Captain Delancey, and 2nd Lieutenant Richard Wasley for strafing runs while two other Corsairs flew cover for the F6Fs. Caswell damaged a Mitsubishi Ki-21 Army Type 97 "Sally" heavy bomber on his first pass, and on their second run his trio shot up a Japanese freighter observed offshore. Wasley had part of his port wing blown away by antiaircraft fire over Yontan but managed to limp back to *Bunker Hill*, where his inoperable flaps caused him to suffer a barrier crash during landing.

Corsairs of *Bennington's* VMF-112 attacked Okinawa's other airfield, Kadena, and managed to catch the Japanese completely by surprise at 0800. Major Herman Hansen's Wolfpack squadron destroyed at least five parked aircraft on its first low-level firing run. "The first pass was strictly on the house, a free ride," said Hansen. As his dozen F4Us made a second firing run, the now fully alert Japanese gunners opened up with heavy antiaircraft fire from the north side of the field.[44]

Japanese shipping also took a pounding on March 1 at several islands. *Lexington's* Air Group 9 was first to find good targets in Kuji Bay at Amami Oshima, where eight ships were discovered at 0810. This was convoy KATA-604, which included the transports *Daia Maru*, *Daishin Maru*, *Kinzan Maru*, and *Hoshi Maru No. 11*; the 828-ton torpedo boat *Tomozuru*; and the supply ship *Kinezaki*. Early morning raiders from TF 58 managed to sink the 1,037-ton *Daishin Maru* and *Kinzan Maru* in addition to damaging three of the other vessels.[45]

Shortly after 1400 *Lexington* and *San Jacinto* warplanes led by Lieutenant Commander Houck returned to Amami Oshima to pound the remaining merchant ships. Houck ordered the *San Jacinto* Air Group 45 fighters and torpedo bombers to attack the Koniya seaplane base on the southern end of the island, while his own Air Group 9 planes scouted the northern coastline of the island. In Naze Ko (Bay) they found three surviving ships from a convoy that was attacked during the morning strike.

The larger ship, apparently *Hoshi Maru No. 11*, was beached near the entrance of a sizable cove on Naze Ko's eastern shore. Houck directed Lieutenant David G. Woodcock's three sections of VB-9 to attack first. Woodcock was the only one to score, his load of 500-pound and 250-pound bombs seen to hit just forward of the transport's bridge. The VBF-9 and VF-9 Hellcats followed, with two pilots being credited with bomb hits.

Lieutenant Commander Byron Cooke led thirteen of his VT-9 Avengers in next to unload salvos of ten 100-pound bombs from each TBM on the largest beached ship. Houck, several fighter pilots, and the Avenger aircrewmen tallied twenty-two small-bomb hits on the hapless transport. The remaining eight Avengers claimed another thirteen hits on the other two ships with their strings of 100-pounders. By the time *Lexington's* strikers departed Amami Oshima, there were few shipping targets worthy of return strikes. The supply ship *Kinezaki* took a bomb hit that resulted in flooding aft, which caused her bow to rise up so that she was vertical before she plunged under the water. *Hoshi Maru No. 11*, badly damaged by bombs, burned throughout the day, then exploded that night and sank in Naze Ko.[46]

The few groups of shipping turned up by TF 58 planes on March 1 created a feeding frenzy. At Okinawa around 0930, returning strike planes reported a merchant vessel and an accompanying destroyer—actually the 828-ton torpedo boat *Manazuru*—off the island's western coast about three miles from the island's capital, Naha. Mitscher immediately ordered a strike group launched to attack these ships.

Bennington sent off a dozen rocket-armed VMF-123 Corsairs under Major Thomas E. Mobley Jr. along with six VB-82 Helldivers under Lieutenant Commander Wood. Other strike groups were dispatched from *Wasp* and *Hornet*, with VF-17 skipper Marsh Beebe as the overall strike coordinator. The three air groups spread into scouting lines to search for the ships. Beebe located the freighter near Kuzu Saki, about three miles north of Naha, and the apparent destroyer dashing into the town's harbor. He ordered his *Hornet* group to shift its focus to the destroyer while directing the *Wasp* and *Bennington* planes in to attack.

Mobley's VMF-123 Corsairs went in first to draw fire for the *Wasp's* SB2Cs, each Marine firing his eight HVARs in salvo. Second Lieutenant Dwight E. Mayo was credited with the day's outstanding performance of slamming the Japanese warship with seven out of eight rockets along its broadside. First Lieutenant Harry J. Bearlund bracketed *Manazuru* with his eight rockets, scoring at least two hits, while 1st Lieutenants James P. Doolan and Arthur C. Schneider were credited with one hit each.

Wood's Helldivers achieved only one direct bomb hit on the torpedo boat's stern around 1203. Lieutenant Commander Robert M. Ware's VB-17 division could do no better than land two near misses. Beebe's first division of VF-17 closed out the attacks on *Manazuru*, with the skipper, Frank Sistrunk, and Bob Coats each claiming rocket hits at the base of the bridge and foremast of the mainmast. The division led by Tommy Harris and Tilly Pool followed, scoring at least two rocket hits in addition to strafing damage. Fuzz Wooley's third division of Fighting Seventeen claimed two direct bomb hits, both observed by Ted Crosby as he circled in his F6F to photograph the attack. Afterward, Lieutenant Commander Wood noted that the enemy warship appeared to have run aground on a shoal to the north of the channel to the inner harbor.

The frenzy of strikes against the Ryukyus on March 1 also turned up worthwhile shipping targets at Miyako Jima. Throughout the morning Lieutenant Commander Ed DeGarmo and his VT-82 pilots had been sitting "bored stiff" in *Bennington's* stuffy wardroom, listening to reports of strike after strike in beautiful bombing weather. When his pilots had about given up hope, word came that two "Sugar Bakers" (merchant ships) had been sighted in the Miyako Jima anchorage. It was just the news they had been waiting for.[47]

Wood—making his second sortie of the day against shipping contacts—led the Air Group 82 procession. In the rush to launch, only two of DeGarmo's Avengers were loaded with torpedoes, with the remaining three TBMs carrying 500-pound bombs. Wood's *Bennington* group rendezvoused with another *Hornet* strike force of twenty-four warplanes and reached the harbor at 1705.

They found the most notable shipping to be a large freighter of about 7,000 tons, a smaller freighter, and what was believed to be a destroyer escort (likely an auxiliary gunship or torpedo boat of about 800 tons). *Bennington's* VF-82 attacked the larger merchant ship, dropping their pairs of 250-pound bombs at around nineteen hundred feet. Three hits were observed, one of which was credited to Lieutenant Benjamin P. Limehouse, whose crippled fighter slammed into the ocean after flak sheared off the entire tail assembly from the fuselage.

Wood led seven *Bennington* Helldivers down on the larger merchant ship as well. His gunner, ACRM Henry H. Reed, observed two of their 500-pound bombs strike forward on the ship. An additional bomb hit created an explosion on the freighter, which began billowing heavy black smoke. Lieutenant Thomas C. Durkin's first division of VT-17, attacking the big freighter at the same time, claimed two Mark 13 torpedo hits. Ensign Herman E. Rauchfuss of VT-82 laid his load of bombs across the vessel from starboard bow to port quarter, causing the ship to explode again violently, sending a column of smoke and flames two thousand feet into the air. As Rauchfuss cleared, the ship was completely concealed by smoke and an oil slick.

Multiple squadrons similarly piled on the fleeing small warship. Two pilots from Lieutenant Steven G. Sullivan's second division of VT-17 reported torpedo hits, and Lieutenant Jesse "W" Naul of VT-82 landed a bomb squarely amidships. Hugh Nicholson's VBF-17 added two rocket hits and numerous near misses with 500-pound bombs. Lieutenant Douglas J. Yerxa of VB-17 landed a 500-pounder forward on the vessel. Lieutenant Charles T. Beall, leading the second division of VBF-17, claimed a direct hit that appeared to blow off its stern section. When last seen by strafing fighter pilots, the little warship was settling by the stern.

The Miyako Jima strike force managed to sink the transports *Toyosako Maru* and *Taiken Maru*, damage *Edogawa Maru*, and finish off an 800-ton torpedo boat. Elsewhere during the day, search planes from *Belleau Wood* located two destroyers in a harbor at Ishigaki Jima, some 250 miles from the task group. A bombing strike was immediately launched by the carrier, with VT-30 skipper Lieutenant Frederick Charles Tothill leading six of his Avengers (each loaded with four 500-pound bombs) and eight Hellcats of VF-30.

Five miles from the island, one of the fighters, piloted by Ensign William Nelson Thomas, water landed due to engine trouble; later attempts to locate him proved fruitless. Tothill continued on to Ishigaki Jima, where his group found three ships at anchor off the island's main town. These appeared to be a new destroyer, an oiler, and a freighter. Tothill was preparing to attack when Lieutenant (jg) William Ernest "Ernie" Delaney spotted another destroyer-type warship 750 yards northwest of the first three ships.[48]

The second warship was just getting under way with a nearby mine-layer, which was putting up heavy antiaircraft fire. The others ships and shore batteries then began firing as well. The fighters went in to strafe and rocket the northernmost destroyer, causing a large explosion on board. Lieutenant (jg) Lewis M. Cobb and Ensign James J. Noel each scored one rocket hit, but Fighting Thirty lost two more pilots to flak while making shipping attacks.

Tothill led his VT-30 division in next, his bombs straddling the target warship forward of its bridge and scoring one hit on the port side amidships. Ensign Charles Dewitt Relyea Jr. and another TBM pilot landed near misses alongside one of the minelayers before Relyea switched to attack the destroyer. Accurate gunfire from shore batteries hit his left wing tank and likely Relyea himself, as the Avenger was seen to plow into the ocean one-half mile offshore at three hundred knots, killing him and his two crewmen.

Lieutenant Jacob Matthew Reisert, Torpedo Thirty's executive officer, led his division in an attack on the destroyer and landed one hit squarely on its forecastle amidships. Reisert's plane was hit in its dive or again immediately upon pullout. The shell exploded in the interior of his open bomb bay and penetrated the center main tank, flooding the cockpit with gasoline and wounding Reisert in both legs. He immediately notified Tothill of his damage and headed for the southern end of the island, fearing that he would have to crash-land in the bay. Reisert made no mention of his severe wounds. Tothill ordered Delaney to jettison his remaining bomb (already having dropped three near the destroyer), join up on Reisert, and set a course for the carriers.

Japanese records indicate that the carrier planes torpedoed and sank the 457-ton minelayer *Tsubame* off Ishigaki Jima. *Belleau Wood*'s strike also damaged the minelayer *Nuwajima* and the 1,020-ton destroyer escort *Fukue*.[49]

Upon leaving the target area, the *Belleau Wood* fighters and Avengers joined up on Reisert and Delaney about twenty-five miles from Ishigaki Jima. Tothill suggested Reisert should set a course for the nearest

A Japanese ship, believed to be a minelayer, sinking after attacks by *Bennington* and *Belleau Wood* (CVL 24) warplanes on March 1, 1945, near Naha Harbor. This vessel is likely the 457-ton minelayer *Tsubame*. NH-89379, NARA

rescue vessel operating off Okinawa. In the meantime the injured pilot had resorted to violent jerking of the stick and pulling the emergency release to shake off his final bomb. Even having done so, it was considered nearly suicidal to attempt a water landing with open bomb-bay doors, so Reisert told his crewmen to prepare themselves for a parachute jump. Tothill's remaining Avengers were too low on fuel to remain with Reisert, whose plane was limping along at 110 knots, so fighter pilots Cobb and Noel, both with belly tanks, were detached to escort him to the rescue vessel.

The submarine *Bluefish* (SS 222), under Lieutenant Commander Charles M. Henderson, was on lifeguard duty south of Honshu, making her seventh war patrol. Henderson received word at 1510 that a plane in distress was heading toward his position, so he put *Bluefish* at flank speed to meet it. Reisert was becoming desperate, his fuel gauges reading empty by the time he caught sight of *Bluefish* at 1558.

Circling above the sub, he ordered his crewmen—AMM3c William P. O'Shea and AMM3c Charles R. McCall—to jump one at a time. The first airman was spotted drifting down in his parachute at 1601 and was hauled safely on board *Bluefish* thirteen minutes later. Reisert, circling with fuel gauges that had read empty for a quarter hour, ordered his second crewman to bail out. *Bluefish* had him safely recovered by 1618.

Reisert, watching above to ensure the rescue of his two men, then put his Avenger into a vertical dive and bailed out. The TBM slammed into the ocean and sank immediately as *Bluefish* headed toward his parachute at emergency speed. Other VT-30 pilots saw the pilot freefall three hundred feet before his chute opened, striking the water while still oscillating. Reisert was dragged in the water by his open chute for six minutes and drowned before the submariners hauled his unconscious body on board at 1627. "He was suffering from a 6-inch shrapnel wound in his left thigh and a smaller wound in his right leg," noted *Bluefish*'s patrol report. "Artificial resuscitation was commenced right on deck as we headed slowly away from the land. Adrenalin was administered, and everything possible was done to revive the patient."[50]

At 1651 Reisert's body was taken below, and *Bluefish* headed to sea at high speed. Reisert was pronounced dead at 1715 from a combination of shrapnel wounds, shock, and drowning. His body was committed to the sea after a brief funeral service. Lieutenant Tothill recommended Reisert for the Navy Cross, although Admiral Mitscher had him written up for the Medal of Honor for his selfless actions in saving his two crewmen. In the end the Navy Board only issued the Navy Cross, despite repeated attempts to have the decoration upgraded.

◆◇◆

The majority of TF 58 began retiring from Okinawa during the evening of March 1, although a surface force bombarded Okino Daito—an islet 195 miles east of Okinawa—during the early hours of the second. The U.S. carrier fleet pulled into Ulithi lagoon on March 4, winding down an eventful two-week combat cruise.

Vice Admiral Mitscher reported to Admiral Nimitz on the statistics of TF 58 for the period of February 16–March 1, 1945. The various squadrons claimed to have shot down 393 enemy planes and reported another 266 destroyed on the ground. His carriers had lost 84 planes, along with sixty pilots and twenty-one aircrewmen, in combat and had lost another 59 planes, with eight pilots and six crewmen, operationally. During this time, his warplanes had flown 5,514 sorties and had dropped 1,118.65 tons of bombs, 218 napalm bombs, 12 torpedoes, and 9,896 rockets. Airstrikes on Japanese surface targets had sunk or destroyed fifty-seven vessels, ranging from picket boats and armed trawlers to one escort carrier, with another sixty vessels damaged. Twenty-seven pilots had been downed in the water during this period, of whom sixteen were rescued successfully.[51]

Although Lieutenant Reisert had perished during his successful efforts to have his two crewmen saved by *Bluefish*, other pilots from the ten U.S. aircraft downed on March 1 had been recovered thanks to the remarkable rescue system in place for TF 58 aviators. Ensign William F. Hahn of *Bennington*'s VF-82, forced to ditch fifteen miles off the northeast coast of Okinawa, was rescued a half hour later by a floatplane.

VMF-451 fighter pilot Lieutenant Albert C. Simkunas from *Bunker Hill* was shot up by antiaircraft fire near Naha Harbor and was forced down about five miles off Okinawa. Two seaplanes from the battleship *South Dakota* (BB 57) were sent out to recover him, with a pair of *Essex* fighters flying cover. They landed just miles off Okinawa, scooped up Simkunas, and returned him to his ship the same day in good condition. "This kind of teamwork played a large part in maintaining the wonderful morale of our aviators," noted Rear Admiral Sherman.[52]

Chapter Seven

OKINAWA PRELUDE

Lieutenant (jg) Billy Watts watched from the deck of his carrier, *Hornet*, as she slipped between the protective torpedo nets into the Ulithi anchorage on March 4 and marveled at the vast assemblage of American war power he observed. The lagoon was soon filled with TF 58's carriers as far as the eye could see, each of their flight decks jammed with aircraft. Anchored around them were dozens of destroyers, cruisers, battleships, repair ships, floating dry docks, tankers, tugs, ammunition ships, landing craft, minesweepers, and other vessels.

After more than a month of nearly constant combat flying, the ten-day period Pete Mitscher's fast-carrier striking group would spend at Ulithi was a godsend for the aviators. The fleet took on fuel, ammunition, bombs, food stores, and all the provisions necessary to carry on its operations in the Pacific, while pilots like Watts took the chance to enjoy some R&R ashore on Mog Mog, the largest island in the archipelago. Thousands of sailors per day were allowed to enjoy the sixty-acre recreational island, which sported a movie theater, a chapel, refreshment stands, and separate officers' areas, where grilled burgers and cold beer (nicknamed "Grog Grog") were less restricted than the two beers generally issued to enlisted men per day.

Fresh bags of mail from home greeted the VF-17 pilots and those of dozens of other squadrons. Lieutenant Jim Pearce was jubilant, having received a letter from home in which his wife announced the safe birth of their son Michael on March 6. "This news relieved me of some anxiety and concern about things back home," said Pearce. *Bunker Hill* Marine pilot Dean Caswell recalled, "The major recreation was hot volleyball games, drinking beer and coke, and running crab races in the hot sand." He became badly sunburned on both his front and back sides on Mog Mog and could hardly wait to get back to his carrier.[1]

By afternoon many TF 58 pilots switched from beer to hard liquor, and the men roughhoused like boys. "There were a few coconut trees pushed over by bulldozers," said Fighting Seventeen's Tilly Pool. "The Marines would back up one side and the Navy on the other, and we'd have coconut fights with each other." The nightly trips from shore on the LCVP (landing craft, vehicle and personnel) were often a sight, as men unaccustomed to heavy alcohol consumption fell overboard, became sick, or even engaged in scuffling on the crowded vessels. "There was a bunch of them that couldn't even climb the ladder to get back onto the ship," recalled Pool. "So, the *Hornet*'s skipper had them scooped up in a cargo net and dumped out onto the flight deck!"[2]

During his time in Ulithi, Vice Admiral Mitscher and his staff worked on reports on the previous war cruise and developed changes for future operations. He remained unimpressed with *Enterprise*'s Night Air Group 90, having canceled most of their heckler mission over Tokyo because of the difficulty in getting the "zipper patrol" (overnight strikes intended to "zip" up a target area already blasted by daytime attacks) back to their carrier base. "Most of the evening was spent homing lost planes of the zipper patrol by the entire task force," wrote Mitscher on March 7. Further, the night-carrier task group took away from the resources of day-carrier task groups, whose planes had to fly cover over Big E during the nights.[3]

Mitscher recommended to Admiral Nimitz to no longer dedicate a full carrier to night operations and distributing only six VFN planes with ten pilots and three VTN Avengers with five aircrews to each fleet carrier. "The night carrier task group has not yet demonstrated that the damage night carriers can inflict on the enemy compensates for the loss of the offensive power of the day carriers required for the protection of the night carrier task group," Mitscher stated.

But in the end *Enterprise* would continue to be the only fully operational night carrier, while each *Essex*-class carrier operated the small contingent of night fighters that Mitscher wanted. *Enterprise*'s Night Air Group 90 took on replacements, including three new ensigns for VF(N)-90: James R. Perkins, Waldo W. West, and Franklin Thomas Goodson. Reporting to *Enterprise* on March 10, Goodson joined the same squadron a former flight-school buddy, Ensign Charles William "Gibby" Gibson, had flown with until he was killed in action on February 1 during a strike on Clark Field in the Philippines. "The strange part was that I was assigned to the same quarters that he had, and his name was still on his locker," wrote Goodson. "I found myself replacing my former roommate who was now missing in action."[4]

TF 58's squadrons went through a number of changes at Ulithi. Four Marine Corsair squadrons were detached from their carriers: VMF-124 and VMF-213 from *Essex* and VMF-216 and VMF-217 from *Wasp*. These were replaced by two Navy Corsair fighter-bomber squadrons, VBF-83 to *Essex* and VBF-86 to *Wasp*, while *Hancock* also received Lieutenant Commander Roland W. Schumann's VBF-6 Corsair squadron. By the end of the air-group shuffling in Ulithi, TF 58 sported thirteen Corsair squadrons—seven Navy and six Marine.[5]

Two new air groups reported for action as well. Commander Edwin B. Parker's Air Group 5 went to *Franklin*, which now included three F4U squadrons: VMF-214, VMF-452, and VF-5. *Intrepid*'s new Air Group 10 included two Corsair squadrons: VBF-10 under Lieutenant Commander Walter Edward Clarke and VF-10 under Lieutenant Commander Wilmer Ernest "Will" Rawie. The "Grim Reapers" of Fighting Ten had transitioned from Wildcats to Hellcats to Corsairs over three combat tours. *Intrepid*'s dive-bomber and torpedo squadrons, VB-10 and VT-10, were also well tenured, having made two Pacific combat deployments since the 1942 Guadalcanal campaign. Torpedo Ten, nicknamed the "Buzzard Brigade," was under a new skipper, Lieutenant Commander John Creig "Larry" Lawrence, who planned to add to his squadron's successful record off Okinawa.[6]

Lieutenant Gene Valencia and wingman Ensign Harris Mitchell learned at Ulithi that their home carrier, *Lexington*, was being sent to the States for overhaul, taking with her *Yorktown*'s Air Group 3, which had seen many long months of combat. *Yorktown* was still in prime fighting shape, so Admiral Mitscher merely swapped out air groups. On March 6 Valencia and his comrades of Air Group 9 boarded *Yorktown*, where they inherited Air Group 3's F6F-5s, SB2C-4s, and TBM-3s. Lieutenant Commander Torrey had been lost during the Tokyo strikes on February 16, so the new CAG 9 became Lieutenant Commander Houck, who had led Fighting Nine until Torrey's death. Houck's replacement as the squadron's skipper was Lieutenant Buster Kitchen. The other Air Group 9 squadrons were VBF-9, under Lieutenant Commander Frank L. Lawlor, a former Flying Tiger; VB-9, under Midway veteran Lieutenant Tony F. Schneider; and VT-9, led by Lieutenant Commander Byron E. Cooke.

Many green young ensigns joining the fleet at Ulithi expected to see their first combat as soon as TF 58 sortied again. "All the pilots were already very naturally excited," said Ensign Roy D. "Eric" Erickson of

Intrepid's VBF-10. "Some now began to be afraid. It was quite noticeable, the change of attitude, but no one said anything about it."[7]

Vice Admiral Ugaki had been waiting to pounce on the American fleet when it finally relaxed from pounding his airbases. He was in the middle of a training meeting with his kamikaze staff on March 9 when a message was received from the Fourth Fleet. A scout plane reconnoitering Ulithi reported six fleet carriers and nine converted carriers in the atoll, with another four carriers approaching from the northeast.

"Judging that most of the enemy task forces had returned there, I decided to carry out the second Tan operation," Ugaki wrote. High winds and a lack of new reconnaissance intelligence compelled him to suspend the planned attack for two more days. In the interim Ugaki invited all of the officers of the Azusa unit to dinner, where he found them to be in "noble and lofty spirit."[8]

The weather was good on Sunday, March 11, and Ugaki ordered out his strike force on its one-way mission to hit the U.S. fleet at anchor in Ulithi. Beginning at 0900, two dozen twin-engine Frances bombers under Lieutenant Naota Kuromaru, each loaded with a 2,000-pound bomb, started on the 1,360-mile journey, each with scarcely enough fuel to make it one way. Thirteen bombers would turn back due to engine troubles, while thunderstorms forced the remaining eleven bombers to circumnavigate the foul weather. They reached Ulithi at dusk, dangerously low on fuel and lacking sufficient light to accurately see their targets.[9]

Ugaki went into a shelter as evening approached, anxiously awaiting news on their success or failure. The kamikazes headed for the anchorage, so low on fuel that planes began dropping into the ocean only miles from the fleet. "Time passed notwithstanding until it was thought to be quite dark over there," he wrote. "Yet nothing was heard except reports of making emergency landings." A number of the aviators would be rescued and returned within days to Kanoya, where they offered details of their mission to the vice admiral.[10]

On board the carrier *Randolph*, a cargo light had been left on in the after portion of the ship, and it served as a homing beacon for the two remaining kamikazes. Two Frances bombers were still airborne, making their final runs toward the U.S. fleet anchorage. One pilot mistakenly plowed into the lighted baseball diamond on Mog Mog, but the other flew hell bent toward the light shining from *Randolph*'s stern. At 2007 the final Frances slammed into the flight deck aft on the starboard side as the ship's crew was enjoying the movie *A Song to Remember* on the forward end of the hangar deck. The kamikaze's 2,000-pound bomb destroyed parked aircraft, creating a large fire on the aft hangar deck that detonated 40-mm and 20-mm ammunition. The explosion lifted Lieutenant Hamilton McWhorter, the Navy's first Hellcat ace, two feet from the chair he was sitting in in his squadron office. Twenty-six men perished in the explosion, and another 105 were wounded.[11]

The kamikaze attack caught thousands of men completely by surprise. On Rear Admiral Jocko Clark's flagship *Hornet*, many of the ship's company were also in the process of enjoying a movie on the hangar deck. Billy Watts had taken his seat and was waiting for the show to begin. One of his buddies, Tilly Pool, was annoyed at the delay. As per custom, it would not start until the admiral was seated, and Jocko Clark was scrambling as fast as his stubby legs would carry him. Pool could not help but be amused.

The carrier *Randolph* (CV 15) was hit by a kamikaze while at anchor in Ulithi Atoll on March 11, 1945. Note the gaping hole in her flight deck as the repair ship *Jason* (AR 8) works alongside. *80-G-344531, NARA*

It took more than an hour for *Randolph*'s crews to control the fires. Admiral Spruance toured the damaged carrier the next day and determined that the damage to her flight deck, including two destroyed arresting-gear engines, would require stateside repairs. The ship's catapult officer, Lieutenant Commander Sam Humphreys, instead convinced his skipper that the sternmost arresting-gear engine could be relocated with the assistance of workmen from the repair ship *Jason* (AR 8). While flight operations would be restored within eighteen days, *Randolph* would nevertheless miss the next combat sortie of TF 58.[12]

Randolph's CAG, Charlie Crommelin, was not content to remain in Ulithi while repairs were effected to his carrier. He requested and received special temporary duty as a strike coordinator for TG 58.1 and was transferred to *Hornet*, thereby ensuring his opportunity to contribute to the upcoming Okinawa invasion.

Mitscher and Captain Burke had been in *Bunker Hill*'s flag plot at the time of the kamikaze attack. Burke had noticed with irritation that a cargo light had been left burning on *Randolph*'s aft portion, and he had heard the incoming suicider. It was Mitscher's firsthand introduction to kamikazes, but he would witness them in even closer fashion in supporting the upcoming Okinawa invasion.

The task-force ships remained on high alert during the next two days, wary of further kamikaze strikes against them while in such vulnerable positions. General Quarters was sounded more frequently, whenever radar indicated suspicious bogies anywhere near the area. Most were relieved when the task force finally began getting under way at 0930 on March 14.

Mitscher's force was bolstered by the inclusion of a British task force under Vice Admiral Sir Bernard Rawlings that included four carriers, two battleships, five cruisers, fifteen destroyers, and 224 planes. The British flattops had metal flight decks and armored hangars and sides, making them less susceptible to the heavy damage that the nonarmored U.S. carriers faced from kamikaze attacks. Rawlings would operate independently with TF 57, his mission to control the area from the southern Ryukyus to Formosa by knocking out airpower in that region.[13]

While in Ulithi, Air Group 4 was disembarked from *Essex* on March 10, its place filled by an eager new group of aviators. *Essex* would be heading to sea with Air Group 83, under Commander Harmon Tischer Utter, an Ohio native who had graduated from the Naval Academy in 1932 and earned his wings four years later. Utter was flying with Patrol Squadron 101 from Manila when the war started; on December 10 the bow gunner of his PBY Catalina flying boat was credited with shooting down a Zero carrier fighter, scoring the Navy's first verifiable air-to-air kill of a Japanese plane in the Pacific War. Utter's *Essex* air group was heading into its first combat with its mix of Corsair and Hellcat fighters.

Ensign Donald McPherson was still learning his way around VF-83. The young Hellcat pilot, who hailed from rural Adams, Nebraska, had put his dreams of being a football coach on hold to follow his brother into the Navy and the V-5 pilot-training program. He had trained with another squadron only to have been picked up in Hawaii as a replacement pilot on February 17 for a pilot lost during carrier-landing practice. McPherson and the rest of Air Group 83 had been ferried to Ulithi on board a British troop transport before making their way on board *Essex* on March 10. The kamikaze explosion on the nearby *Randolph* did not help soothe McPherson's tensions as he prepared to head into enemy waters. "This sure made me wonder what we had gotten ourselves in for," he said.[14]

McPherson had been carrier qualified in November 1944 on Lake Michigan and again in January 1945 with landings on an *Essex*-class carrier. But as the task force prepared to depart Ulithi, he remained a spare pilot, unassigned to any regular F6F division. One of his young VF-83 comrades assigned to a division had the unique distinction of having not yet qualified for carrier landings. Ensign Larry Clark made little noise about his situation but was more than a little anxious when *Essex* put to sea briefly on March 14 to break in her new air group.

Clark, a former varsity quarterback for his Compton Junior College in California, was one of the few married men among the younger Hellcat pilots of VF-83. He had become close friends with Ensign Jack Lyons during the squadron's training days, and they and their wives had shared apartments in both Atlantic City, New Jersey, and in Massachusetts during times when accommodations were tough to find. Both Lyons and McPherson had gone through the regular carrier-landing practice sessions on the converted luxury liners *Wolverine* and *Sable* (IX 81) on Lake Michigan, but Clark had missed his chance to do so.

As the young ensign settled into the groove on March 14 to make his first true carrier landing, his mind raced through a thousand little details. He knew a crash landing could quickly erase his chances of remaining in a first-team division, so the man of faith said a silent prayer as he watched the landing-signal officer's wands direct him in. Clark went through his routines just as he had done previously many times during field carrier-landing approaches. He was careful to set his guns on safety, as he knew the abrupt jerk of his plane lurching forward in the arresting gear had caused more than a few deaths during the war due to accidental firings.

After a successful landing, Clark climbed from his cockpit with an air of relief and satisfaction. His Hellcat, like the other *Essex* aircraft, was painted blue with an inverted diamond symbol on its tail to identify its air group. "I had never been aboard an aircraft carrier before," said Clark. "I got lost several times the first few days."[15]

Several of Clark and McPherson's Air Group 83 comrades were trained in flying both Corsairs and Hellcats. Lieutenant (jg) Ed Pappert had trained in F6Fs with Lieutenant Commander James J. "Pug" Southerland's VF-83 and had proven himself to be an able marksman. After Pappert scored the most hits on a towed gunnery sleeve during his squadron's formation period, he was assigned by Southerland to serve as the squadron gunnery officer. But during final training at Maui, Pappert's division was reassigned to Lieutenant Commander Frank Patriarca's VBF-83, which flew Corsairs.

Once he boarded his new home carrier *Essex*, Pappert was in awe of the ship's size. He was assigned a stateroom in the forward end of the hangar deck with three other VBF-83 pilots—Vern Coumbe, Glen Wallace, and Clem Wear. "We are fortunate to have a room," Pappert wrote. "Many of the new pilots are assigned to one large area." The roommates settled into an evening routine of playing team acey-deucy games. The losing duo would make a midnight run to the wardroom to fetch a pitcher of hot chocolate and a stack of toast with cherry preserves to serve the winning team.[16]

Utter's new air group would have their first chances at striking their enemy within days. Vice Admiral Mitscher, in the meantime, had his hands full with final meetings and preparations for the Okinawa campaign. Throughout his fleet, the carrier squadrons readied themselves while the ships took on supplies and engaged in last-minute drills and gun practice. During the midday on March 15, Mitscher was eating with his staff in the gallery deck flag mess just as *Bunker Hill's* antiaircraft crews began practice on aerial targets. When his flagship's 5-inch guns suddenly boomed, dishes leaped from the table, startling the admiral.

"For Christ's sake, can't they wait until we have lunch?" someone snapped.

"I don't give a damn what they do," said Mitscher, "so long as they learn how to shoot."[17]

Mitscher's next sortie from Ulithi would mark the commencement of Operation Iceberg, the most complex enterprise yet undertaken by

American amphibious forces. The assault on Okinawa had been carefully planned for months, and it would be carried out by four principal commanders. Admiral Spruance and Vice Admiral Mitscher ruled the U.S. Navy's Fifth Fleet and TF 58, charged with paring down Japanese air power and the dreaded kamikazes before the expeditionary force hit the Ryukyus. Their fast carriers and land-based Army Air Forces B-29s were to conduct preliminary strikes against key Japanese bases during the two weeks preceding the actual landings, scheduled for April 1, 1945—officially designated as L-Day in the plans.

Vice Admiral Richmond Kelly Turner commanded the Joint Expeditionary Force and was in charge of all amphibious operations until the Okinawa beachhead was established. The fourth key commander was Lieutenant General Simon Bolivar Buckner Jr., son of a Confederate Civil War hero, commanding the Tenth Army, which would send four divisions of the XXIV Army Corps ashore on Okinawa. The soldiers of Buckner's 27th Infantry Division were veterans of previous assaults on Makin and Saipan; the 7th Infantry Division had helped take Attu, Kwajalein, and Leyte; the 96th Infantry Division had fought on Leyte; and the 77th Infantry Division had been blooded during the landings on Guam. Major General Roy S. Geiger, a figurehead during the 1942 Guadalcanal campaign, would additionally send three Marine divisions ashore. The First Marine Division had fought at Guadalcanal and Peleliu, while his Second Marine Division had been part of the 1944 assaults on Tarawa and Saipan. In contrast, Geiger's Sixth Marine Division would be seeing its first amphibious attack during Operation Iceberg. Buckner's and Geiger's combatants expected to meet strong resistance from roughly 77,000 Japanese troops.[18]

Operation Iceberg was in full swing by March 11, and the landings on Okinawa would exceed anything previously attempted in the Pacific. Ten miles of the island's western Hagushi beaches were to be assaulted by four divisions—two Marine and two Army—which would land eight regiments of soldiers from landing craft on April 1, while another division was to seize the anchorage of Kerama Retto. More than 180,000 troops and 746,850 tons of cargo would be moved in 433 assault ships from eleven ports, while resupply echelons brought tens of thousands of additional troops and their cargo. Another 115,000 service troops were scheduled to land on Okinawa during the coming operation to handle all aspects of sustaining the massive ground campaign. L-Day on Okinawa would be of a scale scarcely imaginable to the young Marines and Army infantrymen who were being hustled toward the last epic Pacific campaign of World War II.[19]

Rain came down in torrents as twenty-year-old machine gunner Corporal Melvin Heckt prepared to deploy from the Solomon Islands on March

11. Heckt, who had already made landings on Emirau and Guam in 1944, was a member of a machine-gun squad of the 1st Battalion, officially Company A, 3rd Platoon, 1st Raider Battalion. At Guadalcanal Heckt's squad boarded *LST 451* at 0830 on March 11 in a downpour. With two of his buddies, Eugene T. "Nap" Napiwoski and Melvin J. Jennings, he "gung hoed" a tent and a tarp so the trio had a somewhat dry "boudoir" for their topside voyage. Once their canvas shanty was complete, Heckt sprawled out to get some sleep.[20]

Many of the Marines piling on board the amphibious vessels were ready for a change, including Private 1st Class Watson Alexander Crumbie. For months his 1st Battalion, 29th Marine Regiment had endured heat exceeding 100 degrees and endless training exercises. To ward off malaria, the nineteen-year-old soldier, who hailed from Dallas, Texas, took daily Atabrine tablets that turned his skin a yellowish color. "You could tell who was not taking his Atabrine, which was a court-martial offense," said Crumbie.[21]

The young Texan had joined the Marines in July 1943, a month before his eighteenth birthday. When he was baptized the Sunday morning before he shipped out, he read from the 23rd Psalm. Crumbie found courage in the words, "Even though I walk through the valley of the shadow of death, you will be with me." He had walked through his own valley of death less than a year later, when he participated in the landings on Saipan in June 1944.[22]

Crumbie had climbed down a cargo net from his transport ship into a Higgins boat that carried him the last 2,000 yards to the shore of Saipan. The sights he saw as he splashed over the side remained imprinted in his mind. "There on the beach were several dead Marines," said Crumbie. "Ants were already in their noses and mouths. A hand was rising and falling with each wave as if to say 'goodbye.'" During his first night ashore, he came face to face with a Japanese soldier who suddenly appeared above his foxhole. A fellow Marine killed the attacker before Crumbie could raise his own rifle. The artillery fire he endured that first night had left him shaken and helpless. "I could only lie there and pray to God as I had never prayed before," he recalled.[23]

Crumbie survived Saipan, subsequent months of training at Guadalcanal, and his mid-March voyage on board the transport *Leon* (APA 48) to Ulithi. This was the final staging area for the Marines before reaching Okinawa. Now a seasoned veteran, Crumbie had some old scores to settle for the brothers in arms he had lost on Saipan.

During the early morning hours of March 21, the Marine-laden troopships were slammed by a storm fierce enough to wash a truck and a jeep over the side of one LST. When Heckt's *LST 451* finally dropped anchor in Ulithi's lagoon on the twenty-second, he was overjoyed to receive mail from his family back home and his first fresh oranges in months. Three days later, on March 25, the U.S. amphibious force got under way for Okinawa. The LSTs were battered again by a storm en route, which created seasickness among the men and caused the ship's crane to break loose and pull down the little boudoir shelter Heckt and company had been sleeping under.[24]

Anticipation ran high among the Marines and soldiers as they prepared to hit the beach, the fateful day being Easter Sunday and ironically codenamed "Love Day." Few expected any love from the enemy ashore. Sprawled on the deck of his pitching LST, Heckt scribbled in his little diary, "May the Lord bless every man who falls in the ensuing struggle."[25]

Chapter Eight

"A WILD DOGFIGHT ENSUED"

Pete Mitscher used the two weeks preceding the Love Day landings to pound Japanese resistance, hitting both kamikaze airfields and warship anchorages. Under way from Ulithi by 0620 on March 14, TF 58 made course for the southernmost home island of Kyushu, whose key airfields were fewer than two hundred miles from Okinawa. After refueling at sea on the sixteenth, the U.S. carriers began their final run toward the Japanese islands, the Bald Eagle intent on launching massive airstrikes roughly ninety miles from Kyushu.

Vice Admiral Ugaki was well aware that the American fleet had sortied from Ulithi on the fourteenth. He correctly deduced that strikes would be made against his airbases by about Sunday, March 18, and therefore he directed his base commanders to disperse their aircraft in order to maintain overall fighting strength. "At 0205, I decided to launch an encountering attack with full strength and ordered activation of the First Attack Method," Ugaki wrote. He began sending off attack planes at 0350, followed at 0600 by a daylight strike force. By about 0650 Ugaki's reconnaissance planes told him he was facing four U.S. carrier task groups. He thus had a fairly accurate count of the total number of flattops arrayed against him.[1]

The day's carrier airstrikes would create problems with Ugaki's plans. Shortly after noon on March 18—once the first waves of morning attackers began departing from the Japanese airfields—Ugaki ordered the Thunder Gods Corps' Ohka-ferrying bombers to prepare to strike. Lieutenant Commander Jiro Adachi readied eighteen Betty bombers, which ground crews began pulling from secret tunnels at Usa Airfield. They were only halfway through the task when a wave of American carrier planes began assaulting nearby Tomitaka Airfield, then arrived over Usa.[2]

Adachi had gathered some of his Ohka pilots at a hangar for a farewell drink before their one-way missions. Ground crews were hauling Ohkas across the runway to the Bettys when U.S. planes began unleashing devastation. Adachi sprinted for an air-raid shelter as Hellcats, Helldivers, and Corsairs ripped into the defenseless Bettys, causing them to erupt into flames as they sat on the runways. By the time the Americans departed, leaving the smoking wreckage behind them, the first would-be launch of the Thunder Gods had been spoiled. Miraculously, none of the Ohkas were hit.[3]

At Tomitaka Airfield the fighter planes from the 306th and 307th Squadrons that did make it into the air were overwhelmed by American fighters. Reserve Sub-Lieutenant Hachiro Hosokawa had planned to follow these two squadrons into battle, but he was prevented from launching by Wing Commander Kunihiro Iwaki, who told him that it made no sense for his men to waste themselves on defensive fighting. "It's hopeless," said Iwaki. "You people should die in Ohka attacks!"[4]

Hosokawa watched helplessly as his comrades tried in vain to resist the American attack. He saw one of his former flight instructors, Petty Officer Umeno, chasing one raider overhead only to be himself jumped by three other American fighters. As Hosokawa looked skyward, he saw Umeno cause a U.S. fighter to begin smoking only seconds before Hellcats and Corsairs shot up his own fighter, which burst into flames and plunged toward the ground.[5]

Alarm sirens wailed throughout the day, as Ugaki weathered the attacks from within an air-raid shelter. He prayed that some of his own planes would survive to punish Mitscher's carriers. "In a shelter on the ground, without fear of sinking," he recorded, "there was nothing to worry about except the damn noise."[6]

March 18 marked the beginning of a two-day raid on Japanese airfields and shipping on and around Kyushu. *Enterprise*'s Night Air Group 90 led the entire operation, with its first three fighters launching around midnight. Night Avengers assaulted Japanese airfields and radar installations, while VF(N)-90's overnight fighters chased bandits away from TF 58. By daybreak they had knocked down four Japanese aircraft near the fleet. "Japs were everywhere, dropping flares trying to locate the fleet," wrote Ensign Franklin Goodson, who tangled with some of the enemy attackers.[7]

One of the Japanese planes managed to damage Big E's deck, forcing the VF(N)-90 pilots to circle until 0940. Poised roughly ninety miles southeast of Kyushu before daybreak, Vice Admiral Mitscher's carriers were alive with action, as deck crews readied the strike planes. Second Lieutenant Dean Caswell figured it would be another big day as he and his fellow aviators shoveled down steak and eggs in the *Bunker Hill* wardroom. When he reached the VMF-221 ready room, Caswell and sectionmates Joe Brocia and Dick Wasley listened to a thorough briefing by division leader Captain John Delancey. Caswell was disappointed at not having seen aerial action in the airstrikes during February, but he would not be disappointed this day.[8]

In Rear Admiral Jocko Clark's flagship *Hornet*, VF-17 skipper Marsh Beebe similarly instructed his division leaders on their morning assignments. During his first aerial battles over Tokyo weeks before, Beebe had secured one and a half kills. Over Kanoya Airfield this day, his individual tally and those of some of his junior pilots would rise dramatically. Section leader Tilly Pool gobbled up a quick breakfast and dressed appropriately for the expected cold weather. "They didn't have winter flight gear on the carrier, so we doubled up by putting on green wool Marine pants, with khakis over that, and our flight suit on top of it all," Pool described. Small groups of night fighters, including four Hellcats of *Essex*'s VF(N)-83, were sent on "zipper missions" to strafe the Japanese airfields before daybreak, but Pool would be among those hitting the enemy with enough daylight to see his targets.[9]

Beginning at 0545, Lieutenant Commander Beebe led twenty Hellcats off *Hornet*'s flight deck. His division was followed by those of Tommy Harris, Bob Coats, Fuzz Wooley, and Willis Parker. VF-17's fighter sweep over Kanoya Airfield was among the first launched from TF 58 to help neutralize the threat of kamikaze attacks. These early sweeps were scheduled to suppress forty-five enemy airfields. "Although the Japanese lacked trained aviators, they had no shortage of aircraft," noted Rear Admiral Sherman, commander of TG 58.3. "Scores of fighters were in the air when our planes arrived."[10]

Beebe's Hellcats had crossed the Japanese coastline by 0715, when division leader Harris and his wingman, Swede Sundberg, swung into action. Harris downed two Zekes and added a probable kill and damage to another Japanese fighter, while Sundberg claimed one Zeke kill and a probable. Ensign Pool, the second-section leader of Harris' division, sprayed a twin-engine bomber with lead as it attempted to lift off from Kanoya, then spotted four grayish-colored Franks parked on the edge of the runway. "I hit those four planes and three of them crumpled down," said Pool.

Beebe's VF-17 flight tangled with a dozen Zekes and Franks over Kanoya, where Lieutenants (jg) Frank Sistrunk and Jack Davis disposed of three enemy fighters. The divisions of Coats and Parker were attacked at the same time. Parker destroyed one Zeke only to find another starting a run on him. Coats slid in and burned the second enemy fighter. Before the two divisions could begin their strafing runs on the airfield, another five Zekes were tallyhoed. Ensign Geremiah J. Foster destroyed one, while division leader Coats pursued the remaining four. Closing to pointblank range on one, he knocked it down, then doggedly pursued the remainder, knocking down one after another until he had destroyed all four, one of which exploded spectacularly in midair. En route to Kagoshima Bay minutes later, Coats achieved ace-in-a-mission status by knocking out a fifth opponent, a Zeke he closed while firing to eight hundred feet until its pilot parachuted out. "We were knocking them down as fast as they would come up," remarked Coats.[11]

Beebe, Good, Pool, and Stan Smith had just recovered from their airfield runs and were beginning a rendezvous orbit when the Japanese attacked them. "I was turning around, and here comes two right at me, firing," recalled Good. He simply aimed right at one Zeke, holding his fire as long as he could, until he finally opened up, his hits causing it to flip over onto its back and dive into the ground.[12]

During his attack run on the airfield, skipper Beebe had heard several tallyhos shouted over the air. "As I pulled out and started to rendezvous with the others, enemy planes were coming down at us in a steady stream," he said. "They really surprised us."[13]

One aggressive Zeke locked onto Beebe's tail, forcing him to throw his Hellcat into a controlled spin. He waited until the last instant to pull out, hoping to fool the enemy pilot into thinking he had been fatally hit. "I still had my belly tank on and I thought that I was so low that I had scraped it on the beach," he said. Beebe quickly recovered, jettisoned his belly tank, and headed right back toward the fighter that had been on his tail. "I caught him flat-footed," said Beebe, who landed bullets in the Zeke's cockpit until it slammed into a low hill.

He was then joined by Tilly Pool, who latched onto a Zeke and began firing. His first kill as a fighter pilot almost seemed too easy. "I gave him a good burst in his cockpit," said Pool. "He just flipped inverted and went right into the water with no flames." Beebe in turn shot another Zeke from Pool's tail, coming to his rescue again moments later when a Frank attacked the ensign. Beebe fired at the Frank head on, closing from one thousand feet to two hundred feet. The blazing plane pulled over the top and crashed into the bay, marking the skipper's third kill of the morning. Beebe missed colliding with the flaming wreckage by mere feet as the enemy plane flashed past him.

All American aircraft rendezvoused and were heading south and climbing when another enemy plane was sighted near the water on an opposite course. The attack signal was given, and Stan Smith fired at maximum range from astern. The Japanese plane countered by firing from a fixed tail gun and then turned right into Beebe, who fired until the burning plane crashed into the bay.

The flight proceeded south and circled while climbing at the mouth of Kagoshima Bay to reform tactical divisions, then headed north on another reconnaissance of the bay, climbing further to eight thousand feet. As the Americans banked to return, three Zekes were sighted attacking Smith. Bud Good heard the old fighter-pilot circus call from Smith of, "Hey, Rube!" followed by, "We've got lots of 'em over the bay here!"[14]

Good turned and applied throttle to join this latest mix, splashing his second Zeke of the morning. Tilly Pool added to the tally by knocking down his second plane of the day, another Zeke, but the third opponent proved to be the most elusive. Sliding in behind the Japanese fighter, Pool managed to get only a few rounds into him before his guns ceased firing. The ensign reached down on the console and pressed the button to hydraulically charge his guns, fired again, but found that only one round was expended. To his disgust, he discovered that he was out of ammunition in his first successful dogfight.

"I stayed on him," said Pool. "I had heard in Germany when the RAF faced those buzz bombers, the pilots would get right up on their tails, tip them up at low altitude, and send them right into the ground with their buzz bombs. So, I thought I'd try that." Pool could see that the Zeke pilot appeared to be dead, slumped over in his cockpit, with his plane gliding down. He moved his Hellcat in close, aspiring to use his own wingtip to lift the Zeke's tail and send his opponent into the ocean. "But when I started slipping under him to get a wing under him, I started getting some incoming hits in my wing."[15]

Pool later admitted that his stunt "was the stupidest thing in the world." In the course of trying to tip over the doomed Zeke, he was flying his F6F straight and level, thereby making himself an easy target. The small-caliber hits in his right wing were enough to convince him to give up the tipping drill and return to the protection of his fighter circle. Out of ammunition, Pool met another Zeke head-on, charging forward on a bluff until forcing his opponent to break off.

Beebe took his flight north after this big scrap and managed to engage five more Japanese planes that were tallyhoed just to the east of Kanoya

Airfield. During this action, the lieutenant commander caught a Frank and, with a deflection shot, cut off a section of its port wing, knocked its wheels down, and started a fire in the fuselage, causing the enemy to crash into the bay. Marsh Beebe had earned the distinction of ace in a mission with five confirmed kills.

Before the *Hornet* Hellcats were finished, Smith knocked another Zeke into the eastern side of the bay entrance. The rest of the Japanese planes fled. After an exhausting half hour of nearly constant combat through 0745, the *Hornet* divisions headed back to their ship. The collective flight was credited with eleven planes destroyed on the ground, three probables in the air, three damaged enemy fighters, and two dozen aerial kills split between eleven VF-17 pilots. Pool and Harris each claimed two of these victories, while Beebe and Coats finished the first fighter sweep of the morning with five kills each.

TF 58's warplanes made repeated strikes against the Japanese homeland airbases throughout the morning of March 18. Rear Admiral Radford's TG 58.4 was assigned the airfields on northern Kyushu, all those on the smaller island of Shikoku, and any enemy shipping discovered in the Inland Sea. Lieutenant Commander Larry Lawrence's veteran VT-10 squadron made bombing runs on Oita Airfield on Shikoku. The Buzzard Brigade Avengers returned intact to *Intrepid*, with the unit's only loss coming as skipper Lawrence missed the arresting wires and plowed into the crash barrier upon landing. Crewman Ralph Hovis deemed their TBM-1C to be "scrap iron once we got through with it," and deck hands quickly gave Lawrence's crushed torpedo bomber the deep six over the side.[16]

Between 0715 and 0745, fighter pilots from other carriers tangled with small groups of Zekes and other Japanese aircraft. Sixteen F6Fs of *Essex*'s VF-83 arrived over Matsuyama West Airfield at 0715 and became embroiled in a scrap with more than two dozen Jacks and Oscars. Lieutenant (jg) Hugh N. Batten and his wingman, Lieutenant (jg) Samuel J. Brocato, each downed two fighters, while three other members of VF-83's fighter sweep achieved a kill apiece.

That morning also proved to be very productive for *Essex*'s VBF-83. Lieutenant (jg) Warren Okey Sigman led thirteen Corsairs against the airfields of Nittigahara, Karashara, and Tomitaka to strafe Japanese aircraft. Sigman and his wingman, Ensign Harry Lamprich, knocked down three Zekes, but Sigman and another VBF-83 pilot, Lieutenant (jg) William Fredrick Garner, failed to return from their first big fight with the Japanese. The VBF-83 flight ended its morning with two lost pilots in return for eight kills claimed and five probables.

The next major *Essex* strike—involving sixteen VF-83 Hellcats, thirteen VB-83 Helldivers, and fifteen VT-83 Avengers—arrived over Nittagahara around 0750. They found it less congested with enemy planes, but intense antiaircraft fire downed the Avenger of Ensign John Lewis Kiernan. *What a hell of a way to spend my twenty-first birthday!* thought Ensign Jack Lyons of VF-83, who endured fierce ground fire as he delivered rockets and bullets to Japanese hangars on his first combat strike. "It made me grow up pretty fast," Lyons recalled.[17]

Hornet's second fighter sweep of the Kyushu raids departed at 0644. It included Lieutenant Commander Charlie Crommelin, CAG 12, who had secured a temporary assignment while his home carrier, *Randolph*, was being repaired for kamikaze damage. Crommelin flew escort for a Hellcat photo-reconnaissance team and destroyed a Zeke fighter near Takayama Airfield.

Commander Ed Konrad, CAG 17, led *Hornet's* third flight off at 0815 with orders to hit Kanoya Airfield near the shore of Kagoshima Bay. In the course of their runs, the twenty VF-17 planes and their fellow dive bombers and torpedo bombers destroyed twenty-one planes, probably destroyed another four, and damaged seven. Billy Watts destroyed two twin-engine aircraft on the ground. Aerial opposition was meager, but Ensign Bill Hardy spotted one Zeke at 0925 making runs on the Helldivers and drove it away with damaging hits.

For division leader Jim Pearce, it was one of the few missions in which his regular wingman, George Johnson, was replaced by Ensign John Paul Wray from Eugene, Oregon. Wray, a more recent replacement pilot for Fighting Seventeen, had grown tired of patrol duty and wanted to see action over Tokyo. His squadronmates had tagged Wray with the nickname "Robespierre" in reference to a Warner Brothers cartoon character, but his desire to fight did not go unnoticed. Bud Good, wingman for skipper Beebe, had finally told Wray, "Go talk to the Old Man."[18]

Beebe allowed Wray to fill an open slot for the Kanoya strike. In his first two strafing passes over the airfield, Lieutenant Pearce destroyed a Judy and a Betty. After making his second strafing run low over parked aircraft on the tarmac and in revetments, Pearce was just commencing his pullout when Wray came up on his right-hand side. His Hellcat had been hit by antiaircraft fire, and his entire engine block was wrapped in flames. Pearce escorted his wingman over Kagoshima Bay until Wray was forced to ditch. His F6F went down with its life raft, but Pearce was able to drop his own raft to the ensign. "He waved to us as we circled overhead and appeared to be uninjured," said Pearce.[19]

He and two squadronmates flew cover over their downed comrade, Pearce and Ernie Vonder Heydon excusing themselves only long enough to dispose of a Nakajima C6N Navy "Myrt" fast-reconnaissance plane. Fuel exhaustion finally forced the lieutenant and company to abandon Wray before an inbound OS2U Kingfisher seaplane could arrive, Pearce departing only after receiving assurance from a friend, VF-18 pilot Bill Stevenson, that his Corsair division would safeguard the downed pilot.

Pearce's division returned at 1140 to *Hornet*, where he was able to use the carrier's communications gang to contact the cruiser that had launched the Kingfisher. To his horror he learned that their OS2U pilot had only managed to retrieve a dead Japanese pilot in a life vest. Distraught over the loss of his wingman, Pearce persuaded Marsh Beebe to allow three divisions to be launched to search for Ensign Wray's life raft.[20]

Hornet's task group came under kamikaze attacks shortly after 1300, as the carrier was preparing to launch further strikes. Its flight deck was packed: a dozen VBF-17 Hellcats were spotted forward and behind them sat another two dozen VB-17 Helldivers and VT-17 Avengers, all loaded for another attack on Kanoya Airfield. Spotted beyond them were three divisions of VF-17, led by Beebe, Harris, and Pearce.

At 1310 a Judy bomber, undetected by radar, suddenly dropped from the clouds, hell bent on crashing into *Hornet's* flight deck. Alert 40-mm and 20-mm gunners took the suicider under fire and damaged the aircraft. "The gunners set that plane on fire but it kept coming in with its left wing on fire," recalled Tilly Pool, who watched helplessly from his cockpit. "The left wing finally burned off, forcing him into a half roll as he went over the flight deck. I swear you could feel the heat when he went over us."[21]

Hornet's deck log recorded that this Judy passed over the flight deck sixty feet forward of the stern—parts of the burning plane rained down on the deck—before it slammed into the ocean one hundred yards off the carrier's port beam and exploded. Having narrowly avoided disaster, Pool's division remained on standby until 1450, launching three hours after returning from their morning strike.

Led by skipper Beebe, the three divisions made strafing and rocket attacks on Chiran Airfield, followed by secondary strikes on two other airfields. During the flight, the VF-17 divisions searched the area of the ocean where Wray had last been seen in his life raft. No trace of their squadronmate was seen, leaving Pearce quite distraught. Weeks later the lieutenant was dumbfounded to find that his buddy had been forced to abandon his circling watch over Ensign Wray. Stevenson's squadron skipper had ordered him to carry on with his assigned target strike and leave the downed aviator for the Kingfisher pilot to find. "Unbelievable!" Pearce later wrote. "Wray was never heard from again, during or after the war."[22]

Second Lieutenant Caswell's Marine squadron had already lost one Corsair during *Bunker Hill's* first fighter sweep of the day. Commander George Ottinger, leading Air Group 84, had taken sixteen fighters down to bomb and strafe the Miyazako Airfield at 0800. During VMF-221's second pass, antiaircraft fire hit Lieutenant Ralph Glendinning's plane and severed his oil line, forcing him to make a water landing fifteen miles west of Miyazaki. His squadronmates circled above, dropping dye markers near his raft, but Glendinning would endure some six hours in the ocean before a Kingfisher from the battleship *New Jersey* (BB 62) recovered him.

Caswell's division, "Viceroy 15," led by Captain Delancey, was part of *Bunker Hill's* second fighter sweep against Kyushu on March 18. Glendinning was still adrift after lunch when the divisions of Captains Delancey, William N. Snider, and Mitchell L. Parks passed nearby en route to attack Japanese airfields. The dozen VMF-221 Corsairs delivered a rocket attack to the Kumamoto Airframe Plant on Kyushu before heading east toward Tomitaka Airfield. Caswell was flying at 13,000 feet with his division when they encountered about twenty-five Zekes and Franks around 1630 on about the same level. The *Bunker Hill* units attacked immediately and began dropping Japanese planes, with Captain Snider and his wingman, 1st Lieutenant Donald MacFarlane, turning in claims for four kills.

After several firing runs, Captain Delancey shot up a Zeke, which fell out of control to crash into the sea. Amid the action, wingman Caswell nosed over and delivered a medium burst to another Zeke maneuvering on Delancey's tail. Caswell's victim was seen to slam into the water. Farther down the coast, the lieutenant polished off two more Zekes in a five-minute interval by attacking each from astern and above. He downed the first with a tail shot and the second with hits in the cockpit. Neither burned, but both were seen to crash, giving Caswell his first three confirmed kills.

The other two pilots of Delancey's division, Lieutenants Brocia and Wasley, tangled with ten Franks and Zekes. Wasley burned one Frank and damaged two other fighters. Brocia downed one enemy fighter and fired head-on into another that appeared intent on ramming him. Brocia pulled over at the last instant, missing his opponent by inches. In the meantime the divisions of Captains Snider and Parks added seven more kills to VMF-221's daily tally before the surviving Japanese fighters took off, apparently dispirited.

Caswell felt certain he had downed a half dozen enemy planes, but he would learn that credits were not easy to come by. In cases where other pilots witnessed an enemy plane explode or crash, a kill was generally granted. In the case of Caswell, his squadron operations officer reviewed his gun-camera film and decided that only those planes shown in flames or exploding would be counted. His camera also captured four other planes that had lost a piece of their tail or wing and were smoking. In the end skipper Ed Roberts made the decision to award the pilot with three kills and three probables. Being only a second lieutenant at the time, Caswell decided not to cause a problem by airing his opinions on his engagements. At the time, too, he had already taken a ribbing from the ordnance folks on his ship for holding down his trigger too long and burning up his guns.[23]

Lieutenant Gene Valencia's first combat strike from his new carrier *Yorktown* that afternoon was particularly memorable thanks to a Japanese kamikaze raid on his task group.

The morning hours had already been busy, as *Yorktown* sent various fighter sweeps, CAPs, and attack groups aloft to tangle with incoming Japanese bogies and to pound airfields on eastern Kyushu, 150 miles to the northwest. At 1000 Valencia's "Mowing Machine" division was launched with two other VF-9 divisions for a strike against Tsuiki Airfield on Kyushu. At 1230, two and a half hours into the flight, the divisions of Lieutenants Jack Kitchen and Edward C. McGowan tangled with two Vals and a Nate while Valencia's division flew high cover for them. They claimed damage to one Val and recorded the other Val and Nate as probable kills before moving on to Tsuiki Airfield, where a smoky haze prevailed from the effects of earlier strikes.

Valencia spotted the airfield through a hole in the clouds and led his division down from 11,000 feet. His wingman, Lieutenant (jg) Harris Mitchell, could see pieces flying off two Mitsubishi F1M Navy Type 0 "Pete" observation seaplanes they shot up on the north edge of the field and proceeded to strafe hangars and buildings on the airfield. Lieutenant (jg) Jim French followed and scored two rocket hits on the largest hangar, strafed another building, damaged a single-engine plane with strafing hits, and destroyed two Japanese biplane trainers, which burst into flames as his .50-calibers chewed through them.

Lieutenant (jg) Clint Smith, flying the "tail-end Charlie" position, tore up two more aircraft with his slugs before Valencia called for the division to rendezvous over the inland sea. A quick check told him that his three companions were running low on fuel, so the lieutenant led his flight back toward *Yorktown*, leaving the divisions of Kitchen and McGowan to make additional strafing runs on Tsuiki. By the time Valencia's division reached their carrier around 1400, Smitty announced that he was desperately low on fuel. Ordered to land first, at 1420 Smith took the cut from *Yorktown* assistant landing-signal officer Lee Spaulding. French trapped his F6F next before Valencia settled into the groove with his section. His approach was normal, but at the last instant Spaulding vigorously waved him off from landing.

Mitchell spotted the problem: the tail hook on Valencia's Hellcat was jammed in the up position, his landing gear having been damaged by light antiaircraft fire over Tsuiki. The lieutenant circled around and made three more landing attempts but was waved off by Spaulding each time due to his tail hook remaining lodged upward. Mitchell was finally directed to land as *Yorktown*'s skipper, Captain Thomas Combs, prepared for extreme measures. Combs was prepared to offer special consideration to Air Group 9's top fighter ace, so he maneuvered his big flattop to allow Valencia to make a barrier crash to get on board.[24]

Mitchell scrambled from his Hellcat once it was chocked to watch the barrier-crash procedure. Valencia had spent a half hour trying to bring his wounded bird down, but *Yorktown*'s radio shack suddenly sent an alert of a large group of bogies some 130 miles out. The task group immediately rang up battle speed of twenty-five knots and made preparations to defend against an air raid. Before Valencia could make it in for his barrier-crash attempt, his ship's combat-information center (CIC) announced another bogey at 1459, this one only 8 miles out and closing fast.

Admiral Ugaki's counterattacks on March 18 had amounted to about fifty planes. The only carrier task group to receive damage was Rear Admiral Radford's TG 58.4, which was operating about 75 miles west of Shikoku. *Enterprise* was hit by a dud bomb in the morning, while *Intrepid*'s gunners splashed a would-be Betty kamikaze so close that the bomber's burning fragments started a fire in the hangar deck that killed two men and wounded forty-three others.

As Valencia cleared the area, it was *Yorktown*'s turn to be the center of enemy attention from three Judy bombers. He was still clawing for altitude as 5-inch, 40-mm, and 20-mm guns erupted in a violent thunder of smoke and fire that caused Mitchell to retreat below decks. The first two diving Judys missed, but one minute later the third Judy scored a hit on the starboard side of *Yorktown*'s signal bridge. The bomb passed through one deck and exploded near the carrier's side, blowing two large holes. Five men perished from the explosion and another twenty-six were wounded.

Yorktown's damage-control parties were still hard at work when Valencia's fuel tanks finally ran dry. He signaled his intentions to ditch at 1509 and settled into a relatively smooth water landing near the task group's screening warships. Valencia scrambled from his cockpit uninjured and was picked up within ten minutes by *McNair* (DD 679). His part in the planned two-day strikes on Japan was over, his only excitement of the late afternoon being that of watching *McNair*'s able gunners detonate a drifting Japanese mine. Valencia would be transferred back to his *Yorktown* on the morning of March 20 via breeches buoy as his carrier refueled.

Ensign Glen Harold Wallace's first combat mission with VBF-83 would prove to be equally successful and tragic. He launched from *Essex* at 1357 on March 18 as wingman for his division leader, Lieutenant James Jenkins "Steve" Stevens, in company with two other Corsair divisions collectively led by Lieutenant Thomas H. Reidy.

"We were the second group to hit Kyushu and figured the Japs were probably stirred up and waiting for us," reported Wallace. As his flight crossed the Kyushu shoreline at 12,000 feet, the ensign looked down and spotted two Japanese torpedo bombers at twelve o'clock. He waved to attract the attention of Stevens and pointed to the left. The lieutenant nodded his okay and led his division into a diving turn. Wallace quickly filled his sights with a Judy and opened fire with all six .50-calibers. The plane came apart, burst into flames, and fell to the ocean.[25]

The other plane escaped. Stevens led his flight on to blast Karashara Airfield with 500-pound general-purpose bombs and to strafe parked planes, hangars, and the runways. The *Essex* flight then proceeded to hit Kumamoto Airfield with the same results. "By then we were pretty cocky, seeing as how this business was so easy and fun, too," said Wallace.

Heading back, Stevens opened up on the radio with, "What the hell? Let's hit another one on the way back."[26]

Stevens led his division to Tomitaka Airfield, but this time they were greeted by some twenty waiting Hamps and Zekes. One of the pilots the lieutenant faced here was a blooded ace, twenty-six-year-old Warrant Officer Takeo Tanimizu, who had joined the IJN flight-training program in March 1942 against the wishes of his mother, a former pearl diver. Tanimizu had seen his first fighter combat in November 1943 over Rabaul and had been shot down by P-51 Mustangs on November 3, 1944. He had parachuted from his doomed fighter at low altitude, was recovered, and spent a month in a Formosa hospital before being ordered back to Japan. Tanimizu's desire to become a kamikaze pilot was rejected, and he was instead sent to the 203rd Air Group.[27]

On the morning of March 18, Tanimizu took to the skies in his Zeke to defend his airfield against the American fighters. "I believe in fate," he later said. "God determines at the time of birth just when and where a person shall die." It was not his turn to die this day, as Tanimizu would make the most of his encounter with Steve Stevens.[28]

The *Essex* fighters made their first run to drop their remaining wing bombs, but there would be no follow-up strafing run. "As we pulled up, the air was suddenly full of meatballs, and a wild dogfight ensued," said Wallace. "We were caught off guard and at low altitude."[29]

Lieutenant (jg) Ed Pappert, leading the second section of Stevens' division, pulled out of his strafing run to find himself confronted by three planes painted dull green with red meatballs. Ensign Vern Coumbe went after one, taking off to the left, while Pappert pulled into one that was pulling up to the right and opened fire. "Two bursts from the six .50-caliber guns and the next thing I knew I was flying through the debris of the Japanese plane," wrote Pappert.[30]

Around 1615 the battle evolved into a wild melee of tail chases, with a Zeke chasing a Corsair with another Corsair chasing that Zeke. Stevens shot up one enemy fighter while Wallace came in to knock another off his tail. The lieutenant was credited with a Zeke kill, and the ensign with a Zeke probable. Just as Wallace flamed his target, another pilot warned him that another Zeke was on his tail. "I saw tracers whizzing by on both sides, so I pulled up into a full-power, straight up, climb until she stalled out and went into a spin," he recorded afterward.[31]

Wallace recovered from his spin and pulled his bent-wing bird right back into the middle of the fight. He spotted Stevens' plane smoking and heading out to sea in a shallow dive toward the position of a known lifeguard submarine. Warrant Officer Tanimizu, who had shot up the F4U, remained on the American's tail, continuing to pour lead into his crippled Corsair. Wallace followed to keep the Zekes off his division leader's back while Stevens ditched. In the meantime Coumbe had flamed a Zeke, and Pappert was credited with one kill and one probable. Flight leader Reidy (a former VB-83 Helldiver pilot) was credited with two Zekes, his VBF-83 group ending the fight with nine total kills and four probables.

Having already lost pilots Garner and Sigman in the unit's morning strike against the airfields, the divisionmates of Stevens were distraught at the prospect of suffering a third downed comrade. Pappert, Coumbe, and Wallace circled above his position, each throwing down a spare life raft to the lieutenant, who made no attempt to retrieve them. Pappert and Coumbe finally left, but Wallace was reluctant to abandon his wingman. He dropped his spare life raft, only to watch it float past his drifting comrade. Wallace then located the duty lifeguard submarine and directed it toward the pilot's bearing before heading for home. Tanimizu had claimed another victim, and he would finish the war with thirty-two aerial victory claims in 1,425 flight hours. Following his victories on the eighteenth, Tanimizu began applying victory markings to his Zeke. He would finish the war tied for fifteenth-best Japanese naval ace.[32]

Wallace returned to *Essex* to find that each of his three shipboard roommates—Coumbe, Pappert, and Clint Wear—had also scored an aerial victory during the mission. But the lifeguard submarine failed to locate Lieutenant Stevens, who officially became yet another MIA of TF 58. His loss created some reshuffling within the squadron, as the following day Wallace, Pappert, and Coumbe were reassigned to fly in a new division with VBF-83 skipper Pat Patriarca—who had lost two of his wingmen on the eighteenth.

Marc Mitscher's carrier aviators closed the day with a combined claim of ninety-seven Japanese aircraft destroyed in aerial combat, with another thirty-two claimed as probables and damaged. The morning strikes had bombed hangars and barracks, while the afternoon strikes had been directed against fields farther inland. Search planes had not turned up prime Japanese warship targets for the aviators during the day. Their luck would change in that regard within hours, resulting in a broad-scale carrier assault of another kind for the following morning.

Chapter Nine

SAVING *FRANKLIN*

Maybe they'll recognize it's too damn bad to fly tonight. The thought often entered the mind of VT(N)-90 pilot Lieutenant (jg) Bill Balden as he sat in his Avenger cockpit on the blackest of nights, one in which the ceiling often dropped to five hundred feet. But it was business as usual at 0030 on March 19, as *Enterprise* sent off five torpedo bombers—"batmen" aviators of her Night Air Group 90—to conduct dangerous zipper raids on enemy airfields and to scour the Inland Sea for shipping targets long before Admiral Mitscher's main carrier strikes were scheduled to launch.[1]

Skipper Charlie Henderson attacked a destroyer escort with his bombs and shot down a Kawanishi H8K Navy Type 2 "Emily" flying boat around 0500. Lieutenant (jg) LaVern F. "Torr" McLaughlin fired rockets into a building on Kurashiki Airfield and bombed the Mitsubishi Mishima plant. Balden, fighting a fouled radar set, started a sizeable fire at Saeki Airfield with his rockets.[2]

The find of the night came from VT(N)-90's Lieutenant (jg) Ernie Lawton, who discovered a *Yamato*-class battleship and an aircraft carrier near eastern Honshu. He dropped two bombs on the carrier and fired his rockets at the battleship from a six-hundred-foot altitude. "It is regrettable that additional VT(N) were not on hand to support this single-plane attack against two capital ships," reported Henderson. Squadronmate Lieutenant (jg) Shannon McCrary attacked two merchant ships at 0345, scoring a direct hit on one that left it burning and settling.

Vice Admiral Mitscher's oft-dismissed Night Air Group 90 had thus stirred up things in the Inland Sea and provided valuable intelligence for the daylight strikers. The presence of a *Yamato* battleship and at least one aircraft carrier would give the morning's raiders plenty of incentive. By the time VT(N)-90's five Avengers were being recovered at 0715, TF 58 had already sent out hundreds of strike planes.[3]

The strike groups began launching at 0628 as *Essex* sent up the first of 42 planes (sixteen F4Us of VBF-83, thirteen SB2Cs of VB-83, and thirteen VT-83 Avengers). *Cabot* put up her 19-plane contribution at 0643, followed two minutes later by 46 planes from *Bunker Hill*'s Air Group 84—raising TG 58.3's total to 110 planes. An additional 252 strike planes and fighters would be launched by 0715 from the other three U.S. task groups, bringing Mitscher's early punch from thirteen carriers to about 385 warplanes. TG 58.3 and 58.1 were to concentrate on warships at Kure, while TG 58.2 aircraft were to hit targets and installations in the Kure Naval Air Depot area and TG 58.4 planes were assigned to Kobe.

As TF 58 was flinging deckloads of strikers skyward, Japanese warplanes slipped in on Mitscher's carriers. Their moment of attack could not have been more deadly, as big damage ensued from small numbers. Two carriers of Rear Admiral Davison's TG 58.2 were hit within moments of each other.

Commander Joe Taylor had to attend a funeral before he could see off *Franklin*'s strike group for their morning attacks. The carrier's popular executive officer, who hailed from Danville, Illinois, stood on the ship's fantail—an area on the hangar level just below the jutting after portion of the flight deck—as Protestant chaplain Grimes Gatlin wrapped up the brief service for a young sailor who had perished from drinking torpedo fluid.[4]

Taylor was a 1927 Annapolis graduate who had earned a Navy Cross at the 1942 Coral Sea battle for leading his *Yorktown* torpedo squadron on two successful attacks against Japanese carriers. He was not about to miss seeing his aviators take off for their own potential strikes against Japanese carriers and other warships that morning. As the wrapped body slid over the side to the bugle's blaring of "Taps," Taylor turned to head topside. It was just minutes before 0700.

Dozens of Hellcats, Corsairs, Helldivers, and Avengers were already turning up their engines in the brisk morning air in preparation for takeoff. The first fighter cleared *Franklin*'s deck at 0657, and a string of others made their way toward the starting line. Commander Edwin "Iceberg" Parker, CAG 5, was among the first eight Corsairs of VF-5 and VBF-5, and he would serve as the strike coordinator for the planes heading for Kobe Harbor. The first F4Us were roaring off the deck as Joe Taylor took a spot beside Lieutenant Fred Harris, *Franklin*'s flight-deck officer, to watch.

Fourteen SB2Cs of VB-5 were spotted next, but the expected launch order had been scrambled. The squadron's skipper, Coral Sea veteran Lieutenant Commander John G. Sheridan, found his dive bomber spotted toward the back of his unit. Lieutenant (jg) Nathan P. Crawford hollered at his gunner, ARM3c Samuel Ferrante, to hurry since their SB2C—scheduled for sixth in takeoff order—had been spotted first. Crawford cleared the flight deck at 0703. "Eight or nine bombers had taken off when there was a terrific blast, which appeared to be about 100 feet forward of the leading plane in the spot," reported Taylor. "I was thrown against the life lines on the starboard side just aft of the island superstructure."[5]

Moments before, the carrier *Hancock* had sent a quick radio warning of a bandit closing on radar, but the aviators and sailors on *Franklin*'s flight deck were caught by surprise. A lone Judy bomber, whose radar pip quickly mixed with the dozens of task-group strike planes beginning to circle above the carriers, suddenly plunged from the clouds at 0708 approximately one thousand yards ahead of the carrier affectionately known to her crew as "Big Ben" in honor of her namesake, Benjamin Franklin. The carrier's Number Three 5-inch turret opened fire, but it was too late. The first 550-pound semi-armor-piercing bomb had already been released.[6]

The bomb crashed through *Franklin*'s flight deck near her forward 5-inch turrets, ripped through wood planking and 1/8-inch steel deck plates, and passed into the hangar deck. Its delayed explosion sent bomb splinters slicing through parked aircraft and mowed down sailors and airmen. The Judy's second bomb pierced the flight deck near the Number Three elevator and burst above Corsairs parked on the hangar deck. The force of its explosion lifted *Franklin*'s Number One elevator platform into the air and dropped it back into its well at a 45-degree canted position.

The big carrier could not have been caught in a more vulnerable position. Five Helldivers were still in the process of taking off, and behind them were spotted fourteen of Lieutenant Commander Allan Christie "Ace" Edmands' VT-5 Avengers, all fully loaded with ordnance and fuel. Aft of the TBMs were another dozen Corsairs, each loaded with Tiny Tim rockets that quickly began cooking off in the conflagration topside. Below on the hangar deck were twenty-two additional ready aircraft: one Helldiver, one Avenger, five Tiny Tim–loaded VBF-5 Corsairs, and another fifteen fighter planes. Lieutenant Commander MacGregor "Mac" Kilpatrick, skipper of VF-5, had just moved from the flight deck to the hangar deck to man his Hellcat when the bombs hit.[7]

Lieutenant (jg) Ridgley D. Radney from Texas had just cleared the flight deck with his Helldiver when the Judy made its bombing attack. Last off *Franklin* was VB-5's Lieutenant Dewayne Hubbard "Ted" Stegner, who had spent two years in dental college in California before joining flight training. Stegner's Helldiver was just lifting off the flight deck when the first bomb exploded. "He was blown off the ship from concussions from the bomb," said Radney. "It knocked his tail hook out of the housing. He had to fly the whole flight and make his dive with his tail hook hanging out the back."[8]

Bombing Five skipper Sheridan was forced to abandon his plane as explosions and heavy black smoke swept the after flight deck. Lieutenant Chester B. Spray, the most senior officer of VB-5 to make it off the deck, would have to assume command of the nine airborne SB2Cs for the mission. The other pilots on deck were suddenly fighting for their lives. The explosions tossed planes about like toys. The Helldiver behind Stegner was just beginning its takeoff roll when the explosion flipped it upside down, forcing its badly startled pilot to release his restraining harness and crawl from his cockpit onto the flight deck.

Torpedo Five's skipper, Ace Edmands, was still warming up his engine when the bomb concussion ripped through his pack of TBMs. Edmands was among the many aviators who perished, blown off the ship by the force of the explosions. Seven other Avenger pilots died on *Franklin* along with seventeen of VT-5's enlisted men.

Another Torpedo Five pilot, Ensign William Richardson from Providence, Rhode Island, had closed his canopy due to the cold morning air, and it offered him some protection from the blast. Parked on the flight deck's port side, Richardson cut his engine, slid back his canopy, and leaped to the flight deck. Planes were exploding around him, and the deck was so filled with choking black smoke that he had to rapidly crawl on his hands and knees toward the island superstructure. "I saw one big orange flash and a rocket whizzed about five feet over my head," said Richardson.[9]

Lieutenant Christos Edgar Mikronis, a *Franklin* landing-signal officer from Baton Rouge, was knocked to the flight deck by the first explosion. He quickly donned a lifejacket and handed another to an alarmed Air Group 5 pilot. "Then one big explosion came right under me," recounted Mikronis. "It broke the ankles of two pilots standing by me. I decided to jump, so over I went." He hit the water far below and spent the next two hours clinging to a floater net with fifteen others—including the two pilots with broken ankles—before they were recovered by the destroyer *Marshall* (DD 676).[10]

The attacking Judy retired to the southeast, pursued by one Hellcat whose pilot fired all of his ammunition while still out of range. Commander Iceberg Parker led his eight F4Us, which had been completing their rendezvous one mile off the port bow of *Franklin*, in pursuit as well. They rapidly overtook the Judy, and Parker opened fire on it just as it entered a cloud formation. When the Japanese pilot made a poorly executed turn to the left, Iceberg hit his plane solidly in the engine and cockpit.[11]

The Judy was observed to crash into the sea. Parker and Lieutenant Spray then rendezvoused their eight Corsairs and nine Helldivers with strike groups from the carrier *Hancock* and light carrier *San Jacinto* before departing for their target area at 0723. The *Franklin* aircraft would not see their task group again for three hours. When they returned, they would be forced to seek refuge on their sister carrier *Hancock*.

Ready Room No. 51 on *Franklin* belonged to VMF-214, the famed Black Sheep Squadron once led by Major Gregory "Pappy" Boyington. Khaki-clad Marine Corsair pilots were taking notes on their clipboards when the bomb explosions forced the center deck of their room to slam violently into the ceiling, crushing their legs and bodies. Only four men out of twenty-eight in the room survived the blast and its ensuing flames, heat, and smoke.

First Lieutenants John Vandergrift and Carroll K. "Bud" Faught were standing close to the bulkhead at the instant of the explosion. They both suffered shattered lower legs and ankles and were slammed against the overhead. "Flames were coming in from every area, through holes in the deck and a part of the ready room that had been torn away," said Vandergrift. "And it was blacker than hell." He, Faught, and two other survivors managed to force open the hatch and crawl on their shattered legs onto the port-side catwalk next to the aircraft elevator near the island.[12]

The fight for survival for the Black Sheep pilots—and many hundreds of men trapped on the fiercely burning carrier—was only just beginning.

One minute after all hell broke loose on *Franklin*, her TG 58.2 sister carrier *Wasp* was hit by another of Admiral Ugaki's pilots. *Wasp* had just completed flight quarters at 0658, having launched ninety strike planes of Air Group 84 under Commander George R. Luker. By 0707 *Wasp* had secured from General Quarters, her aircraft were effecting their rendezvous near the task force, and her Gunnery Department had set conditions to Readiness One.

Two minutes later a Judy plunged through the two-thousand-foot ceiling and dropped a semi-armor-piercing 540-pound bomb that penetrated *Wasp*'s flight deck amidships, smashed through the hangar deck, and exploded after passing through the second deck. It blew a hole sixteen feet by twenty-four feet in the second deck and a similar-size hole in the third deck, completely destroying the carrier's galley and laundry and all related equipment. Many fire mains were ruptured, and Fireroom No. 4 became partially flooded. Two aircraft burned on the hangar deck, four hundred bunks were destroyed, and the hangar deck bulged upward six inches. *Wasp* suffered 101 men killed and 269 others seriously wounded.[13]

Fires on five decks and leaking aviation fuel could have spelled disaster, but damage controlmen had the fires on *Wasp* extinguished in fifteen minutes. Captain Oscar Weller's carrier was recovering planes by 0800. Minutes later another kamikaze missed *Wasp* by mere feet, nicking the exterior plane elevator and exploding alongside her. The carrier would doggedly remain in operation several more days before retiring for repairs.[14]

TG 58.3 was also assailed by Japanese attackers shortly after its strike groups had departed. *Essex* narrowly avoided two Judy kamikazes, one of which landed a bomb close aboard her starboard side. Admiral Mitscher knew the risks in operating only one hundred miles from the Japanese coast, and Ugaki's aviators had drawn blood. In a nod of respect to their skills, Mitscher summed the March 18–19 enemy strikes as "slight in the number of aircraft employed, but the attacks were conducted in an aggressive and determined manner."[15]

The battle to save Big Ben would continue hours after normal operations had resumed on *Wasp*.

Captain Leslie Gehres had his hands full. The force of the first bomb's explosion had knocked him to the deck. As he regained his footing, the skipper saw flames leaping from the forward starboard side of the flight deck, spreading aft. He ordered full right rudder to bring the wind along the carrier's port side to try and keep the flames away from planes on the after flight deck. "At about 0709, the first of a five-hour-long series of heavy explosions occurred on the flight deck," Gehres reported.[16]

Fire, nearly continuous explosions, and choking smoke forced hundreds of *Franklin* sailors trapped in deadly positions to simply leap through the blackness into the ocean. Among them were Black Sheep aviators Budd Faught and John Vandergrift. Faught, having inhaled too much smoke, was aided by VMF-214's Captain Robert M. Jones, who had enough breath to inflate his squadronmate's gravity suit. Given his two broken legs and a fractured arm, the Marine pilot would need the buoyancy in the water to help keep him afloat.[17]

Explosions from the nearby port elevator finally forced Lieutenant Faught to use his one good arm to swing out from a piece of framework

Crewmen battle fires on the forward flight deck of the carrier *Franklin* (CV 13) after she was crippled by a Japanese air attack on March 19, 1945. *80-G-273882, NARA*

and plunge into the sea. When he bobbed to the surface, he witnessed a violent explosion above that killed Captain Jones and others still on the portside catwalk. Faught pushed himself away from *Franklin* and successfully avoided the deadly propeller wash of the speeding carrier's massive screws. Lieutenant Vandergrift, suffering from two shattered legs, was also forced to flop himself over the portside catwalk railing. "The whole area [on board] quickly turned into a griddle, and we were being cooked like marshmallows," he said. "I had to get my ass out of there." Still in shock, he bobbed to the surface as his carrier raced past. "Explosions were ripping the *Franklin* to pieces," he said.[18]

Captain Gehres would later raise the ire of his crew by initiating court-martial proceedings against some of those he claimed had deserted his stricken ship. Two days later a muster found 704 officers and men who had remained aboard *Franklin* through the worst of the inferno. Gehres created the "Big Ben 704 Club," issuing personally signed membership cards to each of the qualifying crewmen. It was a move that would be seared into the memories of hundreds of *Franklin* men who had been blown overboard or forced to leap into the ocean to escape the explosions and suffocating smoke.[19]

Mac Kilpatrick, skipper of VF-5, would earn a Navy Cross for his quick actions in tackling spare ammunition and burning aircraft. "Lieutenant Commander Kilpatrick led parties of men in continuous and valiant fire fighting, jettisoning shells in enclosed mounts, and flooding ready service magazines until forced by a superior officer to leave the ship with his squadron," his citation noted. It was Captain Gehres who finally ordered Kilpatrick from *Franklin*, barking, "You are an aviator, not a fire fighter!"[20]

Many other heroes were in action throughout the stricken *Franklin*. One of them was Lieutenant (jg) Donald Arthur Gary, as assistant engineering officer from Ohio, who headed below decks with an oxygen breather immediately after the bomb explosions. He found three hundred men trapped on the third deck; left them temporarily to map out an escape route through the burning, blackened passageways; and returned to lead ten sailors toward salvation. He followed a twisting path some six hundred feet through six decks to reach a 40-mm gun sponson, where he left his ten shipmates gulping in fresh air. Gary then charged back below and next led a group of fifty survivors topside. For his third evacuation trip, he led the remaining large group of men groping through black smoke and heat to salvation. As the fight for *Franklin* progressed, Lieutenant Gary repeatedly organized firefighting crews and led them against the blazing infernos. He later entered Fireroom No. 3 to direct the raising of steam in one boiler under hazardous conditions. For his actions on March 19, Gary would later be draped with the Medal of Honor.[21]

Gary was not alone in receiving the nation's highest honor for life-saving heroism on board *Franklin*. The ship's Roman Catholic chaplain, Commander Joseph Timothy O'Callahan from Boston, manned firehoses to cool smoking bombs, joined firefighting crews on the flight deck, and helped jettison live ammunition. He also administered last rites to dying sailors and worked and prayed with those seriously injured, even as ready ammunition and Tiny Tim rockets whistled through the air around him. Executive Officer Taylor, busy directing countless damage-control efforts, could not help but notice the courage of his Catholic chaplain. He found O'Callahan to be "a soul-stirring sight. He seemed to be everywhere, giving extreme unction to the dead and dying, urging the men on and himself handling hoses, jettisoning ammunition, and doing everything he could to help save our ship."[22]

Yeoman 2nd Class Robert C. Blanchard experienced the gallantry of both Lieutenant Gary and Father O'Callahan firsthand. Following the bomb hits, Blanchard and another sailor had made their way to the third-deck mess hall, where they and hundreds more were eventually led to safety by Gary. As soon as Blanchard reached the flight deck, his body buckled as he gasped in the better air. He woke up to find Father O'Callahan praying over him. "That was a wake-up call to see him over me, giving me the last rites," said Blanchard. "I'm okay Father, I'll be all right," he declared, "I just inhaled too much smoke." A ship's photographer happened to be snapping pictures on the flight deck as O'Callahan knelt down over the yeoman's prone body. The image, often labeled as the chaplain administering last rites to a dead sailor, became one of the most oft-published images of the

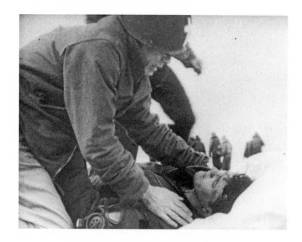

Father Joseph O'Callahan is reportedly offering last rites to a wounded *Franklin* survivor on the flight deck. The man in the photo, Robert Blanchard, actually survived. *80-G-49132, NARA*

entire *Franklin* ordeal. Blanchard would survive and was soon transferred over to the cruiser *Santa Fe* (CL 60).[23]

Rear Admiral Davison and his staff were forced to transfer his flag from the stricken carrier, now drifting just fifty-two miles from the Japanese mainland, while the crew continued to fight the fires. The destroyer *Miller* (DD 535) nestled alongside *Franklin*'s starboard beam, her crew playing firehoses onto the erupting flattop while Davison and his staff evacuated the carrier via a breeches buoy line. By 0900 the admiral radioed the task group from *Miller* that he was afraid *Franklin* would have to be abandoned. A half hour later Captain Harold C. "Hal" Fritz pulled his cruiser *Santa Fe* alongside Big Ben to play thousands of tons of water across the carrier's fires. Two trolley lines were used to transfer the most seriously wounded to the cruiser.

Fritz was forced away from *Franklin*'s side but returned his cruiser at 1050, using his engines to slam his warship against the blazing carrier and hold her in place. Despite the bumping and grinding that punched holes in *Santa Fe* and wrecked some of her upper works, the captain allowed his crew to continue to help fight fires and to evacuate wounded men on litters in one of the most gallant rescue efforts of the war.

Davison reported to Vice Admiral Mitscher that he believed *Franklin* should be abandoned. But Captain Gehres was not about to give up on his ship. Over the TBS (Talk between Ships) system, he called to Mitscher on *Bunker Hill*. "This is the commanding officer of the *Franklin*. You save us from the Japs and we'll save this ship."[24]

Mitscher could see the black smoke on the horizon but had little knowledge of how things were on the stricken carrier. He took Gehres for his word. "You tell him we'll save him," Mitscher told Captain Burke. The vice admiral gave orders for the task group to retire, providing cover for both *Franklin* and *Wasp* as they did so. Captain Fritz's *Santa Fe* took on board 832 officers and men from *Franklin*, while destroyers rescued scores more from the ocean.

By noon Captain Gehres reported the fires on his ship practically under control and the carrier's once heavy list reduced to 13 degrees. *Franklin* was taken under tow by the cruiser *Pittsburgh* (CA 72), which by early afternoon was tugging the shattered carrier at three knots away from the coast of Japan. Lieutenant Gary and others of *Franklin's* engineering gang labored through the night to restore power to their ship. By midmorning on March 20 they had her under way using her own power.

The ultimate survival of the carrier *Franklin* and her return stateside for repairs would prove to be one of the more uplifting stories of World War II. Her losses on March 19 were the third worst for the Navy, with 724 officers and men killed and at least 265 wounded.

While the fight was on to save Big Ben, her air group and hundreds of other TF 58 strikers prepared to unleash their own devastation on enemy warships in Kure and Kobe Harbors.

Early morning fighter sweeps from Mitscher's carriers had already swung into action against the Japanese mainland airfields long before the main strikes reached the harbors at Kobe and Kure. Lieutenant Edwin Conant's five divisions of *Hornet* VBF-17 Corsairs, launched at 0618, were intercepted over the Inland Sea at 0805 by the most formidable aerial opposition the air group had yet encountered.[25]

During the ensuing melee, two dozen Japanese planes were shot down and seven *Hornet* fighters were lost; only one of the American pilots was rescued by a destroyer. Conant downed two Franks and was credited with probable destruction of an Oscar, while eight other VBF-17 pilots scored at least two kills. In VBF-17's action report, Conant noted "the Jap pilots encountered here were superior to those met in the Tokyo area" weeks prior.

En route to strafe Matsuyama Airfield on Shikoku Island, Lieutenant Bert Eckard's VF-9 division from *Yorktown* entered a scrap with Japanese fighters around 0815. The VF-9 sweep claimed five kills in the early morning action, including a Jake reconnaissance floatplane knocked into the sea by Lieutenant Marv Franger—marking the Hellcat ace's eighth victory.[26]

These early air battles were still playing out as the first TG 58.1 warplanes from *Hornet, Wasp, Bennington, Belleau Wood,* and *San Jacinto* approached Kure Harbor at 0745. They found it to be filled with prime targets: carriers, battleships, cruisers, destroyers, and all sorts of other vessels. Among the key ships present were the carriers *Amagi* and *Katsuragi;* light carrier *Ryuho;* escort carriers *Kaiyo* and *Shimane Maru* (tied up alongside a dry dock); battleships *Haruna, Yamato, Ise,* and *Hyuga;* heavy cruiser *Tone;* light cruisers *Oyodo* and *Kitakami;* ancient armored cruiser *Iwate;* and dozens of other vessels, including additional cruisers, destroyers, submarines, and freighters. At the start of the raid, *Kaiyo* was moored in the outer harbor east of and on *Katsuragi's* starboard beam, while *Amagi* was anchored northwest of *Haruna,* tied up at the arsenal.

Commander George Luker, CAG 86, dispersed his collection of twenty-eight *Wasp* planes to attack various targets. Thirteen Helldivers of VB-86 claimed hits on three ships—the battleship *Haruna,* an *Ise*-class battlewagon, and a light carrier—in exchange for one lost Helldiver crew. Lieutenant Commander Lawrence F. Steffenhagen, a veteran of the 1942 Coral Sea carrier battle, and his nine VT-86 Avengers claimed three hits on a light carrier, two hits on another carrier, and three direct hits on a cruiser.

By 0800 Kure Harbor was a hailstorm of flak and explosions as the air groups from *Essex* and *Bunker Hill* began making their attacks. So many bombs rained down on the Japanese warships in short order that ascertaining which group made hits proved nearly impossible. Lieutenant Commander Harry A. Stewart and his VT-83 *Essex* Avenger pilots claimed numerous hits and near misses. VB-83's contingent of thirteen Helldivers was led by two veteran pilots of the Coral Sea, Lieutenant Commander Dave Berry and his executive officer, Lieutenant James Taylor Crawford. Their two divisions appear to have largely concentrated on the light carrier *Ryuho.*

Berry landed a likely near miss on *Ryuho,* but hits were reported by Lieutenant (jg) Sheldon Olney and Lieutenant James Austin Riner, the latter a veteran of the 1942 Santa Cruz carrier battle near Guadalcanal. Lieutenant (jg) Winston Jay Lay was seriously wounded during his dive but managed to release on the carrier before his Helldiver rolled over and crashed into the harbor. Lieutenant Crawford, leading VB-83's second division, was bleeding heavily, his right arm ripped by shrapnel, but persisted in leading his men down on the carrier. Another plane from Crawford's division, flown by Lieutenant (jg) Donald Willis, was seen to be hit and fall off.

Other Bombing Eighty-Three pilots claimed hits on a pair of battleships, with the squadron suffering one downed Helldiver in the process. *Ryuho* was certainly punished during the early attacks on March 19. Berry's rear-seat man, ACRM Joseph Michael Eardley, snapped photographs as VB-83 made its dives. Once developed, they showed *Katsuragi* and another carrier moored nearby, *Kaiyo*, bracketed by explosions. Light carrier *Cabot*'s seven VT-29 Avengers and dozen VF-29 planes also made their presence felt during these early attacks as they claimed hits on a cruiser and a battleship.

Frank Patriarca, skipper of *Essex*'s VBF-83, was flying with wingmen Ed Pappert, Glenn Wallace, and Vern Coumbe. Pappert, Wallace, and Coumbe were forced to fly missions with both the fighter-bomber squadron and VF-83 due to pilot losses. Wallace had decided their division should "adopt a new insignia—'The Free Lancers'—because we are flying both for both squadrons." Patriarca sent one Corsair division to attack a carrier, another to hit a cruiser, and two others to drop bombs on forge and repair shops ashore.[27]

The first Kure strikers encountered enough aerial opposition that a radio call was put out for more fighter cover. Lieutenant Ned Langdon of VF-17 launched with four divisions at 0800 to head for the Japanese harbors. Billy Watts, Tilly Pool, and other Hellcats pilots were still completing their rendezvous near the task group as *Hornet*'s contribution to the early strike force began its attacks on Japanese shipping around 0815.

Commander Ed Konrad, strike leader of the *Hornet* group, split his fighter divisions and led his division to strafe and bomb a carrier in the harbor. Bombing Seventeen suffered the loss of two Helldiver crews but claimed hits on a carrier in the bay, a battleship, and a freighter. *Hornet*'s Avengers claimed two hits on carriers at the cost of one downed TBM crew.

Bennington's Air Group 82 and light carrier *Belleau Wood*'s Air Group 30 also commenced their attacks at 0815. Lieutenant Commander Hugh Wood Jr., the VB-82 skipper and flight commander, was still leading his *Bennington* contingent toward Kure when he sighted the battleship *Yamato* and escort vessels off his port bow in Hiroshima Bay. *Yamato* was under way at about fifteen knots, steaming with seven destroyers and two cruisers. As Wood's dive bombers went into their glide attack from 11,000 feet, the mighty battlewagon opened fire on them. Colored puffs of red, green, purple, yellow, and phosphorous bursts painted the sky with a volume so intense, it was as if a long string of fireworks had been ignited.

Six of VB-82's planes were hit, and Lieutenant Donald D. Worden was forced to make a water landing. Each Helldiver released a pair of 1,000-pound semi-armor-piercing bombs on *Yamato*, resulting in three hits from the first nine dive bombers. "The first bomb dropped hit amidships forward of the after turrett," said Lieutenant Commander Ed DeGarmo, skipper of VT-82, who also noted two more hits and "many near misses." *Bennington*'s fighters joined in, and Lieutenant Richard Earl Britson of VF-82 was credited with a direct hit near the battleship's funnel. DeGarmo,

The Japanese battleship *Yamato* seen under air attack in the Inland Sea on March 19, 1945. *80-G-309662, NARA*

realizing that his Avengers' 500-pound general-purpose bombs would do little damage to the heavily armored *Yamato*, led his squadron in an attack on a 10,000-ton oil tanker, whose stern they left ablaze from a number of direct hits.[28]

Belleau Wood's Air Group 30 moved over Kure Harbor, where Lieutenant Robert F. Regan of VT-30 selected *Oyodo*, anchored offshore, as his target. Regan landed two bombs forward of the light cruiser's bridge, while Lieutenant (jg) Francis E. Hedges walked three of his bombs right up the cruiser's deck. The VF-30 fighters accompanying the strike dumped their own bombs on the cruiser and a nearby battleship, while the final two pilots of Torpedo Thirty claimed hits on an *Ise*-class battleship.

Lieutenant Commander John P. Conn, approaching Kure Harbor from 13,000 feet at 0830, allowed division and section leaders from his *Bunker Hill*–based VB-84 to select their own targets from the bountiful selection. Conn led his section down on the battleship *Hyuga*, anchored near the southern docks and ablaze with antiaircraft fire. The Helldivers of Conn and his wingman, Lieutenant (jg) John Daniel Welsh, were hit during their dives. Welsh's SB2C broke up in midair, killing him and his gunner, ARM2c Donald Milton McKown.

Many of VB-84's pilots concentrated on the larger carrier *Katsuragi*, anchored in the middle of the harbor, and succeeded in starting a fire on her after flight deck. Bombing Eighty-Four's other pilots made their dives

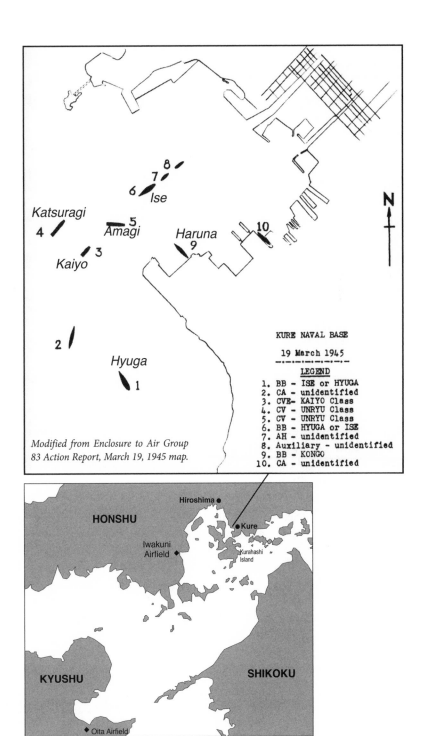

Katsuragi

Amagi

Haruna

Ise

Kaiyo

Hyuga

N

KURE NAVAL BASE

19 March 1945

LEGEND
1. BB - ISE or HYUGA
2. CA - unidentified
3. CVE- KAIYO Class
4. CV - UNRYU Class
5. CV - UNRYU Class
6. BB - HYUGA or ISE
7. AH - unidentified
8. Auxiliary - unidentified
9. BB - KONGO
10. CA - unidentified

HONSHU

Hiroshima ●

Kure ●

Iwakuni Airfield ◆

Kurahashi Island

KYUSHU

SHIKOKU

◆ Oita Airfield

TASK FORCE 58 RAID ON KURE HARBOR, MARCH 19, 1945

on the carrier *Kaiyo*, light carrier *Ryuho*, and heavy cruiser *Tone*. During his dive on *Tone*, Lieutenant (jg) William B. Kornegay's Helldiver was hit by a 20-mm shell that exploded in his rear cockpit. His gunner, ARM2c Vernon C. Rawlings, was wounded by shrapnel in his left arm but kept the nose of the Japanese projectile as a souvenir.

The squadron's "tail-end Charlie" pilot, Lieutenant Charles L. Carper, was hit by antiaircraft fire at the top of his pushover point. Hydraulic fluid began spurting into his front cockpit as his engine commenced smoking on top of the starboard cowling. Despite the fluid spraying into his face and a fouled windshield, the pilot continued his glide toward the dock area and released his bombs over it. With his engine now streaming smoke, Carper radioed that he was heading back for the fleet.

Smoke poured through the floorboards of his plane. "My oxygen mask was lost over the side when I tried to put it on," said Carper, "so it was necessary to keep the hood partially open to clear the smoke." Two F6Fs joined on him and provided escort over Shikoku's mountains before they broke off and headed for their own carrier. Carper headed east on his own, radioing Lieutenant Commander Conn, "I think I can make it home okay."[29]

When he reached *Bunker Hill*, Carper tried in vain twice to land, but his wheels failed to extend. Commander George M. Ottinger, CAG 84, finally instructed the Helldiver pilot to make a water landing near a destroyer. Carper circled twice, instructing his rear gunner, ARM2c Millard Wilcox, to jettison all loose gear, including his twin .30-caliber machine guns. They landed downwind with no flaps, but the impact with the water was disastrous. "The plane bounced, flipped over onto it back, broke in two, and settled," reported Carper.[30]

The Helldiver was gone in twenty seconds, dragging its pilot below the surface before he was able to swim free of the cockpit. The violence of the impact knocked Wilcox unconscious, and although Carper popped his life jacket and held his injured head above the water, it was too late for the gunner. Destroyermen who pulled Carper from the water twenty minutes later performed artificial respiration on Wilcox for four hours to no avail.

In the period between 0830 and 0845, strike planes from *Hancock* and *San Jacinto* attacked two of the Japanese flattops and claimed more hits.

Lieutenant Commander Gordon P. Chase, leading *Hancock*'s VB-6 dive bombers, assigned a Japanese carrier within the breakwater to his Helldivers. Lieutenant (jg) Dale Allen Barrows was hit by heavy antiaircraft fire, and his plane was seen to trail heavy smoke. Barrows still made his dive and was credited with a hit on the bow of the escort carrier. His gunner, ARM2c Frank R. Gordon, then bailed out, landed in the harbor, and was seen to be alive. Barrows managed to ditch his plane a few miles south of Kobe. He and Gordon were covered by *Franklin* Corsairs, but the Marine fighters saw two powered harbor craft moving to capture the downed aviators. Lieutenant Commander Chase's plane also was hit by antiaircraft fire during his dive. His gunner, ACRM Donald H. Hand, was injured in the forehead, knocking him out. He recovered seconds later and, although covered in blood, picked up his camera and snapped several pictures of the stricken Japanese carrier before he resumed strafing fire.

Ensign Paul H. Whitford's dive bomber was hit during his dive, but he managed to ditch nearly seventy miles outside of Kobe Harbor. He and his gunner, ARM3c Vincent R. Smith, were protected by Lieutenant Commander Bud Schumann and his Grim Reapers wingman until they could direct in the lifeguard submarine *Guardfish* (SS 217). Whitford and Smith were saved by the *Guardfish* crew and would spend the next month making their way back to *Hancock*.

The balance of *Hancock's* Air Group 6 attacked two of the carriers in the harbor, claiming four hits on each of their two targets, last seen to be burning and exploding. *San Jacinto's* Air Group 45 moved in during the closing actions of the *Hancock* planes' attacks and claimed an additional hit on each carrier, coupled with many damaging near misses.

The *Hancock* and *San Jacinto* aircraft then made a running rendezvous and retired from the harbor area. But the Japanese warships had little break from the action. Other TF 58 squadrons were moving in.

Lieutenant (jg) Watts arrived over Kure Harbor around 0845 as part of a sixteen-Hellcat fighter sweep. *Hornet's* main strike group was already completing its attacks when Lieutenant Langdon arrived with his four VF-17 divisions. Watts found the antiaircraft fire above the harbor to be the most hellish he had ever encountered. Every pilot in the air that day would agree with him.

Langdon was just preparing his divisions to begin attacking prime warships when some ten to twelve Oscars, Franks, Zekes, and Tonys were sighted over Kiroshima Airfield, ten miles northwest of Kure. The last two *Hornet* F6F divisions, under Lieutenant Jim Pearce and Lieutenant (jg) Tommy Harris, broke away to attack the enemy aircraft. Harris' division released its four bombs over the outskirts of Kure before engaging the fighters. "What ensued was like a WWI dogfight," wrote Pearce.[31]

The Hellcats became engaged with three divisions of Georges from the 407th and 701st Squadrons of the 343rd Air Group, dubbed the "Squadron of Experts" because it had the highest concentration of aces of any unit then in the Japanese navy. The 343rd was under the direction of Commander Minoru Genda, who had masterminded the Pearl Harbor Raid in 1941. Genda's pilots would make heavy claims of downing fifty-three Hellcats and Corsairs plus four SB2C Helldivers on March 19 against the loss of thirteen of their own pilots. Japan would tout Chief Petty Officer Katsue Kato as their top ace of the nineteenth, with nine victories against American pilots that morning.[32]

The Georges faced by the U.S. pilots were often misreported as being Franks or Oscars. Pearce, in the lead of the VF-17 group, was credited with one Frank kill and one shared kill. His wingman, George Johnson, suffered damage to his F6F from a 20-mm shell and a raking of 12.7-mm slugs, while Lieutenants (jg) Chili Crawford and Murray Winfield each shot down a George. Harris' division knocked down four fighters before pursuing another that fled south up a canyon. As the George pilot pulled up to clear the mountains at the head of the canyon, Tilly Pool flamed the plane with a long burst that caused its pilot to bail out.

The other two VF-17 divisions attacked enemy shipping in Kure Harbor. Grandma Langdon led his division down on strafing runs on an anchored carrier and a battleship, paving the way for Watts' division to drop their bombs. "I'd seen a lot of anti-aircraft fire out there, but I saw more this day than I'd seen all my time in two tours of duty," said Watts. "I wondered if I was going to get out. It seemed they had us closed in."[33]

Watts could see *Yamato* in the distance, but his sights were set on the carrier below him. He poured .50-caliber bullets into the flattop as it grew larger by the second, but he was disgusted to find that all four of his Hellcats suffered bombs that hung up due to a mechanical failure. His division recovered over the harbor, rendezvoused with that of Lieutenant Langdon over Aki Nada, and proceeded southeast to attack a *Natori*-class light cruiser just off Osumi Nana. Once again Langdon's Hellcats made strafing runs on the ship while Watts and his three other pilots made bombing runs. Watts found the antiaircraft fire to be less intense over this warship, which he and George Covelly damaged with close near-misses.

Watts and Langdon led their eight Hellcats along the northern coast of Shikoku, where they strafed a small ship and wrecked six parked aircraft at Kanonji Airfield. Four miles north of Kanonji, the formation intercepted a locomotive pulling six cars and destroyed it with a strafing attack. "It was a cold day, and you could see the white smoke coming from that engine," said Watts. Each pilot came in low, his .50-caliber armor-piercing bullets ripping chunks out of the train cars until the locomotive began coasting to a stop.[34]

The *Hornet* pilots next attacked the Takuma seaplane base, where they spotted two Emily flying boats and nine Rufe (Nakajima A6M2-N Navy Type 2 interceptor/fighter-bomber) floatplanes on the water, with an additional nine Emily and Mavis (Kawanishi H6K Navy Type 97) large flying boats on the ramp. In two passes four planes were burned and all of the remaining aircraft were severely damaged. For his relentless attacks on March 19 against an aircraft carrier, a cruiser, enemy airfields, and even a locomotive, Texan Billy Watts would later be pinned with a Navy Cross.

Following its action over Kure, the divisions of Pearce and Harris strafed and bombed a town on the coast of Shikoku and destroyed another locomotive pulling six loaded cars just southeast of the town. Pool arrived back over TF 58 to find one of the fleet carriers blazing and exploding. His momentary fears that his own *Hornet* had been ravaged were replaced by relief when he realized it was the stricken *Franklin*, but his thoughts went out to those in peril in the ocean and on board Big Ben.

Around 0845 the strike planes from TG 58.4—the *Intrepid* and *Yorktown* air groups, led by Commander Johnny Hyland, CAG 10—began their attacks on Kure Naval Base and its air depot.

Two of Hyland's Corsair wingmen, Roy "Eric" Erickson and Robert "Windy" Hill, teamed up to knock down three George fighters in a series of twisting dogfights. Their opponents were led by Lieutenant Naoshi Kanno, commander of the 301st Squadron. Reckless by nature and with a bulldog tenacity, Kanno had graduated in December 1941 from the Etajima Naval Academy and had seen considerable aerial combat prior to being assigned to Genda's 343rd Air Group, thirty kills already to his credit. By the time he was lost in action on August 1, 1945, Kanno would be credited with an additional eighteen victories, making him Japan's top ace from the naval academy.[35]

Kanno's 301st pilots had already engaged VMF-123 Corsairs in the fight over Kure that day, but the George divisions had become separated by the time his pilots met up with Erickson and Hill. Erickson blasted the Japanese plane from astern, forcing Kanno to bail out of his flaming George so close that Erickson could see his astonished face and brand new brown flight suit. Kanno, his hands and face burned, landed in a farm field, where he was advanced upon by a farmer who mistook him for an American pilot. The lieutenant cursed the man soundly in Japanese until he backed off, then appropriated a bicycle to pedal back to base.[36]

Lieutenant (jg) Robert Hal Jackson pushed over into his dive close on the heels of VBF-10 skipper Will Rawie. A native of Denton, Texas, Jackson had finished his undergraduate degree at North Texas State Teacher's College and was attending law school at the University of Texas when Pearl Harbor was attacked, spurring him to sign on for naval-aviation training. Jackson noted that Rawie nearly created his own demise during the firing of his Tiny Tim rockets on the nineteenth. "Our skipper released his in too steep a dive, and it didn't explode, but it knocked his prop out of kilter," said Jackson. "The thing was vibrating like hell." Rawie managed to nurse his plane back to *Intrepid*, but the deck crew would not take him on board, forcing him to ditch near a destroyer. "I noticed in his report that he said he had to land in water because of being low on fuel," Jackson later said with a chuckle.[37]

While the Grim Reapers were thus engaged, two divisions of Lieutenant Commander Bob Buchan's VB-10 Helldivers and ten of Larry Lawrence's VT-10 Avengers made attacks on a battleship, a carrier, and a tanker. Ensign Robert Brinick and his gunner, ARM3c Crawford H. Burnette, were forced down in the harbor and soon became prisoners of the Japanese, while another downed Bombing Ten crew was later picked up by a TF 58 destroyer.

Torpedo Ten's pilots were ordered to attack warehouses and hangars at the air depot, where they found the sky black with antiaircraft fire. "I thought that if I got through a week of this, I would be lucky!" said rookie pilot Harry Hunt. Lieutenant (jg) Grant "Jack" Young, an Illinois native and VT-10 veteran pilot making his second combat tour, found Kure to have the hottest enemy gunfire he had encountered. "It looked like Roman candles going off amongst us and it went right through your wing," he said. Young's Avenger, the only one hit, was not seriously damaged, and he watched with great delight as Lieutenant (jg) Mervin "Bill" Beil of the Grim Reapers attacked a Japanese locomotive chugging toward a mountainside. Beil's Tiny Tim rockets connected with the train, sending parts of the locomotive high into the air.[38]

Yorktown's Air Group 9 followed at 0900, close on the heels of the *Intrepid* SB2Cs and TBMs. Their objective was to smash up hangars, parked aircraft, and other buildings ashore. Ten minutes after their attack commenced, the reduced *Franklin* air group began its attacks. The bomb damage incurred by their carrier had negated more than half of Air Group 5's intended planes from launching, but those that arrived over Kure were ready to extract some vengeance.

Lieutenant Chet Spray led his nine VB-5 Helldivers down on the carrier hull anchored outside the breakwater at Kure, crediting one of his wingmen, Lieutenant (jg) Orson A. Boyce, with landing a string of 500-pound and 250-pound bomb hits. Lieutenant (jg) Nathan Crawford led the other four *Franklin* Helldivers in strikes on the light carrier between the breakwater and the dock area, claiming one hit. Lieutenant Dewayne Stegner and his final pilots believed that they added at least two more hits to the light carrier near the docks.

When Bombing Five's pilots returned to their task group, they found *Franklin* still ablaze and staggering with massive explosions, forcing the SB2C pilots to seek refuge on *Bennington*, *Essex*, and *Hornet*. "I didn't have enough gas left in my tank to measure," said Lieutenant (jg) Radney, whose plane exhausted its fuel upon landing on *Essex*.[39]

The last of the 325 morning strikers to push over into attack dives at 0930 were thirteen fighters and five torpedo bombers from *Bataan* (CVL 29). VT-47 skipper Lieutenant Commander Harold R. Mazza, who had cut his teeth while flying with the first *Lexington*'s VT-2 at the Coral Sea, dumped his load of a dozen 100-pound bombs across the flight deck of a light carrier. Other VT-47 pilots claimed hits on a *Taiho*-class carrier and a tanker.

The Japanese warships in Kure Harbor had a brief hiatus to lick their wounds before secondary fighter sweeps from several of the U.S. fleet carriers moved in to mop up. Thirteen Corsairs from *Yorktown*'s VBF-9 attacked the escort carrier *Shimane Maru* alongside dry dock, with Lieutenant Commander Frank Lawlor and Lieutenant (jg) D. W. Graham claiming rocket hits on her. Ensign Raymond E. Jehli followed through by planting a 500-pound bomb on the forward end of her flight deck.

One of the final groups to attack Kure Harbor was a fighter sweep of eight VF-10 Corsairs from *Intrepid* and another six from VBF-10, all led by Lieutenant Commander Wally Clarke. Arriving at 1100, Clarke found *Shimane Maru* docked at the repair yard at Ino Shima, a small island just east of the harbor. Six of his Grim Reapers dropped their bomb loads on the flattop, with Lieutenant (jg) James H. Dudley being credited with three near misses and one direct hit in the forward part of the flight deck. Ensign Edward Latczas followed by pickling off his four 5-inch HVARs, three of which were seen to hit in the carrier's catwalks.

Clarke was well pleased with the results of his Corsair pilots against *Shimane Maru*. "We put enough holes in it with our bombs and rockets to sink it in port," he said. The flak over Kure was the worst he had experienced, and upon his landing back on board *Intrepid*, the skipper was none too pleased to find that his plane captain had neglected to attach his harness hooks to his parachute. "If I had had to jump, it would be without a parachute," recalled Clarke. "I was quite angry over that."[40]

TF 58's massive strikes against Kure Harbor and the nearby shipping areas failed to sink many prime warships but handed out a heavy amount of damage. *Shimane Maru* had been plastered in her dry dock, hit by bombs on her stern, flight deck, and forward elevator.[41]

The carrier *Ryuho* suffered at least three direct bomb hits and two rocket hits that killed twenty men. *Ryuho* settled six feet aft, with raging fires and a heavily damaged flight deck. The battleship *Haruna* reported one bomb hit on the starboard side, aft of her bridge. The battleship *Hyuga* took three direct bomb hits and many near misses, suffering thirty-seven sailors killed and fifty-two injured. The escort carrier *Kaiyo*, hit directly by one bomb and ripped open by many near misses, listed so heavily by midday that she was moved to shallow water to avoid sinking. The massive battleship *Yamato*, under way during the attacks, suffered only one direct bomb hit with near misses exploding all around her.

The carrier *Katsuragi* was hit by at least two rockets that damaged her flight and hangar decks, while the carrier *Amagi* sustained at least two smaller-size bomb hits. The light cruiser *Oyodo* took three direct bomb hits and several near misses that ruptured her starboard hull plating and killed fifty-two sailors. Down by the bow and developing a 15-degree list, *Oyodo* was towed to Etajima after the attacks and beached to avoid sinking. The cruisers *Tone* and *Iwate* were slightly damaged by strafing attacks and bombs that near-missed their hulls.

The incomplete carrier *Shimane Maru* burns at right in Kobe Harbor on March 19, 1945, with a large cargo ship at left. Photo taken by a *San Jacinto* plane. *NH-95782, NARA*

In a view taken from a *Hornet* attack plane during the strike on Kure Harbor, the carrier *Kaiyo* is seen at extreme right. The burning carrier at bottom is *Amagi* or *Katsuragi*. *80-G-309660, NARA*

TF 58 continued to battle Japanese aircraft attacks while its warplanes pounded the enemy's capital ships in and around Kure Harbor. Vice Admiral Mitscher had his carriers begin retiring from the Japanese mainland shortly after noon, although passing strikes of fighters were flung against Kanoya Airfield—distance 224 miles—where they destroyed more planes and inflicted further damage on ground installations.

Radar picked up more bogies approaching TG 58.3 around 1300. Minutes later Lieutenant (jg) Jack Lyons and another VF-83 pilot were ordered to man two ready Hellcats on the forward catapults. They were still warming up their engines when *Essex* and other ships of their group suddenly began firing at approaching enemy planes at 1317. Lyons would spend what felt to be an eternity trapped in his F6F, unable to be catapulted as his carrier maneuvered radically to avoid Japanese planes. CAP fighters splashed a Judy at 1319, but bogies continued to dot the radar sets. Lyons and his companion were finally able to get out of their planes and run for cover. Minutes later, at 1328, a Zeke dived toward *Essex* and was taken under fire by guns of all caliber. It was hit and burst into flames, crashing just fifteen hundred yards off the port beam.

Ensign Larry Clark was among the VF-83 pilots who contributed to the demise of this wave of Japanese attackers. Launched ninety minutes earlier with his own F6F division and a pair of Corsair divisions from VBF-83,

Clark and seven other pilots were vectored out toward one of the bogies around 1330. Clark's F6F section soon tallyhoed a Judy at 4,500 feet, which he sighted just as she nosed over into her dive. The Judy momentarily vanished into the cloud layer, with the fighters in pursuit, but Clark soon picked it up again at 3,000 feet. Fleet gunners had opened up by then, but the ensign continued his pursuit right into his own ships' antiaircraft fire.

"There were a lot of antiaircraft bursts around me," said Clark. "But you don't pay attention to that when you're in attack mode." At two thousand feet, the Judy executed a split-S, with Clark following closely. He closed to five hundred feet and poured fire from all six .50-calibers into his opponent. Clark continued diving through the hail of friendly antiaircraft fire, clinging doggedly to his opponent until flames erupted from the bomber's cowling and wing root. The flaming Judy plowed into the ocean just off the starboard beam of *Bunker Hill*, and only then did the determined Hellcat pilot pull out, just above the wave tops.[42]

Larry Clark's first aerial victory was credited as a kill that had saved *Bunker Hill* from a direct kamikaze hit. After returning from his flight, he was directed to the bridge to see Vice Admiral Mitscher, who congratulated him on his fine victory. "I was speechless," said the humbled Clark. Mitscher was impressed enough with the young F6F jockey's pursuit of the kamikaze through antiaircraft fire that he had him written up for the Navy Cross.[43]

Lieutenant Tom Reidy's VBF-83 *Essex* CAP division was vectored out around 1430 to engage a Myrt, which Reidy downed after a ten-minute chase. Ensign Don McPherson of VF-83 made his first combat mission on the afternoon of March 19 when *Essex* launched a final ten-F6F fighter sweep against Nittigahara Airfield on Kyushu. Although not regularly assigned since settling on *Essex*, McPherson was swept into VF-83's "Wonder Five" division this day, after another rookie ensign put two Hellcats into the drink within a short period of time. McPherson immediately felt at home flying wing on his new division leader, quiet and confident Lieutenant Carlos Soffe. Their second section was filled out by Lieutenant (jg) Lyttleton "Tom" Ward and Ensign Melton Truax. Soffe's division, making attack runs from southwest of the airfield, caught a number of Japanese aircraft on the ground at Nittigahara, seven of which were tucked into revetments.

"As we rolled into our first rocket run, I could see people running from their barracks to man the antiaircraft guns," said McPherson. He had been instructed to switch from his auxiliary belly tank to a wing tank before his run, but the stress and excitement of his first engagement caused him to forget to make the switch.[44]

McPherson had eyeballed a big Betty bomber on the runway as he came in low. Bright pink streaks of antiaircraft fire zipped past him as he fired his six 5-inch HVARs from three thousand feet. He immediately afterward began strafing the Betty. "I stayed in my dive until I saw the bomber blow up," he said. McPherson then tried to pull up sharply from his dive, only to find that his engine was not pulling enough fuel from the auxiliary belly tank. "The engine quit and I was still going, and the propeller was windmilling from the speed," he said. McPherson was forced to work his "wobble pump"—a hand-powered fuel pump—to get his engine started again. "By that time, I had lost enough speed that the antiaircraft tracer bullets were crossing in front of me," he said. At least one bullet hit his starboard elevator and filled his cockpit with smoke. "I rolled the hatch back to get fresh air," McPherson said. "But I had enough speed left that the air suction pulled my helmet, goggles, and radio earphones off my head."[45]

Left without radio communication, the rookie ensign pulled out over the ocean until he was able to realign on Soffe's right wing. Soffe gave him a thumbs up after a quick inspection, but McPherson had to struggle with his trim-tab controls to keep his Hellcat under control en route back to *Essex*. His VF-83 group was credited with burning seven Japanese aircraft with their rockets and setting fire to another three with their strafing runs. After landing, McPherson's plane captain crawled up to help unbuckle him. "I see you picked up a little lead today," he commented. The sailor pointed to a 20-mm cannon shell hole that had penetrated the F6F's fuselage just a foot behind the pilot's seat, where it severed one of the cables that controlled the vertical rudder. "That's the reason I was flying a little funny," McPherson noted. "After that, I always remembered to switch from the belly tank to the wing tank if I was attacking. I guess I was the luckiest guy in the world."[46]

Pete Mitscher's final strike from TG 58.1 on the nineteenth was launched at 1400 to hit Kanoya and Takayama Airfields in southern Kyushu as the carriers retired from the area. Lieutenant Commander Hugh Nicholson, skipper of VBF-17, led twenty of his Corsairs and VF-17 Hellcats 224 miles to Kanoya to deliver 500-pound bombs.

Lieutenant Bob Coats and his wingmen, Ensign Geremiah Foster and Lieutenant (jg) Bill Colvin, shared one-third credits for the probable destruction of a Tony. Near the airfield the trio would claim probable destruction of six Zekes and a George. Fighting Seventeen's other division destroyed two Zekes, one each falling to Lieutenant Dick Cowger and

Ensign Ernie Vonder Heyden. *Hornet*'s fighters were the deadliest of the day in and near Japan. Beebe's VF-17 claimed 12.5 kills, nine probables, and three damaged enemy aircraft, while Nicholson's VBF-17 claimed 24 kills, nine probables, and three more Japanese planes damaged.

Mitscher's carrier fighters turned in a daily scorecard of eighty aerial victories, twenty-six probable kills, and sixteen more aerial opponents damaged. Numerous other aircraft had been destroyed on the ground, and Japanese shipping in Kure Harbor had paid a heavy price. In return, Vice Admiral Ugaki claimed to have sunk a number of carriers and battleships, but his Thunder Gods in fact had only damaged *Wasp* and *Franklin*.

Chapter Ten

"A FIGHTER PILOT'S DREAM"

Vice Admiral Ugaki was left reeling after the two-day assault by Pete Mitscher's carriers against Japan's harbors and airfields on March 18–19. Many of his assault planes had been dispersed to rear bases during the raids, leaving him "uneasy about continuing attacks." But Ugaki was determined to strike back. "I ordered them to get back quickly to their original or operational bases, where every effort would be made to fix planes for the next operation," he wrote in his diary.[1]

Ugaki's dawn search planes on the twentieth found three groups of U.S. carriers retiring from the area. His available strike planes were limited, but Ugaki sent out several special-attack units to harass TF 58. Rear Admiral Davison's TG 58.2 became the focal point for Japanese counterattacks that afternoon. The destroyer *Halsey Powell* (DD 686) was slammed by a Zeke kamikaze that killed a dozen men and wounded twenty-nine more. The carrier *Enterprise* dodged two near-miss bombs but suffered casualties from friendly fire from other warships shooting at a low-flying attack plane. Big E was further damaged later in the afternoon by one attacker that landed a direct hit on her port bow.[2]

Halsey Powell, badly damaged, suffered a loss of steering control that caused her to nearly collide with the carrier *Hancock*. *Powell*'s skipper then stopped all engines to allow his damage controlmen to repair the issues. The rest of TF 58 pressed on, though, Mitscher eager to retire from Japanese waters and willing to scuttle the damaged warship, if necessary. Captain Burke, the former destroyer-squadron commander, pleaded with the admiral, "You're not going to let one of my favorite ships out there get sunk?"[3]

Mitscher was not initially enthusiastic until Burke stood his ground and insisted that the lone destroyer was as important as any of the Bald Eagle's beloved aircraft carriers. Mitscher finally muttered, "All right," and allowed TF 58 to remain in the vicinity, providing night-fighter cover and daytime CAPs while *Halsey Powell* hauled clear toward Ulithi at greatly reduced speed. "Here was a fleet that would stay and fight for one little ship, and we got the little ship out," said Burke.[4]

Ugaki was not overly pleased with the performance of his strike planes and encouraged them to make more attacks. One of his air-group commanders, angry that he could not participate in the work of his subordinates, threatened the admiral that he would commit hara-kiri. "I just laughed it off," wrote the admiral, "saying that if he could commit hara-kiri for such a thing as that, he had better go ahead and do it."[5]

Japanese planes shadowed TF 58 as it continued to retire that night. In the meantime Ugaki felt that there was a good chance of finally unleashing his Thunder Gods and their Ohka bombs; fair weather the following morning boded well for such activity. The admiral had been waiting since March 18 for just such a moment, "intending to prove its usefulness by any means. If we missed such a chance which presented itself right before us, we'd be forced to attempt another one-way attack upon Ulithi, which has little prospect of success."[6]

Shortly after 0800 on March 21, Japanese reconnaissance aircraft reported two carrier task groups within striking distance in clear weather. In the underground operations room of the 5th Air Fleet, Ugaki met with key members of his staff, corps commander Captain Motoharu Okamura, wing leader Commander Kunihiro Iwaki, and Betty squadron leader Lieutenant Commander Goro Nonaka. Ugaki's chief of staff, Rear Admiral Toshiyuki Yokoi, reported that only twenty-three supporting fighters were available from the 203rd Flying Corps for indirect cover. Although the sighted American carriers were reported to have no CAPs flying above them, the Japanese staff worried that the distance—more than three hundred miles of flight—would prevent any of the mother Bettys from returning even after launching their Ohkas.[7]

"Sir, shall we wait for another chance?" Yokoi asked.

Ugaki was determined. "If we can't use the Ohkas now, in this situation," he said, "we will never have the chance to use them."[8]

The order for launching the first Thunder Gods mission was passed at 0945, and Lieutenant Commander Nonaka, a graduate of the Imperial Naval Academy, selected eighteen of his best pilots for the operation. Fifteen of the eighteen Bettys would carry Thunder Gods and their stubby-winged bombs. Each light-gray Ohka Model 11 carried 2,600 pounds of explosive in its pointed nose and was capable of 400 miles per hour once detached from its mother bomber and its pilot engaged the rocket engine. Each Ohka pilot placed clippings from his hair and fingernails in unpainted wooden boxes that would be delivered to his parents in order to conduct funerals. They all donned new uniforms, burning their old ones, before sitting down to write their individual death statements.[9]

The selected pilots were the men of the 711th Hikotai (HKT), the Jinrai Corps' main attack element, many fresh from pilot-training programs. "My body will collapse like a falling cherry blossom, but my soul will live and protect this land forever," wrote twenty-three-year-old Kansai University graduate Yuzuru Ogata. "I shall fall, smiling and singing songs," wrote Flight Petty Officer 1st Class Ataru Shimamura. "Please do not cry. Make my death meaningful." Nineteen-year-old Flight Petty Officer 2nd Class Naokichi Kameda penned, "The value of being a man is given at the time of his death."[10]

One Ohka pilot carried a tray of celebratory sake drinks across the flight line for a final toast for the brave pilots. One of the Betty pilots had just turned up his engines for a flight check, and its propeller sucked the young suicide pilot into the whirling blades, killing him instantly. A more ominous mood could not have been present as the First Kamikaze Ohka Special Attack Unit—the Thunder Gods Corps (the 721st Naval Flying Corps)—prepared for battle.[11]

Each 711th HKT pilot wore a headband inscribed with the words "Thunder Gods" given to them by Admiral Toyoda, commander in chief of the Combined Fleet. Vice Admiral Ugaki arrived to deliver a final message of inspiration to his young warriors, as tears streamed down his face. Ugaki, Okamura, and other officers exchanged farewell cups of sake with the Betty crews and their Ohka pilots before the planes began warming up for takeoffs. In a booming voice, Lieutenant Commander Nonaka implored his pilots to not hesitate as they attacked the American warships. "Attack aggressively and destroy your target regardless of all else," said Nonaka. "Let us fight to the death! Let us fill the Pacific with our blood!"

Lieutenant Kentaro Mitsuhashi, the twenty-two-year-old leader of the Ohka squadron, announced, "Let us die together!"[12]

Within minutes, around 1135, the airfield was a roar of thundering props and whining engines as the Betty bombers gathered speed and took to the air over Kagoshima Bay. They were followed by dozens of escorting fighter planes, all heading southeast toward the U.S. carrier fleet as Ugaki and his staff headed for their underground operations room to await the results of the first Thunder Gods mission.

"I prayed for their success," he wrote.[13]

✦◇✦

Marsh Beebe's VF-17 *Hornet* pilots would be first to tangle with the unusual Ohkas on March 21. Lieutenant Jim Pearce had spent the morning loafing in the ready room, playing cribbage with his wingman, George Johnson. He then grabbed a Spam sandwich from the wardroom around 1030, half an hour before his division was launched for its afternoon CAP duty. "We droned over the fleet for more than three hours, in what looked to be a typical boring flight to nowhere," Pearce recalled.[14]

At 1350 radar operators in TG 58.1 plotted a sizable blip approaching, distance seventy miles. The fighter-director officer (FDO) issued orders for the available *Hornet* CAP to vector out on course 330 degrees "Buster" (at top speed). Pearce firewalled the throttle of his Hellcat, leading his "Red Five" division and the VBF-17 "Red Twenty-Eight" division of Lieutenant (jg) Henry "Hal" Mitchell in the direction of the enemy. *Hornet* in the meantime scrambled more fighters to replace the two divisions sent on the chase, while *Belleau Wood* also directed eight of its VF-30 Hellcats toward the intercept.

Pearce and Mitchell's divisions flew at full power, climbing to 18,000 feet to be above the bogies. When first tallyhoed at 1418, the enemy planes were about ten miles distant and still some fifty miles from *Hornet*.

The situation had deteriorated quickly for the Thunder Gods. Just a half hour out from base, half of the escorting fighters returned to base due to malfunctioning fuel pumps. These and other malfunctions left only about thirty fighters to escort the Ohka-laden Bettys toward TF 58. Japanese reconnaissance planes brought further bad news: instead of facing only two U.S. carriers without a CAP, three groups of American carrier task groups had been spotted, each believed to have ample fighter coverage. The Betty pilots dutifully maintained radio silence, leaving Vice Admiral Ugaki to ponder long hours over what had become of his first Ohka mission.[15]

Although normally fast-flying planes, the Bettys Pearce found were moving at a relaxed pace. His division was on the right side of the bombers and Hal Mitchell's on their left as the Japanese approached. When the Bettys were about three miles distant, the two *Hornet* Hellcat divisions made U-turns over the top of them to put themselves in ideal attack position from both sides. "The fighter escorts were high above and didn't seem to be paying much attention to the bombers," recalled Pearce. "This looked like a fighter pilot's dream." His Red Five division dropped their belly tanks and prepared to attack. Relaying the word from the fleet FDO, Pearce radioed, "Forget the fighters and go for the bombers!"[16]

Both divisions dove into the big bombers, making high side runs on the formation to avoid getting sucked behind the Bettys, where their tail gunners could punish the F6Fs. Mitchell made twelve firing runs on the formation and downed four of the big Ohka transports. During his last run, he forced a Betty down low over the water and fired until he exhausted his bullets. He bored in from eight o'clock, a mere fifteen feet above the waves, hoping to force the enemy plane into the ocean. Mitchell finally pulled up sharply, clearing the Betty by a matter of feet as the big bomber dropped its nose, caught a wing in a swell, and crashed into the ocean. Mitchell had just become an "ace in a day."

Mitchell's second-section leader, Lieutenant (jg) Carl "Junior" Van Stone, was credited with knocking down a Zeke and two Bettys. Pearce's first victim was the Betty flight leader, which quickly burst into flames as his .50-caliber bullets ripped through the bomber's right nacelle and fuselage. Pearce followed the Betty downward for a few seconds to get a better look at the Baka bomb tucked outside its bomb bay. "Almost immediately, the Betty's right wing blew off, so I cycled up into position to make my second run."[17]

Pearce found that the Bettys maintained formation, going straight ahead, despite the aerial attacks. He alertly picked up muzzle flashes from the bomber's tail gunner, forcing him to knock out this menace before concentrating on the Betty's vulnerable nacelle wing-fuselage juncture. He set his second Betty afire and watched its Ohka bomber suddenly drop free and head for the ocean, along with its crippled mother ship. By this point Pearce could see "Bettys flaming all over the sky."[18]

Pearce's wingman, George Johnson, accounted for three more of the Bettys, while Murray Winfield claimed four more. Aside from the Ohka seen by Pearce to have launched, most of the other Bettys were knocked down before their rocket bombers could be released. The lone loss for the eight *Hornet* fighters was the VBF-17 Hellcat of Lieutenant (jg) Wallace F. "Blackout" Klein, who was missing in action following the melee, presumably picked off by some of the Zeke escorts.

Two CAP divisions of VF-30 joined the fray, led by Lieutenant Commander Douglas Clark, CAG 30. The *Belleau Wood* Hellcats were on station at 10,000 feet forty miles northwest of their task group when radar pinpointed a large formation of bogies approaching from the northwest. "This vector led to an air battle which will go down in squadron history as the 'First Turkey Shoot,'" VF-30's ACIO, Lieutenant (jg) John Pooley, wrote.[19]

Left: Lieutenant Jim Pearce of *Hornet's* VF-17 holds two fingers to indicate the number of Ohka-laden Betty bombers he destroyed on March 21, 1945. *U.S. Navy. Right:* This division (call name "Fighter Bomber 28") of *Hornet's* VBF-17 was highly successful in the "turkey shoot" intercept of the Bettys. *Left to right:* Lieutenant (jg) Carl "Junior" Van Stone, Lieutenant Guye W. Troute, Ensign Michael Skees, Lieutenant (jg) Wallace F. "Blackout" Klein, and Lieutenant (jg) Henry "Hal" Mitchell. Mitchell, who would achieve five victories to become an instant ace, was killed in action weeks later during the Okinawa campaign. *Tilman Pool*

Ensign Johnnie Miller tallyhoed the incoming Japanese group at 1430, and Clark's division climbed to 16,000 feet to take favorable attack position. *Hornet's* VF-17 and VBF-17 were already assailing the Betty formation, which was also jumped by an *Intrepid* VF-10 division, which claimed three more bombers. Clark's Fighting Thirty claimed ten of the Bettys and eleven Zekes in the action that followed. If one trusts all the claims turned in by the *Hornet, Intrepid,* and *Belleau Wood* pilots, more Bettys were downed than were actually present—obviously a case of damaged planes being hit by multiple squadrons.

The VF-30 skipper and his wingman Miller scissored back and forth with a dozen Japanese fighters until Clark finally flamed one Zeke with a burst into its right wing and gas tanks. Clark's F6F was crippled by a 20-mm cannon, but Miller accounted for two Zeke kills and two other fighters damaged before he also headed for base, low on fuel and his own plane winged by enemy fire, in company with three *Hornet* planes.

All eight *Belleau Wood* fighters claimed one or more kills in the vicious dogfighting. Clark and Pooley credited Ensign James Reber with top honors with kills of two Bettys and two Zekes. One of the Zekes Reber ignited exploded at such close proximity that his own engine was left smoking badly from shrapnel damage. Adding in three previous victories, Reber had achieved ace status in the March 21 "turkey shoot."

During the course of the battle with the Thunder Gods bombers, the VF-30 pilots noted the Ohka bombers, which were christened "gizmos" in their action report. Ensign James W. Ward, credited with kills of two Zekes and a Betty, reported that each bomber carried a small aircraft just below its engines. "The fuselage was blunt nosed, tapering to the stern, and appeared to be too small in diameter to be a torpedo," noted the Fighting Thirty report. "No previous reports have been received by this squadron or carrier of the attempted use by the Japanese of such a weapon."[20]

Tilly Pool, a member of Tommy Harris' airborne VF-17 division that was held close to the task force, had been forced to listen to the action over his radio. "We were sitting there drooling, waiting for them to let some of them come through so we could get a shot at them," he said. The reliving of the fight was a period of excitement in Fighting Seventeen's ready room once its divisions had landed on *Hornet*. "We determined that if we had not destroyed this powerful raid before it got close enough to the fleet to launch the bakas, Pearl Harbor would have gone down in history as a 'minor defeat,'" wrote Pearce.[21]

Fighters from *Hornet*, *Intrepid*, and *Belleau Wood* had knocked out Ugaki's first major deployment of Ohka-laden bombers and had shredded much of the Thunder Gods' accompanying fighters in the process. Lieutenant Mitchell of VBF-17 emerged from the fracas as an "ace in a mission," and many other pilots padded their aerial-victory records. The first big "Cherry Blossom" strike of Operation Iceberg had been defeated. "It was an exciting fifteen minutes," admitted Pearce. "It was something we didn't get to do very often—to just sit there and whack away at them as they plowed on toward the task force."[22]

Nine of the Bettys had gone down, along with two special-attack bombers and a number of the escorting fighters. Thunder Gods leader Nonaka and three other Betty crews were last seen by surviving Zero pilots to be diving in unison toward the ocean. The first sortie of the elite bomber group had ended in tragedy, with the loss of some 160 airmen and fifteen Ohka pilots. Japanese leaders blamed the failure on insufficient fighter coverage and began planning how better to deploy such weapons in the future.[23]

The final week of March was occupied by the various task groups making strikes on Japanese bases to keep the kamikaze threat at bay. TF 58 caught its breath on the twenty-second, replenishing fuel loads from fleet tankers. Vice Admiral Mitscher took the chance to reorganize his force into three task groups, leaving TG 58.2 to support the crippled *Franklin*. No enemy aircraft kills were claimed this day, and only five Navy aerial victories were claimed over the next three days.

Mitscher's air groups attacked Naha Airfield on Okinawa and airfields in southern Japan during the next several days, with few enemy aircraft contacts. The night fighters did score four kills overnight on March 26–27. A large enemy flight picked up on radar the following morning necessitated the scramble of some of *Hornet*'s VF-17 planes. Lieutenant Pearce and wingman Chili Crawford were assigned to launch from the hangar deck via experimentally installed catapult launches.

Pearce had experienced the jolt when fired from the longer flight-deck catapults, so he fully expected "an enormous wallop" for a shorter hangar catapult to move his Hellcat to flight speed. The catapult officer signaled full power, so Pearce revved his 2,000-horsepower engine up to maximum before he was catapulted into the predawn darkness. The other thirty-eight Hellcats, all launched from the flight deck by 0630, managed to find some action.[24]

Skipper Marsh Beebe tallyhoed a Jill at 0655 some thirty-five miles from the task group and sent it flaming into the ocean after two firing runs. The only other kill for the large VF-17 contingent went to Lieutenant Willis Parker, who downed a Myrt. Pearce and Crawford failed to find any enemy aircraft to tangle with, leaving the lieutenant to wonder why he had been selected to test the new hangar-deck launches in the dark. "I suspected Admiral Clark might have had something to do with it," he mused.

Lieutenant Frederick Fox of *Yorktown*'s VBF-9 on March 27 earned the distinction of becoming the first American to land on Okinawa. His division was accompanying fifteen TBMs of VT-9, led by the squadron's skipper, Lieutenant Commander Byron Cooke. An Okinawa air coordinator assigned Cooke's Avengers to attack a series of amphibious-boat revetments and dual-purpose batteries along well-defended Kadena Airfield. With clouds solid at 3,500 feet, the first run was made at low altitude, the attack planes jinking constantly to avoid the heavy antiaircraft fire rising up from both Yontan Airfield and Kadena.

Cooke rendezvoused his flight for a second run through the gauntlet of antiaircraft fire. His wingmen were Lieutenants (jg) Bill Patterson and Leon Frankel. Skirting the barrage from Yontan, the flight had reached a point just east of Kadena and was preparing to push over for diving runs when tragedy struck. Frankel, one of only two Jewish pilots in his squadron, was raised in Saint Paul and had attended the University of Minnesota before enlisting in the Navy's flight program. During his flight training, Frankel and his buddy Grady Jean had found the TBM Avenger to be completely versatile. "It could carry bombs, torpedoes, rockets, and machine guns, and could lay mines," noted Frankel. He and Ensign Jean "made up our minds right then and there that we were going to opt for torpedoes" instead of being fighter pilots.[25]

Frankel was flying wing on Cooke's Corsair when two F6Fs of VBF-9, in their dives on the target, came boring toward the formation from the port beam. As Cooke caught sight of them, he threw his plane into a violent bank in an effort to avoid collision. He succeeded in avoiding one Hellcat, but just then an antiaircraft shell burst near the second one, piloted by Lieutenant Fox. The fighter was hurled into Cooke's plane, shearing off the VT-9 skipper's starboard wing. Frankel also maneuvered violently. "I pulled back on the stick as hard as I could, and as I went past, I could feel the heat from the two airplanes," he said.[26]

The stricken planes went down smoking, with Fox's Corsair twirling like a falling leaf. Cooke's TBM exploded on impact with the ground, killing him and his crewmen. Ensign Ray Jehli saw that Fox regained sufficient control to make a belly landing in a field west of Kadena Airfield. He then witnessed the F4U explode about ten seconds after touching the ground and assumed Fox had perished.

But Fred Fox had been thrown clear of the wreckage. For three days he would elude enemy capture on Okinawa, hiding in caves until he obtained a small boat and paddled out from the coastline to attract the attention of U.S. warplanes. The pilot of an OS2U Kingfisher from the cruiser *San Francisco* (CA 38), conducting a search of the areas north of Machinato town, spotted a small native boat aground two hundred yards from the beach with a man in it and green-dye marker on the water around it.

Lieutenant Fred Fox of *Yorktown*'s VBF-9 wades out across a reef during his rescue from Okinawa on March 29, 1945. *U.S. Navy*

The *San Francisco* pilot settled into the ocean to retrieve Lieutenant Fox but damaged one of its floats in the process. Prevented from taking off or even rapid taxiing, the OS2U pilot called for help. A nearby minesweeper, *Heed* (AM 100), arrived at 1230 and towed the Kingfisher and its rescued VBF-9 pilot out to where the cruiser *Birmingham* (CL 62) could assist. An hour later *Birmingham's* crew had used their crane to lift the damaged OS2U on board, along with a much-relieved Fred Fox, who was suffering from a broken nose and multiple bruises.

Yorktown squadronmates who had seen Fox's aircraft explode on Okinawa felt that he had returned from the dead.

The prospect of loss lurked around every corner during late March, as TF 58 pilots continued to soften up Okinawa for the impending landings. *Hornet's* Air Group 17 launched its third strike of the twenty-eighth against gun emplacements and caves on the island's southeast coast. The VF-17 divisions of Marsh Beebe and Billy Watts flew cover for the *Hornet* and *Bennington* Avengers and Helldivers assigned to the strike. Tragedy struck as the F6F divisions delivered their bullets and rockets.

As a pair of VF-17 photo-reconnaissance Hellcats recovered from low-level runs over the beach areas, Ensign Wendell Schurse Harrington's F6F collided with the Hellcat flown by the commander, Carrier Division 5, air coordinator, Commander Charlie Crommelin, the *Randolph* CAG who was on temporary duty with *Hornet*. Watts saw the impact shear off the port wing of Crommelin's F6F and the starboard wing of Harrington's fighter.

Both Hellcats plunged into the bay five hundred yards offshore with no survivors. Crommelin's collision may have been indirectly linked to the impaired vision he

Commander Charles Laurence DeBerniere Crommelin, *Randolph's* CAG, was killed in action during the Okinawa preinvasion strikes on March 28, 1945, while temporarily serving on *Hornet*. U.S. Navy suffered in one eye from the injuries sustained in a November 1943 flight. In any event, he would be sorely missed by Rear Admiral Jocko Clark, on board TG 58.1's flagship carrier *Hornet*, who considered Crommelin "the bravest man I encountered during the entire war."[27]

Clark was already stirring up the ire of Vice Admiral Mitscher at the time Crommelin was killed. Admiral Spruance had messaged at 0933 that morning that a Japanese fleet, presumably including the battleship *Yamato*, was heading southeast of Kyushu toward Okinawa, according to a sighting report from Army Air Force bombers. Admiral Clark collected his morning strikers and turned his task group north at high speed, advising both Mitscher and Spruance that he would attack "unless otherwise directed." A heated exchange ensued over the TBS system, in which Spruance expressed his desire for his battleships to engage the reported *Yamato* force. Mitscher believed his carrier air power could do a better, more economical job on the Japanese fleet and remarked that he would launch a bombing strike regardless of any order to the contrary coming from his boss, Spruance.[28]

Clark's 58.1 carriers raced north and began launching search-strike planes at 1515. No trace of *Yamato* nor any Japanese warship was found, so the planes carried out sweeps over southern Kyushu airfields. Commander Ed Konrad, CAG 17, led nineteen *Hornet* F6Fs to hit an airfield near Kagoshima Bay. As the Hellcats crossed the bay and began dropping altitude, the first signs of enemy fighters aloft were observed. Ned Langdon's second-section leader, Lieutenant (jg) Joe Stenstrom, flamed a Myrt that was finished off by a *Bennington* Corsair.

The *Hornet* flight leveled two hangars with its 500-pound bombs and wrecked a number of parked aircraft by strafing. Watts and wingman, Werner Gaerisch, were each credited with destroying a twin-engine plane. As Fighting Seventeen rendezvoused over Kagoshima Bay at 1700, Watts spotted a Jake about five hundred feet off the water. He dived in for a flat side run, closing the firing distance from one thousand feet to a mere fifty feet, until his bullets sent the Jake spiraling down to crash into the ocean. Watts and his division landed back on *Hornet* at 1830. His excitement of scoring an aerial victory was dampened somewhat to learn that Lieutenant (jg) Wyman Edmund of VF-17 had disappeared during the hop, presumably a victim to Japanese antiaircraft fire.

Another fighter pilot, Lieutenant (jg) Harry William Swinburne Jr. from the light carrier *San Jacinto*, had a harrowing mission during the afternoon. The Iowa native had scored his first aerial victory a week earlier while guarding the damaged *Franklin*. As dusk approached at 1725 on March 28, Swinburne's VF-45 group made a rocket and strafing attack on a group of ten small enemy freighters and 60-foot gunboats.[29]

One of the gunboats was blown up by four rocket hits in VF-45's first run. On his next pass, Swinburne decided to release his rockets at point-blank range. "The two rockets hit almost simultaneously with my pushing the pickle on them," he said. When the lieutenant pulled into a steep, climbing turn to port, the small vessel was smoking, burning, and sinking. The other VF-45 pilots, joined by a division from *Belleau Wood*, pumped bullets and rockets into the merchantmen, leaving six small vessels ablaze and two others sinking.[30]

Swinburne fired his other four rockets on another gunboat and observed solid hits. He continued to make strafing runs on the other ships until he heard Lieutenant Levern Forkner radio, "Lucky Flight, this is Lucky-One. Rendezvous south of the force." Swinburne decided to make one final, minimum-altitude run to strafe one of the fleeing gunboats. "During the completion of my attack, I was so low I had to pull up to clear the mainmast," he said. His new F6F, fresh from the factory, was suddenly struck by a 20-mm round that ripped through his port ammunition box. "The wing burst into flames instantaneously, and all six machine guns went on automatic fire," said Swinburne.[31]

He jettisoned his external fuel tank and opened his canopy to bail out as the fire became more intense. Deciding against ditching among angry Japanese sailors in the waters below, Swinburne climbed for altitude and prayed the fire would burn out as he headed back toward *San Jacinto*. It did, and another pilot accompanied his crippled F6F back toward TG 58.1. Upon reaching the carriers, Forkner and three other VF-45 pilots made night landings on *Belleau Wood*. Swinburne was still circling the fleet when a radio call came in from Admiral Clark.[32]

"Lucky-One-Three, this is Bull Durham. What's your problem?" Swinburne announced that his Hellcat had been hit, he had no flaps or landing gear, and that a large portion of his port wing was gone.

"Lucky-One-Three, this is Bull Durham," the admiral called back. "If you will remain airborne until we get all our airplanes aboard, Arab Base will take you aboard." Swinburne circled until the other fighters had landed, then made his approach on Arab Base, Clark's flagship *Hornet*. At the last instant he realized that, in the pitch blackness, he was attempting to settle onto a destroyer.

On his next try Swinburne was coached in by *Hornet*'s landing-signal officer. He came in fast, exhausted after five hours in the air, and landed hard enough that his left landing-gear strut cut into the deck. Swinburne had only enough time to salvage the Grumman's cockpit clock before sailors pushed his crippled fighter over the side.[33]

Jocko Clark's carriers launched another 146-fighter sweep-search mission that afternoon but failed to find the *Yamato* force. A third search, launched after midnight, did locate the Japanese battleship at dawn on March 29, but it was anchored at the Kure Naval Base.

Three of Mitscher's task groups, operating 120 miles south of Kyushu on the twenty-ninth, launched strikes against the southern airfields, while the Bald Eagle dispatched another large-scale strike from TG 58.4 carriers *Yorktown, Langley, Intrepid,* and *Independence* shortly after dawn to try to catch the reported *Yamato* force.

The massive sweep proved to be nothing more than a wild goose chase, but the air group had gone out loaded for bear. Lieutenant Commander Larry Lawrence's thirteen VT-10 *Intrepid* Avengers each carried aerial torpedoes but were forced to dump them against worthless sampans. Gunner Bill Banta watched the torpedo dropped by his pilot, Lieutenant (jg) Ken Oburn, churn through the bay and slam into the main support of a Japanese bridge. "We blew up a concrete pier," said Banta. "It pretty much destroyed the whole dock."[34]

By day's end the Navy pilots had turned in claims for two dozen aerial kills in a series of small dogfights. March 29 marked the campaign combat debut of Lieutenant (jg) Phil Kirkwood and his division of *Intrepid* Grim Reapers. Kirkwood had achieved four aerial kills during his previous 1944 combat cruise with VF-10, and the Princeton graduate was itching to achieve one more kill to reach the coveted ace status. He had special incentive, as businessman S. S. Ramagos from his hometown of Wildwood, New Jersey, had offered to pay $100 for each additional Japanese plane Kirkwood shot down.[35]

His wingman was a rookie, Ensign Norwald Richard "Dick" Quiel, a twenty-two-year-old from Grand Marais, Minnesota. Quiel had been eager to earn his keep since enlisting in the Navy's V-5 flight-training program in 1942. "I knew that I wanted to fly, having built airplanes for Lockheed before the war," he said. "I was enthusiastic about being part of the war."[36]

Kirkwood and Quiel launched from *Intrepid* at 1400 as part of a mixed twenty-Corsair bunch that included divisions from their VF-10 and sister squadron VBF-10. An hour into their flight, the group crossed the coast of southern Kyushu and were fifteen miles south of Kanoya East when they contacted a force of eight Japanese fighters—seven Zekes and a Jack—proceeding in a northerly direction toward Kanoya.

Kirkwood's division, being nearest, peeled off to engage by executing high side runs from ten thousand feet. "We had a load of 500-pound bombs and eight rockets on and a full load of ammo, and a couple of gas tanks, so we were pretty heavy," noted Quiel. Each pilot—Kirkwood, Quiel, Ensign Horace W. Heath, and Ensign Fred E. Meyer—scored a kill on their first pass. Lieutenant (jg) John Sweeney, in the VF-10 division that followed Kirkwood's, flamed a fifth Zeke in the opening action.[37]

Heath added a second kill by blasting the Jack in a head-on run before it could fire on his wingman, Meyer. Not to be outscored, Kirkwood and Quiel tore into the remaining Zekes. Quiel had tense seconds as one of the Japanese fighters nearly collided with him in midair. "He headed straight for me," said Quiel, who pushed over hard enough that the Zeke narrowly screamed past the top of his canopy. "There was just feet to spare. You could almost see the rivets in the bottom of his airplane."[38]

The Fighting Ten group ended the brief battle with seven kills, including two credited to Kirkwood, achieving the coveted ace status. He could now plan on collecting $200 from his New Jersey bet upon returning stateside, and during the next month off Okinawa, his team would continue to run up that score.

Jocko Clark's aggressive desires to catch the *Yamato* fleet at sea had not panned out. Pete Mitscher, frustrated by the lack of targets his carriers had found on the twenty-ninth, signaled to Clark, "How do you like going on a wild goose chase?"

"It was not a wild goose chase," Clark defiantly replied. "I found the *Yamato*. She has not yet come out. Otherwise, we would have done battle."[39]

Task-force rescue planes were a godsend for downed aviators during the latter part of March, and Kingfisher pilots of the cruiser *Astoria* (CL 90) proved to be exceptional at search-and-rescue missions. On March 24 Lieutenant Charles S. Tanner landed his OS2U at 1834 in very choppy seas and taxied to the life raft of two downed VB-84 *Bunker Hill* airmen, Lieutenant (jg) Judson Charles Davis and ARM3c J. D. Mahoney. Tanner found them nearly three hours into his flight and then had great difficulty getting the exhausted men into his Kingfisher due to heavy seas that tossed their life raft around mightily.

Astoria's rescue pilots were at it again five days later in a coordinated search-and-recovery mission for a downed *Hancock* Helldiver pilot. Commander Henry Miller, CAG 6, led a forty-nine-plane strike from *Hancock* to Kyushu to bomb Kanoya Airfield, nearby docks, and other structures. During his air group's rendezvous after the strike, the dive bomber of Lieutenant (jg) Ronald Lee Somerville from Chillicothe, Missouri, was struck by another Bombing Six SB2C, piloted by Lieutenant (jg) Vernon A. Lileks. "My plane went completely out of control and headed straight for the water in a steep dive," reported Somerville.[40]

Lileks recovered control and returned to *Hancock* with his badly damaged plane. Somerville and his radioman, ARM2c Louis F. Jakubec, had to bail out of their tailless bomber. The lieutenant parachuted out at a mere eight hundred feet and narrowly avoided drowning as his parachute pulled him face down underwater. Surfacing, he scrambled into a dropped life raft and was soon drifting only a mile from the eastern shore of Kanoya. While paddling out from Kagoshima Bay, Somerville witnessed an incredible dogfight above him.

Lieutenant (jg) Louis L. Davis of *Hancock*'s Fighting Six tallyhoed a formation of Japanese planes heading south over the bay, and the fight was on. As Somerville watched, one Hellcat was shot down and five Zekes plunged into the ocean. "One Jap pilot bailed out right over my head about 800 feet," he said. The Japanese pilot was carried downwind from his position and was not seen again. The VF-6 division remained above the downed *Hancock* pilot until another flight arrived, escorting a pair of *Astoria* OS2Us.[41]

One of the Kingfisher pilots, Lieutenant (jg) Jack F. Newman from Battle Creek, Michigan, landed and taxied his floatplane alongside Somerville's raft. The pilot was too weak to pull himself on board via the Jacob's ladder, so Newman grabbed his vest and helped haul him onto the aircraft. Newman then circled around the bay in search of Somerville's gunner, but no trace of him was ever found. During the course of this rescue, another American pilot, Ensign David Kelleher of *Cabot*'s VF-29, was downed by antiaircraft fire near the seaplane base at Ibusuki. Kelleher bailed out at eight hundred feet near Somerville's location and was quickly retrieved from the ocean by the second *Astoria* Kingfisher pilot, Lieutenant (jg) Donald O. Comb from Minneapolis.

Astoria's Kingfisher pilots proved to be the most effective in the task force, as they would successfully retrieve seven downed airmen during late March and early April 1945.

On March 30 and 31, TGs 58.3 and 58.4 launched sweeps and strikes against Okinawa and furnished CAPs for ships in the vicinity. Lieutenant Bob Coats of Fighting Seventeen was also rescued by floatplane when his F6F was hit by an antiaircraft shell, forcing him to ditch near one of Amami Oshima's bays. Bill Hardy and fourteen VF-17 comrades flew air cover over Coats as he struggled in the water and kept shore-based small-arms fire at a minimum with strafing attacks on adjacent villages. Lieutenant Pearce, vividly recalling the loss of wingman John Wray weeks earlier, flew cover over Coats for two hours until a pair of OS2Us from *Vincennes* (CL 64) arrived. He could see mortar shells starting to land close to the scene of the action. "[Lieutenant (jg) Harry] Chief Hanna, Coats' wingman, circling Bob with the rest of us, radioed the rescue pilot that if he left he would be shot down before he got off the water," recalled Pearce. Hanna, part Native American and nicknamed "Chief" by his squadronmates, was determined that his division leader be rescued.[42]

Pearce noted where the mortar fire was coming from and made repeated strafing runs while the Kingfisher pilot moved in closer. The rear-seat man had to swim out and tow Coats, a nonswimmer, out to the OS2U. The fighter pilot made it on board the floatplane, was taken to *Vincennes* at 1300, and was treated for minor abrasions and a lacerated forehead before being transferred back to *Hornet* the same day. "I was happy to see them," said Coats of his rescuers.[43]

Vice Admiral Mitscher's pilots claimed only nine aerial victories during their missions on March 30 and 31, as TF 58 prepared for the main landings on Okinawa the following day. In the week preceding the invasion, Vice Admiral Ugaki's program had undergone intense scrutiny. His Thunder Gods had failed in their first mass sortie on March 21. The mothership Bettys had been chewed up by American CAP patrols due to insufficient Japanese fighter cover. An eighteen-officer study group—including Vice Admiral Jisaburo Ozawa, vice chief of the Naval General Staff, and Rear Admiral Toahitane Takada, vice chief of the Combined Fleet—met for two days to reevaluate the use of the Thunder Gods.[44]

Captain Okamura, Jinrai Corps commander, was livid at the failure of his Thunder Gods and recommended they be used only in individual surprise attacks moving forward. This suggestion was adopted beginning March 23, and the special Ohka squadron was disbanded. Okamura now divided the Thunder Gods into two groups: one to fly special-attack fighter planes loaded with bombs, and the other to fly the Ohka manned bombs launched from Betty bombers.[45]

Okamura met with his pilots on March 24 at the Tomitaka Airfield to explain to them their new roles. Thus far he had lost twenty-seven Ohka pilots—fifteen in the failed attack on the twenty-first and a dozen others in accidents and American air raids. The pilots assigned to fly bomb-laden planes were instructed that they would now use the latest-model Zeke fighters armed with 1,100-pound bombs instead of the 550-pound bombs used previously.[46]

Preparations consumed the next week as the revamped Thunder Gods prepared for their next mission. Operation Heaven No. 1 was put in motion on March 31, on the eve of the Allied invasion of Okinawa. "As many enemy transports swarmed in the sea around the main island of Okinawa, it became apparent that the enemy would attempt a landing," Ugaki wrote on the thirty-first. "I ordered an all-out attack with the whole strength except those saved for the enemy task force."[47]

In a matter of hours, the second assault by the Thunder Gods would determine if Okamura's new plan would be any more successful.

Chapter Eleven

LOVE DAY LANDINGS ON OKINAWA

Flight Chief Petty Officer Keisuke Yamamura climbed out of the truck and joined the formation of aviators assembling before the headquarters building at Kanoya Airfield. The young Ohka pilot was prepared for the mission ahead. Earlier in the year he had resisted orders to join a fighter squadron, stating to his superiors, "Those who leave the *Ohka* squadron are cowards!"[1]

It was 0200 (an hour later than the time being kept by the Americans with TF 58) on April 1, 1945, as Yamamura and five other Ohka pilots stood with the forty-two Betty aircrewmen who would take them out against the American invasion fleet assembled off the coast of Okinawa. Some of the Thunder Gods had placed cherry-tree twigs in the backs of their uniforms, while Yamamura donned a long-tailed kamikaze headband he intended to wear on his final flight. In the heavy predawn mist, the warriors awaited their final instructions.

Vice Admiral Ugaki's 5th Air Fleet was still stinging from losses it had suffered at the hands of Vice Admiral Mitscher's relentless carrier attacks. Reconnaissance planes had confirmed the presence of the U.S. Fleet, but Japanese leaders were busy shuffling aircraft and personnel to bases on Kyushu from which they could stage a major offensive within the week. Ugaki could only send conventional attack aircraft and kamikazes in small numbers during the opening days of the Okinawa invasion. Long before dawn on April 1, he unleashed six Bettys of the 1st and 2nd Flights of Mission K708 from Kanoya Airfield, each bomber carrying an Ohka manned bomb.

Pilot Yamamura and his five Ohka companions listened intently as their commander, Captain Motoharu Okamura, made a short speech. He asked the men to perform their duty but to return to base if they found themselves in a position where they were unable to reach the American warships with a good chance of making a successful strike. Farewell cups of sake were exchanged before the four dozen Japanese airmen boarded the motherships. The first Betty rumbled off the air strip at 0221, followed by the rest at two-minute intervals. As his bomber climbed past the nearby blooming cherry trees at Kanoya, Yamamura was emotional. *I'm going to die!* he thought, as tears flowed down his cheeks.[2]

As the bombers lumbered toward Okinawa, Yamamura slipped out of his life jacket and prepared himself for the coming order to climb through the hatch into his Ohka once over their target area. But fate was not with Yamamura's pilots this morning, as a pair of American fighters cut off their flight well short of its goal.

Lieutenant George Anthony August Jr., a University of Rhode Island graduate who was a member of VF-10's night-fighter detachment, had lifted off from *Intrepid* with his wingman at 2145 on March 31. For nearly three hours their flight had been routine until Anthony was vectored toward bogies moving on Okinawa from Kanoya. The Grim Reaper F6F pilots closed the distance, scanning their radarscopes.

Finally, around 0130, August made radar contact with bandits some three miles away. His targets were flying low above the water at one thousand feet, a good three thousand feet below his own altitude. August and his wingman stealthily closed the distance until he made visual contact with a large Betty bomber, which was now just breaking through a layer of clouds.[3]

August closed to a mere 250 feet, taking a position about 50 feet below the Betty's tail to keep himself clear of the bomber's gunners. The lieutenant then squeezed a short burst from this .50-calibers, hoping to strike the wing-root fuel tanks, a known area of devastation for the big G4M2s. His first burst was right on the money. Lieutenant (jg) Yoshio Sawamoto, pilot of the leading Ohka-laden bomber, had no inclination of the danger sliding on to his tail. His Ohka pilot, Yamamura, was shocked by the sudden burst of machine-gun fire that ripped into the Betty. Sawamoto immediately jettisoned the heavy Ohka to try and outmaneuver the attacking Hellcat.[4]

August could not have been more accurate. His first burst caused the Betty's port engine to burst into flames. Sawamoto was unable to control his bomber as it fell off on its starboard wing and spiraled toward the ocean. As the altimeter wound rapidly toward zero, Yamamura shouted, "Pull up! Pull up!" The Betty slammed into the water at more than two hundred knots, the impact killing several crewmen. Yamamura fought his way free of the wreckage and swam to the flaming surface. Suffering from various wounds and burns, he found a seat mat and clung to it. Within minutes Yamamura found other survivors from the destroyed Betty, and they spent the night clinging to a rubber life raft dropped by a gracious American pilot.[5]

Lieutenant (jg) Sawamoto's Betty had been shot down off Cape Sata, the southern tip of the Osumi Peninsula of Kyushu. Shortly after daybreak on April 1, Yamamura and several enlisted aviators from the Betty crew were plucked from the sea by Japanese fishermen. Only after being treated for his wounds would Yamamura learn that the second sortie of the Thunder Gods had been another great failure. Five of the six Bettys failed to return. Two simply vanished, Sawamoto was shot down, and another crashed against a mountain in the southern part of the Osumi Peninsula. Another of the Bettys managed to land in Taiwan but crashed during its return flight. Fourteen bomber crewmen and three Ohka pilots had perished during the early morning hours of the first.[6]

Yamamura survived his wounds and would return to the Thunder Gods in time to make another Ohka sortie on May 25. Lieutenant August (later awarded a Distinguished Flying Cross for his night victory) and his wingman returned to TF 58 after nearly five hours in the air. They had busted up Ugaki's second effort to strike a blow with the Thunder Gods, with August downing one of the Bettys in an uncommonly conservative fashion. Unable to land on his own *Intrepid*, the lieutenant took refuge on the flight deck of *Yorktown*, where crewmen noted that the Grim Reaper night fighter had only discharged fifteen rounds from each of its .50-calibers. Within weeks, George August would score his second night-fighter victory and earn a second Distinguished Flying Cross.

A mere ninety rounds of ammunition from his F6F in the wee hours of April 1 had been enough to down one Ohka-laden Betty and scatter its accompanying Thunder Gods.

Vice Admiral Mitscher's TF 58 carriers were buzzing with action long before daybreak on Love Day, April 1. Their job was to protect the flotilla of 1,300 ships preparing to deliver Army and Marine Corps personnel en masse to the shores of Okinawa. On board the converted transport *Eldorado*, the amphibious-force flagship of Vice Admiral Richmond Kelly Turner, he sent a traditional radio order at 0406: "Land the landing force."[7]

Forty-five minutes later the bombardment of the landing areas commenced with the flaming eruptions of 5-inch up to 16-inch naval guns. The battleships *Tennessee* (BB 43), *Colorado* (BB 45), *Idaho* (BB 42), *New Mexico*, *Texas* (BB 35), *New York* (BB 34), *Arkansas* (BB 33), and *West Virginia* (BB 48) all joined in the prelanding pummeling of shore targets, their mighty firepower supported by shellfire from numerous cruisers and destroyers. The softening-up shelling would only be halted briefly at times to allow carrier-based aircraft to move in and unleash bombs, rockets, and machine-gun fire against Japanese gun emplacements and other designated targets.

First off the decks on April 1 from Rear Admiral Clark's TG 58.1 flagship *Hornet* was a thirty-plane napalm strike and sweep, utilizing Lieutenant Commander Hugh Nicholson's VBF-17 to soften up landing beaches on Okinawa's western coast. They were followed by Commander Ed Konrad and Lieutenant Jim Pearce's VF-17 divisions at 0545, their mission being that of conducting bomb and rocket strikes on the landing beaches at 0735, when the battleships were under orders to check fire. Throughout the task groups, hundreds of other fighters and fighter-bombers joined the early morning sweeps to soften up the beaches before the Marines put their boots on them.

On *Bunker Hill*'s flight deck, Corsair pilots of VMF-221 eagerly anticipated their chance to support their fellow Marines preparing to storm the beaches. The Fighting Falcons squadron was launching a dozen planes for the first fighter sweep, joining fourteen others from *Bunker Hill*'s VMF-451. For Lieutenant Blaine Imel, April 1 held another special significance—squadron flight officer Luke Snider had given him the new responsibility of stepping up to be a division leader. As he headed for the flight deck, Imel was prepared: in addition to his flight suit, he wore his G-suit, Mae West flotation vest, parachute, jungle backpack, .45-caliber automatic pistol, hunting knife, full canteen, and other gear.[8]

His F4U chocked fifth in launch order, Imel watched with shock as the first two VMF-451 pilots failed to gain proper altitude and crashed off the bow; both men were killed. After a long pause to figure out the issue, flight operations resumed. As he moved into takeoff position, a crewmen jumped onto his port wing and moved his flaps from their normal launch position of 40 degrees to a 20-degree setting. "Don't change it!" the plane captain shouted over the roar of the engine. "As I was flagged down the deck, I was praying mightily as I was pushing the throttle full forward," said Imel.[9]

His plane and those that followed had no problems lifting off. Upon arriving on station near the landing beaches, Imel and his companions made strafing runs and dropped their napalm just ahead of where the troops—still circling in their landing craft—would be going ashore. Upon returning to *Bunker Hill*, Imel learned in the ready room that fins added to their napalm loads had caused an obstruction to airflow when the F4U's flaps were lowered to 40 degrees. "Consequently, when the airplanes took off, the wind pressure would push the flaps back up to their zero degree setting," Imel explained. "Without the help of the flaps, the fully loaded aircraft never reached their required air speed, and they stalled when they left the deck."[10]

Mitscher followed with additional strikes by Helldivers and Avengers, while the Hellcat and Corsair pilots logged thousands more flight hours supporting the Love Day landings. To provide better advance warning against Japanese air attacks, sixteen radar-picket stations had been established around Okinawa, each plotted in reference to "Point Bolo"—Zampa Misaki, the westernmost tip of Okinawa's coast. Each of the eight stations ranged from eighteen to ninety-five nautical miles offshore and was held by two destroyers with highly trained fighter-direction teams on board.[11]

The F6F pilots of *Hornet's* VF-17 were typical of the squadrons deployed from each of Mitscher's fleet carriers. The ready-room chalkboards spelled out the various divisional assignments, varying between routine task-group CAP, radar-picket CAP, and softening-up sweeps over Okinawa. Skipper Marsh Beebe led his division and those of Tommy Harris and Fuzz Wooley on a fighter sweep over the island in the early afternoon. For Tilly Pool, his Love Day flight was his first hop with his Hellcat being loaded with a napalm belly tank.

Beebe led his strikers on a strafing run south of Naha Airfield and made a second pass for his pilots to unload their napalm tanks on gun emplacements and barracks nearby. One pilot's napalm tank failed to release, but the others fell and ignited, creating violent fires in the attack area. Lieutenant (jg) Pool was nearly killed when his napalm tank was hit by antiaircraft fire just as he dropped it on a hangar. Wingman Stan Smith had the unenviable misfortune of flying right through the blast of Pool's napalm.

Lieutenant (jg) Billy Watts and his division made strafing runs on the little island of Ie Shima. He spotted a horse track on the island, where a horse was running wild with fear from the noise of machine-gun bursts. Some division leaders had been briefed to kill everything that might provide food for the Japanese, but Texas farm boy Watts was having none of that. "You don't shoot a horse," he said. "I don't know what ever happened to him, whether he ran himself to death or what."[12]

The fighter pilots aloft that day executed hundreds of strafing and bombing attacks to support the Allied landings but found little action with Japanese attack planes. Only a small number of Admiral Ugaki's

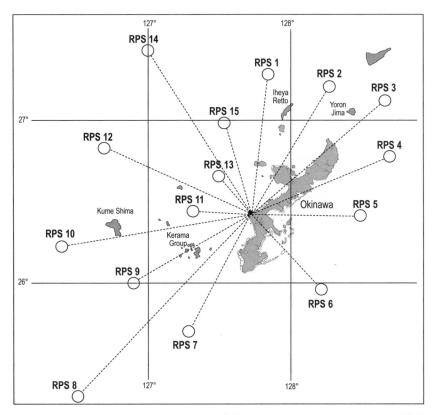

Wartime map of the radar picket stations (RPS) off Okinawa, each starting at Point Bolo. *Modified from Enclosure "6" to Appendix "K" COM PHIBS PAC OP PLAN A1-45*

kamikazes posed threats to the Love Day landings, but a few managed to cause a little excitement during the early morning hours. Radarman 3rd Class Bob Dumont was stationed on the high-speed transport *Kline* (APD 120), a former destroyer escort recommissioned for special duty with such amphibious operations. "The huge invasion armada is preparing to go in," Dumont wrote in his diary. "Planes fill the sky. There are thousands of small landing craft. I am anxious to see just what will take place."[13]

The radarman had little time to wonder. Small numbers of Japanese attack planes appeared during the early morning, and the *Kline* crew observed one enemy aircraft downed by antiaircraft fire to their north at 0608. Twelve minutes later a pair of Val dive bombers were spotted near the transport fleet and taken under fire. *Kline's* gunners fired in earnest and were credited with downing one of the Vals as it approached from her port beam. The bomber burst into flames at 2,500 feet, its bomb falling harmlessly into the sea as the aircraft came apart. "He was diving straight for our ship," Dumont wrote. "Another 200 yards and I wouldn't be writing this."[14]

Mitscher's F6F and F4U jockeys were vigilant in their duties on April 1, even as their minds wondered what kinds of carnage their Marine comrades were enduring as they splashed ashore on Okinawa.

Thousands of grim-faced Marines clutched their rifles in pitching landing craft headed toward their respective beaches. H-Hour was set for 0830, and each wave of amphibious craft was led toward Okinawa's coast by guide boats flying colored pennants to denote the beach name their flock was to descend upon: Green Beach to the north; followed by Red Beach, Blue Beach, Yellow Beach, Purple Beach, Orange Beach, White Beach; and finally the southernmost landing area, Brown Beach. A key landing area, Brown Beach was just to the west of the two Japanese airfields, Yontan and Kadena.

Nineteen-year-old Private 1st Class Watson Crumbie expected the worst when he waded ashore, having witnessed horrific carnage in the bloody fight for Saipan the previous summer. In sharp contrast to that landing, he ran off the ramp of his amtrac through shallow water onto Okinawa's western coast without a single bullet fired at him by the enemy. Thin as a rail and weighing only around 135 pounds, Crumbie hardly looked the part of a seasoned infantry assault-squad leader. By afternoon of the first day, his company had advanced so far that they were already working toward their Day 3 objectives. "We thought the Japanese had abandoned the island," said Crumbie.[15]

Corporal Mel Heckt, a machine gunner for Baker Company of the 4th Marine Division, possessed two items banned by his service, a Browning camera and a personal diary, both of which he would carry throughout the campaign. He hit the beach at 0830 "with very little opposition," noting that only two of his comrades were hit, neither seriously. By day's end, Heckt noted in his diary, only one Marine of another platoon had been killed.[16]

The advance went so well on Love Day that Major General Lemuel Shepherd, commander of the 6th Marine Division, moved his command post ashore. His 22nd and 4th Regiments had already swept across Yontan Airfield, and by nightfall some Marines were a thousand yards to the east. Some of Colonel Alan Shapley's 4th Marines were guarding the captured airfield in the late afternoon when an unsuspecting Zero fighter casually landed on the field and taxied toward the administration building. The pilot climbed out and headed toward the building before he realized he was facing American soldiers. He reached for his pistol but was instantly cut down by bullets that perforated his body and his fighter. "I guess he never got the word," said Heckt.[17]

South of Yontan, Major General Archibald V. Arnold's 7th Army Division swept along two roads from the beach onto Kadena Airfield, filled with broken military aircraft and equipment. They found decoy planes made of canvas over bamboo frames, but the most alarming discovery was at the central airport, where, hidden in earthen bunkers, the soldiers seized four intact Ohka suicide planes. Nicknamed "Baka" (Japanese for "fool") bombers by the Americans, an appropriate sobriquet for an April Fool's Day discovery, the intact aircraft would be packed up and shipped off for intense study by U.S. intelligence personnel.

Lieutenant General Mitsuru Ushijima watched the Americans wade ashore on April 1 from his headquarters at ancient Shuri Castle, a thick, stone-walled fortress atop a labyrinth of ancient caves that were virtually bomb and shell proof on high ground overlooking the Okinawa capital city, Naha. Lean, composed, and sporting a thin mustache, Ushijima was revered by his men as an experienced senior commander who had successfully led his infantry during the Burma campaign. His chief of staff, Lieutenant General Isamu Cho, was stern, burly, and one who enjoyed the finer things of life, including whiskey and women. While Cho possessed a scholarly look from the rounded glasses he wore, he had skirted trouble during his pre–World War II years and was something of a fireball in contrast to Ushijima's more rigid militant disposition.[18]

Ushijima's more than 100,000 troops were not heavily concentrated near the coast where the Marines splashed ashore. Instead, his command staff had taken to higher ground at Shuri Castle. The Japanese 32nd Army had dug in deep, hiding hundreds of soldiers in underground mazes of shelters and caverns that would present a formidable defense once the Americans advanced.

The weather remained favorable throughout April 1 as U.S. forces advanced. Ushijima remained composed, however, little worried until his enemy advanced closer to his dug-in troops. He began the following day with traditional sword-wielding samurai exercises in the mouth of his cavern. The general was content to let his defensive plan proceed, even though his subordinate Cho grew increasingly eager to mount an attack.[19]

Corporal Heckt's squad of Marines hiked a considerable distance in the afternoon of April 2 before finally coming under enemy fire near a ridgeline. Four men fell wounded to Japanese snipers, while Heckt dropped one assailant with a single round from his M1 rifle. That afternoon he helped clear a Japanese sniper from a cavern but later lost his company commander during the overnight hours to another sniper.[20]

Heckt's squad pushed forward on April 3, discarding their heavy helmets in the process. By nightfall he was exhausted, filthy, stinking, and sporting a three-day beard. "I have slept 20 minutes in the last two and a half days," he wrote in his secret journal. Yet the Army and Marine troops had scarcely begun the battle for Okinawa. The enemy assaults Heckt had endured thus far were but a minor glimpse of the hell he would soon face.[21]

"Enemy air opposition was non-existent and it became increasingly apparent that our initial strike on Kyushu facilities had interfered with enemy air operations," Vice Admiral Mitscher noted of the days leading to the Love Day landings. His carrier air groups remained vigilant during the first days of the Okinawa ground campaign, but his fighters registered only ten kills on April 1. TF 58 night fighters had downed three Japanese aircraft before daybreak that day, and two *Essex* VF-83 photo-reconnaissance Hellcats had seen the most significant action shortly before the landings commenced.[22]

The task-force fighters turned in claims for another ten aerial victories on April 2, including two Georges downed by a pair of Marsh Beebe's *Hornet* VF-17 pilots off Okinawa's northwest coast in the late afternoon. Vice Admiral Ugaki's kamikaze corps was silent during the landings but went into action on the second. Four fighter-bombers loaded with 1,100-pound bombs moved to attack the American invasion fleet that day, while another eight were launched for a twilight attack on April 3. Two of the planes returned to base with engine trouble, while another seven were knocked down by U.S. fighter planes and antiaircraft fire. Only three of the dozen attackers over these two days made it through to attempt suicide dives on ships.[23]

Lieutenant Commander Beebe's VF-17 spent April 2 attacking artillery emplacements on Okinawa, a small town harboring Japanese soldiers, and a group of a dozen trucks that were subjected to bombs, rockets, and strafing. The following day Beebe and his executive officer, Ned Langdon, led sweeps to Ishigaki Jima and Sakishima Gunto, where *Hornet* pilots were credited with damaging fourteen parked aircraft. Lieutenant (jg) Watts took care of three single-engine planes and shared credit with his division-mates on four more.

Hornet's air group suffered a significant loss on April 3 with the downing of Lieutenant Hal Mitchell, who had become an "ace in a day" on March 21 while flaming the first Ohka-laden Betty bombers. On the third

Mitchell was making strafing runs on an airfield on the island of Hirara, close to Okinawa, when his F6F was struck by several rounds of medium antiaircraft fire. Despite two large holes in his starboard wing and the loss of his left horizontal stabilizer, he led his VBF-17 division back to *Hornet*.

Since his tail hook had been shot away, preventing him from making a controlled landing on the carrier, Mitchell was directed to climb to eight thousand feet and bail out. He did as ordered, and his divisionmates circled him as Mitchell drifted down in his parachute. Within a minute of the time his chute hit the ocean, a destroyer was there to retrieve him. But Hal Mitchell had disappeared; he was simply gone. Hours spent searching for him were in vain.

TF 58's fighter pilots saw increased action on April 3, claiming a total of forty-five aerial victories. But such success did not come without a cost, as evidenced not only by the loss of Mitchell but also by the experience of Lieutenant (jg) Melvin Cozzens of *Cabot*'s VF-29.

Raised on his family's sheep ranch in rural Powell, Wyoming, Cozzens was a veteran of the October 1944 Philippines campaign and had 3.5 kills to his credit. On April 3 he was launched at 1500 with nine other Hellcats of his squadron, sent to sweep Amami Oshima and Kikai Jima in conjunction with six Corsairs from *Bunker Hill*'s Air Group 86 and a dozen F6F-5s of *Bataan*'s VF-47. The *Cabot* fighters bombed Tokuna Airfield before attacking Wan Airfield on the southwest side of Kikai Jima with strafing runs. Cozzens was flying wing on Lieutenant Uncas L. Fretwell, who began organizing his VF-29 Hellcats in a climbing rendezvous at sea, preparing for a second run on the airstrip.

At that moment, around 1715, the *Cabot* formation was jumped by twenty Zekes and two Tojos, diving on the Americans from out of the sun. The ensuing dogfight was vicious, forcing Fretwell and another pilot to limp back to the fleet with crippled F6Fs. Lieutenant (jg) Robert E. Murray claimed two Zeke kills, and Ensign Richard L. Bertelson hammered three more into the ocean in a series of dogfights. By the time the brief melee was complete, *Cabot*'s pilots had downed ten Japanese fighters and damaged three others. In return two VF-29 Hellcats were so badly shot up that they were later jettisoned. A third, that of Cozzens, failed to return.

When the twenty-two Japanese fighters first struck, Cozzens started a defensive weave, then pulled up to make a head-on run against an approaching Tony. Pressing fire into the enemy's engine to pointblank range, he pulled up into a wingover in time to witness his opponent crash into the sea. Having lost contact with Lieutenant Fretwell, Cozzens tangled with several Zekes on his own. He climbed into one enemy fighter and fired, exploding it in a great mass of flame.

Lieutenant (jg) Melvin Cozzens, second from left, with squadron-mates of VF-29 on the wing of a *Cabot* (CVL 28) Hellcat. On the day he reached ace status over Okinawa, he was forced to bail out of his F6F. *U.S. Navy*

Cozzens then turned his sites on a lone Zeke and created a fire in the starboard side of its engine. The propeller of this third victim began to windmill when the American suddenly found himself being attacked from behind by two other Zekes. Twenty-mm shells slammed into his Hellcat, causing his own engine and port wing to burst into flames. Realizing his plane was finished, the VF-29 pilot—who had achieved ace status during this day's melee—bailed out at 3,500 feet.

As he drifted down in his parachute, Cozzens witnessed his own F6F as well as what he believed was the crippled Zeke crash. He was spared death in the air by a fellow F6F pilot who shot down another Zeke lining up to make a strafing run on him. "After the Zeke fired at me, I pulled my chute so he would miss me, but I was going down so fast that I damn near went to the bottom when I hit the ocean," he said. Cozzens spent the balance of the afternoon drifting in his life raft, nursing serious burns on his arms and watching ten Japanese fighters land at dusk on nearby Kikai Airfield, about two and a half miles distant.[24]

Cozzens was among the fortunate. Shortly after daybreak on April 4, he was scooped up by a Consolidated PBY Catalina flying boat after more than fourteen hours adrift. The pilot was deposited on Kerama Retto, where he began a two-week journey to return to his *Cabot* squadron, rejoining Fighting Twenty-Nine on April 21.

April 3 was also a big day for the new *Essex* squadron VF-83. Ensign Larry Clark had only become carrier qualified on March 14 before scoring his first shoot down on the nineteenth and earning a Navy Cross. Now, two weeks later, he was eager to add to his tally.

Clark launched at 1415 for a routine three-hundred-mile shipping search with ten F6Fs of VF-83 and a pair of VBF-83 Corsairs. Hours of routine flight suddenly changed when large numbers of Japanese planes were encountered on the homeward leg in the area north of Tokuna Shima. Clark and Ensign Joseph Norman Berube were one hundred miles north of the island when they spotted a Judy low over the water. Using his altitude advantage, Clark sent the Judy down in flames to explode on the water. Several minutes later he and Berube chased a lone Val toward the water, and Clark splashed the dive bomber with a 40-degree deflection around its wing roots. The two then responded to calls for help from friendly fighters near Tokuna. En route to assist, each pilot shot down a Tony, pushing Clark's record to three kills in one mission.

In other action, Lieutenant Thomas Conder and his wingman, Lieutenant (jg) John Larkin, shot down a "Sonia" (Mitsubishi Ki-51 Army Type 99 assault aircraft), two Tonys, and a Val near Tokuna Shima. Near Kuchinoerabu Jima, just forty miles southwest of Kyushu, Lieutenant Thad Coleman and his wingman, Ensign Richard Langdon, began a systematic shoot down of seven Sonias. Coleman finished with four kills and, combined with a Frank he had downed four days prior, joined the growing list of Okinawa aces. Fighting Eighty-Three proved to be the deadliest Navy fighter squadron in action on April 3, accounting for sixteen kills.

Not all of the fighter interceptions went smoothly. During one of his CAP missions, 2nd Lieutenant Dean Caswell of *Bunker Hill*'s VMF-221 spotted the contrail of a Myrt photo-reconnaissance plane, a single-engine aircraft with a crew of two. The fast-moving Japanese plane had a slight altitude advantage over Caswell's division, but the pilot then turned into the section of Caswell and John McManus. They found that their 30,000-foot altitude made their Corsairs hard to maneuver and that the extreme cold (estimated at 70 degrees below zero) caused their .50-caliber machine guns to freeze up. Unable to fire, they gave up the chase. "No doubt our enemy was smiling all the way back home with his photos," Caswell later wrote.[25]

TF 58 maintained its presence off Okinawa, sending continual waves of fighters and bombers to work over areas of resistance ashore and against airfields on the surrounding islands. Japanese aerial resistance was lighter on April 4 and 5, when Mitscher's warplanes registered only thirteen total kills. Lieutenant (jg) Harris Mitchell found that the low-level bombing and strafing attacks were as dangerous to his survival as tangling with enemy fighters. His VF-9 division, led by Lieutenant Gene Valencia, found Miyako

Island socked in with foul weather. Valencia led Mitchell, Jim French, and Clint Smith to the island's east coast, where they located a barracks area suitable for their bombs and rockets.

For his first run, Mitchell was trailing several hundred yards behind Valencia, as his division leader made a steep-angle dive toward a group of four barracks buildings on the northeast corner of the group. "As he pulled out, up from under that barracks, I pickled off my bomb," said Mitch, who was credited with flattening some of the buildings.[26]

After pulling up, Mitchell noted Valencia coming around for another attack, again at a steep angle. Gene was still carrying his 500-pound general-purpose bomb, which Mitch figured he would drop on this run. Once again Valencia strafed targets before pulling up to prepare for a third run. *Well, if you're just going to strafe, then I'm going to come in at a flatter angle on the next run so I can strafe, too,* Mitch thought. On their third pass, Mitchell dived in below Valencia to provide himself with a less-steep angle to better strafe the barracks. Nearing the buildings, he looked up to see that Valencia had finally released his bomb. "There I was, just about a hundred feet above the ground," he said. He pulled back hard on his stick and had only gained another hundred feet of altitude when the bomb exploded almost directly beneath him. His Hellcat lurched from the force of the blast. Mitch tested his ailerons and surveyed his wings, which appeared none the worse for the near-fatal blast. "I figured I'd lucked out," he said.[27]

The division proceeded to expend its remaining bombs, rockets, and bullets against shore installations and small vessels on and around Yerabu Jima and Shimoji Jima. By the end of the busy mission, Mitchell had all but forgotten the blast from Valencia's bomb that had rocked his F6F. Upon landing on *Yorktown*, however, he was surprised when his plane captain hopped up on his wing and announced, "Boy, you sure had a narrow escape, didn't you?"

How in the world does he know that? Mitch wondered. "What are you talking about?" he asked.

"Sir, it's right here," said the plane captain, pointing to the root of Mitch's right wing. Just six inches outside his cockpit, a jagged hole about eight inches wide had shredded through the top of his aluminum wing.

"I guess I did have a narrow escape," a shocked Mitchell mumbled.[28]

TF 58's air-support missions continued around the clock during the first days following the Okinawa landings. General Ushijima's troops largely lay in wait, although small-scale firefights erupted as the U.S. Army and

Marines advanced toward Shuri Castle. By April 3 both Yontan and Kadena Airfields could be used for emergency landings by Allied airmen, while amphibious vessels continued hauling supplies and military hardware ashore for the extensive ground fighting that was fully expected to develop.

Isolated kamikaze attacks damaged some warships and transport vessels snugged near the island's coast, but few believed that the reprieve would be long-standing. Vice Admiral Ugaki monitored reports of the Americans' progress on Okinawa during the first days of April. His search planes kept him updated on the movements of the Allied naval forces, but the meager numbers of attack planes he dispatched each day achieved only minor results. He met with military leaders on the second, including Combined Fleet Chief of Staff Ryūnosuke Kusaka and Vice Admiral Minoru Maeda, commander in chief of the 10th Air Fleet. "Heads were well arrayed but planes and skilled flyers weren't," Ugaki observed.[29]

On April 3, plans were issued for Operation Kikusui No. 1, a massed attack on American task forces and convoys that would employ all strength available. Meaning "floating chrysanthemums," *kikusui* was the crest of a famous medieval Japanese samurai, Kusunoki Masashige, who gave his life on a fourteenth-century battlefield against superior forces after stating his regret that he did not have more than one life to give for the emperor. Ugaki rose early on the morning of the fourth and went hunting, bagging a pigeon before he returned to his headquarters at Kanoya to participate in table maneuvers for the Kikusui operation.[30]

Ugaki believed this engagement would require "the utmost care," being that it was an all-out gamble that could not be repeated due to the scarcity of war equipment. The Combined Fleet called for attacks on enemy convoys by carrying out a great air battle. "It was said that its real aim was to spur the Sixth Air Army and Tenth Air Army into more activity," Ugaki noted. He believed that the actions of the Sixth Air Army had been "passive and quite disagreeable toward others." Rear Admiral Minoru Ota, commander of the Okinawa Special Base Force, requested that destruction of U.S. carrier task forces be given top priority, while Chief of Staff Kusaka sent a telegram requesting the army to concentrate its assaults against American forces in the north and central areas to nullify their use of these key positions. "When a war goes wrong, this sort of argument is apt to take place and become a sign of defeat," Ugaki wrote in disgust.[31]

Japanese pilots struggled not only with fuel shortages but also with being sent into combat with, in many cases, outdated and inferior aircraft. Lieutenant Commander Iyozoh Fujita complained about the equipment and armament his pilots had to utilize. "During the early part of the war, we felt that the weapons in our Zeros were adequate, but later on this was not enough," said Fujita. The two 7.7-mm and 20-mm guns in the early Zeros could not match the .50-caliber six-gun firepower now employed by the F6Fs and F4Us. Fujita also requested better sunsights like the ones used by American fighter pilots, but "again, we never received them."[32]

High-level briefings for Operation Kikusui No. 1 continued on April 5, while Ugaki readied his available air groups for the attacks scheduled to commence the following day. During the day he learned that the high command had even issued orders for a fleet centered around the battleship *Yamato* to steam for Okinawa to join the Japanese counterattack.

Ugaki had no doubts as to the importance of the following day's operation. "This is the decisive battle."[33]

Chapter Twelve

"TURKEY SHOOT"

Admiral Nimitz knew it was coming. Messages intercepted from Combined Fleet headquarters on April 4 foretold the Japanese strikes planned for April 6 against Allied convoys and the American carrier task groups. Vice Admiral Mitscher's night fighters were on the prowl early, but the first daylight interception of an enemy aircraft came at 0600, when VF-83's Lieutenant Don Umphres downed a Betty near the northern tip of Okinawa.[1]

Aside from that, it was a quiet morning. The hours ticked away toward noon while divisions of CAP Hellcats and Corsairs crisscrossed the skies, laying down the big blue blanket both for TF 58's carriers and for its radar-picket destroyers. For hours it was beginning to look like the anticipated Japanese counterattack was not going to happen.

Yorktown and other ships of her task group spent the better part of April 6 refueling from the tanker *Lackawanna* (AO 40). Several strike groups and CAP divisions were put into the air; although Eugene Valencia's VF-9 division saw no action, his men did help replenish their air group's aircraft. The escort carrier *Bougainville* (CVE 100), having taken on replacement aircraft at Guam, had spent the previous two days taking on board pilots to ferry badly needed fresh Hellcats, Corsairs, Helldivers, and Avengers to the carriers *Intrepid, Bennington, Essex, Bunker Hill, Bataan, Cabot,* and *Hancock.*[2]

Bougainville rendezvoused with TG 58.4 at 0655 on the sixth and made preparations to swap out planes with *Yorktown* and *Independence.* Due to receive thirteen new F6Fs and a spare Avenger, Air Group 9 flew six of its airworthy "duds" to the escort carrier at 0859 as part of the swap. The pilots of the scrap planes were catapulted from *Yorktown*'s hangar deck, but another eight pilots were needed to ferry to the ship the thirteen new F6F-5s and a TBM-3 it was slated to receive. Lieutenant Valencia, in charge of the Mowing Machine division, and his pilots were included in the group that transferred over to the CVE via breeches buoy from a destroyer. The inevitable rolling of the ships dipped Harris Mitchell's canvas basket so low he was dragged through the water. "There was a moment of decision to ride it or leave it, and I was about to decide the latter when they finally pulled me back out of that water," he said.[3]

Once on board *Bougainville*, Valencia seized the opportunity to thank the escort ship's crew for the vital role they were playing in the war by keeping the fast-carrier fleet properly provisioned with fighting aircraft. He also offered a short speech of what was happening in the combat zone off Okinawa, then took the chance to ask *Bougainville*'s skipper, Captain Charles A. Bond, for permission to entertain his crew with a little show.

After launching in the new Hellcats, Valencia rendezvoused his three wingmen and began climbing to eight thousand feet. Attaining that altitude, the division nosed over, with Jim French's second section splitting away from Gene's lead section. French and Clint Smith then crisscrossed directly in front of the F6Fs of Valencia and Mitchell as all four Hellcats roared over *Bougainville*'s flight deck just fifty feet overhead. The two sections then pulled up into a slow roll before passing close enough to the carrier again to waggle their wings in salute before turning home toward *Yorktown*.

The cheering sailors enjoyed the mini–air show, a minor event amid a war zone, but one that further displayed the proud nature of Valencia's talented aviators.

Vice Admiral Ugaki found weather favorable enough to begin launching attack groups as part of Operation Kikusui No. 1. April 6 would become the fourth-heaviest day of air combat seen by the U.S. Navy during the Pacific War. Ugaki knew there would be no follow-up operation if he failed with the first effort. He therefore gathered every aircraft that could fly, including older Zeros from the 10th Air Fleet that had been serving as training planes. Additional groups of Thunder Gods fighter-bombers, laden with smaller 550-pound bombs, were formed utilizing these planes, with orders to dive on any American warships off Okinawa. The pilots of the Ohkas were to target aircraft carriers and other capital ships.[4]

Kyushu was partially obscured with clouds on the morning of April 6, but the weather was fair over Okinawa. Groups of fighter planes lifted off from Kanoya Airfield during the early morning, while reconnaissance planes swept the ocean ahead of them in search of the U.S. carriers. Once sighting reports began filtering in, Ugaki ordered up sixty navy planes, along with eighteen aircraft from the 3rd Kemmu Squadron of the Jinrai Corps.[5]

Only four of these kamikazes broke through the fighters and antiaircraft umbrella to attempt dives on American warships, but their radio calls spurred Ugaki to continue sending up his warplanes. During the late-morning hours, his bases sent up another sixty army planes and additional 150 navy planes, including the Thunder Gods fighter-bombers carrying 550-pound bombs. Approximately 700 Japanese aircraft would assault the U.S. Fleet, including at least 355 kamikazes and some 340 bombers and escort planes sent to rain down destruction. This would mark the largest one-day air attack by the Japanese of the Okinawa campaign.

Twenty-three-year-old 2nd Lieutenant Kenji Tomizawa, a member of the 62nd Shinbu Special Attack Squadron, lifted off in a Sonia assault plane. Prior to his departure, he inked a farewell letter to his family. "I will summon courage with all my might and will go to strike," he wrote. "Even right now my comrades, believing in those who will follow after them, are striking the enemy. Even though my body dies, I will certainly defend you."[6]

Twenty-five-year-old Ensign Shunsuke Yukawa, flying in the rear seat of a IJN Nakajima B5N Navy Type 97-1 "Kate" carrier attack bomber, had attended Kwansei Gakuin University before joining the Special Attack Group. His final letter included poetry, including this patriotic note:

Time now has come when mountain cherry blossoms must fall
This the path where we will live.
Our lives offered to the Emperor,
Spirits fun-loving as usual.
I offer myself without reserve for a sacred battle,
I will go as the Emperor's shield.[7]

Radar Picket Stations 1, 2, and 3 saw heavy enemy action beginning at the noon hour. Small groups of Japanese planes attacked the destroyers of Stations 1 and 2 during the morning hours but caused no damage. As the lunch hour approached, various groups of bogies began showing up on radar sets on both the picket line and throughout TF 58. The stage had been set for what would become a long afternoon of widely scattered dogfights.

It was a Marine Corsair squadron from *Bennington,* VMF-112, that started the action just after noon. Major Herman Hansen Jr. pursued a Zeke right toward the ocean, pulling out just before the enemy fighter hit the water and exploded. A short while later he charged another Japanese plane until severe G-forces jammed his link ammunition and put five of his six guns out of operation. Hansen narrowly avoided colliding with the enemy plane as he pulled back hard on his stick. "I wasn't more than 12 inches above him," he reported. "I could see the rivets in the plane. I saw the pilot clearly."[8]

After Hansen flashed past, his wingman drove into the Japanese plane with all guns blazing. When he was a mere twenty-five feet away, the enemy plane flamed, rolled over, and crashed into the sea.

Beginning at noon and lasting a full quarter hour, four divisions of *Essex* VF-83 and VBF-83 Hellcats tangled with Zekes and Oscars. Lieutenant (jg) Sam Commella of VF-83 was high scorer, with three Zeke kills, while his comrades brought down another nine Zekes, three Judys, and an Oscar. Near Tokuna Shima, Lieutenant Thad Coleman dropped his wing tanks to pursue a pair of Judys, both of which he shot down into the sea.

The first signs of the really big Japanese raids started showing up on radar shortly after lunch. Lieutenant (jg) Daniel Paul of *San Jacinto*'s VF-45 knocked down a Myrt that was approaching the radar-picket destroyers at 1245. A quarter hour later Marsh Beebe's CAP No. 3 was vectored into action a little more than a half hour after launching from Jocko Clark's flagship *Hornet.* The fleet FDO coached Beebe to ease down from his station at 10,000 feet above the task force and head out fifteen miles toward a bogey shown at about 3,000 feet.

It was Lieutenant (jg) Tilly Pool who tallyhoed two bomb-laden Judys at 700 feet and flying a northerly course toward the task force. Beebe scanned the ocean where Pool was indicating but could not spot the bandits. "Lead us to them!" he called. The *Hornet* CAP dropped down on them, with Lieutenant (jg) Tommy Harris' division making the first attack at 1300. Pool drove toward one Judy, landing hits that caused the plane to burst into flames and slam into the sea. "Those planes apparently had no self-sealing tanks," said Pool. "They burned easily, with a bright orange flame."[9]

Ensign Gooch Cunningham, a squadron rebel who had stirred the ire of his skipper with his shore-leave antics on more than one occasion, moved in to finish off the second Judy. Afterward Beebe's CAP returned to orbit *Hornet* and was vectored 30 degrees almost immediately. Three Tojos flying in a V formation on an opposite course were tallyhoed five miles ahead, at 1500 feet at 1430. Beebe's division made a sharp 180-degree left turn and dropped on the tails of the bandits. The lieutenant commander closed on the starboard plane, raking its cockpit and apparently killing the pilot, whose plane steadily continued down until it crashed into the water.

Beebe had a close encounter with another kamikaze that approached him from straight on. Closing to effective firing range, he opened up. "He didn't give one inch," Beebe said. "We were eye-to-eye, and I thought that I had hit him. It was impossible not to have hit him, but he kept boring right in. He was going to ram me." Beebe pushed over at the last moment; his wingman, Bud Good, told him the Zeke's wing passed just under the skipper's wing.[10]

Lieutenant (jg) Frank Sistrunk attacked the port plane, believed by him to be a Tojo, from above at eight o'clock. The enemy fighter started down to the left, and as Sistrunk slid behind, flames broke out aft of the cockpit. The pilot parachuted before the plane crashed into the sea. Lieutenant (jg) John J. Davis attacked the Tojo formation leader and exploded him in midair.

Sistrunk's victim was Sata Omaichi, a flight instructor who had graduated in late 1944 from Kisarazu and had sortied from Kikai Jima. He was actually flying a Jack fighter when damage caused by Sistrunk forced him to bail out. The destroyer *Taussig* (DD 746) was sent to search for the Japanese pilot seen to parachute into the ocean. En route the "tin can" was attacked by an Oscar that landed a bomb just thirty feet off *Taussig's* port bow. The attacker retired with its engine smoking, then was quickly splashed by CAP fighters just outside the destroyer's gun range.

Taussig located Omaichi in his life raft and pulled him from the water still wearing a silk scarf bearing the inscription (in Japanese) "Kamikaze Special Attack Unit 3." He was transferred to the carrier *Hornet*, where Lieutenant (jg) E. B. Beath, a staff Japanese language specialist, began interrogations. Omaichi bragged that another mass Kikusui attack was scheduled to take place on April 11, one so powerful that it would wipe out the American fleet. This intelligence was quickly passed to Rear Admiral Clark, who in turn relayed the news to Vice Admiral Mitscher.[11]

Fighting Seventeen saw considerable action throughout the day. While Sistrunk and Davis were engaged in their fights, Tommy Harris pursued a lone Tojo and hammered it into the sea. Jim Pearce, leading two divisions on task-force CAP, received a vector in the late afternoon for a bogey approaching the force. His wingman, Lieutenant (jg) George Johnson, and an ensign from the second division combined to flame a Myrt, which exploded brilliantly two hundred feet above the water.

Lieutenant (jg) Billy Watts and his mixed VF-17 and VBF-17 *Hornet* division saw action shortly after Beebe's group had scored. Watts and the division of Lieutenant George McFedries had a quiet patrol over Okinawa for the first few hours. They orbited at nine thousand feet until 1500, when they were vectored out to intercept a single bogey, a Val, which was disposed by Ensign Charles Dikoff of McFedries' division. En route back to station, McFedries sighted the destroyer *Bush* (DD 529) under attack by several Japanese planes. As they approached the vessel, a suicide plane struck the warship and a Kate was seen departing after dropping its bomb.

Ensign Fred Chapman closed the range and burned the Kate, which hit the water and exploded. Chapman then spotted another Kate diving on the crippled destroyer, made a beam run on it, and sent it flaming into the ocean.

The destroyer *Bush* had had its hands full, fighting off swarms of Japanese kamikazes at Radar Picket Station No. 1. Her FDO, Ensign Franklin Coit Butler from Providence, Rhode Island, vectored a division of CAP fighters after the first kamikaze group shortly after 1430. He was relieved to hear their "tallyho" followed by reports of bandits being splashed. Minutes later *Bush*'s gunners downed two aircraft approaching from the port side.[12]

During the first hour, Corsairs and Hellcats from *Bennington*, *Essex*, *San Jacinto*, and *Hornet* had knocked down many of the kamikazes, but there were simply too many. While the VF-17 division of McFedries was engaging some of the fifteen Jills launched from Kushira Naval Air Base on Kyushu, at least one of them made it through, as the American pilot had witnessed.

At 1515 a bomb-toting Jill crashed amidships on *Bush*'s starboard side between the ship's stacks, its bomb exploding in the forward engine room. The tremendous force of the blast threw a five-hundred-pound engine-room blower high enough into the air to knock the ship's SC-2 antenna off the mast. Within minutes, flooding caused the destroyer to list 10 degrees to port. The ship's radio gang called for assistance from the aerial fighters and from other warships as the flooding caused some of her 5-inch and 40-mm guns to go dead.[13]

The destroyer *Colhoun* (DD 801), on duty at nearby Radar Picket Station No. 2, could see Japanese planes swarming over the stricken *Bush* and bent on thirty-five knots to bring her antiaircraft guns to the scene to assist. *Colhoun* was commanded by Commander George R. Wilson, whose previous command, the destroyer *Chevalier* (DD 451), was sunk in October 1943 by a torpedo during a battle with Japanese ships during the Vella Lavella landings. After six months in the hospital, Wilson took command of the new *Colhoun*, then finishing out on the West Coast. His new destroyer had arrived in the combat zone in time to support the landings at Iwo Jima and thereafter the recent Okinawa invasion. *Colhoun* had come to the aid of a Marine Corsair pilot—1st Lieutenant Junius B. Lohan of *Bennington*'s VMF-112—the previous afternoon, April 5, when he was forced to ditch his F4U due to antiaircraft fire received while attacking the Japanese airfield at Tokuna Shima. Lohan was pleased to be plucked from the cold water but was not prepared for the ordeal he would experience on board *Colhoun* during the sixth.[14]

Commander Wilson had a new mission of mercy as he sped westward to aid the *Bush* crew. "It was my intention to drive off these aircraft with gunfire and with the aid of the fighters, then to proceed to help the *Bush* in controlling her fires and flooding," explained *Colhoun*'s skipper.[15]

Ensign Bob Carney, *Bush*'s supply officer, was manning a portside 40-mm gun when the kamikaze hit. "The first strike blew me to the deck with a broken pelvis," he said. The ship's doctor, George Johnson, ordered Seaman 1st Class Ralph L. Carver to inject the ensign with morphine as he was slipped into a metal basket. One of destroyer's husky mess attendants, Solomon Jackson Jr., then placed Carney and his basket into a life raft, offering him a fair chance at survival if their ship was to sink. The ensign never had the chance to thank Jackson, who was killed in action on board *Bush* before the day was out.

Bush's crew managed to restore some power to the motionless ship, and it was spared further destruction from this round of kamikazes thanks to her efficient aerial umbrella. Lieutenant (jg) Watts also responded to *Bush*'s calls for assistance, and his division bent on course 340 to intercept more closing bogies. At three thousand feet Watts tallyhoed two Vals some fifteen hundred feet above them, all heading for the stricken destroyer. He led his division in a climbing turn into the light scattered clouds above, noting that one Val broke for the deck while the other stayed on course.

Watts and wingman Lieutenant (jg) Werner Gaerisch made stern runs together on the Val that was still boring in, set its cockpit ablaze, and watched the bomber crash. Watts' second section of Lieutenant (jg) George Covelly and Ensign Clyde Toburen dived on the other Val, sending it spiraling down to explode on impact with the ocean. The *Hornet* division had saved the lives of destroyer sailors by knocking down some of the would-be kamikazes, but the fight for survival was just beginning for the sailors of *Bush* and *Colhoun*.

Air battles began heating up near Amami Oshima and Tokuna Shima around 1430. During one ninety-minute running battle, *Essex* fighters encountered small formations of Vals, Judys, Kates, and Sonias, escorted by several Zeros and eight Tonys, all heading south toward Okinawa. By the end of the action, the *Essex* squadrons had claimed thirty-two kills.

Lieutenant Carlos Soffe's VF-83 division arrived over Kikai Jima in time to furnish protection against Japanese planes coming down from the north. They encountered two Vals below them at sixty-five hundred feet just west of the island. Soffe attacked them from above and astern, smoking one of the dive bombers, which went into a spin and crashed. The other Val was flamed by Ensign Tom Ward; its pilot bailed out. Soffe's division utilized their rockets to tear up installations on Wan Airfield before continuing to circle the area, looking for trouble.

About thirty minutes later two more Vals were sighted: one just off the water, the other at about five hundred feet. "I spotted them first and I set the nose down and got the sight on them," said Ensign Don McPherson, who led Lieutenant Soffe into the action. McPherson dove in from above, closing on the Val's starboard side before he squeezed his trigger. "I saw the pilot slump forward, so I knew I had killed him," he said. This first Val slammed into the ocean as McPherson did a wingover turn to check on the second bomber. "He was heading for the island that we had just tore up, so I applied full throttle on the Hellcat."[16]

McPherson zeroed in on his prey, closing again from the starboard quarter. In the process he lost focus on how the Val was leading him into the danger zone. Soffe opened up on the radio with a shout, "Get out of there! They're shooting at you with shore batteries!"[17]

Ignoring the warning, McPherson pushed through the gunfire and set his sights on the fleeing dive bomber. He squeezed the trigger for mere seconds before his six wing guns caused the Val to explode and plunge toward the ground. The ensign had scored his first two kills, but his "Wonder Five" division was not finished for the day. Minutes later Soffe's second section of Ensigns Ward and Myron Truax brought down a Kawasaki Ki-48 Army Type 99 "Lily" twin-engine light bomber near Kikai's airfield.

But Air Group 83's action on April 6 was far from over. Southwest of Tokuna Shima, Lieutenant Commander Henry Graham's VBF-83 division tallyhoed six Tonys; Graham disposed of two of the Japanese planes. In other actions near the Tokuna airbase, two other VBF-83 pilots shot down three Zekes. Lieutenant David Robinson's division of Fighting Eighty-Three expended all of its ammunition in downing two Judys and seven Vals, with Ensign William J. Kingston Jr. taking top honors with three of the kills.

Lieutenant Tom Conder's VF-83 division left its search sector upon hearing calls for help from friendly fighters some twenty miles to their northeast. They jumped a quartet of Sonias from astern and picked them off in less than two minutes, one each falling to Conder, Ensign Larry Clark, Lieutenant (jg) John Larkin Jr., and Ensign Joe Berube.

Conder's division then climbed through the overcast to assist four Hellcats in a scrap with twenty Zekes. The lieutenant commander smoked one Zeke but had his own left aileron shot away by another Japanese fighter that latched on to his tail. Conder went into a spin but managed to recover at two thousand feet, dropping his burning belly tank. He was forced to limp back toward *Essex*, while wingman John Larkin downed another Zeke before his F6F was so badly shot up in turn that he joined Conder in retreating to base.

During this time, Conder's second section of Clark and wingman Berube had tangled with another Zeke, which Clark had shot down. With their first section retiring from the action, Clark and Berube found themselves in trouble when they emerged from a cloud mass to find about twenty Zekes. "We were young and foolish and stayed up above the clouds and got into a dogfight," remembered Clark. Both pilots were low on ammunition and outmatched, forced to resort to Thach Weave maneuvers to try and shake their numerous opponents. Thus protecting each other's tail and firing a round or two intermittently to keep the Zekes from closing too rapidly, Clark and Berube made again for the protective covering of the clouds.[18]

Clark's good fortune ran out when a burst of 7.7-mm bullets shattered his instrument panel. The Zeke pilot also completely shot away one of Clark's horizontal stabilizers and punched holes through the rear of his fuselage. The ensign fought to control his battered F6F as other Zekes began landing lethal hits on wingman Berube's plane. By the time the section finally shook their opponents over Tokuna Shima, their planes were in bad shape.

Berube's F6F was smoking badly, its engine was sputtering, his canopy was so badly shattered that the hatch was jammed closed and unable to be jettisoned, and the rest of the plane was riddled with holes. The ensign announced to Clark that he would crash-land on Okinawa. Before friendly territory could be reached, however, his engine died, and Berube was forced to ditch. The impact must have torn off his canopy, for in about twenty seconds he emerged from the cockpit with his Mae West inflated.

Clark circled Berube and broadcast his position over the radio to a lifeguard submarine until an acknowledgment was received. Despite his Hellcat being badly damaged as well, Clark selflessly dropped his own life raft. His heart sank as he saw the deflated raft sink before Berube could reach it. Clark remained in radio contact with the lifeguard sub, finally

Ensign Larry Clark of VF-83, based on *Essex* (CV 9), scored two kills on April 6, 1945. His Hellcat was shot up by Zekes but made it back to the carrier. Wingman Ensign Joseph Berube was forced to ditch his F6F and was lost at sea. *U.S. Navy*

dropping his dye markers as he headed home due to low fuel, joining up with another *Essex* pilot en route. "We said a little prayer and headed in the direction where we were supposed to find the task force."[19]

The two *Essex* pilots located their task group and homed in on their home flight deck around 1830—after four and a half hours in the air. While Clark had landed uninjured, he had scarcely been helped from his cockpit before his crew chief motioned for deck hands to give his fighter the "deep six" to clear the flight deck for other returning warplanes. Although he had chalked up two more victories on April 6, Clark's thoughts and prayers went to wingman Joe Berube. A PBY rescue plane scoured the seas at the last-reported position of the downed VF-83 pilot, but Ensign Berube was never seen again.

The destroyer *Bush* was badly hit, listing, and down by the stern by 1520. Her *Hornet* CAP was replaced by a flight of fourteen *Belleau Wood* VF-30 Hellcats, and during the next ninety minutes—from 1530 to 1700—they engaged more than sixty enemy aircraft in small groups. Commander Wilson's *Colhoun* had arrived on the scene by 1635, and at 1650 *LCS(L) 64* came alongside to help evacuate some of the wounded men. The *Belleau Wood* fighter pilots took their incoming opponents to be kamikazes, as the Val dive bombers they encountered had no tail gunners and continued to fly toward the destroyers even when under attack.

By the end of the battle, VF-30 claimed forty-six Japanese planes shot down. One Fighting Thirty pilot said it felt like "an Easter egg hunt—look under any cloud and there would be Jap plane or two." Ensign Carl Foster of Detroit shot down two Tojos, one Zeke, and four Vals to become high scorer for the squadron, making him another "ace in a day" for April 6. Ensign Kenneth Dahms downed two Zekes, three Vals, and received half

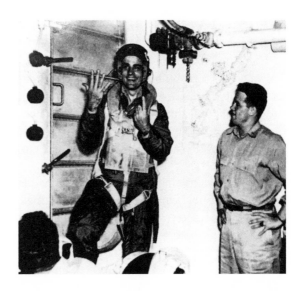

Ensign Carl Foster of VF-30 indicates his seven kills made on April 6, 1945, in the squadron ready room on *Belleau Wood*. According to the carrier's wartime cruise book, "Flight Quarters," a VF-30 squadronmate scribbled on the ready-room chalkboard, "Never fear when Foster is near." *U.S. Navy*

credit for an Oscar kill. Ensign Johnnie Miller tagged five enemy aircraft, producing the squadron's third "ace in a mission." The proud squadron's first big day of the campaign had been against Ohka-laden Betty bombers on March 21. In his action report for April 6, Lieutenant (jg) John Pooley, VF-30's ACIO, triumphantly called this "Turkey Shoot Number Two."[20]

With his pilots claiming nearly four dozen shoot downs on the sixth, *Belleau Wood*'s skipper, Captain William G. "Red" Tomlinson, sent a query to his task-group commander, Jocko Clark: "Does this exceed bag limit?"

Rear Admiral Clark's reply was one for the books. "Negative. This is open season. There is no limit. Well done."[21]

Lieutenants Charles R. Knokey and James B. Cain, leading two divisions of VF-45 Hellcats from *San Jacinto*, entered the shootout at 1545 and remained in heavy action for another hour and a quarter. Cain, who hailed from Georgia, fired at a Val until its pilot was forced to bail out of his blazing dive bomber. As the Japanese aviator floated down toward the ocean, another *San Jacinto* pilot quipped that a few rounds into the chute might be called for. "Hell, no!" Cain replied, before he led his division back above *Colhoun*.[22]

Colhoun's antiaircraft fire exploded close enough to the VF-45 Hellcats to cause some concern, but Lieutenant Cain's F6Fs were soon vectored after another enemy formation approaching from Kyushu. A Tony made a weak firing pass on the *San Jacinto* fighters, but it was enough to stir Cain into pursuing the enemy, even though his 2,500 hours of flight time and experience as a flight instructor told his good senses never to follow a single opponent into a dive. "Good sense, good logic, and good strategy be damned," he later wrote. "I followed the Tony down with all six .50s blazing from dead astern."[23]

Cain chased the Tony for fifteen minutes along the northern mountains and valleys of Kyushu but could only claim it as a probable. He opened up on his radio in an attempt to rendezvous with the balance of his division and soon spotted three fighters in the distance. "I closed from below and was about to reduce throttle when, to my amazement, I saw that the three single-engine aircraft had meatballs on their fuselages," Cain recalled. "They were Zekes!"[24]

The lieutenant charged in with his guns blazing, exploding the flight leader and his port wingman. His F6F sustained some damage from flying debris but emerged from the fight as high scorer for VF-45, with 3.5 kills. Lieutenant (jg) Robert C. Woolverton finished with 2.5 kills, as did Ensigns Henry Nida and Norman Bishop. Four other Fighting Forty-Five pilots shot down two Japanese planes each, and the squadron overall claimed 24 kills for the mission. Lieutenant (jg) Harry Swinburne, who had been forced to make a night landing on *Hornet* with his badly damaged F6F on March 28, was among those claiming two kills.

By 1630 eleven VF-82 *Bennington* Hellcats, led by Lieutenant Richard E. Britson, had reached the scene in response to the aerial battles jamming the radio waves. They arrived above the destroyers *Bush* and *Colhoun* and found their F6Fs were in less danger of being hit by enemy fire than in running afoul of friendly fighter fire or suffering a midair collision. Lieutenant Hayden Gregory tried to keep a tally on his plotting board of the planes he saw crashing. By the time he returned to *Bennington*, he had made twenty-eight marks. Gregory estimated that he had twenty different Japanese planes in his sights during the action and fired on at least a dozen of them. He was credited with three Val kills but had to break off his firing runs on more than one occasion to avoid hitting nearby U.S. fighters.[25]

The eleven *Bennington* pilots each scored at least one kill during the next two hours of dogfighting above the picket destroyers. Lieutenant (jg) Stanley P. Ward shot down a Frank and two Vals, while Lieutenant (jg) Clarence E. Davies was credited with 3.5 kills. Lieutenant Robert H. Jennings Jr. shot down three Vals, one of which he pursued so low toward one of the U.S. destroyers that his own wingtip touched the water.

Echoing the phrase in VF-30's action report, *Bennington*'s ACIO, Lieutenant Wallace D. Lyon, added a similar statement from VF-82: "April 6 will go down in the squadron history as the day of the 'Turkey Shoot.'"[26]

✦◇✦

The massive air battle above the radar-picket stations succeeded in keeping a large number of Japanese planes from hitting the destroyers. The last major carrier squadron group to join the CAP over the pickets on the afternoon of April 6 was a mixed bag of sixteen Hellcats from VF-17 and VBF-17. Launched at 1528, they had been airborne for ninety minutes before the action began heating up. For Ensign Bill Hardy, it would be a big day.

En route to their station ten miles northeast of Ie Shima, Hardy heard many "tallyhoes" broadcast over the air. After reaching station around 1700, the *Hornet* planes were vectored out by the stricken destroyer *Bush's* FDO, Ensign Butler, to intercept a large incoming raid. Ten minutes later they began sighting numerous Japanese planes, all flying singly or in pairs—mostly Vals and Zekes—and heading toward Radar Picket Station No. 1.

Flight leader Dick Cowger quickly exploded one Val and then split his two VF-17 divisions high and low to meet the bogies at whatever altitude they came in. Minutes later a desperate call from their FDO requested help for a destroyer under aerial attack twenty miles from Point Nan. "They were really screaming over the guard channel," recalled Hardy. He implored Cowger that the picket ships needed help, but the ensign found that his division leader was not about to relinquish the lead.[27]

By the time the VF-17 division finally reached Radar Picket Station No. 2, *Colhoun* was under attack by several kamikazes. Between 0247 and 0600 the destroyer had been subjected to eleven bombing attacks and one torpedo dropped by a Betty bomber. *Colhoun* remained undamaged as wave after wave of kamikazes assaulted the destroyers at Stations 1, 2, and 3, in the process hitting *Bush*.

The relentless kamikaze strikes against Station No. 1 finally proved to be overwhelming. Four FM-2 Wildcats from VC-13 joined the melee late, around 1700, and accounted for seven kills and two probables by 1745, when they were forced to return to *Anzio* (CVE 57) due to low fuel and ammunition. *Hornet's* VF-17 Hellcats had no sooner reached their orbiting point than *Bush's* radarmen vectored them out to greet another incoming group of Zekes and Vals. Dick Cowger and his wingman, Lieutenant (jg) Lonnie C. Pace, reached the scene in time to witness the first kamikaze slam into *Colhoun* at 1720; Commander Wilson had ordered left full rudder, but it was too late.

Rescued Marine aviator Junius Lohan, now a passenger on *Colhoun*, was in the uncomfortable position of being stuck on board a destroyer, powerless to stop the Japanese Zeke he saw screaming toward his savior ship. "I stood by the rail on the main deck forward of amidships watching him come in," said Lohan. "It was a horrible sound." The Zeke crashed

The destroyer *Colhoun* (DD 801) is seen burning just sixty seconds after taking a kamikaze hit on April 6, 1945. The smoke cloud in the lower corner is rising above the stricken destroyer *Bush* (DD 529), which has also been damaged by kamikazes at Radar Picket Station No. 1. This photo was taken by *Anzio* (CVE 57) pilot Lieutenant (jg) T. N. Banks. *80-G-317258, NARA*

into the destroyer's starboard side, carrying devastation into the forward fireroom. Its bomb then exploded, breaking *Colhoun*'s keel and causing extensive damage.[28]

All of the men manning 40-mm Mounts No. 3 and No. 4 were mowed down and their guns were destroyed. The main steam line in the forward engine room was pierced, forcing the crew to either abandon the compartment or dive for cover in the bilges. Lieutenant (jg) John A. Kasel Jr. opened the cross-connection valve before diving for the bilges, allowing the after engine to get steam from the forward fireroom and his ship to maintain fifteen knots on its port engine. Other officers directed firefighting crews to extinguish fires with carbon dioxide in the fire-control switchboard, the ship's office, and other areas. All depth charges and torpedoes were jettisoned, and repair crews continued to fight fires. In the forward engine room, Machinist's Mate Joe Orabona also escaped the superheated steam by diving into the bilges. He later scrambled topside on *Colhoun* by wrapping his hands with rags to climb the hot steel rungs of the escape ladders.[29]

High above, Dick Cowger and Lonnie Pace of VF-17 were immediately swept into the intense aerial battles. Pace shot down three Vals and shared credit on a fourth with a *Bennington* fighter pilot, while Cowger dropped two more Vals near the destroyer-minelayers *Emmons* (DMS 22) and *Rodman* (DMS 21). The melee became so wild that Cowger ordered his pilots to operate independently to protect the imperiled ships.

Colhoun, whose damage forced her gunners to fire under manual control, was attacked at 1725 by two more Vals and a Zeke that slipped in past the CAP fighters. The Zeke was knocked into the water 150 yards off the port beam, but one Val slammed into *Colhoun's* after stack, bounced off Turret No. 3, spread gasoline over the decks, and further ripped the destroyer's hull when its bomb exploded in the ocean near the stern.

The other Val missed but continued on into the destroyer *Bush*, slamming the port side of her main deck at 1730 and starting a large fire. As this kamikaze came in, Electrician's Mate 3rd Class Bob Shirey was hollering instructions to volunteers helping operate his 40-mm gun. "We were damn near helpless, with the 5-inch useless and the 40's in manual," said Lieutenant Harry Stanley, *Bush's* gunnery officer. The second kamikaze hit in nearly the same place as the first one, but this time the results were devastating.[30]

The force of the explosion nearly cut the destroyer in half, with her keel seemingly the only thing holding *Bush* together. Repair parties attacked the fresh fires with two operative handy-billy pumps. Gunner Shirey, finding the bridge abandoned by the officers, took advantage of a momentary lull in the action to snatch a can of V8 juice and a couple of the skipper's cigars. "I returned to my gun, having a big old time drinking V-8 juice, smoking a cigar, and shooting at Japs," he said.[31]

The damage-control parties worked on the fires and the newly wounded, but their time was limited. Fifteen minutes after the second kamikaze struck, a Zeke flashed overhead in a strafing run so low that *Bush* crewmen could see the pilot's face. "He seemed to be looking right at us standing on the fantail, turning his head to watch us as he pulled away," recalled Ensign Coit Butler. The Zeke circled back and barreled in toward *Bush's* forward gun mount area, causing some sailors to dive overboard to escape the inevitable destruction.[32]

The gunners kept up a steady fire to the last instant. Nevertheless, the Zeke plowed into the port side of the main deck at 1745 in the vicinity of Turret No. 2 and the wardroom, where casualties being treated were instantly killed or burned to death. Ready ammunition on deck started exploding, and the forward half of the ship began to settle. Boatswain's Mate 1st Class Wesley G. Northey helped fire one of the 40-mm guns until the plane hit, the impact and explosions snapping both of his legs and mortally wounding him.

Brave crewmen battled the damage for another forty-five minutes, but a large swell at 1830 created such tearing and crunching noises that the skipper feared *Bush* would sink. He ordered abandon ship as the angle of the list increased dramatically. Shirey took to the water with two prized possessions, a wooden Saint Christopher plaque he had liberated from the bridge and his lucky silver dollar, both tucked into his life belt. Lieutenant Commander Rollin E. Westholm, *Bush*'s captain, was the last to leave his stricken ship's fantail moments before it disappeared.

Fourteen officers and men had been killed, and another seventy-three were missing by the time *Bush* slipped beneath the waves that evening. "About 200 yards out, I looked back as the ship folded and sank," said Sonarman 2nd Class Al Blakely. "The sizzling sound as the flames were extinguished by the sea were spectacular and loud." *Bush* had earned the unenviable distinction of becoming the first radar picket duty destroyer to be sunk by kamikazes.

Many survivors were in poor shape by the time they were rescued after ten hours in the water. Commander Wilson feared *Colhoun* would soon follow *Bush* to the depths, as his own destroyer was dead in the water and settling, forcing Wilson to order his executive officer to get most of the men off the ship. One of her escorts, *LCS(L) 84*, came alongside *Colhoun* at 1900 and began removing most of the men, leaving only a skeleton crew of about twenty-five sailors and five key officers.[33]

As *LCS(L) 84* approached, *Colhoun*'s executive officer asked if anyone had flashlights to use in the darkness to help guide the gunboat alongside their broken destroyer. Gun captain William S. "Jake" Hurley raced below to his locker to retrieve one, taking the opportunity to grab up some of his personal effects as well—cash, his shaving gear, the watch his parents had given him for graduating high school, and extra socks, among other items—that he stuffed into a pillowcase. Back on deck Hurley assisted with moving the wounded and unneeded hands over to the LCS(L). One of Hurley's buddies, Seaman 2nd Class Frank Joseph Esposito, froze, saying he could not make the jump between the two bobbing warships. "I took Esposito by the butt and when we went down and that LCS came up, I threw him over," said Hurley.[34]

The destroyer *Cassin Young* (DD 793) attempted to tow *Colhoun* that evening, but the strain of the towing line only further increased the breaking up of the ship. "The whole starboard side was awash, the bow was water tight, and the stern went under," reported Wilson.[35] The skeleton crew was finally forced to abandon *Colhoun*. *Cassin Young* was called upon to use her guns to finish off the forward half of the ship, making *Colhoun* the second U.S. destroyer lost to the afternoon's bloody Kikusui No. 1 assault.

✦◇✦

The radar-picket stations' fighter blanket simply could not stop all of the kamikazes on April 6, and two other warships not afforded full fighter coverage became victims. Thirty miles south of *Colhoun* and *Bush*, the destroyer-minelayers *Emmons* and *Rodman* were riding herd on six small minesweepers of Sweep Unit 11 between Iheya Shima and Okinawa's northwest coast when the first Kikusui No. 1 attackers dropped down on them at 1515.

Although Sweep Unit 11 was not officially tended by a radar-picket CAP, some assistance was rendered by *Bunker Hill* VMF-221 Corsairs returning from a reconnaissance sweep over Kyushu around 1500. Captain Bill Snider destroyed a Tony, while his wingman, 2nd Lieutenant William L. Bailey, damaged an Oscar with a head-on run. Captain Frank B. Baldwin's Marine flight tangled with four Zekes, dropping all of them in short order. En route back to *Bunker Hill*, Baldwin's division jumped three Jills and likewise sent all of them into the ocean. VMF-221 thus claimed eight kills in these small encounters, two falling to 1st Lieutenant Blaine Imel and three to 2nd Lieutenant George R. Johns.

Imel, excited to see his first Japanese "meatballs," forgot to arm his gun camera, which he had nicknamed "Jorge," during the initial encounter and was thus robbed of confirmation of his first kill. Arming Jorge afterward, Imel sped to catch up with Baldwin and Johns, in the process running upon a Jill torpedo plane dead ahead. "I doubted if the pilot saw me, but his rear gunner soon did," said Imel, who dropped his second victim into the ocean.[36]

Kikusui No. 1 was in full swing. Radar picket *Macomb* (DD 458) reported two enemy aircraft approaching the destroyer-minelayers at 1515. On the destroyer-minelayer *Emmons*, Lieutenant John J. Griffin's gunners brought all weapons to bear on these enemy aircraft, now closing on his ship's port quarter. "With the range fouled, we saw one plane crash [into] the forecastle of USS *Rodman* and the second carry out an unsuccessful bombing attack," related Griffin.[37]

The first aircraft, a Val dive bomber, slammed into the port side of Commander William H. Kirvan's *Rodman*, with its bomb exploding after it entered the ship at 1532. The other plane crashed close aboard, showering the starboard side of the vessel with a sheet of flame and then a wave of seawater that enveloped the superstructure as high as the gun director. The explosion from the crash ripped a fifteen-foot hole in *Rodman*'s starboard side, creating heavy flooding.

Lieutenant Commander Eugene N. Foss maneuvered his *Emmons* alongside the crippled *Rodman*. Once the fires were brought under control, *Emmons* began circling her to lend antiaircraft support against other attacks. Numerous bogies appeared on radar, and the CAP above was soon very much engaged. "Much credit is due the pilots of the Combat Air Patrol who never hesitated to carry through their attacks, although on many occasions it meant flying directly into friendly anti-aircraft fire," said Griffin.[38]

The Marine Corsairs and several divisions of TF 58 Hellcats could not stop them all, as the air attacks had become rampant by 1600. Kamikazes would continue to work over both *Rodman* and *Emmons* in small waves for nearly three hours. During this time, *Rodman* was further crippled by two more kamikaze hits, one on the port side and another in the captain's cabin. Steering was lost, and *Rodman* was forced to steam in circles at five knots while her crew fought fires and tended to the wounded. The ship would survive the day but suffered sixteen men killed or missing and another twenty men wounded.[39]

The *Emmons* gunners splashed six planes, while another four kamikazes slammed into the ocean within yards of the careening destroyer-minelayer. When the 5-inch gunners in the ship's forward mounts ran out of antiaircraft shells, they began loading common, phosphorous, and even star shells to fire at the circling planes, burning their hands as they did so on the blazing nose cones of the shells and the cork rings on the powder charges.[40]

Emmons was maneuvering radically at 25 knots, with all guns firing, but a kamikaze coming up her wake slammed home at 1732 while making an estimated 235 knots speed. The aircraft and its bomb hit the fantail at about Frame 175, exploding with such violence that the after section of the hull was carried away and badly damaging the port screw so that the port engine was put out of commission.

On the bridge Quartermaster 3rd Class Edwin L. Hoffman could see this kamikaze through the starboard hatch of the pilothouse. He was standing at the engine order telegraph wearing a battle headset, serving as Commander Foss' talker by relaying orders to the engine room and communicating any input from below. Near Hoffman stood Chief Quartermaster Henry O. Thompson, manning the helm to respond to the skipper's course changes. Foss quickly learned that the kamikaze hit had destroyed the steering room and caused the loss of the ship's rudder. "When we found we did not have steerageway, the captain ordered to shift control to after steering, which was a person on manual steering with hand crank on the motors that controlled the rudders," said Hoffman. "When we shifted control to after steering, we didn't know at that time that after steering wasn't there."[41]

At 1734, less than two minutes after the first kamikaze hit, *Emmons* was struck again twice—simultaneously. Hoffman could see one of the

Battle-talker Edwin L. Hoffman was wounded by the kamikazes that hit his destroyer, *Emmons* (DD 457), on April 6, 1945. *Tom Hoffman*

aircraft before it hit, but he had only enough time to grab the pilothouse railing before a blinding flash roared through the bridge. One kamikaze hit two decks below the pilothouse, wiping out the Combat Information Center and killing all hands in that location, including the ship's executive officer, Lieutenant Temple James Lynds. The second bomb-toting warplane hit the starboard side of the bridge, ripping away half of the position, wrecking the pilothouse, and creating large gasoline fires that spread throughout the superstructure.

Commander Foss, who had been standing on the port wing of the bridge, was blown overboard. He came to in the ocean, badly burned and temporarily blinded. Near him landed Chief Quartermaster Thompson, whose neck had been slashed open by shrapnel. The two remained together until they were pulled on board a life raft. Foss would survive the day badly injured, but Thompson did not make it through the night.[42]

"I found myself on my hands and knees on the deck," recalled Hoffman, the only other man to survive from the pilothouse. "I can't remember hearing the explosions." Badly burned, Hoffman moved as fast as he could with a shattered ankle and broken leg. "I made my way out of the flames onto the wing of the bridge on the port side," he said. Hoffman hopped to the after part of the bridge in time to see other sailors scrambling down the ladders through the roaring gasoline fires from the main battery director above.[43]

Gunnery officer John Griffin ordered his crew to head for the main deck, as he had no communication with the main guns he was to direct. He tried to help his assistant gunnery officer, Ensign Ross Tompkins Elliott Jr., but the young man died before first aid could be rendered. Elliott had used his body as a shield to absorb bullets from strafing kamikazes, saving the lives of some of his enlisted shipmates.

As Griffin headed for lower decks, two more kamikazes slammed into *Emmons*, the fourth on the starboard side of the Number Three 5-inch gun, and the fifth near the waterline on the starboard side. The entire bridge structure was destroyed, and fires raged from amidships all the way to the forward 5-inch gun from the main deck upward. Firefighting efforts became treacherous as 20-mm ready-ammunition boxes began exploding.

"Somebody was watching over me," recalled Tony Esposito, a twenty-one-year-old sailor who hailed from Peekskill, New York. Posted at the depth-charge release station on the starboard side of the *Emmons* bridge, Esposito had watched a nearby 20-mm gun crew shoot down one of their attackers. "I was hollering and cursing and everything else," he said as two more kamikazes streaked in low on the starboard quarter. The two hits that blew Commander Foss from the ship knocked Esposito momentarily unconscious. The 20-mm gunner standing in front of him was blown overboard, while the loader adjacent to Esposito, Soundman 3rd Class Cleo Richard Kohl, was killed. "I was very fortunate," Tony admitted.[44]

Gunner's Mate 3rd Class Armond Jolley from Connecticut had fought with his forward 5-inch gun crew until his weapon was rendered useless. As the gun's pointer, Jolley had a clear view of the first kamikaze that hit sister ship *Rodman* early in the action. "I saw the plane come out of the sky straight down for the *Rodman* and it hit," he said. Once his own ship was struck by the kamikazes, fires spread to the forward areas of *Emmons*. "After the plane hit forward, the mount was on fire from all the oil in there," recalled Jolley. He remained on board until orders were passed to abandon ship, at which time he leaped from the forecastle. Jolley was later retrieved by a minelayer whose crew tended to his burned hands with Vaseline gauze.[45]

Before climbing to the main deck, Lieutenant Griffin paused to render aid to another wounded shipmate, battle talker Ed Hoffman. Griffin helped him down the ladder to the weather deck but found that the last ten feet of steel ladder had been ripped away by the explosions. "He dropped down, then he told me to drop down, and I did, and he caught me," related Hoffman. On the main deck Griffin learned that he was senior officer on board and, as such, acting skipper. Some seventy officers and men from *Emmons* had been blown or forced to jump overboard to escape fires and smoke.[46]

Griffin learned that someone had hastily given an abandon-ship order, causing other crewmen to take to the ocean, so he ordered all hands to stand by until the situation could be fully investigated. Some of the wounded men were put into rafts and floats on the water to get them out of harm's way, while the most serious casualties were kept on board. Hoffman was among those helped over the side into the cool ocean water, which offered some relief from his terrible burns. All topside gear was jettisoned, the fire in the superstructure was brought partially under control, and the ship's whaleboat was lowered to pick up the wounded and transfer them to minelayers and other ships.[47]

Tony Esposito regained consciousness on the bridge and scrambled to the main deck without a scratch. "I was very scared and I started looking for my buddies," he said. Esposito and several other sailors lowered the ship's badly holed whaleboat into the ocean as the water was approaching the main deck. "We went around to the starboard side and picked up some of the guys," he noted. Many were badly wounded, including a sailor with a hole all the way through his leg. "I put my life jacket over his legs to keep the saltwater out of his open wounds," Esposito said.[48]

Griffin, five other officers, and fifty-seven enlisted men remained on *Emmons* after the unauthorized abandon-ship order and after all the wounded were moved off. They continue to fight fires and work on damage control until the six surviving officers still on board held a conference at 1800. They decided to officially abandon ship, which Griffin felt was fully justified: the port engine was dead; the rudder was blown off, preventing steerage; the forward fire could not be controlled because of its intensity and lack of water-main pressure; only two 20-mm guns remained operable; and the entire ship was in danger of explosion from its fuel tanks and magazines.[49]

Around 1930 *PGM 11* came alongside to port to render assistance and take on the wounded. The vessel was still alongside when a heavy explosion occurred in Mount No. 2's handling room. Griffin then passed the word to all hands to abandon ship. *PGM 11* took the remaining survivors from *Emmons* on toward the anchorage while other vessels stood guard over the drifting, burning hulk through the night. The following morning *Ellyson* (DMS 19) received orders to scuttle her. It took ninety-six rounds from *Ellyson*'s forward battery to force *Emmons* to finally capsize and sink. Gunner's Mate 3rd Class Ray Quinn, who watched his ship slip below the surface, recalled, "A part of each one of us stayed with her."[50]

The *Essex* Hellcat pilots of VF-83 were not finished with their action on April 6. Lieutenant (jg) Hugh Batten and wingman Sam Brocato vectored to intercept a fresh group of bogies, tallyhoed nine Zekes, and went to work. By the end of their combat, they each accounted for four enemy aircraft, pushing each pilot to ace status (adding in their prior kills) and the award of Navy Crosses.

Ensign Bill Hardy of VF-17 would finish the afternoon with at least some satisfaction that he had done his utmost to spare even more American lives from being lost. In the frenzy of the early vectors from warships like *Bush*, *Colhoun*, and *Emmons*, Hardy and his wingman, Lieutenant (jg) Harrison "Crash" Morgan—who had flown from Guadalcanal on an earlier tour—operated independently from Dick Cowger's first section. Eight miles out on their initial vector, the pair tallyhoed one Zeke and one Judy flying a close formation at twenty-five hundred feet on an opposite course from their own. Hardy led Morgan into a firing pass on the two Japanese planes from above. Executing a high wingover, they slid in behind their foes and opened up with stern attacks, Morgan downing the Judy and Hardy taking out the Zeke, both of which crashed into the water.[51]

During the Japanese kamikaze attack on the two destroyers near Point Nan, Hardy and Morgan sighted four Vals above them, heading for the destroyers at twenty-five hundred feet. "I'll take the tail end man, and you take the next man," Hardy called over the radio to his wingman. "We'll just work our way up to the leader." Morgan made quick work of two of the Vals, while Hardy pumped rounds into the trailing two dive bombers. Two of the Japanese planes burned heavily, including one that Hardy nailed in the fuel tank directly behind the pilot. "I made toast out of him," he said. Within minutes all four Vals had hit the ocean. "I was very democratic," Hardy said of his work with Crash Morgan. "I got two and he got two."[52]

They regrouped over the radar pickets and resumed their shepherding of the embattled warships in the waning hours of daylight. Soon the VF-17 pilots were pressing an attack on a Judy, bracketing it from astern. Morgan fired just three rounds before he exhausted his ammunition. "He had gotten on the trigger too long in his early attacks, and he was now out of ammo," explained Hardy. "I was a little more conservative on my bullets on my first three." Hardy took over the offensive, closing to a mere three hundred feet before he fired a three-second burst aimed between the pilot's and rear gunner's cockpits. "The rear seatman on that plane was giving me hell," he said. "But I got up underneath him where he couldn't get to me. He could see my wingtips but he couldn't get his gun depressed enough to hit me. So, I had him running."[53]

Hardy waited for the right opportunity, pulled up to one side, and put another burst between the crewmen that ignited a blazing fire. He maintained his position, watching as the Judy's pilot stood and prepared to leap from his plane. His parachute apparently deployed prematurely, draping back into the flames and was soon ablaze. "I was flying on his wingtip, watching him trying to get back into his airplane with his parachute burning up," said Hardy. He watched in awe as the panicked pilot leaped back into his seat and tried to regain control of the plane, which was plummeting toward the wave tops.[54]

"We were almost directly on the water," he said. Being so mesmerized by the scene of the pilot trying to save his plane, Hardy had paid little attention to how low they had dropped. At that instant the Judy slammed into the ocean with its bomb-bay doors open, detonating its ordnance as

This painting, *4 of 5 on the 6th*, depicts Ensign Willis "Bill" Hardy of *Hornet's* VF-17 becoming an "ace in a day" by downing five Japanese aircraft. This is his fourth victim, a Judy bomber whose pilot is seen attempting to climb from his blazing cockpit. *Courtesy of artist Roy Grinnell and the American Fighter Aces Association*

it plowed into the concrete-like surface. "All of a sudden, the whole Pacific Ocean came down on me," Hardy said. The explosion blasted a wall of water that engulfed his Hellcat. "As soon as the shower receded, I looked back over my shoulder and there were big bubbles coming up out of the water where he had crashed."[55]

His fourth kill of the mission could well have caused his own demise, but Hardy recovered and climbed for altitude to rejoin Crash Morgan. His wingman was out of ammunition, but he stuck with Hardy to ride out the balance of their time on radar-picket CAP. Minutes later the FDO vectored the *Hornet* section toward a fresh bogey on the radar screen, forty miles from Zampa Misaki. Hardy noted a blazing destroyer below as he scanned the skies for the approaching bandit. He finally tallyhoed another Judy to the south of the FDO's crippled ship. The Americans closed on the Judy after a ten-minute chase. The Japanese pilot, apparently mistaking the overhauling Hellcats for friendlies, started a gentle right turn to enable the F6Fs to join on him. Hardy obliging "joined up" by taking a position on the Judy's wing.

By this point Hardy had hit enough planes on this mission to know right where to aim to hit the gas tank. As the attack began, Morgan turned his bulletless Hellcat in to the Judy on a dummy run, forcing his opponent to turn toward his wingman. Hardy opened up with a short burst. After only a few rounds, he found that his gun needed to be recharged.

As the Judy turned away from him, Morgan pressed in on another feint and drove the Japanese pilot back into the path of his wingman. "I took my foot off the rudder, pushed the gun, and charged it," recalled Hardy. "I got one or two rounds off." The back and forth herding of the Judy continued. "Sometimes, I'd hit the button and I'd get just one round," he noted. "Sometimes, I'd get two." After three such feints, he had managed to land only a handful of hits but could see a small stream of fuel pouring from one side.[56]

Finally, Hardy lowered his flaps, turned inside the Judy on a left turn— all the while charging his one gun with his left foot—and finally flamed it between the cockpits. The Judy nosed down and exploded violently upon impact with the water. It was Hardy's fifth kill, making him an "ace in a day."

Hardy called the FDO to announce that he was out of ammunition and had only fifty gallons of fuel remaining. The fighter director acknowledged and offered the new ace the proper heading back toward his task group. The ensign's biggest challenge of the afternoon became that of finding his carrier in the dark and executing his first night landing on *Hornet* at 1854, ending three and a half hours of action. In his excitement Hardy announced to his plane captain that he had downed five Japanese airplanes on his mission. "Hey, sir, we can't talk," said the sailor. "We've got to get out of the way. There's somebody coming on board right behind you."[57]

Hardy and the plane captain jumped down into the catwalk as Crash Morgan brought his Hellcat up the deck. The two pilots proceeded to the ready room, eager to share their fresh stories, but found no one loitering around to enjoy their escapades. "First thing the next morning, we saw everybody reading the ship's bulletins when we got up," said Hardy. "It turns out I had shot down five airplanes and my wingman had shot down three, so we were pretty popular at breakfast in the wardroom."[58]

By the end of the day, Fighting Seventeen's seven pilots claimed 16.5 victories, with Hardy top of the pack with five kills. His division leader, Dick Cowger, had scored on three planes, while Lonnie Pace had contributed another three and a half victories. Not to be outdone, sister squadron VBF-17 claimed another sixteen planes in the day's actions.

The *Hornet* fighter squadrons ended the day with a staggering total of 41.5 kills. *Belleau Wood*'s VF-30 claimed 47 victories on April 6, but Jock Southerland's VF-83 from *Essex* took top honors for the day with 56 total victories. Four pilots—Carl Foster, Kenneth Dahms, and Johnnie Miller from VF-30 and Bill Hardy of VF-17—chalked up "ace in a day" honors while fighting off the Kikusui No. 1 attackers. April 6, 1945, would go down in history as the U.S. Navy's fourth-heaviest day of aerial combat in the Pacific.

Vice Admiral Mitscher's carrier aviators claimed 257 kills during their "turkey shoot," and island-based Corsairs helped run the day's complete totals to 350 aerial victories—falling just short of Mitscher's first turkey shoot in the Marianas in June 1944. American fighters had faced some 700 attackers on the sixth, half being kamikazes.

"The sea around Okinawa turned into a scene of carnage, and a reconnaissance plane reported that as many as 150 columns of black smoke were observed," Vice Admiral Ugaki logged in his diary. Japanese leaders initially declared that five transports, two battleships, and seven other American warships had been sunk during the day, later raising the claims to add three cruisers and eight destroyers. Based on such lofty interpretations, the Japanese concluded that Kikusui No. 1 was successful enough to warrant additional operations.[59]

Ugaki's combined strikers had hit nineteen ships, thirteen being destroyers, and three had gone down. Two others, *Leutze* (DD 481) and *Newcomb* (DD 586), were so badly damaged that they were towed to the Keramas to spend the balance of the war affecting repairs. The destroyers *Hyman* (DD 732) and *Morris* had been badly damaged by kamikazes, while other suiciders had caused the demise of *Colhoun*, *Bush*, and *Emmons*. By day's end radar-picket casualties added up to 367 men killed and 408 wounded.[60]

As the last dogfights played out on April 6, Japan's surface-force contribution to the kamikaze mission was steaming toward Okinawa.

In midafternoon on April 6, Admiral Toyoda, commander in chief of the Combined Fleet, arrived at Kanoya Airfield from Tokyo. He would take direct command of the final phase of Operation Kikusui No. 1, the dispatching of the *Yamato* fleet. The big battlewagon and her escorting warships got under way that day for their final mission to Okinawa. The suicide sortie had been dubbed Operation Ten-Go, meaning "Heaven No. 1."

By 1524 *Yamato*'s crew had weighed her 12-ton anchor and had the ship under way. The 7,710-ton cruiser *Yahagi* led the formation, with destroyers forming columns on either side of *Yamato*'s beam as she moved out past the northwestern corner of Kyushu, with the pink blossoms of cherry trees visible on the lower slopes of Mount Futago. Numerous enlisted men gathered topside, taking in the views of their homeland, which most assumed they would never see again.[61]

Lieutenant (jg) Takekuni Ikeda, a 1943 graduate of the IJN Academy, was on the bridge of *Yahagi*, a cruiser he had helped put into commission. Prior to departing the anchorage, *Yahagi* was filled with 1,250 tons of fuel despite orders limiting this to a much smaller quantity. "I learned later that even though the Japanese Naval General Staff had instructed the fuel facility to supply oil for only one-way, each ship was filled to capacity," Ikeda declared.[62]

Yamato's force moved into the deeper waters of Bungo Strait that evening, and many of the ship's company were mustered forward. The battleship's executive officer, Captain Jiro Nomura, climbed on top of Turret No. 1 to read a brief order of the day from Vice Admiral Seiichi Ito. The sun was just beginning to set as he described how Operation Ten-Go would be the turning point of the war. "The future of the empire rests on our efforts," read Nomura. "Every man will do his utmost for the glory of the Imperial Navy and of Japan." The statement was met with caps flung skyward and roaring banzai cheers from the crew.[63]

Vice Admiral Charles Lockwood's submarine force was patrolling around the main passages leading from Japan, waiting to send contact reports on any prime warships in the area. At 1956 Commander John J. Foote's *Threadfin* (SS 410) sent urgent contact reports to Pearl Harbor of eight Japanese warships under way, but by the time Foote received confirmation of their receipt, his sub was no longer in a position to launch torpedoes.[64]

Around 2030 the *Yamato* force passed close to another U.S. sub, *Hackleback* (SS 295), whose crew soon broadcast another sighting report that was passed to Nimitz and Lockwood on Guam, then on to Admiral Spruance on board the battleship *New Mexico*, and finally to Vice Admiral Mitscher with TF 58. Like *Threadfin*, the best efforts of *Hackleback*'s crew to line up *Yamato* for a torpedo attack were frustrated by pesky destroyers that charged close enough to prevent the sub from getting into range.[65]

The officers and men of the *Yamato* crew knew what was expected of them. Ensign Sakei Katono lay in a hammock, struggling to read the lengthy book *War and Peace*. Young gunner Masanobu Kobayashi lay in his bunk, feeling confident his gun crews would shoot down their first enemy planes the following day. *Yamato* maintained twenty-two knots after clearing the lurking submarines, making zigzag maneuvers every five minutes to keep any watching enemy skipper guessing. Captain Nomura could not sleep, so he spent time walking about the vast battleship, ensuring that everything was in order.[66]

Sailor Kazuhiro Fukumoto joined other young men in a sake party that evening, listening to records and singing. "We were drunk to the point of staggering," he admitted. While most consumed sake and beer freely, some of the older, married sailors like Naoyshi Ishida resisted. With a heavy heart, he found he had stomach for neither food nor alcohol that night.[67]

Pete Mitscher was chomping at the bit, eager to fling his warplanes against the last great naval force the Japanese had left to assault the Allied fleet. He had three of his four carrier task groups ready for action: Jocko Clark's 58.1, Ted Sherman's 58.3, and Arthur Radford's 58.4, which had just completed refueling. Rear Admiral Davison's 58.2 would not be of service on April 7 as his ships took their turn at refueling.

Contact reports from *Threadfin* and *Hackleback* had reached Mitscher, but the enemy fleet was too far away for any immediate strikes. The admiral finally climbed onto a cot in *Bunker Hill*'s Flag Plot after 0200 and began reading a detective novel until he finally nodded off for a few hours. He was awake again before dawn, taking enough time to shower, shave, and change into a fresh uniform.[68]

Mitscher's pockets included an extra pack of cigarettes for the following day, and he smoked almost ceaselessly throughout the morning of the seventh. He and his chief of staff, Captain Arleigh Burke, conferred in Flag Plot on how best to strike the enemy once the fleet was spotted. Long before dawn, divisions of Hellcats and Corsairs flew out from TF 58 to sweep the seas far ahead toward Kyushu and into the Pacific and China Sea on either side. Mitscher put up CAP divisions early and sent Hellcats and Corsairs from TG 58.1 and 58.3 up at 0530 to begin 325-mile antishipping search legs.

Long after daybreak there was still no further word on the *Yamato* force. The Japanese navy had not sent a serious surface force out to face an American carrier fleet in six months. "We immediately decided that this was another desperate attack," recalled Burke. "They were going to do something that would hurt us the most and make their sacrifice warranted." Burke and other members of Mitscher's staff put in long hours, plotting the likely course of *Yamato* and her consorts. "We decided she would probably go west of the chain of islands of which Okinawa is a part."[69]

Mitscher's weather-worn face showed the obvious strains of how badly he itched for this chance. If search planes ultimately reported that the *Yamato* group had turned and retreated back into a home anchorage, staffers could only imagine the salty tirade the admiral would unleash.

For the moment, all Mitscher could do was light another cigarette and impatiently wait for some word from his search planes.

Chapter Thirteen

GET *YAMATO*

Lieutenant Carlos Soffe of VF-83 was the first to spot Japanese ships on April 7. Far below, the telltale white wake trailed a gray ship on the blue surface, as the leader of the Wonder Five division opened up on his radio to send a contact report. He had discovered a 5,000-ton Japanese tanker, accompanied by two destroyer escorts, heading for Kyushu. But it was not the sighting Vice Admiral Mitscher was itching to hear.

Soffe's report at 0754 was the first of several to come in from *Essex's* Air Group 83. Her VBF-83 had launched eight Corsairs at 0538, along with eleven Hellcats of VF-83, each division being assigned search subsectors of 8 degrees in size. The two F4U divisions took stations at 100 and 200 miles from the task group to serve as communication-relay teams for the F6F pilots, who ventured farther into their assigned sectors. Mitscher's staff would remain huddled around their radio gear for another twenty minutes before the *Essex* teams struck gold.

Four VF-83 searchers, flying the cross leg of their searches at 3,500 feet, finally found the ten-ship *Yamato* fleet around 0815. Lieutenants (jg) Simon Crites Jr. and Gerald Russell "Geb" Schaub each relayed contact reports back to TF 58. Crites spotted *Yamato* about five miles ahead of him, steaming in formation with a light cruiser and seven or eight destroyers. Minutes later Schaub emerged from low cloud cover and eyeballed the massive battleship and her escorts just one and a half miles ahead of him.

A second VF-83 team sighted the *Yamato* group at 0823. Ensign Charles E. "Chuck" Hubenthal, from Lucerne, Indiana, concerned with the heavy cloud cover, snugged in tight on the wing of his section leader, Lieutenant (jg) Jack Lyons. The pair had reached the extreme limits of their search leg when they spotted what appeared to be large rocks or small islands below. "Then we saw several of them in a group and discovered that they were moving," said Lyons. "We immediately turned back and circled the fleet."[1]

Lyons counted the destroyers and larger warships, carefully noting their speed and course before sending the data to the Corsair section relay team for retransmission to TF 58. He and Hubenthal continued circling, content for the moment that the battleship's force had not opened fire on them. Low on gas, his section soon headed for home, having done their part by providing important clarifications on *Yamato's* course. Lyons would receive the Silver Star and Hubenthal the Distinguished Flying Cross for pinpointing the suicide fleet.

Members of the *Essex* VBF-83 relay team paid a heavy price for the air group's success this morning. Four Corsairs that had been flying on oxygen at 20,000 feet above the overcast failed to find *Essex* and TG 58.3 upon their return. All four Marine pilots were forced to ditch and ride out long ordeals on the ocean in their life rafts. The division leader, Captain Thomas M. Tomlinson, lashed his raft to that of 2nd Lieutenant Harold M. Sagers. The pair drifted for some thirty-six hours until they were scooped from the sea by a searching lifeguard submarine, *Sea Devil* (SS 400), at 2108 on the evening of April 8.

Tomlinson reported once on board the sub that his other two VBF-83 pilots were drifting in the vicinity, and *Sea Devil* commenced an intensive search of the area. Nearly two hours later the crew succeeded in recovering a third Corsair pilot, 2nd Lieutenant T. M. Lewis, thanks to the SOS signal he was flashing, but a prolonged search failed to find the fourth pilot, 2nd Lieutenant John Leonard Garlock.[2]

When Lyons made it back to *Essex* after more than five hours in the air, he was called to the bridge to report to Rear Admiral Sherman, who quizzed him about the largest warship of the force. "Being before the admiral for a 21-year-old kid was interesting and kinda scary," Lyons admitted. "I wasn't sure we had found the *Yamato* because the ship was shaped kinda strange, with an open back stern area that looked more like a flight deck." By the time the young VF-83 pilot finished his quiz session with the admiral, Sherman was convinced of the battleship's identity and thanked Lyons for his work.

"That's it," said Sherman. "That's the *Yamato*."[3]

At the time it was first sighted by Americans, the Operation Ten-Go force was performing a zigzag, making her course appear to be 300 degrees.

Mitscher's staff in *Bunker Hill*'s Flag Plot was left to wonder whether the *Yamato* group might be heading for Sasebo. Then came the contact report from Lyons, which put all questions to bed.

Lieutenant (jg) Takekuni Ikeda was on the bridge of the cruiser *Yahagi* at 0600 on April 7, just around sunrise. His ship was leading the force, some 1,500 yards ahead of *Yamato*. While Ikeda munched on a meager rice ball for breakfast, at 0630 he heard a lookout announce that nine Zero fighters were approaching their force.[4]

The fighter escort had been expected, nine Zeros from Flight Squadron 203 sent to fly cover over the *Yamato* group for several hours as they passed from the vicinity of mainland Japan. Shortly after daybreak, *Yamato* catapulted her penultimate seaplane and sent it back to Kagoshima. "From now on, we will see no friendly aircraft," recorded twenty-two-year-old Ensign Mitsuru Yoshida. A former law student at Tokyo Imperial University, Yoshida had been hurriedly pushed through the IJN's Officer Candidate School in late 1943 and had gained months of experience serving as one of *Yamato*'s assistant radar officers.[5]

Yahagi's veteran skipper, Captain Tameichi Hara, had an ominous sense about the morning. "It was a dismal day," Hara wrote, noting the cool weather and heavy clouds that hung low on the sea. His spirits were further diminished when the nearby destroyer *Asashimo* began losing speed and sent signal messages that she was having engine troubles. Hara requested more information, and the ship's skipper, Lieutenant Commander Yoshiro Sugihara, replied that his men were rushing repairs and hoped to rejoin the main body soon. *Asashimo* slowly drifted back out of sight beyond the horizon, her place in the *Yamato* formation assumed by the destroyer *Kasumi*. By 0800 the Japanese were aware of snooping U.S. scout aircraft nearby.[6]

Yahagi dispatched a reconnaissance floatplane from a catapult at 0815. Its pilot soon reported American fighter planes in the vicinity. "At 1016, two enemy PBM seaplanes were detected," wrote Lieutenant Ikeda. "The *Yamato* jammed the frequency of their operational transmission and fired a salvo with her 18-inch guns, but the planes were out of range."[7]

The U.S. seaplanes remained near *Yamato*'s warships, lurking about for hours in almost maddening fashion. "What a pity we did not have fighters available to shoot down this threat to our safety," said Captain Hara. "While we watched wistfully, this plane cruised beyond the range of our antiaircraft guns." The American scouts were still trailing the *Yamato* group when Hara's cruiser picked up a radio report from the Amami Oshima lookout station close to noon that hundreds of enemy planes were heading northward.

"Without even looking at a chart, every bridge officer knew that these enemy planes would be overhead within an hour," said Hara.[8]

Jack Lyons and the *Essex* searchers had pinpointed the *Yamato* fleet, but Pete Mitscher was not yet ready to commit his warplanes to the attack. In June 1944 in the Marianas, he had sent out 240 carrier planes to attack the Japanese fleet in the famous "mission after darkness." They succeeded in causing great damage to aircraft carriers, sinking *Hiyo* as well as two tankers, but more than 100 aircraft were lost. His decision to turn on the lights to land returning strikers long after dark saved many lives, but those who had perished weighed heavily on him.

Mitscher was not prepared to launch against the *Yamato* force at a distance so great that severe aircraft losses might be repeated, this time due to running out of fuel. He was in a quandary. Another long-legged flight might cost him numerous planes, but if he pondered the dilemma too long, the *Yamato* fleet might slip away, damaging his reputation. Mitscher finally turned to Chief of Staff Burke and announced: "Order a full strike for 1000. Target 344 degrees, range 238 miles."[9]

He could only hope the *Yamato* group would continue on its suicide course for Okinawa. The ninety minutes following the last *Essex* contact reports were nail biters for both the task-group brass and the aviators who faced the long attack flights. Captain Burke and his staff had worked through the night, trying to plot *Yamato*'s likeliest course. With the *Essex* reports in hand, Burke could only rely on best instincts when Mitscher's carriers "launched the works" around 1000.[10]

As the pivotal moment approached, Burke found British liaison Charlie Owen to be overly excited and a bit apprehensive. "You don't know where she is," said Owen.

"No," admitted Burke.

"Where are you letting the pilots go?" Owen asked.

"We're launching to the point where we would be if we were the *Yamato*," Burke explained. "We are directing the planes to that spot. We expect her to be there by the time the planes get to this spot." He silently prayed that other search planes would offer fresh intelligence of *Yamato*'s course once the strike planes were airborne.[11]

On *Bunker Hill* Ensign Melvin Guttenberg went to the front of VT-84's ready room and scrawled a simple phrase in large letters across the chalkboard: "GET THE *YAMATO*."[12]

Not everyone in the room was feeling as spirited. Lieutenant (jg) Alan "Al" Turnbull noticed his buddy Lieutenant (jg) Richard John Walsh, with whom he had graduated flight school in Corpus Christi, solemnly smoking in the back of the room. "Bull," Walsh announced, "I am not going to make it back from this strike. I got that feeling."

Turnbull, feeling a certain apprehension about his own fate this day, tried to reassure his friend: "I'll get you back, Dick."[13]

In *Hornet's* ready room VF-17 skipper Marsh Beebe prepared his four divisions to be included in the strike group. Lieutenant (jg) Tilly Pool of Tommy Harris' division was not at ease with this mission. "They told us we were going to launch an attack on this Japanese fleet," said Pool. "They said, 'The bad news is you don't have enough fuel to get there and back, but we're headed there as fast as we can to shorten the distance.' So, they hung wing tanks on our planes and 500-pound bombs."[14]

The added weight of a bomb for such a long-range mission did not soothe Tilly's nerves, but last-minute challenges prevented the deck crews from loading the ordnance on most of Fighting Seventeen's Hellcats.

From TG 58.2, *Bataan's* and *Cabot's* first warplanes roared off the decks precisely at 1000, followed by the first *Essex* planes at 1005, and then the *Bunker Hill* strikers from Vice Admiral Mitscher's flagship. For nearly an hour squadrons effected their takeoffs and rendezvous above TF 58's carrier groups. Light carrier *Belleau Wood* launched her Avengers and Hellcats via catapult, while the fleet carriers dispatched their warriors via conventional procedure. The strikers from TG 58.1 and TG 58.3 led the procession, some 280 aircraft heading toward *Yamato*.

Another large attack wave from TG 58.4 was held in check for a short time. The first planes from *Yorktown* began clawing for altitude at 1045, led by Lieutenant Commander Herb Houck. *Langley's* nineteen planes began launching at 1050, while *Intrepid's* VBF-10 did not clear the deck until 1105. The 106 strike planes from TG 58.4 would be the clean-up crew, arriving on target shortly after TG 58.1 and TG 58.3's planes had gone to work.[15]

The extra forty-five minutes of waiting to launch only increased the excitement on *Yorktown*. In VT-9's ready room there had been a roar of approval when the "Air Plot" ticker had announced, "Load with torpedoes." Lieutenant Tom Stetson's Avenger pilots had not launched an aerial torpedo in six months. As one of his pilots jokingly chalked a picture of a "war fish" on the blackboard, Stetson quipped, "Do you suppose we still know how to drop them?" One of his junior pilots, Lieutenant (jg) Clyde J. Lee, was counting the ticker, noting the hundreds of warplanes already launched ahead of the *Yorktown* air group. "There probably won't be anything left for us to hit when we get there," Lee grumbled.[16]

On board *Intrepid* Lieutenant (jg) Roy "Eric" Erickson of VBF-10 was rousted from his bunk and told to report to the ready room to replace a buddy, Ensign Bill Ecker, who had injured his hand. Erickson hurriedly jotted down "Point Option" on his plotting board, put on his flight gear, and ran to the flight deck.

As he strapped himself him, his plane captain handed him a chocolate bar and a canteen of water. Confused, Erickson asked, "What the hell is this for?"

"Haven't you heard?" said the plane captain. "They've located the Jap fleet!"[17]

Rising into the sky with a 1,000-pound bomb tucked under his Hellcat, Erickson took wing on Lieutenant Wes Hays from Texas, ready to fill in with a division other than his normal one.

Once the strikers were away, Mitscher messaged Admiral Spruance, a black-shoe surface officer, in jest. "Will you take them or shall I?"

The reply back from Spruance brought cackling laughter from Mitscher: "You take them."[18]

The first wave of Mitscher's strikers was en route toward the Japanese fleet with contact information that was nearly two hours old. The *Essex* searchers had long since departed the area of the *Yamato* fleet, but fresh information that Burke's staff so desperately desired was soon available from a pair of Martin PBM-5 Mariner two-engine flying boats.

Pilots Lieutenant Richard L. Simms from Atlanta, Georgia, and Lieutenant James R. Young of Central City, Kentucky, had lifted their flying boats—nicknamed "Dumbos" after Disney's animated flying elephant—from the protected waters of Aka Channel in Kerama Retto early on April 7. Their newly formed squadron, VPB-21, had moved from NAS Tanapag on Saipan on March 29 to the Nansei Islands to operate from Kerama to help support the Okinawa landings.[19]

At a range of eighty miles, the Japanese ships first appeared around 1015 as one big blip on the radarscope in Simms' Mariner. The blip subdivided into smaller shapes on the screen as Young and Simms edged closer through the heavy overcast. Lieutenant (jg) William Graves, Simms' copilot, noted through his binoculars that one destroyer had fallen far astern of the main group, which soon appeared to include a large battleship, two light cruisers, and about eight destroyers. The coded contact report flashed to flagship carrier *Bunker Hill* was just the update that Mitscher had been wanting to receive.[20]

The Dumbo crews continued to stalk the Japanese warships, slipping in and out of the available cloud cover. At 1017 they had moved close enough to draw a salvo of gunfire from *Yamato*'s massive 18-inch guns. The VPB-21 pilots wisely eased their lumbering flying boats farther out of range but maintained station near the warships, with ample fuel supply to lurk about the area for hours to help coach in TF 58's strike groups.

The first of these to reach the area was the 100-plane TG 58.1 force. Commander George L. Heap, *Bennington*'s CAG 82, had been slated to lead the entire force, but only one F4U of VMF-123 had managed to be spotted on deck in time to join the hasty launch. Control of TG 58.1's strikers thus fell to the next senior aviator, *Hornet*'s CAG 17, Commander Ed Konrad. The Helldiver, Avenger, Corsair, and Hellcat pilots faced heavy cloud cover at three thousand feet, but above that the skies were clear, leaving the lower-flying groups to deal with the nasty weather. Nearly two hours passed from the time the first planes had launched before evidence of the enemy ships finally presented itself.

Aviation Chief Radioman Henry H. Reed, holding vigil over his AN/APS-4 radar set in the rear seat of VB-82 skipper Hugh Wood Jr.'s Helldiver, finally broke the silence. "I have a contact, 25 miles, port 25," he announced. The blips on Reed's screen were miles away from where the Japanese position had been estimated, but they were still within easy reach. Woods' SB2Us turned toward the new heading to port, and strike coordinator Konrad signaled for the other squadrons to follow suit.[21]

About four minutes later the leading planes caught glimpses of the enemy ships, about eight miles distant, through breaks in the cloud formations. It was 1217 as *Bennington*'s warplanes approached the enemy fleet and first began drawing fire from the Japanese warships far below. Air Group 82 was quickly joined by the smaller strike groups from *Belleau Wood* and *San Jacinto*, with the *Hornet* strikers bringing up the rear about two miles astern. More minutes ticked away as Konrad carefully sized up the formation below him. Several pilots took photos of the circling ships while bomber and torpedo bomber crewmen tossed out bundles of aluminum foil strips—called "window" (now known as "chaff")—that was designed to confuse the enemy's radar control.

For nearly twenty minutes, TG 58.1's pilots circled about the area while their strike coordinators assessed the situation. The black puffs of anti-aircraft fire clawing up toward them did little to soothe anxious nerves. Tilly Pool of VF-17 was in awe of the size of *Yamato*—"the biggest thing I ever saw"—and was concerned with the 18-inch cannons firing toward the circling aircraft. "Those guns were big enough to throw a Toyota."[22]

During this lengthy pause, TG 58.3's warplanes reached the scene, with those of *Bataan* arriving over the Japanese ships at 1220. Two massive collections of warplanes now filled the skies in the near vicinity of *Yamato's* fleet, creating as much danger for the aircrews as the hot lead being hurled at them by the Japanese warships. As the approach was made, the cruiser *Yahagi* darted ahead of *Yamato*, leading the formation. Four destroyers—*Kasumi*, *Suzutsuki*, *Hamakaze*, and *Yukikaze*—moved about *Yamato's* beam. Three others—*Isokaze*, *Hatsushimo*, and *Fuyutsuki*—were between *Yamato* and *Yahagi*. Twelve miles to the north lay lone destroyer *Asashimo*, seemingly under control but actually struggling with engine trouble. The main fleet was making twenty knots when sighted.

After endless minutes of circling, Ed Konrad was ready for the attack. The various groups of fighters were to assault the escort warships to help suppress their antiaircraft fire. The dive and torpedo bombers from *Hornet*, *Belleau Wood*, and *Bennington* were directed to go after the big battleship and the cruiser, while *San Jacinto's* smaller air group was ordered to hit the straggling destroyer *Asashimo*. Konrad offered opening honors to his own *Hornet* strike force, but they had circled too wide for an immediate attack, consuming precious time their CAG was not prepared to waste as they circled back.[23]

At 1237 Konrad barked at *Bennington's* strike group, ordering its SB2C Helldivers to make an immediate assault on *Yamato*. "Sugar Baker Two Charlies," he called. "Take the big boy!"[24]

Lieutenant Commander Ed DeGarmo, skipper of VT-82 and the *Bennington* flight leader, was surprised by the call. He had initiated a wide orbit with his Avengers to allow room for the *Hornet* group to strike first. He was midway through the turn when Konrad ordered the *Bennington* group to go in, so DeGarmo immediately pushed over toward the Japanese warships, setting his sights on *Yahagi*.

Bombing Eighty-Two skipper Hugh Wood thus took the honors of leading the first Helldivers down to attack *Yamato*, bringing his planes in from astern. His division pushed over from three thousand feet as red tracers curved past their SB2Cs and *Yamato* heeled sharply to port to evade the plunging dive bombers. Wingman Ed Sieber was in awe of the fire coming up at him. He called back to his gunner, ARM3c Antonio "Moe" Santaferra, asking him to watch for any pattern of tracers that was homing in on them. During the attack, his gunner said nothing but later offered: "There was no pattern. There was just fire coming from everywhere."[25]

Wood, Sieber, and Lieutenant (jg) Francis "Fran" Ferry from *Bennington* were the first of any TF 58 planes to attack the *Yamato* force on April 7. Wood's SB2C took small-caliber hits that damaged his port dive flap and severed two oil lines, but he held his course stoically until he pickled his pair of 1,000-pound semi-armor-piercing bombs toward the battleship's stern. Wood flew down the length of *Yamato*'s hull, just missing her bridge tower, before glancing back to see a column of smoke from behind her smokestack.[26]

Wood claimed two hits, which were followed almost immediately by hits from Ferry and from Sieber. Chief Reed, in Wood's plane, observed bombs hit forward of the bridge, one closely aft of the bridge, and a third farther aft. Sieber was credited with a hit amidships, striking *Yamato*'s Turret No. 3. Following their attack, Ferry circled the battleship while taking photos. His buddy Sieber could only think of clearing the area and saving his own skin. He later kidded Ferry: "Fran, you're made of different stuff from me. What was uppermost in my mind was just getting the hell out of there."[27]

Six of the VB-82 Helldivers split to attack some of the escort ships. Ensign Jack Carl Fuller's SB2C was hit by antiaircraft fire during the approach, and two parachutes were seen to blossom. Neither Fuller nor his gunner, ARM3c Charles "T" Williams Jr., were recovered.

Bennington's fighters, led by Lieutenant Commander Ed Hessel, numbered six VF-82 Hellcats and one lone Marine Corsair. Three two-plane sections made runs against various screening destroyers, while Hessel announced that he had carried his 1,000-pound bomb some 260 miles to use on the Japanese and was not about to waste it. His bomb failed to release, however, so he made a secondary attack on a destroyer, finally landing his bomb within twenty-five feet of the twisting warship—only to see that it failed to explode. Two of Hessel's VF-82 sections missed their destroyer targets, but the third—Lt. (jg) Clarence Davies and Ensign Melvin Carter—dropped on a destroyer, and Carter scored a direct hit aft of amidships.[28]

The lone *Bennington* Corsair, piloted by 2nd Lieutenant Kenneth Huntington of VMF-112, made a solo attack against the cruiser *Yahagi*. As he moved in, he saw a Helldiver land a hit on the nearby *Yamato*. Huntington released his bomb at fifteen hundred feet and was credited with a direct hit on *Yahagi*'s forward turret, which silenced its guns and helped clear the way for incoming torpedo planes.

Ed DeGarmo was caught in a quandary when his *Bennington* Avengers were ordered to attack *Yamato*. His torpedoes were set to shallow depth, and many of the TBMs had made the long trip without a radioman. Knowing his warheads would be wasted on the battleship, DeGarmo sent some of his TBMs against the screening warships. His own division dropped on *Yahagi*, and he noted a large explosion on the starboard beam of their target.

As Lieutenant Norman A. Wiese led his VT-82 division against screening vessels, his Avenger was hit four times by gunfire from *Yamato*. An instinctive duck saved his life as a 25-mm shell crashed through his windshield and instrument panel, driving a splinter of shrapnel into his scalp. He was temporarily blinded by a spray of gasoline from his broken fuel-pressure gauge. Another shell exploded in the radio compartment, leaving his radioman, ARM2c Durward E. Blakely, with a chunk of shrapnel in his right arm and a gash in his head. Wiese's wingmen, Lieutenants (jg) Wilfred McDowell and John Walker, dropped on *Yahagi*, one of their torpedoes exploding on her port quarter. Lieutenant Jesse Naul and Lieutenant (jg) Donald Barber of VT-82 also attacked the cruiser and claimed an additional torpedo hit.

Lieutenant (jg) Robert Mini, separated from Naul's division, lined up for a solo run on a destroyer. After he released his torpedo, he was gratified to hear a loud yell of "Bingo!" from his turret gunner, AMM3c William A. Raker. Mini turned around and saw the Japanese destroyer exploding violently amidships and beginning to sink. "This was the most spectacular bull's-eye of the day," reported the VT-82 action report. This target was possibly *Hamakaze*, hit early in the April 7 attacks. The destroyer was struck on the starboard side around 1247 and quickly jackknifed.[29]

Bennington's part in the airstrike against the *Yamato* group was complete, but divisions and sections from several other TF 58 carriers were already in their attack runs before Air Group 82 cleared the area.

TG 58.1 strike coordinator Ed Konrad enjoyed a grandstand view of the action as he circled two miles to the east of the Japanese force. As *Bennington's* air group was finishing its attack runs, he next directed in his own *Hornet* fighters. Throughout the assault, he maintained communication with his friend Harmon Utter, strike leader of the TG 58.3 group that was circling twenty miles to the west, waiting its turn.[30]

Lieutenant Commander Marsh Beebe's VF-17 Hellcats dropped through the cloud cover near a destroyer on the port side of the formation, making strafing runs down to one thousand feet. Climbing back to eighteen hundred feet, Beebe raked *Yahagi* with a two-second burst and pulled out astern of the formation "on the deck." His wingman, Bud Good, and his second section of Frank Sistrunk and Jack Davis strafed a destroyer on the starboard side of the formation and left it burning. Good was in awe of the massive shells fired from *Yamato's* 18-inch guns. "Think of a 50-gallon oil drum coming up at you," he said.[31]

Vice Admiral Marc Andrew Mitscher, seen on board his flagship *Lexington* (CV 16) in June 1944, received the nickname "Pete" during his U.S. Naval Academy days. Mitscher would command TF 58 in its raids against Japanese mainland kamikaze bases and during the Okinawa campaign of 1945. *80-G-236831, NARA*

"Murderers' Row"—U.S. Navy fleet carriers waiting at anchor in Ulithi Atoll in December 1944, shortly before the Okinawa campaign. Seen from foreground moving back are *Wasp* (CV 18), *Yorktown* (CV 10), *Hornet* (CV 12), *Hancock* (CV 19), and *Ticonderoga* (CV 14). Three of these five fleet carriers would suffer bomb or kamikaze damage during TF 58's participation in the Okinawa operation. *80-G-294131, NARA*

Senior U.S. Navy commanders met on board the cruiser *Indianapolis* (CA 35) in February 1945. *Left to right:* Admiral Raymond Spruance (Fifth Fleet commander), Vice Admiral Pete Mitscher (TF 58 commander), Admiral Chester Nimitz (commander in chief, Pacific Fleet), and Vice Admiral Willis A. Lee Jr. (commander, battleships, Pacific Fleet). *NH-49705, NARA*

Admiral Nimitz (*right*) visits with Admiral William F. "Bull" Halsey in 1945. Halsey would assume command of the Third Fleet late in the Okinawa campaign. *NH-58049, NARA*

Commodore Arleigh "31 Knot" Burke (*right*) was chief of staff for Vice Admiral Mitscher. Burke, a former destroyer-squadron commander, is seen with the Bald Eagle in May 1945 on the carrier *Randolph* (CV 15). *80-G-468931, NARA*

Two of Vice Admiral Mitscher's task group commanders are seen together on the carrier *Yorktown* in October 1943. Rear Admiral Arthur W. Radford (*right*) would command TG 58.4 from the carrier *Yorktown* at Okinawa. Rear Admiral Joseph J. "Jocko" Clark, captain of *Yorktown* at the time of this photo, would command TG 58.1 from *Hornet* at Okinawa. *80-G-205661, NARA*

Rear Admiral Frederick C. "Ted" Sherman, seen in November 1943, commanded TG 58.3 from his flagship *Essex* (CV 9). *80-G-44090, NARA*

Rear Admiral Ralph E. Davison commanded TG 58.2 from the carrier *Enterprise* (CV 6). *U.S. Navy*

Grumman F6F Hellcat fighters seen taking off from the carrier *Hornet* in 1945. *Charles Watts*

TF 58 warplanes attacking Japanese airfields and shipping targets at Kure on the island of Kyushu on March 18, 1945. *Record Group 38, Box 347, Carrier Air Group Nine, NARA*

Right: Japanese carriers under attack in Kure Harbor on March 19, 1945, with an *Essex* Helldiver seen in upper right. The carrier in the background is *Kaiyo*, and the light carrier in the foreground is probably *Katsuragi*. *NH-95778, NARA*

Left: Yorktown planes score a direct hit on a Japanese merchant ship at Kure. *Record Group 38, Box 347, Carrier Air Group Nine, NARA*

Vice Admiral Matome Ugaki, commander of the Japanese 5th Air Fleet, was responsible for unleashing ten Kikusui (kamikaze) operations at Okinawa. *Author's collection*

Lieutenant General Mitsuru Ushijima commanded the Japanese Thirty-Second Army and directed the defense of Okinawa ashore until committing suicide late in the campaign. *Author's collection*

Lieutenant General Simon Buckner, at right with camera, commanded Allied ground forces on Okinawa. Here he is seen with Major General Lemuel Shepherd, commander of the 6th Marine Division. *U.S. Marine Corps*

Famous Scripps-Howard newspaper war correspondent Ernie Pyle, seated in center with an army tank crew in 1944, would lose his life on Okinawa. *SC-191704, NARA*

General Buckner stated that Okinawa cliff battles would be won by the use of "corkscrew and blowtorch"—meaning explosives, Marine flamethrowers, and napalm—to extract Japanese defenders from their deep-seated island defenses. *U.S. Marine Corps*

Above: Japanese bomber crews stand by on a Kyushu airfield as a Mitsubishi "Betty" bomber is loaded with an Ohka piloted bomb beneath its fuselage. *NH-73100, NARA*

Above: Captured Japanese MXY7 Ohka suicide rocket-bomb (also called "Baka" by the Americans) being examined by Marines on Okinawa at Yontan Airfield. *208-MO-Box-113-Okinawa-2, NARA*

Above and left: A Mitsubishi G4M Navy Type 1 "Betty" attack bomber, with Baka bomb underneath, under attack and catching fire, as seen through a U.S. fighter pilot's gun camera. *80-G-185585, NARA*

Lieutenant Commander Marshall Beebe, commander of VF-17, with his division on board *Hornet* on February 14, 1945. *Left to right:* Lieutenant (jg) Chester Good, Lieutenant (jg) John Davis, Ensign Leonard Mallon, Lieutenant (jg) David Crist, Lieutenant (jg) Frank Sistrunk, and Marsh Beebe. *U.S. Navy photo via Tilman Pool*

Lieutenant (jg) Tilman "Tilly" Pool of VF-17 was credited with six kills off Okinawa. *Tilman Pool*

Lieutenant (jg) Willis "Bill" Hardy, seen wearing the skull-and-crossbones logo of his "Jolly Rogers" squadron, VF-17, became an "ace in a day" on April 6, 1945. *U.S. Navy*

Lieutenant (jg) Charles "Billy" Watts of VF-17 made 6.5 kills during the campaign. *Charles Watts*

Lieutenant (jg) John "Ted" Crosby became one of VF-17's five "ace in a day" pilots on April 16, 1945. *U.S. Navy*

Ensign Ardon R. Ives of VBF-9 escapes his burning Hellcat on the deck of *Lexington* after hitting the landing barrier on February 25, 1945. *80-G-268191, NARA*

The carrier *Franklin* (CV 13) became an inferno after two Japanese bombs landed among armed strike planes on her flight deck on March 19, 1945. Although she was saved, 724 men were killed and 265 were wounded. *Right: Franklin* sailors scramble to escape falling debris from a bomb explosion. *U.S. Navy*

The VT-82 Avenger of Ensign Robert King en route back to *Bennington* (CV 20) after his crewmen had bailed out near Chichi Jima on February 18, 1945. King's two crewmen were captured by the Japanese and later executed by their cannibalistic captors. *U.S. Navy, NARA*

Left: Ensign Alfred Lerch of VF-10 achieved seven kills in a mission on April 16, 1945. *U.S. Navy*

Right: Ensign Don McPherson of *Essex*'s VF-83 scored three kills on May 4, 1945, defending picket-station destroyers from kamikazes. *Don McPherson*

Above: Second Lieutenant Dean Caswell of VMF-221 squadron, flying Corsairs from *Bunker Hill* (CV 17), was the top-scoring Marine carrier pilot of World War II. *Dean Caswell*

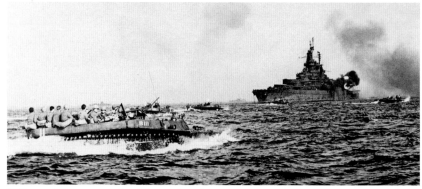

LVT-4 amphibious tractors head for Purple and Orange Beaches as part of the Love Day landings on Okinawa, April 1, 1945, as the battleship *Tennessee* (BB 43) fires her 5-inch secondary batteries at an objective area. *80-G-309930, NARA*

In one of the more dramatic Okinawa campaign photos, a Zeke/Zero kamikaze is about to crash into the battleship *Missouri* (BB 63) on April 11, 1945, as her gun crews fire away. This image was captured by ship's baker Harold "Buster" Campbell, a volunteer photographer. *U.S. Navy*

"Death Rattlers" Corsairs of Major George Axtell's VMF-323 making a rocket strike against Japanese positions south of the front lines on Okinawa. *127-GW-524-12851, NARA*

Above: The cruiser *Yahagi*, part of the Operation Ten-Go fleet with the battleship *Yamato*, is seen under attack by TF 58 carrier planes on April 6, 1945, with near misses straddling her and a bomb exploding on her fantail. *80-G-316084, NARA*

Left: Ensign Jack Lyons of VF-86 received the Silver Star for his tracking and reporting of the *Yamato* fleet's position. *Jack Lyons*

Right: Hornet CAG 17 Ed Konrad led the first strike wave against the *Yamato* fleet. *U.S. Navy*

Below: The world's largest battleship, *Yamato*, seen smoking from a bomb hit and maneuvering frantically as another bomb explodes close to port. *L42-09.06.05, NARA*

In a photograph taken by an *Intrepid* (CV 11) strike plane, the cruiser *Yahagi* sinks at 1405 after numerous bomb and torpedo hits. *NH-62575, NARA*

Above: Lieutenant Commander Will Rawie, VBF-10 skipper, was strike coordinator for the third assault wave of TG 58.4 air groups on the *Yamato* fleet. *U.S. Navy*

Above: Lieutenant (jg) Grant "Jack" Young of *Intrepid*'s VT-10 received the Navy Cross for his successful solo torpedo attack on *Yamato*. *U.S. Navy*

Yamato explodes in a mighty fireball at 1432 as her Number One magazine detonates. Ninety percent of her crew perished as a result of the relentless air strikes by TF 58 warplanes on April 6, 1945. *U.S. Navy*

Japanese student volunteers waving cherry boughs to send off kamikaze strikers from Chiran Airfield, April 12, 1945. Second Lieutenant Toshio Anazawa's Nakajima Ki-43 Army Type 1 "Oscar" fighter is carrying a 550-pound bomb. *Author's collection*

Japanese kamikazes prepare for battle as a comrade tightens the symbolic white *hachimaki* around one pilot's head. *NH-73096, NARA*

Above: Vice Admiral Mitscher's flagship carrier *Bunker Hill* burning after kamikaze hits on May 11, 1945. Sailors scramble to fight the fires that turned their ship into an inferno that claimed 390 lives and left another 264 men wounded. *80-G-323712, NARA*

Below: Many were forced to leap overboard to escape the smoke and flames. *80-G-274261, NARA*

"Hell's Bells" Corsairs of VMF-311 are brilliantly outlined by tracer fire during a night attack on Okinawa's Yontan Airfield. *127-GR-118775, NARA*

Left: Lieutenant (jg) Shunsuke Tomiyasu flips his bomb-laden Zeke on its back seconds before slamming into Pete Mitscher's flagship carrier *Enterprise* on May 14, 1945. *U.S. Navy*

Below: The explosion of Tomiyasu's bomb hurled Big E's forward elevator hundreds of feet into the sky and forced Vice Admiral Mitscher to abandon his second flagship in four days. *U.S. Navy*

Corporal Jim White, G Company, 29th Marines, 6th Marine Division. *James White*

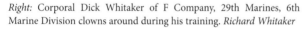

A view from the top of Sugar Loaf Hill, scene of the Okinawa campaign's bloodiest fighting ashore, after its capture on May 23, 1945. Japanese mortar shells burst in background. *127-GW-518-122265, NARA*

Right: Corporal Dick Whitaker of F Company, 29th Marines, 6th Marine Division clowns around during his training. *Richard Whitaker*

Above, left to right: Corporals Ray Courtney, Ed Copeland, Mel Heckt, and Don Exinger were the only four machine gunners not killed or wounded on Okinawa from B Company, 4th Marines, 6th Marine Division. *Melvin Heckt photo via Barb Kenutis*

Right: The image of Heckt shows Marines enjoying a rare moment in the trenches while not under Japanese assault. *Melvin Heckt photo via Barb Kenutis*

Down by the stern, the battered destroyer *Laffey* (DD 724) is seen after surviving damage from six kamikazes and four bombs that killed thirty-two and wounded seventy-one men on April 16, 1945. *NH-78233, NARA*

Aaron Ward (DM 34) remained afloat after sustaining six kamikaze hits on May 3, 1945, that killed forty-five men and wounded another forty-nine. *80-G-330113, NARA*

Above: Vice Admiral Mitscher (*left*) seen meeting with his relief, Vice Admiral John "Slew" McCain, on the carrier *Shangri-La* (CV 38) on May 27, 1945. *U.S. Navy*

Right: A Marine F4U Corsair fires rockets into enemy positions on the crest of a mountain at Okinawa in June 1945. *127-GW-520-126420, NARA*

Gene Valencia's VF-9 "Flying Circus" division was the Navy's top-scoring fighter division, with fifty combined kills. *Left to right:* Lieutenant Valencia (twenty-three kills), Lieutenant (jg) Harris Mitchell (ten kills), Lieutenant (jg) Clint Smith (six kills), and Lieutenant (jg) Jim French (eleven kills). Valencia's division served on both *Lexington* and *Yorktown* during the Okinawa campaign. *U.S. Navy*

Dick Whitaker and Tom McCarthy (*right*) of F Company, 29th Marines, 6th Marine Division, hold a captured Japanese flag in May 1945. Fellow graduates of New York's Saugerties High School, both Marines were wounded in action on Okinawa. *Richard Whitaker*

Above: Vice Admiral Ugaki, unwilling to surrender, led Japan's final kamikaze flight at 1630 on August 15, 1945. He is posing in a dark green uniform before his plane, a Yokosuka D4Y Navy Type 2 Suisei ("Judy") dive bomber, on Oita Airfield. *Right:* Ugaki seated in the Judy's rear seat as his pilot prepares to taxi away on their final flight. *Imperial Japanese Navy*

Lieutenant Willis Parker's fourth VF-17 division, carrying 500-pound bombs, made a bombing run on a new type destroyer, probably *Hamakaze*, and two of his wingmen claimed hits. The targeted destroyer was soon seen to explode, although a torpedo was believed to have caused the final explosion of *Hamakaze*.

The third VF-17 division, under Lieutenant (jg) Harris, strafed a destroyer on the starboard side of the formation. Tilly Pool, Harris' second-section leader, made a glide-bombing run on *Yahagi*, watching it through his guide until it disappeared below his F6F's cowling. He counted to three and released his 1,000-pounder toward the Japanese cruiser. "I broke away to see [the result], but the cruiser had done a hard left turn as I released. My bomb hit just off his stern, and I heard later in the reports that this cruiser suffered rudder damage from an early near miss." Pool later felt consolation that his miss may well have contributed to the demise of *Yahagi*.

The *Hornet* fighters also fired rockets at the ships, which appeared to result in good hits to them. But after the battle, the destroyer *Fuyutsuki* reported being struck several times by what proved to be dud rockets. Commander Konrad's division escorted the two photo-reconnaissance planes recording the action and stayed behind to coordinate the remainder of the airstrike as the other *Hornet* planes rendezvoused and returned to base.[32]

Battleship *Yamato* under attack on April 7, 1945, as photographed from a *Hornet* plane. *80-G-320642, NARA*

Eight Avengers of VT-17 from *Hornet* moved in against the port side of *Yamato* around 1240, following the *Bennington* dive bombers. Lieutenant Thomas C. Durkin's pilots claimed four torpedo hits, although these were likely double counted. The "tail-end Charlie" TBM, piloted by Ensign Lee O'Brien, suffered a direct hit that destroyed its engine, causing the plane to crash just off the bow of *Yamato*. O'Brien and his two crewmen—AMM3c Jacob Elijah Ricketson and ARM3c James Lorelle Opheim—perished in the high-speed crash.

Lieutenant Henry E. Clark's division of Torpedo Seventeen attacked one of the screening destroyers and claimed one hit. It is possible that Clark's Avengers hit the luckless *Hamakaze*, although the demise of this destroyer was primarily credited to *Bennington's* torpedo unit.

Yamato's worries of more torpedoes were through for the moment, as only *Bennington* and *Hornet* Avengers from the TG 58.1 strike group were carrying war fish. But *Hornet's* Helldivers made their plunges on the battleship on the heels of the *Bennington* SB2Cs, and they were not to be taken lightly. Four of Lieutenant Commander Robert Ware's VB-17 bombers were badly damaged by antiaircraft fire during their attacks. Ware's left foot was ripped by shrapnel during his dive, but he claimed two bomb hits, one aft of the smokestack and one on the battlewagon's superstructure. Lieutenant Clifford G. Van Stone claimed one hit on *Yamato's* bow, while Lieutenant (jg) Jesse M. Bristow claimed another aft of her stack.

The other *Hornet* Helldivers attacked various destroyers and *Yahagi*, claiming hits on three destroyers and the cruiser. One of Ware's battle-damaged Helldivers was forced to make a water landing near TF 58, while two other SB2Cs were so badly wrecked that they would be jettisoned upon return to *Hornet*.

Lieutenant Commander Douglas A. Clark, VF-30 skipper and strike leader of *Belleau Wood's* fourteen-plane group, had circled the area while the *Bennington* and *Hornet* planes made the first assaults on the *Yamato* group. Around 1245 Clark led his divisions down against the screening warships.

The eight VF-30 planes made rocket and bombing attacks on a "light cruiser" to the starboard of the formation. Ensign Michele Mazzocco, a hero of the previous day's turkey shoot, had never seen such massive main guns as those carried by *Yamato*— it was "like looking into a volcano." Mazzocco made his run, released his bomb, and felt sure he had scored a hit, although there was no way to properly assess. Fighting Thirty's target was most likely the destroyer *Fuyutsuki*. Ensign William R. McAllister narrowly missed with his 1,000-pounder, as did three other F6Fs carrying bombs, but McAllister watched two of his rockets slam into the destroyer's stern. *Fuyutsuki* would later report being hit by two dud rockets during this early strike.[33]

Lieutenant Robert F. Regan wasted no time with his six torpedo bombers, each loaded with four 500-pound bombs. A veteran of thirty-two prior missions with VT-38—all land-based sorties during the Bougainville and northern Solomons campaign of 1944—Regan had only joined *Belleau Wood*'s air group in early March 1945 at Ulithi. Two weeks later, on the eighteenth, the squadron's skipper, Lieutenant Frederick Tothill, had been killed during an airfield attack on Japan. Elevated to acting commander of VT-30, Regan had led a strike against Japanese warships in Kure Harbor the following day.[34]

Now three weeks later, Regan had his sights set on the biggest prize of the IJN. He led VT-30 into a cloud bank, intending to accompany *Bennington*'s dive bombers in their attack on *Yamato*, but when the Avengers emerged from the clouds, half of the *Bennington* dive bombers had vanished, and Regan's second division had become separated. The lieutenant dived on a destroyer instead. An antiaircraft shell exploded in his Avenger's bomb bay and belly, tearing a foot-square hole in the fuselage at the base of the bomb-bay window. His radioman, ARM3c Clarence A. Conner, narrowly cheated serious injury due to the fact that he was crouching over a camera at the tunnel-gun port. Shrapnel shredded radio gear and only missed ripping Conner thanks to a spare life-raft assembly.

Lieutenant Ernie Delaney, second in command of Torpedo Thirty, wished he was celebrating his second wedding anniversary back home with his wife in Detroit. Having lost sight of Regan's first division and his own wingmen during the run in toward *Yamato*, Delaney opted to make a solo bombing run against the cruiser *Yahagi*. He again entered a cloud bank, preparing his crew for their attack, but when he emerged from the cumulus, he found that he had overshot *Yahagi* and was looking down at *Yamato* instead. He proceeded with his run, toggling his bomb load at 1,600 feet and also jerking the emergency release.

"I was at 500 feet, indicating 250 knots, and was still heading for the water when we were hit," said Delaney. The shell ripped through his closed bomb-bay doors and starboard wing stub, creating a fire that filled his cockpit with smoke almost instantly. He ripped the hatch open, burning his arm in the process, and leveled his TBM out at 1,000 feet. Delaney ordered his crewmen—AMM2c William Tilley and ARM3c Edward Jackson Mawhinney—to jump, waiting only long enough for them to strap on their parachutes and leap free. "By then, the smoke in the cockpit was choking me pretty badly and I couldn't see a thing," he said. "The seat was too hot to sit on much longer, and I knew I had to get out of there." Delaney climbed onto his left wing, pulled his ripcord with his right hand, and dived off the edge of his wing to miss the tail surfaces. As his chute opened, he saw Mawhinney's parachute a little below him, close enough that he could see his radioman's face.[35]

Once Delaney hit the water, he lost track of his crewmen. Tilley, a jovial senior member among VT-30's enlisted men, was remembered by a fellow airman as being unphased by his potential fate in combat. When asked about his chances for survival, Tilley would often quip, "A man can die but once. We owe God a death, and let it go which way it will."[36]

Delaney inflated his Mae West and then his life raft but opted to stay in the water alongside it, for fear the Japanese sailors would see him. He looked at his wristwatch and noted the time to be 1300. Five weeks prior he had flown wing on Jake Reisert when his TBM was crippled, helping escort him to a lifeguard submarine. Now, however, Delaney was on his own in the ocean near the Japanese fleet. For the moment he was thankful that the enemy warships were preoccupied with the final TG 58.1 warplanes finishing their attacks.

TG 58.1's strike group had shot three-quarters of its bolt within ten minutes against *Yamato*, *Yahagi*, and many of the destroyers. Accurately assessing all of the reported versus actual damage caused by the three task groups of TF 58 would later prove to be nearly impossible. To confound the situation, at least one squadron from *Bunker Hill* became overzealous and ended up attacking the Japanese fleet not only before the rest of its TG 58.3 planes but also before *San Jacinto*'s group of TF 58.1 had even finished.

Bunker Hill's VB-84, carrying mainly 1,000-pound bombs, was led by its skipper, Lieutenant Commander John P. Conn. After endless circling of the enemy fleet, Conn decided to attack a lone destroyer due to his dwindling fuel situation. The ship they attacked at 1245 was miles from the scene of the battleship, leaving only *Asashimo* (meaning "Morning Frost" in Japanese) as the probable target. At least one VF-84 pilot—Lieutenant (jg) James C. Dixon from Parsons, Kansas—joined the VB-84 group in assailing *Asashimo*. Dixon's bomb was seen to score a direct hit, and Conn's Helldiver pilots claimed another three direct hits.[37]

San Jacinto's air group, last of the TG 58.1 strikers to commence runs, largely took on *Asashimo* at the same time *Bunker Hill*'s eager dive bombers were working her over. Lieutenant Charles Knokey's seven F6Fs released their half-ton bombs around two thousand feet and achieved only near misses. Knokey and his two wingmen returned to strafe the decks of *Asashimo*, which was last seen by the *Bunker Hill* and *San Jacinto* strikers to be slowing down, belching white smoke from her forward stack.

Lieutenant John Piegari led *San Jacinto*'s torpedo planes in on the heels of the dive bombers and fighters. A survivor of the sinking of *Liscome Bay*, Piegari had been awarded the Navy and Marine Corps Medal for helping save the life of a fighter pilot who was still recovering from an appendectomy seven days prior to that attack on the escort carrier. Piegari's VT-45 pilots now were right on the money in their attack runs, and he believed that two torpedoes struck the damaged destroyer. Squadronmates were certain that Lieutenant (jg) John L. Mason launched the torpedo that hit *Asashimo* squarely amidships around 1305. Lieutenant (jg) William B. Kornegay and two other VB-84 pilots observed a terrific explosion aft of Turret No. 3. Within three minutes *Asashimo*'s bow plunged under the waves, her stern reared out of the water momentarily, and then she slid smoothly down to the depths. She was gone within minutes, taking down Captain Hisao Kotaki, commander of Destroyer Division 21, and all hands with her.[38]

TF 58.1's strikers moved clear, with the exception of *Hornet* coordinator Ed Konrad and his wingmen. The *Hornet, Belleau Wood, Bennington,* and *San Jacinto* aviators claimed some ten torpedo hits, at least nineteen bomb hits, as well as rocket and strafing damage. Added to their tally were VB-84's three bomb hits claimed while jumping into the fight early with TG 58.1. More hits were claimed than were actually made, but there was no doubt the first-wave strikers had inflicted serious damage on the *Yamato* fleet.

Captain Hara called for full power as the first American carrier planes attacked. His 7,590-ton light cruiser surged ahead of *Yamato* in a valiant effort to draw some of the American planes to attack it. Hara, who had taken command of *Yahagi* in December 1944, stood on his bridge with an old friend, Rear Admiral Keizo Komura, commander of the Japanese Destroyer Squadron 2. The endless trail of U.S. warplanes descending on his cruiser would shake many an officer's spirits, but Hara was "determined now to fight to the last."[39]

The captain put his cruiser hard to starboard as a quartet of bombers landed near misses that soaked *Yahagi*'s upper decks with ocean water. Hellcats moved in next, raking the warship with bullets that exploded one of *Yahagi's* floatplanes as it lay strapped to its catapult. Hara later wrote that the "thud of machine gun bullets beat like hail through the length of the ship."[40]

Lieutenant (jg) Takekuni Ikeda stood on the bridge in his role as target-designating officer, reporting exact bearings and ranges of enemy aircraft to *Yahagi's* gunnery officer and to her navigator, Commander Ryoichi Kawazoe. Bullets felled one young sailor near Ikeda, while another orderly, experiencing his first combat, crumpled to the deck in fear but physically unharmed. "My earplugs were blown out, and my eardrums were damaged," recalled Ikeda.[41]

Hara dodged bombs from the first four groups of warplanes, but *Yahagi* was soon bracketed by torpedo bombers from both sides. One torpedo caught his cruiser amidships, knocking out her engines, wiping out the entire engine-room gang, and killing all electrical power, leaving *Yahagi* nearly helpless against the other incoming planes. By 1246, just twelve minutes into the American attack, *Yahagi* had taken two torpedoes. "It was inconceivable that a speeding warship of her size could be brought so suddenly dead in the water," Hara wrote.[42]

In the meantime *Yamato* was absorbing her fair share of punishment from the initial American assault group. The great ship opened fire at 1234 with her two forward main turrets and antiaircraft guns. A minute later her skipper ceased zigzagging and increased speed to twenty-four knots as her arsenal of weapons opened up. Her nine 18-inch guns fired Sanshikidan beehive shells, adding to the flak produced by two dozen 127-mm antiaircraft guns and 152 smaller 25-mm antiaircraft guns as American warplanes dived in.

At 1240 the first *Bennington* Helldivers landed at least two 1,000-pound semi-armor-piercing bombs. One wiped out two 25-mm mounts and exploded two decks below, killing every member of the after port damage-control team. Another bomb knocked out *Yamato's* air-search radar, creating more casualties. There was no respite in the action, as *Bennington* and *Hornet* Helldivers came in from the port side. The battleship was still moving at flank speed when two 1,000-pound bombs struck. The first exploded in the crew's quarters abaft the Type 13 Radar shack, while the second semi-armor-piercing bomb penetrated the port side of the aft command station, exploding between the 155-mm gun magazine and main-gun Turret No. 3's upper powder magazine. The force ripped a sixty-foot hole in the weather deck and created a raging fire.[43]

Ensign Mitsuru Yoshida was standing watch on the bridge as the first Helldivers came in. His whole body tingling with excitement, he gritted his teeth and broke into a grin as *Yamato's* antiaircraft guns began pounding away. Moments later his smile was gone as F6F bullets ripped through nearby shipmates, adding the peculiar smell of blood to the heavy odor of gunpowder choking the air. Yoshida flung himself to the deck several times to avoid incoming fire from F6Fs. A nearby gun crew cheered as their tracers knocked down one of the *Bennington* Helldivers, which crashed and exploded off the battleship's port bow.[44]

At 1243 a division of five low-flying VT-17 Avengers commenced torpedo runs from *Yamato's* port side. The battleship, now making twenty-seven knots, heeled to starboard in evasive action, but one of the war fish slammed into her port side near the forward windlass room. One of the Avengers was shot down by *Yamato's* crew, but the TBM pilots had scored at least one hit. *Yamato's* escorts suffered as well during the first assault wave. *Hamakaze* took a near miss at 1247 off her starboard quarter that disabled her starboard shaft. Two minutes later at least one torpedo struck the destroyer aft of amidships on her starboard side, causing the ship to jackknife and plunge to the bottom. *Fuyutsuki* was slammed by dud rockets, while *Suzutsuki* took a 500-pound-bomb hit to starboard abreast her Number Two gun mount.[45]

After *Yamato's* first bomb hits, Ensign Yoshida raced from the bridge to the aft radar compartment, one of his normal posts. He found there "instruments scattered in all directions," unrecognizable debris cluttered with charred hunks of human flesh that felt "like the bark of a rough tree." Seeing no one left alive in the radar compartment, Yoshida dashed back toward the bridge before the second American assault commenced.[46]

By 1250 the first attack wave was retiring. They had sunk one destroyer, damaged others, left *Yahagi* dead in the water, and had hit *Yamato* with bombs and at least one torpedo. The battleship maintained flank speed, using the precious respite from combat to shore up damage and haul casualties to aid stations. But the break would be short, for within twelve minutes the second American assault began.

Dave Berry was no stranger to attacking Japanese shipping. The brash Kentuckian had participated in the first carrier battles in 1942, Coral Sea and Midway, where he earned three Navy Crosses as a dive-bomber pilot. The lieutenant commander's VB-83 had most recently participated in the March 19 strikes on enemy shipping in Kure Harbor, where he had earned a Distinguished Flying Cross. He and his men now had their sights on the world's largest warship prize, the battleship *Yamato*.

Lieutenant Commander David Render Berry, skipper of *Essex*'s VB-83. Berry earned three Navy Crosses during 1942 and two Distinguished Flying Crosses in 1945 for leading his Helldivers in attacks against Japanese shipping, including the *Yamato* fleet. Berry was killed in action during the Okinawa campaign. *U.S. Navy*

The former Dauntless pilot now headed his own Helldiver unit, based on the carrier *Essex*. A dozen of his SB2Cs had launched from TG 58.1 that day, flying in company with eight F6Fs of VF-83, five Corsairs of VBF-83, another two photo-reconnaissance Hellcats, and fifteen TBMs of VT-83. The *Essex* air group was led by its CAG, thirty-five-year-old Ohio native Commander Harmon Tischer Utter, who was appointed TG 58.3 strike coordinator.

Berry's VB-83 was flying at six thousand feet toward the Japanese fleet when Chief Joe Eardley called up from the rear seat. He had picked up the *Yamato* fleet at thirty miles. His continued position reporting helped Berry coach CAG 83 Utter in to the fleet. En route to the target, *Hancock*'s strike group had gotten off course after making a late takeoff; they would miss the *Yamato* fleet entirely.[47]

The *Essex* planes, in company with the strike groups from *Bataan*, *Bunker Hill*, and *Cabot*, arrived on the scene while TG 58.1 was still attacking. The collective formation began circling at a safe distance to avoid cluttering the target area, although overeager VB-84 pilots from *Bunker Hill* had already mixed in with the first strike wave's attacks. The first strike group cleared the area by 1250, but Commander Utter held his warplanes in check for another ten minutes as they cued up.

Ed Konrad, the TG 58.1 strike coordinator, handed control over to Utter but remained on the scene for a while to watch the next group go in. By this point the cruiser *Yahagi* was practically dead in the water, listing to port, and burning heavily as she fell astern of the main formation, with only the destroyer *Isokaze* to assist her. The wounded *Yamato* was still surging ahead at full speed, with destroyers chasing about her flanks like sheep dogs. Utter passed orders for the execution of TG 58.3's assault: all torpedo bombers and dive bombers were to attack the *Yamato*, while the fighter pilots were to bomb, strafe, and rocket the destroyers.

Utter called for his own *Essex* dive bombers to move in first on *Yamato*, followed by the *Bunker Hill* warplanes. Berry's VB-83 was preceded by the five Corsairs of VBF-83, each carrying a 1,000-pound bomb, in order to draw some of the battlewagon's antiaircraft fire away from the dive bombers. Lieutenant (jg) George A. Gibbs Jr. scored a hit on *Yamato*, while other VBF-83 pilots attacked nearby destroyers.

While the F4Us drew fire and created their own damage, Berry's Helldivers moved in over *Yamato* at sixty-two hundred feet. Going into their attack dives, Berry's wingman, Lieutenant (jg) Shelby W. Mitchell, was credited with making a direct hit near *Yamato*'s bridge tower. Ensign Thomas D. Samaras landed another direct hit near Turret No. 1, Ensign William H. Wellen planted his ordnance slightly forward of the tower, and Lieutenant (jg) Robert R. Goodrich was credited with a hit forward, also near Turret No. 1.

Lieutenant (jg) Kermit Quentin "Kirby" Ellis was making his glide approach when a shell ripped through his left wing tank. "White-hot flames occurred immediately, which burned a three-foot hole in the wing," said his gunner, ARM3c Frank Edward Guptill. Ellis completed his drop before calling back to his rear-seatman, "Gup, we're on fire."[48]

The fire burned out, but Ellis struggled with a rough engine as he cleared the *Yamato* force. Lieutenant (jg) Sheldon Olney joined up on his SB2C and flew wing until Ellis announced that he was ditching due to another fire that was making the cockpit untenable. The landing broke his SB2C in half and pitched gunner Guptill clear of the wreckage. He regained consciousness underwater, fighting his way to the surface, where Lieutenant Ellis assisted him into a life raft that Olney's rear gunner had tossed down and Ellis had already inflated.

When last seen by VB-83, *Yamato* was smoking but still under way. Lieutenant Thad Coleman's VF-83 division became separated from the strike group in bad weather, so they joined six SB2C's attacking *Yahagi*. The skipper and another of his pilots suffered antiaircraft damage to their planes, but Coleman's bomb was reported to hit amidships on the cruiser's starboard side.

Lieutenant Commander Harry White, the skipper of VT-83, led his planes on *Yamato*, approaching with divisions on each side of her bow. The majority of his pilots claimed direct hits on the now-struggling battleship. Ensign William E. Barrett's torpedo missed her stern but was seen by Grant Harris of VBF-83 to go straight into the stern of a nearby destroyer, which exploded and sank. VT-83 triumphantly claimed eleven torpedo hits from fifteen drops, including sinking one destroyer, although their claims were certainly exaggerated in the heat of the action.

CAG 83 Utter, circling the scene as strike coordinator, was thoroughly impressed with the valor displayed by his aviators, some seen to clear the warships' superstructures by mere inches. "The Japanese ships squirmed like a nest of snakes," he recorded.[49]

Utter continued flying lazy circles with his three VBF-83 wingman—Ed Pappert, Glen Wallace, and Vern Coumbe. "We had a ring-side seat for the whole show," recalled Wallace. "The *Yamato* tried to hit us with those big 18-inch guns. We could look right down the barrels, and when they fired, it looked like red-hot molten metal coming out of the muzzles." Following Air Group 83's runs, Utter next ordered the nine *Bataan* Avengers to attack without delay to help finish the fight.[50]

Lieutenant Commander Harold Mazza, the VT-47 skipper and former quarterback of the University of San Francisco's varsity football team for the 1932 and 1933 seasons, was a veteran of the Coral Sea, where his torpedo planes had helped finish off the light carrier *Shoho*. He had also earned a Navy Cross for putting a torpedo into *Yokohama Maru* off Lae in an early 1942 raid. Mazza's TBMs now approached *Yamato* three hundred feet above the waves and began releasing their war fish at fifteen hundred yards. During his retirement from the scene, Mazza and his gunner, Lieutenant (jg) Joseph N. Ambrogi (a radar officer flying with him), saw two torpedo hits to starboard.

Lieutenant William T. Williams led in VT-47's second division. Ensign Joseph Schmidt dropped at one thousand yards and then flew directly down the length of *Yamato*, so close he could see the antiaircraft mounts tracking him as they fired ordnance that looked like "purple popcorn balls." Schmidt's gunner, ARM3c William S. Armstrong, fired back and watched some of his tracers bounce off the heavily armored battleship. The second-division pilots believed that two or three of their torpedoes hit *Yamato*'s starboard side.[51]

While clearing the battleship, Lieutenant William N. Collins' Avenger was hit by two 25-mm explosive shells. One exploded in his bomb bay, breaking out his canopy glass and cutting the back of his neck. The other shell passed through his right wing. His hydraulic system was punctured, and Collins was unable to close the doors. Upon returning to *Bataan*, only his left gear would lower, forcing him to make a skillful one-wheel landing. His TBM was jettisoned after he and his gunner crawled free of the wreckage.

During VT-47's attack runs, *Bataan*'s VF-47 Hellcats had dropped their pairs of 500-pound general-purpose bombs on *Yamato* and three escorts. Lieutenant John W. Wright Jr.'s division claimed one direct hit on a destroyer just off the battleship's starboard bow, likely *Suzutsuki*. Lieutenant Raymond L. Podsednik's VF-47 division attacked a bomb-damaged destroyer on *Yamato*'s starboard quarter, likely *Kasumi*. Podsednik and Lieutenant (jg) Walter Trigg were credited with hits. Trigg's Hellcat sustained damage from an antiaircraft shell that would force him to ditch near a task-force destroyer upon his return to *Bataan*. Three other VF-47 Hellcats were badly shot up in their attacks, but Ensign Richard Stephansky was credited with a solid hit on the starboard side amidships of one of the destroyers.

As *Bataan*'s air group hauled clear of the Japanese warships, the time was approximately 1309—just ten minutes after the assault by TG 58.3 had commenced.

Strike coordinator Utter next ordered in *Bunker Hill*'s VT-84. Lieutenant Commander Chandler Swanson knew exactly what his squadron would be doing. During his briefing in the ready room that morning, he had stressed the fact that Torpedo Eighty-Four would attack *Yamato*. Only in the case of absolute necessity was any of his pilots to attack any other ship.

Swanson's squadron had circled with the rest of the *Bunker Hill* group until 1250, when Commander Utter ordered his task group to prepare for attack. The TBMs eased down from five thousand feet and spotted *Yamato* five miles away. A veteran torpedo pilot from the 1942 Coral Sea battle, Swanson wisely intended to catch the battleship simultaneously from two directions. "Puffs of purple, red, yellow, and green flak blanketed the sky," Swanson described later. "It would have been beautiful if you didn't know it was so deadly."[52]

Six of the Avengers were struck during their approach. Lieutenant Bernard F. "Buck" Berry received a 40-mm burst in his port wing about three feet from the tip, "which almost flipped me on my back." The TBMs of Ensign Clint "Mouse" Webster and Lieutenant Phil Wainwright were also hit by shells, but they continued their runs. Lieutenant (jg) Al Turnbull was just preparing to pickle his torpedo when he felt an explosion to his right and saw a ball of fire where his buddy Dick Walsh had been flying. Apprehensive that he would not survive this attack, Walsh indeed perished when his TBM was hit in the belly before he could drop. His Avenger slammed into the ocean, exploding on impact, killing Walsh and his crew-men, ARM2c Glen E. Heath Jr. and AMM2c Clayton Vencil Whiteman.[53]

Swanson's first division moved in on *Yamato*'s starboard side, taking heavy fire. His wingman, Ensign Francis Melvin Guttenberg, was just releasing his torpedo when a 20-mm round burst in the fuselage just aft of his turret. Shrapnel ripped through the Avenger, tearing into ARM3c Thomas F. Kelly's right arm, back, and right shoulder. The turret gunner, ARM3c Edward D. Duffy, was knocked unconscious and lay near a wide opening where their hatch door had disintegrated. Burning oil from a severed hydraulic line seared Kelly's good left arm as he held Duffy from sliding out the opening until the gunner regained his senses.[54]

During this time, the battleship accentuated its turn to starboard, and the torpedo planes began dropping at an average range of 1,570 yards. Swanson's first division claimed at least two hits on *Yamato*'s starboard side, while Buck Berry's port-side Avengers were equally effective. Al Turnbull, flying wing on Phil Wainwright in the fifth and final section of VT-84, flew directly over the battleship so low that his radioman, George Gelderman, could see sailors running across the deck. Jack Weincek, firing the .30-caliber stinger gun in Turnbull's tail, blasted away at the battleship and then a Japanese destroyer that filled his rearward vision during his pilot's retreat.[55]

The other Avenger crews strafed the destroyer screen during their exodus through the hail of antiaircraft fire. Lieutenant Judson Davis noted, "On the way in, I was working for the Navy, and on the way out, I was working for myself and my crew." Mouse Webster's TBM was hit in the starboard wing root, but he would return to *Bunker Hill*, though with only seven gallons of gas remaining. Lieutenant (jg) Dewey F. Ray made the entire flight and attack with his landing gear jammed in the down position but managed to land his shot-up Avenger on the carrier with only fifteen gallons of gas remaining.[56]

Chan Swanson's torpedo squadron claimed as many as nine hits, although only two were certain. Lieutenant Commander Roger Hedrick's VF-84 Corsairs, each toting a 500-pound bomb and eight HVARs, made their runs on *Yamato* in concert with *Bunker Hill*'s TBMs. As they dropped from the clouds, Lieutenant (jg) Andrew S. Bearwa's F4U was hit and suddenly went into a steep dive, killing him instantly when he slammed into the sea. In conservative fashion, as compared to other squadrons that attacked *Yamato* this day, Hedrick only claimed one certain 500-pound bomb hit for VF-84.

At 1312 Harmon Utter sent in his final planes, those from *Cabot*, which were making their fifth strike against Japanese warships. Lieutenant John W. Adams Jr.'s ten VF-29 Hellcats, each toting a 1,000-pound bomb, singled out a lone destroyer six miles away from the main warship cluster and landed one bomb directly amidships. The sections of Lieutenants Alfred J. Fecke and Max G. Barnes bracketed the isolated destroyer *Isokaze* with a pair of near misses. Adams led his *Cabot* fighters back toward their ship intact, with Ensign Gene Broome managing to shoot down a snooping Judy en route, some sixty miles from their task group.[57]

Lieutenant Jack Anderson's VT-29 division was credited with scoring two torpedo hits on *Yamato*'s starboard side. Lieutenant (jg) Howard H. Skidmore's second division of VT-29 attacked the battleship about five minutes after Anderson's division cleared. The "tail-end Charlie" of Skidmore's division was Lieutenant (jg) John P. Speidel, who had been worried about making this strike, as his wife was due to give birth that week. His crewmen watched Speidel's torpedo during its entire course and witnessed the explosion as it hit near the bridge structure. Speidel would return to *Cabot* to receive the welcome news that his wife had given birth to a baby boy.[58]

Cabot's planes thus closed out the efforts of the second assault wave from TG 58.3. Claims for bomb and torpedo hits again surpassed what was actually suffered by the Japanese ships, but the air groups had nailed *Yamato* with as many as another five torpedo hits. Strike coordinator Utter, now low on fuel, radioed his three Corsair wingmen that they should go in and get a hit on the battleship before they departed. "Since we were the only targets in sight, every ship opened up on us, even those on their sides," recalled Glen Wallace. "It was a solid curtain of gunfire and almost certain curtains for us."[59]

Commander Utter quickly gave up the idea, ordering his VBF-83 wingmen to do a 180 and dump their 1,000-pound bombs into the sea. "Let's get the hell out of here!" he called.

"We weren't going to argue with him," recalled Ed Pappert.[60]

In his action report, Utter was quick to hand out credit to all carrier air groups. "No air group or task group can claim a major part or all of the credit," he wrote. "Each pilot who dropped a bomb or torpedo deserves a portion of the credit."[61]

Downed *Belleau Wood* Avenger pilot Ernie Delaney had a front-row seat during the second American strike on the *Yamato* force. He was still in the water, clinging to the side of his life raft, as he watched the show from about five miles away. "I could see quite heavy smoke coming from the battleship after these attacks," he said. "A great deal of underwater turbulence could be felt where I was." His position was even more obvious from the air than his bright raft due to dye-marker packets dropped around him by fellow pilots.[62]

Delaney witnessed the end of the destroyer *Asashimo*, which went up with a tremendous explosion. "There was one huge orange ball of flame that seemed to come straight up out of the superstructure," he said. Around 1420 an undamaged destroyer passed uncomfortably close to his raft, coming within four hundred yards. "I hid behind the raft and prayed," recalled Delaney. He breathed easier when the tin can made a sharp turn to port and moved back closer to *Yamato*.[63]

✦✧✦

At 1302 *Yamato*'s radar clearly showed the second American attack group incoming, and lookouts soon had more than fifty *Essex* and *Bataan* planes in view. The battleship still sported an impressive array of functional guns, and the torpedo damage sustained so far scarcely slowed her down. Captain Hara's *Yahagi* had fallen far astern, dead in the water, with the destroyer *Isokaze* maintaining cover for her. The destroyer *Asashimo* had disappeared after the attack of the first assault group, but six destroyers remained near the big battleship.

On *Yamato*, gunner Masanobu Kobayashi heard a petty officer shout, "Here they come again!" The antiaircraft guns roared into action as Helldivers and Corsairs began the second main attack on *Yamato*. At 1322 an *Essex* Corsair landed a 1,000-pound bomb on the superstructure in the port-bow area. Helldivers next landed several hits near *Yamato*'s bridge and Turret No. 3. Kobayashi felt the heat from one of the explosions and an intense shockwave. A gunner near him fell mortally wounded, so Kobayashi took his place and helped maintain fire at the incoming American planes. Machine-gun bullets clanged off the steel gun mounts, sending a six-inch shard of metal ripping through Kobayashi's forehead. He pulled out the shrapnel, bandaged his own wound at an emergency station, and then selflessly tended to a shipmate who was bleeding out from a bullet that had shattered his thigh.[64]

In the minutes that followed, at least three more torpedoes ripped into *Yamato*'s port side amidships, flooding two firerooms. The dead and dying lay everywhere as damage controlmen fought to stem the flooding that soon began slowing the giant from twenty-two knots down to eighteen knots. Kazuhiro Fukumoto, a young sailor attached to the damage-control parties, was sent down to the second-lowest deck with his crew shortly before these torpedoes began hitting *Yamato*. He suddenly found himself in pitch darkness, with water surging up from below. Rising air pressure helped Fukumoto and his comrades swim toward the light of a hatch above them, allowing them to escape from drowning.[65]

Back on the bridge during the second wave, Ensign Yoshida cheated death when an explosion sent shrapnel ripping through the area. Behind him, in front of him, and to his left side, two sailors and Ensign Tatsuo Nishio were fatally wounded by the hot steel splinters, but their bodies sheltered Yoshida from serious injury. His uniform splattered crimson with their blood, he watched an incoming bomb rapidly increase in size as it approached. "Just as I hold my breath thinking it will land right on top of us, it whizzes past, barely missing our heads," Yoshida wrote.[66]

Yamato's escorting destroyers were not spared. *Kasumi* was badly damaged by bombs that caused her to momentarily lose steering control.

She staggered toward *Yamato*, narrowly avoiding collision before falling away on the battleship's port quarter. *Suzutsuki* was hit at 1308 by a bomb that ripped a large hole in the destroyer, killing fifty-seven men and injuring thirty-four others. Another bomb landed close enough aft to create further chaos.

Captain Hara's *Yahagi*, drifting without headway, also was assaulted by the second American attack wave. Near misses further ripped open her hull, while another bomb landed on the forecastle, killing a dozen men and blowing the bodies of a half dozen more sailors into the air. Minutes later another torpedo hit *Yahagi's* starboard bow, further increasing her list. Another bomb hit Turret No. 1, wiping out the entire gun crew and creating additional casualties on the forecastle.[67]

Lieutenant Ikeda, temporarily deaf from earlier explosions, thought that "it was as if I were watching a silent movie. I felt my whole body shaking heavily. Columns of water jumped up around the ship, one after another, taller than the mast. The bloody odor of our dead and wounded sailors mixed with the smell of gunpowder."[68]

Lieutenant Commander Takeshi Kameyama, *Yahagi's* torpedo officer, requested permission to dump the ship's torpedoes overboard before they exploded. Captain Hara agreed, and Kameyama's crew had just finished dumping the ordnance with the ship's amidships crane when more bombs burst among the torpedo tubes, bringing down the mainmast and wrecking the aircraft catapult. "The ruins of twisted iron looked like melting candy bars," Hara wrote.[69]

Ensign Shigeo Yamada abandoned his wrecked aft radio room, where close friends lay dead around him. As he moved near *Yahagi's* bridge, another explosion bruised and burned him as additional radiomen were cut down. "There were explosions and fires all over the place," observed Yamada. His cruiser was almost unrecognizable to him as the ensign picked his way past gun mounts littered with dying comrades.[70]

American Avengers swept in and began launching their torpedoes toward the blazing *Yahagi*. Three or more direct hits rocked the ship, transforming her into a listing pile of junk. "Our dying ship quaked with the detonation," said Hara. By the time the second assault wave began clearing the immediate area, Rear Admiral Komura knew that it was time to shift his flag to a ship with some fight left in it. Captain Hara passed the word to abandon ship, and signalmen flashed for *Isokaze* to come alongside. More planes arrived as *Isokaze* approached, however, forcing the destroyer to take radical evasive actions.[71]

Near misses shattered the ocean all around *Isokaze* as she dodged each attacker. As the smoke cleared the destroyer was heavily damaged but still afloat. Admiral Komura then called Hara's attention to the east, where a third large group of American planes were forming up and beginning to head their way. Some sailors began jumping overboard from *Yahagi* as water began reaching the decks on the starboard side. The relative quiet from the lack of explosions was now filled with the sound of the approaching aircraft engines of the third American attack wave.

The time was 1342.

Ensign Leon Frankel was eager to make his first live torpedo drop. His Torpedo Nine had thus far only flown into combat during the Okinawa campaign with bomb loads. On April 7 *Yorktown*'s VT-9 was finally loaded with torpedoes, and their targets were the best available ships of the IJN. Frankel was flying wing on Lieutenant Clyde Lee, leader of the squadron's second division, who had grumbled earlier that they would arrive to the party too late to find any warships to torpedo. Thirteen TBMs were included in the *Yorktown* strike group, led by Lieutenant Tom Stetson, who had taken acting command of the squadron following their skipper's loss days before.

Yorktown's contribution to TG 58.4's strike force included thirteen TBMs, eight VBF-9 fighter-bombers, a dozen VF-9 Hellcats, and thirteen Helldivers of VB-9. The 107 warplanes of 58.4's third wave included 42 planes from *Intrepid* and 19 from *Langley*. Each of the three torpedo squadrons included in the third wave were carrying torpedoes, and their final attacks on the *Yamato* group would largely determine how many ships escaped the fury of Mitscher's carrier assault group.

ACRM Chester Ruxer, manning the radarscope in Torpedo Ten skipper Larry Lawrence's TBM, picked up the enemy fleet thirty miles away and provided his pilot the proper navigational course. Lawrence transmitted the information to "Red One," Lieutenant Commander Will Rawie, the VBF-10 skipper and, as senior aviator present, strike coordinator for the collective TG 58.4 force.

Flying about two miles ahead of Air Group 10's main contingent, Rawie was first to spot the *Yamato* fleet at 1330. TG 58.4's three air groups were spread out due to the weather and staggered launching, but they arrived just as the second attack wave was finishing its business. The stricken *Yahagi* was spotted miles astern of the main group, shepherded by *Isokaze*. The badly battered *Yamato* was still making headway, ringed by her surviving destroyers. Taking in the scene, Lawrence later remarked, "It was kinda like the old western Indian attacks where they were circling the wagons—meaning the screen surrounding the *Yamato* in the center."[72]

VBF-10 pilots after returning to *Intrepid* (CV 11) from their attacks on *Yamato* and *Yahagi*. *Standing, left to right:* Ensign Percy Liles, Lieutenant Commander Will Rawie, Ensign Lee Thompson, Ensign Roy Erickson, and Ensign James Clifford. *Kneeling, left to right:* Ensign Gerald Stahl, Lieutenant Hal Jackson, Ensign Mervin Beil, and Lieutenant (jg) Ralph Jacobsen. *U.S. Navy*

Rawie directed that his *Intrepid* Air Group 10 would lead the assault, followed in turn by the squadrons from *Yorktown* and *Langley*. He led his own VBF-10 against *Yahagi*, and his F4U division claimed two hits and a near miss. "We pulverized that cruiser," remarked Rawie. The pounding flak caused great concern for Ensign Percy Liles. "My mouth turned so dry that my tongue seemed to ricochet back and forth against the roof of my mouth," he said. Lieutenant Hal Jackson led his VBF-10 division on *Yamato*, chalking up one 1,000-pound hit and two near misses.[73]

Lieutenant (jg) Wes Hays' division—including Ensigns Roy Erickson, Jim Hollister, and Salvatore "Russ" Carlisli—made runs on the cruiser, claiming three hits and one very near miss. "It was tailor-made," Hays said of the attack. "My pipper was right on the after section of the island of a cruiser. All I did was give a burst of shells and then drop my bomb." Erickson found the tracers were so close he could smell the cordite. Black flak bursts tossed his Hellcat around as he pulled out and circled back to fire his guns into *Isokaze*.[74]

Torpedo Ten in the meantime drove in relentlessly on *Yahagi*. Lieutenant (jg) Sid Overall, flying wing on skipper Lawrence, noted that it looked like "the whole side of *Yamato* went up in a wall of [antiaircraft] fire." Overall's TBM took several light rounds through the fuselage, and Ensign George Smith's Avenger was holed by a 5-inch shell during their runs. Three Buzzard Brigade pilots—Lawrence, Overall, and Ensign Orbie Guthrie—would later receive the Navy Cross for torpedo hits credited to them.[75]

Only one VT-10 pilot failed to drop on the squadron's assigned target. Lieutenant (jg) Grant "Jack" Young had been flying wing on skipper Lawrence as well, but his plane was forced out of position when his lead section made an abrupt turn to attack. Young circled back to make another approach and found himself within the destroyer screen, with *Yamato* dead ahead of him. He wasted no time, although the antiaircraft fire was fierce. "My plane was holed in five places by 20 millimeter shells," he said.[76]

Young bore in straight for the crippled battleship, and other pilots saw his torpedo explode on *Yamato*'s starboard side amidships. As he jinked wildly to dodge the wall of antiaircraft fire from the screening destroyers, Young struggled to see through a splattering of oil across his windshield. "About halfway around the Jap force, I noted a pair of F6F Hellcats with checkerboard-painted tails making a casual pursuit curve against us," said Young.[77]

The Hellcats moved in against Young's TBM, even as he flipped his radio selector to the guard frequency to warn them that he was a friendly plane. At that instant the leading F6F opened fire on the Torpedo Ten warplane with a long burst of .50-caliber bullets. Young began screaming frantically the identity of his "turkey" torpedo bomber over the guard frequency, "I'm a turk! I'm a turk!" The second Hellcat fired a burst at Young as well before his calls caught their attention. Horrified at their near-fatal mistake, the F6F pilots joined up on Young and escorted him back to the squadron's rendezvous point to avoid further mishap. One of the Hellcat pilots managed only a sheepish single word of "sorry" to acknowledge his mistake. "Luckily, he was a lousy shot," said Young.[78]

Lieutenant Cloyd D. Rauch Jr., leading *Intrepid*'s fourteen Helldivers of VB-10, led one division of seven planes in a glide-bombing attack against the bow of *Yamato*. Lieutenant (jg) Erling E. Jacobsen's second division circled to the north and came in over the battleship's stern. En route they passed right over a screening destroyer. Aviation Chief Radioman James Bernard "Buck" Buchanan, rear gunner for Hubert Grubiss, looked down at the blazing guns on the tin can, appearing big enough to him to be a light cruiser. "Hot damn!" Buchanan hollered. "We're past the cruiser. The *Yamato* can't be far ahead."[79]

As Bombing Ten released their 1,000-pound bombs, Lieutenant (jg) Carl N. DeTemple's Helldiver was hit by a 3-inch shell that sheered two feet off his right wing, leaving the fabric blistered and torn. "It peeled back like a banana," he said. With the aid of the automatic pilot, DeTemple succeeded in bring his SB2C back to land on *Intrepid*.[80]

Lieutenant Rauch's crews felt certain their bombs helped wreck *Yamato*. "What moments earlier had been a massive, zigzagging platform of blazing guns bent on destroying us, was now a stalled, flaming inferno," wrote Buchanan.[81]

Langley's air group, the smallest unit of the TG 58.4 attack, arrived over the target area led by Lieutenant Commander Merlin Paddock. He singled out *Yahagi* and her escort *Isokaze* for his two squadrons. As Paddock formed his planes for attack, *Yorktown*'s VT-9 moved in to execute an attack on the *Yahagi*'s starboard side.

Captain Hara remained on the bridge of his dying ship as bullets hissed all around him, one of which hit his left arm. Completely dazed, he gritted his teeth and mumbled, "All right, you Yankee devils, finish us off!"[82]

Division leader Clyde Lee brought seven of his torpedo-armed TBMs in on *Yahagi*, just behind fighters and Helldivers that were working her over from above. Preceding the *Yorktown* TBMs were seven VF-9 Hellcats, directed by *Yorktown* strike leader Herb Houck to attack *Yahagi*. Bill Bonneau and his fellow F6F pilots unloaded their 500-pound bombs on the drifting cruiser and claimed four direct hits. Houck claimed a hit on a destroyer before turning his attention to strafing Japanese survivors and lifeboats in the water. Next in were the Corsairs of VBF-9, which split their efforts against *Yahagi* and her escort *Isokaze*. Ensign Raymond May's 500-pound bomb exploded astern amidships on *Yahagi*, while aerial witnesses credited Ensign Raymond G. Jehli with a direct hit on her port quarter.[83]

At 1345 strike coordinator Rawie called for Lieutenant Tony Schneider's thirteen VB-9 Helldivers to concentrate on *Yahagi*. Lieutenant Harry Wiltsie Worley broke his section off from the main flight and attacked first from the cruiser's port beam. No hits were observed by his section, but Schneider's remaining ten SB2Cs were effective. Schneider's bombs hit near the bridge on the port side. Both of Lieutenant (jg) Robert L. Verrall's bombs landed near the bridge, and Ensign Jack Greenwall scored hits on the fantail. Lieutenant (jg) Leo Martin and Ensigns Winthrop R. Hanawalt and William H. Sigman, all from VB-9's last section, were credited with direct hits aft and amidships on the cruiser.

Lieutenant Lee swept in behind Schneider's bunch, splitting his seven TBMs into two lines abreast, with wingmen Ensign Frankel and Lieutenant (jg) William Patterson snugged in tight with him. Frankel called back to his radio operator, ARM3c Harry E. Kistler Jr., who had a radarscope. "I told him to let me know when we hit fifteen hundred yards," he said. Frankel bored straight in, listening to the nervous voice of Kistler until he heard the magic range and pickled his war fish.[84]

Frankel's TBM jumped up a little as the 2,000-pound weapon fell free and began its run on *Yahagi*. At 240 knots speed and a mere two hundred feet above the wave tops, the pilot was unable to divert from his course, which took him right over *Yahagi*. "I could see guys running around the ship," recalled Frankel. "I almost hit the mainmast of the cruiser."[85]

Frankel and four other pilots were credited with torpedo hits, which were deemed by their squadron's report to be "the death blow" for *Yahagi*. "She began erupting," said pilot Stew Bass. "Flames belched through holes in her deck, and great holes were blown in her portside." Clyde Lee and

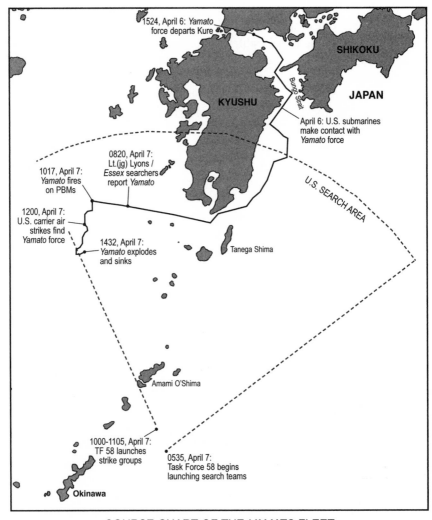

COURSE CHART OF THE *YAMATO* FLEET

John Page, whose torpedoes failed to release on the cruiser, swung around and charged through a gauntlet of antiaircraft fire to deliver their fish against the lone destroyer, *Isokaze*. His weapon again failed to release, forcing him to make a third attack run before he was finally able to shake it off. Aerial witnesses credited VT-9's final drop with scoring a direct hit on the starboard bow of the Japanese warship. During their runs, Lee and Page were given strafing support by VB-9 Helldiver pilot Harry Worley, whose SB2C was slammed by a shell from the destroyer in the process. The Helldiver burst into flames and crashed into the ocean about ten feet off *Isokaze*'s starboard bow, killing Worley and his gunner, ARM1c Earl William Ward.[86]

Yahagi was wrecked by the explosions of VT-9's torpedoes even as *Langley*'s dozen VF-23 Hellcats came in right behind the *Yorktown* Avengers. Lieutenant Leslie H. Kerr's division missed a wildly maneuvering destroyer, but Lieutenant Commander Paddock's division claimed a hit on *Yahagi*'s fantail. As he recovered, Paddock saw five torpedoes launched by VT-23 explode on the cruiser.[87]

Lieutenant Howard L. Grimmel's VF-23 division worked over the oft-targeted *Isokaze* with bombs and machine-gun bullets. Lieutenant Don Pattie's VT-23 executed a coordinated attack on *Yahagi* with near-textbook precision less than a minute after VT-9's war fish had slammed home. Without power, the cruiser was a sitting duck. Circling the scene, *Langley* CAG 23 Paddock believed as many as six more torpedoes hit the floundering warship.

Yahagi was seen by Torpedo Twenty-Three's pilots and aircrewmen to be dead in the water with fire blazing on her bow as they went in. Within one minute after the last war fish slammed home, the cruiser was observed by many to sink and disappear. Ensign Frankel, circling the area after his VT-9 division attacked *Yahagi*, noted of his target ship, "It just busted up in pieces."[88]

Yorktown's Air Group 9 had already claimed the destruction of a destroyer and a number of the torpedo hits that finished *Yahagi* before her final division of Avengers swept in to seal the fate of mighty *Yamato*.

Lieutenant Stetson circled his six VT-9 Avengers about four and a half miles from the battleship and called for his tunnel gunners to reset the depth setting on their warheads from ten feet to between twenty and twenty-two feet. Aviation Ordnanceman 2nd Class Harvey S. Ewing, turret gunner for Lieutenant Collins' TBM, recalled, "Using a key like a rollerskate key, I felt for the lug and then made the necessary turns to make the fish run deeper."[89]

Within minutes all six Avenger crews had adjusted their settings and ducked through the clouds to make their drops off *Yamato*'s starboard bow. Stetson believed that three members of his division, perhaps four, delivered hits. As he circled, the VT-9 skipper noted that the battleship's list had increased, and *Yamato* was beginning to heel over less than five minutes after his Avengers had delivered the final hits on her.

Yahagi was hit by an estimated dozen bombs and at least a half dozen torpedoes before she capsized to port at 1405. Captain Hara had jumped into the water and was pulled under the waves by the suction his sinking cruiser created. He fought his way to the surface, emerging covered in thick black oil, and soon found Rear Admiral Komura swimming near him. Hara clung to a log with a young *Yahagi* sailor, watching the final minutes of the distant *Yamato* as tears streamed down his face.[90]

Lieutenant Ikeda, having left the bridge to help on the main deck, was blown into the ocean by an explosion shortly before *Yahagi* went under. Temporarily deafened and suffering from powder burns to his face, he swam hard to escape his sinking ship's sucking whirlpool. American warplanes zoomed in low to strafe survivors for some time, after which Ikeda was left clinging to an empty wooden box. "The cold seawater chilled me to the bone, and I felt fatigue extending through my entire body," he wrote.[91]

Yahagi's executive officer, Captain Uchino Nobuichi, and 445 sailors of the cruiser's complement of about 1,000 men perished. Hara and Komura were the senior survivors rescued by *Hatsushimo* and *Yukikaze*. "I grieved at the loss of my cruiser and I grieved doubly the loss of the world's greatest battleship," declared Hara.[92]

In the final assault wave on his *Yamato*, Ensign Yoshida found the American pilots' precision to be "virtually surgical." *Yamato*'s skipper, Captain Kosaku Ariga, continued shouting encouragement to his crew until all hope was lost. Vice Admiral Seiichi Ito finally retired to his cabin and locked the door as the battleship lost headway.[93]

Yahagi had already gone down, and the third American assault wave ravaged the nearby destroyer *Isokaze*. "We fired back with our guns but we stood no chance," recalled gunner Takeo Hashimoto. His position in a small compartment on *Isokaze*'s bridge was suddenly pitched into darkness and seawater flooded in as bombs rocked the destroyer. Another shockwave slammed Hashimoto's face into his gun-sighting device, knocking him momentarily senseless. With blurred vision, he stumbled from the compartment and grabbed a handrail on the bridge. A short distance away, he watched in grief as *Yamato* began sinking before his very eyes.[94]

Riji Inoue, an eighteen-year-old helmsman, was forced to evacuate his navigation station as *Isokaze* began flooding heavily. American aircraft were still making strafing runs as Inoue headed toward the bridge, forced to crawl on his stomach through slippery pools of clotted blood. En route he met a companion who had joined the destroyer with him in January 1944. His friend had blood gushing from a bullet wound in his chest, as a senior petty officer yelled at him, "Come on! Get a grip on yourself!"[95]

Isokaze was mortally wounded, foundering under relentless strafing and bombing while sailors like Hashimoto and Inoue fought to survive. The ordeal of those on *Yamato* was even more severe. As more bombs and torpedoes from the final assaults exploded, the battleship began to sink. Captain Ariga finally granted his executive officer, Captain Jiro Nomura, orders for the men to abandon ship. *Yamato*'s main battle flag was still flying, but waves were lapping over the topside gun mounts. By a conservative count, the battleship had suffered at least a dozen direct bomb hits and taken seven torpedoes, although the true count was believed to be higher by some survivors.[96]

Damage controlman Fukumoto, having escaped from the flooding and carnage below decks, found equal mayhem topside. He noted a sixteen-year-old machine gunner named Yoshifuji lying on the deck, blood pumping out of a nasty head wound with every breath. The doomed sailor alternately moaned, "Long live the Emperor," and begged for water. "They said if we gave him water, he'd die," recalled Fukumoto, who watched the horribly wounded man being transferred to a medical station on a stretcher.[97]

A large explosion blew some men from the decks and into the water. Fukumoto jumped overboard as *Yamato* continued to drift forward very slowly. "I was drawn into the whirlpool from the propeller and pushed backwards," he said. Several times he was sucked into the vortex as the five-yard-long blades forced him under the surface where he swallowed saltwater. "I eventually popped up some distance away from the ship," Fukumoto said. He grabbed a big log and held on, bobbing in the swells with dozens of other survivors.[98]

When Ensign Yoshida finally left the battered bridge of *Yamato*, only a few officers remained alive there. The ship's navigation officer lashed himself to the chart table, committed to going down with the ship. Yoshida was finally compelled to abandon ship by the Second Fleet chief of staff, Rear Admiral Nobii Morishita, who struck him and ordered him to leave. "What are you doing?" Morishita growled. "You young ones, swim!"[99]

Yoshida crawled out a lookout port and stood on the starboard bulk-head of the bridge as *Yamato*'s list grew alarmingly steeper. His last sight of Captain Ariga was of him binding himself to the bridge, displaying "iron nerves without equal." Ocean water crept up the starboard side of the bridge until Yoshida was swept into a large whirlpool that pulled him under the surface. As *Yamato* sank she exploded violently, the force of which thrust the ensign back to the surface, "crashing into a thick yet undulating wall overhead." The suction pulled him back down until a secondary explosion again forced Yoshida to the surface, burned and suffering from a nasty head wound.[100]

Numerous sailors leaped from the decks as the battleship began sinking at 1421. Wounded gunner Kobayashi was flung from the ship by a violent explosion. Captain Nomura suffered severe internal injuries and was found barely alive, floating in a coma. At 1432 *Yamato* exploded in a mighty fire-ball from her Number One magazine that shot columns of smoke and red flames high into the sky. The cloud of smoke and fire could be seen one hundred miles away.[101]

The final blasts from *Yamato* punctured her floundering survivors with more shrapnel. "A piece of metal hit me underwater and snapped a tendon in my hip," Naoyshi Ishida said. "When I surfaced, I was shattered." Ishida thought of his infant son and his young wife, then grabbed floating debris to sustain him until rescue ships might find him.[102]

The final explosions of *Yamato* were almost surreal. "It looked like Old Faithful erupting," said Lieutenant Wilbert P. Popp of VT-17. "She just lifted up out of the water four or five feet, and that was the end of it," said VT-10 skipper Larry Lawrence. "This huge mushroom cloud rose up," said Avenger pilot Leon Frankel. "The sky was just blood red from horizon to horizon."[103]

Damage controlman Fukumoto clung to his log for two hours before joining others on a large emergency raft. A half hour later the destroyer *Yukikaze* approached, and sailors tossed down rope ladders and lines for the survivors to climb. "All of us were black with oil from head to toe, so it was a struggle just to hold on," Fukumoto recalled. According to the senior surviving *Yamato* officer, Captain Nomura, only 269 officers and men were saved—less than 10 percent of the crew. Another 3,055 had perished, along with some 1,187 men from *Yahagi* and the escorting destroyers. Total casu-alties were 3,721 sailors killed and 459 injured.[104]

Destroyers *Yukikaze* and *Fuyutsuki* plucked survivors of *Yamato*, *Yahagi*, and *Kasumi* from the water. Lieutenant Ikeda, one of the few officers to survive from *Yahagi*, struggled to climb the oil-covered lines to make his way on board *Fuyutsuki*. "The uninjured were laying the wounded in a passage on the deck so as not to hinder the crew of the *Fuyutsuki*," wrote Ikeda. "But some of those injured comrades were corpses by the next morning."[105]

Kasumi and *Isokaze*, too badly damaged to be salvaged, were finished off with torpedoes from their sister destroyers. Two other destroyers, *Asashimo* and *Hamakaze*, had already gone under. *Suzutsuki* struggled back to port late the following day by steaming in reverse. She was preceded to Kagoshima by only three other ships of the fleet: *Fuyutsuki*, *Yukikaze*, and *Hatsushimo*.

Survivors like Fukumoto were transported to Sasebo, then later taken by train to Kure. They remained there for a month, as Japanese officials tried to hide the truth of what had happened to the *Yamato* fleet. When Fukumoto was finally allowed to return home to see his parents and younger sister, he wondered why he had survived. "I guess God kept me alive so I could properly mourn the dead and take care of their families," he reckoned.[106]

The American carrier strike forces had lost ten aircraft and a dozen aviators, but several men were still alive in the ocean long after the demise of *Yamato*. Lieutenant Ernie Delaney of *Belleau Wood*'s VT-30 clung to his life raft several miles from the position of the remaining *Yamato* force, watching destroyers move about picking up survivors.

Shortly after 1500 he spotted a pair of PBMs approach and begin circling the area, looking for survivors. They went south of him quite a distance, then split and came back at five hundred feet, searching the water. "By this time, I had broken out a new dye-marker and climbed into the raft and was waving like a madman," Delaney said. His PBM rescue pilots were Lieutenants Dick Simms and Jim Young, whose crews had been stalking the *Yamato* fleet since around 1015.[107]

Young made a water landing at 1515, and his crew hauled the VT-30 pilot on board their flying boat. Japanese destroyer gunfire landed uncomfortably close before Young hauled clear with his passenger and made for Kerama Retto. Delaney then began his journey to Okinawa's Yontan Field and finally back to *Hornet*, hitch-hiking in a TBM.

Other survivors remained in the water. Lieutenant (jg) Kirby Ellis and his gunner, Frank Guptill, tied a line between their life rafts and drifted throughout the night. By morning they could see a distant island and decided to paddle toward it. "Blood from our wounds was in the water, and in five minutes the sharks were there, slowly circling, and their fins were about six inches above the surface," recalled Guptill.[108]

While watching the sharks, the VB-83 crew became aware of aircraft circling them in the distance. Soon afterward the airmen heard the thump-thump sound of a distant diesel engine, which eventually turned into the shape of a submarine approaching with its deck awash. "Kirby stood up in his raft and started waving," noted Guptill. "I was worried that he would fall to the sharks." Minutes later the two were being pulled on board the life-guard submarine *Tench* (SS 417), which was headed for Guam to complete its war patrol. By April 28 Ellis and Guptill were moved via destroyer on a breeches buoy high line back to *Essex*, where they resumed flight duties for the Okinawa campaign.

The returning TF-58 strike groups were jubilant. Some narrowly made it back. VB-10 pilot Hubert Grubiss landed on *Intrepid* with mere fumes. "The engine coughed, the prop stopped just as we hooked number one cable," wrote his rear gunner, Buck Buchanan. "Had it been a few drops of gas less, we would have slammed into the ship's fantail, or into the ship's turbulent wake."[109]

Ensign Eric Erickson on *Intrepid* found that his VBF-10 division was credited with three hits and a near miss on their cruiser target. Unable to determine who made the miss, three of the pilots were asked to draw playing cards from a deck to determine who would record the miss. "Low card would receive that honor!" said Erickson. "Turning the cards over, I discovered I had drawn the deuce of hearts!" The high-card drawer was later awarded the Navy Cross, and Erickson, as low-card holder, later received the Distinguished Flying Cross.[110]

Pete Mitscher sent congratulatory messages to his beloved aviators, and by 1632 his intelligence officers on *Bunker Hill* were offering freshly exposed prints of the demise of *Yamato* and its consorts. With a trademark cigarette hanging from his lips, he examined them carefully as his staff awaited some grand pronouncement on the day's success. To their surprise the craggy admiral turned and walked to his cabin without a word to take a nap.[111]

Chapter Fourteen

"LIKE WOLVES AT A KILL"

In his diary, Vice Admiral Ugaki recorded, "The Surface Special Attack Force met a tragic end before reaching its destination." His beloved *Yamato*—on which he had served a full year as Fleet Admiral Yamamoto's chief of staff and from which Ugaki had commanded the First Battleship Division from May 1944 through the Leyte Gulf battles—was no more. Telegrams from the destroyer *Hatsushimo* first relayed news that *Yamato* and *Yahagi* had been badly hit, followed later by the alarming news that *Yamato* had exploded and sank.[1]

Ugaki had been opposed to the whole operation, believing it "superficial" to consider a mighty battlewagon useless due to Japan's fuel scarcity. His only recourse was to continue with a second day of his Kikusui No. 1 operations on April 7. The previous day his warplanes had succeeded in sinking three U.S. destroyers, the first ships destroyed by kamikazes while on radar-picket duty. Twenty-two American warships were on such duty on the morning of the seventh, when Ugaki sent sixty army planes and ten navy aircraft to attack them. Another forty navy planes, along with a dozen fighter-bombers from the 4th Kemmu Squadron, Thunder Gods Corps, carried out an attack against U.S. ships in the vicinity of Kikai Jima, between Okinawa and the main island of Kyushu. They would suffer heavy losses to U.S. fighters.[2]

The destroyer *Bennett* (DD 473), assisting at Radar Picket Station No. 1, was subjected to a series of kamikaze attacks during the early morning. Her gunners and the vigilant CAP fighters accounted for most of the enemy aircraft, but by midmorning she had been struck by one suicider that escaped the CAP and slammed into her starboard side amidships, handing out devastation in her engineering spaces. *Bennett* was escorted back to the anchorage, having suffered three men killed and eighteen wounded.[3]

Between 0930 and 1000, Lieutenant Commander Frank Lawlor's VBF-9 splashed four Vals fifty miles north of Okinawa, and in the next hour fighters from *Bennington*'s VF-82 knocked down another five Franks and a George while defending the destroyer *Gregory* at Radar Picket Station No. 3. Lieutenant Armand G. Manson shot down a George and a Frank, while his VF-82 comrades accounted for the other four Franks. Lieutenant Commander Willard Eder's two VF-29 CAP divisions from *Cabot* assumed the duties over *Gregory* around 1130 and soon after had knocked down a pair of attacking Judys. *Cabot*'s second fighter division downed an additional Judy, sparing *Gregory* from damage.[4]

Around 1234 *Gregory*'s crew witnessed a tragedy above their picket station as four Corsairs from *Intrepid*'s VF-10 Grim Reapers squadron were en route back to their carrier. Lieutenant Commander Wally Clarke, skipper of the famed squadron, suffered a midair collision with another F4U, piloted by Ensign Donald Howard Croy from Detroit. The junior pilot's Corsair spun into the drink, killing him, but Clarke was able to fight and restore stability to his aircraft. "I unbuckled my parachute harness and was getting ready to jump when I found, with two hands on the stick, I could get control of the aircraft," said Clarke. He managed soon after to effect a safe water landing in the relatively calm sea. "The aircraft skipped across the water like little flat stones we used to throw when we were kids," recalled Clarke. He scrambled into his life raft and bobbed in his Mae West until *Gregory*'s crew retrieved him via a Jacob's ladder. The pilot had suffered facial injuries from slamming into the gunsight during his ditching, but he was patched up by the destroyer's medical officer.[5]

Hours later the Grim Reapers skipper was transferred from *Gregory* to the destroyer *Cassin Young*, which transported him to Kerama Retto. He remained on *Cassin Young* during the next week and experienced a kamikaze attack on April 12, when a Val crashed into the destroyer's upper works. *Cassin Young* returned to Kerama Retto on the thirteenth for repairs, and Clarke made his way back to *Intrepid* via an Avenger crew.

A special flight of four VF-83 Hellcats and eight VBF-83 Corsairs—launched from *Essex* at 0907 to track the *Yamato* fleet until TF 58's strike groups arrived—saw action during the early afternoon hours. Lieutenant (jg) George Minar splashed a Sally bomber at 1130 before it could reach the fleet, while two other *Essex* fighter pilots each claimed a Judy fifteen miles from the *Yamato* fleet. Lieutenant William Wood's division, on task-force CAP duty, shot down four other Judys, running the *Essex* fighters' score to eight kills on the day in two different actions.[6]

Throughout the day on April 7, Navy fighters claimed forty-eight kills from these Japanese attackers, while Marine pilots added more victories. Vice Admiral Kelly Turner, commander of Okinawa's amphibious forces, was filled with confidence by the *Yamato* sinking and was pleased that his vessels had escaped the brunt of the kamikaze efforts this day. "I may be crazy, but it looks like the Japanese have quit the war, at least in this sector," he cabled Admiral Nimitz in Hawaii. The succinct reply from the commander in chief of the Pacific Fleet read simply, "Delete all after 'crazy.'"[7]

The best efforts of Mitscher's fighters failed to prevent one of Admiral Ugaki's Thunder Gods from finally connecting with an American flight deck on the seventh. As fate would have it, the victim was the luckless *Hancock*, whose *Yamato* strike group had been the only TF 58 force to fail to find the Japanese fleet. Captain Robert F. Hickey sent his crew to General Quarters at 1210, when a bogey was reported twelve miles out and closing fast.[8]

Hancock's gunners scarcely had time to open fire before the enemy aircraft turned and landed a 550-pound semi-armor-piercing bomb right through the flight deck. The kamikaze followed the course of his bomb and slammed his plane into the flight deck, where it cartwheeled into aircraft spotted on deck, setting them ablaze. Thirteen planes on the flight deck were destroyed, and fires erupted among those housed on the hangar deck.

Two 40-mm quads were damaged and both forward catapults were rendered inoperable from this attack, with *Hancock*'s damage-control crews spending more than an hour fighting to get all the fires contained. The carrier suffered twenty-nine sailors killed in action, thirty-five missing, and another seventy-one wounded, but her crew patched her flight deck sufficiently to land her errant strike group by 1630. *Hancock* remained on duty with her task group until April 9, when Mitscher ordered her back to Ulithi for repairs in company with the light carrier *Cabot*, which was due to return to the States for an overhaul after constant Pacific duty since November 1943.

Lieutenant Harris Mitchell, the newest member of Gene Valencia's VF-9 Mowing Machine division, proved his worth to his skipper on the afternoon of April 7. Flying monotonous radar-picket CAP duty near one destroyer off Point U—west of the northern tip of Okinawa—Mitch's boredom evaporated when their FDO suddenly issued orders for Valencia's division to move north to investigate a bogey. Minutes later,

Mitch suddenly spotted a small shape on the horizon. "Tallyho!" he shouted over the radio. "Ten o'clock high! Close in."[9]

Their opponent was a Frances, grayish brown in color and with dull red meatballs on its fuselage and wings, flying on an almost opposite course. Valencia's division began a sharp break to the left. In the process Ensign Jim French's second section came sliding under Valencia so close that Mitchell was forced to make a radical maneuver to avoid a collision. His choices were few: slide back, nose down, or pull straight up. *I've waited too long to see another one of those Rising Sun emblems*, he thought. *I'm not about to be squeezed out of this action!*[10]

Mitchell pointed the nose of his Hellcat sharply down and dove fast after the Frances, which was twenty-five hundred feet ahead and moving fast just feet above the wave tops. Making 256 knots with his abrupt dive, Mitch could see the propellers of the Frances ahead of him picking up spray from the ocean. Even after four minutes of hot pursuit, he was gaining little distance on his quarry. Mitch calculated the range and drift, figured his best guestimate, and then put his pipper on that spot by pulling up slightly and squeezing off about three rounds per gun. He watched his .50-caliber tracers burn out and hit the water just behind his adversary.

Correcting for his error, Mitchell squeezed off a few more rounds. His attention was suddenly taken by red tracers soaring just over his cockpit. "Needless to say, it scared the hell out of this young man," he said. He found the bullets were coming from his divisionmates, trailing behind him and all hoping to make the same long-range luck shot Mitch had already attempted.[11]

Valencia's team made additional long-range lobs until the Frances began to make a shallow turn to the left. Mitchell crossed over from the right to the left of Valencia and got a short burst. As he closed, his next bursts scored hits in the left side of the fuselage, wings tops, and both engines. The Japanese plane lost air speed as its right engine caught fire, and the Fighting Nine pack closed rapidly. "In an instant, we were on him like wolves at a kill," said Mitch. His next burst caused the Frances to slam into the ocean, tearing off its left wing in the process. The VF-9 division circled the scene for a few minutes as Mitchell savored his second aerial victory.[12]

TF 58 fighters accounted for four dozen aerial victories on the seventh, the final kill of the day going to VF-17's Lieutenant (jg) Billy Watts, who had launched from *Hornet* at 1430 with wingmen George Covelly and Werner Gaerisch, along with five VBF-17 Hellcats. After hours of uneventful task-force CAP duty, Watts was vectored to intercept a bogey twenty miles out from the carriers. He caught the lone intruder, chopped his throttle, and caused the Japanese fighter to burst into flames as he stitched it from five hundred feet astern. The Zeke splashed into the sea, raising the total victories for young Watts to 2.5 aerial kills.

In the wake of the *Yamato* sinking, Vice Admiral Mitscher was not himself on board his flagship *Bunker Hill*. Chief of Staff Burke's first indication of the Bald Eagle's troubles came when their staff physician, Captain Raymond W. Hege, came to announce that the admiral did not feel well. "I've advised him to stay in bed," reported Dr. Hege. When Mitscher did appear later, "he looked like hell," according to Burke. Although Hege said nothing along such lines, Burke believed that Mitscher might have suffered a minor heart attack. "He was tired and he didn't have his old time energy." The captain and the other TF 58 staffers simply ran the show when Mitscher was not on the bridge. Nothing was spoken about the admiral's listlessness during this period.[13]

Fortunately, the operations of the fleet were well planned by Burke, and daily missions continued on their scheduled pace until Mitscher recovered. The Okinawa campaign was already going well enough that permanent Marine fighter squadrons had begun moving ashore on April 7. They operated from recently captured former Japanese airfields to lend permanent cover to ground forces, amphibious vessels, and radar-picket warships.

An advance echelon of Marine Aircraft Group 31 was ferried to Yontan Airfield from the escort carriers *Breton* (CVE 23) and *Sitkoh Bay* (CVE 86) in the early afternoon of the seventh. The first Marine aircraft were all fighters, F4Us of VMF-441, VMF-214, and VMF-311, plus elements of a night-fighter F6F squadron, VMF(N)-542. Colonel John C. "Toby" Munn would direct Tenth Army Tactical Air Force efforts from Yontan, while additional Marine units would quickly be deployed to nearby Kadena Airfield. Land-based Okinawa squadrons would be commanded by Major General Francis P. Mulcahy, a Marine leader whose tactical air arm would soon consist of three Marine aircraft groups and three Army Air Forces fighter groups.[14]

Breton was first to begin launching F4Us of VMF-214 and VMF-311 shortly after noon. The ship's FDO detected a bogey approaching the task group and at 1519 issued a "buster" to two divisions of VMF-311 Corsairs circling the force. Captain Ralph G. McCormick's leathernecks intercepted a Lily on a kamikaze run toward the escort carriers. McCormick and his wingmen made runs on the twin-engine bomber, setting it afire as it neared *Sitkoh Bay*, still actively engaged in launching Marine fighters. The Japanese aircraft, bathed in flames from the Marine Corsair assault, began disintegrating in midair and slammed into the ocean one hundred yards off the port bow of *Sitkoh Bay*, where it exploded on impact. McCormick and 1st Lieutenant John J. Doherty were credited by VMF-311 with a half kill each for their squadron's first aerial victory. *Breton*'s antiaircraft gunners felt certain they deserved at least half credit on the kamikaze kill.[15]

Few men felt greater relief than 1st Lieutenant Bill Farrell, whose Corsair was loaded in one of *Sitkoh Bay*'s catapults as the kamikaze assault commenced. "They just left me up on the catapult dead with no place to run," said Farrell. He was elated to see the bomber explode in the ocean nearby, followed by raucous cheers throughout the carrier force. "I think I was yelling louder than anybody," Farrell declared.[16]

Marine squad leader Watson Crumbie was beginning to wonder by April 8 if his Charley Company of the 29th Marine Regiment, 6th Marine Division would see any fighting at all. His men were advancing onto the Motobu Peninsula when Japanese machine-gun fire and mortars suddenly rained down on them. The surprise attack was effective in felling a number of Marines, and Crumbie found himself frustrated, firing back at Japanese soldiers so well fortified that he could not even see their faces.

Crumbie realized that he was in for a different kind of fight on Okinawa, one where guerrilla tactics and surprise assaults soon become the norm. His company faced Japanese hit-and-run tactics as they assaulted Mount Yae Take over the next two days, during which time the Marines suffered 207 men killed and 757 wounded.[17]

Lieutenant General Simon Buckner, who still maintained his command post on Kelly Turner's flagship *Eldorado*, went ashore each day to confer with his field commanders—Major General Roy Geiger of the Marines and Major General John Hodge of the Army. Buckner's Tenth Army had encountered Japanese resistance on southern Okinawa in the form of a line drawn across the narrow isthmus leading into the southern peninsula, Chinen. The 6th Marine Division had advanced swiftly in the north, but the fighting was beginning to take on a new intensity.[18]

The Army faced its most severe conflict yet on Okinawa, beginning on April 9, in the form of the Kakazu Ridge on the island's west coast. Colonel Edwin T. May's soldiers of the 383rd Regiment, 96th Division faced Colonel Munetatsu Hara's 13th Independent Infantry Battalion, which had dug in for months along the rugged coral ridge. Kakazu Ridge and the adjoining Kakazu West were infested with tunnels and bristling with concrete-fortified artillery and mortar positions. As the first two battalions of the 383rd Infantry advanced on Kakazu, they were pinned down when Hara's defenders suddenly sallied from underground bunkers with vicious assaults of bullets, grenades, and satchel charges.[19]

Private 1st Class Edward J. Moskala from Chicago would earn the Medal of Honor for his valor this day, beginning with his work in silencing two Japanese machine guns with his Browning automatic rifle. When his battalion was forced to abandon the Kakazu Ridge that morning, Moskala was the last man off the hill as he helped bring a wounded comrade to safety. Two more times this day, the private made trips to save lives before losing his own to an enemy attack during his third venture into harm's way.[20]

Airstrikes, artillery, and naval gunfire were employed to pound the ridge before a renewed Army assault commenced on the morning of the tenth. Additional attempts to hold the ridge continued but failed for the next three days against the seemingly impregnable Japanese stronghold. By April 12 the Army had suffered 451 soldiers killed, another 241 missing, and more than 2,000 wounded, yet Kakazu remained solidly in Japanese possession.[21]

General Ushijima, convinced that *Yamato*'s Ten-Go operation and Admiral Ugaki's Kikusui No. 1 attacks had seriously weakened the American defense, finally gave his subordinate, Lieutenant General Cho, the green light to execute powerful counterattacks during the night of April 12–13. Three red flares over General Hodge's soldiers around 1900 were followed by more than a thousand rounds of artillery shells falling on the Army's 381st Infantry Division. More than twelve hundred shells rained down on Colonel Mays' 383rd troops in their deep entrenchments.

These artillery barrages were followed by charging Japanese infantrymen, who advanced swiftly under cover of darkness. These assaults cost Ushijima many good soldiers while inflicting fewer American losses. The so-called banzai charges also exposed a weakness for the Japanese on Okinawa. Ushijima's men were vulnerable in exposed attacks, yet they were well protected when defending from their almost impregnable network of fortified caverns. The U.S. Army learned during mid-April that they were in for a long fight on the bloody volcanic island.

The fighting at Kakazu Ridge and the evening infantry charges brought a new intensity to the ground fight for Okinawa just as the air action simmered to a low boil in the wake of Kikusui No. 1. From April 8 through April 10, Vice Admiral Mitscher's carrier aviators only registered seven victories in aerial combat. During this time, he sent his fighters on more sweeps against enemy airfields in the area, and by early afternoon of the eleventh, his pilots ran into aerial opponents in small numbers while looking for such trouble.

Two VF-84 *Bunker Hill* divisions downed three bomb-loaded Zekes around 1415 near Tokuna Shima. *Yorktown* scrambled eight Hellcats at 1350 as some of the Japanese planes began appearing on task-force radar. Lieutenant Valencia's VF-9 group was vectored out to intercept by their FDO, and Jim French soon tallyhoed a lone Zeke fighter five hundred feet below them. Clint Smith registered his second aerial victory shortly afterward, the only action for the flight, by igniting the Zeke's cockpit and fuselage, sending his opponent curling into the water.

Some of the Japanese attackers broke through TF 58's CAP fighters to press their attack on TG 58.3's *Essex*, *Bunker Hill*, and *Enterprise* shortly after 1400. One Zeke was downed at 1409 just fifteen hundred yards off Big E's starboard quarter. One minute later a Judy managed to dive into *Enterprise*'s after 40-mm gun mounts, although its bomb carried over the side and exploded in the water under the carrier. In the ensuing minutes antiaircraft fire brought down two more kamikazes, one of which crashed near *Bunker Hill*. At 1501 another Judy narrowly missed scoring another hit on Big E, this one crashing off her starboard bow close enough to set fire to a Hellcat strapped to the starboard catapult. The wreckage of the Judy, including a sheared-off wing, clattered across the flight deck. "I was almost hit by shrapnel," Ensign Franklin T. Goodson of VF(N)-90 wrote in his diary. "It burst into flames and came streaking down, crashing and scattering its parts everywhere."[22]

TG 58.3 was harassed for the next several hours by small groups of kamikazes, several of which were splashed uncomfortably close. *Enterprise* shook off her damage, including the blazing Hellcat, which had to be launched off the starboard catapult and into the water, but eleven crewmen had been injured, most by shrapnel from the explosions of near misses. Rear Admiral Radford's TG 58.4 drew the attention of several kamikazes during the afternoon of April 11, with *Yorktown* scrambling two divisions of Hellcats at 1355 to intercept a fresh bogey contact forty-eight miles to the north. FDO Commander Carl J. Ballinger Jr. watched the opposing blips merge on his radarscope at twenty-eight miles but was surprised when the F6F jockeys reported no contact.[23]

The latest bandits were from a flight of sixteen Zeros of the 5th Kemmu Squadron, Kamikaze Special Attack Corps that had departed from Kanoya Airfield. The eight pairs of Japanese fighters had taken on varying targets, the most successful attack being made by a Zero that plunged into the destroyer *Kidd* (DD 661), killing thirty-eight sailors and wounding fifty-five more. Shortly after 1400 only two of the Zero pilots—Flight Petty Officers 2nd Class Kenkichi Ishii and Setsuo Ishino—were still searching for U.S. warship targets. Prior to departing, nineteen-year-old Ishino had left a final message to his parents: "Today's mission is something I have long awaited. All that's left for me now is to crash straight on into some enemy aircraft carrier."[24]

Ishino telegraphed back to base at 1438 that he had spotted the American fleet. Two minutes later, while approaching TG 58.4 from the south, he reported having sighted enemy fighters. One of the two Zeros was spotted coming in low on the water, apparently heading for either *Intrepid* or *Yorktown*. Nearly every gunner in the task group opened fire as the kamikaze zipped over the cruiser *San Diego* (CL 53) and barreled straight in on the battleship *Missouri*.

Captain William McCombe Callaghan was on the bridge of *Missouri* when either Ishino or his wingman Ishii set his sights on the massive battle-wagon. The forty-seven-year-old Callaghan was a devout Roman Catholic from San Francisco whose family had already scarified for their country in World War II. His brother, Rear Admiral Dan Callaghan, had been post-humously awarded the Medal of Honor for his action on the cruiser *San Francisco* in November 1942 during a surface battle with Japanese warships off Guadalcanal. At 1443 on April 11 Captain Callaghan was staring into an oncoming Zero fighter, strapped with an 1,100-pound bomb, plunging through a hail of gunfire that might just have his number.[25]

Several sailors armed with cameras were also shooting at the kami-kaze with their less-than-lethal instruments. Near the main deck Seaman 1st Class Leonard J. Schmidt was snapping away. Seventy feet above the main deck, two other *Missouri* photographers stood ready on the bridge with their cameras: Seaman 2nd Class Pasquale J. "Pat" Ferrigno, holding an F-56, and Baker 2nd Class Harold I. "Buster" Campbell, with a K-20 camera. One plane was hit and exploded, but the kamikaze that made its final dive on *Missouri* at 1443 had Campbell's full attention. "He kept coming in through the greatest ack-ack I've ever seen—5[-inch], 40s, and 20mm," Campbell wrote. "About 100 yards off the starboard quarter, he was hit slightly but kept coming. I kept shooting pictures."[26]

The Zero pilot missed the bridge but plowed into *Missouri* just below the main deck level of the starboard gun deck, sheering off its port wing to crash into 5-inch Mount No. 3 and starting a fire. Wreckage from the plane sprayed across the starboard side of the ship, leaving half of the pilot's body on deck before most of the wreckage carried over the side. By some miracle, the Zero's bomb did not explode and not a single sailor was killed. "This I really believe is a miracle," Campbell noted in his diary. "I was shaking but felt relieved after he hit. I took a beautiful shot of him as he hit. No one knows I took the picture except some of my friends, as I told Pat to take the credit." Buster Campbell's photo would become one of the most famous last-minute photos ever taken of a Japanese kamikaze in World War II.[27]

The following morning Captain Callaghan made the unorthodox move of paying respect to his enemy. Officers and crew were gathered at attention as a bugler played "Taps," a Marine honor guard fired a three-rifle volley, and ship's chaplain Roland Faulk said, "Commend his body to the deep." The torso section of the kamikaze pilot, wrapped in a hastily sewn Japanese flag, was buried at sea—an honorable ceremony that did not sit well with all of the *Missouri* crew at the time. Although this attacker was believed to be Setsuo Ishino, no conclusive evidence exists, as antiaircraft fire downed the second Zero minutes later.

The second Zero may well have fallen to Grim Reapers pilots launched with *Intrepid*'s third CAP of the day. Lieutenant (jg) James H. Dudley and his VF-10 wingman, Lieutenant Frank M. Jackson, each downed a Zeke near their task force, and another Japanese fighter that evaded the Corsair pilots was shot down by a destroyer before the kamikaze could complete his attack.

Minor brushes with Japanese planes persisted into the evening hours. By midnight TF 58's pilots had turned in claims for two dozen victories. Lieutenant Dallas E. Runion of *Enterprise*'s VF(N)-90 downed a Tony near Okinawa at 1905, while Lieutenant Ralph Waldo Cummings of VT(N)-90 splashed a Showa/Nakajima L2D Navy Type O "Tabby" transport north of the island at 2023. Big E night-fighter pilots would be credited with three Betty bomber shoot downs by 0200 on the twelfth. *Intrepid*'s VF-10 night fighters added two more kills, including a Betty downed by Lieutenant Mark Orr, a thirty-year-old Texan who pursued his opponent through friendly antiaircraft fire to splash the bomber short of reaching the carrier *Yorktown*.

The late afternoon and early evening attacks were evidence of an increased level of enemy activity, spurring speculation among the men of TF 58 that the rumored second Kikusui operation might indeed take place on April 12.

Chapter Fifteen

CHERRY BLOSSOM FIRES

Vice Admiral Ugaki wrote in his diary on April 12, "I want to wipe them out by any means." His morning searches pinpointed three groups of American aircraft carriers some eighty miles east of the northern tip of Okinawa. To achieve his goal of inflicting maximum damage to Pete Mitscher's TF 58, Ugaki unleashed Kikusui No. 2, an assault force consisting of 354 Japanese naval aircraft and 124 army planes.[1]

Ugaki had originally planned to strike two days prior, but foul weather had caused him to postpone the operation. Misled by many exaggerated reports that claimed as many as sixty-nine American ships had been sunk on April 7–8, he planned to use 185 kamikazes for these new attacks, including 60 from the army and 125 from the navy.[2]

The fighter forces of Kikusui No. 2 would be divided into four waves, including thirty-four Shiden fighters of the 343rd Air Group under Commander Mamori Genda. Ugaki would also dispatch nine Ohka-carrying Bettys from Kanoya Airfield to attack battleships. The launching of kamikaze forces from Chiran Airfield proved emotional. Schoolgirls, ranging in age from twelve to fifteen years old, from Chiran Girls' School had stripped bare a cherry tree in the neighborhood Shinto shrine. One of them, Shoko Maeda, also carried an armload of blossom-laden boughs from a big cherry tree in her grandfather's backyard.[3]

Maeda and the other girls passed out blossom boughs to the Ohka pilots, knowing that each young man, many only a few years older than the schoolgirls themselves, was willingly heading toward his own death in defense of their country. Newspaper cameramen and reporters documented the Chiran event. Requiring two and a half-hours of flight time to reach targets off Okinawa, it would be one of the last daylight launchings of a kamikaze unit from the airfield.

Maeda spoke with a Corporal Fuke about his younger sister, whom he hoped would grow up to be a fine Japanese woman. Second Lieutenant Miyazaki gave young Maeda his fountain pen, with which she promised to write to Miyazaki's sister about her brother's brave sortie. The young girl was also moved by a Corporal Iwama, who wrote, "All that lives is born to die, and cherry blossoms will always blow away in the wind."[4]

One of the memorable photos from the April 12 launch was that of 2nd Lieutenant Toshio Anazawa, a twenty-three-year-old graduate of Chuo University, revving up the propeller of his Oscar. Anazawa waved from his fighter, which was loaded with a 550-pound bomb, to the Chiran schoolgirls as they pointed their boughs skyward. Before his final flight, the young lieutenant wrote to his fiancée: "I only wish your happiness. Do not mind the past. You are to live from moment to moment in reality. I, Anazawa, no longer exist in the world of reality."[5]

Among the Ohka pilots was Reserve Sub-Lieutenant Saburo Dohi, who climbed on board the second Betty making up the 3rd Ohka Squadron. Two hours after launching, the Bettys were engaged by American fighters, which fought through the Japanese escort fighters and tore through the bombers' ranks. Throughout the melee, crewmen on Dohi's Betty noted that he looked almost asleep as he sat silently with his eyes closed and his arms folded across his chest, preparing for the moment his rocket-powered bomb would be launched.[6]

Ugaki spent the day keeping track of radio reports from his operations room, hoping for successful results against the American fleet. Determined fighter pilots like those of VF-17 and VBF-17 had downed the first flight of Ohka bombers on March 21, but the "Cherry Blossoms" would not be denied on April 12.

TF 58 night fighters accounted for five enemy planes destroyed during the predawn hours of April 12, but it was past noon before the action began heating up. It would prove to be another banner day of combat for U.S. fighter pilots. The first unit to begin tangling with Japanese fighters was *Bennington*'s VF-82 at 1230, about ten miles north of Amami Oshima. Lieutenant Armand Manson's flight accounted for three kills in exchange for one pilot who ditched his Hellcat and was rescued by an OS2U Kingfisher from the cruiser *Miami* (CL 89).

Beginning at 1300, two *Hornet* fighter squadrons began tangling with Japanese fighters off Kikai Jima in a running series of battles that would last nearly an hour. Lieutenant Edwin S. Conant's dozen F6Fs of VBF-17, acting as an interceptor CAP over Kikai, were attacked by fourteen Georges, Zekes, Tonys, Tojos, and Jacks. Ensign Raymond Grosso was shot down almost immediately, but Conant's divisions claimed thirteen victories and three enemy aircraft damaged in a wild melee.

Lieutenant Commander Marsh Beebe was in the area with three divisions of his VF-17. As their radios crackled with reports from VBF-17 of the large melee in progress, Beebe swung his Hellcats down the northwest coast of Kikai to join the fight. "The boys from the [other] squadron were having another heyday, and I was to relieve them on station," he said. "There were airplanes splashing every place when I came upon the situation," he said. "The battle was about over."[7]

Beebe, wingman Bud Good, and Lieutenant (jg) Frank Sistrunk were quickly caught in a swirling blend of slashing aircraft. Beebe and Sistrunk pursued an aggressive Jack flying at full speed. "I guessed the Japanese pilot figured he'd run us out of gas," offered Beebe. The Jack eventually began making very slight skid turns, allowing Beebe the chance to finally fire a 20-degree deflection shot on its tail. Beebe hung tight until his bullets began causing pieces of metal to shear off the Japanese fighter. More than eight minutes into the chase, the Fighting Seventeen skipper finally had the satisfaction of seeing his foe slam into the water and disintegrate. Beebe felt that if he had encountered another such opponent in a one-on-one battle, "I would have had my hands full."[8]

In the interim Sistrunk had burned a Zeke, while the divisions of Tommy Harris and Dick Cowger had been equally busy. Harris and wingman, Lieutenant (jg) Swede Sundberg, the latter forced to head back to the ship with a balky engine, were jumped by a pair of Georges. Sundberg downed one, while Harris disposed of the other as it made a run on his wingman. Harris then turned into a Kate torpedo bomber, burning it with one burst. Its torpedo fell free, a chunk of fuselage came off, and the plane's wreckage hit the ocean flaming. "As I flew through the debris, I didn't see anything big enough to hurt my F6F," said Harris.[9]

Lieutenant (jg) Tilly Pool, leading the remaining section of Harris' division, headed toward the melee to catch up with Cowger's Hellcats. Approximately ten miles east of the north tip of Amami, at 8,000 feet, Pool spotted four Franks heading west at 11,000 feet. He fired into the belly of one fighter from 900 feet, causing it to flame and fall to the ocean. As Pool and wingman Stan Smith approached the combat area, Smith downed a lone Zeke spotted flying on an opposite course.

Hornet's "Fighting Two" division of VF-17. *Left to right:* Lieutenant (jg) Harry "Swede" Sundberg, Ensign Robert F. Cunningham, Lieutenant (jg) Tilman E. "Tilly" Pool, Lieutenant (jg) Tommy Harris, and Ensign Stan Smith. *Tilman Pool*

Cowger's division got into the fight about ten miles off the west coast of Kikai. Lieutenant (jg) Bill Hardy dropped one Tojo and teamed with a *Bennington* VMF-112 Corsair to finish off a second. Around 1330 Cowger tallyhoed four Zekes flying south at 4,000 feet. In a matter of seconds, all four were splashed. Cowger, Lieutenant (jg) Morgan, and Ensign Vonder Heyden each destroyed one opponent, while Tilly Pool claimed the fourth Zeke.

Following this action, Heyden, whose Hellcat was suffering engine problems, was escorted back to the carrier by Hardy. They were jumped by a Frank en route, but Hardy drove it off and was credited with damaging it. Cowger's division and Pool's section remained over Kikai long enough for Cowger to dispose of another Zeke. Division leader Harris could hear the melee over his radio as he raced to join the action after escorting Sundberg most of the way back to base. En route he engaged a George pilot in a duel of scissoring maneuvers. "This turned into a sequence like a dog shaking a rat," explained Harris, who eventually landed enough hits to cause the George to stall and nose toward the water.[10]

By the end of the action on the twelfth, *Hornet's* VF-17 and VBF-17 pilots had turned in claims for an impressive 32.5 kills, two probables, and six planes damaged.

Second Lieutenant Dean Caswell's division of Fighting Falcons joined in the action near Kikai on the afternoon of April 12. Led by Captain John Delancey, his *Bunker Hill* division had flown escort for photo Hellcats over Tokuna Shima before heading to help a group of *Bennington* fighters engaged in a dogfight at Kikai Jima.

The VMF-221 Corsairs arrived about 1500 to find that the Japanese airfield on Tokuna had launched Zekes and Franks into the scrap. Delancey, with wingmen Joe Brocia and Caswell, dived down on three Zekes flying about one thousand feet off the water. The captain stitched the cockpit and starboard wing root of one Japanese fighter that was seen to crash on the edge of the island. Caswell was amazed by the mottled colors of these Japanese planes, some painted in greens, yellows, and light blues. In his first dive he hit the canopy of a Tojo that had just lifted off the runway. He passed within three feet of the army fighter as he swept past at high speed. "The pilot was still in the cockpit—with no head," he said. "I received no credit for that one. My gun camera did not pick that up."[11]

Caswell then picked up a Zeke making a climbing left turn right ahead of the Tojo. He carefully led his quarry—just like he had done a decade earlier while duck hunting as a boy—and gave him a burst with all six guns. Caswell's gun camera did catch this Zeke bursting into flames, and his victim was seen to crash on the north end of the Wan Airfield at Kikai. Divisionmate Joe Brocia downed another Zeke, while John McManus, flying "tail-end Charlie" for the division, jumped on a Frank that was being pursued by *Bennington* Hellcats. McManus doggedly stayed on the enemy fighter, flying through heavy antiaircraft fire over the airfield while landing more hits. McManus finally broke off his attack shortly before Caswell saw the Frank execute a steep wingover, plunge into the ground, and burn. "It was a good fight," said Caswell.[12]

Another Corsair division, led by VF-10 executive officer Lieutenant Commander John Sweeny, swung onto the tail of some Zekes over Tokuna that afternoon. Sweeny's efforts were spoiled by malfunctioning .50-calibers, but two of his divisionmates—Ensign Jack Twedell and Lieutenant (jg) Lester Gray—each downed a Zeke with their functioning guns.[13]

Gray, a veteran of the Grim Reapers from its early days and credited with four prior kills, achieved ace status with this shoot down, but he was not finished. Minutes later he caught another lone Zero, pursued him over Amami Oshima, and shot him down with a two-second burst. Sweeny, disgusted with his nonfunctioning guns, headed back for *Intrepid* with his Grim Reapers wingman, leaving Les Gray and his wingman, Ensign Jack Halbe, to complete their CAP duty. A half hour later a lone Jack fighter surprised the pair with a diving pass from out of the sun.

Bullets ripped through Halbe's cockpit, one penetrating his knee, and punctured his fuel tank. His Corsair went into a violent spin, but the ensign managed to parachute out safely. Gray gave lengthy chase to the crafty Jack before turning back to fly cover over his downed wingman until a PBY rescue seaplane retrieved him from the ocean an hour later.[14]

✦◇✦

Shortly after 1400 Vice Admiral Ugaki's kamikazes of Kikusui No. 2 began playing hell upon the ships manning Radar Picket Station No. 1 off Okinawa. Of these six ships—destroyers *Cassin Young* and *Purdy* (DD 734) and *LCS(L)s 33, 57, 114,* and *115*—five would be hit by kamikazes by the end of the day's onslaught.

Due to detected incoming raids, *Cassin Young* had three divisions of *Intrepid* VF-10 Corsairs under her direction by early afternoon. The first raid of fifteen Vals and Nates was assailed by two Fighting Ten divisions, those of Lieutenant Wally Schub and 1st Lieutenant William A. "Nick" Nickerson—the latter one of four Marine Corsair pilots who had volunteered to augment *Intrepid's* F4U squadron. In mere minutes eight Grim Reapers had slashed a dozen of the fifteen kamikazes from the sky, leaving the other three to flee.

The third division of VF-10 was an equal mix of Navy and Marine Corsair pilots, led by heavyset Lieutenant Frank Jackson. His division was vectored to greet another wave of kamikazes, this one proving to be the more sleek and dangerous Oscar and Zeke fighters. Jackson and his wingman each disposed of a Zeke in a series of sharp maneuvers and blazing guns above the radar-picket warships. Grumman F4F Wildcat fighters from VC-93 off the escort carrier *Petrof Bay* (CVE 80) joined the battle and claimed kills, but the squadron suffered its own losses.[15]

Ensign Paul R. Baumgartner of VC-93 was shot up by a Zeke and then was taken under fire by the Radar Picket Station No. 1 destroyers as he attempted to ditch. Fortunately, Baumgartner was quickly plucked unhurt from the ocean by *Purdy*. Two other pilots, Lieutenant Jackson of VF-10 and Ensign Charles Joseph Janson of VC-93, collided in midair while making diving passes on the same Zeke. Each plane suffered one wing sheared off. Janson was killed in the subsequent crash, while Jackson was picked up uninjured by a destroyer.[16]

The six picket ships were attacked by forty Vals, Kates, Zekes, Oscars, and Bettys from Kanoya and Kushira Airfields, and some of the kamikazes made it through the CAP. *Cassin Young* was crashed in her starboard quarter at 1337 by a diving Val. Nick Nickerson's VF-10 division came to the aid of *Purdy* as another ten Jill torpedo bombers, Vals, and Judys moved in on the destroyer and her support ships. Nickerson downed a Jill and a Val, but the dive bomber's rear gunner slammed a burst of 7.7-mm machine-gun bullets into his engine, blackening his windshield with oil. Nickerson, able only to see by looking out the side of his canopy, glided his crippled Corsair down into the ocean and was rescued by one of *Purdy's* LCS gunboats.[17]

One kamikaze slammed into the forward 40-mm gun tub of *LCS(L) 57*, and at 1352 a Nate exploded ten feet from the ship, blowing an eight-foot hole in her side. As the *57*'s crew struggled with a 10-degree list and crippled steering ability, another Nate crashed into her forward single 40-mm gun mount at 1430, forcing the ship's skipper to make a run for port to make repairs. Having suffered three kamikaze hits, *LCS(L) 57*'s crew had downed four Nates but was knocked out of the war. *Purdy*'s gunners shot down four kamikazes by 1500 but was damaged by a Val that was splashed twenty feet shy of the destroyer. The dive bomber itself skipped off the water and into *Purdy*, its bomb exploding inside the ship, killing thirteen and wounding another fifty-eight sailors.

Another radar-picket gunboat, *LCS(L) 33*, was slammed amidships by a Val, knocking out the ship's power and creating a 35-degree list. Minutes later another kamikaze struck the ship forward of amidships, spraying gasoline over the decks and impacting with such force that the ship's skipper suffered a broken vertebra. "Then came a terrific crash when the plane struck and suddenly, for me, there was only darkness, stillness and emptiness," wrote Lieutenant (jg) Frank C. Osterland. "There was a deep dent in my helmet that hadn't been there before, and I knew that I'd received a hard blow to my head and that my nose was bleeding."[18]

Osterland was among the seventy survivors who were picked up from *LCS(L) 33* after the order to abandon ship was given at 1505. The hulk of the gunboat was scuttled by gunfire from *Purdy* that afternoon, making *LCS(L) 33* the fourth ship sunk and the first gunboat lost on radar-picket duty off Okinawa.

Radar Picket Stations No. 1 and No. 2 seemed specially targeted on the twelfth, with another raid picked up by radar around 1620. Vectored in to intercept it was Captain Frank B. Baldwin's division of VMF-221 Corsairs. First Lieutenant John E. Jorgensen flamed one of the approaching Vals, while 1st Lieutenant Arthur B. Imel disposed of another. Other VMF-221 pilots accounted for another Val and two Zekes in the vicinity of the damaged *Purdy*.

Corsairs, Wildcats, and Hellcats from fleet carriers and escort carriers battled kamikazes throughout the afternoon off Okinawa as the aircraft comprising Kikusui No. 2 continued to swarm with a vengeance. The *Petrof Bay* VC-93 Wildcat division of Lieutenant Ralph E. Friedrich knocked down ten enemy planes in a running series of battles, but some of the kamikazes made it through the CAP. Off Radar Picket Station No. 2, the destroyer *Stanly* (DD 478) was slammed by an Ohka launched from one of the nine Thunder Gods Bettys that had taken off from Kanoya. The rocket-propelled plane came in so fast that it literally ripped through

Stanly's starboard bow before exploding in the ocean to port. *Stanly* was damaged enough to keep her out of action for the next week.[19]

Belleau Wood's VF-30 saw considerable action on April 12. Lieutenant (jg) Bob Carlson of Beaver Falls, Pennsylvania, downed a Tony and two Zekes, one of which he doggedly pursued right through the gunfire of task-group warships. Near Radar Picket Station No. 14, another division of Fighting Thirty came to the aid of the destroyer *Mannert L. Abele* (DD 733) and her two gunboat companions. Lieutenant Lloyd G. Rygh's *Belleau Wood* fighters shot down four Vals and one Oscar, but *Abele* suffered a direct hit around 1415 from a Zeke that crashed into her starboard side, its bomb exploding in the after engine room. "All guns were still firing when the plane crashed into the starboard side at the after engine room, causing a tremendous explosion," reported Lieutenant Peter J. Murphy Jr., *Abele*'s gunnery officer.[20]

Ten men were killed, and *Abele* began to lose power and headway. At 1445 another of the Ohka-laden Bettys from Kanoya was moving in against the crippled destroyer. Flight Petty Officer Zenjiro Sugano had spotted the wakes of American ships on the horizon. The Ohka pilot, Reserve Sub-Lieutenant Dohi, had continued resting in an almost trancelike state. At the announcement of warship targets, Dohi opened his eyes, took off his aviator's cap, and tied his Thunder Gods band around his head. He removed his life jacket and handed his waist pistol to Sugano, asking that it be given to a comrade. Sugano opened the floorboard hatch leading to the Ohka plane suspended beneath the Betty, and Dohi lowered himself into the tiny cockpit.[21]

Dohi signaled that he was ready, even as close antiaircraft fire rocked the Betty mothership. Sugano tapped out a signal to Kanoya that their bomber was ready to launch its Ohka. Lieutenant Kitataro Miura, the Betty's chief pilot, pushed the button to detach the flying bomb, but it failed to release, forcing Petty Officer Sugano to yank the emergency tripwire holding the rocket plane. Lieutenant Dohi fired his rockets and screamed toward his target ship at 500 miles per hour. Sugano watched the Ohka streak toward the distant destroyers, leaving a trail of smoke in its wake. Seconds later he saw a rising column of thick black smoke that marked the impact of Dohi's Ohka into an American warship. It was the destroyer *Mannert L. Abele*.[22]

Pilot Miura nursed his crippled Betty back to Kanoya around 1745 that evening. Ground crews found that more than fifty shrapnel holes, some more than a foot in diameter, had riddled the plane. The Betty crew was hustled to Vice Admiral Ugaki's underground operations room for the 5th Air Fleet, where they were the first surviving Betty crew to return with eyewitness reports of the launching of an Ohka flying bomb. Lieutenant Miura and his officers were criticized for being unable to specifically identify the type of warship that Dohi had slammed into, but the Thunder Gods had finally crashed into an American warship with one of their rocket planes.[23]

Abele gunnery officer Pete Murphy observed Dohi's Baka coming in fast on his ship's starboard beam and realized that his two forward gun mounts did not have time to finish training in the proper direction to bring it under fire. "It was faster than any of our planes," noted Murphy, who had only enough time to note the jet plane's solid light gray color and rounded wingtips. "It looked like a flying torpedo," said Seaman 1st Class James L. Morris. "I had no idea what it was."[24]

The Cherry Blossom pilot slammed into *Abele*'s hull at 1446 with a terrific explosion amidships, near the topside torpedo tubes. The damage-control officer, 1st Lieutenant George L. Way, was blown overboard but managed to grab a line hanging from the forward boat davit and haul himself back on board. Way immediately organized all available men forward and had them begin cutting loose life rafts. He then broke off a jammed dog on the port hatch to the forward engine room using a crowbar, with the help of Electrician's Mate 2nd Class Henry S. Paulman, allowing some ten men to escape from below.[25]

The ship was felt to buckle badly, and the executive officer, Lieutenant Commander Harry W. Burns Jr., was ordered to hurry aft to help 1st Lieutenant Way direct repair parties. "By the time I reached the main deck, starboard side, the ship was listing to port and sinking rapidly," wrote Burns. He and Way ordered everyone they could see to abandon ship before they also jumped overboard.[26]

At 1448, two minutes after the Ohka hit, *Abele*'s bow and stern sections parted. In a matter of seconds the water was up to the after-bridge deck gratings, and the last men on the bridge pushed themselves out into the water. One minute later the destroyer disappeared below the surface. Seaman 1st Class Leonard A. Hartley was fortunate. Just the previous day he had requested duty below decks but had been denied. "I would have been dead," reflected Hartley. "I could hear the people who were trapped below deck banging on the walls and yelling as it sank."[27]

A Zeke dropped a bomb among the swimming survivors, killing and injuring more sailors. First Lieutenant Way felt pains in his stomach from the concussion of the underwater blast. Other Japanese planes briefly strafed the survivors, who were further challenged by the sighting of shark fins as they clung to wreckage. Seventy-nine sailors on *Abele* were killed and another thirty-five were wounded by the kamikaze strikes. At least 108 of her survivors were picked up by *LSM(R) 189*, a rocket gunboat that was herself seriously damaged on the twelfth by a direct kamikaze strike.[28]

◆◇◆

Commander Thomas E. Chambers' destroyer-minelayer *Lindsey* (DM 32) narrowly survived the relentless kamikazes on April 12. His picket ship, named for VT-6 torpedo-bomber squadron skipper Lieutenant Commander Eugene Lindsey, who was killed at Midway while attacking the Japanese carriers, came under assault around 1445 six miles off Aguni Shima, south and west of Okinawa.[29]

Lindsey's gun crews chewed pieces from a Val kamikaze as it raced in three hundred feet above the wave tops, but the remains slammed into the warship at the base of the bridge superstructure on the starboard side. Shrapnel tore holes in the bridge and pilothouse, demolished the wardroom and galley, and killed a nearby 20-mm gun crew. Within a minute a second Val slammed into *Lindsey*'s port side near the forward 5-inch gun mount. The detonation of the plane's bomb created a tremendous explosion that ripped the forward sixty feet off the destroyer's bow.

Lindsey was still amazingly afloat. Skipper Tom Chambers immediately ordered full reverse, an action that prevented the pressure of the inrushing sea from collapsing the fireroom bulkhead and sinking his ship. Other vessels helped tow the stricken vessel some twenty miles to the Kerama Retto anchorage, arriving there by nightfall. The final casualty tally was fifty-seven men wounded and fifty-seven others lost, but *Lindsey* had been saved.

One of the last enemy intercepts of the afternoon again involved the Grim Reapers of *Intrepid*'s VF-10. Lieutenant (jg) Phil Kirkwood's Corsair division had been flying radar-picket CAP for more than two hours when he spotted a Betty at 1630, ten miles ahead and several thousand feet below them. Kirkwood landed the first punishing blows in the bomber's

The destroyer-minelayer *Lindsey* (DM 32) was towed back to the Kerama Retto anchorage on April 12, 1945, after losing sixty feet of her bow to kamikaze attacks. *U.S. Navy*

starboard engine. The Japanese pilot immediately pushed over into a dive, but Ensign Dick Quiel closed to one thousand feet on the Betty's starboard side and set the already damaged engine ablaze. The crippled bomber went into a spin to the right as all four Reapers continued pouring streams of lead into it all the way down.

Quiel watched with satisfaction as the big bomber slammed into the ocean and exploded, marking his second confirmed kill. The Grim Reapers finished the day with 26 kills from among Vice Admiral Ugaki's Kikusui No. 2 aircraft, taking single-squadron honors, although *Hornet's* two fighter squadrons had collectively downed more planes. Navy fighter pilots closed out April 12 with claims of 144 kills, three probable victories, and eight Japanese aircraft damaged. Marine Corps fighter pilots claimed 77 kills that day, with 17 falling to shore-based units and the other 60 being dropped by carrier-based leathernecks.[30]

The first two weeks of radar-picket duty off Okinawa had cost the U.S. fleet three destroyers and one LCS(L) sunk, another dozen ships damaged, 235 men killed, and 304 wounded. Other kamikazes had slipped through to hit ships anchored in the Hagushi and Kerama Retto anchorages as well as adjacent waters. During this same period, an additional 946 sailors had been killed and 1,496 men wounded.[31]

Vice Admiral Ugaki's Thunder Gods had made a lasting impression upon the U.S. fleet on April 12. Few rational minds believed they had seen the last of the deadly kamikazes.

Chapter Sixteen

"I'LL NEVER ABANDON SHIP"

"A ttention, all hands. President Roosevelt has died. Our supreme commander is dead." Hellcat ace Hamilton McWhorter was sitting in his
cockpit on *Randolph* preparing to launch for a strike when he heard the
announcement over the ship's loudspeaker. The news from Washington
was received throughout TF 58 and was filtered down through the ranks
of Army and Marine soldiers fighting from their foxholes on Okinawa on
April 13.[1]

The passing of Franklin Delano Roosevelt was mourned with simple
memorial services both ashore and afloat by many, while those currently
under siege simply acknowledged the grim news and continued firing.
Harry S. Truman was sworn in as the new U.S. president while combat
raged on and around Okinawa. "In the midst of fighting, we were unable to
spend much time considering what effect this tragic event would have on
the war," said TG 58.3 commander Ted Sherman.[2]

Lieutenant Gene Valencia and his VF-9 wingman Harris Mitchell had
another reason to recall April 13, 1945. Their division was flying target
CAP over Okinawa when Valencia noticed his oil pressure running low
and asked Mitch to inspect his plane. "The whole bottom of his fuselage
was covered with oil, so he was instructed to land at Yontan for repairs,"
said Mitchell. Marine Air Group 31 had been operating from Yontan Airfield since the seventh, making the former Japanese base ideal for carrier
pilots struggling with maintenance emergencies.[3]

Mitchell and Valencia found that cooking there was done over open
fires, with hot coffee available, but most of the meals still came from

K rations and C rations, as construction of the Marine field camp at Yontan was still ongoing. Marine plane handlers were unable to repair Valencia's oil leak before the close of darkness, so the Navy officers were invited to make themselves at home for the night. The VF-9 pilots were assigned to a six-man tent shared by men from an LST. Mitch found their stories to be interesting, but he was exhausted from a long day of flight duty. He and Valencia stripped down to their skivvies, carefully rolling their clothes, flight gear, and shoes into a bundle that they stowed at the foot of their cots.

Mitchell had just dozed off when he was startled by the high-pitched tone of a soldier's voice. "Don't turn that bomb over!" Mitch heard a loud hissing sound. In one swift move he leaped from his cot, grabbed his clothing, bounded from the tent, and sprinted as far from the bomb as his legs could carry him. He was a hundred yards away before he heard the shouts of his comrades. "Stop! It's just a mosquito bomb!"[4]

Mitchell sheepishly returned to his tent amid howls of laughter. Men explained to him that they had merely been setting off a mosquito bomb to rid their vicinity of the biting insects. Everyone had a good laugh at the Navy pilot's expense, but the weary Mitchell was again snoring soundly within ten minutes.

Another Fighting Nine pilot was forced to land on Yontan with engine trouble on the morning of April 14. By afternoon all three *Yorktown* pilots were able to take off with repaired planes for the flight back to their home carrier, where they shared plenty of tales with their fighter comrades about their adventures ashore on Okinawa.

Vice Admiral Ugaki considered his Kikusui operations on April 12 to have been a success. He spent the following day monitoring intelligence of his enemy's activities and learned that President Roosevelt had died. Ugaki took advantage of some rare downtime that afternoon to take a drive and go bird hunting. Despite the presence of vivid green trees and high wheat, he found no targets, noting, "Maybe it is time for me to give up shooting."[5]

In the past month of action, the Thunder Gods Corps had lost some 172 men. The remaining Ohka pilots were shifted from Tomitaka to Kanoya Airfield on the twelfth, its roster reduced to only 70 men—two division leaders, five reserve officers, and sixty-three petty-officer pilots. The five reserve officers, the last of an original group of twenty-one that had been first to join the corps, chided each other over their fates while eating dinner on the evening of April 13. Among them were Katsuhei Terashita and Hachiro Hosokawa, who listened as one of their fellow pilots commented on how their number had dwindled. "Now there are only five of us left."[6]

"Until tomorrow. Then there will be only four," said another pilot as he stared at reserve officer Hisaki Nakane, who was destined to lead an Ohka flight the following morning. Terashita tried to soothe the tension by offering: "It won't make any difference whether you hit your target or crash into the sea. We'll all meet at Yasukuni Shrine. So, Nakane, you go first and wait for us at the shrine."

Nakane, prepared for his fate, stood up and announced that he was going to take a bath. "I don't want to show up at Yasukuni so grimy my friends will laugh at me," he declared.[7]

April 14 dawned bright and clear, paving the way for the launch of Nakane and his fellow Ohka pilots to execute a daylight attack. Seven Betty bombers and two squadrons of fighter-bombers, each carrying 550-pound bombs, were sent against the American fleet. Among the fighters flying cover for the mission was Captain Genda, one of the key planners of the Japanese surprise attack on Pearl Harbor nearly four years earlier. Genda's planes mistakenly began attacks against another Japanese fighter squadron they were to rendezvous with. By the time the mess was sorted out, the Ohka-carrying Bettys were left flying without fighter cover toward twenty Hellcats of *Hornet*'s VF-17.[8]

CAG 17 Ed Konrad's five divisions had launched at 1205 for a strike against airfields on Tanega Shima, twenty miles to the south of Kyushu. Division leader Billy Watts was about fifty miles north of Kikai Jima when he tallyhoed a Betty at 11,000 feet at 1310. The big Japanese bomber was heading south, carrying a large torpedo-like Ohka under its belly.

After announcing his contact, Watts was directed by Konrad, "Go get him!"

Watts made a high side run on the Betty, flaming its starboard engine immediately. As he recovered below his quarry, he saw the Baka pilot detach from the Betty, his Ohka dropping straight down and exploding on impact with the ocean. During Watts' second run, the flaming starboard engine dropped out of the mothership's wing and fell into the sea. The lieutenant (jg) made his third and final run from astern and above the Betty, sending its flaming wreckage into the ocean. Watts believed he should have also received credit for downing the piloted rocket. "That *baka* bomb should have been worth two kills," he groused.[9]

Lieutenant (jg) George Covelly of Watts' division downed another Betty, though not before its Ohka pilot jettisoned his rocket bomb. Other VF-17 pilots found action close to their task group when *Hornet* scrambled two divisions at 1330 to intercept a pair of bogies closing on the carriers.

Dave Crist and Bud Good combined to kill a Zeke, while Frank Sistrunk and Jack Davis downed a bomb-laden Judy.

Belleau Wood's VF-30 encountered three Ohka-carrying Bettys and a Zeke escort around 1410 some twenty-five miles from their task group. Ensign Harris A. Lee disposed of the fighter, while Ensign James Jacob Noel and two other pilots dropped the Bettys in sequence. One of the bombers was seen to release its gray-colored Ohka, which glided down to the ocean without exploding.

Twenty miles west of Okinawa, three other VF-30 divisions found three Zekes and a Tony approaching the beach. Lieutenants (jg) Bob Carlson and Robert H. Baldwin and Ensign Arlo I. Lunder each downed a Zeke, while Ensign Johnnie Miller—who had become an ace in a day during the big April 6 turkey shoot—added to his scorecard by taking down the Tony. Snugged in on the Japanese fighter's tail, he fired into its wing-root gas tanks until the plane exploded and broke in two. "There wasn't enough left to make a splash," Miller quipped upon his return to *Belleau Wood*.[10]

TF 58 pilots claimed forty-five victories on April 14, and *Belleau Wood*'s VF-30 pilots finished second highest, with eight combined kills. *Hornet*'s Air Group 17 took the top-performance honors that day, with three kills for VF-17 and another fifteen for sister squadron VBF-17. Lieutenant (jg) John Mitchell Johnston, a graduate of Oregon State College, was high scorer for VBF-17. Short in stature and nicknamed "Super Mouse" by his squadronmates, Johnston was a former member of Medal of Honor–recipient Edward "Butch" O'Hare's VF-3 squadron. Johnston was no meager mouse on the fourteenth, as he flamed three Zekes, leaving him one kill short of becoming an ace. He would surpass this goal in a mere two days.

Vice Admiral Ugaki designated April 15 and 16 to be the dates he would launch his third kamikaze assault, Kikusui No. 3. He planned to use 165 suicide aircraft, drawing 120 from the navy and 45 from the Sixth Air Army, pulling his strike planes from fields north of Okinawa on Kyushu and Tokuna Shima as well as from Taiwan to the south. Another 300 aircraft would fly as fighter support and as conventional strike planes.[11]

Poor weather forced a delay in the planned morning strike schedule, and before any afternoon kamikaze launch could take place, the Kyushu airfields were visited by warplanes from TF 58. Among those sweeping in was 2nd Lieutenant Dean Caswell, who launched from *Bunker Hill* at 1318 with two divisions of his VMF-221 Corsair squadron along with ten VF-84 fighters.

Lieutenant Joe Brocia developed engine trouble soon after takeoff and was forced to make a deadstick water landing near the destroyer *Erben* (DD 631). Caswell and the remaining seven Fighting Falcons pilots attacked aircraft and installations on two airfields at Kanoya. Captain Delancey splashed the lone Jill found airborne, while his fellow pilots destroyed one single-engine aircraft on the ground and damaged another dozen. By the time Caswell's flight returned to *Bunker Hill* around 1656, he found that downed pilot Brocia had been returned to their carrier an hour earlier. Major Ed Roberts, the squadron skipper, was on hand to greet his lost aviator as soon as he swung back on board via a breaches buoy shot across from the rescuing destroyer. "I thought now I would get a few days off to catch up on some sack time, but this was not to happen," recalled Brocia. "I was flying the next day as usual. The war goes on!"[12]

Lieutenant Commander Robert "Doc" Weatherup, skipper of VF-46, led his *Independence* strikers against Kanoya Airfield on April 15. As the Hellcats roared in to rocket aircraft revetments, Japanese pilots raced for two fighters at one end of the flight line. Among them were Chief Petty Officer Shoichi Sugita—one of Japan's top-five naval aces—and his wingman, Petty Officer 2nd Class Toyomi Miyazawa. Another ace pilot, Ensign Saburo Sakai, yelled at Sugita to take cover, but his warning was ignored.[13]

Sugita lifted off and was just climbing through two hundred feet when Doc Weatherup dived in again with his guns blazing. He had waited until Sugita's wingspan filled his sights before opening up. Seeing the tracers, Sugita attempted to relax his turn, but .50-caliber slugs ripped through his armor and caused his George to nose over while trailing a thin plume of smoke; the plane crashed at the end of the airfield in a ball of fire. Seconds later Weatherup blasted wingman Miyazawa to a similar fate.

Sugita was posthumously promoted two ranks to ensign. Commander Genda would credit him with achieving seventy individual and forty shared aerial victories. Fellow ace Sakai, who would meet Doc Weatherup at a 1982 reunion, said of his downed friend, "He was a great ace but a little reckless."[14]

Essex Air Group 83 participated in an afternoon sweep over Kanoya East Airfield and destroyed six enemy planes in the air. Lieutenant (jg) Glen Wallace of VBF-83 was frustrated to find no bogies as he maintained a boring tactical CAP flight over Okinawa while this action took place over Kyushu. "Tomorrow we have the same thing!" Wallace logged in his diary with frustration. "To hell with that place."[15]

The Navy strikers claimed twenty-nine shoot downs near the southern Kyushu airfields on April 15 in addition to fifty-one aircraft destroyed on the ground. Vice Admiral Ugaki sent dozens of strike planes to bomb and strafe the Okinawa airfields of Yontan and Kadena, but little long-term damage resulted. Other attackers moved in over the radar-picket warships, but most were taken down by vigilant antiaircraft fire and effective CAP fighters.[16]

Ugaki had held back the bulk of his kamikaze forces, but he would not flinch from unleashing them with a fury the following morning.

The sixteenth of April was taxing on both Navy and Marine fighter pilots flying from Okinawa, as the carrier fleet's blue umbrella fought the second phase of Kikusui No. 3 strikes. At dawn Ugaki sent out eight planes to attack Allied-controlled airstrips and another fifty-eight Zeros to challenge air supremacy over Okinawa. Between 0600 and 0700 he sent another forty dive bombers and fighter-bombers plus a dozen twin-engine Frances bombers and six Ohkas. Between 0830 and 1000, numerous pilots radioed that they were making their final dives on U.S. ships. In addition, sixty-five army fighters and special-attack planes were launched to add to the assault force even as U.S. carrier planes raided his airbases in southern Kyushu. "Now they came to attack us while we were attacking them over there," Ugaki wrote. "Let's go and get them!"[17]

Langley's Air Group 23 lost its fighter skipper, Lieutenant Commander Merlin Paddock, during its morning strikes on Kagashima Airfield. Paddock led two VF-23 divisions along with a dozen Hellcats from *Yorktown's* VF-9. Once over Kyushu at 1100, CAG 9 Herb Houck sent in his VF-9 fighters first for a combined strafing and rocket attack. Gene Valencia's division rocketed hangars and buildings, while Houck's division shot up parked aircraft. *Langley's* Hellcats followed, but Paddock's F6F was hit by antiaircraft fire, forcing him to bail out. The Fighting Twenty-Three skipper was still drifting down in his parachute when Gene spotted a Judy dive out of the cloud layer, apparently intent on strafing the downed American.

Diving at high speed, Valencia flew toward the Judy, which executed first a left and then a sharp right turn. As the lieutenant was just reaching optimal firing range, the Japanese plane executed a split-S maneuver but failed to recover. He watched in amazement as the inexperienced Judy pilot slammed his aircraft into the ground. Valencia would later express regrets at not having time to open fire. His aggressive approach had caused the Japanese pilot to panic and crash his plane, but the fact that no bullets were fired negated Gene from receiving credit for its destruction.

Kanoya Airfield was assaulted by strikers from *Essex*, *Bunker Hill*, and *Bataan*. Lieutenant Tom "Ham" Reidy took command of the fourteen VBF-83 Corsairs after his skipper and a wingman, Glen Wallace, turned back with engine problems. "I could only get three guns to fire and Ham only one!" Wallace logged in his diary. The only two Japanese planes encountered in the air over Kanoya, a Judy and a Zeke, were shot down by Reidy and Lieutenant Jack Tripp. Two VBF-83 planes, those of Ensigns Clint Wear and James Milton Bouldin, were forced down by flak. Wear was rescued by a PBY of Rescue Squadron 3 the following day, but Bouldin was last seen lying on the ground one hundred feet from the burning wreckage of his plane. He would survive the war as a prisoner of the Japanese. Lieutenant (jg) Ed Pappert was given the somber task back on board *Essex* of inventorying Bouldin's personal effects for shipment to his family.[18]

Ensign Tommy Ward of VF-83 was also lost when his F6F took a shell in the engine. He took to his life raft after being forced to ditch and had the good fortune of being retrieved after four hours in the ocean by another Rescue Squadron 3 seaplane, a PBM-5 piloted by Lieutenant Commander R. R. "Hawk" Barrett Jr. from Kerama Retto.

Ugaki was pleased with his Kikusui No. 3 assault pilots. "One reported ramming on a carrier, five on a battleship, three on enemy vessels, and two on transports, while the release of one *Ohka* was reported," he logged for April 16. "All considered, two battleships or cruisers seem to have been almost surely sunk." As usual, Ugaki overestimated his fliers' success, but his Cherry Blossom warriors would hand out heavy destruction to the radar-picket warships.[19]

Dick Quiel's Grim Reapers division had its finest hour during the frantic morning of April 16 while helping repel Kikusui No. 3's second-phase aircraft. He was again flying wing on Lieutenant (jg) Phil Kirkwood, whose second section composed Ensign Horace "Tuck" Heath and Ensign Al Lerch, a baby-faced newlywed from Coopersburg, Pennsylvania. The latter had only been assigned to VF-10 by chance in January after missing deployment with his own unit, VF-87 on *Ticonderoga* (CV 14), while recovering from a broken leg.[20]

Kirkwood's team, launched from *Intrepid* at 0645 with two other Grim Reapers divisions, was assigned a target CAP station over northern Okinawa. Twenty minutes into orbiting over a radar-picket destroyer, Kirkwood vectored to intercept incoming kamikazes. Tuck Heath, finding his radio to be inoperable, turned over command of the second section to Al Lerch, normally the "tail-end Charlie" pilot of the division. As the quartet headed toward Amami Oshima, Lerch tallyhoed a flight of four Nate fighters and two Val dive bombers.

Quiel locked on to the rearmost Nate and opened fire, causing it to burn almost instantly. Kirkwood and Lerch each shot down one of the Vals. Heath, separated from his group due to his malfunctioning radio, caught the remaining Nates as they ducked into a cloud bank and splashed one before they disappeared. He was then able to rejoin Lerch and proceed back to their orbit point. Kirkwood and Quiel similarly regrouped and were proceeding back to orbit when they heard the radar-picket destroyer calling for help.

When they arrived overhead, they saw that the ship had already been hit by one suicide plane. Quiel and Kirkwood intercepted seven Nates and Vals coming in twenty miles north of the tin can and attacked immediately. "They were low wing monoplanes," said Quiel. "Then I saw their gear hanging down, which meant they were either Val dive bombers or obsolete Nate fighter planes. I steamed into them."[21]

Quiel was on his own, as Kirkwood made his own initial assault from lower altitude. Phil quickly dropped one of the dive bombers, while Quiel set his sights on one of the fighters. "I made a climbing pass from their rear," said Quiel. "That way it would slow down my speed differential and I would be in their blind spot. It was just a matter of picking one out and squeezing the trigger on my six .50-calibers to blow him up." The ensign shifted his aim to another of the fighters, which refused to break formation and merely continued their incoming flight. Within short order he had dispatched three Nates toward the ocean, pushing his morning's tally to four kills. Breaking into a clear patch of sky, Quiel spotted another Nate hell-bent for the damaged destroyer in the distance. "I could see my rate of closure was too fast," he said. "So, I cut back on the throttle and did anything I could to stop my airplane."[22]

Quiel's Corsair closed on the enemy fighter until he was no more than forty feet from his opponent, flying parallel for a brief moment. He glanced over into the open Nate cockpit, staring at the enemy pilot wearing a fur-lined helmet. "He never even looked at me. He just looked straight ahead." The Japanese airman was in an almost trancelike state, peering intently ahead at the destroyer he intended to crash. *I'm so close*, thought Quiel. *I don't even have to lead him. I can shoot him with my Smith and Wesson .38.* He reached for his revolver, rolled back his canopy, and prepared to fire.[23]

At that instant the destroyer opened up on the two inbound planes with its 5-inch guns, creating concussive black clouds all around them. Frazzled by the nearby explosions, Quiel was unable to react before the Nate pushed into his dive and slammed into the destroyer's forward gun turret. Quiel

A division from *Intrepid's* "Grim Reapers" squadron downed twenty enemy planes in one mission on April 16, 1945. The division leader, Lieutenant (jg) Phil Kirkwood (*left*), accounted for six kills, while Ensign Norwald "Dick" Quiel (*right*) destroyed four Nates. *U.S. Navy*

was pleased to see that the rugged destroyer absorbed this second kamikaze hit and continued steaming at high speed. He rendezvoused with Phil Kirkwood, who in the past hour of action had shot down two Vals and three Nates before they could reach the picket destroyers.

The two *Intrepid* pilots observed antiaircraft fire from another group of small picket boats and went over to help. Kirkwood sighted a Nate just starting a dive from four thousand feet and caught up with it just over the water. He hit the Nakajima fighter with three short bursts and splashed it just short of the destroyer it was attempting to ram. The Grim Reapers section had shot down ten enemy planes in one mission, and Kirkwood (now a double ace) relished the prospect of collecting another $600 in bounties from his New Jersey benefactor for his six latest kills.

The second section of Tuck Heath and Al Lerch proved to be equally deadly on the sixteenth. They had each already downed a Val in their first battle, but after that point the two were on their own, separated from Kirkwood and Quiel by miles. They returned to their rendezvous point but did not have long to circle before tall, thin Lerch spotted approximately thirty Nate fighters, each carrying bombs under their wings, heading for the picket stations.[24]

With Heath following, Lerch charged in for an immediate attack, and each pilot splashed one of the fighters before the Nates scattered. The Japanese pilots appeared unorganized, milling around close to the water, where they became sitting ducks for the Grim Reapers section. Lerch slid in behind three of them. Firing from dead astern, he sent two of them smoking to crash into the water and then exploded the third. Lerch said it was "the first time I really got a crack at them. They were all loaded down with bombs, and none of them made any effort to jettison." The young ensign had just become an ace in a day.[25]

Lerch had lost sight of Heath as he climbed back to altitude, but he quickly spotted three more Nates skirting the northern tip of Okinawa. He was just opening fire when another blue Corsair suddenly flashed in with its .50-calibers blazing. Lerch swerved, narrowly avoiding a collision with his sectionmate, whose radio was still inoperable. Heath splashed one Nate while Lerch maneuvered to get behind one of the other two. He opened fire from close astern, and the bomb-laden fighter exploded in brilliant fashion so close that his own F4U was struck in the wings and cowling by bits of wreckage. The Nate "blew up under my nose and just about creamed me," admitted the ensign.[26]

Lerch found that his engine was still running smoothly, and within minutes he and Heath were teaming up to chase another lone Nate. Lerch was quicker to fire, setting the fighter aflame before Heath added some final bullets to send the Nate diving into the ocean. By the time they cleared the sky in their area, Heath had three kills and Lerch had downed seven airplanes in a single mission—an accomplishment only four other U.S. pilots in history could claim. "I ran out of ammunition or I might have been able to get more," he told a radio interviewer weeks later.[27]

Phil Kirkwood's Grim Reapers division had downed a stunning twenty Japanese airplanes in one mission.

Thirty-seven-year-old Commander Julian Becton expected to battle the kamikazes on April 16. Sixteen months earlier he had been the executive officer of the destroyer *Aaron Ward* (DD 483) when his ship survived being hit by nine shells during a November 1942 battle with Japanese warships off Guadalcanal. One mile astern of *Aaron Ward*, the destroyer *Laffey* (DD 459) had gone down fighting after sustaining severe damage. Becton, now skipper of the new *Laffey* (DD 724), remembered the example set by its namesake's valiant crew during her final minutes and vowed to have his new ship perform as admirably in combat. He made sure that his crew had been properly fed on the morning of sixteenth, in expectation of suicide attacks on the radar pickets and wanted everyone to be alert. Fleet CAP fighters and his ship's gunners chased away the first would-be suiciders. Becton was on *Laffey*'s bridge when radarman Philip Nulf announced at 0820 that a large formation of bogies was approaching fast from the north. The skipper sounded the general alarm and rang up full speed.[28]

Four Vals were spotted inbound at 0830, all of which were shot down by *Laffey*'s gunners and those on the nearby LCS(L) 51. Baker Robert C. Johnson, one of the ammunition handlers at Mount No. 41—the forward

40-mm guns on *Laffey*'s starboard side—had jumped from his bunk and raced to his station upon hearing the battle-stations alarm. The nineteen-year-old from Farmfield, Virginia, had been with his ship for a year, having joined the Navy in February 1944 on his eighteenth birthday. Once at his station, Johnson rapidly passed the clips of four shells to the 40-mm gun crew above him as they blazed away at the incoming planes.[29]

Seaman Robert Dockery, sight setter for Mount No. 52, was stationed inside the mount, checking dials on the starboard side that monitored the gun's movement. His gun captain, Warren Walker, watched the action with the upper third of his body exposed through the hatch. Dockery could only listen to the sounds of the battle and feel his ship heeling side to side as Commander Becton dodged incoming kamikazes. Once the 40-mm and 20-mm guns began firing, he knew the action was getting too close for comfort.[30]

The opening minutes of *Laffey*'s battle went as well as the crew could hope. The ship's gunners took down the first four suiciders, and the next two—a pair of Judys—were also destroyed, although the sixth attacker crashed so close to the ship's port side that its detonating bomb wounded some of the sailors and knocked out *Laffey*'s SG radar. With only a short respite, the destroyer was attacked by a seventh kamikaze at 0839. Taken under fire, the Val managed to strike a glancing blow off 5-inch Mount No. 3 (Mount No. 53) before exploding in the water aft of the ship.

"I was told to stay in local control and pick my own targets while the bridge controlled Mounts One and Two in the forward part of the ship," said Gunner's Mate 2nd Class Larry Delweski, gun captain of Mount No. 53. Shortly thereafter a Judy came in from astern slightly to starboard. Pointer Calvin Cloer and trainer Jim LaPointe locked on to the target and opened fire. "Splash one kamikaze for Mount Three on our own," announced Delweski as the Japanese plane slammed into the water.[31]

Another Judy, the ninth kamikaze since 0827, came in from the port bow and crashed into the area near Mount Nos. 43 and 44, putting those guns out of action. The impact spread burning gasoline over the positions and began cooking off 40-mm and 20-mm ammunition stacked nearby. Just two minutes later, at 0847, Delweski yelled to "Frenchy" LaPointe to train on a bearing of 135 degrees to hit the next incoming kamikaze, a Val dive bomber. "While the mount was still turning, we took a direct hit from the starboard quarter," said Delweski. He regained consciousness to find himself draped over a K-gun, a depth-charge launching device, fifteen feet forward of his mount.[32]

Kamikaze number eleven, another Val, hit right behind the previous Val, releasing its bomb mere seconds before it crashed into *Laffey*. The

Trial by Fire. This Tom Freeman naval print depicts the destroyer *Laffey* (DD 724) under attack on April 16, 1945, having already been hit by kamikazes. *U.S. Naval Institute photo archive*

plane and its bomb created further devastation on the after decks of the destroyer. Ripped by shrapnel, Delweski raced back to Mount No. 3, where he found Coxswain Chester Flint pinned in the starboard hatch by parts of the most-recent kamikaze's engine. "I tried to free him but he died in my arms," remembered Delweski. Four of the gun captain's men—including LaPointe and Cloer—perished, while others of the mount they adoringly called "Ole Betsy" were badly wounded.[33]

The twelfth kamikaze, another Val, dropped a bomb that punctured *Laffey*'s after deck and exploded in a 20-mm ammunition room before the Japanese pilot fled over the horizon. The rear third of the destroyer was now a blazing wreck, with dying men strewn across her decks and a rudder now jammed so that *Laffey* steamed in circles.

Commander Becton sent Quartermaster Ari "Greek" Phoutrides down to the main deck to make a quick inspection. Near one of the 20-mm gun mounts on the fantail, he saw a sight that he could never forget. "There was a man still in his straps with both legs gone, bleeding," said Phoutrides. The sailor, whose severed legs lay nearby, was still alive and beginning to be released from his straps, but he succumbed before he could be freed. Phoutrides continued his inspection before returning to the bridge to deliver his sobering report to the skipper.[34]

Lieutenant Elvin A. "Al" Henke, *Laffey*'s engineering officer, could hear the explosions from his station in the forward engine room. Throughout the booming of guns and shudders from direct hits, he silently repeated the Psalm 23. "My Christian faith provided me with a means of finding peace of mind in the midst of all the stress," affirmed Henke.[35]

Laffey's crew was blessed with a brief break in the intense action, during which time her engineers and damage-control crews raced to put out fires, create a makeshift steering method, and tend to the wounded. Two more kamikazes barreled in at 0920, hitting the crippled port after section of the destroyer and creating tremendous explosions and new fires.

Marine Corsairs, Navy Hellcats, and even FM-2 Wildcats from the escort carrier *Shamrock Bay* (CVE 84) tore into fresh groups of kamikazes that approached Radar Picket Station No. 1 during this time, but they were not able to down them all. One F4U from VMF-441 pursued an Oscar right through the fire of *Laffey*'s gunners, the pair of planes zooming over the bridge so low they clipped the mast that held the bedspring-like radar equipment. The Oscar, the fifteenth kamikaze, splashed in the water just off *Laffey*'s starboard side while the Marine Corsair pilot was seen to eject from his crippled fighter.[36]

Sonarman 1st Class Cyril C. Simonis was part of a repair party on deck spraying a 2.5-inch firehose on Mount No. 53, as the latest suicider came in. "One of our Corsairs knocked the SC antenna off the top mast," said Simonis. "It landed about six feet from [Signalman 3rd Class] Bill Kelly and me. By that time, I didn't think anything could scare me, but that did."[37]

Amid such chaos occurred one tiny incident that inspired those who witnessed it. The Corsair and Oscar had also clipped *Laffey*'s port yardarm, sending the American flag fluttering to the deck. Signalman 2nd Class Thomas McCarthy, ignoring the deadly bullets and shrapnel topside, retrieved a new flag and climbed the ship's mast to attach it with line as the kamikaze onslaught continued.[38]

Laffey was attacked by an additional seven suiciders between 0920 and 0946, although several were knocked down by her efficient remaining gunners. One was hit in the engine by a shell from Mount No. 52, creating an enormous explosion that incinerated the plane and its pilot. Seaman Robert Johnson, passing shells up to the 40-mm gunners, had a clear view of the dissolving plane. "We got the son of a bitch!" shouted Chief Gunner's Mate Warren Walker, Mount No. 52's gun captain. "What a beautiful sight!"[39]

Commander Frederick Julian Becton, skipper of the destroyer *Laffey*, vowed, "I'll never abandon ship as long as a gun will fire." *NARA, No. 333787*

During one brief lull in the action, Lieutenant Frank Manson, *Laffey's* assistant communications officer, appeared on the bridge to report to Commander Becton how badly battered their ship was. "Do you think we'll have to abandon ship?" Manson asked.

The destroyer's skipper felt a momentary flush of anger but quickly calmed himself to offer encouragement to his junior officer. "Hell, no, Frank," said Becton. "We still have guns that can shoot. I'll never abandon ship as long as a gun will fire!"[40]

Laffey's battering continued as a Val landed another bomb that exploded behind Mount No. 53. Seaman 1st Class Felipe Salcido, a bridge lookout, tackled Commander Becton to the deck as the twenty-first kamikaze, another Val, splintered the bridge with machine-gun bullets. Marine fighter pilot Marion Ryan downed the dive bomber, though not before it sent its bomb into *Laffey's* forward gun platforms, shredding more sailors with the blast and tearing a large hole through the deck. Shrapnel ripped through *Laffey's* wardroom below, slicing off the tips of two of Lieutenant (jg) Matthew Darnell's fingers, who bandaged his hand and continued treating more-severely wounded sailors.[41]

The final kamikaze, number twenty-two of the attack, was splashed off *Laffey's* port bow, where it exploded and sprayed shrapnel around the forward 20-mm gunners. Commander Becton was stunned as the ship's radar was suddenly free of bogies, and he gazed skyward in silent thanks for the Navy and Marine fighters now circling above his crippled destroyer, ready to take on any more Japanese fliers who dared to go after the stricken vessel. They would maintain their blue umbrella over *Laffey* while Becton and his crew tended to their wounded and damage control until tugs could help escort the smoldering tin can back to the relatively safe anchorage at Kerama Retto.

Laffey's gunners expended 7,090 shells and bullets in eighty minutes against twenty-two kamikazes, shooting down nine on their own and assisting with three other kills. The ship had been smashed by six airplanes and grazed by a seventh, while another five attackers had landed bomb hits or sprayed shrapnel across her decks. Thirty-two men had perished, and another seventy-one lay wounded, but *Laffey* stubbornly remained afloat. The fighting spirit of the destroyer and her crew remained unbroken. "What guns we had left in working order—and there were damned few of them—were kept fully manned," wrote Commander Becton. The skipper lovingly referred to his *Laffey* as "the ship that would not die."[42]

Laffey's survival against twenty-two attacking kamikazes became a source of inspiration throughout the fleet. Naval historian Samuel Eliot Morison, a participant in the Okinawa campaign, wrote, "Probably no ship has ever survived an attack of the intensity she experienced." Rear Admiral Turner Joy noted that *Laffey's* performance "stands out above the outstanding."[43]

Commander Becton, a hero to his crew, had issued a declaration amid the kamikaze fight that was as uplifting as any battle cry John Paul Jones, the so-called "Father of the American Navy," might have spoken: "I'll never abandon ship as long as a gun will fire."

Corsairs and Hellcats tangled with the seemingly endless waves of kamikazes throughout the day near the radar picket. Grim Reapers skipper Wally Clarke added to VF-10's high score for the day with three kills, while another division leader, Chuck Farmer, turned in four victories.

Land-based Marine squadrons from VMF-311, VMF-312, VMF-323, and VMF-441 also battled kamikazes over the picket ships on April 16, splashing thirty-six planes. Major Bob White's Yontan-based VMF-441 responded to calls for help from the destroyer *Laffey* after she was already hit by several suiciders. Aided by VMF-311, White's Corsairs accounted for seventeen kamikazes at the cost of four Marine F4Us lost in action.[44]

Beginning around 0946, during the height of the action over *Laffey*, 2nd Lieutenant Marion I. Ryan and 1st Lieutenant Charles H. Coppedge splashed a Val that had just dropped its bomb near the destroyer. Ryan was also credited with knocking down another Val after it had planted its bomb on one of *Laffey's* 20-mm gun groups. His F4U was then shot down in the ongoing dogfights, but he was later picked up by a patrol boat. Another of his VMF-441 squadronmates, 2nd Lieutenant Larry Friess, was killed. Lieutenant William W. Eldridge was top-scorer from the Marine group,

VMF-441 Corsair pilots who shot down 15.5 kamikazes over the radar pickets during the destroyer *Laffey*'s ordeal with 22 kamikazes. *Kneeling, left to right:* Captain Floyd Kirkpatrick and 2nd Lieutenants Clay Whitaker and Charles Coppedge. *Standing, left to right:* 2nd Lieutenants Will Dysart, William Eldridge, and Selva McGinty. The Marine aces are posing in front of Kirkpatrick's Corsair No. 422, nicknamed "Palpitatin' Paulie." *208-AA-PAC-10046, NARA*

with four kills, while Captain Floyd C. Kirkpatrick and 2nd Lieutenant Selva E. McGinty each claimed three victories. Second Lieutenants Will H. Dysart and Clay H. Whitaker finished their fight over *Laffey* with one and a half kills, while Coppedge shot down two.[45]

Hornet's Fighting Seventeen had another banner day on the sixteenth, including notable performances by Billy Watts and Ted Crosby, the latter becoming his squadron's latest "ace in a day." Among the pilots downed by VF-17 over Amami Oshima this day was Warrant Officer Katsue Kato, who had claimed nine victories over Kure Harbor on March 19 while flying with Commander Genda's "Squadron of Experts."[46]

At 0730 the divisions of Lieutenants Watts and Jim Pearce were directed to fly to the southern end of Kikai Jima to intercept an incoming raid. As they awaited the approaching Japanese, Pearce charged his guns for action. "To my chagrin, only one gun fired about two rounds and then silence with the gun trigger pulled in hard," he said. To his frustration, he would be going into a gunfight without his guns.[47]

Pearce called Watts and asked him to take the lead for the mission. Moments later Pearce tallyhoed the incoming flight of about forty Japanese fighters, mostly Franks, Zekes, and Oscars. "There was just a big circle that stretched out at least half a mile," recalled Watts. The Japanese were approaching at 18,000 feet—about 3,000 feet above the VF-17 Hellcats—so Watts and Pearce's divisions climbed and attacked. Gunless, Pearce nonetheless made mock firing runs on one Japanese fighter after another, hoping to chase them from his harmless F6F toward the waiting guns of a comrade. This worked to some degree until Pearce found himself in a split-S contest with an Oscar.[48]

Each time Pearce got behind his opponent, the Oscar did a split-S (half a loop downward), while the American followed him. This continued until they were a mere one thousand feet above the wave tops. Apparently unaware of his altitude, the Japanese pilot went into another split-S and slammed straight into the ocean. "Scratch one Oscar!" said Pearce. "It was apparent, and sad in a way, that we were not engaging experienced fighter pilots."[49]

In the meantime Billy Watts moved in on a Frank and began landing hits at eight-hundred-feet distance. "I know they never saw us," he observed. "They didn't make any movements as I slid in behind this old boy." As Watts closed to two hundred feet, the Frank began smoking, flipped to the right, and spun down out of control into the water. The division leader locked on to another Frank, closed to three hundred feet, fired, and sent it crashing into the sea three miles west of Kikai. By this point the action had become wildly scattered. "As soon as we started firing, they took off like a bunch of hornets off a nest and it all broke loose," Watts said.[50]

Lieutenant (jg) Werner Gaerisch, Watts' wingman, destroyed one Jack and received probable credit for the destruction of a Frank. Watts' second section of Lieutenant (jg) George Covelly and Ensign Joe Friedman shot down one Oscar, damaged three others, and also caused a Jack to begin smoking from bullet hits. Pearce's division knocked down one Jack and two Franks and damaged a third Frank.

At the close of the action, the *Hornet* divisions had been airborne for nearly four hours and were low on fuel. Pearce called for a rendezvous but managed to only collect his wingman, George Johnson, plus Watts and Gaerisch. They returned around 0930 to find their *Hornet* at General Quarters and were directed to land on the nearby *Bennington*. The gunnery department on *Bennington* informed Pearce that his malfunctioning wing guns were brand new and had not been cleaned of the Cosmoline in which they had been packed for shipment. "They had no chance of operating with that heavy grease coating," noted Pearce.[51]

East of the northern tip of Okinawa, VF-17 skipper Marsh Beebe and three of his divisions began intercepting incoming kamikazes that morning. Frank Sistrunk destroyed a Val that narrowly missed a suicide-ramming attempt on Beebe's Hellcat. Shortly after 0845 Lieutenant Fuzz Wooley's division tallyhoed twenty Jacks and Zekes near Iheya Shima. Wooley made three passes, shooting down two Jacks and damaging a third.

Lieutenant (jg) Ted Crosby approached one of the Jacks head-on with all six of his .50-calibers blazing. "The impact of the bullets blew him apart," Crosby noted. "Part of his engine and propeller, with the prop still turning, flew right over my head." He picked out another target, a Zeke, which was apparently loaded with explosives for a kamikaze mission. "When you hit one, they would really explode!" he said. As he pulled away Crosby maneuvered to avoid the airborne "garbage and debris."[52]

After downing his second opponent, Crosby was attempting to find division leader Wooley when he noticed tracer bullets zipping past his Hellcat. Ironically, he found the quick burst had been fired in error by the lieutenant, who had momentarily mistaken Crosby's F6F for an enemy plane in the frenzy of the action.

"Did I get you, Ted?" Wooley called sheepishly.

"No," radioed Crosby. "But let's settle down and get more of these guys!"[53]

The division continued to assail the big group of Japanese planes, and in short order Crosby had flamed a Zeke and a Jack. Wooley's wingman, Lieutenant (jg) Jack Garrett, downed a Zeke and a Betty bomber, while Crosby's wingman, Lieutenant (jg) Bill Osborn, dropped two Vals. Fuzz Wooley returned to the division's rendezvous point and splashed a Val recovering from its dive on a destroyer. Wooley joined with Crosby and Osborn to assault a lone Val approaching the picket ships. Crosby executed a split-S maneuver and came down vertically on the Japanese dive bomber, landing solid hits in its engine and cockpit. He broke off his attack as he came within range of a destroyer's antiaircraft fire, but the Val was seen by the three pilots to crash into the beach of a nearby island.

Beebe's three divisions turned in claims for fourteen shoot downs plus a probable and one damaged. Crosby, who had become VF-17's latest "ace in a day" with this combat, would later receive the Navy Cross for this mission, although he did later experience some remorse at killing opponents who appeared to be less skilled than himself and his squadronmates. Crosby did feel better "when I was told the extent of the damage they did on ships, and by shooting them down, I was saving American lives."[54]

The four orphaned VF-17 pilots—Pearce, Johnson, Watts, and Gaerisch—were only on board *Bennington* for half an hour before they were scrambled again at 1000. Radar had picked up a quantity of bogies in the vicinity of the task force, so the quartet was launched to supplement the regular CAP already in the air, along with eight *Bennington* VF-82 Hellcats. Watts was impressed with the *Bennington* crewmen who had replaced and loaded guns on both his F6F and that of Pearce while the pilots wolfed down a quick lunch.

At 1200 Pearce's mixed division received a vector to fly at 24,000 feet to intercept a raid closing on the task force. Sixty miles out, the division tallyhoed two Frances fighter-bombers below at 4,000 feet on an opposite course. After a ten-minute chase, Gaerisch sent the leading Frances plunging into the ocean. Watts tailed the second Frances, opening fire into its starboard wing root and engine. "He didn't even know I was back there," recalled Watts. "He wasn't trying to turn." The plane started burning, went into a shallow right turn, flipped over on its back, and crashed. Watts noted that the Frances burned on the water, marking the spot of his third kill of the day.[55]

The flight logbook of Lieutenant (jg) Billy Watts includes Rising Sun emblems drawn by the VF-17 squadron yeoman to represent his kills during April 1945. *Author's photo*

No further bogies were encountered, so the Watts and Pearce sections were directed at 1300 to land on *Belleau Wood*, as *Hornet* was once again unable to receive them. Once on board the quartet went below for a quick meal, during which time their VF-17 skipper, Marsh Beebe, teamed with Frank Sistrunk to knock down a lone Judy that was stalking task-force destroyers.

Watts, Pearce, and their wingmen were soon launched on their third CAP mission of the long day, each of the three having commenced from the flight deck of a different carrier. By the time Pearce finally landed on *Hornet* at 1621, he noted that he had "spent a frustrating ten hours and fifteen minutes in the air that day."[56] He received no kill credits for his three hops, although he had helped an Oscar crash, while his comrades had enjoyed success. The greatest consolation for Pearce, Watts, and their two wingmen was the ability to sleep in their own bunks that night.

Vice Admiral Ugaki's Kikusui No. 3 had taken a toll on the radar-picket vessels. *Laffey* had taken the brunt of the assault, but other ships had been damaged, including *LCS 51*, *LCS 116*, and the destroyer *Bryant* (DD 665)— the latter taking a kamikaze that crashed into the base of her bridge, killing thirty-four men. The destroyer *Pringle* (DD 477), working Radar Picket Station No. 14, had been crashed by a Val that created such an explosion that the ship broke in two and sank within five minutes, taking down sixty-five sailors. Other kamikazes took on the destroyer-minesweepers *Hobson* (DMS 26), *Bowers* (DE 637), and *Harding* (DMS 28), killing seventy-four more men and wounding dozens of others.

Phil Kirkwood and Al Lerch of the Grim Reapers had banner days on April 16, but they would soon be without a flight deck. Five members of the Divine Wind came upon *Intrepid* shortly after 1330. Three were downed by antiaircraft fire and a fourth narrowly missed the flight deck to crash into the ocean. But the fifth suicider held true to target.

In VT-10's Ready Room No. 4, more than a dozen pilots were passing the time, and skipper Larry Lawrence had just triumphantly thrown an acey-duecey. At the same moment a bomb-laden Zeke crashed *Intrepid's* flight deck aft of the Number Three elevator. Many airmen had to fight their way topside through dense smoke and jammed hatches. Lieutenant (jg) Johnny Adams waded into knee-deep water on the hangar deck to help push good airplanes over the side to prevent them from catching fire and exploding. Turret gunner Bill Banta found the reality of war sobering as he viewed the bodies of shipmates strewn across the steel decks. *Intrepid's* damage-control teams fought the fires for nearly an hour, during which time their ship took a bomb close aboard.[57]

Repair parties managed to patch the flight deck enough for the last Grim Reapers pilots circling overhead to land. But *Intrepid* was badly damaged and forced to retire to Ulithi for repairs for the next two weeks. By May 4 the decision was made to send her and Air Group 10 back stateside for more extensive repair work. The Japanese Divine Wind had thus robbed TF 58 of the services of yet another carrier during the Okinawa campaign.

U.S. Navy squadrons finished April 16 with claims of 157 kills—the sixth-highest haul of the war—with fourteen more listed as probables or damaged. Okinawa Marine pilots added another 35 kills, with no claims for probable kills or damaged planes.[58]

Three Kikusui assaults had taken a toll on the Allied ships off Okinawa, a campaign that was already promising to push the time frame of carrier support to new limits for such an amphibious operation. After seventeen days of boots on the island's rocky soil, the Army and Marine foot soldiers were learning that Operation Iceberg would have no quick ending.

Chapter Seventeen

FLYING CIRCUS IN ACTION

Gene Valencia was roused from his deep sleep two hours before dawn on April 17, 1945. Fighting Nine's leading ace dropped to the deck to do his customary forty push-ups before donning his flight gear and strapping on his .45-caliber pistol. He followed his morning exercise routine with a stroll to the wardroom for breakfast, aware that his division was scheduled for an early mission.[1]

The lieutenant had caused the downing of an enemy aircraft the previous day without even firing a bullet. This day Valencia had higher hopes of achieving some shoot downs based on the magnitude of the kamikaze raids experienced by the radar pickets on the sixteenth. He visited with VF-9's ACIO, Lieutenant Ralph Murphy, who advised him to expect another dose of aerial assaults from the Japanese.

Valencia's division was already spotted on deck, ready to launch into the predawn sky on a day that would prove fair, with only broken clouds. He was scheduled by Lieutenant Commander Cooper Bright, the air officer, to be flight leader over three divisions, including those of Lieutenant Glenn Phillips and Lieutenant (jg) James Caldwell. Each blue Hellcat was packed with 2,400 rounds of .50-caliber bullets as the dozen pilots scrambled into the air at 0520 to take their stations between the task force and the kamikaze airfields on Kyushu. The first two divisions, those of Valencia and Phillips, were stationed approximately fifty miles north of the task force and saw nothing during their first two hours of patrol. Then at 0817 Commander Carl J. Ballinger Jr.'s CIC radars on *Yorktown* registered many incoming blips about seventy-eight miles out.[2]

Yorktown's fighter directors issued a vector. The call to action was electric to Lieutenant (jg) Harris Mitchell. "Ruler, four-one, vector 320, angels 15, buster." To Mitchell, the order was clearly understood. It meant to fly on a heading of 320 degrees magnetic, climb to 15,000 feet, and "bend that throttle forward." Glenn Phillips and his quartet of F6F jockeys maintained station 5,000 feet below that of Valencia's team. Mitch felt that his division "jolted like a young colt stung by a bee and started grabbing that blue as fast as we could." His division was still clawing for altitude when a second transmission from the *Yorktown* FDO announced that he had lost contact with the bogey but that the fighters should orbit in that area.[3]

Valencia duly turned his division 360 degrees to the left. A third transmission was received from the FDO, who now reported only a small target. Caldwell's division was detached to return to base. Mitchell felt sorry for some of his fellow pilots, who would likely miss out on any action with the anticipated small bunch of Japanese planes. The thought went through Mitch's mind, *They're going to be sitting ducks for the four of us!*

Valencia led his flight in the general direction of the contact for some fifty miles without a bogey to be seen. Everything changed at 0830, when Gene called: "Tally-ho! Ten bogies, 12 o'clock, twenty miles low."

We're outnumbered now, but what the hell, thought Mitch. *There's four of us, and I'm feeling pretty confident.* His confidence dwindled as his division leader began seeing the true numbers they were about to face. "Change that tally-ho to 15," Valencia corrected. He was quickly back on the air to change his tallyho count to twenty-five enemy planes, urgently calling for support. The division of Phillips, lower in altitude, quickly turned around and bent their throttles to come to the aid of Valencia's men.

Valencia finally counted thirty-eight total enemy aircraft: brown camouflage Franks, Zekes, and Oscars, all sporting bright red meatball insignias. Flying at about 15,000 feet, the clusters of planes were still sixty-two miles from *Yorktown*. Valencia and Mitchell could clearly see bombs carried externally on many of the Franks and Zekes. *This is it!* Mitch thought excitedly.[4]

His division was outnumbered nine to one, but when Mitchell stole a glance at Lieutenant Valencia, he was amused. To him Gene's face bore the expression "of a young child who had, just that moment, spotted his favorite toy under the Christmas tree." Valencia led Mitch on a fast climb to attack the two higher-cover Franks. "We met them at the top and a short burst from Gene's guns exploded his first target," Mitchell reported. His own Frank target proved to be a tougher opponent, but Mitch twisted and pursued it until the Japanese fighter was plummeting in flames to the ocean. He then charged the main group of planes, hoping to regain position on Valencia. As he approached, a determined Zeke fighter slid out of formation onto Gene's tail. Mitch poured on the throttle and cut straight across the middle of the formation. The Zeke pilot alertly detected the incoming F6F and decided to take him on first. "He turned away from Gene and headed straight for me, head on," said Mitch.[5]

Mitchell opened up with a short burst from his six .50-calibers, producing flames in the Zeke's wings and fuselage. But his opponent continued his head-on run, even as Mitch's tracers ripped through the cowling of the aircraft. As they flashed past each other, the Zeke pilot attempted to ram the F6F. Mitch broke hard left, and the Japanese fighter roared past him with only a few feet to spare. The Zeke continued straight up into the sky, burning profusely, before finally exploding, its charred wreckage plunging toward the water.

During the initial encounter, Jim French and Clint Smith provided cover for Valencia's section as they made the first attacks. Valencia and Mitchell then covered their second section, allowing French and Smith to join in the fight. But after the first runs, the Japanese planes broke formation and started flying in a compact left-hand circle, losing altitude. Valencia's four Hellcats made repeated attacks on the enemy aircraft from the center and above, covering each other as much as possible with their "Mowing Machine" tactics.

Mitchell watched in awe as his division leader tore into their opponents. "Just to watch him in action instilled confidence in me." Valencia managed to shoot down a Frank that had moved into position on Smitty's tail. French downed four Zekes, while Smith was credited with destroying one Frank and the probable destruction of a second.[6]

Valencia's third opponent was a fighter he identified as a Frank as he opened fire from one hundred yards. The plane began smoking, and as the pilot attempted to escape, his fighter exploded. With three victories in the bag, Valencia charged into a formation of three Japanese fighters. A burst of tracers zinging past his own cockpit momentarily distracted him, but his F6F was not hit. The lieutenant turned his attention back to his three targets, confident that Mitchell would cover his tail. Valencia pursued and fired on his fourth victim, a Frank that burst into flames and spiraled down.[7]

One by one the Japanese planes dwindled as Valencia's quartet picked them off. Mitchell blasted two more Zekes off his leader's tail, although one blazing victim not seen to crash was only credited to him as a probable. Valencia similarly could only claim a probable on a Frank that he fired into until forced to pull up hard to avoid ramming it.[8]

Valencia attacked three remaining Japanese fighters, dropping one as Mitchell shot another off his division leader's tail. Gene fired on the single

Lieutenant Gene Valencia joined the "ace in a day" club by downing six Japanese planes and adding a probable kill on April 17, 1945. His VF-9 "Flying Circus" division achieved seventeen victories during the mission. Valencia posed for this publicity photo—beside the cockpit of a Hellcat marked with twenty-three total victories—near the end of VF-9's Okinawa cruise. *U.S. Navy photo via Edward M. Young*

remaining Frank, which caught fire and exploded, giving Valencia his fifth kill within minutes. Pulling up from his last attack, Gene spotted another Japanese fighter closing on two F6Fs below him. Diving in, he laced its fuselage full of lead until his sixth Frank of the morning exploded. Valencia additionally fired on an already smoking Frank that flew past him and watched it belch even heavier smoke as it fell away. Counting this one as only damaged, the division leader still emerged from the fight with six solid kills and a probable—his best day of the war.[9]

Little more than eight minutes had passed since Valencia had tallyhoed the big formation. In the closing minutes of the battle, his division was joined by that of Glenn Phillips, which chalked up three kills and a probable. Clint Smith counted four Japanese pilots drifting down in their parachutes at the same time. "It was the kinda thing you read about or dream about," Smith admitted later. "It was the prettiest sight I have ever seen."[10]

Valencia and Phillips led their divisions for base, low on fuel after more than three hours in the air. En route to *Yorktown* Gene encountered another Japanese fighter. He maneuvered into position and squeezed his gun button only to discover that he had already exhausted all 2,400 rounds of his ammunition.

The two *Yorktown* VF-9 divisions had claimed seventeen aerial kills and were given additional credit for four probable kills and one plane damaged. Valencia took top honors with six kills, one probable, and one damaged. Mitchell finished the flight with three kills and a fourth Zeke as a probable.

Smith claimed one Frank destroyed and another probable, while French was credited with four Zeke kills. Mitchell and French thus both became an ace on this mission, leaving only Smitty shy of reaching this status in their Mowing Machine division.

As Valencia and Mitchell settled their F6Fs on *Yorktown*, they were swarmed by plane captains eager to hear of their latest exploits. *Yorktown* executive officer Walter F. Boone was ecstatic, remarking aloud on Valencia's six kills: "It wasn't so long ago that stuff like that was getting the Congressional Medal!" Valencia would instead receive the Navy Cross for his work on April 17.[11]

Mitchell was astonished that not one of their Hellcats had been scratched. Valencia made a point to thank Mitch for saving his rear several times by shooting Zekes off his tail. Mitchell appreciated the praise, especially after months of being barked at during his training phase. "I should thank him for teaching me how."[12]

On board *Yorktown* as a special guest of Secretary of the Navy James Forrestal was Henry Luce, the publisher of *Time*, *Life*, and *Fortune* magazines. He met with Valencia's team after their record intercept on the seventeenth and was so impressed with their efficiency that he gave them a new nickname, "Valencia's Flying Circus."[13]

Randolph's VF-12 enjoyed almost as much success during the same hour on April 17. Divisions led by Lieutenant Commander Fred Michaelis and Lieutenant Harold Vita intercepted fourteen Oscars and Georges near Tokuna Shima and Kikai Jima. They disposed of the entire lot within ten minutes at the cost of only one battle-damaged F6F.

By midmorning the fighter actions near the fleet had subsided, with Navy pilots turning in claims for forty-seven kills that day. Larry Clark of *Essex's* VF-83 scored his seventh and final victory of the Okinawa campaign shortly after 0945. His division attacked a Betty bomber, with Clark given the credit for exploding this opponent.

On board his flagship *Bunker Hill*, Vice Admiral Mitscher's personal physician, Doctor Ray Hege, told Commodore Burke on the seventeenth that Mitscher was not feeling well and that he had advised the admiral to stay in his bunk. Burke later noted that the Bald Eagle came to the bridge anyway, "but he looked like hell. He was tired. This was after days and days of combat. What I think happened was that the admiral had a small heart attack." Doctor Hege never reported such, so Burke could only be left guessing.[14]

Mitscher's carriers maintained their vigil off Okinawa during the ensuing days, providing the big blue blanket over their own task groups while sending scores of attackers to bomb and rocket targets of opportunity on the island. With the damaged flattops *Enterprise, Intrepid,* and *Hancock* being released to effect repairs, Rear Admiral Radford's TG 58.4 was reshuffled to include the fleet carrier *Yorktown* and three light carriers—*Independence, Langley,* and *Bataan.* Within a week *Bataan* was exchanged for a brand-new *Essex*-class carrier, *Shangri-La* (CV 38).

The aerial victories enjoyed by Mitscher's fliers had been earned with a cost since the fleet's last sortie from Ulithi. Glen Wallace of VBF-83 noted in his diary for April 18 that a squadronmate, Lieutenant William A. Rach, was killed in a water landing created by a defective catapult launch from *Essex.* "Today we have been in combat one month and have lost 9 pilots in the F4U squadron alone—17%," recorded Wallace somberly.[15]

Casualties continued to mount ashore on Okinawa as well. Vice Admiral Turner and Lieutenant General Buckner had advanced the target date for the seizure of the smaller Ie Shima to April 16, with the 77th Division having landed two battalions following three days of naval and aerial bombardments. The troops moved forward swiftly, overrunning the Japanese airfield on the island, but ran into strong resistance near the Iegusugu pinnacle, a 607-foot dead volcano with built-in Japanese strongpoints that proved as tough to overcome as Iwo Jima's Mount Suribachi had been.[16]

The strongest resistance near Ie town on Ie Shima was a rise soon nicknamed "Bloody Ridge" by the soldiers. Progress was measured in yards as platoons fought their way house by house toward Bloody Ridge on April 18. The Army was joined ashore on the island that day by famed war correspondent Ernie Pyle, whose wartime books had highlighted his exploits of U.S. forces in the previous invasions of North Africa, Sicily, Italy, and Normandy.

During the morning of the eighteenth, Pyle joined Lieutenant Colonel Joseph B. Coolidge, commander of the 305th Infantry, for a jeep tour to the frontlines near Ie town. A Japanese machine gunner forced the two and their driver to dive into a nearby ditch for cover, but the enemy gunner soon found his mark. Pyle was struck in the left temple, and America's famed correspondent was gone. He was buried in the 77th Division cemetery wearing his helmet in a casket constructed of salvaged packing crates. A wooden marker over his grave read: "On this spot, the 77th Division lost a buddy, Ernie Pyle, 18 April, 1945."[17]

By the time General Buckner's troops had secured Bloody Ridge and Ie Shima, 218 American soldiers had been killed and another 1,000 wounded, while 4,700 Japanese were killed and 409 taken prisoner. Meanwhile, the Army's XXIV Corps made little progress on Okinawa between April 14 and 19 due to the enemy's carefully planned defensive system, and complaints in the Navy were that the Army was dragging its feet. The Army responded on the nineteenth by attacking along a line running across the island from a point about four miles north of Naha. The ancient capital of Shuri was a key point in the Japanese defense, enduring assaults by Navy and Marine planes as well as a sustained naval bombardment. Assault platoons swept forward but were stopped in their tracks by Japanese defenders who came up out of their sheltering caves. Progress was measured only in yards during the next five days.

Admiral Nimitz, commander in chief of the Pacific Fleet, landed at Okinawa's Yontan Airfield on April 22 to learn why the campaign was dragging out so long. In the past three weeks, Japanese warplanes had sunk or crippled some sixty vessels and killed more than 1,100 of his men. On the twenty-third Nimitz met with Lieutenant General Buckner, commander of the Tenth Army; Admiral Ray Spruance, commander of the Fifth Fleet; General Alexander Vandegrift, commandant of the Marine Corps; and Nimitz's own chief of staff, Vice Admiral Forrest Sherman. Buckner offered Nimitz a tour of the captured sectors of Okinawa and was presented with a bottle of liquor from the admiral, who stated, "May you walk in the ashes of Tokyo."[18]

The fact that a navy commander held overall command of a land campaign created tense moments as Nimitz pushed Buckner to break the impasse with whatever tactics were required, even another amphibious landing behind the Japanese lines. Buckner, the bold son of a Civil War Confederate general, responded that the ground war was the Army's job and that he would take care of things. "I'm losing a ship and a half a day," Nimitz snarled. "If this line isn't moving within five days, we'll get someone here to move it so we can all get out from under these stupid air attacks."[19]

The debate between the top brass dragged out, but Buckner held his ground, insisting that he would continue a classic frontal assault that would save lives in the long run. Nimitz did not desire another Army-Navy fracas over another fired general. When he left Okinawa, Buckner remained in command of the Tenth Army, albeit with the added pressure that the Navy's top commander in the Pacific had placed on him.

Marine fighter squadrons operating from Yontan and Kadena Airfields continued to prove their value during April. Major George Axtell's VMF-323 "Death Rattlers" at Kadena was credited with a record 24.75 victories in

General Alexander Vandegrift and Major General Francis Mulcahy congratulate three VMF-323 pilots at their Okinawa airfield who each became an "ace in a day" on April 22, 1945. *Left to right:* Major George Axtell, Vandegrift, Mulcahy, Major Jeff Dorroh, and 1st Lieutenant Jerry O'Keefe. *U.S. Marine Corps*

one mission on the twenty-second. Axtell and his executive officer, Major Jeff Dorroh, were serving afternoon CAP duty when their two divisions of F4Us were vectored toward a group of nearly three dozen Val dive bombers threatening U.S. shipping north of Aguni Shima.[20]

Within fifteen minutes Axtell had attacked eight Vals with beam runs from slightly above. The skipper became the Death Rattlers' first instant ace by downing five of the dive bombers and damaging three more. Axtell's second-section leader, 1st Lieutenant Jerry O'Keefe, flamed four Vals from a pointblank six-o'clock position, then fired his guns at a fifth Val that came at him head-on, intent on ramming him. "It was one of the most exhilarating, brief moments of my life," declared O'Keefe, who had to pull up violently to avoid a collision with his fifth victim.[21]

"I could see it was going to be a long day, so I switched off two guns," explained Major Dorroh, who burned five Vals within twenty minutes via his conservative ammunition use. En route back to Kadena, the VMF-323 executive officer achieved his sixth victory of the day by setting another dive bomber afire. "We just tore them wide open," skipper Axtell said. "We were shooting so much lead I was afraid we'd start shooting each other up."[22]

Another eight Japanese planes were downed on April 22 by two other Marine Corsair squadrons, Major Jim Poindexter's VMF-224 "Wildcats" and Major Bob White's VMF-441 "Black Jacks," both based from Yontan. In its first three weeks of flying CAP missions from Kadena, Axtell's Death Rattlers would log 656 combat missions, turning in claims for 54.75 Japanese aircraft destroyed plus six probables and six damaged enemy planes.[23]

On April 23, Marine machine-gunner Mel Heckt's squad boarded trucks with the rest of the 1st Platoon to represent the 4th Marine Regiment in an official flag-raising ceremony upon securing the northern and central part of Okinawa. General Vandegrift, wearing a fleece-lined jacket, khaki pants, and a summer-service cap, was introduced, and the flag was raised to the sounds of the "Marine Corps Hymn." Corporal Heckt carried two forbidden items with him on Okinawa—a small diary and a Browning camera. He managed to snap only four photos during this ceremony before a captain threatened to take away his camera if he did not cease.[24]

By the evening of April 23, Lieutenant General Ushijima's outer lines had been penetrated in several places, forcing the Japanese commander to withdraw his forces to their next line of defenses around the old Shuri Castle. His men fell back silently under cover of darkness, fog, and an artillery barrage. The Americans who advanced the next morning found only a few stragglers remaining. But time would show that the Japanese had merely abandoned one position and taken up in strength in another.

Life ashore on Okinawa was an experience few of the Marines not yet blooded in island fighting prior to Operation Iceberg could imagine. Corporal Jim White of the 29th Marines, 6th Marine Division, had joined the Corps in the summer of 1944 at age eighteen, one year after graduating from Benson High School in Omaha, Nebraska. His dungaree utility jacket and pants, made of a cotton twill and gray-green in color, were filthy and ragged, covering his fouled green skivvy shirt and shorts. When cooler weather settled over his foxhole at night, White often pulled on a wool sweatshirt to maintain body heat.[25]

In his foxhole White chose not to eat the newer C-ration can that was labeled pork and rice. "When I opened a can of pork and rice and looked at the contents, I couldn't convince myself that the grains were not moving," he recalled. "With hunks of gray meat nestled in a mass of white rice grains, the appearance was similar to that of the gray rotting flesh, abounding with writhing white maggots, of a human body torn by artillery fragments and exposed too long to the weather and the flies."[26]

The primitive living conditions, irregularity of meals, and lack of sanitation had its effect on the human body. "My solid waste excretionary system either failed to function or it performed altogether too well," wrote White.

"There didn't seem to be an in between. I was either bound up or loose as a goose."[27]

To ground troops like Jim White, even small progress was measured as positive. By April 28 General Buckner spread the word that the 1st Marine Division would relieve the 27th Infantry Division on the western flank in two days, with the 6th Marine Division following as the Marines took responsibility for that end of the Shuri line by May 7. Private 1st Class Watson Crumbie had been moving steadily with the 6th Division across northern Okinawa, engaged in running periodic battles that he deemed "guerrilla type warfare." He had stayed in no one place for any great length of time thus far. "We moved every day," said Crumbie. "At first crack of dawn, we were out of our foxholes, heating our rations, and then we were moving on."[28]

Crumbie sensed that the military brass were eager to close the circle on their holed-up adversaries. Gunner Heckt's diary entry for this period reflects the mood of the common soldier on Okinawa: "The Army has begun to push. Perhaps Nimitz put a spark up Buckner's butt."[29]

Chapter Eighteen

"THE FLAG WAS STILL THERE"

TF 58's fighter action trailed off significantly in the wake of the forty-seven kills registered on April 17. During the next ten days, only thirty-seven successful shoot downs took place, the lull suggesting to Pete Mitscher that his adversary, Vice Admiral Ugaki, was toiling to build his air arsenal for another violent kamikaze assault in the coming days.

Aircraft losses and B-29 raids over his bases challenged Ugaki, but by April 28 he was ready to launch his fourth Kikusui attack. Down to only 115 suicide planes to fly against Allied shipping, he dispatched a dozen special-attack planes and waves of fighters that evening. They were met by U.S. Marine and Navy fighters over Okinawa and Ie Shima, resulting in an increased number of dogfights near the radar-picket ships.[1]

Two U.S. destroyers were slightly damaged by near misses, while the hospital ship *Comfort* (AH 6) was more heavily damaged by a direct kamikaze hit. Marine Corsairs operating from Okinawa's Yontan and Kadena Airfields were efficient in knocking down many of the early evening Japanese aircraft. Lieutenant General Buckner was appreciative of the Marine squadrons, as noted in a message he sent to Major General Francis P. Mulcahy, commanding general of the Tenth Army Tactical Air Force. "I desire to commend you and your command and air crews for decontaminating the Okinawa atmosphere and turning thirty-five more Jap aviators over to the tender mercies of the attraction of gravity," Buckner wired.[2]

Some of Buckner's praise could have been shared with carrier-based Marine fighter pilots, as 2nd Lieutenant Dean Caswell enjoyed one of his best fights during the late afternoon of April 28. Four divisions of VMF-221 Fighting Falcons launched at 1430 from *Bunker Hill*. Caswell's division leader, Captain Joe Delancey, was forced to return to the carrier with engine problems, leaving Lieutenant Joe Brocia to take acting command of Lieutenants Caswell and John McManus.

As was often the case, position meant everything. The divisions of Major Ed Roberts and Captain Jim Swett orbited 30 miles north of Aguni Shima, where the VMF-221 pilots encountered nothing at all. The other seven Corsairs composing the divisions of Captain Don Balch and Lieutenant Brocia were orbiting some 25 miles west of Izena Jima when the action began. Caswell's division, "Viceroy 15," had been assigned to fly cover duty at 12,000 feet above two picket destroyers located roughly 120 miles from their carrier fleet. Shortly before 1600 Brocia received a warning from their fighter director of high-altitude bogies 30 miles to the north.

Brocia and Balch kicked their flights into high gear, climbing to reach 20,000 feet. As they reached altitude, Caswell found the visibility to be poor due to a high-level haze. He was unable to see the enemy fighter formation, estimated to number thirty planes, until they were almost upon them.[3]

Balch's division attacked the highest planes, shooting down three Zekes. Second Lieutenant William L. Bailey was forced to make an emergency landing on Yontan Airfield due to battle damage, while another VMF-221 pilot had to bail out of his riddled Corsair. Lieutenant Brocia expended considerable ammunition chasing a Zeke in a downward plunge, enduring G-forces so strong they caused him to gray out several times from the pressure.

Caswell almost immediately found himself on a head-on run against an enemy fighter, which he believed to be a Tony (although likely a Zeke). The Japanese plane was coming straight at him, firing, until it almost filled his sights. Dean opened fire with all six guns. His wingman, McManus, having already flamed one Zeke, was climbing back to 10,000 feet when he spotted Caswell's engagement, while a second Zeke was latched on to the lieutenant's tail.

"Break right! There's a Zero on your tail!" McManus shouted.[4]

But Caswell was solidly locked on to the Zeke ahead of him and quickly filling his gunsight. As he squeezed the trigger, tracers flew past his canopy from two directions: from his head-on opponent and from the Zeke on his tail. A split second later the Zeke ahead of him exploded, and he flew through pieces of the destroyed plane. McManus, who had opened up with a three-second deflection shot on the Zeke shooting at Caswell from behind, also exploded his quarry. "I got the Zero on your tail!" McManus shouted.[5]

Dean's Tight Spot depicts 1st Lieutenant Dean Caswell in his VMF-221 Corsair as he narrowly avoids a Tony fighter exploding in front of him. Caswell scored three kills on April 28, 1945, and became the U.S. Marine Corps' top-scoring carrier pilot of all time. *Courtesy of artist Roy Grinnell and the American Fighter Aces Association*

McManus and Caswell went into a defensive Thach Weave, protecting each other's tails while they lined up on the numerous enemy targets. Caswell felt certain he smoked another Zeke before he and his wingman engaged a formation of Zekes headed back home. He took the stragglers on the right while McManus went after those to the left. McManus eased up behind the first one and exploded him, then chased another one down to the water, where the Zeke blew apart after a long burst.

Caswell, closing in on the stragglers to the right, achieved his second kill by hitting the pilot and sending his plane into the water. The twisting action was intense, with enemy fighters moving against his team from every direction. "I was sweating profusely and certainly was not at ease," Caswell admitted. "I was feeling so scared that I could throw up and I had already wet my pants."[6]

The fight was far from over, though. Caswell executed an overhead snap shot, which reminded him of his early days of duck hunting. His rounds walked into the belly of a Zeke, his long burst causing it erupt into flames and then explode. He then chased another Zeke, got within range, and started firing. Pieces flew off the fighter, but its pilot made a split-S that Caswell was unable to match.

The fourteen VMF-221 pilots who returned to land on *Bunker Hill* at 1758 claimed fourteen Zeke kills and another probable. McManus was high scorer with four kills. Caswell felt certain he had made four kills and three more probables, but his gun camera had run out of film. In the end he would be credited with only three kills and a probable. "Who cares?" Caswell said. "I was unhurt and alive, and my pants could go to the wash."[7]

Lieutenant Caswell's victories on April 28 pushed his wartime total to seven kills and one probable, making him the top-scoring U.S. Marine Corps carrier pilot of all time.

Ugaki's Kikusui No. 4 had been largely a failure, as only three destroyers and a few other vessels had sustained combat casualties. The carrier-based fighter squadrons saw less action in the ensuing days, although on April 29 *Yorktown* Hellcats splashed four Zekes and a Judy that approached the task force.

With the luxury of operating multiple carrier task groups, Vice Admiral Mitscher took the opportunity to give Rear Admiral Jocko Clark's TG 58.1 a breather from the action. Clark's flagship *Hornet*—in company with *Bennington*, *Belleau Wood*, *San Jacinto*, and their screening warships—anchored in Ulithi on the afternoon of April 30, having been at sea since March 14 for six weeks of combat. The task group would enjoy two weeks of replenishment and recreation for the crews and take on board replacement aircraft for their air groups from Falalop Island. Fighting Seventeen skipper Marsh Beebe felt good to be taken off the line briefly "to get some much-needed upkeep and rest at Ulithi."[8]

Air-group personnel enjoyed ample beer parties ashore at Mog Mog and even had the chance to celebrate the return of a few members who had been downed in previous actions. For VF-17 ace Billy Watts, the Ulithi break was most memorable for the return of close friend and former shipboard roommate Lieutenant (jg) Joe Farrell, who had been rescued by the submarine *Pomfret* on February 17, 1945, during their first strikes against Kyushu. "Joe was happy to be back," said Watts, "but he was a little ticked off that Bob Coats and I had drank his case of beer when we figured he was not coming back for this tour."[9]

Even the pilots still at sea with their task groups found occasional opportunities to blow off steam. Caswell and his VMF-221 wingman John McManus were still basking in their seven kill mission from April 28 days later when *Bunker Hill* completed taking on fuel from the tanker *Mascoma* (AO 83). The weather began to deteriorate throughout that afternoon until further flights by the air group were curtailed. Visibility had collapsed, winds picked up to twenty-four knots, and the seas had become swollen as a solid line of thunderstorms moved through. To celebrate their recent victories, VMF-221 squadron commander Ed Roberts allowed McManus and Caswell, who were both written up for the Silver Star for their mission, to break out a bottle of their favored White Horse scotch for the evening.

When *Bunker Hill* was preparing to depart the West Coast for the Pacific theater, Admiral Mitscher had allowed liquor to be brought on board the carriers for use by the aviators when approved by their skipper. "He decreed each pilot could bring aboard ship six bottles of their favorite beverage, but placed under lock and key," noted Caswell. "Each squadron commanding officer would be responsible for its use, at an appropriate time."[10]

Following evening mess in the height of the storm, Caswell and McManus retired to their junior officers' stateroom, a compartment that held bunks for fifteen pilots far forward on the anchor deck, just below *Bunker Hill's* flight deck. After allowing their companions to take several tugs on the bottle of White Horse, McManus and Caswell decided to slip away with their favored libation to enjoy it more thoroughly on their own.

The two Marine aviators "opened the hatch and went out on deck in the driving rain to escape the unwanted attention," according to Caswell. They "dodged the huge waves washing over the bow, ignoring [their] sopping wet clothes." Fully inebriated, the pilots sang songs and took hits from the scotch bottle until a forceful wave carried away their booze and left the lieutenants clinging "to the anchor chain for dear life." McManus and Caswell finally stumbled back into their bunkroom, where they were "checked over by a medic and put to bed dry" to sleep off what would soon produce for Caswell "the miserable pangs of a hangover."[11]

In the early morning hours of April 30, the batmen were the only aviators on patrol. From *Yorktown's* VF-9, Ensign John Orth downed both a Nakajima J1N Navy Type 2 "Irving" night-reconnaissance fighter and a Betty bomber. During the next several days, TF 58 fighters would only down five enemy snoopers. The relative quiet could only mean one thing: the Japanese were likely building up for another massive assault.

Things were anything but quiet on Okinawa for the U.S. Army, whose divisions had suffered heavy losses in the weeks of pushing past Kakazu Ridge, two hills with a connecting saddle that formed part of Shuri's outer defenses. But Lieutenant General Ushijima's troops had merely taken up station in a new defensive area, stretching from the vicinity of Conical Hill and Kochi Ridge on the east across the Urasoe-Mura escarpment toward the west.

The Army's 27th Division began attacking the west end of the Urasoe-Mura escarpment on the morning of April 26. The caverns below were large enough to hold entire companies of Japanese troops, and they were linked to numerous firing ports and apertures on both faces of the ridge. Casualties were heavy among the Americans, who began referring to the cliff as "Hacksaw Ridge." One man who stood out among the many heroes fighting to take the bloody hilltop was twenty-seven-year-old Private 1st Class Desmond Thomas Doss, a Seventh Day Adventist from Virginia, who was classified as a conscientious objector—a soldier who refused to handle duties on the Sabbath Saturday and who would not carry a weapon. But Doss proved to be the only medic who remained atop Hacksaw Ridge's cliff, treating injured men and dragging others to safety. Time and again he pulled the wounded to the edge of the cliff, tied them to rope slings, and lowered them down to waiting hands.

After each successful delivery, he reportedly prayed, "Dear God, let me get just one more." By nightfall he was credited with saving no less than seventy-five lives. "You made yourself as small a target as you could and just hoped and prayed [the Japanese] didn't hit you," Doss later stated. A member of B Company, 1st Battalion, 307th Infantry, he was again with his comrades when they were forced to scale Hacksaw Ridge's cliff again the next morning to continue the assault.[12]

By the time the Japanese defenders began retiring deep inside the escarpment on May 4, Colonel Stephen S. Hamilton, commanding the 307th Regiment, called over a battle telephone to his regimental commander, "You can have this goddam thing back any time you want it." Lieutenant General Buckner summed up such Okinawa cliff battles as being won only by use of "corkscrew and blowtorch," meaning explosives, flamethrowers, and napalm, which proved to be the more effective means of extracting his Japanese opponents.[13]

Kikusui No. 5 commenced on May 3 and would run for two days, during which time Vice Admiral Ugaki would sent out 449 planes against the Okinawa invasion fleet, including 160 kamikazes. The action was sparse on the third, as Ugaki sent reconnaissance flights to check out the Allied positions. He was still suffering from a bout of diarrhea, which he dryly noted in his diary had "served to clean up my insides."[14]

Marine ace Dean Caswell was among the TG 58.3 pilots charged with catching Ugaki's air strength lying idle on the ground that afternoon. His *Bunker Hill* division was part of a fourteen-Corsair strike, under VMF-221's Captain Swett, that bombed Kikai Jima's Wan Airfield before moving on to Tanega Shima to finish unleashing their remaining rockets on the Japanese installations there.

As they swept in, Caswell noted Zeros, Tonys, and Tojos on the ground, all painted in mottled colors of greens, yellow, and light blue. As he pulled out of his first dive, the lieutenant fired a quick burst into the canopy of a Tojo that was attempting to take off, hitting the pilot in the head. "I received no credit for that one," he said. "My gun camera did not pick that up."[15]

Noting the numerous planes in revetments and others attempting to take off, Captain Delancey decided that his division should make another firing pass. Caswell was apprehensive. The squadron's leading ace, Captain Swett, had cautioned them that making another pass over a highly defended target was a "no, no," but Delancey was determined. He led his division in for a maximum-speed pass. While his men destroyed three planes in the process, it came at a high cost. Three VMF-221 Corsairs were lost due to the accurate antiaircraft fire.

Lieutenant Edward K. Nicolaides had a 40-mm shell explode in his radio gear, just aft of the cockpit seat. He was uninjured and made it back to the ship, where his F4U was pushed overboard. Delancey's plane was hit solidly by enemy shells, and his F4U plowed into the ocean at high speed. As Caswell circled, he noted that the captain made no effort to escape before his Corsair quickly sank beneath the waves.[16]

Second Lieutenant Walt Goeggel's Corsair was also hit, but he nursed his plane two hundred miles back toward the carrier. Swett's flight was greeted

Bunker Hill's VMF-221 lost two Corsairs on May 3, 1945. *Left:* 2nd Lieutenant Walt Goeggel (*left*) with his rescuer, pilot Lieutenant Charlie Tanner, beneath Tanner's OS2U Kingfisher seaplane on the cruiser *Astoria* (CL 90). *U.S. Navy. Right:* Captain John Delancey was less fortunate, unable to escape his sinking F4U off the coast of Tanega Shima. *Dean Caswell*

near the task group by an OS2U Kingfisher from *Astoria* (CL 90). Its pilot, Lieutenant Charles Tanner, had only recently returned to his cruiser after being lost during a January rescue mission off Formosa in which he had helped direct a lifeguard submarine in picking up two downed aviators. Tanner had been forced to bail out over Luzon, where Filipino guerrillas helped guide him into the hands of the U.S. Army. He would spend more than another month securing passage back to his cruiser.[17]

Goeggel's engine quit short of the task force, but he made a safe water landing. Tanner was right on hand to taxi his OS2U up toward the Marine pilot before his plane could even submerge. "Walt wouldn't have gotten his feet wet if he hadn't slipped on the wing getting off," joked Swett. Tanner made it back to *Astoria* with Lieutenant Goeggel, who was returned the next day to *Bunker Hill*, but only after the cruiser's skipper collected the customary forty gallons of ice cream from the carrier—standard payment for the return of a downed airman.[18]

The lion's share of Vice Admiral Ugaki's kamikaze assault on May 3 came in the late afternoon, directed toward the unfortunate ships at Radar Picket Station No. 10: destroyer-minelayer *Aaron Ward* (DM 34), destroyer *Little* (DD 803), *LSM(R) 195*, *LCS(L) 14*, *LCS(L) 25*, and *LCS(L) 83*. The first major threat appeared at 1833, two bogies that slipped past the four Hellcats on CAP at that station a little more than a half hour before sunset.

It was an evening that would fully test the skills of Commander William Henry Sanders Jr., a San Diego native, and his *Aaron Ward* crew. The Hellcats caught up to the two Vals only as they came within range of the ship's gunners. One was splashed a hundred yards to starboard at 1829, but debris ricocheted off the water, sending the plane's engine, part of a wing, and its propeller onto the vessel's deck.[19]

The second Val was gunned down twelve hundred yards to port. Less than a minute later, at 1831, a Zeke came in from the port side and released its bomb just before the plane crashed into *Aaron Ward*. The bomb penetrated below the water line, exploding in the after engine room and causing severe flooding that slowed the ship and jammed her rudder to port, leaving her circling to port. The Zeke crashed into the superstructure below Mount No. 44 and exploded on impact, completely covering the area and the men nearby in gasoline and inducing ammunition explosions.

Aaron Ward had been badly hit and was forced to steam in circles, making only twenty knots. This tight action was followed by about twenty minutes during which no kamikazes pressed attacks on her. This enabled

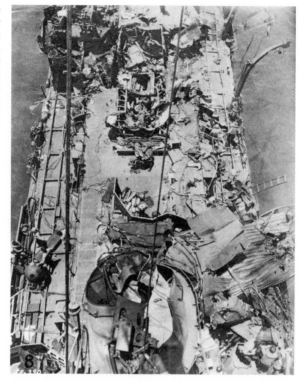

Twisted wreckage topside on the destroyer-minelayer *Aaron Ward* (DM 34), seen in Kerama Retto on May 5, 1945, following her kamikaze ordeal. This view is taken looking down and aft from *Aaron Ward*'s foremast, with her greatly distorted forward smokestack in the lower center. *80-G-330107, NARA*

repair parties to isolate damaged areas of the ship, attend to the wounded and dying, and fight fires. The crew also made efforts to set up manual steering and reestablish directional control.

While *Aaron Ward*'s men used the respite wisely, destroyer *Little* began catching the heat from Kikusui No. 5. At 1843, only fourteen minutes after *Aaron Ward* had suffered her first damage, a kamikaze crashed into the port side of *Little*. Seconds later she was hit by another suicider in nearly the same spot. At 1845 a Zeke crashed her starboard side at almost the same instant that another Zeke slammed into her in a vertical dive. The four successive hits in two minutes were lethal, spreading uncontrollable fires and causing *Little* to begin flooding. Her keel was broken, and she listed heavily to starboard. Abandon ship was ordered at 1851, just eight minutes after the first kamikaze hit. Four minutes later *Little* sank in 850 fathoms of water.

Shortly after *Little* slipped beneath the waves, another kamikaze raid was reported to be approaching the radar-picket stations. *Aaron Ward* became the bull's eye for this fresh wave of Japanese planes that approached at 1859. The initial kamikaze damage had played hell below decks, where the force of the blast had hurled engine-room personnel against machinery and burned them severely.[20]

Fireman 1st Class Eddie Strine from Maryland, who had volunteered for black-gang duty, was checking the pressure on his boilers when the first plane hit. He heard a loud bang, looked down in a daze, and saw bare bone showing on his right hand where the skin had been burned away in an instant. Strine began praying. Badly burned and in shock, he remembered little of the next minutes other than the fact that lifesaving hands helped force him up the escape-hatch ladder toward the upper decks.[21]

As the next attack wave moved in at 1859, *Aaron Ward's* wardroom had become an emergency triage center. The ship's medical officer, Lieutenant Jack Barbieri, worked diligently with his corpsmen: Chief Pharmacist's Mate Orville Tedford, Pharmacist's Mates Clair Crider and John James Kennedy, and Seaman 2nd Class Farrell Ronald Fletcher. At the height of the renewed attack, Fletcher was killed while running to his station, but the others worked tirelessly to save lives.[22]

Sunset was fast approaching as a lone Val commenced a suicide run on *Aaron Ward* from about eight thousand yards out. First the big 5-inchers roared, joined by the barking of the 40-mms as the dive bomber barreled in, and finally the chattering of the 20-mms told all below decks that they were in serious jeopardy. At a mere two thousand yards the Val was destroyed by a direct hit from a 5-inch shell. *Aaron Ward's* gunners had splashed four kamikazes by this point.

Around 1905 a Betty bomber closed to five thousand yards before *Aaron Ward's* able 5-inch guns also brought it down. Minutes later a pair of Vals appeared off the port bow pursued by Marine CAP fighters, which downed one of them. The second dive bomber, damaged by antiaircraft fire, clipped the top of *Aaron Ward's* Number One stack and broke off the ship's radio antenna. Another Val came in at 1913, was hit repeatedly, but crashed into the main deck aft of Gun Captain George O. Larson's Mount No. 42. Its bomb exploded a few feet to port, holing the hull near the forward fireroom. This kamikaze caused flooding of the forward fireroom, and the ship gradually lost headway as its power failed.

The force of the explosion knocked the ship's gunnery officer, Lieutenant David M. Rubel, and his assistant, Lieutenant Lefteris Lavrakas, to the deck. Rubel picked himself up in time to see a Val a thousand yards away that slipped in unopposed to slam into the destroyer's after superstructure close to the prior hit.[23]

These two Val hits caused devastation among the gun crews. The first loader for Mount No. 44, Machinist's Mate 3rd Class John Brantley Rawlins, had been wounded and blown off his mount by the kamikaze hit twenty minutes earlier. He had then rushed to Mount No. 25, replaced a seriously wounded gunner, and kept firing this gun until the Vals slammed home. At 1916, about one minute after the dual hits, *Aaron Ward* was approached by a lone Zeke on her port quarter. The big 5-inch guns were unable to bear on the fighter, but Larson's Mount No. 42, firing manually, took him under fire. It was not enough.

The Zeke, carrying a belly tank, crashed into the base of Mount No. 43, demolishing it, knocking Mount No. 25 and Mount No. 27 out of action, and setting fire to the 40-mm and 20-mm clipping rooms. Several gunners, including Rawlins, and loaders in the area were killed or blown over the side of the ship. At 1921 another kamikaze slammed into the base of *Aaron Ward*'s Number Two stack with a fiery blast of its bomb and gasoline, toppling the stack, a searchlight, and two gun crews.[24]

Heroes were abundant on the blazing warship throughout her over-hour-long ordeal with kamikazes. Mineman 2nd Class Joseph Edward Zaloga perished saving others, willingly running into the burning 40-mm clipping rooms and stowage racks to help wounded comrades. Radar Technician 2nd Class James L. Reichard climbed *Aaron Ward*'s foremast and worked amid diving and strafing planes to repair antennae. One of the ship's few black steward's mates, Eddie Gaines, helped with damage control and then volunteered to assist Doctor Barbieri in the wardroom, tending to wounded throughout the night.[25]

Another steward's mate, twenty-nine-year-old Carl E. Clark, was equally valiant. The first suicide plane wiped out seven men near him, but Clark struggled back to his feet, wounded. He spent the evening fighting fires with a hose that normally required the strength of four men to control, and his efforts to help save the ship were noted by skipper Bill Sanders. Clark was later ignored by the awards board for seven decades until his valor was finally recognized in 2012, when the then ninety-five-year-old was pinned with the Navy and Marine Corps Commendation Medal with Combat Distinguishing Device.[26]

By 1922 *Aaron Ward* had been crashed by five kamikazes, two of which carried bombs, and her upper works had been damaged by a sixth plane that had caromed off her Number One stack. The ship was dead in the water, raging with fires, and her upper decks and superstructure resembled a floating junk pile. Darkness had settled over the ocean, but the fight to survive had just begun as the last kamikazes cleared the radarscopes.

The situation was grim. "We were starting to sink by the fantail," said Sonarman Bob Potter. *Aaron Ward*'s main deck was only inches above the water, as numerous compartments—engine rooms, firerooms, the crew's bunkroom, and the machine shop—were all flooded. Bucket-brigade parties worked at bailing out compartments, while other sailors fought fires and helped toss hot ammunition overboard.[27]

Corpsmen worked through the night, administering first aid to their burned and bleeding shipmates. Pharmacist Kennedy happened upon boiler-room survivor Eddie Strine on the fantail in the darkness. Eddie's uniform had been burned completely off him, and he lay unconscious, his skin blistered red and his hair singed from his scalp. Sailors moved about, gathering human remains and zipping them into body bags. Fortunately for Strine, Kennedy—whom he recognized to be from his own home state of Maryland—knelt beside him to check his vitals one last time and detected a weak pulse. He shouted for help, and Strine immediately began receiving medical attention.[28]

Aaron Ward stubbornly remained afloat throughout the early evening, although two of her radar-picket sisters had lost their fights for survival. The destroyer *Little* had gone down due to the successive kamikaze strikes on her, and escort gunboat *LSM(R) 195* had been crashed by a kamikaze that started explosions in the forward rocket magazines. At 1920 the order was given to abandon ship, and *LSM(R) 195* sank fifteen minutes later. Two other warships had been damaged at Radar Picket Station No. 1, where a total of eighty-six lives were lost that day. Farther away, at Radar Picket Station No. 9, *Macomb* was hit by a kamikaze at 1830 that day that killed seven and wounded twice as many.

The successful fight to save *Aaron Ward* would prove to be an inspiration to many throughout the U.S. Navy. Once the kamikazes cleared and it was completely dark, *LCS(L) 83* came alongside at 1935 to help fight fires. Severely wounded casualties were moved in stretchers over to her on the port side and to *LCS(L) 14*, which came alongside the starboard side. By 2024 the two ships and *Aaron Ward*'s damage-control crews had put out the fires, and within the next hour the destroyer-minelayer *Shannon* (DM 25) had taken the badly mauled destroyer-minelayer under tow for the five-knot overnight trip back to safe harbor at Kerama Retto. Upon *Aaron Ward*'s arrival there, skipper Bill Sanders was greeted by a message from Admiral Nimitz himself: "We all admire a ship that can't be licked. Congratulations on your magnificent performance."[29]

As she neared Kerama Retto shortly after sunrise on May 4, *Aaron Ward* was met by a flotilla of small craft from *Gosper* (APA 170), which removed the remaining casualties in an expeditious manner. Fireman Eddie Strine could see other severely wounded shipmates lying near him as his canvas stretcher was hustled toward one of *Gosper*'s waiting boats, but what gave him inspiration was the sight of his ship's battle flag, blackened and singed, still flying high above him. Familiar words from the "Star Spangled

Fireman Eddie Strine, badly burned, was moved by the sight of the U.S. flag still flying on his *Aaron Ward. Eddie Strine via Jim Horan*

Banner" now passed through his mind, now with a new, special meaning to him.

> And the rockets' red glare,
> the bombs bursting in air,
> gave proof through the night
> that our flag was still there.

Strine had survived the night, as had his ship. "As I was going down, I could see well enough that the flag was still there," he recalled years later. He knew that the best the Japanese Divine Wind could throw at his ship had not been enough to put her and her crew under the waves before the dawn's early light.[30]

But the hell endured by Eddie Strine and his brave *Aaron Ward* shipmates was but a preview of what the radar-picket warships would face from Kikusui No. 5 the following day.

Chapter Nineteen

"BE ALERT AND
KEEP THEM SPLASHING"

American military intelligence had predicted May 4 to be an active day
of kamikaze attacks thanks to successful intercepts of radio traffic.
Additionally, the presence of enemy search planes on the evening of the
third indicated the Japanese were attempting to pinpoint ship locations for
strikes the following day.[1]

Yorktown's night fighters saw signs that a new Japanese Kikusui operation was beginning to stir during the early hours of May 4. Lieutenant Dale L.
Knopf of VF-9 closed on an Emily in the moonlight and sent it plunging
into the water with such an intense blaze that it was visible nineteen miles
away on his home carrier.[2]

Meanwhile, Ensign Franklin Goodson was strapped into his Hellcat,
waiting for takeoff from *Yorktown.* "While sitting on the catapult, my radar
just would not function properly," Goodson wrote. "My plane was removed
from the catapult and my alternate, backup, Ensign John Orth, was moved
in to the vacated position." The twenty-three-year-old Orth, who had
downed two aerial opponents on the morning of April 30, would be the
next VF-9 pilot to score. A series of vectors from *Randolph's* FDO, helped
him make radar contact at 0345 and destroy a Betty bomber after multiple
firing runs. Orth made contact with another Betty at 0422, flamed its port
engine, and watched in satisfaction as the big bomber hit the water.[3]

Orth's next radar contact was established at 0455. His third victim was
soon in flames and seen to explode on impact with the ocean. When the
ensign returned to base an hour later, he was *Yorktown's* newest ace, with
six night kills to his credit. Only four other night fighters would achieve ace

Lieutenant (jg) John Orth of *Yorktown*'s VF-9 made six kills while serving as an F6F night fighter. *U.S. Navy*

status in Hellcats during World War II. Goodson, whose F6F had been removed from the catapult, wrote in his diary that Orth received congratulations from Vice Admiral Mitscher and the skippers of several ships; he would later receive the Navy Cross. "All that I got was a good night sleep," Goodson logged.[4]

Fifteen minutes after Orth's final kill, three divisions of VF-9 were launched from *Yorktown* to take station over the radar pickets. Counting the four predawn kills by Fighting Nine's batmen, May 4 would prove to be the squadron's best of the Okinawa campaign.

The divisions of Lieutenants Gene Valencia, Bert Eckard, and James H. Caldwell were assigned to CAP duty above Radar Picket Station No. 1, due north of Okinawa. This station was patrolled by the destroyers *Morrison* (DD 560) and *Ingraham* (DD 694) along with *LCS(L) 21*, *LCS(L) 23*, *LCS(L) 31*, and *LSM(R) 194*. Beginning at 0600, *Yorktown*'s dozen F6Fs began alternating altitudes, as directed by *Morrison*'s FDO, to be ready for any incoming kamikazes.

The VF-9 pilots would soon face elements of Vice Admiral Ugaki's fifth Kikusui mission, scheduled to coincide with a ground counterattack on Okinawa. The JAAF sent out some fifty special-attack planes, with an escort of thirty-five Frank fighters, while the IJN added seventy-five special-attack aircraft, with an escort of thirty-five George and forty-eight Zero fighters. Adding in seven Ohka bombers, Ugaki's early morning strike groups winging toward Okinawa would play hell on the radar-picket warships.[5]

Valencia and wingman Harris Mitchell were two hours into their radar-picket CAP at 0800 as they began dropping altitude so they could remove their oxygen masks. Valencia suddenly spotted a twin-engine Dinah with a Frank fighter escort, both planes heading toward the picket ships. "I'll take the fighter," Gene called to Mitch. "You take the small twin."[6]

Mitchell paused long enough to see Valencia lock on to the Frank, following the Japanese pilot's every maneuver. The Frank tried to lose the Hellcat by executing a tight loop, but Valencia remained with him all the way. He sprayed the Japanese fighter with two long bursts right at the top of the loop, causing the Frank to burst into flames. "This was something most fighter pilots thought couldn't be done, but believe me, I'm a live witness," Mitchell later stated. Valencia had one final hair-raiser from the Frank pilot, who remained in his blazing cockpit and pulled up sharply in an attempt to ram the F6F. Gene pulled his Hellcat in an equally violent maneuver before he watched the blazing Frank splash into the ocean.[7]

Mitchell in the meantime turned his attention on the Dinah, which was jinking up and down from fifty to two hundred feet. This looked to be the opportunity to make his easiest kill yet, and Mitch opted to try something he had heard about from a squadronmate. On VF-9's previous tour, Lieutenant Hamilton McWhorter had achieved the near-miraculous feat of downing a Betty bomber on November 19, 1943, near Tarawa with only eighty-six rounds from his six machine guns. Squadron skipper Phil Torrey had thereafter dubbed him "One Slug" McWhorter for his sparse use of ammunition and keen shooting. "I learned later that my roommate and wingman, Gene Valencia, was shouting to himself, 'Miss it, Mac! Miss it!' He wanted that bomber for himself," recalled McWhorter.[8]

As Valencia and others would later relate McWhorter's "one shot" kill on the Betty to him, the legend of the Navy's first Hellcat ace seemed almost unachievable to young Mitchell, unaware that McWhorter had actually dispensed 86 rounds in the kill. "It takes a mighty soft touch to squeeze off just one round, but I made up my mind that is what I was going to try for," Mitch said, knowing that the Hellcat's six .50-caliber machine guns fired at a rate of 850 rounds per minute. "I purposely safetied all but my two inboard guns and settled down to getting that Dinah just where I wanted her to be in my gunsight. I actually slowed my Hellcat down so I could maneuver into position for a try at a one-shot kill."[9]

The Dinah was directly ahead and scarcely fifty feet above the wave tops as Mitchell moved in. He gently squeezed the trigger of his two inboard guns and immediately released it. Mitch was unable to restrict it to just one slug each, but "not over three or four came out." His tracers hit at the Dinah's wing root, causing the twin to abruptly roll left. Mitch fired another short burst that caused the plane's wings to burst into flames before it plunged into the water, its bomb exploding on impact. Mitch was well pleased when Jim French called in a "well done" to him over their intercom. In attempting to match the legend of "One Slug" McWhorter's kill, Lieutenant Mitchell had achieved his own shoot down with fewer bullets expended.[10]

Mitchell rendezvoused with Valencia, French, and Clint Smith over the picket ships to resume their CAP, and soon the FDO vectored their division to intercept large numbers of approaching Japanese aircraft. French shot up an inbound Oscar that was seen to hit the ocean just beyond one of the picket destroyers. Valencia raked an incoming Val dive bomber and exploded it before he could commence a second pass on it. Wingman Mitchell found the whole scene one of "mass confusion" as *Morrison*, *Ingraham*, and their gunboats put up a heavy blanket of flak. "The Japs were coming in singly and from all angles and directions," said Mitchell. "So, we split up and each took a quadrant."[11]

Two miles north of the Radar Picket Station No. 1 warships, Mitchell closed near the tip of a Frank's tail before unleashing his .50-calibers and sending it into the drink. Valencia and Mitch had scarcely resumed station at two thousand feet above the destroyers before they tallyhoed another small group of Vals. Valencia dispatched a bombless Val while Mitchell flamed a Japanese army fighter that passed twenty feet over a nearby destroyer's deck before crashing into the water beyond—a kill that marked Mitch's eighth aerial victory of the war. Jim French, struggling with only two operable machine guns, ripped a Frank and sent it plunging two thousand feet into the ocean with a violent explosion. He also received an assist for a kill on a Zeke that he and several other F6F pilots shot up.[12]

As Valencia returned to altitude above *Ingraham* and *Morrison*, he caught sight of several Franks under antiaircraft fire as they drove in on the destroyers. He would receive one-half credit for a Frank kill he shared with other Hellcat pilots. Minutes later, and ten miles north of the embattled destroyers, Valencia, French, and Smitty attacked a Nate. As he closed to fire, Valencia discovered that he had expended all of his ammunition. His divisionmates responded to his calls for help, with French receiving credit for destroying the Nate with hits that sheared off one of its wings.

Mitchell engaged Japanese kamikazes until the fire from Radar Picket Station No. 1's warships became too hot for his personal safety. Lieutenant French was credited with an additional assist while his wingman, Clint Smith, downed a Frank and a Judy over the next twenty minutes. By the end of their action above *Ingraham* and *Morrison*, the various *Yorktown* divisions had shot down twenty-six kamikazes, including seven Franks, six Vals, and five Oscars. Valencia led the scoring with 3.5 kills, while French and Mitchell each tallied three kills. Adding in two kills made by Smitty, VF-9's Flying Circus division had turned in another outstanding day, with 11.5 kills between the quartet.

The sky duels over the destroyers *Morrison* and *Ingraham* and their gunboats at Radar Picket Station No. 1 was one Ensign Don McPherson of *Essex*'s VF-83 squadron would never forget. His "Wonder Five" division was

The "Wonder Five" division of *Essex*'s VF-83. *Left to right:* Ensign Don McPherson, Lieutenant Carlos Soffe, Lieutenant (jg) Tom Ward, and Ensign Myron Truax. The four Hellcat pilots finished the Okinawa campaign with twenty combined kills. *Don McPherson*

on radar-picket CAP just off Izena Shima when it received its first vector around 0730. The single bogey was first spotted at 3,300 feet by Lieutenant Soffe's second section of Lieutenant (jg) Tom Ward and Ensign Myron Truax. Calling out a tallyho on the plane they identified as an Oscar, Ward and Truax found that their opponent made an immediate split-S maneuver and dived for the water, heading for a destroyer.[13]

Ward followed, popping the wheels and flaps on his Hellcat to keep from overrunning the Oscar. He opened fire from astern and continued his pursuit, even as the destroyer's gunners opened up on them. Ward remained on the Oscar's tail, watching it flame and finally splash just over the destroyer's bow. Truax claimed an assist by joining several Marine Corsairs in exploding a Val before it reached the picket ship. A low-flying Zeke near-missed one destroyer with his bomb but was shot down by Truax as the Japanese pilot turned to make a second run on the ship.

The Kadena-based VMF-323 Death Rattlers took on a group of Vals approaching the already damaged destroyer *Morrison*. First Lieutenant John W. Ruhsam was credited with downing four Vals and damaging three others, while 1st Lieutenant Bob Wade downed at least two opponents before the two Marines exhausted their ammunition. Yontan-based VMF-224 Corsair pilots claimed an additional ten kamikaze kills during the hellacious battles.[14]

Two Zekes got through the American fighters shortly after 0825, and both slammed into *Morrison*. The first hit the base of the forward stack, exploding its bomb in the process, while the second Japanese fighter hit the deck near the Number Three 5-inch gun. *Morrison*'s Number One boiler exploded, sections of the bridge were heavily damaged, power and lights on the ship went out, the engine rooms were seriously damaged, and heavy fires broke out in several places.

Separated from his VF-83 companions, Ensign Truax joined on a pair of VMF-224 Corsairs around 0825 to attack a group of about ten Naka-jima E8N Navy Type 95 "Dave" seaplanes—constructed largely of wood and fabric—that had launched from Ibusuki. Truax was credited with two kills and an assist, while the other Marines accounted for five more of the nimble floatplanes.[15]

The severely damaged *Morrison* was hit at 0834 by another Dave that made it through the Marine and Navy fighter pilots. It crashed into her Number Three 5-inch gun, igniting the powder in the upper handling room and causing a massive explosion. A second Dave landed in *Morrison*'s wake to evade a Marine Corsair pursuing it. The seaplane only made a touch-and-go landing five hundred yards astern before taking off and coming in low over *Morrison*'s fantail. The pilot then crashed into *Morrison*'s Number Four 5-inch gun and ignited its powder. Water quickly rushed into the crippled destroyer, and she rolled over to starboard.

Morrison's engineering officer, Lieutenant Jesse W. Franklin Jr., found that the explosions left all members of the after engine room dead or missing. He noted four major explosions before he was forced to pass the word to abandon ship to help preserve lives. *Morrison* sank in 325 fathoms of water, taking 152 men down with her.[16]

The ship's medical officer, Lieutenant (jg) Charles N. Hoyt, had only ten minutes to treat patients between the time the first kamikaze hit the *Morrison* and when his ship went down. "The chaos and annihilation cannot be described," said Hoyt. One of his corpsmen was killed, and another suffered a compound fracture of his right tibia, leaving only Hoyt and one assistant to swim from group to group of survivors to assess their flash burns and shrapnel wounds until they could be rescued.[17]

Ensign Truax flew north to find his VF-83 section leader, Lieutenant (jg) Ward, after the sinking of *Morrison*. En route he encountered a Val, which he flamed with a head-on run. The surviving destroyer *Ingraham* helped the Hellcat pilots designate incoming bogies by firing its 5-inch guns at the kamikazes. Truax and Ward followed one of these bursts and spotted a Dave, whose low airspeed caused the ensign to overshoot it in his pursuit. Ward coolly popped his wheels and flaps, slid in astern, and hammered the floatplane into the sea.

In the meantime division leader Carlos Soffe had downed a Dave and a Val near *Ingraham*. Shortly thereafter, he and Don McPherson were able to rejoin Ward and Truax. The reunited Wonder Five division then tallyhoed a flight of six Daves to the southeast. Soffe and Ward each downed one aircraft, while Truax shot down two of the seaplanes, making him an ace in a mission and then some, with six confirmed kills.

McPherson misjudged the slow speed of his floatplane target and over-shot it, adjusting in time to shoot down the next Dave. The action near Radar Picket Station No. 1 had become so mixed that Soffe finally opened up on the radio, "Guys, just split up and get onto every one you can get." McPherson soon dropped another of the floatplanes, bringing his career kills to four.[18]

Returning above the embattled *Ingraham*, the Wonder Five division again followed a 5-inch salvo bursting to the north and tallyhoed another flight of eight floatplanes. They were joined in battle by another VF-83 division led by Lieutenant Robert B. Garrard. His division had destroyed five enemy planes in the preceding half hour, and Garrard's team downed another three planes in this melee. McPherson closed on another Dave as the nimble floatplane bore in on the damaged *Ingraham*. Ignoring the friendly fire from the destroyer, he splashed his third kill of the mission well short of *Ingraham* before banking away to clear the picket ship's deadly antiaircraft fire.

McPherson's Wonder Five division shot down sixteen enemy planes, and other VF-83 pilots pushed the squadron's total victories to two dozen in the vicinity of the embattled *Morrison* and *Ingraham*. McPherson had achieved ace status in the process, while divisionmate Truax joined the fleet's "ace in a day" club. Unaware of the identity of the warships he helped defend, McPherson was shocked many years later to receive a signed photo from thirty-five crewmen of *Ingraham*. The sailor who contacted him had long desired to find the identity of the Hellcat pilots who had braved friendly antiaircraft fire to battle the kamikazes. "He said if they'd taken another hit, it would have sunk them," said McPherson. "He wanted to thank us for saving their ship."[19]

Gene Valencia's Flying Circus division remained in the fight over Radar Picket Station No. 1 until all four pilots were low on fuel and ammunition. Valencia, French, Smitty, and Mitchell headed for Yontan Field to refuel, picking up Ensign Martin Lally of VF-9 en route. Near Okinawa the *Yorktown* quartet spotted three Val fixed-gear dive bombers. Mitchell realized they "would have been easy prey for the Hellcat, but we didn't have enough gas to even attempt one pass at them."[20]

Mitchell's Hellcat ran out of fuel once on the ground, and Marines had to tow him from the runway. Smith landed with a mere ten gallons remaining. The division had spent five hours and twenty-five minutes in the air, with about two hours of that time at full throttle in wild combat. Once the ground crews had pumped fuel into the F6Fs' starved tanks, Valencia led his bunch on the hour and forty-five minute flight back to their *Yorktown* home. It took all off Mitch's stamina to get through the necessary debriefing with the VF-9 ACIO, Lieutenant Ralph Murphy. "It didn't take me long to crawl into my sack and wander off to slumberland," admitted Mitchell.[21]

Following the loss of the destroyer *Morrison*, the surviving six ships at Radar Picket Station No. 1 continued battling the suiciders of Kikusui No. 5 for hours on May 4. *LCS(L) 21* suffered minor damage from a kamikaze that skimmed the gunboat at 0832. Another gunboat, *LSM(R) 194*, was hit in the stern at 0838 by a Val that caused such a tremendous boiler explosion that the ship began settling by the stern.[22]

The surviving crew took to the water, the men suffering further injuries when *LSM(R) 194*'s magazine exploded underwater, rocking nearby rescue gunboats. Once the skies were somewhat cleared by 0940, other gunboats picked up survivors from the *Morrison* and *LSM(R) 194*. The remaining kamikazes in the area turned their attention toward the destroyer *Ingraham*, already damaged by one near miss. Corporal Kanichi Horimoto, an eighteen-year-old pilot of one of the Frank fighters, had vowed to sink a ship this day by giving his life. As ground crews warmed up his aircraft that morning on Miyakonojo East Airfield, Horimoto handed a farewell note for his family to maintenance worker Saburo Otani. "I will do my utmost," he vowed. "I am determined to blossom as a flower at the end."[23]

Beginning at 0838, *Ingraham*'s gunners splashed four more planes, but a fifth, piloted by Corporal Horimoto, crashed into her port side near the waterline. Its bomb exploded in the forward diesel room, creating heavy damage and knocking out power to her forward 5-inch gun mounts. The nearby *LCS(L) 31* suffered two sailors killed by a Zeke that clipped that ship's pilothouse. Moments later a Val crashed into *LCS(L) 31*'s main deck, crippling her effective firepower. The badly damaged *Ingraham* was taken under tow by a tug that afternoon and pulled back to Kerama Retto for repairs. The action was also intense over Radar Picket Station No. 7, where waves of attackers continued to arrive until nightfall. Around 1920 three planes swept in on a group that included the jeep carrier *Sangamon* (CVE 26), which was hit in her flight deck by a diving Nick. Escort ships moved in to help battle the fires on *Sangamon*, which was saved through valiant damage control efforts.[24]

The kamikazes of Kikusui No. 5 were relentless against the picket ships stationed at Radar Picket Station No. 12 shortly after 0800. One Val crashed into the water close aboard the starboard side amidships of the destroyer *Luce* (DD 522), its bomb explosion temporarily knocking out power to the ship. A second Val, its wing sheared off by gunfire, crashed into the ship's Number Three 5-inch gun at 0811. Other kamikazes ravaged *Luce*, so badly devastating the destroyer that she was listing heavily and settling rapidly by the stern within minutes. At 0814 her skipper, Commander Jacob Wilson Waterhouse, was forced to pass the order to abandon ship.[25]

Luce's list became more rapid and her bow rose sharply into the air. Five minutes after the first kamikaze strike, *Luce* disappeared under the water, followed thirty seconds later by a severe underwater explosion that killed and injured more swimming sailors. Fewer than 100 of *Luce*'s crew of 335 escaped death or injury.

Moments after *Luce* was hit, Captain Bill Van Buskirk's VMF-323 division splashed a Dinah heading for the crippled destroyer. Van Buskirk then flamed an incoming Val, but the crippled dive bomber plunged into a 5-inch gun mount on the nearby *LSM(R) 190*, killing the ship's gunnery officer and wounding her skipper. Minutes later another Val crashed into *LSM(R) 190*, and another Japanese pilot landed a direct bomb hit. Orders were passed to abandon ship, and by 0840 *LSM(R) 190* had slid beneath the waves, with the loss of thirteen men killed or missing in action.[26]

The radar-picket destroyers that day also faced seven twin-engine Dinah bombers loaded with rocket-powered Ohkas from the 7th Cherry Blossom Unit from Kanoya, accompanied by twenty bomb-laden fighters and ten Kate attack planes. This group was joined in flight by twenty-eight reconnaissance seaplanes from the seaplane base at Ibusuki and from Kushira Airfield. In the sky above Radar Picket Station No. 14, Sub-Lieutenant Susumu Ohashi climbed into his Ohka and was released from his Dinah mothership at 0856 as U.S. fighters tore into the bomber.[27]

The picket ships maneuvering below Ohashi's Baka included the destroyer-minelayer *Shea* (DM 3), destroyer *Hugh W. Hadley* (DD 774), and four gunboats. Around 0830 a division of VC-90 FM-2 Wildcat fighters from the escort carrier *Steamer Bay* (CVE 87) intercepted incoming bogies and downed one twin-engine Dinah. Lieutenant (jg) Edward E. McKeever witnessed the bomber's crew release the Ohka, but he was left behind as Ohashi kicked in his rockets and streaked toward *Shea* at 0856. McKeever observed that once a "*baka* starts its jets and gets underway, it is too late to catch it."[28]

Sailors on board *Shea* had no view of the incoming rocket-bomb until five seconds before it impacted the starboard side of the bridge superstructure. Lieutenant (jg) William Kuyper, *Shea*'s damage-control officer, saw the Baka coming in from the starboard side and shouted at shipmates to take cover. The Ohka ripped right through the thin-skinned destroyer-minelayer's hull and exploded about fifteen feet from the ship. "I guess that's why they call tin cans 'tin cans,' because the bulkheads up around the chart house are sheet metal, almost like paper," noted Kuyper. "The *baka* bomb went completely through the ship and came out the port side. The concussion went up my pants legs and blew the seams out of my pants."[29]

The slashing Ohka and its external blast buckled frames and plates on the ship, killed 27 men, and wounded another 130 men. *Shea's* skipper, Commander Charles C. Kirkpatrick, kept his destroyer-minelayer under way, and his crew's valiant damage-control efforts allowed her to limp back to the Hagushi anchorage for repairs. *Shea* was only the second U.S. warship to be struck by a manned Ohka of the Thunder Gods Corps.

Several other kamikazes were shot down while attacking the destroyer *Hopkins* (DD 249) and the minesweeper *Gayety* (AM 239). Higher Flight Petty Officer Masayoshi Ishiwata bore in on the *Gayety* at more than 400 miles per hour, even as U.S. gunners began disintegrating his Baka with direct hits. Ishiwata's plane slammed into the sea fifteen yards off *Gayety's* port bow and exploded with enough force to knock out her port 40-mm gun and wound three sailors. The Dinah crew that had launched Ishiwata's Ohka saw smoke rising from the explosion and believed that his targeted ship had been sunk.[30]

Only one Ohka-carrying Dinah crew returned to base, pushing the death toll of the Thunder Gods Corps to 587 men. Vice Admiral Ugaki was pleased with the results of his Kikusui No. 5 operation on May 4, believing his special attackers had sunk several cruisers and destroyers and had damaged two battleships, three other cruisers, and five unidentified ships. "We achieved a great deal of success," he logged.[31]

Kikusui No. 5 had indeed taken a heavy toll on the radar-picket ships off Okinawa. Some 475 U.S. sailors had lost their lives, and another 484 men had been wounded. *Morrison*, *Little*, *Luce*, *LSM(R) 190*, *LSM(R) 194*, and *LSM(R) 195* had been sunk, and nine other radar-picket warships had been subjected to varying degrees of damage.[32]

Vice Admiral Mitscher could only point toward the saving grace that his TF 58 fighters had registered 105 kills that day off Okinawa. In an effort to maintain positive spirits for his fleet, the Bald Eagle messaged: "Today, we in this force have reached and well passed one thousand enemy aircraft shot out of the air by aircraft and ships' gunfire since 1 April. The enemy cannot take it at such a murderous rate much longer. Be alert and keep them splashing."[33]

Chapter Twenty

"I WILL GO SMILING"

Lieutenant Gene Valencia's VF-9 division was the most seasoned killing machine in the fleet. Following their latest victories on May 4, the team boasted forty-one confirmed kills and three probables. With his latest kills, Valencia had reached quadruple-ace status in two tours, surpassing Lieutenant Pat Fleming of *Hancock*'s VF-80, who previously held the TF 58 kill record with eighteen victories.

Valencia advised his divisionmates to temper their cockiness around others from the squadron. But he was not opposed to letting his comrades have some fun with VF-9's ACIO, Lieutenant Ralph Murphy. His division flew a pair of four-hour CAP hops on May 5 and May 6 that were each void of enemy action. At the end of one such fruitless mission, Valencia's team landed back on *Yorktown* and made their way to the ready room, where Lieutenant Murphy assaulted them with questions.

"Old Murphy would pounce on us with a big pad and a packet full of pencils, expecting a long, exciting tale of how we had engaged and destroyed the enemy," said VF-9's Harris Mitchell. Valencia gave the ACIO a real hairraiser of a story. Mitchell, French, and Smitty jumped in on the storytelling as if they had rehearsed the tale a dozen times. Mitch found himself nearly doubled over with glee as Murphy scribbled out an impressive action report and turned to scurry toward the bridge to report to Rear Admiral Radford. Valencia halted Murphy and informed him they were pulling his leg. "We didn't see a single enemy plane all day," they announced. The Flying Circus quartet burst into laughter as their ACIO cursed, tore his report into shreds, and stormed out of the ready room.[1]

✦◇✦

Admiral Nimitz and Vice Admiral Turner remained frustrated with the stalemate ashore on Okinawa. But Lieutenant General Buckner's troops continued to slowly flush deeply entrenched Japanese soldiers from their coral caverns. The 1st Marine Division alone suffered 649 men killed, wounded, and missing on May 4 and May 5, added to the 687 casualties suffered by the Army's 7th and 77th Divisions for the same two days.[2]

Vice Admiral Mitscher's carriers enjoyed a relative lull in the kamikaze action in the days following the May 4 Kikusui No. 5 push. His Navy fighters would only claim four aerial victories during the next six days. Word flashed through the task force on the eighth that Germany had surrendered unconditionally to the Allies, but it was little consolation for the ground troops struggling on Okinawa. "Nazi Germany might as well have been on the moon," thought Eugene Sledge of the 1st Marine Division's K Company, 3rd Battalion, 5th Regiment, which was in the process of taking casualties near the Shuri lines.[3]

Vice Admiral Ugaki and Admiral Toyoda ordered the few remaining Ohka pilots to prepare for action on May 11, the date when Kikusui No. 6 was scheduled to be unleashed. The Thunder Gods Corps had been badly whittled down by the time the attack force began launching at 0500. Sub-Lieutenant Shibata, leader of the 10th Kemmu Squadron, boasted to other Thunder Gods pilots that he would skim the surface of the ocean and crash into the center of his target during this next round of attacks.[4]

Ugaki's strike force included nearly every serviceable plane on Kyushu: eighteen Judy dive bombers, with fighter cover, and sixty-five army and navy kamikazes (including Ohkas and their mothership bombers), the latter force escorted by some seventy-five long-range fighter-bombers. As the various strike groups took off and headed toward Okinawa, Ugaki added poetry to his diary to honor their sacrifices:

Flowers of the special attack are falling,
When the spring is leaving.
Gone with the spring
Are young boys like cherry blossoms,
Gone are the blossoms,
Leaving cherry trees only with leaves.[5]

✦◇✦

Pete Mitscher crawled from his bunk at 0200 on May 11 as the General Quarters alarm sounded throughout the carrier *Bunker Hill*. His flagship was marking her fifty-ninth consecutive day on the kamikaze front lines while steaming some seventy-six miles east of Okinawa. The Bald Eagle pulled on a light robe and donned his trademark ball cap. He was still weak from his sickness or possible light heart attack, unable to ascend or descend ladders without help, and his weight was down to a mere hundred pounds. His mind was still clear, and he returned to his bunk within the hour, catching another nearly two hours of sleep before he was awakened again at 0441 by dawn General Quarters. His staff finally convinced the admiral to at least wear a steel helmet and Mae West life preserver when he was on the wing bridge. The Bald Eagle rotated between his cabin, the Flag Plot transom, and his favored swivel chair throughout the day.[6]

Task force FDOs were busy through the early morning, coaching out fighters to intercept the bogies beginning to dot the radar scopes. Many of Ugaki's kamikaze pilots slipped in toward Okinawa by flying low over the water, hoping to avoid both the waiting CAP fighters and the probing reaches of the American radar sets. The early intercepts on May 11 were made by Okinawa-based Marine fighter pilots.

Around 0830 1st Lieutenant Edward C. Keeley and 2nd Lieutenant Larry N. Crawley of VMF-323 engaged eleven incoming bandits in the vicinity of Radar Picket Station No. 15, claiming kills on a Tojo, a Dinah, and five Nates. They exhausted their final ammunition chasing another suicider through friendly fire as it made a run on the destroyer *Hugh W. Hadley*. The Corsairs flew so close in pursuit of the kamikaze that the enemy plane was forced off course and was seen to splash on the other side of the destroyer. The skipper, Commander Baron J. Mullaney recorded, "I am willing to take my ship to the shores of Japan if I could have these Marines with me."[7]

Mullaney and his U.S. Naval Academy classmate, Commander Robert J. Archer, held Radar Picket Station No. 15 with their respective destroyers, *Hadley* and *Evans* (DD 502), along with LCS(L) 82, LCS(L) 83, LCS(L) 84, and LSM(R) 193. Ensign Doug Aitken, a twenty-two-year-old radar officer from Ohio working in *Hadley*'s CIC, estimated from his radarscope that his picket station was assailed by more than 150 attackers in five distinct waves of attacks in less than two hours. Between 0830 and 0900, *Hadley*'s gunners splashed a dozen attackers, while four VF-85 Corsair divisions from the carrier *Shangri-La* downed eight planes and claimed two more probables.[8]

But there were simply too many incoming kamikazes. Around 0905 a Tony slammed *Evans* at the waterline on the port side, flooding part of the ship. Two more kamikazes hit the destroyer in the minutes that followed, exploding her boilers, leaving her afloat but dead in the water. The *Evans* crew, having lost thirty men killed and twenty-nine wounded, fought fires with extinguishers and bucket brigades through the morning until gunboats and tugs helped tow their crippled ship to the Kerama anchorage.[9]

Carrier-based Marine fighters also joined the fight against the kamikazes near Radar Picket Station No. 15, including seven *Bunker Hill* Corsairs led by Captain Jim Swett of VMF-221. Swett damaged a Frances that 1st Lieutenant Walt Goeggel finished off. A short while later he downed an incoming Jill before it could crash into *Hadley*. "He didn't have a prayer," remarked Swett. This Jill would prove to be his final victory, running his wartime tally to 15.5 kills and four probables. At 0855 Swett's Corsairs intercepted an Ohka-carrying Betty, whose ultimate demise was credited to 1st Lieutenant Ralph Glendinning.[10]

Gene Valencia's Flying Circus division, in company with VF-9 divisions led by Lieutenants Bert Eckard and Marv Franger, soon joined the battle above Radar Picket Station No. 15. Directed by an FDO on board the headquarters ship *Panamint* (AGC 13), the *Yorktown* fighters were joined by three VF-47 Hellcat divisions from the light carrier *Bataan*. Shortly after 0800, while orbiting over Point Yoke on Yoron Jima, Valencia tallyhoed a group of Japanese planes flying in the opposite direction about four thousand feet above them. Although wingman Harris Mitchell was straggling behind with a balky F6F, Valencia dispatched his second section of Jim French and Clint Smith to hit the four leading planes of the first group while he tackled the next bunch on his own.

French came in on the tail of an Oscar, set fire to its engine and wing roots, and watched it head for the water smoking and burning. Within minutes he had also downed a pair of Franks. After the initial action, Smith joined French to circle a downed F6F pilot, Lieutenant Max C. Replogle of *Bataan*'s VF-47, who had been forced to ditch after his engine froze up. Prior to ditching, Replogle had taken down a Tojo, while other members of his VF-47 laid claims to eight other Tojos and two Zekes. *Bunker Hill*'s VF-84 was also active during the early hours off Kikai Jima, where the pilots downed eight Nates and three Zekes.

Valencia started his own run-in against two planes of this group that appeared to be attacking from out of the sun. Upon closing the distance, however, Gene found them to be a pair of F6Fs embroiled in a battle with some Tonys. As Valencia pulled away, a Tony sliced in and shot down one of the two F6Fs. Valencia then tangled with the offending Tony until he landed hits from a near-head-on run that caused a large part of the enemy's wing to fall off. Valencia's first kill of the mission was seen to plunge toward the ocean. He quickly followed this victory by setting ablaze an Oscar from a group of Japanese planes under attack by some Corsairs.

Harris Mitchell, left alone while his three divisionmates did battle, was still climbing through 18,000 feet when he found three Tonys closing fast on his tail from below. Mitch dropped his left wing and "horsed back on that stick with all my might." The Tonys followed, and sent tracers walking right up Mitchell's tail. The VF-9 ace flipped over on his back, executed a half roll, and pulled back to the vertical and headed for the deck at full throttle. "My airspeed indicator was so far past the red line it was difficult to determine just how fast I was going," he said, "but the buffeting effect told me I was in close proximity to the sonic barrier."[11]

Mitchell recovered a mere two hundred feet above the wave tops and climbed back into a cloud layer, hoping to rejoin his VF-9 division. As he approached he spotted a Corsair chasing a Tony low on the water. Mitch set himself up for a high side run, dove down on to the Tony's tail, and fired until his opponent exploded and crashed into the ocean.

The Flying Circus pilot turned back for the destroyer pickets only to find that he was being trailed by another Tony. At the same moment his intercom finally crackled with the voice of Gene Valencia, calling for his lost wingman to come join him on station at about 10,000 feet. Mitch announced that a Tony was on his tail, adding, "I'll join you as soon as I splash this fellow."[12]

Mitchell and the Tony dodged through the overcast for more than fifteen minutes and covered some seventy miles. Mitch finally achieved good target range as the Japanese pilot set his sights on a radar-picket destroyer. As he neared the warship, the enemy started into a turn, allowing Mitchell to cut across his path. Once his .50-calibers caused the Tony to burst into flames and crash, the exhausted VF-9 pilot headed back toward the picket destroyer, only to be challenged by a Corsair CAP division. "I started rocking my wings so they could recognize me and they passed me almost too close for comfort," Mitchell stated.[13]

Too far separated from his own division, Mitchell joined with Franger's VF-9 division for the return to *Yorktown*. As he debriefed with squadron ACIO Murphy, he was shaken to realize how many brushes with death he had cheated in one mission. But his two aerial victories this day had pushed Harris Mitchell to double-ace status, with ten confirmed kills.[14]

Gene Valencia's day was far from over when his wingman became separated from him. He had already downed a Tony and an Oscar, but his attempts to reach second-section leader Lieutenant French on the radio were in vain. Valencia joined with a pair of F6F pilots from another carrier and soon found himself closing on the tail of a single-engine Japanese fighter, painted brown with red meatball insignias.[15]

Lieutenant Valencia made a flat side run from about seven o'clock, achieved hits in its engine, and saw the Japanese plane explode from the engine back to the cockpit then fall out of control. Now with three kills on the morning, Valencia found himself alone, still unable to raise his VF-9 comrades on the radio. Gene tallyhoed a group of eight to ten Zekes and Oscars. As he closed and came up under one of them, two divisions of F6Fs attacked the same aircraft from above. Valencia disengaged and followed a Zeke into a dive, blasting pieces from the fighter until he was forced to break off, receiving credit for only a probable on this one. Valencia finally managed to rendezvous with French and Smith, who had spent time flying cover over the downed VF-47 fighter pilot.

The VF-9 trio encountered a Frances near Izena Shima, but when Valencia started a run on it, he found that his Hellcat was out of ammunition. Smitty chased the fighter-bomber down toward the water, landing hits that caused the propeller to rip away from the plane's right engine. Valencia saw the Frances hit the ocean one thousand yards from a radar-picket destroyer-escort. As the Japanese plane bounced off the concrete-like ocean, it exploded violently enough to knock Valencia's radio set loose and freeze his elevator. TF 58's leading ace was forced to seek refuge on Ie Shima to effect repairs on his damaged Hellcat but was later able to make his return to *Yorktown*.

The divisions of Lieutenants Franger and Eckard also found action on May 11. Franger managed to shoot down a Tony, the only kill for his division, while Eckard's four Hellcats were especially deadly. Eckard became an "ace in a day" by downing five opponents and damaging another. His wingman, Ensign Joe Kaelin, shot down three Zekes, damaged two, and probably destroyed one other. By the end of the action, three divisions of VF-9 had collectively bagged twenty kills, adding two probables and three damaged aircraft to their tally.[16]

By the time Gene Valencia made his triumphant return to *Yorktown*, he had secured a place for himself in naval history. His three kills and one probable pushed his wartime tally to twenty-three victories, another plane he had forced to crash without firing a shot, two probables, and two aircraft damaged. This placed Valencia solidly in the number-two position for top Navy ace of World War II. But his division—including Mitchell, French, and Smith—combined to give the Flying Circus unique honors. The four

Hellcats pilots had achieved an astounding total of fifty shoot downs, making them the most successful fighter division in U.S. Navy history.

By 1100 on May 11, Navy carrier pilots had claimed sixty-eight Japanese shoot downs plus four probables. It was a big day by anyone's standards, but their valiant efforts were simply not enough to spare a number of warships from grievous damage.

At Radar Picket Station No. 15, the destroyer *Evans* had been knocked out of action by three kamikaze hits. Commander Baron Mullaney's *Hugh W. Hadley* escaped serious damage during the early attacks but became the focal point for the next waves of kamikazes. *Hadley's* gunners destroyed ten attackers that swarmed the ship from all sides around 0920, but her luck ran out with the next attack wave. During these assaults, *Hadley* was struck aft by a bomb, hit aft by a diving kamikaze, and nearly derigged by a third plane. Her most severe damage came from a Betty bomber that approached from astern and released an Ohka. The pilot of the rocket-powered missile came in from about six hundred feet altitude and hit *Hadley's* starboard side between the engine room and the forward fireroom, the explosion raising some of the destroyer's decks twenty inches and breaking the knees and ankles of some of her crewmen.

Ensign Doug Aitken, directing the fighter efforts from *Hadley's* CIC, felt the high-speed impacts of the direct strikes. Once power was lost, he went onto the open deck and witnessed the smoke, fires, and commotion topside, where twenty-eight sailors lay dead and another sixty-seven wounded. Commander Mullaney passed the word to abandon ship, leaving only a skeleton crew of fifty men on board to assist the gunboats that came alongside to help fight fires and rescue sailors still trapped below decks. Aiken noted that such gunboats "were popularly referred as pallbearers, because when a destroyer got hit, they closed up to help us, and they became pallbearers for us."[17]

Evans and *Hadley* had absorbed the brunt of the kamikaze action at Radar Picket Station No. 15, but both destroyers would be towed to Kerama Retto for repairs. Vice Admiral Ugaki's Kikusui No. 6 had played hell on the radar-picket destroyers, but TF 58 also drew the attention of about fifty kamikazes in what would prove to be a dark day for the Bald Eagle's flagship *Bunker Hill*.

Pete Mitscher and Arleigh Burke were called to Flag Plot around 1000, when CIC radar operators detected apparent Japanese planes mixed in with returning strike planes. Captain Swett's seven VMF-221 Corsairs, having downed suiciders above the stricken destroyer *Hadley*, returned to their task group just in time to see kamikazes attacking their own carrier. Swett spotted two planes diving on *Bunker Hill* and screamed a warning over his radio to his ship. First Lieutenant Glendinning started up after the Zeke and Judy—so close that he could see their large red meatballs—but it was too late. "The first plane dove diagonally down and crashed with a giant fireball amidst all the bomb and rocket-laden planes waiting to take off," reported Glendinning. Swett's pilots, forced to circle the task group until they could land on *Enterprise*, had unwittingly flown their last CAPs of the war.[18]

Among *Bunker Hill*'s attackers was twenty-year-old Sub-Lieutenant Yasunori Seizo, whose squadron had launched from the Kanoya Airbase on southern Kyushu. At 1002 he dove his Zero fighter, machine guns blazing, toward the deck of *Bunker Hill*, releasing his bomb seconds before his plane smashed through the flight deck. The 550-pound bomb pierced the flight deck, gallery deck, and hangar deck before exploding just outside the ship's port waterline. Another Zero pilot, twenty-two-year-old Ensign Kiyoshi Ogawa radioed, "I see the enemy aircraft carrier." Two minutes later he send his final words, "I am nose-diving into the ship." Thirty seconds later after the first Zero hit, Ogawa released a semi-armor-piercing 550-pound bomb that smashed through the flight deck twenty-five feet port of amidships. His plane then plowed into *Bunker Hill*, creating a brilliant explosion near the island structure. In his last letter to his parents, Ogawa had promised, "I will go smiling."[19]

Admiral Mitscher's flagship *Bunker Hill* blazes heavily after sustaining two kamikaze hits on May 11, 1945. *80-G-274266, NARA*

The two kamikazes tore through thirty fully loaded planes assembled on the flight deck. Another four dozen aircraft were being fueled and armed on the hangar deck. The engine from one of the suicide planes flew up into the flag office, killing three officers and eleven men of Mitscher's staff. Chief of Staff Burke, on the flag bridge at the moment of impact, was stunned by the carnage. "The whole deck exploded and fire spread over the whole deck, gasoline all over the place, [with] tremendous amounts of smoke," he recalled.[20]

Burke helped Mitscher up the ladder one deck to confer with Captain George Seitz. Staff officer Jimmy Flatley raced from CIC for the bridge after the first kamikaze hit. He was still climbing up when the second Zero's bomb exploded, causing sheets of flames to scorch his back. He reached Flag Plot to find Burke and others fighting through the smoke from the blazing CIC below. Flatley, Burke, and Lieutenant Commander Frank Dingfelder helped drag injured occupants from the radio room. The chief of staff then rushed back up the ladder to the smoke-filled flag bridge while Flatley descended to the gallery deck toward the CIC to help rescue others.[21]

The two kamikazes and their bombs created a living hell for the airmen who had been standing by in their ready rooms. Marine Corsair pilot Blaine Imel felt his carrier shudder twice before the lights went out and VMF-221's ready room began filling with smoke. He and other Marines, including Don Balch, Norman D. Smith, Neylon Murphy, and Leo Pambrun, crawled toward the hatch to the steel passageway outside their compartment only to find the area impassable, with glowing orange-hot steel. Imel and others then crawled to a second escape hatch that opened onto a narrow catwalk on the carrier's port side.

The pilots made their way onto the catwalk, where they faced a new danger from .50-caliber ammunition belts that were cooking off. Captain Balch organized several pilots in a line to help toss overboard aircraft rockets stored in a nearby ordnance locker room. "The heat was unbearable," recalled Balch, who gave his own life vest to a steward's mate on the catwalk who could not swim. Within minutes the Fighting Falcons pilots and the steward's mate realized they were trapped. "We had done all we could do and now it was time to think of our lives," said Imel.[22]

Perched some seventy-five feet above the ocean, they leapt from their blazing carrier. Imel, wearing a Mae West, held his nose with one hand, covered his privates with the other, and jumped overboard. He, Balch, and their companions popped to the surface and swam hard away from the giant screws of their warship, turning to watch *Bunker Hill* race past at twenty knots. They were among the fortunate. Many other pilots and enlisted men did not escape the smoke-filled passageways. The gallery deck was in shambles near the CIC, and the bodies of twenty-two pilots of VF-84 were later found among the wreckage.

Second Lieutenant Dean Caswell and his Viceroy Fifteen wingman, John McManus, had just left the ready room to have coffee in the officers' mess just below the hangar deck. They heard the explosions and felt the rocking of the kamikaze hits before the lights went out. Blowers pulling fresh air to the lower decks now caused their area to fill with rolling black smoke. Caswell and McManus pulled on their gas masks, still draped around their necks from a recent General Quarters, and searched for a way out.

"We had always questioned the need to carry the masks," noted Caswell. "Now we found a perfect use for them." He and McManus began crawling through the adjoining passageway, heading toward a ladder that led to the hangar deck. They groped their way by memory through the blackened passageway, their movement inhibited by the bodies of shipmates who had choked to death on the oily black smoke. The VMF-221 lieutenants pushed their way through the corpses to the ladder leading to the hangar deck above.[23]

Caswell scrambled up the ladder, still holding a battle lantern that had proven useless in the heavy smoke. He knew his gas mask only had minutes of air supply remaining, so desperation set in when Caswell found the hatch above him to be dogged down tight. His only option was to pound on the hatch with the metal lantern and shout for help. His energy was nearly spent when his banging finally captured the attention of a sailor above, who undogged the hatch. "It was just in time because those poor

Dozens of pilots and aviation personnel perished in the smoke-filled passageways of *Bunker Hill* in the minutes after the kamikaze hits. Dean Caswell and his VMF-221 wingman were among the few to escape the terrifying ordeal below decks. *U.S. Navy*

masks had about ceased being useful," declared Caswell. He, McManus, fellow pilot Charlie Nettles, and one other man crawled out onto the hangar, nearly asphyxiated, to lay gulping in the semifresh air.[24]

But *Bunker Hill's* hangar deck was no safe haven. Flames had begun cooking off ready ordnance, sending .50-caliber rounds and even ten-foot Tiny Tim rockets zipping over their heads. Once they had recovered for a few minutes, McManus and Caswell hurried to lend a hand to several sailors who were struggling to control a gyrating firehose. McManus discovered a silver firefighter's suit—complete with an oxygen mask and glass facemask—and announced that he would go back below to see if anyone from their fighter squadron had survived the inferno and smoke.

Caswell tried to argue him out of the dangerous maneuver, but McManus donned the gear and began crawling down the ladder as shipmates sprayed him with the firehose. Below decks, he was unable to find any other aviators still living in the horrific scene in the corridors and ready room. Twelve enlisted men from VMF-221 alone would be classified as dead or missing by day's end. McManus and Caswell spent hours helping damage controlmen tackle *Bunker Hill's* fires until both Marines were nearly overcome with exhaustion and the pains of backs sprained by wrestling the firehoses.

Chief of Staff Burke sent Captain Gus Read to gather Vice Admiral Mitscher's staff on the bridge to offer input to *Bunker Hill* skipper Seitz. The news that filtered in to the Bald Eagle was all bad, especially learning how many of his staff members had been killed in the kamikaze attack. His flight surgeon, Captain Ray Hege, died from asphyxiation while sleeping in the bed Burke would have occupied had he opted to use that compartment. Mitscher's flag secretary, Lieutenant Commander Charlie Steel, had also perished, along with Lieutenant Commander Frank Quady, the assistant operations officer. In addition to the three flag officers, Mitscher found that eleven enlisted men of his staff, roughly half of the compliment, were also gone. He sighed deeply as the horrifying intelligence was passed to him.

"Are you okay, sir?" Read asked.

Mitscher merely sighed, "Yes."[25]

Adding insult to injury, Burke also relayed to the admiral that his sea cabin had been destroyed, incinerating all of his clothing and most of his personal papers. Mitscher scarcely raised an eyebrow at the news but instead grinned and quipped, "That seems to be the usual show now. They always get the Admiral's quarters and the Admiral's pantry."[26]

Once it was clear *Bunker Hill* could no longer serve as the flagship of TF 58, Mitscher sent a signal to Rear Admiral Sherman on *Essex* to take acting command. The destroyer *English* (DD 696) soon came alongside to transfer Mitscher's staff. "He didn't have the strength," Burke said of the admiral, so he helped him over the high bulwark. "That man didn't weigh a hundred pounds. I picked him up and put him over on the ladder and he went down. Then I crawled up and over and went down, and had him carried down the Jacob's ladder to the destroyer."[27]

Mitscher, Burke, and their surviving staff members moved via breeches buoy to *English* and then on to the carrier *Enterprise*. From Big E's Flag Plot—located one deck higher than that of *Bunker Hill*'s admiral territory— the Bald Eagle would be able to supervise TF 58's night-carrier operations firsthand. He would resume full command of TF 58 from Sherman the next morning, but he could only sadly watch his former flagship smolder on the horizon through the afternoon of the eleventh.

Captain Seitz assisted his firefighters by turning his carrier onto a course designed to blow smoke and flames broadside to his ship, allowing her to heel into the turn enough to wash an inferno of gasoline, water, oil, and foam from the hangar deck over the port side. Firefighting work consumed some five and a half hours, but *Bunker Hill* would become the second-worst-hit carrier of World War II to survive, with some 400 men dead or missing and another 250 wounded. Her sister ship *Franklin* had survived an even more deadly ordeal less than two months earlier during this same violent campaign.[28]

Bunker Hill would clear the Okinawa area and make its way across the Pacific to Bremerton, Washington, for repairs. When she approached the stateside port, the civilian dock workers were on strike, leaving only a few volunteers to help dock the blackened carrier. "We had been in fierce combat, lost a bunch of fine young men fighting for our country," wrote fighter ace Dean Caswell darkly. "We were deeply angry at the docking situation and ready to consider the striking dock workers our enemy. We would have gladly shot the strikers if we had rifles."[29]

Chapter Twenty-One

"GET THE CARRIERS"

Lieutenant General Buckner commenced a new offensive push on May 11, just as Vice Admiral Ugaki was attempting to knock out Vice Admiral Mitscher's carriers with Kikusui No. 6. Buckner ordered his staff to make a coordinated attack to break Lieutenant General Ushijima's Shuri bastion, with four divisions sweeping in at 0700 immediately on the heels of a half-hour precision artillery bombardment.[1]

The leathernecks of the 6th Marine Division were charged with breaking the Japanese line on the west by crossing the Asa River, bypassing Naha, and crossing the Kokuba Hills into the Kokuba River valley behind Ushijima's stronghold. The 1st Marine Division would have to smash through a deadly series of hills and draws to the east of the 6th Division. The Army's 77th Division would move across flatter terrain south of Maeda in the center of the island to reach Shuri Castle and the underground caverns housing Ushijima's command staff. The Army's 96th Division was to break the enemy's eastern flank by smashing through the Japanese 89th and 22nd Infantry Regiments to take Conical Hill, a five-hundred-foot cone rising above Okinawa's narrow eastern coastal flat.[2]

The four-pronged assault that began on May 11 was met with stiff resistance. Once soldiers seized the forward slope of a hill, the more tedious and deadly process of flushing all of Ushijima's soldiers from the tunnels and caves commenced. The 22nd Marines of the 6th Division moved a considerable distance that first day until challenged with advancing into the hilly ground between Naha and Shuri, a one-thousand-yard-wide corridor. Buckner would soon find that this would be one of the toughest advances of the Okinawa campaign, taking his Marines through hilly grounds centered by a series of three clay hills with fairytale-like names.[3]

The Marines called the small rise in the center Sugar Loaf Hill because of its general shape. To either side of Sugar Loaf lay Horseshoe and Half Moon (also called Crescent) Hills. All three were highly fortified with Japanese artillery, mortar positions, pillboxes, and deep underground tunnels packed with soldiers. Lieutenant Colonel Horatio C. Woodhouse Jr.'s 2nd Battalion, 22nd Marine Infantry was initially charged with taking Sugar Loaf Hill, but his G Company was shredded by two thousand Japanese soldiers, heavy artillery fire from Shuri, and embedded 47-mm antitank guns. A frustrated Woodhouse on May 14 ordered F Company to advance again at 1630 with the remnants of G Company on Sugar Loaf, hoping his Marines could take the hilltop by nightfall.[4]

By sunset, however, only forty-four officers and men of Company F remained at the base of Sugar Loaf, where Major Harry A. Courtney Jr. called for volunteers to storm the top of the hill. Joined by twenty-six other Marines, Courtney led the leatherneck charge up the slopes. As the sun rose on the fifteenth, less than twenty men from F and G Companies remained effective. Courtney was killed during the assault; he would be awarded the Medal of Honor posthumously.[5]

Shortly after 1130, fifteen surviving able Marines were forced to abandon the Sugar Loaf hilltop, below which lay the blazing hulks of three Sherman tanks and the bodies of more than one hundred 6th Division Marines. General Ushijima reinforced Sugar Loaf with another regiment, determined to hold this area. As the survivors retreated down the hill at midday on May 15, Private 1st Class Watson Crumbie's 252-man C Company, 29th Marines was advancing on nearby Half Moon Hill. His Charley Company had three platoons that would be going in to replace the 29th's Able Company, which had been badly shot up the previous day.

The first two squads of the 3rd Platoon to advance on Half Moon were nearly wiped out by Japanese machine-gun and rifle fire. Charley Company's 3rd Platoon, which included Crumbie, pushed forward toward the top of the hill, where they weathered a hellish storm of bullets, mortars, satchel charges, and artillery rounds. Crumbie clung to his faith, reciting prayers and Psalm 23 as men died around him during the explosions and periodic banzai charges by sake-fueled Japanese soldiers.[6]

By nightfall the company was cut off from the rest of the division and unable to move back for fear of snipers. Crumbie was trading hand grenades with the Japanese near the top of the hill, trying to avoid having his foxhole overrun, when a powerful explosion shattered his world. His bazooka man, James P. Thompson, took the brunt of the shrapnel from the artillery explosion, but the blast also left Crumbie unconscious, with internal injuries and a concussion.

Crumbie and Thompson were both evacuated from Half Moon Hill, but the former would remain under hospital care for only three days before, wracked with guilt, he was granted permission to return to the ongoing battle for Sugar Loaf, Half Moon, and Horseshoe Hills. The 6th Marine Division had uncovered the western anchor of General Ushijima's main defensive position, but the heavily fortified terrain would see many more days of fighting.

Admiral Spruance was frustrated with the damaging results of Vice Admiral Ugaki's latest two Kikusui operations. By the end of May 11, the latest kamikaze attacks had killed or wounded more than 1,000 sailors, sunk three destroyers and three rocket ships, and damaged seven other destroyers and destroyer-minelayers, LSM(R)s, and LCS(L)s. The commander in chief of the Fifth Fleet ordered Vice Admiral Mitscher to take his carrier task force and work over the kamikaze airfields again. Mitscher steamed northward with two task groups to blast eighteen airfields on Kyushu and five on Shikoku with repeated carrier strikes.

Lieutenant Gene Valencia's VF-9 Flying Circus division had reached fifty kills on the eleventh, but his team would not be part of the action over Kyushu this time. *Yorktown* and her task group briefly retired from the Okinawa combat scene on May 12 for reprovisioning in Ulithi, where she dropped anchor on the fourteenth. *Yorktown* had spent sixty-one straight days at sea and had been under aerial attack almost exactly half of those days.[7]

Mitscher, now based on board the night carrier *Enterprise*, would use Night Air Group 90 to make sure Ugaki had no respite during the darkness. "The best defense against the kamikaze is to offensively blanket his airdromes at all times and prevent enemy aircraft from taking the air," reported CAG Night 90 Bill Martin.[8]

The air group commenced its heckling of Kyushu's airfields by launching three groups of VT(N)-90 Avengers during the overnight hours of May 11–12 to keep the Japanese air forces continually pinned down. Fifteen TBM crews participated, with CAG Martin leading the five-plane group that launched at 0100 on the twelfth. Each flight spent from one and a half to three hours over the airfields at Minami Daito, Kikai Jima, and Tokuna Shima, where the TBMs bombed and strafed targets of opportunity. In addition to these fifteen hecklers, VT(N)-90 skipper Charlie Henderson led another four Avengers against Kyushu's airfields.[9]

Henderson arrived over Kanoya Airfield at fifteen hundred feet to find that his Avenger, tracked by enemy radar as he approached, had been mistaken as friendly. Red, green, and white runway and obstruction lights had been turned on, and his plane was flashed with blinker code from a control tower. Henderson circled the base for more than five minutes, and the airfield lights were not extinguished until his load of 100-pound bombs began exploding along the western side of the field.

The success of the hecklers ensured the such missions would be repeated over the Japanese kamikaze fields over the ensuing nights. *Enterprise's* night group launched seven VF(N)-90 Hellcats at 0230 on May 12 for a dawn patrol over Kyushu. Lieutenant Owen D. Young achieved 4.5 kills, while other *Enterprise* night fighters helped bring the night hecklers' score to 8 kills over Kyushu by daybreak.[10]

During the night of May 12 going into the morning of May 13, Henderson's VT(N)-90 launched sixteen Avengers on four different heckler missions to button up the Kyushu airfields until dawn. During his return to the carrier from Omura, Henderson chased a George fighter for forty miles but was only credited with damage to his opponent. Minutes later he locked on to a Rufe. "After a long dogfight, I managed to turn inside him thanks to wheels and flaps down," described Henderson. "He plunged into the sea." In two tours as a torpedo-bomber pilot, Henderson had narrowly missed achieving ace status. He was credited with four aerial victories, making him the most successful Avenger pilot of World War II against enemy aircraft.[11]

As Night Air Group 90's hecklers winged back for their task force after daylight on May 13, hundreds of Corsairs, Hellcats, Avengers, and Helldivers were roaring northward toward the Kyushu and Shikoku airfields. Earlier strikes had targeted Kyushu's southern fields. Now Spruance and Mitscher were rightly convinced that Ugaki was staging some attacks from northerly fields as well, so these were scheduled for carrier strikes.[12]

Rear Admiral Sherman's TG 58.3, built around his flagship *Essex* plus the *Randolph* and *Bataan* air groups, was operating about one hundred miles east-southeast of the southern tip of Kyushu on the morning of May 13. Sherman's three flattops contributed more than 300 aircraft this day to fighter sweeps, photo-reconnaissance work, and strike missions against airfields and installations at Kumamoto, Kikutomi, Kikuchi, Waifu, and Omura Airfields. More than one hundred other sorties were made as Hellcat and Corsair divisions carried out their routine task-force-protection CAP duties. From *Randolph* alone, the carrier boasted 189 takeoffs during the day, even thirty-one straight landings at one point without a wave off, setting new flight records for the proud deck crewmen.[13]

Although enemy aircraft were not found aloft to battle above Kyushu, Lieutenant Hamilton McWhorter's dawn CAP near the carrier *Randolph* proved productive. His VF-12 Hellcat division was vectored thirty-five miles west of TF 58 to greet a bogey, a Myrt, that was riddled by two passes from the lieutenant. The Japanese plane crashed into the sea, marking the final kill of the war for McWhorter and pushing his career victories to an even dozen.[14]

Operational losses were light for Sherman's TG 58.3 on May 13, but one loss was sorely felt by the *Essex* air group. Lieutenant Commander Dave Berry, veteran of the 1942 Coral Sea battle, the March Kure Harbor attack on the carrier *Unryu*, and the *Yamato* attack in April, made his last mission as part of a forty-five-plane strike launched at 0528 against the Saeki sea-plane base. As his VB-83 division released their bombs on airfield hangars, intense and automatic antiaircraft fire opened up on his Helldivers.

Berry's SB2C was hit and caught fire under its starboard wing root. The skipper recovered control and was about a mile northeast of the field when his gunner, ACRM Joe Eardley, was seen to toss out his camera and then jump. Eardley's parachute opened fully, but he made a fast descent into the ocean, where a dye marker was later observed. The skipper's Helldiver was observed to make a gentle turn for the water before dropping its wing and plunging into the bay. In an almost ironic letter he penned in 1942, Berry had written his own epitaph to his family in Kentucky, "There are no thrills that match those of the dive bomber. In the air is a wonderful place to fight. There is no mud or filth of trenches—no forced marching—no personal contact. You make your own theater to fight in, the fighting is clean, impersonal, fast, and beautiful. The sea is an adequate burial marker for those who lose—the incessant waves form a permanent marker."[15]

Rear Admiral Jocko Clark's TG 58.1, operating about eighty miles southeast of southern Kyushu at daybreak on May 13, concentrated on a different group of Japanese airfields, namely Kanoya, Izumi, Saeki's seaplane base, Kokubu, Oita, and Chiran. Warplanes from the *Hornet*, *Bennington*, *Belleau Wood*, *Monterey*, and *San Jacinto* air groups flew some 424 combat and photo sorties against the Kyushu airfields during the day in addition to the standard task-force CAPs.

Clark's TG 58.1 had been joined on May 9 by the light carrier *Monterey* (CVL 26), fresh from Pearl Harbor and sporting a revamped air group. It included Ensign Dick Schwendemann, who had survived kamikaze dam-age to his previous carrier, *Saratoga*, on February 21. In the reshuffling at Pearl Harbor, his VF-53 was reorganized as VF-34, and May 13, 1945, marked Schwendemann's return to combat action. He flew escort for eight bomb-armed Avengers of VT-34 during their runs against targets at the Saeki airfield and seaplane base, where heavy antiaircraft fire holed three of the TBMs.

The only squadron of TG 58.1 to register aerial kills over Kyushu on the thirteenth was *Bennington*'s VF-82, all three kills falling to one pilot. Lieutenant Commander Ed Hessel led three divisions to bomb and strafe Izumi Airfield before heading down the western coastline, where his Hellcats shot up two trains. Hessel led his division on to reconnoiter Inujo Airfield on Tanega Shima, where antiaircraft fire removed the tip of his F6F's port wing. There, two of Hessel's pilots, Ensign John B. Hoag and Lieutenant Phil Perabo Jr., were jumped by a dozen Frank and George fighters. Hoag shot down two opponents and forced a third to crash into the ocean, but Perabo was shot down. Pursued for some time by four Japanese fighters, Hoag eventually crash-landed his battle-damaged F6F onto *Bennington*'s flight deck, his engine remaining behind as the balance of his fuselage slid over the side. Hoag escaped his sinking Hellcat in time to be scooped up by a plane-guard destroyer.[16]

Kikusui No. 6 had officially commenced on May 11, the day Mitscher's flagship *Bunker Hill* had been knocked out of the campaign. The Japanese had launched 345 planes on the first day, of which 86 were kamikazes. Ugaki's airmen continued the operation for four more days, deploying 237 strike planes (including 47 kamikazes) from May 12 through May 15. Aerial dogfights were heaviest on the eleventh, when Navy fighter pilots alone claimed sixty-eight shoot downs compared to only eight victories claimed the following day. Mitscher's two carrier task groups pounded Kyushu throughout the thirteenth but turned in claims for only nine aerial victories—one-third of them having been accomplished by John Hoag.

Okinawa-based Marine fighter squadrons added their own kills on May 13. Yontan-based VMF-224 scrambled to defend Radar Picket Station No. 9 from kamikazes, where Captain Ernest F. Chase's Corsair division knocked down three suiciders, while the gunfire of destroyers *Cowell* (DD 547) and *Bache* (DD 470) downed at least two others. *Bache*'s radar team detected more bogies ten minutes later, at 1840, and her FIDO coached in a pair of VMF-311 "Hell's Belles" Corsairs to intercept. Captain Raymond F. Scherer and his wingman downed four Petes, but *Cowell* and *Bache* were soon assailed by two groups of Vals.[17]

Four kamikazes were downed by the picket warships' gunfire, but another dive bomber was seen making an attack on *Bache*. First Lieutenant Forest E. Warren of the VMF-322 "Cannonballs" followed the Val through the flak to within five hundred yards of the ship, collecting enough antiaircraft damage himself that he was forced to ditch his F4U just off-shore of Kadena. Warren's opponent plowed into *Bache*'s Number Two stack at 1850, and its 500-pound bomb exploded just above the deck. *Bache* suffered forty-one killed and thirty-two injured and had to be towed into port as a result.

"Unless we sleep in shelters, we no longer can sleep soundly," Vice Admiral Ugaki scribbled in his diary. "We shall have to revert to the primitive life of cavemen." Army bombers had commenced pounding Japanese mainland bases and installations on May 11, and *Enterprise*'s night-heckler missions had commenced the following evening.[18]

As of May 12, the Japanese Combined Air Force and the 3rd Air Fleet combined under the new designation of Tenth Air Force, all under Ugaki's command. "How much we can increase our fighting strength and how far we can take advantage of this new setup has to be seen," logged Ugaki. Mitscher's carrier strikes against Kyushu on the thirteenth further frustrated Ugaki, who had but two operational scout fighters with which to search for the U.S. fleet. His reconnaissance efforts were soon successful in locating a wealth of American carriers, battleships, and cruisers, so Ugaki activated his "First Attack Method." His first force—sixteen heavy bombers with fighter escort—launched during the late hours of May 13. Shortly before dawn on the fourteenth, he sent out twenty-eight fighter-bombers in company with forty fighter planes to counter Mitscher's persistent carrier task groups.[19]

The twenty-eight assembled kamikaze pilots would each fly Zeke fighters of the 6th Tsukubu, 11th Kemmu, and 8th Shichisho Squadrons, each aircraft being loaded with an 1,100-pound armor-piercing, delayed-action bomb. Among the anxious Floating Chrysanthemum pilots was twenty-two-year-old Lieutenant (jg) Shunsuke Tomiyasu, who had graduated in 1943 from Waseda University with a degree in politics and economics. He had joined the special Zeke kamikaze corps on March 28, and his instructions at the Kanoya Airfield on the morning of May 14 were direct: "Get the carriers." The first dozen kamikazes clawed their way into the air at 0525, with the balance following at 0619. Lieutenant Tomiyasu's final note to his sisters and parents reflect his mindset: "I surely am determined to achieve excellent battle results."[20]

Six of the twenty-eight bomb-laden kamikazes would return to base with mechanical issues, but twenty-two of these strikers would press home their attacks to the end. Their flights to TF 58 covered more than 130 miles to the southeast, roughly a ninety-minute journey. Lieutenants Keijiro Hiura and Takuro Fujita made their final communications after 0657, the moment when Lieutenant Tomiyasu made a fateful intercept with Vice Admiral Mitscher's flagship carrier *Enterprise*.[21]

Ugaki's evening strikers began showing up on TF 58 radar hours before midnight on May 13, sending the batmen of *Enterprise*'s Night Air Group 90 to work. Lieutenant (jg) George A. Oden, following vectors from *San Jacinto*'s FDO, doggedly pursued a Dinah snooper that he splashed in flames at 2300. One hour into May 14, VF(N)-90 squadronmate Lieutenant (jg) Charles H. "Sandy" Latrobe brought down a Betty bomber.[22]

Fifteen VF(N)-90 Hellcats and fourteen VT(N)-90 Avenger crews helped keep the Kyushu and Shikoku airfields locked down once again before dawn on the fourteenth. The controllers in the Kanoya tower had still not learned caution at night, as the first TBM to arrive was again blinkered with landing instructions. Three Oscars attacked VF(N)-90's Kyushu group, but Lieutenant (jg) Lamar F. Harrison chased one of them into the ground and forced the other two to flee.[23]

Despite Big E's heckling, at least twenty-two of the suiciders of the Kikusui No. 6 attack approached Mitscher's carriers. Some were engaged by American strike groups en route to their morning airfield targets, while others were greeted as they neared TF 58's ships. Lieutenant (jg) George Pete Taylor, returning from VF(N)-90's night-heckler attacks over Kyushu, downed a Zeke near the task force at 0615. Taylor's squadronmate Ensign Franklin Goodson was vectored after another bogey, which he chased for forty minutes to within one and a half miles without any contact on his radar. At that point "the Fighter Director Officer advised me that I had merged with the enemy plane on the ship's radar screen," Goodson noted in his diary.[24]

The ensign chopped his throttle, looking up for the enemy plane that his FDO said was right on him. "I felt an in-rush of air on my head," he wrote. "I felt back about a foot from my head on the port side and found a large hole in my canopy." When he reported his plane had been hit, Goodson was recalled to his ship. He landed at 0600 and went to see the FDO, asking why he had been recalled. "He told me that they had intercepted a message from a twin engine Betty that I was tracking that stated they had a night fighter on their tail and were opening fire. He stated that within one minute, I radioed in that I did not know whether I had been hit or not, but I had a hole in my canopy. He immediately called me back."

334 | Chapter Twenty-One

Goodson was back on board *Enterprise* for less than an hour before tragedy struck.[25]

At 0653 the carrier's antiaircraft guns opened up on a single Zeke that was seen ducking in and out of the clouds as Captain Grover Hall maneuvered his flattop to put the enemy plane dead astern. Lieutenant Tomiyasu, the pilot of the approaching fighter, paralleled *Enterprise*'s course for some time, closing to two miles before he doubled back into a cloud and then opened the range to three miles.[26]

Tomiyasu waited until 0656, when Big E's stern swung past the cloud bank he had entered, before he pushed his fighter into a fast, shallow dive straight for the carrier's flight deck. Five-inchers, 40-mm mounts, and 20-mm gunners opened fire until the whole port side of *Enterprise* was yellow with smoke. Watch officer Gus Read had gathered Vice Admiral Mitscher's team in Flag Plot as the air attacks commenced. Jimmy Flatley had stepped out on the bridge to take a look and saw Tomiyasu's Zeke coming straight in. He ducked back in to where Mitscher stood and shouted, "Hit the deck."[27]

Tomiyasu's brown-green Zeke nearly missed its mark, but halfway up *Enterprise*'s flight deck he rolled left onto his back at 0657 and dived inverted right through the carrier's forward elevator. His bomb erupted five decks down, the force of the blast lifting the Number One elevator atop a cap of gray and white smoke more than four hundred feet into the sky. "There was a tremendous explosion and heavy concussion," Ensign Goodson wrote in his diary. His squadron skipper was knocked unconscious and lay on the ready-room deck for a few minutes.[28]

In the exposed Flag Plot, chunks of metal and wood banged against the bulkheads as *Enterprise* shuddered from stem to stern. "After the explosion, I cautiously looked around from my prone position," wrote Flatley. "There stood the Admiral in the midst of all of us with his arms folded and perfectly calm."[29]

Lieutenant (jg) Shunsuke Tomiyasu dove his bomb-carrying Zeke into the flight deck of *Enterprise* (CV 6) on May 14, 1945, and knocked Marc Mitscher's flagship out of the war. *Kan Sugahara photo via U.S. Naval Institute*

Admiral Mitscher's flagship *Enterprise* is hit by Lieutenant Tomiyasu's kamikaze on May 14, 1945. *80-G-323565, NARA*

The commander picked himself rather sheepishly as Mitscher quipped, "Son, if the radio is working, tell the task force that my flag is still flying but that if the Japs keep this up they are likely to grow hair on my bald head yet."[30]

Commodore Burke was uninjured by the explosions that flung debris through Flag Plot, although one man beside him was killed and communications officer Frank Dingfelder, on his other side, was hit in the face by shrapnel. Admiral Mitscher remained calm, even when news reached him that his own quarters on the gallery deck had been wrecked again. Parts of the suicide pilot and his possessions were recovered, and many, including Mitscher, claimed souvenirs, such as the pilot's calling cards, a rubber stamp, and pieces of the Zeke's wreckage. A translation error caused Lieutenant Tomiyasu's identity to be listed as Tomi Zai for years.[31]

Repair parties went to work immediately with firehoses and rescue breathers, tossing hot projectiles overboard while dragging wounded shipmates to safety. Seventeen minutes after being hit, *Enterprise's* fires were under control and were out in another thirteen minutes. Her casualties amounted to only thirteen men killed and sixty-eight wounded. The destroyer *Waldron* (DD 699) retrieved eight men blown overboard by the kamikaze's blast, some of whom were found drying out while standing on a fifteen-foot floating section of the carrier's ejected elevator.[32]

Vice Admiral Marc Mitscher seen making a transfer via boatswain's chair to the carrier *Randolph* on May 14, 1945, due to damage to his flagship *Enterprise*. It was the Bald Eagle's second time to transfer his flag in a week due to kamikaze attacks. 80-G-320987, NARA

The loss of the forward elevator made it clear to Mitscher that he would have to move his flag yet again. The following day, May 15, Mitscher, Burke, Flatley, seventeen other officers, and twenty-five enlisted men were transferred by the destroyer *Hickox* (DD 673) at 1636 to the carrier *Randolph*—the Bald Eagle's third flagship within a week.[33]

TF 58 fighters prevented other elements of Ugaki's Kikusui No. 6 strikers from reaching the carriers that morning. *Hornet*'s VF-17 Hellcats were vectored from their radar-picket CAP duties to intercept various bogies. Lieutenant Dick Cowger's division mixed with a formation of fifteen Franks, Zekes, and Oscars. Ensign Ernie Vonder Heyden shot down one Zeke, while Cowger and his wingman, Lieutenant (jg) Bill Hardy, became engaged in a violent clash with several other Japanese fighters. Cowger was credited with a Zeke probable kill and damage to an Oscar, while Hardy took down a Frank with a long burst into its cockpit that appeared to kill the pilot.[34]

Lieutenant Billy Watts' division, also sent after a single bogey, made visual contact with a Judy ten miles south of TG 58.1. Watts overshot his quarry, but wingman Werner Gaerisch took care of the Judy with bursts into its cockpit and fuselage. Marsh Beebe led three other of his VF-17 divisions to bomb Tachiarai Airfield on northern Kyushu, where they had no aerial intercepts. *Hornet*'s afternoon sweep against Kyushu's Kushira Airfield was a different story.

Around 1445 *Bennington* fighters tallyhoed twenty Frank fighters near the eastern shore of Kagoshima Bay. Strike leader Jim Pearce downed one Frank, whose pilot was seen to parachute out wearing a maroon flying suit. Lieutenant John C. Moore's VBF-17 division went to work too, knocking down six other Franks. *Hornet's* Air Group 17 finished May 14 with top honors from TF 58, having downed eleven of the forty-two kills that Mitscher's carrier pilots claimed for the day.[35]

Okinawa-based Marine squadrons chalked up their own victories against Kikusui No. 6 this day. First Lieutenant Herbert F. Pfremmer of the VMF-123 Flying Eight Balls scored the squadron's final wartime kill that morning by downing a Sally near the Kumamoto Aircraft Factory. His F4U was hit by antiaircraft fire, but Pfremmer managed to ditch near a task-force destroyer to be rescued.[36]

VMF-112's Wolfpack fighters scored their final four kills of the war on the afternoon of May 14 on a strike against Izumi Airfield on Kyushu. Major David C. Andre's three divisions tallyhoed a group of Tonys flying in parade formation into Kyushu and attacked. Andre and 1st Lieutenants John M. Callahan and Junie Lohan—the latter a survivor of the sinking of the destroyer *Colhoun* by kamikazes on April 6—each destroyed a Tony with aggressive head-on runs. Minutes later the Wolfpack spotted a large group of brown-colored Frank fighters loaded with 500-pound bombs and ferry tanks—another ferry flight cruising in parade formation.[37]

Once the Frank pilots realized their danger, they dropped their wing tanks and led the VMF-112 pursuers on a chase across Kagoshima's antiaircraft defenses. The fast Japanese aircraft began splitting off and mostly outran the Marines, but 2nd Lieutenant Carroll V. King was wily enough to hammer one Frank into the ocean. The *Bennington* pilots noted that not one of their surprised opponents made an effort to fight, suggesting they were less-seasoned pilots caught ferrying fresh aircraft in for the kamikaze corps.

Vice Admiral Ugaki's Kikusui No. 6 operation continued through May 15, although almost-daily bombing attacks would continue on Allied warships afterward. On May 17 off Radar Picket Station No. 9, the destroyer *Douglas H. Fox* (DD 779) was hit by an Oscar that also unleashed its bomb on deck moments before crashing between two gun mounts.

By the end of that day, Vice Admiral Turner, commander of TF 51, reported that his picket ships had endured 560 raids from 2,228 enemy planes since April 1. Five picket destroyers had been sunk, thirteen other ships had been seriously damaged, and another five had minor damage from kamikaze crashes.[38]

These losses were in addition to what had been endured by TF 58 warships. Vice Admiral Mitscher had been forced to move his flag twice due to his flagship carrier being crippled by kamikazes. The relentless pace of battling Ugaki's suiciders was taking its toll on the Bald Eagle. On May 18 he informed Admiral Spruance that the continued support of Okinawa by TF 58 held doubtful value and recommended that his task force be relieved. Spruance felt otherwise and initiated steps to give the Bald Eagle himself a break from the constant strain of aerial action.[39]

Chapter Twenty-Two

WEATHERING ICEBERG'S FINAL WEEKS

By the time Vice Admiral Ugaki's sixth Kikusui operation was winding down on May 15, 1945, U.S. Marines were still heavily embroiled in the battles near Shuri Castle to secure Half Moon, Horseshoe, and Sugar Loaf Hills. Thousands of lives had been shattered in the contest to control the region, and Allied troops were making little headway in seizing the embattled slopes.

The 29th Marines suffered heavily during the offensive. By the morning of May 17, C Company, 3rd Platoon, 29th Marines had only about 50 men still fighting of the 252 Marines who had commenced the assault on Half Moon Hill days earlier. Corporal Jim White's G Company, 3rd Battalion, 29th Marines was sent with I Company to assault Half Moon Hill. White and fellow Marine Francis West dug a foxhole together the first night. West's helmet had already been creased by one Japanese bullet that hit near the top, passing through both steel and plastic liners. "I then and there lost any faith in a helmet's ability to protect against anything more powerful than a thrown rock," said White.[1]

Company G would sustain heavy casualties during their next three days of fighting. One of White's fellow Marines, Private 1st Class Clyde T. Busy, who carried a Browning automatic rifle and had played baseball in high school, caught incoming Japanese grenades and lobbed them back at their opponents. White and two other uninjured soldiers took turns catching naps while around-the-clock watches were maintained to prevent their grave-like foxhole from being overrun. At one point the call of nature forced White to do the only thing he could do while under enemy fire. "I pulled my pants down, crapped in my skivvy shorts, cut them off on the sides with my K-Bar, wadded it up, wiped myself, and then flung it out toward the enemy," he said. By the time his company was relieved on Half Moon Hill and fell back to its starting point on Charlie Hill, "there were just twenty of us kicking."[2]

Private 1st Class Dick Whitaker's Fox Company, part of the 6th Marine Division, was sent into the attack on Sugar Loaf Hill on the afternoon of May 17. His machine-gun section was attached to the 2nd Rifle Platoon under Lieutenant Charlie Behan, a big man who had played end for the Detroit Lions before joining the Marines. Whitaker was shaken when Behan was killed by a mortar round while leading a charge up Sugar Loaf. Riding out the night in his foxhole, Whitaker leaned forward at one point to light a cigarette and was hit in the hand by a Japanese bullet. Sent to an aid station the next day, he later reflected: "I spent two days there, sleeping on a cot. I was on Okinawa 101 days and those were the only two days I did not sleep in a hole I had dug myself or had found."[3]

After more than a week of fighting for Sugar Loaf Hill, the 6th Marine Division had suffered 2,662 combat and 1,289 noncombat casualties (exhaustion and battle fatigue), the largest percentage being men from the 22nd and 29th Regiments. On May 15 alone, Marines had rushed to the top of Sugar Loaf's summit several times, only to be driven back by withering enemy grenade, rifle, and mortar fire. A final push on the eighteenth enabled Marines to finally secure the top of the bloody height. Combat correspondent Elvis Lane wrote that the fighting on that hill "must be the

Men of 1st Battalion, 4th Marine Regiment set up camp on Sugar Loaf Hill on May 26, 1945. Sugar Loaf and its adjacent hills saw some of Okinawa's bloodiest fighting during May. *U.S. Marine Corps*

bloodiest triumph in Corps history. I've lost count of how many times Sugar Loaf was seized by us, by them, and how many times we've been there."[4]

The fact that Marines had seized Sugar Loaf on May 18 did not end the combat for the hills near Shuri Castle by any means. Major General Roy Geiger released the 4th Marines from the III Amphibious Corps reserve to relieve the 29th Marines and consolidate the gains that made thus far. Corporal Mel Heckt had already spent a month and a half on Okinawa by the time his Baker Company was sent into the Sugar Loaf and Horseshoe Hill actions on May 20. During the week that followed, Heckt's company suffered heavy casualties as it advanced toward Naha.

By the end of May 23, Heckt's machine-gun squad had only four men remaining—eight had been killed, nine others had been wounded, and one man had cracked under the pressure. Of the original 3,512 Marines of the 29th Regiment that landed on the island on April 1, only 691 would survive unharmed. That night Heckt, who had not slept the past two nights, scribbled his thoughts in his little diary: "This artillery gets on one's nerves. I now duck at every shell, whereas I used to laugh as they went over. This day and May 21 I shall remember as long as I live as being the closest to death and most similar to hell. We who remain have God and only God to thank for our being alive."[5]

The U.S. Army's 306th and 307th Infantry Regiments struggled with stubborn pockets of Japanese resistance at their own bloody hills, named Chocolate Drop, Wart Hill, and Flattop Hill, while the Marines fought for Sugar Loaf, Half Moon, and Horseshoe Hills. By the evening of May 21, Colonel Stephen S. Hamilton's 307th Regiment had pushed past these hills, but Company B became heavily engaged with Japanese soldiers at other positions.

Corpsman Desmond Doss refused to carry a weapon but saved more than seventy-five lives on Okinawa at Hacksaw Ridge. He continued treating downed men during heavy fighting in late May even after he had been seriously wounded. Doss is seen being pinned with the Medal of Honor by President Harry Truman at the White House on October 12, 1945. *U.S. government photo*

Private 1st Class Desmond Doss, the conscientious objector from Virginia who had saved seventy-five lives weeks before on Hacksaw Ridge, scrambled to assist wounded comrades once again. He was wounded in the legs by an exploding mortar but treated his own wounds while waiting five hours for stretcher bearers to reach him. Enemy fire soon forced the corpsmen to leave him behind as they took cover. Doss rolled himself off his stretcher, crawled over to a seriously wounded man nearby, and treated him. Doss was hit again as he did, suffering a compound fracture of his arm. He splinted the arm with a rifle stock and crawled an additional three hundred yards rearward to an aid station. The young man who had refused to carry a weapon would later be pinned with the Medal of Honor.[6]

Heavy fighting along numerous hilltops and key frontline points in every sector on Okinawa created severe casualties for Japanese and American forces alike during the bloody period of May 11–21. The 77th Division had suffered 239 killed, 16 missing, and 1,212 wounded, while the 96th Division had lost 138 killed, 9 missing, and 1,059 wounded. Lieutenant General Buckner's plan to blockade and eliminate Lieutenant General Ushijima's stubborn army was further set back by a steady rain that began falling on May 21. This turned roads to mud and terrain into filthy ooze that trapped Sherman tanks, which forced cursing Marines to wade in stinking mire up to their waists to attempt to free them.[7]

An English-language broadcast from Tokyo days later attempted to drain the spirits of the Allied soldiers fighting for Okinawa by calling out the irony of the candy-like names they had given hills—Sugar Loaf, Chocolate Drop, and Strawberry—that had become deadly positions of combat. "The only thing red about these places is the blood of Americans," stated the propaganda broadcaster. "These are the names of hills in southern Okinawa where the fighting's so close that you can get down to bayonets and sometimes your bare fists. . . . Only those who've been there know what they're really like."[8]

Gene Valencia, the Navy's top fighter ace of 1945, was far removed from such hell by late May 1945 as the ground troops scarified to gain crucial yards on Okinawa. The lieutenant's Flying Circus division had gone ashore with *Yorktown's* Air Group 9 shortly after reaching Ulithi on the fourteenth to enjoy some downtime, drink beer on Mog Mog, play daily softball games, catch up on mail from home, and relax to nightly movies.

While the task group relaxed and recovered in the fleet anchorage, the U.S. Navy took the chance to help build morale back home with positive

Four decorated veterans of the *Yorktown's* Air Group 9 being interviewed by the media on May 19, 1945, on Guam. *Left to right:* Lieutenant Gene Valencia, Commander Herb Houck, Lieutenant Bert Eckard (describing one of his dogfights), and Lieutenant Angus Morrison. *80-G-329439, NARA*

news from the Pacific War's violent Okinawa campaign. Four heroes of Air Group 9—Lieutenant Angus Morrison of VT-9, CAG 9 Herb Houck, VT-9 ace Lieutenant Bert Eckard, and the fleet's leading active ace, Lieutenant Valencia—were flown to Guam on May 19 to be interviewed by journalists. Morrison told tales of how he had maneuvered his Avenger to down a Japanese plane on April 17, using his wing to shear off its rudder. Houck recounted his air group's part in the successful destruction of the battleship *Yamato* on April 7, while Eckard described how he became an "ace in a day" on April 17, the same day that Valencia scored six kills.

The interviews were widely published in U.S. newspapers the following day—along with a feature story of the 6th Marine Division's epic battle for Sugar Loaf Hill and Admiral Nimitz's assessment of the campaign for Okinawa, one in which American forces since March 18 had sustained 30,526 casualties. But the aviators' accounts helped press the point that progress was being made toward ending the war in the Pacific. Valencia described how Japanese kamikazes made "fine turkey shoot targets," having lost fourteen of their number to his VF-9 division on April 17. "That's an indication," the lieutenant stated, "that the Jap pilots we're running into now are pretty mediocre."[9]

Pete Mitscher's other carrier task groups were still heavily embroiled in daily support actions off Okinawa during this time, making strikes against Japanese resistance on the island and shipping. Mitscher warned his fleet on May 23 to expect another all-out effort from the kamikaze corps at any time. Vice Admiral Ugaki had originally scheduled his Kikusui No. 7 to commence on May 14, but foul weather and American carrier strikes on his airbases had forced the operation's postponement for more than a week.

In the end Ugaki scraped together 165 special-attack planes, drawing 65 from his navy and another 100 from the army. More than 200 other aircraft flew bombing missions against the Allied-occupied Okinawa airfields and Allied shipping beginning on May 23, the heaviest concentration being on the twenty-fifth.[10]

Rear Admiral Clark's TG 58.1 conducted fighter sweeps over the southern Kyushu airfields during the afternoon of May 24, where Hornet's fighter squadrons found only a modest amount of action. Marsh Beebe led VF-17 Hellcats on a 298-mile flight with belly tanks to assault Miyazaki Airfield, where Lieutenant Edward George Verhelle was hit by antiaircraft fire and crashed on the base. Beebe, Dick Cowger, Howard Johnson, Bud Good, and Bill Hardy shared claims for damaging a Zeke, but Cowger's F6F was hit by antiaircraft fire over Miyazaki. Cowger was forced to ditch near the entrance to Ariake Bay, but his comrades flew cover over him until a PBM from VH-3 effected his recovery.[11]

Kikusui No. 7 included a most unusual and aggressive mission flown by a dozen Sally bombers that had been stripped of their guns for a special commando raid by the Giretsu Raiding Unit. The army units lifted off on the afternoon of May 24 in an attempt to land suicide soldiers on the Marine airfields at Yontan and Kadena to destroy as many Allied aircraft as possible. Several of the troop-carrying bombers were shot down, four turned back after becoming lost or suffering engine trouble, leaving only four to attempt the raid at Yontan. As the four Sallys approached the Okinawa airfield around 2225, antiaircraft fire brought down three of them in flames. One bomber slammed into an antiaircraft site, killing two Marines, but the final aircraft made a wheels-up belly landing on the airfield.[12]

One Marine was killed and eighteen others were wounded before the surprise commando raid could be subdued, the last Japanese commando not hunted down until the following afternoon near MAG 31's headquarters. In the tracer-lit confusion on Yontan, the Giretsu assault managed to destroy nine planes, damage twenty-eight others, and explode a 70,000-gallon high-octane-fuel supply cache. At nearby Kadena Airfield later that day, Major George Axtell assembled his VMF-323 pilots and aircrewmen to warn them to be prepared for a similar assault.[13]

Okinawa-based Marine fighters were ready for the main kamikaze attacks of Kikusui No. 7, which were launched on the morning of May 25. VMF-312's "Checkerboards" intercepted a large formation of Zekes shortly before 0800 about sixty miles north of Kadena, splashing thirteen of the Japanese planes. Minutes later VMF-322 and VMF-323 were vectored against another large formation near the offshore islands, where they claimed sixteen more kills. Sporadic combat lasted until noon, when

VMF-312 wrapped up the action. Among the day's forty-two Marine claims, 2nd Lieutenant James Webster of VMF-322 took top honors, with three confirmed kills and one probable.[14]

Achievements for the Japanese were small compared to previous such operations, with Kikusui No. 7 resulting in one transport sunk, a destroyer damaged, and one escort carrier damaged. The Marine Corsair squadrons had intercepted the lion's share of the attackers, as only four carrier-based Navy fighter pilots made individual claims for kills near TF 58 and the radar-picket stations on May 25.

By May 27 Vice Admiral Mitscher had weathered seven of Ugaki's Kikusui operations and had had two of his flagships blasted by kamikazes. But his resolve remained unshaken. "He was a stubborn little man," noted Arleigh Burke, his chief of staff. "As long as he lived, he would fight." On board *Randolph*, however, Mitscher was forced to operate with a reduced staff, many of them borrowed from Rear Admiral Jerry Bogan's flagship. Task-force operations continued without any serious hitches, although Burke admitted that "each of the task group commanders [were] fighting without much help from us."[15]

Admiral Spruance came out on May 27 to relieve Mitscher's tattered staff and to give the vice admiral a rest. At midnight on May 27, Admiral William "Bull" Halsey signified his assumption of overall command of the Okinawa operation by firing nine rounds of 16-inch shells toward Ushijima's lines from the battleship *Missouri*. Admiral Nimitz already had replaced Vice Admiral Kelly Turner ten days earlier and now judged that more than two months of intense aerial and naval fighting off Okinawa was enough for any commander and staff. Pete Mitscher transferred on board *Shangri-La* via boatswain's seat on the twenty-seventh for a closed-door meeting with Vice Admiral John S. "Slew" McCain to discuss the Okinawa campaign and what the new carrier-task-force commander could expect. The following day, May 28, the sixty-year-old McCain officially assumed command of TF 38, with *Shangri-La* as his flagship.[16]

Mitscher, Burke, and the surviving staff members returned with *Randolph* to Guam, where the Bald Eagle enjoyed a fresh shower and a day to recover before proceeding on to Pearl Harbor to write official reports on the Okinawa campaign. On May 28 the Fifth Fleet officially became the Third Fleet, and TF 58 switched its identity back to TF 38. Spruance, Turner, and their staffs could now begin planning for the expected invasion of Kyushu, while Admiral Halsey and Vice Admiral McCain mopped up off Okinawa. Halsey sent Mitscher a fond farewell message: "With deep regret, we are watching a great fighting man shove off. All luck to you and your magnificent staff from me and every last member of my staff and the whole fleet."[17]

McCain would have no downtime from the relentless kamikaze fury, as Vice Admiral Ugaki's next operation commenced on May 27, as TF 58 was preparing to revert back to TF 38. Kikusui No. 8 would run through the following day and involve 217 navy planes and 71 army planes, of which 108 were kamikazes. Ugaki remained overly optimistic in recording numbers of ships sunk in his diary entry for the twenty-seventh. During that afternoon, he took the chance to survey some of his airfields on horseback, noting that destruction to his airbases and to civilian housing "was worse than I had heard about. Almost nothing original is left, and bomb craters, big and small, are dangerous to the horse's legs. We returned at 1700, man and horse both sweating."[18]

Kikusui No. 8 reached its peak on May 28, when several merchant ships were damaged and one destroyer was sunk. At Radar Picket Station No. 15, Marine Corsairs assailed kamikazes that moved in against the destroyers *Drexler* (DD 741) and *Lowry* (DD 770) and two gunboats. First Lieutenant Russell C. Brown and 2nd Lieutenant James B. Seaman tore into the Japanese aircraft as they began their runs on *Drexler* and *Lowry*, managing to explode one of the attackers. Seaman hit another of the Kawasaki Ki-45 Army Type 2 two-seat, twin-engine "Nick" fighters in the cockpit, but the determined Japanese pilot continued his dive toward *Drexler*. At the last instant the Nick leveled sufficiently to slam directly into the destroyer's starboard side at 0702, slightly forward of the starboard 40-mm quad mount.[19]

At 0702 a Frances exploded in *Drexler's* after fireroom, damaging both engine rooms in the process and starting large gasoline fires. Less than one minute later, a third suicide plane slammed into her Number Two stack just abaft the amidships passageway. "There was a tremendous explosion which rocked the ship violently from stem to stern," said her skipper, Commander Ronald Lee Wilson. "Parts of the ship were blown hundreds of feet in all directions."[20]

Wilson passed the word to abandon ship, but survivors were already jumping overboard on their own initiative. *Drexler* turned over flat on her starboard side and sank stern first, disappearing from site a mere forty-nine seconds after the third kamikaze hit. Her swift sinking left some Navy brass to debate whether the Japanese had deployed some special new explosive device, but *Drexler's* loss was merely the result of three devastating hits that ripped her open in spectacular fashion. Commander Wilson and 50 other sailors were wounded, and another 158 men of the 350 on board perished.

The month of May 1945 had been deadly for TF 58/38 and for the radar-picket ships off Okinawa. Four destroyers and three gunboats had been sunk by kamikazes, with another twenty damaged. The destroyers *Aaron Ward, Hugh W. Hadley,* and *Evans* were so badly wrecked that they would be decommissioned and scrapped once the war ended. Naval personnel losses on the radar-picket ships amounted to 870 killed and 834 wounded throughout May. During the last two weeks of the month, seventeen other ships had been hit, including two of Mitscher's flagship carriers.[21]

By the time Bull Halsey resumed command of TF 38, Pete Mitscher's former fleet had weathered eight of Ugaki's Kikusui assaults. Okinawa had already proven to be the most costly naval campaign of the war, with ninety ships either sunk or damaged badly enough to be out of action for more than a month. Correspondents in Washington took the chance to criticize Lieutenant General Buckner's tactics, with one labeling Okinawa as "a worse example of military incompetence than Pearl Harbor."[22]

During June 2–3, Jocko Clark's TG 38.1 provided air cover for Okinawa while Rear Admiral Radford's TG 38.4 sent more fighter sweeps over the Kyushu airfields. *Shangri-La's* VF-85 achieved ten kills in the mopping-up actions but lost several Hellcats in the process. *Shangri-La's* Corsair squadron, VBF-85, claimed three Tonys and an Oscar on June 3 in exchange for three F4Us that failed to return to the carrier. Elements from *Yorktown's* VF-9 became embroiled in the dogfights over Kyushu as well on the third.

TF 38's top ace, Gene Valencia, returned to action by leading three divisions in bombing and strafing Kyushu airfields. Over Kanoya Airfield, Howard Hudson and his wingman, Lieutenant (jg) Bill Brewer, knocked down a Zeke and a George (the latter misidentified by the pair as a Frank). Hudson's fourth aerial victory was achieved by knocking the George, piloted by Petty Officer 1st Class Kiyoshi Miyamoto from the Sento 407th Hikotai, into Kagoshima Bay.[23]

During the afternoon of June 4, Clark's task group began battling the effects of an approaching typhoon. As the weather worsened, VF-17's Jim Pearce and wingman George Johnson were launched from Clark's flagship *Hornet* to search for a *Shangri-La* Corsair pilot who had gotten lost from his strike group while returning from Okinawa. By the time Pearce and Johnson returned with the lost VF-85 pilot, *Hornet* was bobbing like a cork in the worsening seas. Surface winds increasing from fourteen to forty knots effectively shut down any further flight operations.[24]

By 0500 on June 5, *Hornet* was nearing the eye of the typhoon. Rear Admiral Clark was forced to run his TG 38.1 through heavy rain, ninety-knot wind gusts, and mountainous seas, with waves fifty to sixty feet from crest to trough. "*Hornet* was gyrating in every direction, cracking and creaking," recalled Marsh Beebe. "We were taking green water over the bow constantly." Pilot Tilly Pool, whose junior-officers cabin was far forward, recalled, "The ship would go up, shudder, come back down, and those dang anchors would bang against the sides."[25]

Shortly before dawn, Clark's flagship carrier was slammed by monster waves that collapsed the flight deck from the forward edge back some twenty-four feet. Lieutenant Pearce felt as if *Hornet* "had hit a stone wall." Task-force destroyers had rolled as much as 60 degrees, and the cruiser *Pittsburgh* had her entire bow structure ripped away at 0604. Once the worst of the storm had passed, nearly every ship of Jocko's group was left with damage. *Bennington*'s forward flight-deck section had similarly collapsed, destroying a catapult and forcing her to jettison six damaged airplanes. *Belleau Wood* lost her starboard forward catwalk, while *San Jacinto* suffered minor hull damage and some flooding. Six men from TF 38 were killed or washed overboard, and another four were seriously injured. Halsey's force suffered thirty-three aircraft washed overboard, thirty-six jettisoned, and another seven damaged beyond feasible repair.[26]

By early afternoon of June 6, Jocko Clark ordered *Hornet* to resume flights despite the carrier's mangled forward flight deck. "I had severe misgivings about flight operations," said Marsh Beebe. He went to *Hornet* skipper Artie Doyle and recommended flights be suspended, but

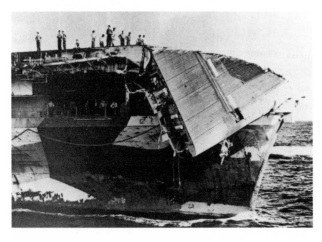

The damaged bow of the carrier *Hornet* following typhoon damage received on June 5, 1945. *80-G-700122, NARA*

A VF-17 Hellcat is seen making a rare launch in reverse. The carrier *Hornet* is steaming 18.5 knots in reverse on June 6, 1945, due to typhoon damage to her bow. *Tilman Pool*

his warning went unheeded. The first plane launched at 1414, the orphaned *Shangri-La* Corsair, which was hit by turbulence over the damaged bow and slammed into the ocean. Jim Pearce of VF-17 was greatly disturbed to find that Clark refused to halt the unsafe plane launchings. "They could have had my wings, but damned if I was going to place any of my pilots in a similar situation," Lieutenant Commander Beebe declared. "Using smoke bombs, I proved that there was an erratic airflow caused by the crushed bow. The airflow reversed and produced a void at the forward end of the flight deck."[27]

Within the hour, Beebe had *Hornet*'s skipper turn the carrier and proceed at 18.5 knots in reverse. Lieutenant (jg) Hardy, among the two dozen Hellcat pilots preparing to make his first reverse takeoff, was apprehensive of the chewed-up rear end of the flight deck, chock full of divits from heavy planes slamming down during hundreds of recent landings. "That deck was like a country road back there, rough and full of ruts where the wood was all eaten out from three cruises worth of people landing on the *Hornet*," explained Hardy.[28]

Lieutenant Billy Watts found enough wind over the stern during his launch that it felt almost as easy as a normal bow launch. His flight succeeded in locating *Pittsburgh*, plowing along slowly minus its bow section. Upon VF-17's return, Tilly Pool was pleased to make a normal stern landing as he found *Hornet* "heading into the wind with the bent-down bow."[29]

U.S. forces made significant advances into Japanese-held territory on Okinawa during late May and early June. This photo shows Marine lieutenant colonel Richard P. Ross Jr. raising the U.S. flag over Shuri Castle on May 29, 1945. *National Archives, FMC 42043*

Simon Buckner's infantrymen and Marines ashore on Okinawa were weathering their own storms during early June. After two months of bitter fighting, the Tenth Army had secured the island's capital, Naha, on May 27. Two days later the Japanese Thirty-Second Army began its withdrawal from Shuri's ruins. Buckner's soldiers and his Marines began the drive on June 1 to prevent Lieutenant General Ushijima's forces from escaping into the base of the Chinen Peninsula's rugged hills.

In the meantime the 6th Marine Division embarked on the important secondary mission of seizing the Oruku Peninsula, which jutted into the water just south of Naha. Major General Geiger opted to outflank the enemy by landing Major General Lemuel C. Shepherd's 6th Marines across two small beaches at Oruku's northern tip on June 4 using seventy-two amtracs (LVTs). The peninsula was defended by some two thousand troops, under Rear Admiral Minoru Ota, armed with more than two hundred machine guns and light cannon.[30]

Corporal White's G Company was hit by Japanese 47-mm shells as it advanced on June 5 toward an enemy-infested hill. "I was hit in the right thumb, the left forearm, the left knee, and left hip," reported White. Most of his shrapnel wounds were small, but his ripped right thumb required wrapping with a rag before he could continue. White and the 6th Marines pushed forward despite heavy losses. The corporal killed a Japanese sniper the following day after a bullet ripped through the pack on his back. "The bullet missed me, but really messed up a carton of Lucky Strike cigarettes in my pack," quipped White.[31]

By June 9 White was enduring his seventieth day on Okinawa as his 3rd Platoon advanced on a hill his comrades nicknamed "Flat Top."

"We were running out of hills to take and Japanese to take them from," remarked White. "We were running out of us, too." Several of his platoon were downed in this assault, and the Marine was hit in both legs by a Japanese 7.7-mm bullet. "On the right side of my right calf was a half-dollar sized hole, bleeding heavily and rythmically," he recounted. "I noticed what looked like bits of fresh hamburger on the inside of my pants."[32]

The 3rd Platoon was relieved the following day, and White was loaded by stretcher onto the hospital ship *Relief* (AH 1). He was down to a scrawny 128 pounds, having dropped 22 pounds during his seventy days of fighting on Okinawa. His G Company had suffered 61 Marines killed on the island plus another 224 men who received the Purple Heart. "Many wounds were treated only by a corpsman, with no Purple Heart awarded," noted White. "Of the original members of G Company who landed on April 1, 1945, almost all had been killed or had been wounded at least once by the end of the battle."[33]

Corporal Mel Heckt's machine-gun squad was assailed by saber-wielding Japanese soldiers who charged the Marine foxholes, yelling "Banzai!" and "Marine, you die!" Heckt's sand-fouled M1 rifle jammed during one such assault, but other Marines dropped the charging Japanese within fifteen yards of his position. The following night Private 1st Class Edwin H. "Danny" Maczko was shocked when a Japanese soldier jumped into his foxhole and grabbed one of his grenades. Maczko wrestled away the grenade, beat the enemy soldier with a club, and stabbed him with his Marine K-bar knife before he finished the job with his rifle.[34]

By June 11 Rear Admiral Ota's forces on the Oroku Peninsula had been compressed into a small section between Oroku town and Tomigusuku. Ota radioed a final message to Lieutenant General Ushijima at Thirty-Second Army headquarters, "Enemy tank groups are now attacking our cave headquarters. The Naval Base Force is dying gloriously at this moment." The 6th Marine Division had paid heavily during this lengthy engagement, suffering more than 1,600 killed and wounded. After mopping up on the thirteenth, the Marines finally discovered Ota's headquarters under a hill near Tomigusuku. Deep in the labyrinth of underground tunnels, they located a concrete-lined room in the center of the complex, where the bodies of Ota and five of his officers were found. Each commander was dressed in full military uniform, with swords and dress sabers, lying prone on the spots where each had allowed their throats to be slit in order to avoid capture.[35]

Near Okinawa's southern tip, Ushijima's final defensive line lay in a solid wall of coral as Lieutenant General Buckner's Tenth Army continued its advance. By nightfall of June 17, Buckner predicted to newsmen that his forces were "down to the final kill." The following day the general went to the front lines to visit a newly arrived combat unit, Colonel Clarence Wallace's 8th Marine Regiment of the 2nd Marine Division.[36]

Buckner watched the Marines advance across a valley for about an hour and was preparing to leave Wallace's observation post around 1315 to visit another front. At that instant five Japanese artillery shells—among the last fired in the Okinawa campaign—exploded nearby and blasted jagged hunks of coral into the air. General Buckner was felled by pieces of shrapnel that punctured his chest and abdomen, leaving the senior Allied commander on Okinawa helpless to stop the blood flow. Buckner died within ten minutes.

Major General Geiger would assume acting command of the Tenth Army for the time being and in so doing became the first Marine to command a field army. It was a bitter irony that the oft-criticized Buckner had his life pass from his body just two miles and four days short of his goal, the capture of Okinawa.[37]

The massive air battle that had raged for more than two months during the Okinawa campaign was winding down by the second week of June 1945. Vice Admiral Ugaki's Kikusui No. 9, staged between June 3 and June 7, included 367 navy planes and 71 army planes (of which 23 navy and 31 army planes were kamikazes). Okinawa-based Marine Corsairs were efficient in downing a large number of the suiciders, along with Army Air Forces P-47N Thunderbolt pilots. The net result of this Floating Chrysanthemum was damage to one battleship, one escort carrier, and one heavy cruiser. By the time the last kamikaze hit the water on the seventh, Allied forces on Okinawa had taken Naha, and the remaining Japanese troops defended only the southernmost tip of the island.

Ugaki's air strength was dwindling from the long campaign. By June 7 he wrote that the combined number of planes belonging to both the 5th and 3rd Air Fleets had "reached a few thousand on paper, of which only 700 were available, and of which, in turn, 570 planes were in operational condition." In response to Ugaki's demand that these operational forces be more active, he was greeted with the excuse that many pilots were unable to fly at night due to their poor skill. "It's very distressing," the admiral logged.[38]

The end was in sight for kamikaze threats, and Vice Admiral McCain's TF 38 would see little aerial combat moving forward. On June 8 Rear Admiral Radford's TG 38.4 and Rear Admiral Clark's TG 38.1 launched attacks against the southern Kyushu airfields. It was only fitting that the final Navy fighter kills of the Okinawa campaign for TF 38 would come from VF-9, a unit whose "Flying Circus" division already had taken top honors for the war. Lieutenant Valencia's division flew five final CAPs between June 6 and June 11 but enjoyed no further aerial victories.

Henry Champion and Bill Brewer of VF-9 shared the honors of closing out the campaign with the final kills made by Halsey's carrier aviators. Each pilot downed a Zeke fighter, with Champion becoming the last carrier-based ace of the Okinawa campaign. During its third combat cruise on the carriers *Lexington* and *Yorktown*, VF-9 claimed 128.75 Japanese planes destroyed in aerial combat, an additional 18 probables, and 52 more damaged. Their strafing attacks resulted in another 47 planes destroyed, 58 probably destroyed, and 209 damaged on the ground. Ten Fighting Nine pilots achieved ace status during this combat cruise.[39]

Yorktown's air group flew its final missions on June 9, whereupon TF 38 sailed for the new advance base of Leyte in the Philippine Islands to take a break. Although Kikusui No. 9 had run its course, sporadic kamikaze attacks still posed a menace for the radar pickets off Okinawa in the days that followed. On the tenth a lone Val dive bomber eluded Marine Corsairs and the antiaircraft fire of Radar Picket Station No. 15A's warships to crash alongside the after engine room of *William D. Porter* (DD 579). The Val exploded directly beneath the destroyer, creating such extensive damage that *Porter* rolled over and sank within hours.[40]

Even before Slew McCain's carrier fleet moved into Leyte Gulf on June 13, the pilots of Valencia's Flying Circus division had become celebrities, whether the fame was desired or not. Valencia, Harris Mitchell, Jim French, and Clint Smith were surrounded by photographers on June 10. Sporting leather flight jackets, their colorful flight helmets, and goggles, the quartet

The destroyer *William D. Porter* (DD 579) rolls over and sinks after a kamikaze attack on June 10, 1945. *80-G-490027, NARA*

The Navy's deadliest fighter division poses for publicity photos at the close of the Okinawa campaign on June 10, 1945, holding a scoreboard of their combined fifty aerial victories. *Left to right:* Harris Mitchell, Gene Valencia, Clint Smith, and Jim French of VF-9. *80-GK-5990, NARA*

posed under a Hellcat on the flight deck along with a freshly created sign that sported fifty Rising Sun emblems—one for each kill the division had achieved in the Pacific War. On the reverse side of the sign, another fifty Rising Suns had been arranged to create the numeral "50" for additional photos.

Lieutenant Valencia and his Air Group 9 were detached from *Yorktown* on June 16 for passage back to the United States on *Hornet*, along with Air Group 30 from *Belleau Wood*, also being relieved. Jack Kitchen's Fighting Nine was among the best squadron in the fleet, sporting many aces. Gene Valencia led the pack with 23.5 kills (12.5 on *Yorktown*), followed by Jim French with 11, Harris Mitchell with 10, Marv Franger with 9, Bill Bonneau with 8, Bert Eckard with 7, Ed McGowan with 6.5, and three VF-9 pilots with 6 kills: Clint Smith, Les DeCew, and Johnny Orth, the latter achieving his victories as a night fighter. Rounding out the ace club were Herb Houck, Henry Champion, and Howard Hudson, each with 5 kills.

Once on board *Hornet*, Valencia, French, Smith, and Mitchell met with George E. Jones of the *New York Times* and Malcolm Johnson of the *New*

York Sun. Sporting a wispy black mustache and a confident grin, Valencia spouted forth praise on his men and their achievements as the flashbulbs popped. Some of his quips were widely printed, such as his admiration for the Grumman Hellcat. "It's a great airplane," he said. "If it could cook, I'd marry it."[41]

Johnson nicknamed the VF-9 division the "Valencia Turkey Shoot Club," but publisher Henry Luce's "Flying Circus" moniker would prove to be everlasting. For the moment, all Harris Mitchell could think of were the prospects of family and liberty back in California. He signed off his final logbook entry for June 1945 with his heartfelt desire: "That's all, Brother. Frisco, here we come."[42]

EPILOGUE

The battle for Okinawa was in its final stages as *Hornet* got under way for Pearl Harbor on June 19, 1945. The naval forces remaining off Okinawa were then amid Vice Admiral Ugaki's final Floating Chrysanthemum operation, Kikusui No. 10, conducted from June 16 to June 22. Only sixty-seven kamikazes took to the air during this final effort, and their results were equally meager: only two ships suffered casualties and heavy damage. Nine land-based Marine Corsair squadrons claimed the final thirty-three victories of the Okinawa campaign on June 22, pushing total Marine Corps fighter-squadron victories during Operation Iceberg to 490.[1]

The fighting ashore also reached its final climax, including heavy combat along Kunishi Ridge, as Ugaki's airmen carried out Kikusui No. 10. By June 21 the Japanese had been driven to the southernmost point of the island, at which time Major General Geiger declared Okinawa secured. Early the next morning Lieutenant General Ushijima and his chief of staff, Lieutenant General Cho, dressed in ceremonial uniforms. Each man thrust a short dagger into his own belly before a sword-wielding captain standing behind them beheaded the generals. Their few remaining soldiers fled down the cliff to meet the American soldiers once they learned of the deaths of their commanders, signifying the end of organized resistance by the Thirty-Second Army.[2]

But Ushijima's death did not translate to a quick end to hostilities on Okinawa. Corporal Mel Heckt's Baker Company, 4th Marine Regiment, 6th Marine Division suffered more casualties during the mopping-up actions that followed. His closest buddy, Captain Ed Dunham, was killed on June 23 while leading a charge over a ridgeline. "I had tears in my eyes for the first time during the operation," wrote Heckt. "Dunham was the most brave and courageous man I've ever known." The captain was one of

52 Marines of B Company who perished on the island. More than 1,700 Marines from the 6th Division also had been killed. The eighty-three-day Okinawa campaign resulted in more than 12,000 American deaths, numbering nearly 5,000 U.S. Navy fatalities and 7,300 men from the four U.S. Army and the two U.S. Marine Corps divisions.[3]

Major air battles over Okinawa ended by late June as Japanese air strength was withdrawn to other bases in northern Kyushu, Honshu, and Shikoku to prepare to defend the homeland. The number of radar-picket stations near Okinawa was reduced during early July, and the last serious attack on the radar-picket ships took place on July 29–30. The final American warship lost off the island was the destroyer *Callaghan* (DD 792), hit by a kamikaze whose bomb created severe fires and secondary explosions that doomed the ship.

Lieutenant Harris Mitchell was upbeat as the carrier *Hornet* completed its eight-thousand-mile homeward voyage on July 8, 1945, by passing under the Golden Gate Bridge. Mitch, Lieutenant Gene Valencia, and other VF-9 pilots went ashore to NAS Alameda the following day to receive numerous campaign awards. Mitch made a rush on the ship's service store to buy ribbons and stars for his jacket. "It was a job trying to arrange them in their order of seniority and very few of us had them all placed in their correct position," observed Mitchell. "But we really didn't give a damn."[4]

Valencia appeared on several radio broadcasts and was ordered to Washington, D.C., for further awards and recognition. It was not until August that he was able to return home on a forty-day leave to reunite with his wife, Jeanne, and to meet his four-month-old son, Jerry Anthony, for the first time. His air group was soon split up with new orders, but Valencia's Flying Circus would long be remembered for its accomplishments during the Pacific War. It remains the U.S. Navy's most successful fighter division of all time.

Vice Admiral Matome Ugaki struggled with the final months of the war, as Allied bombing attacks against ports, airfields, and major cities increased. News of the atomic bombs dropped on his country in early August 1945 distressed him, but the lack of positive orders to counterattack the Americans was even more disturbing. Ugaki felt that officials considering Japan's surrender were nothing more than "selfish weaklings who don't think seriously about the future of the nation." He much preferred to continue guerilla warfare and resolved to entrust his body to defend the empire "until death takes me away."[5]

By the morning of August 15, Ugaki heard reports that Japan had surrendered unconditionally and that Emperor Hirohito would address the nation in a noon broadcast. The admiral felt shame as Hirohito gave his speech, and he decided to lead one final kamikaze mission to crash American ships off Okinawa. At 1400 he completed his final diary entries, left the documents in care of a military classmate, and joined his 5th Air Fleet headquarters staff for a round of farewell toasts. Clutching a ceremonial sword given to him by the late Fleet Admiral Yamamoto, Ugaki headed for Oita Airfield by car, where he found eleven Suisei (Judy) dive bombers warming up, their engines whipping the midsummer grasses into a frenzy.[6]

Ugaki shook hands with his staff members and posed for photos, wearing a dark green Type 3 uniform with a pair of binoculars around his neck. He then climbed into the rear seat of the Judy piloted by Lieutenant Tatsuo Nakatsuru, commander of the 701st Air Group's Oita detachment. Warrant Officer Akiyoshi Endo, scheduled to lead the flight, was unwilling to remain behind and crammed himself into the bomber's rear seat along with Ugaki. Nakatsuru's bombers roared down the Kanoya airstrip at 1630 and headed south into a gathering dusk on August 15.

Three of the ten Judys would abort due to engine trouble, but the other seven would not return. Ugaki's final note to his staff read, "Having a dream, I will go up into the sky." En route to Okinawa, Ugaki radioed a last message in which he announced his own failure at having destroyed the American military during the past six months. "I am going to proceed to Okinawa, where our men lost their lives like cherry blossoms, and ram into the arrogant American ships, displaying the real spirit of a Japanese warrior," declared Ugaki. "All units under my command shall keep my will in mind, overcome every conceivable difficulty, rebuild a strong armed force, and make our empire last forever. The emperor *Banzai!*"[7]

At 1924 Warrant Officer Endo transmitted Ugaki's final radio message that their plane had begun its dive on an American ship. None of the war's final kamikaze aircraft caused any damage, as all appear to have been downed by antiaircraft fire. The following day the crew of *LST 926* located wreckage of one aircraft that contained three bodies inside. One of the occupants was clad in a dark green uniform, his head crushed and his right arm missing. The Americans buried the bodies on the beach of Okinawa, the likely final resting place of Matome Ugaki.[8]

On the day that Vice Admiral Ugaki gave his life in the war's final kamikaze mission, his principal opponent at Okinawa, Vice Admiral Pete Mitscher, was making the rounds in Washington, addressing the media in his new role as deputy chief of naval operations for air. "Carrier supremacy defeated Japan," Mitscher announced, giving credit to the "balanced, integrated air-surface-ground team" that had combined forces to win the battle for the Pacific.[9]

Mitscher spent the fall of 1945 making speeches, acting on various boards, and performing his duties as a leading military air boss. On March 1, 1946, he was promoted to full admiral (four stars) at age fifty-nine and returned to sea as the commander of the Eighth Fleet on board his new flagship carrier *Lake Champlain* (CV 39). He was greatly relieved to be joined with his old comrade Captain Arleigh Burke, the once-gritty relationship of the two officers having grown as tight as that of father and son during their campaigns in the Pacific.[10]

Burke continued with Mitscher as the admiral next became commander in chief, U.S. Atlantic Fleet, on March 1, 1946, but he noted the Bald Eagle's declining health. By fall Mitscher had become concerned with getting his affairs in order, and he even requested Burke to destroy two filing cabinets filled with his Pacific War personal papers. He explained that there were "statements critical of people I now wish I hadn't written" and other carelessly written documents "capable of misinterpretation by someone for his own advantage or to vent a grudge." The loss of such important documents pained Burke, but he felt it was clear the admiral knew he was dying.[11]

Mitscher celebrated his sixtieth birthday in Norfolk, Virginia, on January 26, 1947, with his wife, Frances. By that afternoon he complained to her of feeling ill. He was admitted to the base naval hospital the next day, where it was announced he was suffering from bronchitis, although his illness was soon properly diagnosed as a heart attack. Just days later, in the early morning hours of February 3, Marc Mitscher passed away due to a coronary thrombosis. The admiral was buried on February 5 with full military honors in Arlington National Cemetery.[12]

The *Baltimore Sun* wrote that Admiral Mitscher had implemented "revolutionary change" in bringing aviation to the forefront for the U.S. Navy. The *Washington Post* hailed him as "Raider of the Pacific." Admiral of the Fleet Chester Nimitz told the press, "I always had the feeling of confidence and security when Admiral Mitscher was out with Task Force 58." President Harry Truman added, "The Armed Forces have lost a brave and gallant leader."[13]

Pete Mitscher's role in advancing naval aviation could not be denied, and his record was never brighter than the period when he had led the world's mightiest carrier fleet against the Divine Wind of Japan's kamikaze corps off Okinawa. Vice Admiral Ugaki's ten Kikusui special operations had sortied no fewer than 1,465 of the 1,900 suicide planes sent against the Allied forces between April and June 1945, sinking 26 Allied ships and damaging 164 more, some never able to return to service.[14]

Prior to Okinawa, the Marianas Turkey Shoot of June 1944 had been the crowning glory for naval fighter pilots. When Mitscher led his fleet against the Japanese mainland on February 16, 1945, his fleet air wing was well on its way to ensuring the demise of the Imperial Japanese war machine that had ravaged the eastern and central Pacific during the war's early years. Six of his pilots became instant aces that day.

From the start of the Okinawa aerial offensive campaign on March 18 through the island being declared secure on June 22, another twenty pilots would be credited with enough enemy aircraft destroyed in aerial combat to classify them as "aces in a day." In this time Navy, Marine, and Army Air Forces pilots would claim some 2,326 aerial victories during the *tetsu no ame* (rain of steel) operation. This figure is further broken down with 1,594 Japanese aircraft claimed in aerial combat by U.S. Navy pilots, another 631 claimed by Marine fighter pilots, and 101 by U.S. Army Air Forces pilots. An astonishing sixty-nine Navy, twenty-two Marine, and five Army Air Forces pilots—ninety-six total—would each down five or more enemy aircraft off Okinawa. At least another thirty-four U.S. fighter pilots achieved ace status during the Okinawa campaign by adding new victories to their previous combat credits.[15]

Land-based Marine fighter squadrons claimed 491 shoot downs between April 7 and June 22, 1945, with eighteen aces crowned during this period. Eleven of these men came from Major George Axtell's VMF-323 Death Rattlers squadron. The ten carrier-based Marine Corsair squadrons were credited with an additional 201 Japanese planes in aerial combat.[16]

During the Okinawa campaign, Tactical Air Force Marines lost 139 Corsairs and sixteen Hellcats through June 22, when the island was declared secure. Twelve Marine Corsair and three night Marine Hellcat squadrons worked from Okinawa's Kadena and Yontan Airfields and from nearby Ie Shima from April to July 1945. Seventeen Marine aces were crowned over these eighty-three days. Major Archie Donahue of *Bunker Hill*'s VMF-451 became the U.S. Marine Corps' only carrier-based "ace in a day." The top-three victory totals from Marine squadrons participating in the Okinawa campaign were VMF-323, with 124.5 kills; VMF-311, with 67 victories; and VMF-312, with 60.5 claimed aerial successes. The leading U.S. Army Air Forces squadron to participate in Operation Iceberg was the 19th Fighter Squadron, 318th Fighter Group, with 59 victories.[17]

Only four U.S. Marine Corps fighter pilots achieved ace status while serving with the fast-carrier fleet, and all four made their kills while flying from the carrier *Bunker Hill* during the Okinawa campaign. Archie Donahue (14 total kills with VMF-112 and VMF-451) was VMF-451's lone carrier-based Marine ace, achieving five kills off Okinawa in aerial combat. He retired as a reserve colonel in 1958, worked in the realty business in Texas, and spent many years flying restored World War II aircraft with the Commemorative Air Force. Donahue passed away at age eighty-nine on July 30, 2007.

The other three carrier-based Marine fighter pilots to reach ace status flew with *Bunker Hill*'s VMF-221 Fighting Falcons. John McManus, who achieved six kills before his carrier was knocked out of action by kamikazes, later logged eighty combat missions during the Korean War and retired from the Marine Corps as a major. William Snider shot down 6.5 Japanese planes off Okinawa, bringing his wartime victory to total to 11.5 kills. He and Donahue were the only Marines to become both shore- and carried-based aces during the war. Snider returned to civilian life in Mississippi, where he died in March 1969.[18]

Dean Caswell of VMF-221 was the top-scoring U.S. Marine Corps carrier pilot of all time, with seven aerial victories achieved during the Okinawa campaign. Following his combat tour on board *Bunker Hill*, Caswell served two tours flying night fighters during the Korean War and retired as a colonel in 1968. In recent years he authored several books on his service and that of his leatherneck fighter-ace comrades. His home in Texas is something of a military museum—one he graciously allowed me and my brother-in-law, David Hunt, to enjoy during an interview with

him in 2017. Every night before bed Colonel Caswell turns on a light for his "Case of Aces" so his fallen Marine comrades are never in darkness.

The author visiting with Dean Caswell, the U.S. Marine Corps' top-scoring carrier-based fighter ace, in his museum-like Texas home. *Photo by David Hunt*

Among the photos in this display is that of double ace Archie Donahue, whom Caswell's current wife, Mary, was married to until his death in 2007.

The top-scoring Navy Corsair squadron off Okinawa was *Essex*'s VBF-83, which produced three aces and claimed eighty-six aerial victories between March 18 and June 22, 1945. The *Intrepid*-based Grim Reapers of VF-10 achieved seventy-eight shoot downs flying F4Us and produced five aces. The deadliest Fighting Ten division off Okinawa was that of Lieutenant (jg) Phil Kirkwood and Ensigns Dick Quiel, Horace Heath, and Al Lerch. Lerch, who downed seven aircraft in his April 16 "ace in a day" mission, passed away in March 2000 at the age of seventy-seven in Pennsylvania. Tuck Heath, with seven aerial victories, was killed on July 8, 1945, in a Corsair accident. Kirkwood, who finished the war with a dozen kills, returned to service during the Korean War; he passed away at age ninety-four in Texas in 2015. Dick Quiel (six kills) returned to combat flying the F4U during the Korean War and retired from the Navy as a commander in August 1966. He passed away at age ninety in Carlsbad, California, on July 5, 2013.

TF 58/38 Navy Hellcat squadrons claimed 837.25 victories during the Okinawa campaign, and *Essex*-based VF-83 led the pack with 122 kills. The squadron produced ten aces between March 18 and June 22, the leader being VF-83 skipper Thad Coleman, with eight kills. Larry Clark of VF-83 finished the war with seven kills, retired from the Naval Reserves as a lieutenant commander in 1968, and passed away in California in 2017.[19]

Myron Truax, who finished with seven kills and was a VF-83 "ace in a day," returned to civilian life in Texas and passed away in November 1984. His divisionmate Don McPherson (five kills) spent his final flights in August 1945 flying cover for the signing of the Japanese surrender in Tokyo Bay and charting prisoner-of-war camps. McPherson retired home to Adams, Nebraska, to enjoy civilian life as a rural mail carrier and farmer.[20]

The second-highest-scoring Hellcat squadron was VF-9, credited with 93.25 kills during the Okinawa campaign while serving on board the carriers *Lexington* and *Yorktown*. Gene Valencia led the squadron with 12.5 kills at Okinawa, raising his wartime tally to 23 kills plus two probables. He became the U.S. Navy's third-highest-scoring ace of all time and the top-scoring Navy fighter pilot of 1945.

Retiring from the Navy as a commander in August 1962 at age forty-one, Valencia also served as vice president of the American Fighter Aces Association. He began compiling a comprehensive history of all aces—even traveling to Germany to meet with Luftwaffe aces—and was instrumental in organizing an international organization of fighter pilots from all nations who participated in World War II. He served as a technical adviser for a movie on the career of Marine ace and Medal of Honor recipient Joe Foss to be called "Brave Eagle," which was filmed in Hawaii in 1955, with John Wayne playing the role of Foss, but was never released.

Valencia was actively involved in interviewing aces and helped former Japanese fighter pilots organize the Zero Fighter Pilot Association in Tokyo. By the early 1970s, Gene had collected audiotaped interviews from 102 fighter aces from several countries. While attending the American Fighter Aces Association meeting in San Antonio, Texas, Valencia suffered a heart attack on Friday evening, September 15, 1972. He died at Baptist Memorial Hospital the following morning at age fifty-one.

Gene Valencia's Flying Circus division of VF-9 was the most successful in U.S. naval history, accounting for fifty combined kills during World War II. His second-division leader, Jim French, finished the war with eleven victories. Afterward, French formed his own crop-dusting company and later became a distributor for the Grumman AgCat. He passed away on January 2, 1996, in Bakersfield, California. His wingman, Clint Smith, who had achieved five kills with VF-9, later operated a successful auto-repair business. Smith died of a heart attack on January 11, 1972.[21]

Valencia's able wingman, Harris Mitchell, considered himself the "last of the Mohicans" after the deaths of his other three famous Flying Circus comrades. Mitch was credited as a double ace, with nine of his kills occurring during the Okinawa campaign. He served again during the Korean War and retired as a Naval Reserve commander in 1959. Mitchell and his wife settled in San Marcos, Texas, where he enjoyed playing golf and attending reunions until he passed away in May 2006.

The third-highest-scoring Hellcat squadron of the Okinawa campaign, netting 89 victories, was *Hornet*'s VF-17. A dozen F6F pilots scored at least five kills between March 18 and June 22, 1945, led by their skipper, Marshall Beebe, with nine planes downed during this period and 10.5 victories for his wartime total. Beebe later commanded Carrier Air Group 5 on board *Essex* during the Korean War and retired as a captain in 1963. Marsh served as a technical adviser on the popular film *The Bridges at Toko-Ri* (1954), the book of the same name having been dedicated to him by author James Michener. Beebe died at age seventy-seven on March 18, 1991, in Orange County, California.[22]

Jim Pearce (5.25 kills with VF-9) later became the first man to break the sound barrier, flying an F-86 as an engineering pilot for Grumman. An assistant program manager for the Apollo space program, Pearce later penned his autobiography, was the first recipient of the James H. Doolittle Award, and was inducted into the Carrier Aviation Test Pilots Hall of Fame in 1989. Pearce passed away at age ninety-one on February 9, 2011.[23]

The author with Navy ace Tilman "Tilly" Pool in his Houston home. *Photo by Charles "Billy" Watts*

Ted Crosby (5.25 kills with VF-18 and VF-17) flew missions during the Korean War and retired from the Navy as a commander in 1969. Ted retired to California and passed away in 2014 at the age of ninety-three. Bill Hardy (6.5 kills with VF-17) retired from the Navy as a commander in 1959 and enjoyed a successful second career in aerospace. Hardy, an active member of the American Fighter Aces Association, passed away peacefully in California at age ninety-seven on September 15, 2017.[24]

Tilman Pool destroyed six enemy aircraft with VF-17 off Okinawa. Released from active duty in 1947, Tilly remained with the Naval Reserves until 1966. He helped organize an advertising and printing corporation in civilian life in Tulsa, Oklahoma, from which he retired in 1993. Pool earned the Distinguished Flying Cross with three gold stars and the Air Medal with four gold stars. Pool lives in Houston, Texas.

Charles Watts (8.75 kills, VF-17) remained in the Naval Reserves until his retirement in November 1959 as a lieutenant commander. Billy graduated from Southern Methodist University in 1947 and worked in the oil industry until his retirement in 1982. He was among the U.S. fighter aces to participate in a White House ceremony in May 2015 for the awarding of a Congressional Gold Medal to the American Fighters Aces Association. My last talk with him was during Christmas time in 2017, when he enthusiastically answered more questions on some of his memorable flights. Billy passed away weeks later on January 12, 2018, in Baytown, Texas.

President Barack Obama congratulates Okinawa ace Charles "Billy" Watts at a White House ceremony in 2015 to award the Congressional Gold Medal to the American Fighter Aces Association. *White House photo via Charles Watts*

The above covers only a portion of the elite aces of the Okinawa campaign. To those who shared some of their combat experiences, I am eternally grateful. Tilly Pool credits his fellow U.S. pilots with achieving air superiority over the Japanese by the end of the Okinawa campaign, "because we did have complete air power at the end." Most who achieved ace status rarely bragged about it among their squadronmates. "The fact of being an ace didn't really enter your thinking until it was all over," said VF-83's Don McPherson. "You were as happy for the next guy if he got one than if you got one yourself. It meant that you were helping to win the war."[25]

Pete Mitscher's carrier aviators had answered the call off Okinawa in top fashion, going above and beyond the call of duty in their efforts to help win World War II in an aerial campaign the likes of which this world will never experience again.

ACKNOWLEDGMENTS

Clifford Neve of the American Fighter Aces Association contacted me to request a signed copy of one of my previous World War II aviation books for one of his Pacific War fighter-ace veterans. It was not long after our first conversations that Cliff invited me to meet a couple of his friends, men who had fought the war against the kamikazes off Okinawa in 1945.

A short time later, in June 2017, I met Cliff in Houston, Texas, at the home of VF-17 ace Tilman "Tilly" Pool. We were joined by Tilly's *Hornet* squadronmate Charles "Billy" Watts. The hours that followed were thrilling, as I watched the two aging men relive their battles in the skies from more than seven decades earlier. Billy and Tilly were back in their youthful days as Hellcat jockeys, trading stories of fellow pilots, tragic losses, Baka bombs, and even battling a typhoon.

From that first interview session, the seeds of a full project on the Okinawa campaign were sewn. The following month I met with retired U.S. Marine colonel Dean Caswell in his Austin-area home, where he walked me through his private aviation museum and recounted stories of battling kamikazes with his *Bunker Hill*–based Corsair. Caswell's books on his service and his squadronmates were enlightening, and I truly appreciate the time he shared.

From the American Fighter Aces Association, other individuals I must thank are Jema Hayes, Ali Lane, Dr. Frank Olynyk, and Ed Garland. Olynyk's books on the Marine and Navy fighter victories of World War II are priceless in terms of cobbling together which pilots and which squadrons were involved in various actions during the ten Kikusui operations of Okinawa. My friend Bill Shinneman, coauthor of my first book in 1996, helped put me back in touch with the USS *Enterprise* CV-6 Association, where Grace Hay Neie helped me track down surviving Big E veterans who had taken part in the 1945 actions.

During the 1990s, Shinneman and I had interviewed a large number of *Intrepid* Air Group 10 aviators for our Torpedo Ten project. Fortunately, I was able to reconnect with several of these Okinawa veterans for this project, including John Adams, Bill Banta, and Don Warner. Other World War II veterans I must thank for their contributions are Robert Carlson, Dean Caswell, Charles Coleman, Watson Crumbie, Richard Cumberworth, Robert Dockery, Willis "Bill" Hardy, Melvin Heckt, Robert Johnson, Armond Jolley, Jack Lyons, Don McPherson, Ed Pappert, Tilly Pool, Richard Schwendemann, Eddie Strine, Billy Watts, Richard Whitaker, and Jim White.

A number of the Okinawa veterans' children also lent their support to this project, including Tony Valencia, Cheryl Valencia Icard, Tom Hoffman, Mike Esposito, and Dennis Jolly. Barb Kenutis made great efforts to reproduce photographs, papers, and the diary from the collection of her father, Marine veteran Melvin Heckt. Mary Frances Mitchell was kind enough to share papers, tapes, and photographs from the collection of her late husband, Harris. Her neighbor, Charles Blankenship, went above and beyond to help copy papers and reproduce an audiotape for my research.

Several others deserve special thanks for helping track down reports and papers regarding the fighter aces of Okinawa. Patrizia Nava of the Special Collections and Archives Division, Eugene McDermott Library, The University of Texas at Dallas was very helpful in retrieving aviation research material. Dr. Dave Thompson, Ann Greer, and Frank Castner of the Palm Springs Air Museum, California, assisted my research by reviewing the oral-history archives of their museum. George White and Ron Lepper of the Emil Buehler Library in the Naval Aviation Museum in Pensacola, Florida, pulled various books and squadron-history folders for my review.

Copy editor Kevin Brock earned my gratitude for his skill, particularly in helping make the frequent air battles—riddled with dozens of pilot names and aircraft code names—easier to follow for the reader. Finally, I must thank Richard Russell and Susan Brook of the Naval Institute Press for believing in this project and their work in pushing it forward in time to celebrate the 75th anniversary of the last Pacific War campaign of World War II—a long and bloody fight the likes of which we can only hope our nations will choose never to undertake again.

APPENDIX

U.S. Aces of the Okinawa Campaign: March 18–June 23, 1945
(Listed by Kills Made during Operation Iceberg)

Name	Rank	Unit	Kills	Prob. Kills	Total Kills	Branch
Valencia, Eugene Anthony*	Lt.	VF-9	12.5	2	23	USN
French, James Barber	Lt.(jg)	VF-9	10	-	11	USN
Reber, James Valentine, Jr.	Ens.	VF-30	10	-	11	USN
Beebe, Marshall Ulrich*	Lt. Cdr.	VF-17	9	-	10.5	USN
Mitchell, Harris Edlow	Lt.(jg)	VF-9	9	1	10	USN
Foster, Carl Clifford*	Ens.	VF-30	8.5	-	8.5	USN
Coleman, Thaddeus Thornton, Jr.	Lt.	VF-83	8	-	10	USN
Johnston, John Mitchell	Lt.(jg)	VBF-17	8	-	8	USN
Kirkwood, Philip Leroy*	Lt.(jg)	VF-10	8	-	12	USN
Miller, Johnnie Gamble*	Ens.	VF-30	8	-	8	USN
Reidy, Thomas Hamil	Lt.	VBF-83	8	-	10	USN
Hibbard, Samuel Bushnell	Lt.	VF-47	7.33	-	7.33	USN
Brown, William Perry, Jr.	2Lt	VMF-311	7	-	7	USMC
Caswell, Dean	2Lt	VMF-221	7	1	7	USMC
Clark, Lawrence Arthur	Ens.	VF-83	7	-	7	USN
Eckard, Bert*	Lt.(jg)	VF-9	7	-	7	USN
Harris, Thomas Switzer	Lt.(jg)	VF-17	7	1	9	USN
Heath, Horace Walker	Ens.	VF-10	7	-	7	USN
Lerch, Alfred*	Ens.	VF-10	7	-	7	USN
O'Keefe, Jeremiah Joseph*	1Lt	VMF-323	7	-	7	USMC
Quiel, Norwald Richard	Ens.	VF-10	7	-	7	USN
Ruhsam, John William	1Lt	VMF-323	7	-	7	USMC
Truax, Myron Melton*	Ens.	VF-83	7	-	7	USN
Wade, Robert	1Lt	VMF-323	7	-	8	USMC

(continued on next page)

369

Name	Rank	Unit	Kills	Prob. Kills	Total Kills	Branch
Wolfe, Judge Edmund	Capt.	318th FG	7	-	9	USAAF
Hardy, Willis Everett*	Lt.(jg)	VF-17	6.5	1	6.5	USN
Watts, Charles Edward	Lt.(jg)	VF-17	6.5	-	8.75	USN
Dillard, Joseph Valentine	1Lt	VMF-323	6.33	3	6.33	USMC
Durnford, Dewey Foster, Jr.	2Lt	VMF-323	6.33	-	6.83	USMC
Terrill, Francis Andell	1Lt	VMF-323	6.08	-	6.08	USMC
Axtell, George Clifton*	Maj.	VMF-323	6	-	6	USMC
Baird, Robert	Capt.	VMF(N)-533	6	-	6	USMC
Barnes, James Malcolm	Ens.	VF-83	6	-	6	USN
Batten, Hugh Nash	Lt.(jg)	VF-83	6	-	7	USN
Brocato, Samuel Joseph	Lt.(jg)	VF-83	6	-	7	USN
Clark, Robert Allen	Ens.	VBF-17	6	-	6	USN
Coats, Robert Charles*	Lt.	VF-17	6	4	9.33	USN
Cowger, Richard Dustin	Lt.	VF-17	6	1	6	USN
Dahms, Kenneth John*	Ens.	VF-30	6	-	7	USN
Dorroh, Jefferson David*	Maj.	VMF-323	6	2	6	USMC
Eberts, Byron Arthur	Lt.(jg)	VBF-17	6	-	6	USN
Freeman, Doris Clyde	Lt.	VF-84	6	-	9	USN
Hamilton, Robert Morrill	Ens.	VF-83	6	-	6	USN
Jennings, Robert Harvey, Jr.	Lt.	VF-82	6	-	9.5	USN
Kingston, William John, Jr.	Ens.	VF-83	6	-	6	USN
McManus, John	1Lt	VMF-221	6	-	6	USMC
Mollard, Norman Wesley, Jr.	Lt.(jg)	VF-45	6	-	6	USN
Orth, John	Ens.	VF-9	6	-	6	USN
Pool, Tilman Ellison	Lt.(jg)	VF-17	6	1	6	USN
Smith, John Malcolm	Lt.(jg)	VF-84	6	-	10	USN
Snider, William Nugent	Capt.	VMF-221	6	1	11.5	USMC
Sturdevant, Harvey Willard	Lt.(jg)	VF-30	6	1	6	USN
Umphres, Donald Eugene	Lt.	VF-83	6	-	6	USN
Valentine, Herbert James*	Capt.	VMF-312	6	1	6	USMC
Winfield, Murray*	Lt.(jg)	VF-17	6	-	6	USN
Yeremian, Harold	Ens.	VBF-17	6	-	6	USN
Cain, James Bernice	Lt.	VF-45	5.5	-	8	USN
Hood, William Leslie, Jr.	1Lt	VMF-323	5.5	-	5.5	USMC
Kirkpatrick, Floyd Claude	Capt.	VMF-441	5.5	-	5.5	USMC
Humphrey, Robert Jay	Lt.(jg)	VF-17	5.33	-	5.33	USN
Alley, Stuart Cecil, Jr.	2Lt	VMF-323	5	-	5	USMC
Anderson, Richard Hinman	1Lt	318th FG	5	-	5	USAAF
Bolduc, Alfred George	Lt.	VBF-12	5	-	5	USN
Conant, Edwin Stanley	Lt.	VBF-17	5	1	7	USN
Crosby, John Theodore*	Lt.(jg)	VF-17	5	-	5.25	USN

(continued on next page)

Name	Rank	Unit	Kills	Prob. Kills	Total Kills	Branch
Davies, Clarence "E"	Lt.(jg)	VF-82	5	-	5	USN
Donahue, Archie Glenn*	Maj.	VMF-451	5	1	14	USMC
Drake, Charles William	2Lt	VMF-323	5	1	5	USMC
Farrell, William	1Lt	VMF-312	5	1	5	USMC
Gildea, John Turner	Lt.(jg)	VF-84	5	-	7	USN
Godson, Lindley William	Lt.(jg)	VBF-83	5	-	5	USN
Hoag, John Bannatyne	Ens.	VF-82	5	-	5	USN
Johannsen, Delmar Karl	Ens.	VBF-12	5	-	5	USN
Kaelin, Joseph	Ens.	VF-9	5	2	5	USN
Kincaid, Robert Alexander	Lt.	VBF-83	5	-	5	USN
Kostik, William John	Ens.	VBF-17	5	-	5	USN
Lustic, Stanley	1Lt	318th FG	5	-	6	USAAF
Maberry, Lewin Ardell	Lt.(jg)	VF-84	5	-	5	USN
Manson, Armand Gordon	Lt.	VF-10	5	-	7	USN
Mathis, William Henry	1Lt	318th FG	5	-	5	USAAF
Mazzocco, Michele Albert	Ens.	VF-30	5	-	5	USN
McClure, Edgar Bradford	Lt.	VBF-9	5	-	5	USN
McGinty, Selva Eugene	1Lt	VMF-441	5	-	5	USMC
McPherson, Donald Melvin	Ens.	VF-83	5	-	5	USN
Mitchell, Henry Earl, Jr.*	Lt.(jg)	VBF-17	5	-	6	USN
Olsen, Austin LeRoy	Ens.	VF-30	5	-	5	USN
Pearce, James Lano	Lt.	VF-17	5	-	5.25	USN
Philips, David Patterson, III	Ens.	VF-30	5	-	5	USN
Sistrunk, Frank	Lt.(jg)	VF-17	5	0.5	5	USN
Smith, Clinton Lamar	Lt.(jg)	VF-9	5	1	6	USN
Stone, Carl Van	Lt.(jg)	VBF-17	5	-	5	USN
Swinburne, Harry William, Jr.	Lt.(jg)	VF-45	5	-	5	USN
Vogt, John Edward*	Capt.	318th FG	5	1	5	USAAF
Ward, Lyttleton Thomas	Ens.	VF-83	5	-	5	USN
Wells, Albert Phillip	1Lt	VMF-323	5	-	5	USMC
Woolverton, Robert Clifford	Lt.(jg)	VF-45	5	-	6	USN

* "Ace in a day" (five or more aerial victories in a single day).
"Prob. Kills" indicates probable kills credited to pilot.
"Total Kills" indicates all aerial victories during the pilot's service in World War II.

Note: Twenty pilots achieved "ace in a day" status during the period March 18–June 23, 1945, by downing five or more enemy aircraft in a single day of combat. Another six pilots earned this distinction during TF 58's raids of February 16–17, 1945, against the Kyushu airfields.

Key Sources: Olynyk, *USN Credits for the Destruction of Enemy Aircraft*; and Olynyk, *USMC Credits for the Destruction of Enemy Aircraft*.

GLOSSARY

ACIO	air-combat intelligence officer
angels	altitude in thousands of feet
Baka	Yokosuka MXY7 Navy Ohka suicide attacker
bandit	aircraft identified as a hostile
Betty	IJN Mitsubishi G4M Navy Type 1 land-based attack bomber
bogey	unidentified aircraft
buster	direction to go as fast as possible, as in closing a bandit
CAG	commander, Air Group
CAP	combat air patrol
CIC	combat information center
Claude	IJN Mitsubishi A5M Navy Type 96 fixed-gear fighter
CV	fleet aircraft carrier
CVE	escort aircraft carrier
CVL	light aircraft carrier
Dave	IJN Nakajima E8N Navy Type 95 reconnaissance seaplane
Dinah	JAAF Mitsubishi Ki-46 Army Type 100 reconnaissance airplane
division	a formation of four airplanes
Emily	IJN Kawanishi H8K Navy Type 2 large flying boat
FDO	fighter-director officer; also FIDO
Frances	IJN Yokosuka P1Y Ginga twin-engine fighter-bomber
Frank	JAAF Nakajima Ki-84 Army Type 4 fighter
George	IJN Kawanishi N1K-J Navy interceptor fighter
Hamp	IJN Mitsubishi A6M3 Navy Type 0 carrier fighter Model 32
HVAR	high-velocity aircraft rocket
IJN	Imperial Japanese Navy
Irving	IJN Nakajima J1N Navy Type 2 night-reconnaissance fighter
JAAF	Japanese Army Air Force
Jack	IJN Mitsubishi J2M Navy interceptor fighter
Jake	IJN Aichi E13A Navy Type 0 reconnaissance seaplane

jg	junior grade
Jill	IJN Nakajima B6N Navy carrier attack bomber
Judy	IJN Yokosuka D4Y Navy Type 2 carrier attack bomber
Kate	IJN Nakajima B5N Navy Type 97-1 carrier torpedo bomber
LCI	landing craft infantry
LCS(L)	landing craft support (large)
Lily	JAAF Kawasaki Ki-48 Army Type 99 twin-engine light bomber
LSM	landing ship medium
LST	landing ship tank
MAG	Marine air group
Mavis	IJN Kawanishi H6K Navy Type 97 large flying boat
Myrt	IJN Nakajima C6N Navy carrier reconnaissance aircraft
NAS	Naval Air Station
Nate	JAAF Nakajima Ki-27 Army Type 97 fixed gear fighter
Nick	JAAF Kawasaki Ki-45 Army Type 2 two-seat, twin-engine fighter
Ohka	Yokosuka MXY7 Navy rocket-powered, human-guided kamikaze attack aircraft; Japanese for "cherry blossom"
Oscar	JAAF Nakajima Ki-43 Army Type 1 fighter
PBM	Martin two-engine seaplane
Pete	IJN Mitsubishi F1M Navy Type 0 observation seaplane
Rufe	IJN Nakajima A6M2-N Navy Type 2 interceptor/fighter-bomber floatplanes
Sally	JAAF Mitsubishi Ki-21 Army Type 97 heavy bomber
section	a formation of two planes
Sonia	JAAF Mitsubishi Ki-51 Army Type 99 assault aircraft
Tabby	Showa/Nakajima L2D Navy Type O transport
TF	task force
TG	task group
Tojo	JAAF Nakajima Ki-44 Army Type 2 fighter
Tony	JAAF Kawasaki Ki-61 Army Type 3 fighter
Val	IJN Aichi D3A Navy Type 99 fixed-gear dive bomber
VB	prefix for dive-bomber squadron
VBF	prefix for fighter-bomber squadron
VC	prefix for composite squadron
VF	prefix for fighter squadron
VF(N)	prefix for night-fighter squadron
VMF	prefix for Marine fighter squadron
VT	prefix for torpedo-bomber squadron
VT(N)	prefix for night-torpedo-bomber squadron
Zeke/Zero	IJN Mitsubishi A6M Navy Type 0 carrier fighter

NOTES

PROLOGUE

1. Marshall U. Beebe interview, July 2, 1965.
2. Beebe interview.
3. Y'Blood, *Little Giants*, 2.
4. Noles, *Twenty-Three Minutes to Eternity*, 161–62.
5. Beebe, "Sis–*Liscome Bay* and Toko-Ri."

CHAPTER 1. BALD EAGLE'S WINGS

1. Cleaver, *Pacific Thunder*, 71.
2. Taylor, *Magnificent Mitscher*, 13–20.
3. Taylor, 21–22.
4. Taylor, 25.
5. Frances Smalley Mitscher interviews, Jan. 23–24, 1971, 7, 43.
6. Mitscher interviews, 8–9, 13.
7. Taylor, *Magnificent Mitscher*, 38–40.
8. Frances Smalley Mitscher interviews, 16–17, 19, 25.
9. Taylor, *Magnificent Mitscher*, 139–45.
10. Frances Smalley Mitscher interviews, 36.
11. Mitscher interviews, 12, 49–50.
12. Marc Mitscher, press conference, Dec. 28, 1944, transcript, 4, NARA via Fold3.com.
13. Taylor, *Magnificent Mitscher*, 245.
14. Burke, "Reminiscences," 242–43.
15. Burke, 261–62, 269.
16. Aircraft Action Report, USS *Lexington*, Apr. 23, 1944, NARA via Fold3.com; Burke, "Reminiscences," 270–71.
17. Burke, "Reminiscences," 337–38.
18. Burke, 341–42.
19. Jones and Kelley, *Admiral Arleigh (31-Knot) Burke*, 137–38.

20. Tillman, *Hellcat*, 198.
21. "The History of Fighting 23," VF-23 War History, Feb. 9, 1945, 52, NARA via Fold3.com.
22. Sherman, *Combat Command*, 333.
23. Ewing, *Reaper Leader*, 195–96, 202–3.
24. Ewing, 204–5.
25. Ewing, 206.
26. Ewing, 222–24.
27. Commander, Fast-Carrier Task Force, Pacific, "Action Report," Feb. 10–Mar. 4, 1945, Enclosure C, 1, Serial 0045, NARA via Fold3.com.
28. Commander, Fast-Carrier Task Force, Pacific, 4.
29. Caswell, *Fighting Falcons*, 94.
30. Tilman E. Pool interview, June 30, 2017.
31. Pyle, *Last Chapter*, 47, 51.
32. Jimmy Flatley letter, *Saturday Evening Post*, Dec. 18, 1947.
33. Reynolds, *Fighting Lady*, 227.
34. Coletta, *Admiral Marc A. Mitscher*, 301.

CHAPTER 2. UGAKI'S THUNDER GODS

1. Thomas, *Sea of Thunder*, 9.
2. Goldstein and Dillon, *Fading Victory*, xii.
3. Goldstein and Dillon, 330.
4. Goldstein and Dillon, 355–60.
5. Scott, *Rampage*, 32.
6. Kuwahara and Allred, *Kamikaze*, 121.
7. Goldstein and Dillon, *Fading Victory*, 503.
8. Scott, *Rampage*, 51, 32.
9. Goldstein and Dillon, *Fading Victory*, 531–36.
10. Timenes, *Defense against Kamikaze Attacks in World War II*, 23–25.
11. Timenes, 28, 45.
12. Sears, *At War with the Wind*, 177–78.
13. Sears, 192.
14. Sears, 198, 245.
15. Naito, *Thunder Gods*, 50.
16. Naito, 63, 70.
17. Goldstein and Dillon, *Fading Victory*, 537–38.
18. Belote and Belote, *Typhoon of Steel*, 41–42.
19. Belote and Belote, 42.

CHAPTER 3. HELLCATS, CORSAIRS, AND THE BIG BLUE BLANKET

1. Marshall U. Beebe interview, July 2, 1965.
2. Charles E. Watts interview, June 30, 2017.

3. Watts interview.
4. Watts interview.
5. Ewing, *Reaper Leader*, 205, 228.
6. Tillman, *Hellcat*, 153–54.
7. Cleaver, *Pacific Thunder*, 46; Tillman, *Corsair*, 9–10.
8. Tillman, *Corsair*, 12–13.
9. Tillman, 19.
10. Tillman, 117–20.
11. Tillman, 124, 129; Tillman, *Hellcat*, 198.
12. Hammel, *Aces against Japan II*, 281.
13. Caswell, *My Taking Flight*, 81.
14. Dean Caswell interview, July 22, 2017.
15. Machado, "Meet a WWII Flying Ace!," 14.
16. Pappert, *Landing Was the Easy Part*, 19.
17. Tillman, *Hellcat*, 200.

CHAPTER 4. OPERATION ICEBERG AND THE "MOWING MACHINE"
1. Young, *F6F Hellcat Aces of VF-9*, 40; Bureau of Naval Personnel, *All Hands Naval Bulletin*, 28.
2. Anthony Valencia interview, Sept. 30, 2017; Cheryl Valencia Icard conversations and correspondence, Nov. 16, 2017–Jan. 11, 2018.
3. Carter, "Armitage Field Aviator Knocks Down 24 Jap Planes."
4. Johnson, "Hot Combat Team Is Custom Built," 1.
5. Tillman, *Hellcat*, 201.
6. Harris Mitchell Memoirs, 2.
7. Mitchell Memoirs, 2.
8. Mitchell Memoirs, 1.
9. Mitchell Memoirs, 1.
10. Harris E. Mitchell interview, Jan. 1999.
11. Harris Mitchell Memoirs, 2.
12. Harris E. Mitchell interview, Jan. 1999.
13. Harris Mitchell Memoirs, 3.
14. Harris E. Mitchell interview, Jan. 1999.
15. Harris Mitchell Memoirs, 4.
16. Mitchell Memoirs, 4.
17. Johnson, "Hot Combat Team Is Custom Built," 1.
18. Harris Mitchell Papers, 5.
19. Tillman, *Hellcat*, 201; Johnson, "Hot Combat Team Is Custom Built," 1.
20. Harris Mitchell Papers, 6.
21. Burke, "Reminiscences," 372–73, 360, 431.
22. Harris Mitchell Memoirs, 7.

CHAPTER 5. ACES OVER KYUSHU

1. Caswell, *Fighting Falcons*, 105.
2. Commander, Fast-Carrier Task Force, Pacific, "Action Report," Feb. 10–Mar. 4, 1945, 19, Serial 0045, NARA via Fold3.com.
3. Hammel, *Aces at War*, 82.
4. Mikesh, *Japanese Aircraft Code Names and Designations*, 170–81.
5. Tillman, *Hellcat*, 203.
6. VF-80, War Diary, Feb. 16, 1945, NARA via Fold3.com.
7. Young, *F6F Hellcat Aces of VF-9*, 65.
8. Pearce, *20th Century Guy*, 155.
9. Pearce, 155.
10. Tilman E. Pool interview, June 30, 2017.
11. Harris Mitchell Memoirs, 7; Harris E. Mitchell interview, Jan. 1999.
12. Harris Mitchell Memoirs, 7.
13. Mitchell Memoirs, 8.
14. Mitchell Memoirs, 8.
15. Mitchell Memoirs, 8.
16. Mitchell Memoirs, 9.
17. Mitchell Memoirs, 9.
18. Tilman E. Pool interview, June 30, 2017.
19. Robert C. Good interview, n.d.
20. Good interview.
21. Valencia, *Knights of the Sky*, 137.
22. Robert C. Good interview, n.d.
23. Valencia, *Knights of the Sky*, 137.
24. Tilman E. Pool interview, June 30, 2017.
25. Pool interview.
26. Tillman, *Hellcat Aces of World War 2*, 64.
27. VF-45, Action Reports, Feb. 16, 1945, NARA via Fold3.com; Tillman, *Hellcat Aces of World War 2*, 64.
28. Tillman, *Corsair*, 130–31.
29. Caswell, *Fighting Falcons*, 97–98.
30. Charles E. Watts interview, June 30, 2017.
31. Watts interview.
32. Olynyk, *USMC Credits for the Destruction of Enemy Aircraft*, 54; Olynyk, *USN Credits for the Destruction of Enemy Aircraft*, 132–41; Tillman, *Hellcat*, 206.
33. Pearce, *20th Century Guy*, 155.
34. Harris Mitchell Memoirs, 10.
35. Mitchell Memoirs, 10.
36. VBF-3, Aircraft Action Report 5, USS *Yorktown*, Feb. 17, 1945, NARA via Fold3.com; Reynolds, *Fighting Lady*, 233.
37. Valencia, *Knights of the Sky*, 138.
38. Niderost, "Ace in a Day."

39. Valencia, *Knights of the Sky*, 138.
40. Pearce, *20th Century Guy*, 156.
41. Pearce, 156.
42. Olynyk, *USMC Credits for the Destruction of Enemy Aircraft*, 53–55; Olynyk, *USN Credits for the Destruction of Enemy Aircraft*, 132–43; Tillman, *Hellcat*, 207; Tillman, *Corsair*, 132; Morison, *Victory in the Pacific*, 25.

CHAPTER 6. CRUEL FORTUNES AT CHICHI JIMA
1. Goldstein and Dillon, *Fading Victory*, 538.
2. Goldstein and Dillon, 539.
3. Goldstein and Dillon, 540.
4. Reynolds, *Fighting Lady*, 174–76; Bradley, *Flyboys*, 263–68.
5. Bradley, *Flyboys*, 268.
6. Bradley, 269–72, 484–86.
7. Hyams, *Flight of the Avenger*, 107–19.
8. Bruce and Leonard, *Crommelin's Thunderbirds*, 71.
9. Bradley, *Flyboys*, 294–95.
10. Park, "Ace of San Juan"; Willis E. Hardy interview, June 27, 2017.
11. Willis E. Hardy interview, June 27, 2017.
12. VT-82, Aircraft Action Report 4-45, USS *Bennington*, Feb. 18 1945, NARA via Fold3.com.
13. Morison, *Victory in the Pacific*, 34.
14. Tillman, *Corsair*, 132.
15. Dye and O'Neill, *Road to Victory*, 224.
16. Caswell, *My Taking Flight*, 87.
17. Morison, *Victory in the Pacific*, 50.
18. "Last Letter of Flight Petty Officer 2nd Class Kunio Shimizu to His Parents," Kamikaze Images, trans. Bill Gordon, May, August 2018, www.kamikazeimages.net/writings/shimizu-kunio/index.htm.
19. Richard (Schwendemann) Mann interview, Oct. 25, 2017.
20. Y'Blood, *Little Giants*, 331.
21. Y'Blood, 332.
22. Y'Blood, 333–34.
23. Robert M. Campbell oral history, n.d., 9–17.
24. Graff, *Strike and Return*, 51.
25. Coletta, *Admiral Marc A. Mitscher*, 304.
26. Morison, *Victory in the Pacific*, 54.
27. Donald L. Warner interview, Sept. 1, 2018.
28. [Anonymous], "Nite Life," 2-31–2-32.
29. MacGlashing, *Batmen*, 28.
30. MacGlashing, 19–20.
31. Harris Mitchell Memoirs, 10.
32. VMF-112/123, Aircraft Action Report 15-45, USS *Bennington*, Feb. 23, 1945, NARA via Fold3.com.

33. Bradley, *Flyboys*, 219–23.
34. Bradley, 223–24.
35. Bradley, 225–28.
36. Bradley, 232–46.
37. Bradley, 281–88.
38. VMF-112/123, Aircraft Action Report 16-45, USS *Bennington*, Feb. 25, 1945, NARA via Fold3.com.
39. Caswell, *My Taking Flight*, 85.
40. Tillman, *Corsair*, 133–34.
41. "Cracked by Flak," Statement on Survival by Lieutenant James S. Moore, Jr., Mar. 10, 1945, VT(N)-90, Pacific Fleet, NARA via Fold3.com; CAG 90 (Night), "Report of Air Operations against the Bonin Islands, 2/24/45–3/9/45," Mar. 11, 1945, NARA via Fold3.com.
42. "Nite Life," 2-36.
43. Morison, *Victory in the Pacific*, 57–58.
44. VMF-112/123, Aircraft Action Report 17-45, USS *Bennington*, Mar. 1, 1945, NARA via Fold3.com.
45. Hackett, Kingsepp, and Cundall, "IJN *Kinezaki*."
46. Hackett, Kingsepp, and Cundall.
47. VT-82, Aircraft Action Report 10-45, USS *Bennington*, Mar. 1, 1945, NARA via Fold3.com.
48. VT-30, Aircraft Action Report 22, USS *Belleau Wood*, Mar. 1, 1945, NARA via Fold3.com.
49. Hackett, Kingsepp, and Cundall, "IJN Minelayer *Tsubame*."
50. USS *Bluefish* (SS-222), "Report of War Patrol Number Seven," Mar. 24 1945, 7, NARA via Fold3.com.
51. Commander, Fast-Carrier Task Force, Pacific, "Action Report," Feb. 10–Mar. 4, 1945, 3–4, Serial 0045, NARA via Fold3.com.
52. Sherman, *Combat Command*, 342.

CHAPTER 7. OKINAWA PRELUDE

1. Pearce, *20th Century Guy*, 159; Caswell, *My Taking Flight*, 90.
2. Tilman E. Pool interview, Aug. 8, 2017.
3. Commander, TF 58, "Action Report of Operations of U.S.S. *Enterprise* in Support of the Amphibious Assault on Iwo Jima, 10 February to 23 February 1944—Phase I," Mar. 7, 1945, Serial 0343, NARA via Fold3.com.
4. [Cunningham], "Franklin Thomas Goodson," Mar. 13, 1945.
5. Tillman, *Corsair*, 134–35.
6. Tillman, 135–36.
7. Erickson, *Tail End Charlies!*, 76.
8. Goldstein and Dillon, *Fading Victory*, 547–48.
9. Goldstein and Dillon, 551; Kennedy, *Danger's Hour*, 190–92.
10. Goldstein and Dillon, *Fading Victory*, 550–51.

11. Bruce and Leonard, *Crommelin's Thunderbirds*, 84–87.
12. Bruce and Leonard, 89.
13. Coletta, *Admiral Marc A. Mitscher*, 306–7.
14. Donald McPherson interview, July 25, 2017; Hammel, *Aces at War*, 77.
15. Lawrence A. Clark interview, Nov. 24, 2006.
16. Pappert, *Landing Was the Easy Part*, 2, 7.
17. Taylor, *Magnificent Mitscher*, 277.
18. Morison, *Victory in the Pacific*, 86–90.
19. Belote and Belote, *Typhoon of Steel*, 37.
20. Belote and Belote, 22.
21. Watson A. Crumbie interviews, Aug. 14, 15, 2017.
22. Crumbie, "My Time as a Marine. Chapter One."
23. Crumbie, "My Time as a Marine. Chapter Two."
24. Melvin Heckt, "Pacific Diary," 23, Heckt Papers.
25. Heckt, 24.

CHAPTER 8. "A WILD DOGFIGHT ENSUED"

1. Goldstein and Dillon, *Fading Victory*, 552–54.
2. Naito, *Thunder Gods*, 93–94.
3. Naito, 94.
4. Naito, 94.
5. Naito, 94–95.
6. Goldstein and Dillon, *Fading Victory*, 555.
7. MacGlashing, *Batmen*, 22; [Cunningham], "Franklin Thomas Goodson," Mar. 18, 1945.
8. Caswell, *My Taking Flight*, 99.
9. Tilman E. Pool interview, Aug. 8, 2017.
10. Sherman, *Combat Command*, 353.
11. Robert C. Coats interview, n.d.
12. Robert C. Good interview, n.d.
13. Valencia, *Knights of the Sky*, 139.
14. Robert C. Good interview, n.d.
15. Tilman E. Pool interview, Aug. 8, 2017.
16. Ralph C. Hovis interview, 1995.
17. Jack M. Lyons interview, July 23, 2018.
18. Robert C. Good interview, n.d.
19. Pearce, *20th Century Guy*, 161.
20. Pearce, 161.
21. Tilman E. Pool interview, Aug. 8, 2017.
22. Pearce, *20th Century Guy*, 163.
23. Caswell, *My Taking Flight*, 99, 101.
24. Reynolds, *Fighting Lady*, 252.
25. Wallace, "War Diary," Mar. 18, 1945. See also Wallace, *Wally's War*, 13.

26. Wallace, "First Time Out!"
27. Sakaida, *Imperial Japanese Navy Aces*, 81–85.
28. Sakaida, 81, 85.
29. Wallace, "First Time Out!"
30. Pappert, *Landing Was the Easy Part*, 11.
31. Wallace, "First Time Out!"
32. Sakaida, *Imperial Japanese Navy Aces*, 85, 104.

CHAPTER 9. SAVING *FRANKLIN*
1. MacGlashing, *Batmen*, 28.
2. CAG 9, Action Reports, Mar. 19 1945, NARA via Fold3.com.
3. Night Air Group 90, Aircraft Action Reports, "Operations against Enemy Targets on Kyushu and the Inland Sea, 18–20 March 1945," 46–50, NARA via Fold3.com.
4. Hoehling, *Franklin Comes Home*, 26.
5. Carroll, "Sam Ferrante's Lucky Day Is March 19," 1A; Cdr. Joe Taylor, "Report to Commanding Officer," Apr. 11, 1945, USS *Franklin*, Report of Air Operations, Enclosure C, 45, NARA via Fold3.com.
6. Springer, *Inferno*, 198.
7. USS *Franklin*, Report of Air Operations, 65, NARA via Fold3.com; Satterfield, *Saving Big Ben*, 65, 86.
8. Ridgley D. Radney oral history, n.d.
9. McCoy, "Eyewitness Describes Wreck," 3.
10. McCoy, 3.
11. VF-5, Aircraft Action Report, Mar. 19, 1945, NARA via Fold3.com.
12. Springer, *Inferno*, 201–2.
13. USS *Wasp*, War Diary, Mar. 1–31, 1945, 10, NARA via Fold3.com; *The Waspirit* 29, no. 4, 2004, 2. *The Waspirit* is the quarterly publication of the USS *Wasp* Association.
14. Morison, *Victory in the Pacific*, 57, 94–95.
15. Commander TF 58, "Action Report from 14 March through 28 May 1945," June 18, 1945, 3, Serial 00222, NARA via Fold3.com.
16. USS *Franklin*, Report of Air Operations, Mar. 19, 1945, 4, NARA via Fold3.com.
17. Hoehling, *Franklin Comes Home*, 64–65.
18. Springer, *Inferno*, 231.
19. Springer, 297–98.
20. MacGregor Kilpatrick Navy Cross citation, Hall of Valor Project, valor.militarytimes.com/hero/19310; Hoehling, *Franklin Comes Home*, 81.
21. Hoehling, *Franklin Comes Home*, 53, 69–70.
22. Joseph Timothy O'Callahan Medal of Honor citation, Congressional Medal of Honor Society, www.cmohs.org/recipient-detail/2921/o-callahan-joseph-timothy.php; Cdr. Joe Taylor, "Narrative of Action 19 March 1945," USS *Franklin*, Report of Air Operations, Enclosure C, 2, NARA via Fold3.com.

23. Robert Blanchard oral history, n.d. (video removed).
24. Taylor, *Magnificent Mitscher*, 278.
25. Aircraft Action Reports, USS *Hornet*, Mar. 19, 1945, NARA via Fold3.com.
26. Young, *F6F Hellcat Aces of VF-9*, 73–74.
27. Wallace, *Wally's War*, 20.
28. Air Group 82, Aircraft Action Report, USS *Bennington*, Mar. 19, 1945, NARA via Fold3.com.
29. "Statement of Lt. Charles L. Carper," VB-84, Action Report, in CAG 84, Action Reports, USS *Bunker Hill*, Mar. 19, 1945, NARA via Fold3.com.
30. "Statement of Carper."
31. Pearce, *20th Century Guy*, 164.
32. Sakaida, *Imperial Japanese Navy Aces*, 78.
33. Charles E. Watts interview, June 30, 2017.
34. Watts interview.
35. Sakaida, *Imperial Japanese Navy Aces*, 92–93.
36. Sakaida, 93.
37. Robert Hal Jackson oral history, July 24, 1997, 55.
38. Harry F. Hunt interview, 1995; Sidney R. Overall interview, 1995; George F. Smith interview, 1995; Grant C. Young interviews, 1995; Moore, *Buzzard Brigade*, 252.
39. Ridgley D. Radney oral history, n.d.
40. Walter E. Clarke interview, Jan. 1990, 8.
41. Hackett and Cundall, "IJN *Shimane Maru*."
42. Lawrence A. Clark interview, Nov. 24, 2006.
43. Clark interview.
44. Hammel, *Aces at War*, 79–80; Donald McPherson interview, July 25, 2017.
45. Hammel, *Aces at War*, 80.
46. Donald McPherson interview, July 25, 2017.

CHAPTER 10. "A FIGHTER PILOT'S DREAM"
1. Goldstein and Dillon, *Fading Victory*, 556.
2. Goldstein and Dillon, 557.
3. Burke, "Reminiscences," 435–36.
4. Burke, 436.
5. Goldstein and Dillon, *Fading Victory*, 558.
6. Goldstein and Dillon, 558.
7. Naito, *Thunder Gods*, 96–97.
8. Naito, 97.
9. Naito, 97–98.
10. Naito, 98–99; Sheftall, *Blossoms in the Wind*, 149.
11. Naito, *Thunder Gods*, 99–100.
12. Naito, 101.
13. Goldstein and Dillon, *Fading Victory*, 558.

14. Hammel, *Aces at War*, 83.
15. Naito, *Thunder Gods*, 102–3.
16. Hammel, *Aces at War*, 84; Pearce, *20th Century Guy*, 166.
17. Hammel, *Aces at War*, 84.
18. Hammel, 85.
19. VF-30, Aircraft Action Report, Mar. 21, 1945, NARA via Fold3.com.
20. VF-30, Aircraft Action Report.
21. Pearce, *20th Century Guy*, 168.
22. Hammel, *Aces at War*, 85.
23. Naito, *Thunder Gods*, 103–6.
24. Pearce, *20th Century Guy*, 169–71.
25. Leon Frankel oral history, n.d., 13, 20–21.
26. Frankel oral history, 38.
27. Reynolds, *On the Warpath in the Pacific*, 411.
28. Reynolds, 411–12.
29. VF-45, Action Report, USS *San Jacinto*, Mar. 28, 1945, NARA via Fold3.com.
30. Hammel, *Aces against Japan*, 258.
31. Hammel, 259.
32. Hammel, 259–61.
33. Hammel, 262–65.
34. Sidney Overall interview, 1995; William M. Banta interview, Aug. 31, 2018.
35. Dopking, "Navy Pilots Find Good Hunting," 3.
36. Norwald Richard Quiel interview, Feb. 20, 2004.
37. Quiel interview.
38. Quiel interview.
39. Reynolds, *On the Warpath in the Pacific*, 412.
40. Lt. (jg) Ronald Lee Somerville statement, in Air Group 6, Aircraft Action Report, NARA via Fold3.com; VB-6, Aircraft Action Report 11, in CAG 6, "Squadron ACA Reports on Air Operations against Japan, Ryukyus and Jap Task Force, 3/18/45–4/7/45," ibid.; VT-6, Aircraft Action Report 11, ibid.; CAG 6, Aircraft Action Report 11, ibid.
41. VF-6, Action Report 17, Mar. 29, 1945, NARA via Fold3.com.
42. Pearce, *20th Century Guy*, 172–73.
43. Robert C. Coats interview, n.d.
44. Naito, *Thunder Gods*, 105.
45. Naito, 105–7.
46. Naito, 107–9.
47. Goldstein and Dillon, *Fading Victory*, 566.

CHAPTER 11. LOVE DAY LANDINGS ON OKINAWA

1. Naito, *Thunder Gods*, 72–73, 112–13.
2. Naito, 112–13.
3. VF-10, Aircraft Action Report 39, Mar. 31, 1945, NARA via Fold3.com.

4. Naito, *Thunder Gods*, 113.
5. Naito, 113–15.
6. Hackett, "IJN Ohka Type 11 Operations at Okinawa."
7. Belote and Belote, *Typhoon of Steel*, 64.
8. Caswell, *Fighting Falcons*, 128.
9. Caswell, 129–30.
10. Caswell, 130.
11. Tillman, *Hellcat*, 211.
12. Charles E. Watts interview, June 30, 2017.
13. Robert Eugene Dumont, Personal Diary, Apr. 1, 1945.
14. Dumont, Personal Diary, Apr. 1, 1945.
15. Watson A. Crumbie interview, Aug. 14, 2017.
16. Melvin Heckt, "Pacific Diary," 24, Heckt Papers.
17. Belote and Belote, *Typhoon of Steel*, 71–72; Mel Heckt, interview by Al Zdon, 6, Heckt Papers.
18. Belote and Belote, *Typhoon of Steel*, 27–29.
19. Belote and Belote, 78–79, 88–90.
20. Heckt, "Pacific Diary," 24–25, Heckt Papers; Mel Heckt interview, 6.
21. Heckt, "Pacific Diary," 24–25.
22. Commander, TF 58, "Action Report from 14 March through 28 May, 1945," June 18, 1945, 7, Serial 00222, NARA via Fold3.com.
23. Naito, *Thunder Gods*, 117–18.
24. Hammel, *Aces against Japan II*, 252.
25. Caswell, *My Taking Flight*, 105.
26. Harris E. Mitchell interview, Jan. 1999.
27. Mitchell interview.
28. Mitchell interview.
29. Goldstein and Dillon, *Fading Victory*, 570.
30. Goldstein and Dillon, 571; Sheftall, *Blossoms in the Wind*, 65.
31. Goldstein and Dillon, *Fading Victory*, 571.
32. Sakaida, *Imperial Japanese Navy Aces*, 79–80.
33. Sakaida, 572.

CHAPTER 12. "TURKEY SHOOT"
1. Rielly, *Kamikazes, Corsairs, and Picket Ships*, 109.
2. USS *Bougainville*, War Diary, Apr. 1945, 3–4, NARA via Fold3.com.
3. Harris Mitchell Memoirs, 14.
4. Naito, *Thunder Gods*, 120.
5. Naito, 121.
6. "Last letter of Second Lieutenant Kenji Tomizawa," trans. Bill Gordon, May 2012, Kamikaze Images, www.kamikazeimages.net/writings/tomizawa/index.htm.
7. "Last letter of Ensign Shunsuke Yukawa," trans. Bill Gordon, March 2018, Kamikaze Images, www.kamikazeimages.net/writings/yukawa/index.htm.

8. VMF-112, Aircraft Action Report, Apr. 6, 1945, NARA via Fold3.com.
9. Tilman E. Pool interview, July 2, 2017.
10. Valencia, *Knights of the Sky*, 142.
11. Gandt, *Twilight Warriors*, 222–23; Reynolds, *On the Warpath in the Pacific*, 412–13.
12. Sears, *At War with the Wind*, 312.
13. Rielly, *Kamikazes, Corsairs, and Picket Ships*, 112; USS *Bush*, Action Report, "Okinawa Operation, 15 March to 6 April 1945," Apr. 24, 1945, NARA via Fold3.com.
14. Rielly, *Kamikazes, Corsairs, and Picket Ships*, 108.
15. Cdr. George R. Wilson, interview, May 11, 1945, 8, U.S. Navy Personal Interviews, Fold3.com.
16. Donald McPherson interview, July 25, 2017.
17. McPherson interview, July 25, 2017.
18. Lawrence A. Clark interview, Nov. 24, 2006.
19. Clark interview.
20. VF-30, Aircraft Action Report 35-45, USS *Belleau Wood*, Apr. 6, 1945, NARA via Fold3.com.
21. Reynolds, *On the Warpath in the Pacific*, 413.
22. Cleaver, *Tidal Wave*, 177.
23. Cleaver, 178.
24. Cleaver, 178.
25. VF-82, Aircraft Action Report, Apr. 6, 1945, NARA via Fold3.com.
26. VF-82, Aircraft Action Report, Apr. 6, 1945.
27. Willis E. Hardy interview, June 27, 2017.
28. Rielly, *Kamikazes, Corsairs, and Picket Ships*, 108.
29. Sears, *At War with the Wind*, 316, 318.
30. "Third Set of Memories: Lost at Okinawa," USS *Bush*—DD529.
31. "Third Set of Memories: Lost at Okinawa."
32. Coit Butler recollections, in "Third Set of Memories: Lost at Okinawa."
33. Mann, "Heroes among Us," 1.
34. William S. Hurley interview, Mar. 1, 2006.
35. Cdr. George R. Wilson, interview, May 11, 1945, 10, U.S. Navy Personal Interviews, Fold3.com.
36. Caswell, *Fighting Falcons*, 131.
37. Lt. John J. Griffin, "Action and Report of Sinking of USS *Emmons* (DMS 22), 6 April 1945," 2, NARA via Fold3.com.
38. Griffin, 2.
39. USS *Rodman*, Action Report, Apr. 6, 1945, NARA via Fold3.com.
40. Belote and Belote, *Typhoon of Steel*, 110.
41. Edwin Hoffman, "USS Emmons Testimonial."
42. Billingsley, *Emmons Saga*, 337–39.
43. Hoffman, "USS Emmons Testimonial."
44. Anthony Esposito interview, Apr. 8, 2019.

45. Armond Jolley interview, Aug. 19, 2018.
46. Hoffman, "USS Emmons Testimonial."
47. Hoffman.
48. Anthony Esposito interview, Apr. 8, 2019.
49. Lt. John J. Griffin, "Action and Report of Sinking of USS *Emmons* (DMS 22), 6 April 1945," 3, NARA via Fold3.com.
50. Herr, "Doomed."
51. Willis E. Hardy interviews, June 27, July 8, 2017.
52. Hardy interviews.
53. Hardy interviews.
54. Hardy interviews.
55. Hardy interviews.
56. Hardy interviews.
57. Hardy interviews.
58. Hardy interviews.
59. Belote and Belote, *Typhoon of Steel*, 116.
60. Sears, *At War with the Wind*, 326.
61. Spurr, *Glorious Way to Die*, 172.
62. Ikeda, "Imperial Navy's Final Sortie," 34–36.
63. Spurr, *Glorious Way to Die*, 173.
64. Spurr, 181–84.
65. Spurr, 185–86; Blair, *Silent Victory*, 806.
66. Spurr, *Glorious Way to Die*, 200–203.
67. Bang, "Matter of Honor"; Bang, "Thoughts of a Young Sailor."
68. Spurr, *Glorious Way to Die*, 200–203, 216–17.
69. Burke, "Reminiscences," 441–42.

CHAPTER 13. GET *YAMATO*

1. Charles Hubenthal interview, May 7, 2011; Jack M. Lyons interview, July 23, 2018.
2. Campbell, *Save Our Souls*, 487.
3. Jack M. Lyons interview, July 23, 2018.
4. Ikeda, "Imperial Navy's Final Sortie," 34–43.
5. Yoshida, *Requiem for Battleship* Yamato, xxii–xxiii, 47.
6. Hara, *Japanese Destroyer Captain*, 287–88.
7. Ikeda, "Imperial Navy's Final Sortie," 34–43.
8. Hara, *Japanese Destroyer Captain*, 288–90.
9. Spurr, *Glorious Way to Die*, 218.
10. Burke, "Reminiscences," 442–43.
11. Burke, 443.
12. Sears, *At War with the Wind*, 331–32.
13. Kennedy, *Danger's Hour*, 204–5.
14. Tilman E. Pool interview, Aug. 8, 2017.

15. Key sources for this chapter are the individual action reports for each air group involved. Those used for this section are Air Group 82, Aircraft Action Reports, USS *Bennington*, Apr. 7, 1945, NARA via Fold3.com; VF-45, Aircraft Action Report 56-11, USS *San Jacinto*, Apr. 7, 1945, ibid.; Air Group 17, Aircraft Action Reports, USS *Hornet*, Apr. 7, 1945, ibid.; and VF-30 and VT-30, Aircraft Action Reports, USS *Belleau Wood*, Apr. 7, 1945, ibid.

16. Reynolds, *Fighting Lady*, 272.

17. Erickson, *Tail End Charlies!*, 110.

18. Spurr, *Glorious Way to Die*, 220–21.

19. VPB-21, Squadron History, Mar. 1–June 1, 1945, 7–8, NARA via Fold3.com.

20. Spurr, *Glorious Way to Die*, 225–26.

21. VB-82, Aircraft Action Report 37, USS *Bennington*, Apr. 7, 1945, NARA via Fold3.com.

22. Tilman E. Pool interview, Aug. 8, 2017.

23. Spurr, *Glorious Way to Die*, 235–36.

24. Spurr, 236.

25. Lollar, "Pilot Recalls Sinking of Battleship *Yamato*," 1.

26. Spurr, *Glorious Way to Die*, 243.

27. Lollar, "Pilot Recalls Sinking of Battleship *Yamato*."

28. CAG 83, Action Reports, USS *Bennington*, Apr. 7, 1945, NARA via Fold3.com.

29. VT-82, Aircraft Action Report 37, USS *Bennington*, Apr. 7, 1945, NARA via Fold3.com.

30. Spurr, *Glorious Way to Die*, 245–46.

31. Robert C. Good interview, n.d.

32. Spurr, *Glorious Way to Die*, 245.

33. Spurr, 248–49.

34. VT-37, VF-37–45, VT-30, and VF-30, Aircraft Action Reports, USS *Belleau Wood*, Apr. 7, 1945, NARA via Fold3.com.

35. Statements of Lt. (jg). W. E. Delaney, in VT-37, VF-37–45, VT-30, and VF-30, Aircraft Action Reports, USS *Belleau Wood*, Apr. 7, 1945, 4, NARA via Fold3.com.

36. Ford, *Torpedo-Squadron-30*, 64–65.

37. CAG 84, Aircraft Action Report, Apr. 7, 1945, NARA via Fold3.com.

38. Nevitt, "IJN *Asashimo*."

39. Hara, *Japanese Destroyer Captain*, 269, 282.

40. Hara, 291.

41. Ikeda, "Imperial Navy's Final Sortie," 34–43.

42. Hara, *Japanese Destroyer Captain*, 292.

43. Hackett and Kingsepp, "IJN Battleship *Yamato*."

44. Yoshida, *Requiem for Battleship* Yamato, 64.

45. Hackett and Kingsepp, "IJN Battleship *Yamato*."

46. Yoshida, *Requiem for Battleship* Yamato, 68–72.

47. CAG 83, Aircraft Action Report, Apr. 7, 1945, NARA via Fold3.com.

48. Guptill, "Notes of the Attack on the *Yamato*."

49. Spurr, *Glorious Way to Die*, 264.
50. Wallace, "Wally's War," 19.
51. Air Group 47, Aircraft Action Report, USS *Bataan*, Apr. 7, 1945, 3, NARA via Fold3.com.
52. Astor, "Japanese Battleship *Yamato* Makes Its Final Stand."
53. Air Group 84, Aircraft Action Report, Apr. 7, 1945, NARA via Fold3.com.
54. Kennedy, *Danger's Hour*, 206.
55. Kennedy, 207–8.
56. Air Group 84, Aircraft Action Report, Apr. 7, 1945, NARA via Fold3.com.
57. CAG 29, Aircraft Action Report, Apr. 7, 1945, NARA via Fold3.com.
58. Hudson, *History of the USS* Cabot, 104; Astor, *Operation Iceberg*, 213–14.
59. Wallace, "Wally's War," 19.
60. Edward Pappert interview, Aug. 1, 2018.
61. Air Group 83, Aircraft Action Report, Apr. 7, 1945, NARA via Fold3.com.
62. Statements of Lt. (jg) W. E. Delaney, in VT-37, VF-37–VF-45, Aircraft Action Reports, USS *Belleau Wood*, Apr. 7, 1945, 5, NARA via Fold3.com.
63. Statements of Lt. (jg) W. E. Delaney.
64. Spurr, *Glorious Way to Die*, 273–74; Hackett and Kingsepp, "IJN Battleship *Yamato.*"
65. Bang, "Thoughts of a Young Sailor."
66. Yoshida, *Requiem for Battleship* Yamato, 85–86, 92–94.
67. Hara, *Japanese Destroyer Captain*, 293.
68. Ikeda, "Imperial Navy's Final Sortie," 34–43.
69. Hara, *Japanese Destroyer Captain*, 294.
70. Spurr, *Glorious Way to Die*, 280–81.
71. Spurr, 294–95.
72. Moore, *Buzzard Brigade*, 275; John C. Lawrence interview, 1995.
73. McWilliams, "Pilots Tell about Sinking Jap Battleship," 16; Erickson, *Tail End Charlies!*, 112–13.
74. Wesley Hays interview, Apr. 28, 2016.
75. Sidney R. Overall interview, 1995; Ralph D. Botten interview, 1995; Robert Rock interview, 1995; Harry F. Hunt interview, 1995.
76. McWilliams, "Pilots Tell about Sinking Jap Battleship," 16.
77. Grant C. Young interview, 1995.
78. Young interview.
79. Buchanan, *Helldiver's Vengeance*, 263.
80. McWilliams, "Pilots Tell about Sinking Jap Battleship," 16.
81. Buchanan, *Helldiver's Vengeance*, 268.
82. Hara, *Japanese Destroyer Captain*, 297.
83. CAG 10, Aircraft Action Report, Apr. 7, 1945, NARA via Fold3.com.
84. Leon Frankel oral history, n.d., 31.
85. Frankel oral history, 31.
86. Reynolds, *Fighting Lady*, 275–77; VT-9, Aircraft Action Report, Apr. 7, 1945, 5, NARA via Fold3.com.

87. Air Group 83, Aircraft Action Report, Apr. 7, 1945, NARA via Fold3.com.

88. Leon Frankel oral history, n.d., 32.

89. Reynolds, *Fighting Lady*, 279.

90. Hara, *Japanese Destroyer Captain*, 297–99.

91. Ikeda, "Imperial Navy's Final Sortie," 34–36.

92. Hara, *Japanese Destroyer Captain*, 299; Hackett and Kingsepp, "IJN *Yahagi*."

93. Yoshida, *Requiem for Battleship* Yamato, 98–102.

94. Sasaki, "Wartime Sailors Recall Loss of Japanese Fleet's *Isokaze, Yamato*."

95. Sasaki.

96. Spurr, *Glorious Way to Die*, 290–91.

97. Bang, "Thoughts of a Young Sailor."

98. Bang.

99. Yoshida, *Requiem for Battleship* Yamato, 107–8.

100. Yoshida, 113–21.

101. Spurr, *Glorious Way to Die*, 296.

102. Bang, "Matter of Honor."

103. Astor, "Japanese Battleship *Yamato* Makes Its Final Stand"; John C. Lawrence interview, 1995; Leon Frankel oral history, n.d., 32.

104. Spurr, *Glorious Way to Die*, 308; Hackett and Kingsepp, "IJN Battleship *Yamato*"; Ikeda, "Imperial Navy's Final Sortie," 34–43.

105. Ikeda, "Imperial Navy's Final Sortie," 40–43.

106. Bang, "Matter of Honor."

107. Statements of Lt. (jg) W. E. Delaney, in VT-37, VF-37–VF-45, Aircraft Action Reports, USS *Belleau Wood*, Apr. 7, 1945, 6, NARA via Fold3.com.

108. Guptill, "Notes of the Attack on the *Yamato*," 2.

109. Buchanan, *Helldiver's Vengeance*, 274.

110. Erickson, *Tail End Charlies!*, 112.

111. Spurr, *Glorious Way to Die*, 312.

CHAPTER 14. "LIKE WOLVES AT A KILL"

1. Goldstein and Dillon, *Fading Victory*, 575.

2. Naito, *Thunder Gods*, 123.

3. Rielly, *Kamikazes, Corsairs, and Picket Ships*, 122.

4. Rielly, 123–24.

5. Walter E. Clarke interview, Jan. 1990, 7, 8.

6. Air Group 83, Aircraft Action Report, Apr. 7, 1945, NARA via Fold3.com.

7. Sears, *At War with the Wind*, 337.

8. USS *Hancock*, War Diary, Apr. 1945, 7 NARA via Fold3.com.

9. *Hancock*, War Diary, Apr. 1945, 12.

10. *Hancock*, War Diary, Apr. 1945, 12.

11. Harris Mitchell Memoirs, 14–15.

12. Mitchell, 15.

13. Burke, "Reminiscences," 445–46.

14. Commander, Naval Air Bases, War Diary, Apr. 7, 1945, Serial 3256, NARA via Fold3.com; Sambito, *History of Marine Attack Squadron 311*, 7.
15. USS *Breton* (CVE 23), Action Report, "Capture of Okinawa," Apr. 7, 1945, NARA via Fold3.com.
16. William Farrell interview, Aug. 1989, 5.
17. Watson A. Crumbie interviews, Aug. 14, 15, 2017; Crumbie, "My Time as a Marine. Chapter Three: Okinawa."
18. Gandt, *Twilight Warriors*, 217.
19. Belote and Belote, *Typhoon of Steel*, 131–32.
20. Belote and Belote, 135–39.
21. Belote and Belote, 144.
22. MacGlashing, *Batmen*, 26.
23. Reynolds, *Fighting Lady*, 285.
24. For a summary of how author Akira Kachi determined the identity of the two kamikaze pilots who attacked the *Missouri*, see review of *Senkan mizuri ni totsunyu shita reisen* (Zero fighter that crashed into battleship *Missouri*; Kojinsha, 2005), Kamikaze Images, www.kamikazeimages.net/books/japanese/kachi/index.htm.
25. Troy, "American Who Buried a Kamikaze Enemy."
26. Troy.
27. Troy.

CHAPTER 15. CHERRY BLOSSOM FIRES
1. Goldstein and Dillon, *Fading Victory*, 580.
2. Rielly, *Kamikazes, Corsairs, and Picket Ships*, 128–30.
3. Sheftall, *Blossoms in the Wind*, 268, 279–80.
4. Sheftall, 268, 281–83.
5. Cole, "USS *Missouri* Hosts Kamikaze Artifacts," 1.
6. Naito, *Thunder Gods*, 125.
7. Valencia, *Knights of the Sky*, 142.
8. Hammel, *Aces against Japan II*, 260.
9. Hammel, 260.
10. Hammel, 261–62.
11. Caswell, *My Taking Flight*, 107.
12. Caswell, 107.
13. Gandt, *Twilight Warriors*, 239.
14. Gandt, 241.
15. Gandt, 237–38.
16. Rielly, *Kamikazes, Corsairs, and Picket Ships*, 132.
17. Gandt, *Twilight Warriors*, 237.
18. Rielly, *Kamikazes, Corsairs, and Picket Ships*, 136–37.
19. Rielly, 139–42.
20. "Gunnery Officer's Report," USS *Mannert L. Abele*, Action Report, Mar. 20–Apr. 12, 1945, App. 2, Enclosure B, 2, NARA via Fold3.com.

21. Naito, *Thunder Gods*, 125–26.
22. Naito, 126.
23. Naito, 127–28.
24. "Gunnery Officer's Report," USS *Mannert L. Abele*, Action Report, Mar. 20–Apr. 12, 1945, App. 2, Enclosure B, 3, NARA via Fold3.com; "Kamikazes," episode 1, season 2, of *Dogfights*.
25. "First Lieutenant's Report," USS *Mannert L. Abele*, Action Report, Mar. 20–Apr. 12, 1945, App. 5, Enclosure B, 1, NARA via Fold3.com.
26. "Executive Officer's Report," USS *Mannert L. Abele*, Action Report, Mar. 20–Apr. 12, 1945, App. 1, Enclosure B, 1–2, NARA via Fold3.com.
27. Veesenmeyer, *Kamikaze Terror*, 67–68.
28. "Assistant First Lieutenant's Report," USS *Mannert L. Abele*, Action Report, Mar. 20–Apr. 12, 1945, App. 6, Enclosure B, 1, NARA via Fold3.com.
29. USS *Lindsey*, Action Report, Mar. 24–Apr. 12, 1945, NARA via Fold3.com.
30. Tillman, *U.S. Marine Corps Fighter Squadrons of World War II*, 74.
31. Rielly, *Kamikazes, Corsairs, and Picket Ships*, 153–54.

CHAPTER 16. "I'LL NEVER ABANDON SHIP"
1. McWhorter, *First Hellcat Ace*, 174–76.
2. Sherman, *Combat Command*, 360.
3. Harris Mitchell Memoirs, 14.
4. Mitchell Memoirs, 14.
5. Goldstein and Dillon, *Fading Victory*, 583–84.
6. Naito, *Thunder Gods*, 131.
7. Naito, 132.
8. Naito, 132–33.
9. Charles E. Watts interview, June 30, 2017.
10. VF-30, Aircraft Action Report, Apr. 14, 1945, NARA via Fold3.com.
11. Rielly, *Kamikazes, Corsairs, and Picket Ships*, 157.
12. Caswell, *Fighting Falcons*, 122.
13. Sakaida, *Imperial Japanese Navy Aces*, 91.
14. Sakaida, 91.
15. Wallace, *Wally's War*, 21.
16. Rielly, *Kamikazes, Corsairs, and Picket Ships*, 158–59.
17. Goldstein and Dillon, *Fading Victory*, 587–88.
18. Wallace, *Wally's War*, 21; Pappert, *Landing Was the Easy Part*, 72.
19. Goldstein and Dillon, *Fading Victory*, 588.
20. Gandt, *Twilight Warriors*, 255.
21. Norwald Richard Quiel interview, Feb. 20, 2004.
22. Quiel interview.
23. Quiel interview.
24. VF-10, Aircraft Action Report, in Air Group 10, Aircraft Action Report 82, Apr. 16, 1945, NARA via Fold3.com.

25. Alfred Lerch interview, May 1945.
26. Lerch interview.
27. Lerch interview.
28. Becton, *Ship That Would Not Die*, 237.
29. Robert C. Johnson interview, Aug. 22, 2018.
30. Robert W. Dockery interview, Aug. 22, 2018.
31. Larry Delweski oral history, accessed May 10, 2018.
32. Delweski oral history.
33. Delweski oral history.
34. Wukovits, *Hell from the Heavens*, 178–79.
35. E. A. "Al" Henke oral history, accessed May 10, 2018.
36. Wukovits, *Hell from the Heavens*, 192–93.
37. Cyril C. Simonis Jr. oral history, accessed May 10, 2018.
38. Becton, *Ship That Would Not Die*, 252.
39. Robert C. Johnson interview, Aug. 22, 2018; Wukovits, *Hell from the Heavens*, 198.
40. Becton, *Ship That Would Not Die*, 255.
41. Becton, 201–3.
42. Becton, 262, 278.
43. Morison, *Victory in the Pacific*, 235–37.
44. Tillman, *Corsair*, 146; Tillman, *U.S. Marine Corps Fighter Squadrons of World War II*, 75.
45. Rielly, *Kamikazes, Corsairs, and Picket Ships*, 165–66.
46. Sakaida, *Imperial Japanese Navy Aces*, 92.
47. Pearce, *20th Century Guy*, 174.
48. Charles E. Watts interview, July 7, 2017.
49. Pearce, *20th Century Guy*, 175.
50. Charles E. Watts interview, July 7, 2017.
51. Pearce, *20th Century Guy*, 175.
52. Niderost, "Ace in a Day."
53. Niderost.
54. Niderost.
55. Charles E. Watts interview, July 7, 2017.
56. Pearce, *20th Century Guy*, 176.
57. Moore, *Buzzard Brigade*, 281; John E. Adams interview, 1995; William M. Banta interview, Aug. 31, 2018.
58. Tillman, *U.S. Marine Corps Fighter Squadrons of World War II*, 75.

CHAPTER 17. FLYING CIRCUS IN ACTION

1. Sims, *Greatest Fighter Missions*, 227.
2. Reynolds, *Fighting Lady*, 288–89.
3. Harris Mitchell Memoirs, 15.
4. Mitchell Memoirs, 15–16.

5. Mitchell Memoirs, 16.
6. Mitchell Memoirs, 16.
7. Young, *F6F Hellcat Aces of VF-9*, 79.
8. Reynolds, *Fighting Lady*, 289.
9. Young, *F6F Hellcat Aces of VF-9*, 79.
10. Johnson, "Hot Combat Team Is Custom Built."
11. Sims, *Greatest Fighter Missions*, 239.
12. Harris Mitchell Memoirs, 17.
13. Valencia, *Knights of the Sky*, 20.
14. Coletta, *Admiral Marc A. Mitscher*, 320.
15. Wallace, *Wally's War*, 22.
16. Morison, *Victory in the Pacific*, 240–41.
17. Gandt, *Twilight Warriors*, 290; Belote and Belote, *Typhoon of Steel*, 190.
18. Hallas, *Killing Ground on Okinawa*, 10.
19. Potter, *Nimitz*, 375.
20. Tillman, *U.S. Marine Corps Fighter Squadrons of World War II*, 76; Wolf, *Death Rattlers*, 134–35.
21. Wolf, *Death Rattlers*, 135.
22. Tillman, *U.S. Marine Corps Fighter Squadrons of World War II*, 76; Wolf, *Death Rattlers*, 134, 136–37.
23. Wolf, *Death Rattlers*, 148.
24. Melvin Heckt, "Pacific Diary," 29, Heckt Papers.
25. James S. White interview, Aug. 19, 2017.
26. White, "On the Point of the Spear," 9.
27. White, 9.
28. Watson A. Crumbie interviews, Aug. 14, 15, 2017.
29. Hallas, *Killing Ground on Okinawa*, 13; Heckt, "Pacific Diary," 29, Heckt Papers.

CHAPTER 18. "THE FLAG WAS STILL THERE"

1. Goldstein and Dillon, *Fading Victory*, 597.
2. Rielly, *Kamikazes, Corsairs, and Picket Ships*, 197.
3. Caswell, *My Taking Flight*, 110.
4. Caswell, 112.
5. Caswell, 112.
6. Caswell, 112.
7. Caswell, 112.
8. Valencia, *Knights of the Sky*, 142.
9. Charles E. Watts interview, June 30, 2017.
10. Caswell, *Looking Back*, 44.
11. Caswell, 45.
12. McLellan, "Desmond Doss, 87," 1.
13. Belote and Belote, *Typhoon of Steel*, 228.

14. Goldstein and Dillon, *Fading Victory*, 603.
15. Caswell, *My Taking Flight*, 107.
16. Caswell, 107.
17. "Rescue Mission off Formosa," 1–5.
18. Caswell, *Fighting Falcons*, 100.
19. USS *Aaron Ward*, USS *Little*, Action Reports, May 3, 1945, NARA via Fold3.com.
20. Lott, *Brave Ship, Brave Men*, 171.
21. Edward S. Strine interview, Dec. 9, 2017.
22. Lott, *Brave Ship, Brave Men*, 167, 173.
23. "Gunnery Officer Report," in *Aaron Ward*, Action Report, May 3, 1945, Enclosure C, 3, NARA via Fold3.com.
24. Lott, *Brave Ship, Brave Men*, 192.
25. *Aaron Ward*, Action Report, May 3, 1945, 21, NARA via Fold3.com.
26. Boyd, "World War II Hero Carl E. Clark Honored," 1.
27. Robert Edward Potter interview, July 29, 2003.
28. Edward S. Strine interview, Dec. 9, 2017.
29. Morison, *Victory in the Pacific*, 252.
30. Edward S. Strine interview, Dec. 9, 2017.

CHAPTER 19. "BE ALERT AND KEEP THEM SPLASHING"
1. Rielly, *Kamikazes, Corsairs, and Picket Ships*, 204.
2. VF-9, Aircraft Action Report 94-45, USS *Yorktown*, May 3–4, 1945, NARA via Fold3.com.
3. [Cunningham], "Franklin Thomas Goodson," May 4, 1945; VF-9, Aircraft Action Report 95-45, USS *Yorktown*, May 4, 1945, NARA via Fold3.com.
4. Tillman, *Hellcat*, 244; [Cunningham], "Franklin Thomas Goodson," May 4, 1945.
5. Goldstein and Dillon, *Fading Victory*, 604; Young, *F6F Hellcat Aces of VF-9*, 82.
6. Harris Mitchell Memoirs, 19.
7. Mitchell Memoirs, 19.
8. McWhorter, *First Hellcat Ace*, 107.
9. Harris Mitchell Memoirs, 19.
10. Mitchell Memoirs, 20.
11. Mitchell Memoirs, 20–21.
12. VF-9, Aircraft Action Report 96-45, USS *Yorktown*, May 4, 1945, NARA via Fold3.com.
13. VF-83, Aircraft Action Report 75, USS *Essex*, May 4, 1945, NARA via Fold3.com.
14. Rielly, *Kamikazes, Corsairs, and Picket Ships*, 210–11.
15. Rielly, 211; VF-83, Aircraft Action Report 75, USS *Essex*, May 4, 1945, NARA via Fold3.com.

16. "Statement of Engineering Officer," in USS *Morison*, Action Report, Mar. 21–May 4, 1945, 19–20, NARA via Fold3.com; Gordon, "2007 USS *Morison* (DD-560) Reunion."

17. "Statement of Medical Officer," in USS *Morison*, Action Report, Mar. 21– May 4, 1945, 21–23, NARA via Fold3.com.

18. Donald McPherson interview, July 25, 2017.

19. Liewer, "One of Two Living Fighter Aces in Nebraska Reflects on His Service," 1.

20. Harris Mitchell Memoirs, 21.

21. Mitchell Memoirs, 21.

22. Rielly, *Kamikazes, Corsairs, and Picket Ships*, 212.

23. "Last Letter of Corporal Kanichi Horimoto to His Parents," Kamikaze Images, trans. Bill Gordon, July 2018, www.kamikazeimages.net/writings/ horimoto/index.htm.

24. Rielly, *Kamikazes, Corsairs, and Picket Ships*, 213–14.

25. Rielly, 227–28.

26. Rielly, 229.

27. Rielly, 233.

28. VC-90, Aircraft Action Report 190, USS *Steamer Bay*, May 4, 1945, NARA via Fold3.com.

29. William Kuyper interview, n.d.

30. Naito, *Thunder Gods*, 145.

31. Naito, 145; Goldstein and Dillon, *Fading Victory*, 604.

32. Rielly, *Kamikazes, Corsairs, and Picket Ships*, 234.

33. Coletta, *Admiral Marc A. Mitscher*, 321.

CHAPTER 20. "I WILL GO SMILING"

1. Harris Mitchell Memoirs, 22–23.

2. Belote and Belote, *Typhoon of Steel*, 245.

3. Sears, *At War with the Wind*, 367.

4. Naito, *Thunder Gods*, 145–46.

5. Goldstein and Dillon, *Fading Victory*, 610.

6. Coletta, *Admiral Marc A. Mitscher*, 321.

7. Rielly, *Kamikazes, Corsairs, and Picket Ships*, 243–44.

8. Rielly, 242; Doug Aitken oral history, Sept. 16, 2005.

9. Belote and Belote, *Typhoon of Steel*, 277–78.

10. Caswell, *Fighting Falcons*, 147, 161.

11. Harris Mitchell Memoirs, 23.

12. Mitchell Memoirs, 24–25.

13. Mitchell Memoirs, 25.

14. Mitchell Memoirs, 26.

15. VF-9, Aircraft Action Report 106-45, USS *Yorktown*, May 11, 1945, NARA via Fold3.com.

16. VF-9, Aircraft Action Report 106-45.
17. Doug Aitken oral history, Sept. 16, 2005.
18. Caswell, *Fighting Falcons*, 147, 161.
19. Kennedy, *Danger's Hour*, 264–66, 284–94; "Last Letter from Ensign Kiyoshi Ogawa to His Parents," Kamikaze Images, trans. Bill Gordon, June 2010, www.kamikazeimages.net/writings/ogawa/index.htm.
20. Burke, "Reminiscences," 447.
21. Tuohy, *America's Fighting Admirals*, 341; Ewing, *Reaper Leader*, 237–38.
22. Caswell, *Fighting Falcons*, 151, 155.
23. Caswell, *My Taking Flight*, 119; Dean Caswell interview, July 30, 2017; Caswell, *Fighting Falcons*, 154, 156–57.
24. Dean Caswell interview, July 30, 2017; Caswell, *My Taking Flight*, 119.
25. Ewing, *Reaper Leader*, 239.
26. Taylor, *Magnificent Mitscher*, 279.
27. Burke, "Reminiscences," 449–50.
28. Belote and Belote, *Typhoon of Steel*, 279.
29. Caswell, *My Taking Flight*, 120.

CHAPTER 21. "GET THE CARRIERS"
1. Belote and Belote, *Typhoon of Steel*, 255–56.
2. Belote and Belote, 256.
3. Belote and Belote, 258.
4. Belote and Belote, 259.
5. Belote and Belote, 259–60.
6. Watson A. Crumbie interviews, Aug. 14, 15, 2017.
7. Reynolds, *Fighting Lady*, 296.
8. CAG 90, Aircraft Action Reports, "Support of Operation Okinawa, 7 to 14 May 1945," 19 May 1945, NARA via Fold3.com.
9. CAG 90, VT(N)-90, Aircraft Action Reports 30 and 31, May 11–12, 1945, NARA via Fold3.com.
10. CAG 90, Aircraft Action Report 52, May 12, 1945, NARA via Fold3.com.
11. CAG 90, VT(N)-90, Aircraft Action Report 32, May 12–13, 1945, NARA via Fold3.com; Tillman, *Avenger at War*, 117.
12. Belote and Belote, *Typhoon of Steel*, 280.
13. USS *Randolph*, War Diary, May 1945, NARA via Fold3.com.
14. McWhorter, *First Hellcat Ace*, 186–89; VF-12, Aircraft Action Report 55, May 13, 1945, NARA via Fold3.com.
15. Air Group 83, Aircraft Action Report, May 13, 1945, NARA via Fold3.com; "Lt. Cmdr. David Render Berry."
16. VF-82, Aircraft Action Report 93, USS *Bennington*, May 13, 1945, NARA via Fold3.com.
17. Rielly, *Kamikazes, Corsairs, and Picket Ships*, 256–57.
18. Goldstein and Dillon, *Fading Victory*, 610.

19. Goldstein and Dillon, 610–11.
20. Stafford, *Big E*, 486–87; "Last letter of Lieutenant Junior Grade Shunsuke Tomiyasu to His Family," Kamikaze Images, trans. Bill Gordon, Dec. 2007, www.kamikazeimages.net/writings/tomiyasu/index.htm; Sugahara, "Who Knocked the *Enterprise* Out of the War?"
21. Sugahara, "Who Knocked the *Enterprise* Out of the War?"
22. CAG 90, VF(N)-90, Aircraft Action Report 53, May 13–14, 1945, NARA via Fold3.com.
23. Belote and Belote, *Typhoon of Steel*, 280–81; CAG 90, VF(N)-90 Aircraft Action Report 54, May 14, 1945, NARA via Fold3.com.
24. [Cunningham], "Franklin Thomas Goodson," May 14, 1945.
25. [Cunningham], May 14, 1945.
26. Stafford, *Big E*, 486–87; "Last letter of Lieutenant Junior Grade Shunsuke Tomiyasu."
27. Stafford, *Big E*, 487; Ewing, *Reaper Leader*, 240.
28. [Cunningham], "Franklin Thomas Goodson," May 14, 1945.
29. Jimmy Flatley letter, *Saturday Evening Post*, Dec. 18, 1947, quoted in Ewing, *Reaper Leader*, 354.
30. Ewing, *Reaper Leader*, 354.
31. Taylor, *Magnificent Mitscher*, 298.
32. Stafford, *Big E*, 500.
33. Burke, "Reminiscences," 453; Ewing, *Reaper Leader*, 241.
34. VF-17, Aircraft Action Report 146, USS *Hornet*, May 14, 1945, NARA via Fold3.com.
35. Pearce, *20th Century Guy*, 177.
36. VMF(CV)-112–VMF(CV)-123, Aircraft Action Report 99-45, USS *Bennington*, May 14, 1945, NARA via Fold3.com.
37. VMF(CV)-112–VMF(CV)-123, Aircraft Action Report 103-45, USS *Bennington*, May 14, 1945, NARA via Fold3.com.
38. Rielly, *Kamikazes, Corsairs, and Picket Ships*, 265.
39. Taylor, *Magnificent Mitscher*, 299.

CHAPTER 22. WEATHERING ICEBERG'S FINAL WEEKS

1. Moore, "Harold Tayler—Marine at Okinawa"; White, "On the Point of the Spear," 18.
2. James S. White interview, Aug. 19, 2017.
3. Richard A. Whitaker interview, Mar. 27, 2013; Hallas, *Killing Ground on Okinawa*, 154.
4. Hallas, *Killing Ground on Okinawa*, 171; Wheeler, *Special Valor*, 433–34.
5. Melvin Heckt, "Pacific Diary," 31–33, Heckt Papers.
6. Belote and Belote, *Typhoon of Steel*, 266.
7. Belote and Belote, 271–73.
8. Belote and Belote, 271.

9. "Alameda Ace Jeers Jap 'Zoot Suit' Fliers," 1.
10. Rielly, *Kamikazes, Corsairs, and Picket Ships*, 270–72.
11. VF-17, Aircraft Action Report 167, USS *Hornet*, May 24, 1945, NARA via Fold3.com.
12. Belote and Belote, *Typhoon of Steel*, 268.
13. Tillman, *U.S. Marine Corps Fighter Squadrons of World War II*, 78; Wolf, *Death Rattlers*, 171.
14. Tillman, *U.S. Marine Corps Fighter Squadrons of World War II*, 78.
15. Burke, "Reminiscences," 454.
16. Belote and Belote, *Typhoon of Steel*, 287.
17. Commander, Third Fleet, War Diary, Feb. 1–May 31, 1945, June 22, 1945, 11, Serial 00204, NARA via Fold3.com.
18. Goldstein and Dillon, *Fading Victory*, 619.
19. Rielly, *Kamikazes, Corsairs, and Picket Ships*, 285.
20. "Fantastic Feat of Suicide Plane Sank USS *Drexler*," USS *Drexler* War History, 1, NARA via Fold3.com; Action Report, "Involving Loss of U.S.S. *Drexler* (DD741)," 5, NARA via Fold3.com.
21. Rielly, *Kamikazes, Corsairs, and Picket Ships*, 288.
22. Morison, *Victory in the Pacific*, 272–73; David Lawrence articles, *Washington Evening Star*, May 30, June 4, 1945.
23. Young, *F6F Hellcat Aces of VF-9*, 88–89.
24. Pearce, *20th Century Guy*, 179.
25. Valencia, *Knights of the Sky*, 143.
26. Pearce, *20th Century Guy*, 180; Morison, *Victory in the Pacific*, 305–7.
27. Valencia, *Knights of the Sky*, 144; Pearce, *20th Century Guy*, 182.
28. Willis E. Hardy interview, June 27, 2017.
29. Tilman E. Pool interview, Aug. 8, 2017.
30. Belote and Belote, *Typhoon of Steel*, 302–3.
31. White, "On the Point of the Spear," 24–25.
32. White, 30–32.
33. White, 40.
34. Heckt, "Pacific Diary," 36–37, Heckt Papers.
35. Belote and Belote, *Typhoon of Steel*, 303–4.
36. Belote and Belote, 303–17.
37. Morison, *Victory in the Pacific*, 272–76.
38. Goldstein and Dillon, *Fading Victory*, 629.
39. Young, *F6F Hellcat Aces of VF-9*, 91.
40. Rielly, *Kamikazes, Corsairs, and Picket Ships*, 304–6.
41. Johnson, "Hot Combat Team Is Custom Built."
42. Harris Mitchell flight logbook, June 1945, Harris Mitchell Memoirs.

EPILOGUE

1. Tillman, *U.S. Marine Corps Fighter Squadrons of World War II*, 79.
2. Morison, *Victory in the Pacific*, 276.

3. Melvin Heckt, "Pacific Diary," 39–40, Heckt Papers.
4. Harris Mitchell Memoirs, 26–27.
5. Goldstein and Dillon, *Fading Victory*, 659.
6. Goldstein and Dillon, 663–65.
7. Goldstein and Dillon, 665–66.
8. "D4Y Judy Tail Code 701-122," Pacific Wrecks, last update June 29, 2019, www.pacificwrecks.com/aircraft/d4y/ugaki.html.
9. Taylor, *Magnificent Mitscher*, 312–15.
10. Taylor, 319, 327–28.
11. Potter, *Admiral Arleigh Burke*, 291.
12. Taylor, *Magnificent Mitscher*, 338–40.
13. Taylor, 342–43.
14. Tillman, *U.S. Marine Corps Fighter Squadrons of World War II*, 79–80.
15. Young, *American Aces against the Kamikaze*, 89.
16. Tillman, *U.S. Marine Corps Fighter Squadrons of World War II*, 80; Tillman, *Corsair*, 152. Barrett Tillman lists seventeen Marine fighter aces, but his tally does not count 1st Lt. William Farrell, VMF-312, who was officially credited with five kills during the Okinawa campaign.
17. Tillman, *U.S. Marine Corps Fighter Squadrons of World War II*, 73, 81.
18. Boyce, *American Fighter Aces Album*, 419.
19. Boyce, 130.
20. Boyce, 444.
21. Boyce, 198.
22. Boyce, 85.
23. Boyce, 129, 360.
24. Boyce, 140.
25. Tilman E. Pool interview, Aug. 8, 2017; Donald McPherson interview, July 25, 2017.

BIBLIOGRAPHY

The vast majority of the war diaries of ships and squadrons used for researching this book come from Archives II, the National Archives at College Park, Maryland. This series of 2,199 rolls of microfilm has been digitized from 114 linear feet of textual records, and much of it can be accessed at the Fold3.com research site operated by Ancestry.com. I used documents from the following National Archive record groups: RG 18, Records of the Army Air Forces; RG 24, Records of the Bureau of Naval Personnel; RG 38, Records of the Chief of Naval Operations; and RG 127, Records of the U.S. Marine Corps.

INTERVIEWS, ORAL HISTORIES, AND PERSONAL PAPERS

Adams, John E. VT-10, USS *Intrepid*. Telephone interviews by author, 1995, and August 31, 2018.

Aitken, Doug. USS *Hugh W. Hadley*. Oral history, September 16, 2005. National Museum of the Pacific War, Fredericksburg, TX.

Balden, William H., Jr. VT(N)-90, USS *Enterprise*. Telephone interviews by and correspondence with author, 1995–96.

Ball, Dr. Lyle E. VT-10, USS *Intrepid*. Telephone interview by author, 1995.

Banta, William M. VT-10, USS *Intrepid*. Telephone interview by author, August 31, 2018.

Beebe, Marshall U. VF-17. Interview by Eugene Valencia, July 2, 1965. American Fighter Aces Association Oral Interviews. Museum of Flight, Seattle, WA.

Blanchard, Robert. Oral history. https://www.youtube.com/watch?v_SvOR Plz5Xro. Video removed.

Botten, Capt. Ralph D., USN (Ret.). VT-10, USS *Intrepid*. Telephone interviews by author, 1995–96.

Burke, Arleigh. "The Reminiscences of Adm. Arleigh Burke, USN Retired. Volume 1, Special Series on Selected Subjects." U.S. Naval Institute, Annapolis, MD.

Campbell, Robert M., USN. USS *Bismarck Sea*. Oral history, n.d. Transcript 03177. National Museum of the Pacific War, Fredericksburg, TX.

Carlson, Robert B. VF-30, USS *Belleau Wood*. Telephone interview by author, June 30, 2017.

Caswell, Col. Dean, USMC (Ret.). VMF-221, USS *Bunker Hill*. Interview by author, July 22, 2017. Telephone interview by author, July 30, 2017. Email correspondence with author, June 29–July 11, 2017.

Clark, Lawrence A. VF-83, USS *Essex*. Interview by Dave Thompson, November 24, 2006. Lawrence A. Clark Collection (AFC/2001/001/75543). Veterans History Project, American Folklife Center. Library of Congress, Washington, DC.

Clarke, Walter E. VF-10. Interview, January 1990. Transcript. American Fighter Aces Association Oral Interviews. Museum of Flight, Seattle, WA.

Coats, Robert C. Interview by Eugene Valencia, n.d. American Fighter Aces Association Oral Interviews. Museum of Flight, Seattle, WA.

Coleman, Charles W. VB-86. Telephone interview by author, October 23, 2017.

Crosby, John T. Interview by Eric Hammell, December 3, 1996. American Fighter Aces Association Oral Interviews. Museum of Flight, Seattle, WA.

Crumbie, SSgt. Watson A., USMC (Ret.). Telephone interviews by author, August 14, 15, 2017. Email correspondence with author, August 14–September 7, 2017.

Cumberworth, Richard E. VT-23, USS *Langley*. Telephone interview by author, January 6, 2018.

Delweski, Larry. Oral history. USS *Laffey* Association. www.Laffey.org/Oral%20 Histories/ohlarde.htm.

Dockery, Robert W. USS *Laffey*. Telephone interview by author, August 22, 2018.

Driver, James. VBF-6, USS *Hancock*. Oral history, March 21, 1999. Transcript 1390. Oral History Collection. University of North Texas, Denton.

Dumont, Robert Eugene. Personal Diary, 1944–45. In possession of Robert Dumont.

Esposito, Anthony S. USS *Emmons*. Telephone interview by author, April 8, 2019.

Farrell, William. VMF-312. August 1989 interview. Transcript. American Fighter Aces Association Oral Interviews. Museum of Flight, Seattle, WA.

Frankel, Leon. VT-9, USS *Yorktown*. Interview by Thomas Drake, n.d. Leon Frankel Collection (AFC/2001/001/85978). Transcript. Veterans History Project. American Folklife Center. Library of Congress, Washington, DC.

French, James, with Clinton Smith, Henry Champion, and David Hill. Group interview by Eugene Valencia, circa 1970. American Fighter Aces Association Oral Interviews. Museum of Flight, Seattle, WA.

Fuentes, John. VT-10, USS *Intrepid*. Telephone interview by author, 1995.

Good, Robert C. VF-17, USS *Hornet*. Interview by Gary Rhay, n.d. Robert C. Good Collection (AFC/2001/001/11079). Veterans History Project. American Folklife Center. Library of Congress, Washington, DC.

Guthrie, Orbie C. VT-10, USS *Intrepid*. Telephone interviews by author, 1995.

Hardy, Willis E. VF-17, USS *Hornet*. Telephone interviews by author, June 27, July 8, 2017. Email correspondence with author, July 3, 2017.

Harris, Thomas S. Interview by Eugene Valencia, n.d. American Fighter Aces Association Oral Interviews. Museum of Flight, Seattle, WA.

Hays, Wesley. Interview with Jessica Williams, April 28, 2016. *Intrepid* Sea, Air, and Space Museum, New York, NY.

Hebert, Gilbert J. VT-10, USS *Intrepid*. Telephone interview with author, 1995.

Heckt, Melvin. U.S. Marines. Papers (including "Pacific Diary" and photographs) Copies in author possession, courtesy of Barb Kenutis.

Henke, E. A. "Al." Oral history. USS *Laffey* Association. www.Laffey.org/Oral%20 Histories/ohhenke.htm.

Hovis, Ralph C. VT-10, USS *Intrepid*. Telephone interview with author, 1995.

Hubenthal, Charles. Interview with Amy Conrad, May 7, 2011. Uploaded July 5, 2011. wikimarion.org/Charles_Hubenthal_Interview.

Hunt, Harry F., Jr. VT-10, USS *Intrepid*. Telephone interview with author, 1995.

Hurley, William S. USS *Colhoun*. Interview by Peter Kraley, March 1, 2006. William S. Hurley Collection (AFC/2001/001/42478). Veterans History Project. American Folklife Center. Library of Congress, Washington, DC.

Icard, Cheryl Valencia. Telephone conversations and email correspondence with author, November 2017–January 2018.

Jackson, Robert Hal. VBF-17, USS *Hornet*. Oral history, July 24, 1997. Transcript 1195. Oral History Collection. University of North Texas, Denton.

Johnson, Merle. Oral history. USS *Laffey* Association. www.Laffey.org/Oral%20 Histories/ohmjohn.htm.

Johnson, Robert C. USS *Laffey*. Telephone interview by author, August 22, 2018.

Jolley, Armond J. USS *Emmons*. Telephone interview by author, August 19, 2018.

Jones, Howard. USS *Bunker Hill*. Oral history, May 18, 2007. National Museum of the Pacific War, Fredericksburg, TX.

Karr, Robert I. Oral history. USS *Laffey* Association. www.Laffey.org/Oral%20His tories/ohrkarr.htm.

Klesack, Franklin James. USS *Wasp*. Interview by Thomas Swope, March 4, 2004. Franklin James Klesack Collection (AFC/2001/001/20704). Veterans History Project. American Folklife Center. Library of Congress, Washington, DC.

Kuyper, William. USS *Shea*. Interview by Theodore Gardner, n.d. William Kuyper (AFC/2001/001/56567). Veterans History Project. American Folklife Center. Library of Congress, Washington, DC.

Lacouture, Capt. John E., USN (Ret.). VF-5, USS *Franklin*. Oral history, October 9, 2000. National Museum of the Pacific War, Fredericksburg, TX.

Largess, Clifton R. VT(N)-90, USS *Enterprise*. Telephone interviews by author, 1995–96.

Lawrence, Capt. John C., USN (Ret.). VT-10, USS *Intrepid*. Telephone interview by and correspondence with author, 1995.

Lerch, Alfred. VF-10, USS *Intrepid*. Radio interview, May 1945. Transcribed by Ann Stegina. Accession P2012.80.09. *Intrepid* Sea, Air, and Space Museum, New York, NY.

Lyons, Lt. (jg) Jack M., USN (Ret.). VF-83, USS *Essex*. Telephone interview by author, July 23, 2018. Email correspondence with author, through Lynn Powers, Lyons' daughter, July 29, 2018.

Mann, Joe. Email correspondence with author, November 7–December 7, 2017.

Mann (Schwendemann), Richard E. USN (Ret.). VF-53, VF-34. Personal, interview by author, October 25, 2017.

McPherson, Donald. VF-83, USS *Essex*. Telephone interviews by author, July 25, August 18, 2017. Correspondence with author, August 2017.

Mitchell, Harris E. VF-9, USS *Lexington*, USS *Yorktown*. Audiotaped interview by Jack Stovall, January 1999. Courtesy of Mrs. Mary Frances Mitchell and her friend Charles Blankenship.

———. Memoirs (including papers and photographs). Copies in author's possession, courtesy of Mary Frances Mitchell through Charles Thompson.

Mitchell, Mary Frances. Telephone interview by author, September 16, 2017.

Mitscher, Mrs. Frances Smalley. Interviews by John T. Mason Jr., January 23–24, 1971. Transcript. Oral History Collection. U.S. Naval Institute, Annapolis, MD.

Molleston, Robert D. VB-6, USS *Hancock*. Oral history, February 27, 2012. National Museum of the Pacific War, Fredericksburg, TX.

Moore, Oral L. VB-8, USS *Hornet*. Telephone interview by author, June 2, 2011.

"Nite Life." 1945. Anonymously written unofficial wartime history of VT(N)-90. Copy in author's possession, courtesy of William J. Shinneman (from Joseph McMullen).

Overall, Sidney R., Jr. VT-10, USS *Intrepid*. Telephone interviews by and correspondence with author, 1995.

Pappert, Edward. VBF-83, USS *Essex*. Telephone interview by author, August 1, 2018.

Pool, Tilman E., USN (Ret.). VF-17, USS *Hornet*. Personal interview by author, June 30, 2017. Telephone interviews by author, July 2, August 8, September 30, December 3, 2017; February 9, 2018; March 24, 2019. Email correspondence with author, June 29, 2017–March 7, 2018.

Potter, Robert Edward. USS *Aaron Ward*. Interview by Judith Rosenkotter, July 29, 2003. Robert Edward Potter Collection (AFC/2001/001/07362). Veterans History Project. American Folklife Center. Library of Congress, Washington, DC.

Quiel, Cdr. Norwald Richard, USN (Ret.). VF-10, USS *Intrepid*. Interview by Fran Foley, February 20, 2004. Norwald Richard Quiel Collection

(AFC/2001/001/14823). Veterans History Project. American Folklife Center. Library of Congress, Washington, DC.

Radney, Lt. Cdr. Ridgley D., USN (Ret.). VB-5, USS *Franklin*. Oral history, n.d. National Museum of the Pacific War, Fredericksburg, TX.

Rock, Robert. VT-10, USS *Intrepid*. Telephone interview with author, 1995.

Schroeder, Arlo E. VT-10, USS *Intrepid*. Telephone interviews by and correspondence with author, 1995–96.

Simonis, Cyril C., Jr. Oral history. USS *Laffey* Association. www.Laffey.org/Oral%20Histories/ohcysim.htm.

Smith, George F. VT-10, USS *Intrepid*. Telephone interview by author, 1995.

Snider, Bernie G. USS *Hancock*. Oral history, June 10, 2002. Transcript 1441. Oral History Collection. University of North Texas, Denton.

Strine, Edward S. USS *Aaron Ward*. Telephone interview by author and James Horan, December 9, 2017, and follow up.

Swedlund, Harold D. USS *Aaron Ward*. Interview by Gale Beal and William R. Cook, March 24, 2005. Harold D. Swedlund Collection (AFC/2001/001/32753). Veterans History Project. American Folklife Center. Library of Congress, Washington, DC.

Turner, Charles W. VT-10, USS *Intrepid*. Telephone interview by author, 1995.

Valencia, Anthony (son of Eugene Valencia). Telephone interview by author, September 30, 2017. Email and mail correspondence and telephone conversations with author, July–October 2017.

Waite, Steve. Oral history. USS *Laffey* Association. www.Laffey.org/Oral%20Histories/ohwaite.htm.

Wallace, Glen H. VBF-83, USS *Essex*. "War Diary of Glen H. Wallace, [October 13, 1942–May 29, 1947." Veterans History Project. American Folklife Center. Library of Congress, Washington, D.C. memory.loc.gov/diglib/vhp/story/loc.natlib.afc2001001.11540/pageturner?ID=pm0002001.

———. "Wally's War." Personal diary kept by Glen Wallace in 1945. See kilroywashere.org/003-Pages/GlenWallace.html.

Warner, Donald L., Jr. VT(N)-90, USS *Enterprise*. Telephone interview by author, September 1, 2018.

Watson, Russell E. USS *Mannert L. Abele*. Interview by Homer Lynch, August 25, 2004. Russell E. Watson Collection (AFC/2001/001/27856). Veterans History Project. American Folklife Center. Library of Congress, Washington, DC.

Watts, Charles E., USN, (Ret.). VF-17, USS *Hornet*. Personal interview by author, June 30, 2017. Telephone interviews by author, June 28, July 7, December 3, 7, 2017.

Whitaker, Richard A., USMC, (Ret.). Interview by Chris Sakmar, March 27, 2013. Transcript. Krause Center. The Citadel, Charleston, SC.

———. Telephone interview by author, August 27, 2017.

White, James S. "On the Point of the Spear: Experiences of a Marine Rifleman during the Battle for the Island of Okinawa in April, May, and June of 1945." Unpublished memoir. Copy in author's possession, courtesy of James S. White.
———. Telephone interview by author, August 19, 2017. Email correspondence with author, August 18–19, 2017.
Young, Capt. Grant C., USN, (Ret.). VT-10, USS *Intrepid*. Telephone and personal interviews by author, 1995–96.

ARTICLES AND VIDEOS
"Alameda Ace Jeers Jap 'Zoot Suit' Fliers." *Oakland Tribune*, May 20, 1945, 1.
Astor, Gerald. "Japanese Battleship *Yamato* Makes Its Final Stand." *World War II Magazine* online, July 28, 2015. www.warfarehistorynetwork.com/daily/wwii/japanese-battleship-yamato-makes-its-final-stand/.
Bang, Keiko. "A Matter of Honor: An Interview with *Yamato* Veteran Naoyoshi Ishida." *Sinking the Supership*. Translated by Risa Okamoto. Edited by Susan K. Lewis. Nova online, September 2005. http://www.pbs.org/wgbh/nova/supership/surv-ishida.html.
———. "Thoughts of a Young Sailor: An Interview with *Yamato* Veteran Kazuhiro Fukumoto." Translated by Risa Okamoto. Edited by Susan K. Lewis. *Sinking the Supership*. Nova online, September 2005. http://www.pbs.org/wgbh/nova/supership/surv-fukumoto.html.
Baumgartner, Dawn. "WWII Veteran Remembers the Sinking of USS *Colhoun*." *Durham Herald-Sun*, November 15, 2009, B6.
Beebe, Marshall U. "Sis–*Liscome Bay* and Toko-Ri." Naval Aviation Museum *Foundation*, Spring 1984, 2–5, 62–66.
Boyd, Herb. "World War II Hero Carl E. Clark Honored before His Death." *New York Amsterdam News*, May 11, 2017, 1.
Brick, Gene. "Sinking of the USS *Drexler* DD-741." Kamikaze Images. wgordon.web.wesleyan.edu/kamikaze/stories/brick/index.htm.
"'Buster' Campbell's Account." Battleship *Missouri* Memorial. https://ussmissouri.org/learn-the-history/world-war-ii-1/buster-campbells-account.
Carroll, Louise. "Sam Ferrante's Lucky Day Is March 19." *Ellwood City (PA) Ledger*, 1A, March 16, 2015.
Carter, Don. "Armitage Field Aviator Knocks Down 24 Jap Planes; Is Second Navy Ace." Clipping from unidentified newspaper, ca. June 1945.
Cole, William. "USS *Missouri* Hosts Kamikaze Artifacts Never Seen before outside Japan." *Honolulu Star-Advertiser*, April 11, 2015, 1.
Crumbie, Watson A., Jr. "My Time as a Marine. Chapter One: Pearl Harbor to Camp Tarawa." Stories by Sixth Division Marines. Sixth Marine Division, June 2012–June 2013. https://www.sixthmarinedivision.com/16StoryCrumbie1.html.

———. "My Time as a Marine. Chapter Two: Saipan." Stories by Sixth Division Marines. Sixth Marine Division, June 2012–June 2013. https://www.sixth marinedivision.com/16StoryCrumbie2.html.

———. "My Time as a Marine. Chapter Three: Okinawa." Stories by Sixth Division Marines. Sixth Marine Division, June 2012–June 2013. https://www.sixth marinedivision.com/16StoryCrumbie3.html.

[Cunningham, Kathryn Goodson, comp.]. "Franklin Thomas Goodson, from Ensign to Lieutenant Sr. Grade, January 1945–September 1955." [Diary]. American Veterans Center. www.americanveteranscenter.org/2017/02/franklin-thomas-goodson-ensign-lieutenant-sr-grade-january-1945-sep tember-1955/.

Dopking, Al. "Navy Pilots Find Good Hunting as Jap Suicide Planes Strike." *Jefferson City (MO) Sunday News and Tribune*, May 6, 1945.

Esposito, Anthony. "USS Emmons Testimonial: Tony Esposito." Crew Member Testimonials. USS *Emmons* DD457/DMS22 Association (https://www.ussem mons.org/testimonials). September 20, 2014. https://www.youtube.com/watch?v=XG3-upG1Su4&feature=youtu.be.

Fenoglio, Y3c Melvin. "This I Remember." USS *Little* DD 803. https://dd803.org/crew/stories-from-the-crew/melvin-fenoglio-account/.

Gordon, Bill. "2007 USS *Morison* (DD-560) Reunion." Kamikaze Images. http://www.kamikazeimages.net/stories/morrison/index.htm.

———. "Censored Suicide." Kamikaze Images, ca. May 2006. https://wgordon.web .wesleyan.edu/kamikaze/stories/fujii/index.htm.

Guptill, Frank, ARM2c. "Notes of the Attack on the *Yamato*." USS *Essex* WWII Air Groups, Their Squadrons, and Their Aircraft. www.ussessex.org/Air_Groups .htm.

Hackett, Bob. "IJN Ohka Type 11 Operations at Okinawa, 1944–1945." The Imperial Japanese Navy Page, 2015–16. http://www.combinedfleet.com/Ohka%20 Type%2011.htm.

Hackett, Bob, and Peter Cundall. "IJN *Shimane Maru*: Tabular Record of Movement." The Imperial Japanese Navy Page, 2010. http://www.combinedfleet .com/Shimane_t.htm.

Hackett, Bob, and Sander Kingsepp. "IJN *Yahagi*: Tabular Record of Movement." The Imperial Japanese Navy Page, 1997–2016. http://www.combinedfleet .com/yahagi_t.htm.

———. "IJN Battleship *Yamato*: Tabular Record of Movement." The Imperial Japanese Navy Page, 2000–2016. www.combinedfleet.com/yamato.htm

Hackett, Bob, Sander Kingsepp, and Peter Cundall. "IJN *Kinezaki*: Tabular Record of Movement." The Imperial Japanese Navy Page, 2007–15. www.combined fleet.com/Kinezaki_t.htm.

———. "IJN Minelayer *Tsubame*: Tabular Record of Movement." The Imperial Japanese Navy Page, 2005–19. www.combinedfleet.com/tsubame_t.htm.

Hensel, Jack. "My Experiences as an Aircrewman." USS *Franklin* Museum Association, August 28, 2012. www.ussfranklin.org/?p=27.

Herr, Ernest A. "Doomed: The Last Day of the USS *Emmons* in the Battle of Okinawa." www.angelfire.com/planet/solomon0/Okinawa.html.

Higgins, Nina Sue Cresap, "The Dan Haywood Fowler Story." Togetherweserved.com (subscription). https://navy.togetherweserved.com/usn/servlet/tws.webapp.WebAPP?cmd=shadowBoxProfile&type=Person&ID=291249.

Hoffman, Edwin. "USS Emmons Testimonial: Ed Hoffman." Crew Member Testimonials. USS *Emmons* DD457/DMS22 Association (https://www.ussemmons.org/testimonials). September 20, 2014. https://www.youtube.com/watch?v=OOArLFW__Dc&feature=youtu.be.

"Hoosier Seaman Cheats Death as Jap Suicide Plane Sinks Ship." *Indianapolis Star*, June 28, 1945, 2.

Ikeda, Takekuni. "The Imperial Navy's Final Sortie." *Naval History Magazine* 27, no. 5 (October 2007), 34–43.

Johnson, Malcolm. "Hot Combat Team Is Custom Built." *New York Sun*, August 1945.

Jolley, Armond. "USS Emmons Testimonial: Armond Jolley." Crew Member Testimonials. USS *Emmons* DD457/DMS22 Association (https://www.ussemmons.org/testimonials). September 20, 2014. https://www.youtube.com/watch?v=v_VEPj8Qv5c&feature=youtu.be.

"Kamikazes." Episode 1, season 2 of *Dogfights*. Aired July 13, 2007, on The History Channel.

Knapp, Tom. "For Memorial Day, US Navy Veteran Recounts Heroic Battle with Kamikaze Planes at Okinawa." *Lancaster Online*, May 29, 2017. https://lancasteronline.com/news/local/for-memorial-day-us-navy-veteran-recounts-heroic-battle-with/article_659580e6-3f16-11e7-91fc-ff9f62546635.html.

Langworthy, Irv. "Doyle Kennedy Account." USS *Little* DD 803, March 20, 1999 (last updated November 25, 2005). https://dd803.org/crew/stories-from-the-crew/doyle-kennedy-account/.

Liewer, Steve. "One of Two Living Fighter Aces in Nebraska Reflects on His Service." *Omaha World-Herald*, March 30, 2015, 1.

Lollar, Kevin. "Pilot Recalls Sinking of Battleship *Yamato*." *Fort Myers (FL) News Press*, February 23, 2004.

"Lt. Cmdr. David Render Berry." AviationMuseumKY channel, YouTube, October 17, 2018. https://www.youtube.com/watch?v=ndFn9lXGYrA&t=2s.

Machado, C. J. "Meet a WWII Flying Ace! Colonel Dean Caswell, USMC, Retired." *Homeland Magazine*, October 2015, 12–15.

Mann, Angie. "Heroes among Us—WWII Veteran." *Mille Lacs (MN) Messenger*, November 13, 2017, 1.

McCoy, Alvin S. "Eyewitness Describes Wreck, Close Escapes on Carrier." *Salt Lake Tribune*, April 18, 1945, 3.

McLellan, Dennis. "Desmond Doss, 87; WWII Hero Who Refused to Carry a Gun." *Los Angeles Times*, March 26, 2006, 1.

McWilliams, George. "Pilots Tell about Sinking Jap Battleship." *Lima (OH) News*, July 5, 1945, 16.

Moore, Don. "Harold Tayler—Marine at Okinawa." *War Tales* (blog), April 14, 2010. https://donmooreswartales.com/2010/04/19/harold-tayler/.

Nevitt, Allyn D. "IJN *Asashimo*: Tabular Record of Movement." The Imperial Japanese Navy Page, 1998. www.combinedfleet.com/asashm_t.htm.

Niderost, Eric. "An Ace in a Day: Ted Crosby's Air War in the Pacific." *World War II Magazine* online, December 22, 2018. https://warfarehistorynetwork.com/daily/wwii/an-ace-in-a-day-ted-crosbys-air-war-in-the-pacific/.

Park, Brian, "The Ace of San Juan." *Capo Dispatch* (San Juan Capistrano, CA), February 22, 2013.

"Rescue Mission off Formosa, January 1945." *Mighty Ninety* 2, no. 1 (June 2010), 1–5.

Roberts, William. "Change of Tides: The William Roberts Story." Crew Member Testimonials. USS *Emmons* DD457/DMS22 Association (https://www.ussemmons.org/testimonials). January 17, 2015. https://www.youtube.com/watch?v=R_lSPzHVeD4&feature=youtu.be.

Sasaki, Yasuyuki. "Wartime Sailors Recall Loss of Japanese Fleet's *Isokaze, Yamato*." *Asahi Shimbun* (Osaka, Japan), May 19, 2018. www.asashi.com/ajw/articles/AJ201805190006.html. Site removed.

Sugahara, Ken. "Who Knocked the *Enterprise* Out of the War?" *Naval History Magazine* 22, no. 2 (April 2008). https://www.usni.org/magazines/naval-history-magazine/2008/april/who-knocked-enterprise-out-war.

"Third Set of Memories: Lost at Okinawa." Recollections. USS *Bush*—DD529. www.ussbush.com/memory3.htm.

Troy, Gil. "The American Who Buried a Kamikaze Enemy." *Daily Beast*, December 4, 2016 (last updated July 8, 2019). https://www.thedailybeast.com/the-amer-ican-who-buried-a-kamikaze-enemy.

Wallace, Glen. "First Time Out!" Supplemental account to "War Diary," Mar. 18, 1945. Kilroy Was Here: Remembering the War Years, www.kilroywashere.org/003-Pages/GlenWallace/45-03-18.htm.

BOOKS AND OTHER PUBLICATIONS

Astor, Gerald. *Operation Iceberg: The Invasion and Conquest of Okinawa in World War II*. New York: Dutton, 2015.

Becton, Rear Adm. F. Julian, USN (Ret.). *The Ship That Would Not Die*. Englewood Cliffs, NJ: Prentice-Hall, 1980.

Belote, James H., and William M. Belote. *Typhoon of Steel: The Battle for Okinawa*. New York: Harper & Row, 1970.

Billingsley, Edward Baxter. *The* Emmons *Saga: A History of the USS* Emmons *(DD457-DMS22).* New York: iUniverse, 2005.

Blair, Clay, Jr. *Silent Victory: The U.S. Submarine War against Japan.* Philadelphia: J. B. Lippincott, 1975.

Boyce, Col. J. Ward, USAF (Ret.), ed. *American Fighter Aces Album.* Mesa, AZ: American Fighter Aces Association, 1996.

Bradley, James. *Flyboys.* Boston: Little, Brown, 2003.

Bruce, Lt. Cdr. Roy W., USNR (Ret.), and Lt. Cdr. Charles R. Leonard, USN (Ret.). *Crommelin's Thunderbirds: Air Group 12 Strikes the Heart of Japan.* Annapolis, MD: Naval Institute Press, 1994.

Buchanan, Buck. *Helldiver's Vengeance.* Victoria, Canada: Trafford, 2001.

Bureau of Naval Personnel. *All Hands Naval Bulletin.* May 1945.

Campbell, Douglas E. *Save Our Souls: Rescues Made by U.S. Submarines during World War II.* Privately published, Lulu.com, 2016.

Caswell, Col. Dean, USMC (Ret.). *Fighting Falcons: The Saga of Marine Fighter Squadron VMF 221.* Austin, TX: Privately published, 2004.

———. *Looking Back: True Stories and Essays.* Austin, TX: Privately published, 2013.

———. *My Taking Flight.* Austin, TX: Privately published, 2010.

Cleaver, Thomas McKelvey. *Pacific Thunder: The US Navy's Central Pacific Campaign, August 1943–October 1944.* Oxford, UK: Osprey, 2017.

———. *Tidal Wave: From Leyte Gulf to Tokyo Bay.* Oxford: Osprey Publishing, 2018.

Coletta, Paolo E. *Admiral Marc A. Mitscher and U.S. Naval Aviation: Bald Eagle.* Lewiston, NY: Edwin Mellen, 1997.

Dye, Dale, and Robert O'Neill. *The Road to Victory: From Pearl Harbor to Okinawa.* Oxford, UK: Osprey, 2011.

Erickson, Lt. (jg) Roy D. "Eric," USNR. *Tail End Charlies! Navy Combat Fighter Pilots at War's End.* Paducah, KY: Turner, 1995.

Ewing, Steve. *Reaper Leader: The Life of Jimmy Flatley.* Annapolis, MD: Naval Institute Press, 2002.

Ford, Donald. *Torpedo-Squadron-30 Air Combat: First Tokyo Strikes after Doolittle, Iwo Jima Conquest, Okinawa Liberation, End of Japanese Fleet.* Self-published, Amazon Digital Services, 2014. Kindle.

Gandt, Robert. *The Twilight Warriors.* New York: Broadway Paperbacks, 2010.

Goldstein, Donald W., and Katherine V. Dillon, eds. *Fading Victory: The Diary of Admiral Matome Ugaki, 1941–1945.* Pittsburg: University of Pittsburg Press, 1991. Reprint, Annapolis, MD: Naval Institute Press, 2008.

Graff, Cory. *Strike and Return: American Air Power and the Fight for Iwo Jima.* North Branch, MN: Specialty Press, 2006.

Hallas, James H. *Killing Ground on Okinawa: The Battle for Sugar Loaf Hill.* Westport, CT: Praeger, 1996.

Hammel, Eric. *Aces against Japan. Vol. 1 of The American Aces Speak.* Novato, CA: Presidio, 1992.

——. *Aces against Japan II. Vol. 3 of The American Aces Speak.* Pacifica, CA: Pacifica, 1996.

——. *Aces at War. Vol. 4 of The American Aces Speak.* Pacifica, CA: Pacifica, 1997.

Hara, Capt. Tameichi. *Japanese Destroyer Captain.* New York: Ballantine Books, 1961.

Hoehling, A. A. *The* Franklin *Comes Home: The Saga of the Most Decorated Ship in Naval History.* New York: Hawthorn Books, 1974.

Hudson, J. Ed. *A History of the USS* Cabot *(CVL-28): A Fast Carrier in World War II.* Privately published, 1986.

Hyams, Joe. *Flight of the Avenger: George Bush at War.* San Diego, CA: Harcourt Brace Jovanovich, 1991.

Jones, Ken, and Hubert Kelley Jr. *Admiral Arleigh (31-Knot) Burke: The Story of a Fighting Sailor.* Annapolis, MD: Naval Institute Press, 2001.

Kennedy, Maxwell Taylor. *Danger's Hour: The Story of the USS* Bunker Hill *and the Kamikaze Pilot Who Crippled Her.* New York: Simon & Schuster, 2008.

Kuwahara, Yasuo, and Gordon T. Allred. *Kamikaze: A Japanese Pilot's Own Spectacular Story of the Famous Suicide Squadrons.* New York: Ballantine Books, 1957.

Lott, Arnold S. *Brave Ship, Brave Men.* Annapolis, MD: Naval Institute Press, 1986.

MacGlashing, John W. *Batmen: Night Air Group 90 in World War II.* St. Paul, MN: Phalanx, 1995.

McWhorter, Hamilton. *The First Hellcat Ace.* With Jay A. Stout. Pacifica, CA: Pacifica Military History, 2009.

Mikesh, Robert C. *Japanese Aircraft Code Names and Designations.* Atglen, PA: Schiffer, 1993.

Moore, Stephen L. *The Buzzard Brigade, Torpedo Squadron Ten at War: Carrier Warfare in the Pacific from Guadalcanal to Okinawa with One of the Navy's Most Famous Avenger Squadrons.* With William J. Shinneman and Robert W. Gruebel. Missoula, MT: Pictorial Histories, 1996.

——. *Pacific Payback: The Carrier Aviators Who Avenged Pearl Harbor at the Battle of Midway.* New York: NAL Caliber, 2014.

Morison, Samuel Eliot. *Victory in the Pacific, 1945.* Vol. 14 of *History of the United States Naval Operations in World War II.* Boston: Little, Brown, 1990.

Naito, Hatsuho. *Thunder Gods. The Kamikaze Pilots Tell Their Story.* New York: Dell, 1989.

Noles, James L., Jr. *Twenty-Three Minutes to Eternity: The Final Voyage of the Escort Carrier USS* Liscome Bay. Tuscaloosa: University of Alabama Press, 2004.

Olynyk, Frank. *Stars and Bars: A Tribute to the American Fighter Ace, 1920–1973.* London: Grub Street, 1995.

——. *USMC Credits for the Destruction of Enemy Aircraft in Air-to-Air Combat, World War 2.* Aurora, OH: privately printed, 1981.

———. *USN Credits for the Destruction of Enemy Aircraft in Air-to-Air Combat, World War 2.* Aurora, OH: privately printed, 1982.

Pappert, Edward. *Landing Was the Easy Part.* Bloomington, IN: 1st Books Library, 2002.

Pearce, Jim. *A 20th Century Guy.* Goodyear, AZ: Sonya Steiner Associates, 2007.

Potter, E. B. *Admiral Arleigh Burke.* New York: Random House, 1990.

———. *Nimitz.* Annapolis, MD: Naval Institute Press, 1976.

Pyle, Ernie. *Last Chapter.* New York: Henry Holt, 1946.

Reynolds, Clark G. *The Fighting Lady: The New Yorktown in the Pacific War.* Missoula, MT: Pictorial Histories, 1986.

———. *On the Warpath in the Pacific: Admiral Jocko Clark and the Fast Carriers.* Annapolis, MD: Naval Institute Press, 2005.

Rielly, Robin L. *Kamikazes, Corsairs, and Picket Ships: Okinawa, 1945.* Philadelphia: Casemate, 2008.

Sakaida, Henry. *Imperial Japanese Navy Aces, 1937–1945.* London: Osprey, 1998.

Sambito, Maj. William J., USMC. *A History of Marine Attack Squadron 311.* Washington, DC: History and Museums Division, U.S. Marine Corps, 1978.

Satterfield, John R. *Saving Big Ben: The USS Franklin and Father Joseph T. O'Callahan.* Annapolis, MD: Naval Institute Press, 2011.

Scott, James M. *Rampage: MacArthur, Yamashita, and the Battle of Manila.* New York: W. W. Norton, 2018.

Sears, David. *At War with the Wind: The Epic Struggle with Japan's World War II Suicide Bombers.* New York: Kensington, 2008.

Sheftall, M. G. *Blossoms in the Wind. Human Legacies of the Kamikaze.* New York: NAL Caliber, 2005.

Sherman, Frederick C. *Combat Command: The American Aircraft Carriers in the Pacific War.* Boston, MA: E. P. Dutton, 1950.

Sims, Edward. *Greatest Fighter Missions of the Top Navy and Marine Aces of World War II.* Ballantine Books, 1962.

Sloan, Bill. *The Ultimate Battle: Okinawa 1945—The Last Epic Struggle of World War II.* New York: Simon & Schuster, 2007.

Springer, Joseph A. *Inferno: The Epic Life and Death Struggle of the USS Franklin in World War II.* St. Paul, MN: Zenith, 2007.

Spurr, Russell A. *A Glorious Way to Die: The Kamikaze Mission of the Battleship Yamato, April 1945.* New York: Newmarket, 1981.

Stafford, Edward P. *The Big E: The Story of the USS Enterprise.* Illustrated ed. Annapolis, MD: Naval Institute Press, 2015.

Surels, Ron. *DD 522: Diary of a Destroyer. The Action Saga of the USS Luce from the Aleutian and Philippine Campaigns to Her Sinking off Okinawa.* Plymouth, NH: Valley Graphics, 1994.

Taylor, Theodore. *The Magnificent Mitscher.* 1954. Annapolis, MD: Naval Institute Press, 1991.

Thomas, Evan. *Sea of Thunder: Four Commanders and the Last Great Naval Campaign 1941–1945*. New York: Simon & Schuster, 2006.

Tillman, Barrett. *Avenger at War*. Annapolis, MD: Naval Institute Press, 1990.

——. *Corsair. The F4U in World War II and Korea*. Annapolis, MD: Naval Institute Press, 1979.

——. *Hellcat: The F6F in World War II*. Annapolis, MD: Naval Institute Press, 1979.

——. *Hellcat Aces of World War 2*. London: Osprey, 1996.

——. *Helldiver Units of World War 2*. London: Osprey, 1997.

——. *TBF/TBM Avengers Units of World War 2*. Oxford, UK: Osprey, 1999.

——. *U.S. Marine Corps Fighter Squadrons of World War II*. Oxford, UK: Osprey, 2014.

Timenes, Nicolai, Jr. *Defense against Kamikaze Attacks in World War II and Its Relevance to Anti-Ship Missile Defense*. Operations Evaluation Group Study 741. Department of the Navy, November 1970.

Tuohy, William. *America's Fighting Admirals: Wining the War at Sea in World War II*. St. Paul, MN: Zenith, 2007.

Valencia, Jerry. *Knights of the Sky*. San Diego, CA: Reed Enterprise, 1980.

Veesenmeyer, Jeffrey R. *Kamikaze Terror: Sailors Who Battled the Divine Wind*. Cambridge, WI: Jeffrey Marketing, 2017.

Wallace, Glen H. *Wally's War, 1942–1947*. Pensacola, FL: Privately published, 1971. Available online at Veterans History Project, American Folklife Center, Library of Congress, memory.loc.gov/diglib/vhp/story/loc.natlib.afc2001001.11540/pageturner?ID=pm0001001.

Wheeler, Richard. *A Special Valor: The U.S. Marines and the Pacific War*. Annapolis, MD: Naval Institute Press, 2006.

Wilde, E. Andrew, Jr. (ed.). *The U.S.S. Drexler (DD-741) in World War II: Documents, Photographs, Recollections*. Neeham, MA: Privately published, 2003.

Wolf, William. *Death Rattlers: Marine Squadron VMF-323 over Okinawa*. Atglen, PA: Schiffer Military History, 1999.

Wooldridge, E. T., (ed.). *Carrier Warfare in the Pacific: An Oral History Collection*. Washington, DC: Smithsonian Institution Press, 1993.

Wukovits, John. *Hell from the Heavens. The Epic Story of the USS Laffey and World War II's Greatest Kamikaze Attack*. Boston: Da Capo, 2015.

Y'Blood, William T. *The Little Giants: U.S. Escort Carriers against Japan*. Annapolis, MD: Naval Institute Press, 1987.

Yoshida, Mitsuru. *Requiem for the Battleship Yamato*. Annapolis, MD: Naval Institute Press, 1999.

Young, Edward M. *American Aces against the Kamikaze*. Botley, Oxford: Osprey, 2012.

——. *F6F Hellcat Aces of VF-9*. Oxford, UK: Osprey, 2014.

Zdon, Al. *War Stories III: Further Accounts of Minnesotans Who Defended Their Nation*. Mounds View, MN: Moonlit Eagle, 2017.

INDEX

ABOUT THE AUTHOR

Stephen L. Moore, a sixth-generation Texan, is the author of nineteen previous books on World War II and Texas history. He graduated from Stephen F. Austin State University in Nacogdoches, Texas, where he studied advertising, marketing, and journalism. A marketing director by trade, he is the author of three previous Naval Institute Press books, including the most recent *Uncommon Valor: The Recon Company That Earned Five Medals of Honor and Included America's Most Decorated Green Beret*. He lives north of Dallas in Lantana, Texas, with his wife and three children.